# Applied Network
# Security Monitoring

# Applied Network Security Monitoring

## Collection, Detection, and Analysis

**Chris Sanders**

**Jason Smith**

**David J. Bianco, Technical Editor**

ELSEVIER

AMSTERDAM • BOSTON • HEIDELBERG • LONDON
NEW YORK • OXFORD • PARIS • SAN DIEGO
SAN FRANCISCO • SINGAPORE • SYDNEY • TOKYO

Syngress is an imprint of Elsevier

**Acquiring Editor:** *Chris Katsaropoulos*
**Editorial Project Manager:** *Benjamin Rearick*
**Project Manager:** *Punithavathy Govindaradjane*
**Designer:** *Matthew Limbert*
**Copyeditor:** *Ellen Sanders*

*Syngress* is an imprint of Elsevier
225 Wyman Street, Waltham, MA 02451, USA

**Library of Congress Cataloging-in-Publication Data**
Application submitted

**British Library Cataloguing-in-Publication Data**
A catalogue record for this book is available from the British Library

ISBN: 978-0-12-417208-1

14  15  16  17  18      10  9  8  7  6  5  4  3  2  1

Working together
to grow libraries in
developing countries

www.elsevier.com • www.bookaid.org

For information on all Syngress publications, visit our website at *store.elsevier.com/Syngress*

This book is a product of strength gained through love. This book is dedicated to God, my wife Ellen, and all those who continue to love and support me.

"But those who hope in the Lord will renew their strength. They will soar on wings like eagles, they will run and not grow weary, they will walk and not be faint."
Isaiah 40:31 (NIV)

# Contents

# SECTION 2    DETECTION

# Acknowledgements

2 Corinthians 12 says, "But he said to me, 'My grace is sufficient for you, for my power is made perfect in weakness.' Therefore I will boast all the more gladly about my weaknesses, so that Christ's power may rest on me."

Writing *Applied NSM* was nothing short of a testament to God's power being made perfect in weakness. This book was easily one of the most difficult projects I've ever taken on, and it was faith in Him that allowed me to persevere. Because of Him, this book and everything I do is possible, and I sincerely hope that my work here can serve as a witness to God's awesome power.

This book was made possible through the direct and indirect contributions of a great number of people. I'd like to take this opportunity to acknowledge them.

Ellen, you are my love, my support, my strength, and my biggest fan. None of this would be possible without you. I want to thank you for putting up with the stress, the despair, the crazy hours, and the overall madness that comes from the book writing process. I also want to thank you for helping to copyedit the book. I suppose that English major finally came in handy. I love you, and I'm so proud to be your husband.

Mom and Dad, I am the person I am because of your influence. Everything I do is, and will continue to be, a tribute to the character you both exhibit and the love you both shared. I love you, Dad. RIP, Mom.

Sanders Family, although we are a small group, the love shared between us is something that is immense, and is so important to me. Even though we are far apart, I know you love and support me and I'm thankful for that.

Perkins Family, The way you've welcomed me into your lives has been truly amazing, and I'm blessed to have your love and support.

Jason Smith, you are quite literally the smartest person I've ever had the pleasure of meeting. More than being a great co-worker and co-author, you've always proven to be a great friend. I don't hesitate to say that you've been like a brother to me. I'm eternally grateful for it all.

David Bianco and Liam Randall, I can't thank you enough for contributing to this book. Your contributions are valued more than you can imagine.

Regarding my coworkers (past and present), I've always believed that if a person surrounds himself with good people, he will become a better person. I have the good fortune of working with some great people who are some of the best and brightest in the business. I want to give special thanks to my InGuardians family: Jimmy, Jay, Suzanne, Teresa, John, Tom, Don, Rad, Larry, Jaime, James, Bob, and Alec. I want to extend special appreciation to Mike Poor, who wrote the foreword for this book and continues to be one of my packet ninja idols.

Syngress staff, thank you for allowing me the opportunity to write this book, and helping this dream become a reality.

The technical content and direction of this book is a product of more individuals than I could possibly name, but I'm going to try anyway. In addition to those listed above, I'd like to thank the following people for their contribution; whether it was reviewing a chapter or letting me bounce some ideas off of you, this wouldn't be possible without all of you:

Alexi Valencia, Ryan Clark, Joe Kadar, Stephen Reese, Tara Wink, Doug Burks, Richard Bejtlich, George Jones, Richard Friedberg, Geoffrey Sanders, Emily Sarneso, Mark Thomas, Daniel Ruef, the rest of the CERT NetSA team, Joel Esler, the Bro team, Mila Parkour, Dustin Weber, and Daniel Borkmann.

**Chris Sanders**

# About the Authors

## Chris Sanders, Lead Author

Chris Sanders is an information security consultant, author, and researcher originally from Mayfield, Kentucky. That's thirty miles southwest of a little town called Possum Trot, forty miles southeast of a hole in the wall named Monkey's Eyebrow, and just north of a bend in the road that really is named Podunk.

Chris is a Senior Security Analyst with InGuardians. He has extensive experience supporting multiple government and military agencies, as well as several Fortune 500 companies. In multiple roles with the US Department of Defense, Chris significantly helped to further the role of the Computer Network Defense Service Provider (CNDSP) model, and helped to create several NSM and intelligence tools currently being used to defend the interests of the nation.

Chris has authored several books and articles, including the international best seller "Practical Packet Analysis" form No Starch Press, currently in its second edition. Chris currently holds several industry certifications, including the SANS GSE and CISSP distinctions.

In 2008, Chris founded the Rural Technology Fund. The RTF is a 501(c)(3) non-profit organization designed to provide scholarship opportunities to students from rural areas pursuing careers in computer technology. The organization also promotes technology advocacy in rural areas through various support programs. The RTF has provided thousands of dollars in scholarships and support to rural students.

When Chris isn't buried knee-deep in packets, he enjoys watching University of Kentucky Wildcat basketball, being a BBQ Pitmaster, amateur drone building, and spending time at the beach. Chris currently resides in Charleston, South Carolina with his wife Ellen.

Chris blogs at http://www.appliednsm.com and http://www.chrissanders.org. He is on Twitter as @chrissanders88.

## Jason Smith, Co-Author

Jason Smith is an intrusion detection analyst by day and junkyard engineer by night. Originally from Bowling Green, Kentucky, Jason started his career mining large data sets and performing finite element analysis as a budding physicist. By dumb luck, his love for data mining led him to information security and network security monitoring, where he took up a fascination with data manipulation and automation.

Jason has a long history of assisting state and federal agencies with hardening their defensive perimeters and currently works as a Security Engineer with Mandiant. As part of his development work, he has created several open source projects, many of which have become "best-practice" tools for the DISA CNDSP program.

Jason regularly spends weekends in the garage building anything from arcade cabinets to open wheel racecars. Other hobbies include home automation, firearms, monopoly, playing guitar, and eating. Jason has a profound love of rural America, a passion for driving, and an unrelenting desire to learn. Jason is currently living in Frankfort, Kentucky.

Jason blogs at http://www.appliednsm.com. He is on Twitter as @automayt.

## David J. Bianco, Contributing Author

Before coming to work as a Hunt Team Lead at Mandiant, David spent five years helping to build an intelligence-driven detection and response program for a Fortune 5 company. There, he set detection strategies for a network of nearly 600 NSM sensors in over 160 countries and led response efforts for some of the company's most critical incidents, mainly involving targeted attacks. He stays active in the security community, blogging, speaking, and writing.

You can often find David at home watching Doctor Who, playing one of his four sets of bagpipes, or just goofing around with the kids. He enjoys long walks nearly anywhere except the beach.

David blogs at http://detect-respond.blogspot.com. He is on Twitter as @DavidJBianco.

## Liam Randall, Contributing Author

Liam Randall is the Managing Partner with San Francisco based Broala LLC- the Bro Core Teams consulting group. Originally, from Louisville, KY, he worked his way through school as a sysadmin while getting his Bachelors in Computer Science at Xavier University. He first got his start in security writing device drivers and XFS based software for Automated Teller Machines.

Presently he consults on high volume security solutions for the Fortune 50, Research and Education Networks, various branches of the armed service, and other security focused groups. He has spoken at Shmoocon, Derbycon, MIRcon and regularly teaches Bro training classes at security events.

A father and a husband, Liam spends his weekends fermenting wine, working in his garden, restoring gadgets, or making cheese. With a love of the outdoors, he and his wife like competing in triathlons, long distance swimming, and enjoying their community.

Liam blogs at http://liamrandall.com/. He is on Twitter as @Hectaman.

# Foreword

Learning how to build and operate a network security monitoring infrastructure is a daunting task. Chris Sanders and his team of authors have crafted a framework for NSM, and provide the reader with a codified plan to put network security monitoring into practice.

Medium and large organizations are being crushed by the amount of data they are collecting. With event counts exceeding 100 million events in some instances, having a monitoring infrastructure and standard operating procedures that can scale is critical.

Seek and ye shall find: the inverse is also true. It makes no sense to collect data, and potentially even do the detection, but skip on the analysis. This book you hold in your hands gives you the keys to each of the steps in the NSM cycle: collection, detection and analysis.

In the late 1930's, many civilian pilots argued for the right to use their skills in defense of their country. The time has come again for civilians to take a more active role in the defense of our nation. We are under attack; make no mistake. Manufacturing, chemical, oil and gas, energy, and many critical sectors of our civilian society are bearing the brunt of a coordinated and systematic series of attacks. While pundits ponder on the future possibility of cyber war, the practitioners on the front line are neck deep in it.

My call is not one to arms, but one to analysis. Got root? Then you must analyze your logs. Most cyber attacks leave traces, and it is up to each and every system operator to review their logs for signs of compromise. That said, the operator should be reviewing logs for the purpose of improving system performance and business analytics. Improving system performance alone can help provide a return on investment to the business, not to mention what business analytics can do in the right hands.

At InGuardians, we get called in to do incident response in cases of large data breaches. Most organizations currently log relevant data from core network devices, proxies, firewalls, systems and applications. That data is stored for an extended period of time, with no apparent ROI. In many cases we are able to identify current and previous breaches through log analysis alone.

The next time you are at your console, review some logs. You might think. . . "I don't know what to look for". Start with what you know, understand, and don't care about. Discard those. Everything else is of interest.

*Semper Vigilans,*
**Mike Poor**

# Preface

I love catching bad guys. Ever since I was a little kid, I wanted to catch bad guys in some fashion or another. Whether it was adorning a cape made from the nearest towel I could find or running around the house playing cops and robbers with my childhood friends, I lived for the thrill of serving justice to wrongdoers of all sorts. As hard as I tried however, I was never quite able to channel my rage into an ability that would allow me to grow into a giant green monster, and no matter how many spider bites I received I never developed the ability to shoot web from my wrists. I also realized pretty quickly that I wasn't quite cut out for law enforcement.

Once these realities set in and I realized that I was nowhere near rich enough to build a bunch of fancy gadgets and fly around at night in a bat suit, I ended up turning my attention to computers. Several years later, I've ended up in a position where I am able to live my childhood dreams of catching bad guys, but not in the sense that I had originally imagined.

I catch bad guys through the practice of network security monitoring (NSM). That's what this book is about. NSM is based upon the concept that prevention eventually fails. This means that no matter how much time you invest in securing your network, eventually the bad guys win. When this happens, you must be organizationally and technologically positioned to be able to detect and respond to the intruder's presence so that an incident may be declared and the intruder can be eradicated with minimal damage done.

*"How do I find bad stuff on the network?"*

The path to knowledge for the practice of NSM typically begins with that question. It's because of that question that I refer to NSM as a practice, and someone who is a paid professional in this field as a practitioner of NSM.

Scientists are often referred to as practitioners because of the evolving state of the science. As recently as the 1980s, medical science believed that milk was a valid treatment for ulcers. As time progressed, scientists found that ulcers were caused by bacteria called Helicobacter pylori and that dairy products could actually further aggravate an ulcer.[1] Perceived facts change because although we would like to believe most sciences are exact, they simply aren't. All scientific knowledge is based upon educated guesses utilizing the best available data at the time. As more data becomes available over time, answers to old questions change, and this redefines things that were once considered facts. This is true for doctors as practitioners of medical science, and it is true for us as practitioners of NSM.

Unfortunately, when I started practicing NSM there weren't a lot of reference materials available on the topic. Quite honestly, there still aren't. Aside from the occasionally bloggings of industry pioneers and a few select books, most

---

[1]Jay, C. (2008, November 03). *Why it's called the practice of medicine.* Retrieved from http://www.wellsphere.com/chronic-pain-article/why-it-s-called-the-practice-of-medicine/466361

individuals seeking to learn more about this field are left to their own devices. I feel that it is pertinent to clear up one important misconception to eliminate potential confusion regarding my previous statement. There are menageries of books available on the topics TCP/IP, packet analysis, and various intrusion detection systems (IDSs). Although the concepts presented in those texts are important facets of NSM, they don't constitute the practice of NSM as a whole. That would be like saying a book about wrenches teaches you how to diagnose a car that won't start.

This book is dedicated to the *practice* of NSM. This means that rather than simply providing an overview of the tools or individuals components of NSM, I will speak to the process of NSM and how those tools and individual components support the practice.

## AUDIENCE

Ultimately, this book is intended to be a guide on how to become a practicing NSM analyst. My day-to-day job responsibility includes the training of new analysts, so this book is not only to provide an education text for the masses, but also to provide a book that can serve as the supportive text of that training process. That being the case, my intent is that someone can read this book from cover to cover and have an introductory level grasp on the core concepts that make a good NSM analyst.

If you are already a practicing analyst, then my hope is that this book will provide a foundation that will allow you to grow your analytic technique to make you much more effective at the job you are already doing. I've worked with several good analysts who were able to become great analysts because they were able to enhance their effectiveness with some of the techniques and information I'll present here.

The effective practice of NSM requires a certain level of adeptness with a variety of tools. As such, the book will discuss several of these tools, but only from the standpoint of the analyst. When I discuss the Snort IDS, the SiLK analysis tool set, or other tools, those tasked with the installation and maintenance of those tools will find that I don't speak too thoroughly to those processes. When the time arises, I will reference other resources that will fill the gaps there.

Additionally, this book focuses entirely on free and open source tools. This is not only in effort to appeal to a larger group of individuals who may not have the budget to purchase commercial analytic tools such as NetWitness or Arcsight, but also to show the intrinsic benefit of using open source, analyst designed tools that provide more transparency in how they interact with data.

## PREREQUISITES

The most successful NSM analysts are usually those who have experience in other areas of information technology prior to starting security-related work. This is because they will have often picked up other skills that are important to an analyst, such as an understanding of systems or network administration. In lieu of this experience, I've created a brief listing of books I really enjoy that I think provide insight into some important skills useful to the analyst. I've tried my best to write this book so that a significant amount of perquisite knowledge isn't required, but if you have the means, I highly recommend reading some of these books in order to supplement information provided in Applied Network Security Monitoring.

*TCP/IP Illustrated, Vol 1, Second Edition: The Protocols* by Kevin Fall and Dr. Richard Stevens (Addison Wesley 2011)

A core understanding of TCP/IP is one of the more crucial skills required to practice NSM effectively. The classic text by the late Dr. Richard Stevens has been updated by Kevin Fall to include the latest protocols, standards, best practices, IPv6, security primers by protocol, and more.

*The Tao of Network Security Monitoring*, by Richard Bejtlich (Addison Wesley, 2004).

Richard Bejtlich helped to define a lot of the concepts that underlie the practice of NSM. As a matter of fact, I will reference his book and blog quite often throughout Applied NSM. Although Richard's book is nearly ten years old, a lot of the material in it continues to make it a relevant text in the scope of NSM.

*Practical Packet Analysis*, by Chris Sanders (No Starch Press, 2010).

I'm not above shameless self-promotion. Whereas Dr. Stevens book provides a thorough in-depth reference for TCP/IP, *PPA* discusses packet analysis at a practical level using Wireshark as a tool of choice. We will examine packets in this book, but if you've never looked at packets before then I recommend this as a primer.

*Counter Hack Reloaded*, by Ed Skoudis and Tom Liston (Prentice Hall, 2006).

I've always thought this book was one of the absolute best general security books available. It covers a bit of everything, and I recommend it to everyone regardless of their level of experience. If you've never done security-related work, then I'd say Counter Hack Reloaded is a must read.

## CONCEPTS AND APPROACH

Applied NSM is broken down into three primary sections: Collection, Detection, and Analysis. I will devote individual chapters to the discussion of tools, techniques, and procedures related to these core areas. I'm a simple country boy from Kentucky, so I try my best to write in a simple tone without a lot of added fluff. I also try to take typically advanced concepts and break them down into a series of repeatable steps whenever possible. As with any book that addresses generalized concepts, please keep in mind that when a concept is presented it will not cover every potential scenario or edge case. Although I may cite something as a best practice, this book ultimately constitutes theories based upon the collective research, experience, and opinions of its contributors. As such, it may be the case that your research, experience, and opinions lead you to a different conclusion regarding the topic being presented. That's perfectly fine; that's why NSM is a practice.

Chapter 1: The Practice of Applied Network Security Monitoring
The first chapter is devoted to defining network security monitoring and its relevance in the modern security landscape. It discusses a lot of the core terminology and assumptions that will be used and referenced throughout the book.

**Part 1: Collection**

Chapter 2: Planning Data Collection
The first chapter in the Collection section of ANSM is an introduction to data collection and an overview of its importance. This chapter will introduce the Applied Collection Framework, which is used for making decisions regarding what data should be collected using a risk-based approach.

Chapter 3: The Sensor Platform
This chapter introduces the most critical piece of hardware in an NSM deployment: the sensor. First, we will look at a brief overview of the various NSM data types, and the types of NSM sensors. This will lead us to discuss important considerations for purchasing and deploying sensors. Finally, we will cover the placement of NSM sensors on the network, including a primer on creating network visibility maps for analyst use.

Chapter 4: Session Data
This chapter discusses the importance of session data, along with a detailed overview of the SiLK toolset for the collection of NetFlow data. We will also briefly examine the Argus toolset for session data collection and parsing.

Chapter 5: Full Packet Capture Data
This chapter begins with an overview of the importance of full packet capture data. We will examine several tools that allow for full packet capture of PCAP data, including Netsniff-NG, Daemonlogger, and Dumpcap. This will lead to a discussion of different considerations for the planning of FPC data storage and maintenance of that data, including considerations for trimming down the amount of FPC data stored.

Chapter 6: Packet String Data
This chapter provides an introduction to packet string (PSTR) data and its usefulness in the NSM analytic process. We will look at several methods for generating PSTR data with tools like Httpry and Justniffer. We will also look at tools that can be used to parse and view PSTR data, including Logstash and Kibana.

**Part 2: Detection**

Chapter 7: Detection Mechanisms and Indicators of Compromise, and Signatures
This chapter examines the relationship between detection mechanisms and Indicators of Compromise (IOC). We will look at how IOCs can be logically organized, and how they can be effectively managed for incorporation into an NSM

program. This will include a system for classifying indicators, as well as metrics for calculating and tracking the precision of indicators that are deployed to various detection mechanisms. We will also look at two different formats for IOC's, OpenIOC and STIX.

Chapter 8: Reputation-Based Detection
The first specific type of detection that will be discussed is reputation-based detection. We will discuss the fundamental philosophy of reputation-based detection, along with several resources for examining the reputation of devices. This discussion will lean towards solutions that can automate this process, and will demonstrate how to accomplish this with simple BASH scripts, or by using Snort, Suricata, CIF, or Bro.

Chapter 9: Signature-Based Detection with Snort and Suricata
The most traditional form of intrusion detection is signature-based. This chapter will provide a primer on this type of detection and discuss the usage of the Snort and Suricata intrusion detection systems. This will include the usage of Snort and Suricata, and a detailed discussion on the creation of IDS signatures for both platforms.

Chapter 10: The Bro Platform
This chapter will cover Bro, one of the more popular anomaly-based detection solutions. It will review of the Bro architecture, the Bro language, and several practical cases that demonstrate the truly awesome power of Bro as an IDS and network logging engine.

Chapter 11: Anomaly-Based Detection with Statistical Data
This chapter will discuss the use of statistics for identifying anomalies on the network. This will focus on the use of various NetFlow tools like rwstats and rwcount. We will also discuss methods for visualizing statistics by using Gnuplot and the Google Charts API. This chapter will provide several practical examples of useful statistics that can be generated from NSM data.

Chapter 12: Using Canary Honeypots for Detection
Previously only used for research purposes, canary honeypots are a form of operational honeypot that can be used as an effective detection tool. This chapter will provide an overview of the different types of honeypots, and how certain types can be used in an NSM environment. We will look at several popular honeypot applications that can be used for this purpose, including Honeyd, Kippo, and Tom's Honeypot. We will also briefly discuss the concept of Honeydocs.

**Part 3: Analysis**

Chapter 13: Packet Analysis
The most critical skill an NSM analyst can have is the ability to interpret and decipher packet data that represents network communication. To do this effectively requires a fundamental understanding of how packets are dissected.

This chapter provides that fundamental backing and shows how to break down packet fields on a byte by byte basis. We demonstrate these concepts using tcpdump and Wireshark. This chapter will also cover basic to advanced packet filtering techniques using Berkeley Packet Filters and Wireshark Display Filters.

Chapter 14: Friendly and Threat Intelligence
The ability to generate intelligence related to friendly and hostile systems can make or break an investigation. This chapter begins with an introduction to the traditional intelligence cycle and how it relates to NSM analysis intelligence. Following this, we look at methods for generating friendly intelligence by generating asset data from network scan and leveraging PRADS data. Finally, we examine the types of threat intelligence and discuss some basic methods for researching tactical threat intelligence related to hostile hosts.

Chapter 15: The Analysis Process
The final chapter discusses the analysis process as a whole. This begins with a discussion of the analysis process, and then breaks down into examples of two different analysis processes; relational investigation and differential diagnosis. Following this, the lessons learned process of incident morbidity and mortality is discussed. Finally, we will look at several analysis best practices to conclude the book.

# IP ADDRESS DISCLAIMER

Throughout this book, several examples are provided where IP addresses are mentioned, in both raw data and in screenshots. In most every case, and unless otherwise specified, these IP addresses were randomized using various tools. Because of this, any reference to any public IP address belonging to an organization is purely coincidental, and by no means represents actual traffic generated by those entities.

# COMPANION WEBSITE

There were quite a few things we wanted to include in this book that we simply weren't able to fit in or find a place for. As a result, we created a companion website that contains all kinds of additional thoughts on various NSM topics, along with code snippets and other tips and tricks. If you like what you read in the coming chapters, then consider checking out the companion website at http://www.appliednsm. com. While it wasn't updated too much during the production of the book, we plan to provide regular contributions to this blog after the book's release. Any errata for the book will also be located here.

# CHARITABLE SUPPORT

We are incredibly proud to donate 100% of the author royalties from this book to support five unique charitable causes.

## Rural Technology Fund

Rural students, even those with excellent grades, often have fewer opportunities for exposure to technology than their urban or suburban counterparts. In 2008, Chris Sanders founded the Rural Technology Fund. The RTF seeks to reduce the digital divide between rural communities and their urban and suburban counterparts. This is done through targeted scholarship programs, community involvement, and the general promotion and advocacy of technology in rural areas.

Our scholarships are targeted at students living in rural communities who have a passion for computer technology and intend to pursue further education in that field. A portion of the royalties from this book will go to support these scholarship programs, and to provide Raspberry Pi computers to rural schools.

More Info: http://www.ruraltechfund.org

## Hackers for Charity

Established by Johnny Long, HFC employs volunteer hackers (no questions asked) and engages their skills in short "microprojects" designed to help charities that cannot afford traditional technical resources. In addition to this, HFC is also on the ground in Uganda, East Africa to support aid organizations working to help some of the world's poorest citizens. They provide free computer training, technical support, networking services, and more. They have supported many local schools with the addition of computers and training software. In addition, HFC also provides food to East African children through their food program.

More Info: http://www.hackersforcharity.org

## Kiva

Kiva is the first online lending platform that allows people to donate money directly to people in developing countries through multiple field companies. Kiva includes personal stories of each person who requests a loan so that donors can connect with those individuals. Simply put, Kiva facilitates loans that change lives. Funds donated from the sale of Applied NSM will go to provide these loans.

More Info: http://www.kiva.org

## Hope for the Warriors®

The mission of Hope For The Warriors® is to enhance the quality of life for post-9/11 service members, their families, and families of the fallen who have sustained physical and psychological wounds in the line of duty. Hope For The Warriors® is dedicated to restoring a sense of self, restoring the family unit, and restoring hope for our service members and our military families.

More Info: http://www.hopeforthewarriors.org

## Autism Speaks

Autism is a very complex condition characterized in varying degrees by difficulties in social interaction, communication, and repetitive behaviors. The U.S. Centers for Disease Control Estimate that 1 in 88 American children have some form of autism.

Autism Speaks is an organization dedicated to changing the future for all who struggle with autism spectrum disorders. They accomplish this through funding biomedical research related to the causes, prevention, treatment, and cure of autism. Autism Speaks also provides autism advocacy and support for families of autistic individuals.

More Info: http://autismspeaks.org

## CONTACTING US

My contributing authors and I put a lot of time and effort into our work, so we are always excited to hear from people who have read our writing and want to share their thoughts. If you would like to contact us for any reason, you can send all questions, comments, threats, and marriage proposals directly to us at the following locations:

Chris Sanders, Lead Author
E-mail: chris@chrissanders.org
Blog: http://www.chrissanders.org; http://www.appliednsm.com
Twitter: @chrissanders88

Jason Smith, Co-Author
E-mail: jason.smith.webmail@gmail.com
Blog: http://www.appliednsm.com
Twitter: @automayt

David J. Bianco, Contributing Author and Tech Editor
E-mail: davidjbianco@gmail.com
Blog: http://detect-respond.blogspot.com/; http://www.appliednsm.com
Twitter: @davidjbianco

Liam Randall, Technical Contributor
E-mail: liam@bro.org
Blog: http://liamrandall.com; http://www.appliednsm.com
Twitter: @liamrandall

# The Practice of Applied Network Security Monitoring

# 1

## CHAPTER CONTENTS

The current state of security for Internet-connected systems makes me think of the Wild West. The West represented a lot of things to Americans at that time. As a mostly untapped resource, the west was seen a vast undiscovered land of opportunity. As more and more people journeyed west, small communities were established and individuals and families alike were able to prosper. With this prosperity and success, inevitably there came crime. Towns were dispersed and law was exclusively localized, allowing rogue groups of desperados to roam from town to town, robbing and pillaging local resources. The lack of coordination and communication between "the law" in these towns meant that the desperados rarely got caught unless they happened to be gunned down by a local sheriff.

Fast-forward to the modern era and the picture isn't painted too differently. The Internet represents a similar land of untapped opportunity where someone is only a domain name and a little elbow grease away from achieving the American dream. Just like the West however, the Internet is not without its own group of desperados. Whereas the West had bank robbers and hijackers, we now contend with botnet masters and click jackers. We are also currently suffering from similar problems with localized law enforcement. The threat we face is global, yet every country, and in some cases individual states, operate within their own disparate set of laws.

In the West, the crux of the issue was that the criminals were organized and law enforcement wasn't. Although the computer security field has improved drastically over the past ten years; on a global scale, defenders are still playing catch up to the groups who are able to operate global criminal networks. Unfortunately, this isn't something that is fixable overnight, if ever.

This reality puts the focus on the individuals in the trenches to do whatever is possible to defend computer networks and the data contained within them from these criminals. It is my belief that the most effective way to do this is through the practice of Network Security Monitoring (NSM).

NSM is the collection, detection, and analysis of network security data. Information security has traditionally been divided into many different focus areas, but I tend to lean most towards the way the United States Department of Defense (US DoD) categorizes the domains of Computer Network Defense (CND) per DoD 8500.2.[1] These are:

*Protect.* The protect domain focuses on securing systems to prevent exploitation and intrusion from occurring. Some of the functions that typically occur within this

---

[1]US Department of Defense Instruction 8500.2, Information Assurance (IA) Implementation (6 February 2003) - http://www.dtic.mil/whs/directives/corres/pdf/850002p.pdf.

domain include vulnerability assessment, risk assessment, anti-malware management, user awareness training, and other general information assurance tasks.

*Detect.* This domain centers on detecting compromises that are actively occurring or have previously occurred. This includes network security monitoring and attack sense and warning.

*Respond.* The third domain focuses on the response after a compromise has occurred. This includes incident containment, network and host-based forensics, malware analysis, and incident reporting.

*Sustain.* The final CND domain deals with the management of the people, processes, and technology associated with CND. This includes contracting, staffing and training, technology development and implementation, and support systems management.

As you may have guessed, this book deals primarily in the Detect domain, but if done correctly, the benefits of proper NSM will extend to all domains of CND.

## KEY NSM TERMS

Before diving in, there are several terms that must be defined due to their extensive use throughout this book. With NSM and network security being a relatively new science, it's hard to find common, discrete definitions for a lot of these terms. The sources I've chosen most closely align with US DoD documentation, CISSP certification literature, and other NSM text. They have been mostly paraphrased, and directly quoted and cited as appropriate.

### Asset

An asset is anything within your organization that has value. At an easily quantifiable level, this may include computers, servers, and networking equipment. Beyond this, assets will also include data, people, processes, intellectual property, and reputation.

When I refer to an "asset" I will generally be referring to something within the scope of your trusted network. This may also include networks that are separate from yours, but still considered trusted (think of government allies, subsidiary organizations, or supply chain partners). I will use the terms asset, good guy, target, victim, and friendly interchangeably.

### Threat

A threat is a party with the capabilities and intentions to exploit a vulnerability in an asset. A threat is relative, as a threat to a civilian might be different than a threat to a large corporation. Furthermore, a threat to an emerging nation might be different than that of a global superpower.

Threats can primarily be classified in two categories: structured and unstructured.

A structured threat utilizes formal tactics and procedures and has clearly defined objectives. This often includes organized criminals, hacktivist groups, government intelligence agencies, and militaries. These are typically groups of individuals; although, it's not unheard of for a single individual to represent an structured threat. A structured threat almost always pursues targets of choice, chosen for a specific reason or goal.

An unstructured threat lacks the motivation, skill, strategy, or experience of a structured threat. Individuals or small loosely organized groups most often represent this type of threat. Unstructured threats typically pursue targets of opportunity, which are selected because they appear easily vulnerable.

Regardless of the scope or nature of the threat, they all have something in common: they want to steal something from you. This can be stolen money, intellectual property, reputation, or simply time.

I will use the terms threat, bad guy, adversary, attacker, and hostile interchangeably.

## Vulnerability

A vulnerability is a software, hardware, or procedural weakness that may provide an attacker the ability to gain unauthorized access to a network asset.

This might take the form of improperly written code that allows for exploitation via a buffer overflow attack, an active network port in a public area that presents the opportunity for physical network access, or even an improperly devised authentication system that allows an attacker to guess an victim's username. Keep in mind that a human can also be considered a vulnerability.

## Exploit

An exploit is the method by which a vulnerability is attacked. In the case of software exploitation, this may take the form of a piece of exploit code that contains a payload that allows the attacker to perform some type of action on the system remotely, such as spawning a command shell. In a web application, a vulnerability in the way the application processes input and output may allow an attacker to exploit the application with SQL injection. In another scenario, an attacker breaking into an office building by tailgating off of another user's access card swipe would be considered an exploit.

## Risk

The study of risk management is extensive, and as such there are several different definitions for risk. In relation to NSM, I think the most appropriate definition of risk is the measurement of the possibility that a threat will exploit a vulnerability. Although most managers desire some quantifiable metric, often times quantifying risk is a fruitless endeavor because of the intrinsic difficulty in placing a value on network and data assets.

I will frequently discuss things that may add or decrease the level of a risk to an asset, but I won't be speaking in depth on calculations for quantifying risk beyond what is necessary for defining a collection strategy.

## Anomaly

An anomaly is an observable occurrence in a system or network that is considered out of the ordinary. Anomalies generate alerts by detection tools such as an intrusion detection systems or log review applications. An anomaly may include a system crash, malformed packets, unusual contact with an unknown host, or a large amount of data being transferred over a short period of time.

## Incident

When an event is investigated, it may be reclassified as part of an incident. An incident is a violation or imminent threat of violation of computer security policies, acceptable use policies, or standard security practices[2]. More simply stated, an incident means that something bad has happened, or is currently happening on your network. This might include the root-level compromise of a computer, a simple malware installation, a denial of service attack, or the successful execution of malicious code from a phishing e-mail. Keep in mind that all incidents include one or more events, but most events will not directly represent an incident.

## INTRUSION DETECTION

Prior to the coining of the term NSM, the detect domain was typically described simply as Intrusion Detection. Although NSM has been around for nearly ten years, these terms are often used interchangeably. These are not synonyms, but rather, intrusion detection is a component of modern NSM.

The detect domain built solely around the old paradigm of intrusion detection often had a few distinct characteristics:

*Vulnerability-Centric Defense.* The most common model of the computer network attacker breaking into a network is by exploiting a software vulnerability. Since this model is so simple and clear cut, it's what most early intrusion detection programs were built around. The intrusion detection system (IDS) is deployed with the goal of detecting the exploitation of these vulnerabilities.

*Detection in Favor of Collection.* The majority of effort placed on this domain lies within detection. While data collection was occurring, it was often unfocused and collection strategies weren't tied to detection goals. A lack of focus on collection often fostered the mindset "too much data is always better than not enough" and "capture everything and sort it out later".

*Mostly Signature-Based.* The exploitation of a software vulnerability is often a fairly static action that can be developed into an IDS signature rather easily. As such, traditional intrusion detection relied on having knowledge of all known vulnerabilities and developing signatures for their detection.

*Attempts to Fully Automate Analysis.* The simplistic vulnerability-centric intrusion detection model lends itself to the belief that most IDS generated alerts can be trusted with reasonably high confidence. As such, this paradigm often relies on little involvement by human analysts, and attempts to automate post-detection analysis as much as possible.

While moderately successful in its time, the current state of security has led us to a point where traditional intrusion detection isn't effective. The primary reason for this is the failure of the vulnerability-centric defense.

Bejtlich provides one of the better explanations for this.[2] Consider a scenario where several houses in a neighborhood experience break-ins. When this happens, the police could respond by putting up barbed wire fences around the other houses in the neighborhood. They could also install large steel doors on all of the houses or put bars on all of the windows. This would be considered a vulnerability-centric approach. It's not surprising that you don't often hear of law enforcement doing such things. That's because the criminals will simply find other vulnerabilities in the houses to exploit if they are determined and are targeting that specific neighborhood.

## NETWORK SECURITY MONITORING

NSM has advanced in large part thanks to the military, which has traditionally been one of the biggest proponents of this defensive mindset. That's no real surprise given the military's extensive use of information technology, the critical importance of their operations, and the high confidentiality of the data they generate.

United States Information Operations (IO) doctrine[3] mentions that a commander's IO capabilities should be used to accomplish the following:

- Destroy: To damage a system or entity so badly that it cannot perform any function or be restored to a usable condition without being entirely rebuilt.
- Disrupt: To break or interrupt the flow of information.
- Degrade: To reduce the effectiveness or efficiency of adversary command, control, or communication systems, and information collection efforts or means. IO can also degrade the morale of a unit, reduce the target's worth or value, or reduce the quality of adversary decisions and actions.
- Deny: To prevent the adversary from accessing and using critical information, systems, and services.
- Deceive: To cause a person to believe that which is not true. Seeking to mislead adversary decision makers by manipulating their perception of reality.
- Exploit: To gain access to adversary command and control systems to collect information or to plant false or misleading information.
- Influence: To cause others to behave in a manner favorable to friendly forces.

---

[2] Bejtlich, Richard, TaoSecurity Blog, "Real Security is Threat Centric" (Nov 2009). http://taosecurity. blogspot.com/2009/11/real-security-is-threat-centric.html
[3] United States Department of Defense Joint Publication 3-13, "Information Operations" (13 February 2006). http://www.carlisle.army.mil/DIME/documents/jp3_13.pdf

- Protect: To take action to guard against espionage or capture of sensitive equipment and information.
- Detect: To discover or discern the existence, presence, or fact of an intrusion into information systems.
- Restore: To bring information and information systems back to their original state.
- Respond: To react quickly to an adversary's or others' IO attack or intrusion.

Many of these goals are interconnected. The majority of NSM is dedicated to Detect in an effort to better Respond. On occasion, this may include elements of other areas. In this book, we will touch on deception and degradation to some extent when we talk about honeypots.

The detect portion of this IO doctrine also lines up with the US DoD definition of Attack Sense and Warning (AS&W).[4] AS&W is the detection, correlation, identification and characterization of intentional unauthorized activity, including computer intrusion or attack, across a large spectrum coupled with the notification to command and decision-makers so that an appropriate response can be developed. AS&W also includes attack/intrusion related intelligence collection tasking and dissemination; limited immediate response recommendations; and limited potential impact assessments.

NSM is considered the new paradigm for the detect domain and has its own set of characteristics that are drastically different than traditional intrusion detection:

*Prevention Eventually Fails.* One of the hardest realities for an individual with the defender's mindset to accept is that they will eventually lose. No matter how strong your defenses are or what proactive steps have been taken, eventually a motivated attacker will find a way to get in.

Beyond information security, the reality is that the defender will always be playing catch-up. When the defender builds a stronger bunker, the attacker builds a bigger bomb. When the defender starts using a bulletproof vest, the attacker starts using armor-piercing bullets. It should be no surprise that when a defender deploys enterprise grade firewalls or ensures that his servers are fully patched, the attacker will utilize social engineering attacks to gain a foothold onto the network or utilize a zero-day exploit to gain root access to your patched server.

Once someone accepts that they will eventually be compromised, they can shift their mindset to one that doesn't solely rely on prevention, but rather, puts an additional focus on detection and response. In doing this, when the big compromise happens, your organization is positioned to respond effectively and stop the bleeding.

*Focus on Collection.* The previous mindset where all data sources that are available were collected and thrown into a central repository has resulted in deployments that are incredibly cost ineffective to manage. Not only that, but they don't provide

---

[4] United Stated Department of Defense Directive O-8530.1, "Computer Network Defense (CND)" (8 January 2001). http://www.doncio.navy.mil/uploads/0623IYM47223.pdf

any real value because the right types of data aren't available and the detection tools can't scale with the amount of data they are forced to contend with.

If an ounce of prevention is worth a pound of cure, then I wouldn't hesitate to say that an ounce of collection is worth a pound of detection. In order to perform any type of detection or analysis, you must have data to parse. If you can perform the same level of detection with less data, then you are saving CPU cycles and being more efficient. Furthermore, if you can provide the human analyst with only the data they need, they can make sound decisions much faster, which can make the difference in a small compromise or a full on data breach.

*Cyclical Process.* Old paradigm intrusion detection is a linear process. You receive an alert, you validate the alert, you respond as necessary, and then you are done. This linear process is both naive and irresponsible. Placing every network security incident in a vacuum does not serve the purpose of defending the network. Although some compromises do take place in a matter of seconds, skilled attackers are often slow and methodical, sometimes taking months to manifest the goals of their attack.

In order to move away from this vacuum approach, it is necessary that the process of detecting and responding to intrusion be cyclical. That means that collection should feed detection, detection should feed analysis, and analysis should feed back into collection. This allows the defender to build intelligence over time that may be used to better serve the defense of the network.

*Threat-Centric Defense.* All of the characteristics I've discussed thus far have led to the concept of threat-centric defense. Whereas vulnerability-centric defense focuses on the "how", threat-centric defense focuses on the "who" and "why". Specifically, you must ask yourself who would be interested in attacking your network, and why would they stand to gain from such an action?

Threat-centric defense is a much harder to perform than its predecessor. This is because it requires two things: extensive visibility into your network, and the ability to collect and analyze intelligence related to the intent and capability of attackers. The former of these is incredibly easy to accomplish for just about any organization with a proper time investment. The latter is much harder when you are operating in any industry other than the federal government, but it is certainly not impossible.

Consider the scenario we discussed previously of robberies in a neighborhood. Instead of a vulnerability-centric approach that may involve additional prevention mechanisms such as barbed wire fences and steel doors, in a threat-centric approach, the police closely examine the houses that were broken into. They look for similarities, or indicators that are common amongst the break-ins, to include a determination of the attacker's perceived goals. With this intelligence, the police can build a profile of the criminals. Combining this intelligence into something resembling a threat profile, law enforcement can then check prior arrest records to see if they can locate criminals who have used similar tactics in the past. This type of analysis combined with other forms of attribution can ultimately lead to the arrest of the criminal, preventing further break-ins. This approach is the essence of threat-centric defense and NSM.

## VULNERABILITY-CENTRIC VS. THREAT-CENTRIC DEFENSE

Consider a hockey match where your goal is defended by either a brick wall or a goalie. Initially, the brick wall might seem like the best option. Someone who thinks vulnerability-centric prefers a brick wall. The brick wall seems solid at first because it protects most of the goal and the attacker can only get in if they break through it. Over time however, shots do break through the brick wall. Eventually, entire bricks might get knocked out. Sure, you can replace the bricks, but while you are replacing one brick, another might get knocked loose.

Someone who thinks threat-centric prefers to have a goalie backing them up. Sure, it's very important that the goalie stops all of the shots. However, when the occasional shot does beat the goalie, the goalie will notice that the shot was low and on the stick side. The next time the goalie encounters the same shooter, you better believe that they will be keeping an eye on the low stick side and will be a lot less likely to allow that to happen again.

The key difference is that the brick wall never changes its tactics and never learns. The goalie, on the other hand, learns the habits of a particular shooter. The goalie learns, the goalie adapts, and the goalie thrives.

Although vulnerability-centric defense and threat-centric defense both seek to defend the network, they attempt it in different ways. Table 1.1 outlines the differences I've just discussed.

**Table 1.1** Vulnerability-Centric vs. Threat-Centric Defense

| Vulnerability Centric | Threat Centric |
| --- | --- |
| Relies on prevention | Knows that prevention eventually fails |
| Focus on detection | Focus on collection |
| Assumes universal view of all threats | Knows that threats use different tools, tactics, and procedures |
| Analyzes every attack in a vacuum | Combines intelligence from every attack |
| Heavy reliance on signature-based detection | Utilizes all-source data |
| Minimal ability to detect unknown threats | Stronger ability to detect adversarial activities beyond known signatures |
| Linear process | Cyclical process |

## THE NSM CYCLE: COLLECTION, DETECTION, AND ANALYSIS

The NSM Cycle consists of three distinct phases: Collection, Detection, and Analysis. This book is organized into three sections for each of these phases (Figure 1.1).

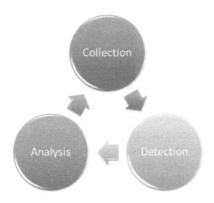

**FIGURE 1.1**

The NSM Cycle

## Collection

The NSM cycle begins with its most important step, collection. Collection occurs with a combination of hardware and software that are used to generate, organize, and store data for NSM detection and analysis. Collection is the most important part of this cycle because the steps taken here shape an organization's ability to perform effective detection and analysis.

There are several types of NSM data and several ways it can be collected. The most common categories of NSM data include Full Content Data, Session Data, Statistical Data, Packet String Data, and Alert Data. Depending on organizational needs, network architecture, and available resources, these data types may be used primarily for detection, exclusively for analysis, or for both.

Initially, collection can be one of the more labor-intensive parts of the NSM cycle due to the amount of human resources required. Effective collection requires a concerted effort from organizational leadership, the information security team, and network and systems administration groups.

Collection includes tasks such as:

- Defining where the largest amount of risk exists in the organization
- Identifying threats to organizational goals
- Identifying relevant data sources
- Refining collection portions of data sources
- Configuring SPAN ports to collect packet data
- Building SAN storage for log retention
- Configuring data collection hardware and software

## Detection

Detection is the process by which collected data is examined and alerts are generated based upon observed events and data that are unexpected. This is typically done through some form of signature, anomaly, or statistically based detection. This results in the generation of alert data.

Detection is most often a function of software, with some of the more popular software packages being the Snort IDS and Bro IDS from a network intrusion detection system (NIDS) perspective, and OSSEC, AIDE or McAfee HIPS from a host intrusion detection system (HIDS) perspective. Some Security Information and Event Management (SIEM) applications will utilize both network and host-based data to do detection based upon correlated events.

Although the bulk of detection is done by software, some detection does occur by manual analysis of data sources. This is especially the case with retrospective analysis.

## Analysis

Analysis is the final stage of the NSM cycle, and it occurs when a human interprets and investigates alert data. This will often involve gathering additional investigative data from other data sources, researching open source intelligence (OSINT) related to the type of alert generated by the detection mechanism, and performing OSINT research related to any potentially hostile hosts.

There are multitudes of ways that analysis can be performed, but this may include tasks such as:

- Packet analysis
- Network forensics
- Host forensics
- Malware analysis

Analysis is the most time consuming portion of the NSM cycle. At this point an event may be formally escalated to the classification of an incident, wherein incident response measures can begin.

The loop on the NSM Cycle is closed by taking the lessons learned from the detection and analysis phase for any given anomaly and further shaping the collection strategy of the organization.

## CHALLENGES TO NSM

As with any paradigm shift, the introduction of NSM and threat-centric security has been met with a fair share of challenges. The primary issue is that NSM is an immature science in itself, and it exists within another immature science that is information technology as a whole. While some effort has been put forth to standardize various nomenclature and protocols, there is still a wide disparity in what is written and what is actually implemented. This is evident in the operating systems we use, the applications that run on them, and the protocols they talk to each other with.

Focusing on information security specifically, a conversation about the same topic with three different people may use three different sets of nomenclature. This is incredibly limiting from a training perspective. One of the reasons the medical field is so successful in training of new physicians is that regardless of what medical school someone graduates from, they all (in theory) have the same baseline level of knowledge prior to entering residency. Further, based upon standardization of residency program requirements and medical board testing, all resident physicians are expected to maintain a similar level of competency in order to practice medicine as an attending physician. This is all based upon acceptance of common theory, practice, and requirements. The fact that NSM lacks this regulation means that we have a group of practitioners that often speak on different wavelengths. Furthermore, although these practitioners are saying the same thing, they are often speaking different languages. Again, medicine has a few thousand years of a jump start on NSM, so it's something that we have and will continue to make great strides in, but for now, it's a problem that won't likely be going away soon.

Another issue plaguing NSM is the amount of skill required to practice effectively. Simply put, there aren't enough people with the experience and knowledge required to meet demand. In a struggling economy where a large number of people are having difficulty finding employment, it is staggering to see the large number of jobs available for someone with NSM or other similar skills. Although NSM can certainly be an entry-level security job, it requires experience to be done at a senior level in order to guide junior staff members. These mid to senior level staffers are quite hard to keep employed as they often end up in higher paying consulting roles, or migrating to some sort of management position.

A final issue worth mentioning as a large challenge to the advancement of NSM is the cost required to establish and maintain an NSM program. Although this high cost of entry is usually associated with the hardware required to collect and parse the amount of data generated from NSM functions, the bulk of the cost is commonly a result of the workforce required to do the analysis portion of NSM, and to support the NSM infrastructure used by the analysts. This is compounded for larger organizations that require $24 \times 7 \times 365$ NSM. Unfortunately, another cost point is added for organizations that require the use of commercial SIEM software. Although these packages aren't always necessary, when they are deemed an organizational "must" they can often be accompanied with six to seven figure price tags.

## DEFINING THE ANALYST

The biggest defining characteristic of an NSM program is the human analyst. The analyst is the individual who interprets alert data, analyzes and investigates that data along with related data, and determines whether the event is a false positive or requires further investigation. Depending on the size and structure of the organization, an analyst may also take part in the incident response process or perform other tasks such as host-based forensics or malware analysis.

The human analyst is the crux of the organization. It is the analyst who is poring through packet captures looking for a single bit that's out of place. This same analyst is expected to be up to date on all of the latest tools, tactics, and procedures that the adversary may use. The simple fact is that the security of your network depends on the human analysts' ability to do their job effectively.

## Critical Skills

There are several important skills that an analyst should have. I generally define baseline knowledge that is good for all analysts to possess, and then define areas of specialization that will set an analyst apart. In an ideal world, an analyst would have two or three areas of specialization, but practically when I've managed teams I ask for them to have at least one.

### Baseline Skills
- Threat-Centric Security, NSM, and the NSM Cycle
- TCP/IP Protocols
- Common Application Layer Protocols
- Packet Analysis
- Windows Architecture
- Linux Architecture
- Basic Data Parsing (BASH, Grep, SED, AWK, etc)
- IDS Usage (Snort, Suricata, etc.)
- Indicators of Compromise and IDS Signature Tuning
- Open Source Intelligence Gathering
- Basic Analytic Diagnostic Methods
- Basic Malware Analysis

### Specializations

There are several specializations that an analyst might possess. Some of these include:

*Offensive Tactics.* This specialty generally focuses on penetration testing and security assessments. Analysts specializing in this area will attempt to gain access to attack the network in the same way an adversary would. These types of exercises are crucial for identifying weaknesses in the way other analysts perform their duties. In addition, analysts who are knowledgeable in offensive tactics are typically better equipped to recognize certain attacker activity when performing NSM analysis. Specific knowledge and skills useful to the offensive tactics specialty include network reconnaissance, software and service exploitation, backdoors, malware usage, and data exfiltration techniques.

*Defensive Tactics.* The defensive tactician is the master of detection and analysis. This specialty usually involves the analyst conceptualizing new development tools and analytic methods. This analyst will also be counted on to keep abreast of new tools and research related to network defense, and to evaluate those tools for use within the organization's NSM program. Specific knowledge and skills useful to the defensive tactics specialty include a more detailed knowledge of network communication, extensive knowledge of IDS operation and mechanics, IDS signatures, and statistical detection.

*Programming.* Being able to write code is a useful ability in almost any facet of information technology, especially in information security and NSM. An analyst who is proficient in programming will be able to develop custom detection and analysis solutions for an NSM team. Additionally, this person will often be very good at parsing large data sets. Generally, someone who chooses to specialize in programming for the purposes of NSM should have a very strong understanding of the Linux BASH environment. Once they have done this, they should become well versed in an interpreted language such as Python or PERL, a web language such as PHP or Java, and eventually, a compiled language such a C or C++.

*Systems Administration.* Although systems administration itself is a more general skill, it is possible to specialize in systems administration as it relates to NSM. Analysts with this specialty are heavily involved with collection processes such as configuring IDS and moving data around so that it may be properly ingested by various detection software packages. An analyst may also perform sensor hardening and the development of friendly host intelligence collection. An in-depth knowledge of both Windows and Linux platforms is the basis for the specialization, along with an adept understanding of data and log collection.

*Malware Analysis.* Performing NSM will frequently result in the collection of known and suspected malware samples. It should be expected that any analyst could do basic malware sandboxing in order to extract indicators, but if an organization ever detects the use of targeted malware, it is immensely valuable to have someone with the ability to perform a higher level of malware analysis. This includes knowledge of both dynamic and static analysis.

*Host-Based Forensics.* An individual specializing in host-based forensics gains intelligence from an asset that has been compromised by doing a forensic analysis of the host. This intelligence can then be used to refine the collection processes within the organization. This knowledge can also be used to evaluate and implement new host-based detection mechanisms, and to generate new indicators of compromise based upon the analysis of host-based artifacts. Useful skills in this specialty include hard drive and file system forensics, memory forensics, and incident time line creation.

## Classifying Analysts

Generally, I've seen most organizations classify analysts as either junior or senior level based upon their years of experience. I prefer a more discrete method of classifying analysts based upon three levels of ability. This is useful for hiring and scheduling, as well as providing analysts achievable goals to advance their careers. This type of model doesn't necessarily fit within every organization, but it provides a good starting point.

### Level One (L1) Analyst

The entry-level analyst is considered to be at L1. This analyst possesses a reasonable grasp on several of the baseline skills listed previously, but will likely not have settled into any particular specialization. A typical L1 will spend the majority of their time reviewing IDS alerts and performing analysis based upon their findings. The biggest factor that can contribute to the success of an L1 is getting more experience under their belt. The more protocols, packets, and events that are seen, the better an analyst is equipped to handle the next event that comes down the wire. This can be related to the career advancement of a surgeon, who becomes better with every surgery they perform. In most organizations, the majority of analysts fall within the L1 classification.

### Level Two (L2) Analyst

The L2 analyst is one who has a solid grasp of the majority of the baseline skills. Usually, this analyst has selected at least one specialization and has begun to spend time outside of normal event review and investigation trying to enhance their skills in that area. The L2 serves as a mentor to the L1, and will begin to identify 'best practices' within the scope of an organization's NSM program. The L2 will become increasingly involved with helping to shape the detection processes within the team by creating signatures based upon other network events or OSINT research. The L2 analyst also develops the ability to look through various data sources manually to attempt to find potential events instead of solely relying upon automated detection tools.

### Level Three (L3) Analyst

The level three (L3) analyst is the most senior analyst within an organization. These analysts are adept at all of the baseline skills and at least one specialty. They are the thought leaders within the organization and rather than spending their time reviewing events, they are primarily tasked with mentoring other analysts, developing and providing training, and providing guidance on complex investigations. The L3 analyst is also primarily responsible for helping to develop and enhance the organization's collection and detection capabilities, which may include conceptualizing or developing new tools, as well as evaluating existing tools.

## Measuring Success

Measuring the success or failure of an NSM program is often handled incorrectly by most organizations. If a compromise occurs, senior management views this as a critical failure of their security team as a whole. Under a vulnerability-centric model where prevention is relied upon fully, this might be an appropriate thought pattern. However, once an organization accepts that prevention eventually fails, they should also expect compromises to occur. Once this mindset becomes prevalent, you should not measure the effectiveness of an NSM program by whether a compromise occurs, but rather, how effectively it is detected, analyzed, and escalated. In the scope of an intrusion, NSM is ultimately responsible for everything that occurs from detection to escalation, with the goal of geting the appropriate information to incident responders as quickly as possible once it is determined that an incident has occurred. Of course, in anything but larger organizations the NSM team may also be the incident response team, but the functions are still logically separate. Ultimately, instead of asking "why did this happen?", the questions leadership should be asking your NSM team after a compromise are, "how quickly were we able to detect it, how quickly were we able to escalate it to response, and how we can adjust our NSM posture to be better prepared next time?"

Most readers of this book will be analysts rather than managers, but I've included this section so that its contents may be shared with management, and in the hopes that readers may one day be in a position to impact some of these changes.

The most important part of an NSM program, and the people who will ultimately be responsible for answering these questions, are the human analysts. I've had the privilege to work with and observe several security teams from organizations of all sizes, and I've seen several good programs and several bad programs. There are a lot of ways to create a great NSM team, but all of the organizations that I've witnessed failing at providing effective security through NSM have one thing in common: they fail to recognize that the human analyst is the most important facet of the mission.

Rather than investing in and empowering the analysts, these organizations invest in expensive software packages or unnecessary automation. Two years down the road when a large compromise happens, the stakeholders who made these decisions are left wondering why their SIEM solution and its seven figure price tag didn't catch a compromise that started six months prior.

Worse yet, these organizations will scrimp on staffing until they only utilize entry-level staff without the required experience or background to perform the task at hand. Although some entry-level staffers are expected, a lack of experienced technical leadership means that your junior level analysts won't have an opportunity to grow their expertise. These are often the same organizations that refuse to provide adequate training budgets, whether this is financial budgeting or time budgeting.

There are several common traits amongst successful NSM teams:

### Create a Culture of Learning

NSM thrives on ingenuity and innovation, which are the products of motivation and education. It is one thing to occasionally encourage education with periodic training opportunities, but it is a completely different animal to create an entire work culture based on learning. This means not only allowing for learning, but facilitating, encouraging, and rewarding it.

This type of culture requires overcoming a lot of the resistance associated with a typical workplace. In a traditional workplace, it might be frowned on to walk into an office and see several employees reading books or working on personal technical projects that don't relate to reviewing events or packets. It might even be unfathomable for the majority of the staff to abscond from their desks to discuss the finer points of time travel in front of a whiteboard. The truth of the matter is that these things should be welcomed, as they increase morale and overall happiness, and at the end of the day your analysts go home with an excitement that makes them want to come back with fresh ideas and renewed motivation the next day.

Although some members of the old guard will never be able to accept such a work environment, it's proven to be very successful. Google is an example of an organization that has created a successful culture of learning, and a large portion of their success is directly related to that.

This mantra of a culture of learning can be summed up very simply. In every action an analyst takes, they should either be teaching or learning. No exceptions.

### Emphasize Teamwork

It's a bit cliché, but the team dynamic ensures mutual success over individual success. This means that team building is a must. Ensuring team cohesiveness starts with hiring the right people. An individual's capacity to perform is important, but their ability to mesh with existing team members is of equal importance. I've seen multiple instances where one bad apple has soured the whole bunch.

At some point, something bad is going to happen that requires an extensive time commitment from all parties involved. Analysts who trust each other and genuinely enjoy spending time together are going to be much more effective at ensuring the incident is handled properly. As an added bonus, a cohesive team will help promote a learning culture.

### Provide Formalized Opportunities for Professional Growth

One of the biggest fears of managers is that their staff will become highly trained and certified and then leave the organization for greener pastures. Although this does happen, it shouldn't steer an organization away from providing opportunities.

In interviewing NSM analysts who have left various organizations, it's rarely ever something as simple as a higher salary that has caused them to jump ship. Rather, they almost always cite that they weren't provided enough opportunity for growth within their organization. Generally, people don't like change. Changing jobs, especially when it involves relocating, is a big step and something people would generally like to avoid if at all possible. This means that you are likely to keep your staff if you can provide opportunities for professional certifications, advancements in position, or migrations to management roles. Simply having a clearly defined path for this type of advancement can often make the difference. This is one of the reasons why having something like the L1/L2/L3 classification system can benefit an organization.

### Encourage Superstars

Information security is notorious for having a culture of people with incredibly large egos. Although there is something to be said for being humble, you can't change the personal traits that are built into someone and you have to do your best to work with it. If your organization has an employee with a big ego, then turn him into a superstar. People who have an excessive amount of confidence typically desire to succeed in a big way, so if you can make this happen then they will thrive. This is done by challenging them, providing learning opportunities, and instilling responsibility in them. A superstar is rare, so some will flounder when it's crunch time. If this happens, then the reality check often serves to lessen a big ego. If the person continually succeeds, then you've found your superstar.

Once you have a superstar, people will want to imitate their success. Their greatness pushes others to be more than they thought they were capable of, and everybody benefits. As long as your superstar isn't negatively impacting others by being rude, abrasive, or otherwise overbearing, then he is an asset. The difference between Allen Iverson and Kobe Bryant is that Allen Iverson played great, where as Kobe Bryant made everyone around him great. That's why Iverson's 76ers didn't have any championships, and Bryant's Lakers had 5 under their respective tenures. Make your superstar into a Kobe Bryant.

### Reward Success

Positive reinforcement can be a monumental difference maker in morale. If an analyst finds something that nobody else found, everybody should know about it. Furthermore, if an analyst stays late for five hours to follow up on an incident, you should let them know you appreciate their efforts. The mechanism for reward doesn't particularly matter as long as it is something desirable.

### Learn from Failure

Analytical work can get mundane quickly. This is especially the case in a smaller environment where there simply just aren't as many events or significant attacks occurring. When this occurs, it becomes very easy for analysts to miss something. Instead of punishing the entire group, take this as another learning opportunity.

---

**FROM THE TRENCHES**

One of my favorite ways to promote learning from failure is another concept taken from the medical field. Many times when a patient dies and the death could have been medically prevented, the treating physician and a team of additional physicians will convene for a meeting called Morbidity and Mortality (M&M).[5] In this meeting, the treating physician will present how the patient was cared for and the additional physicians will provide constructive questioning and thoughts on alternative steps that could have been taken. These sessions are often feared, but when moderated effectively and kept positive, they can enact a great deal of positive change when similar situations come back around. This concept will be discussed in depth in the Analysis section of this book.

---

### Exercise Servant Leadership

The most successful organizations I've had the privilege to work with are those who practice the concept of servant leadership. Servant leadership is something that has been around for quite a while, and I was introduced to it as a University of Kentucky basketball fan from UK coach John Calipari.

---

[5]Campbell, W.B., "Surgical Morbidity and Mortality Meetings" (1988). http://www.ncbi.nlm.nih.gov/pmc/articles/PMC2498614/?tool=pmcentrez

The premise of servant leadership is that rather than establishing leadership based upon a title or some given authority, servant leaders achieve results by giving priority to the needs of their colleagues. This humble mindset is one in which you look to help others achieve their mission so that the organization will prosper. This has the potential to breed an organization that isn't anchored by one strong leader, but rather, a group of leaders with different strengths and weaknesses working in harmony to achieve a common mission. Although it sounds like a lofty goal, with the right mindset and buy in from all parties involved, this type of environment can become a reality.

## SECURITY ONION

Moving forward, this book will go beyond theory and contain several practical demonstrations and examples. To level the playing field, I've chosen to do all of these demonstrations using Security Onion, a Linux distribution designed for intrusion detection and NSM. Security Onion is the product of Doug Burks and a handful of contributors, and is one of my absolute favorite teaching and learning tools. With its simple setup process, you can have a full NSM collection, detection, and analysis suite deployed in less than 15 minutes. The value of Security Onion goes well beyond that of an educational tool, as I've seen several smaller organizations leverage it for production use as well. As a matter of fact, I use for my home office and personal networks.

### Initial Installation

If you plan on following along with the exercises in this book, then I recommend downloading and installing Security Onion (SO). It already has several of the tools I will discuss preinstalled, including Snort, Bro, Argus, and more. If you have an old physical machine laying around and a couple of extra network cards, then you can actually place it on your home network to examine real traffic. However, for the purposes of this book, installing Security Onion into a virtual machine is perfectly acceptable. VMWare Player or VirtualBox work great for this.

Once you have virtualization software setup, you will want to download the Security Onion ISO file. The latest version of this file can be found linked from http://securityonion.blogspot.com/. This page also contains a great number of helpful resources for installing and configuring various aspects of Security Onion. Once you've completed the download, follow these steps in order to get Security Onion up and running:

1. Create a new virtual machine within the virtualization platform you are using. It is recommended that you provide at least 1 GB of RAM for each monitored network interface, and a minimum of 2 GB total. You should also ensure your network interfaces are connected to the virtual machine at this time.

2. Mount the downloaded ISO as a virtual CD/DVD drive in your virtualization software.
3. When you start the VM, allow it to boot to fully into the live operating system. Once this process completes, select the "Install SecurityOnion" icon on the desktop to begin installing the operating system to the virtual disk.
4. Follow the prompts presented to you by the XUbuntu installer. During this installation, you will be asked for a number of items, including how you would like to configure disk partitioning, the time zone you are located in, Internet connectivity, the name of the system, and a username and password for your user account (shown in Figure 1.2). These options can be configured to your liking, but it is important that you do not choose the option to encrypt your home folder, and that you do not enable automatic updates. These options are disabled by default. Once you have completed XUbuntu installation, you will be prompted to reboot the system.

**FIGURE 1.2**

Configuring User Information During Security Onion Installation

This completes the operating system installation process.

## Updating Security Onion

Once you've completed the operating system installation and the machine reboots, the next step is ensuring Security Onion is up to date. Even if you've just downloaded the ISO, it is likely that there are updates to SO packages. An update can be initiated by issuing the following command from a command prompt:

```
sudo apt-get update && sudo apt-get dist-upgrade
```

This process may take a while depending on the number of updates released since the last ISO was generated. Once this is finished, you should then have a fully up to date installation of Security Onion.

## Running NSM Services Setup

In order to get NSM services up and running on Security Onion you must complete its automated setup process. Once you have logged into SO, follow these steps:

1. Initiate the setup process by clicking the "Setup" icon on the desktop.
2. After entering your password again, you will be prompted to configure /etc/network/interfaces. Select "Yes." If you have multiple interfaces, you will be prompted to choose one interface as the management interface, which is the interface you will use to access the system. If you only have a single interface, that interface will be used for management. Proceed through this process by choosing the static IP address option and configuring the interface's IP address, subnet mask, default gateway, DNS server address, and local domain name. You will be asked to confirm this information, and the system will be rebooted.

---

**FROM THE TRENCHES**

Even if you would normally configure your interfaces manually, it is highly recommended that you allow SO to perform this step for you. In doing so, it will perform several optimization steps to ensure that your monitor interfaces are properly configured to capture all possible network traffic.

---

3. Initiate the setup process again by clicking the "Setup" icon on the desktop.
4. Skip the network configuration process since that has already been completed.
5. Choose "Quick Setup." (You can select advanced setup, but the quick setup will suffice for our purposes here. Feel free to explore more advanced setup options on your own.)
6. If you have multiple interfaces, you will be prompted to select a monitoring interface. Select the appropriate interface(s).
7. Enter a username and password for use by various NSM services.

8. When prompted to enable ELSA, choose "Yes."
9. Finally, you will be prompted to confirm the configuration of the sensor (Figure 1.3). Selecting "Yes, proceed with the changes!" will instruct SO to apply the changes.

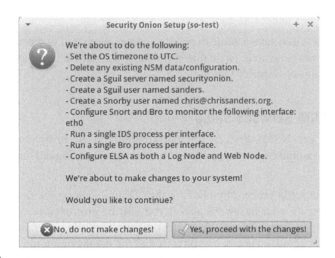

**FIGURE 1.3**

Confirming the Setup Changes

Once you've completed this setup, Security Onion will provide you with the location of several important log and configuration files. If you encounter any issues with setup or notice that a service hasn't started correctly, you can examine the setup log at /var/log/nsm/sosetup.log. The remainder of this book will assume you completed this setup with the quick setup configuration unless otherwise specified.

## Testing Security Onion

The fastest way to ensure that NSM services on Security Onion are running is to force Snort to generate an alert from one of its rules. Prior to doing this, I like to update the rule set used by Snort. You can do this by issuing the command `sudo rule-update`. This will used the PulledPork utility to download the latest set of rules from Emerging Threats, generate a new sid-map (used to map rule names to their unique identifiers) and restart Snort so that the new rules are applied. The partial output of this command is shown in Figure 1.4.

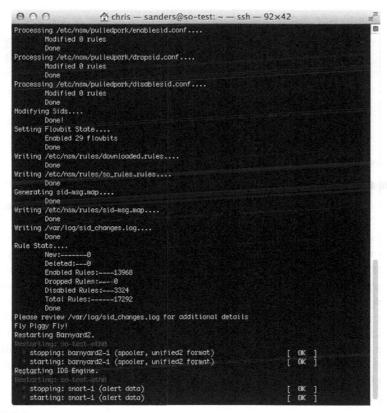

**FIGURE 1.4**

Output of the Rule Update

To test the functionality of the NSM services, launch Snorby by selecting the Snorby icon on the desktop. You will be prompted to login with the e-mail address and password you provided during the setup process. Next, click the "Events" tab at the top of the screen. At this point, it's likely this window will be empty.

In order to generate a Snort alert, open another tab within the browser window and browse to http://www.testmyids.com.

Now, if you switch back over to the tab with Snorby opened and refresh the Events page, you should see an alert listed with the event signature "GPL ATTACK_RESPONSE id check returned root" (Figure 1.5). If you see this alert, then congratulations! You've successfully setup your first NSM environment with Security Onion! Feel free to examine the alert by clicking on it and viewing the output in Snorby. We will return to examine Snorby more closely in later chapters.

**FIGURE 1.5**

The Test Snort Alert Shown in Snorby

This alert should appear pretty quickly, but if you don't see it after a few minutes, then something isn't working correctly. You should reference the Security Onion website for troubleshooting steps, and if you are still running into trouble you should try the Security Onion mailing list or their IRC channel #securityonion on Freenode.

These processes are up to date as of Security Onion 12.04, which was the newest version available during the writing of this book. If you find that this process has changed since the book's writing, then you should reference the SO wiki for up to date procedures: https://code.google.com/p/security-onion/w/list. We will come back to Security Onion many times throughout the course of this book, but if you'd like to learn more about it in the meantime, the SO wiki is the best resource.

## CONCLUSION

This chapter introduced NSM and threat-centric security, along with several other related concepts. We also looked at Security Onion and detailed the process of installing and configuring an NSM environment in only a few minutes. If you are new to NSM, then it is incredibly important that you understand the concepts presented in this chapter, as they provide the foundation for the rest of Applied NSM. The remainder of this book is broken into the three parts of the NSM Cycle: collection, detection, and analysis.

# Collection

# Planning Data Collection

2

## CHAPTER CONTENTS

Collection occurs with a combination of hardware and software that are used to generate and collect data for NSM detection and analysis. If you are an analyst reading this book, you may think this section isn't entirely relevant to you. That is all too wrong. An effective analyst can be described in a lot of ways (I prefer Packet Ninja), but ultimately, the analyst must be a master of their data. This means knowing what data is available, where that data comes from, how it is collected, why it is collected, and what you can do with it. A good analyst can make bad data useful and good data great.

All too often, analysts tend to pass the buck on collection. This typically results in an NSM team where collection is a process owned by a separate systems or networking group, or where a single analyst serves as "the collection guy". Segmenting this knowledge to another group or creating isolated pockets of knowledge doesn't serve the NSM mission and results in analysts who don't fully understand the data they are analyzing.

Most organizations fit into one of three categories:

- Organizations with no NSM infrastructure in place that are just beginning to define their data collection needs.

- Organizations that already perform intrusion detection, but have never taken an in-depth look at the data they are collecting.
- Organizations that have invested a great deal of time in defining their collection strategy, and are constantly evolving that strategy as a part of the NSM Cycle.

This section is dedicated to collection from scratch in hopes that all three types of organizations can benefit from the concepts discussed.

## THE APPLIED COLLECTION FRAMEWORK (ACF)

Abraham Lincoln said, "If I had six hours to chop down a tree, I'd spend the first four hours sharpening my axe." I can't think of a more fitting quote to describe the importance of data collection.

I stated earlier that a skilled analyst must be a master of their data. This is often hard to do because many organizations don't fully understand their data. They didn't take a structured approach to defining the threats to their organization, but rather, simply grabbed whatever ad-hoc data they had available to build their program around. This over abundance of data can lead to servers with an insufficient amount of disk resources for data retention, where excess staffing is required to sift through too many events and false positives, or where detection and analysis tools can't scale effectively with the amount of data they are expected to parse.

Playing the role of network defenders, we generally hate surprises. Although we often think that surprise is a function of uncertainty, it is also a function of complexity.[1] Having an over abundance of data that may not be relevant to realistic organizational threats is a fast way to increase complexity.

Decreasing the complexity of data collection is where the Applied Collection Framework (ACF) comes into play (Figure 2.1). The ACF is a loose set of steps that help an organization evaluate what data sources should be the focus of their collection efforts.

**FIGURE 2.1**

The Applied Collection Framework (ACF)

The ACF is not completed in a vacuum. To be successful, it requires collaboration with senior leadership right from the start. The security team and other stakeholders will be responsible for taking information gleaned from these early

[1]Bracken, P. (2008). *Managing strategic surprise*. Cambridge, MA: Cambridge University Press.

meetings and making it actionable. The ACF involves four distinct phases: Identify threats to your organization, quantify risk, identify relevant data feeds, and refine the useful elements.

## Define Threats

In order to practice threat-centric security you must have some ability to define what threats you face. In this case, I don't mean general threats such as rival companies, script kiddies, hacktivism groups, or nations. Instead, you should identify threats specific to organizational goals.

When identifying threats associated with your organization, you should always start with the question, "What is the worst case scenario as it relates to the survivability of the organization?" The answer must come straight from the top, which is why it is crucial that information security personnel work with senior leadership during the initial phases of defining collection requirements.

It helps to frame these threats by whether they negatively impact confidentiality, integrity, or availability. Consider the following examples:

- A manufacturing organization relies on their production occurring on a $24 \times 7 \times 365$ basis to meet demand by creating the products that generate revenue. When something occurs that interrupts production, it costs the organization dramatically. Therefore, production interruption might be the biggest threat to the organization. This is a threat to availability.
- A law firm expects that its information will remain confidential. Often times, legal firms handle information that could cost organizations millions of dollars, or even cost people their lives. The conversations between legal partners and their clients are of the utmost importance. The threat that a third party could intercept these conversations could be the biggest threat a law firm faces. This is a threat to confidentiality.
- An online reseller relies on website sales in order to generate revenue. If their website is inaccessible for even a few minutes, it may result in a large number of lost sales and revenue. In this case, inability to complete sales might be the biggest threat to the organization. This is a threat to availability.
- A commodity trading company relies heavily on the ability to communicate information to overseas partners during the trading day in order to execute trades that generate revenue. If this information is inaccurate, it could cause a ripple effect resulting in millions of dollars in losses based upon automated trading algorithms. The biggest threat to this organization would be a deliberate or accidental error in data fed into these algorithms. This is a threat to integrity.
- A biomedical company focuses all of its effort on researching new pharmaceuticals. The data generated from this research is the nest egg of the organization, and represents the combined results of the money provided by their investors. Should a competitor gain access to the information, it could potentially

cause the entire organization to fail. The threat of theft of intellectual property could be the biggest threat faced by this biomedical company. This is a threat to confidentiality.

In reality, most organizations will have several threats that they are concerned about. In these cases, senior leadership should prioritize all of these threats so that they can be considered appropriately.

Once threats have been identified, it is up to information security personnel to dig deeper into these organizational threats so that the technology underlying them can be addressed. This is done by understanding the infrastructure within the network and asking the right questions to the primary stakeholders involved with the identified business processes.

Let's more closely examine the biomedical company mentioned in the last bullet point above. This company is heavily invested in its intellectual property, and has identified that the greatest threat to its organization's survivability is the loss of that intellectual property. Considering that, the following questions, could be asked:

- What devices generate raw research data, and how does that data traverse the network?
- From what devices do employees process raw research data?
- On what devices is processed research data stored?
- Who has access to raw and processed research data?
- Is raw or processed research data available from outside the network?
- What paths into the internal network are available externally?
- What level of access do temporary employees have to research data?

Depending on the answers provided, you should be able to start building a picture of what assets within the network are most critical to protecting this sensitive data. The goal is to systematically determine the methods by which the network could be compromised, possibly leading to a theft of the intellectual property. A broad resultant list may look something like this:

- Web Server Compromise
- Database Server Compromise
- File Server Compromise
- Disgruntled Employee Data Exfiltration

## Quantify Risk

Once a list of potential technical threats has been identified, those threats must be prioritized. One way to achieve this is to calculate the risk posed by each potential threat by determining the product of impact and probability. This is represented by the equation Impact (I) $\times$ Probability (P) $=$ Risk (R).

Impact takes into consideration how a given threat, should it manifest itself, could affect the organization. This is measured on a scale of 1 to 5, with 1 meaning that the threat would have little impact, and 5 meaning that the threat would have a large impact. Determining impact can take into account things such as financial loss, the ability to recover lost data, and the amount of time required to resume normal operations.

Probability represents the likelihood that a threat will manifest itself. This is also measured on a scale of 1 to 5, with 1 meaning that there is a low probability that the threat will manifest itself, and 5 meaning that the threat has a high probability of manifestation. The determination of probability can include consideration of an asset's exposure or attack surface visible to the threat, the level of intimacy with the network required to execute an attack, or even the likelihood that someone would be able to gain physical access to an asset. Over enough time, the probability of a vulnerability being exploited increases. When we create probability rankings they represent the moment in time in which they are created, which means that they should be revisited over time.

The product of impact and probability is the level of risk, or the "risk weight" the threat poses to the security of the network in relation to the organization's business goals. This is measured on a scale of 1 to 25. This is broken down into three categories:

- 0-9: Low Risk
- 10-16: Medium Risk
- 17-25: High Risk

In performing this assessment for the biomedical company, our prioritization of the technical threats could look like Table 2.1.

**Table 2.1** Quantifying Risk for a Biomedical Company

| Threat | Impact | Probability | Risk |
|---|---|---|---|
| Web Server Compromise | 3 | 4 | 12 |
| Database Server Compromise | 5 | 3 | 15 |
| Disgruntled Employee Data Exfiltration | 5 | 4 | 20 |
| File Sever Compromise | 5 | 4 | 20 |

Although impact and probability are meant to provide some ability to quantify metrics associated with threats, these numbers are still subjective. Because of this, it is important that these numbers are generated by committee and that the same group of individuals participate in the ranking of all identified threats. Some organizations choose to elicit third parties to help quantify these risks, and I've seen this done successfully in conjunction with network penetration tests.

## Identify Data Feeds

The next phase of the ACF involves actually identifying the primary data feeds that might provide NSM detection and analysis value. Starting with the technical threat that has the highest risk weight, you must consider where evidence of the threat's manifestation can be seen.

Let's examine the threat of File Server Compromise. While defining this threat, you should have identified this server's architecture, its location on the network, who has access to it, and the pathways that data can take to and from it. Based upon this information, you can examine both network-based and host-based data feeds. This list might end up looking something like this:

- Network-Based:
  - File Server VLAN - Full Packet Capture Data
  - File Server VLAN – Session Data
  - File Server VLAN - Throughput Statistical Data
  - File Server VLAN - Signature-based NIDS Alert Data
  - File Server VLAN - Anomaly-based IDS Alert Data
  - Upstream Router - Firewall Log Data
- Host-Based:
  - File Server - OS Event Log Data
  - File Server - Antivirus Alert Data
  - File Server - HIDS Alert Data

You'll notice that this is broad, but that's okay. The goal here is just to begin identifying valuable data sources. We will get more granular in the next step.

## Narrow Focus

The final phase of the ACF is to get intimately granular with the data sources you've selected. This can be the most technically in-depth step, and involves reviewing every data source individually to gauge its value. You may find that some data sources have such a high storage, processing, or management overhead compared to the value they provide, that they aren't worth collecting. Ultimately, your organization will have to perform a cost/benefit analysis of the desired data sources to determine if they value they provide is worth the cost of implementation and maintenance. From the cost perspective, this analysis should take into account the amount of hardware and software resources, as well as the support staff that are required to maintain the generation, organization, and storage of the data resource. To analyze the benefit side of this equation, you should examine the number of documented occurrences in which the data source in question was referenced or desired in an investigation. Your time spent performing this process might include doing things such as defining what types of PCAP data you explicitly want to capture or which Windows security log events are the most important to retain.

Common questions you will ask during this process might include:

- What can you filter out of PCAP traffic from a specific network segment?
- Which system event logs are the most important?
- Do you need to retain both firewall permits and denies?
- Are wireless authentication and association logs valuable?
- Should you retain logs for file access and/or creation and/or modification?
- Which portions of the web application do you really need web logs for?

You should also begin to define the amount and duration of each data type you would like retain. This can be phrased as an operational minimum and an operational ideal. The operational minimum is the minimum required amount necessary to perform near real-time detection, and the operational ideal is the preferred amount of data needed for retrospective detection and as an investigative data source for analysis.

Given the broad list we established in the previous phase, getting granular could result in this list:

- Network-Based:
  - Full Packet Capture Data
    - All ports and protocols to/from file server
    - All SMB traffic routed outside of VLAN
  - Session Data
    - All records for VLAN
  - Data Throughput Statistical Data
    - Long-term data throughput statistics for file server
    - Daily, Weekly, Monthly averages
  - Signature-Based NIDS Alert Data
    - All alerts for the segment
    - Rules focusing on Windows systems and the SMB protocol
  - Anomaly-Based NIDS Alert Data
    - Alerts focusing on file server OS changes
    - Alerts focusing on rapid or high throughput file downloads
  - Firewall Log Data
    - Firewall Denies (External → Internal)
- Host-Based:
  - System Event Log Data
    - Windows Security Log
      - Logon Successes
      - Logon Failures
      - Account Creation and Modification
    - Windows System Log
      - File System Permission Changes
      - Software Installation
      - System Reboots

- Antivirus Alert Data
  - Detected Events
  - Blocked Events
- OSSEC Host-Based IDS
  - Alerts Related to Critical System File Changes
  - Alerts Related to Rapid Enumeration of Files
  - Alerts Related to Account Creation/Modification

Given this list, you should be able to provide the details of what data you need to the appropriate systems and networking teams. At this point, infrastructure will need to be appropriately engineered to support your data collection requirements. Don't worry too much about infrastructure cost at this point. That is a business decision to be made once you've completed the ACF. The goal of this framework is to identify the data you want to collect, and exactly how important you think it is. If budget limitations won't allow for ideal collection, you should at least have a playbook that will tell you what you can sacrifice. This can be based upon a cost/benefit analysis as described earlier. They key here is that you can justify your collection needs by relating them directly to business goals and threats to business continuity.

If you've not had a lot of experience with NSM collection, then you may not know exactly how much value certain data sources can provide. This experience will come, and in the mean time you will run into instances where you decide there are certain data feeds that can be ditched, or where you find it pertinent to start collecting additional data in one form or another. The documents generated from this process are never finalized. It is crucial to understand that you are never "finished" with NSM collection. NSM collection is a living, breathing process, and as you do more detection and analysis and as your network grows you will constantly need to revisit your collection strategy.

The companion website to this book provides the templates shown in the images above that should help you perform the steps of the ACF. Once you've completed their first iteration, these templates are an excellent resource for your analysts to familiarize themselves with the data being collected.

## CASE SCENARIO: ONLINE RETAILER

Let's examine a scenario where an online retailer is establishing an NSM capability for the first time. Our fictitious company, Purple Dog Inc. (PDI), uses their website to market and sell crafts and knick-knacks produced by other suppliers. They have no traditional brick-and-mortar stores, so their entire revenue stream depends upon their ability to make sales from their website.

I've included a diagram of the PDI network in Figure 2.2. This is a fairly typical network design with publicly accessible servers in a DMZ behind an edge router. Users and internal network servers reside in various VLANs behind a core router.

You'll notice that this diagram doesn't include any sensors. That is because we have yet to establish our collection requirements.

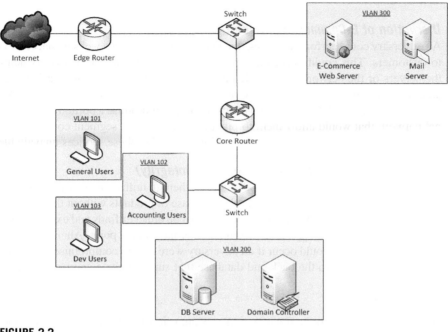

**FIGURE 2.2**

Purple Dog Inc. Network Diagram

## Identify Organizational Threats

Since PDI produces no goods of their own, they are essentially a middleman for the sale and distribution of a product. If you were to ask their executive management what their worst fears are, it would probably result in a list like this:

Fear 1: "All of our customers credit card information getting stolen. We will have to pay huge fines, our customers won't trust us anymore, and business will suffer."

Fear 2: "Something bad happens to our website causing it to be inaccessible for an extended time. At a certain point, this might threaten the continuity of the business."

Fear 3: "An individual finds a bug that allows them to place orders on the website without paying for them. This could result in lost revenues."

Now, let's convert those fears from "executive speak" to actual threats.

### *Theft of Customer PII (Confidentiality)*

The PDI e-commerce site collects and stores customer Personally Identifiable Information (PII) data that includes credit card information. This database is not directly accessible from the Internet. In one scenario, an attacker could compromise the database that stores this information through a vulnerability in the web application connected to it. Alternatively, an attacker could access this information by compromising the workstation of an employee who can access this database, such as a developer.

### Disruption of E-Commerce Service (Availability)

An adversary could perform an attack that makes the e-commerce website inaccessible to customers. This could occur through a denial of service attack that overwhelms the servers or the network they reside on. This could also occur if an attacker were able to compromise an externally facing asset and orchestrate an action that makes these services unavailable. Lastly, an attacker could compromise a portion of the internal network that would allow them to pivot into the network segment containing the e-commerce servers, and orchestrate an action that makes these services unavailable.

### Unintended Use of E-Commerce Service (Integrity)

An attacker could perform an attack that allows them to utilize the web application in an unintended manner, which includes the purchase of products without the exchange of money. The most likely scenario would be that an attacker finds and exploits a bug in the e-commerce web application from an external vantage point. Alternatively, an attack of this manner could occur if an adversary were able to compromise an internal user who had access to the back-end database that supports the e-commerce site.

## Quantify Risk

With a list of threats to the organization, we can prioritize these threats based upon the probability of a threat manifesting itself, and the impact of the threat should it come to reality. Based upon the threat identified in the previous step, the risk associated with each threat in this scenario is calculated in Table 2.2.

**Table 2.2** Quantified Risk for PDI Threats

| Threat | Impact | Probability | Risk |
|---|---|---|---|
| Theft of customer PII—web application compromise | 4 | 4 | 16 |
| Theft of customer PII—internal user compromise | 4 | 2 | 8 |
| Disruption of e-commerce service—DoS | 4 | 2 | 8 |
| Disruption of e-commerce service—external asset compromise | 5 | 3 | 15 |
| Disruption of e-commerce service—internal asset compromise | 5 | 2 | 10 |
| Unintended use of e-commerce service—web application compromise | 2 | 4 | 8 |
| Unintended use of e-commerce service—internal asset compromise | 2 | 1 | 2 |

Now that this list has been created, it can be prioritized, as shown in Table 2.3.

| Table 2.3 Prioritized Risk for PDI Threats | | | |
|---|---|---|---|
| Threat | Impact | Probability | Risk |
| Theft of customer PII—web application compromise | 4 | 4 | 16 |
| Disruption of e-commerce service—external asset compromise | 5 | 3 | 15 |
| Disruption of e-commerce service—internal asset compromise | 5 | 2 | 10 |
| Unintended use of e-commerce service—web application compromise | 2 | 4 | 8 |
| Disruption of e-commerce service—DoS | 4 | 2 | 8 |
| Theft of customer PII—internal user compromise | 4 | 2 | 8 |
| Unintended use of e-commerce service—internal asset compromise | 2 | 1 | 2 |

Based upon this table, we are now able to say that the greatest threat to the organization is the disruption of e-commerce services from the compromise of an externally facing asset, and the least concerning threat of these listed is the unintended use of e-commerce services as a result of an internal asset being compromised. We will use this information to shape the choices we make in the next step.

## Identify Data Feeds

With priorities established, it is possible to identify the data sources that are useful for NSM detection and analysis. For the sake of brevity, we will look at just a few of the higher risk threats.

### Theft of Customer PII – Web Application Compromise

The threat presenting the most risk to the organization is customer PII being stolen as a result of a web application compromise. This presents a potentially large attack surface from the perspective of the web application, but a rather small attack surface from the perspective of network assets.

Starting with the network side of the house, it's crucial that we can collect and inspect web server transactions with external users so that we can detect any anomalous behavior. In order to do this, a sensor can be placed at the network edge to collect full packet capture data, session data, or packet string data. This will also allow for the use of signature and anomaly-based NIDS.

We can also gain visibility into the actions of the web server by collecting its application-specific log data.

Because the web application provides indirect user access to a back-end database, it is also critical that these transactions are inspected. The database server resides in the internal network, so this will require a second sensor placed so that it has visibility here. Again, this provides for collection of full packet capture data, session data, and packet string data, and allows the use of signature and anomaly-based NIDS.

Finally, the database server will likely generate its own application-specific logs that can provide visibility into its actions.

The result of this planning produces a list of the following data sources:

- DMZ Sensor – Full Packet Capture Data
- DMZ Sensor – Session Data
- DMZ Sensor – Packet String Data
- DMZ Sensor – Signature-Based NIDS
- DMZ Sensor – Anomaly-Based NIDS
- Internal Sensor – Full Packet Capture Data
- Internal Sensor – Session Data
- Internal Sensor – Packet String Data
- Internal Sensor – Signature-Based NIDS
- Internal Sensor – Anomaly-Based NIDS.
- Web Server Application Log Data
- Database Server Application Log Data

### *Disruption of E-Commerce Server – External Asset Compromise*

The next threat of high concern is that an externally facing asset will be compromised, leading to the disruption of e-commerce services. Since this could include a web application compromise, this aspect of the attack surface will be included in this assessment.

At PDI, the only two externally facing assets are the e-commerce web servers themselves, with ports 80 and 443 open for web services, and the company mail servers, with port 25 open for SMTP.

Starting with the existing network infrastructure, the collection of firewall logs can be incredibly useful as an investigative data source.

Next, because of the importance of these systems in the context of this threat, it is critical that a sensor exists to collect network data traversing their interfaces. The DMZ sensor described when assessing the last threat provides adequate placement for the coverage needed here.

If these systems are compromised externally, it will likely be done through the compromise of one of the externally facing services. In order to provide adequate detection and analysis of this type of issue, application specific logs will be collected. This includes web, database, and mail server logs.

Beyond the addition of another type of server, the concern of a compromise at the system level is what greatly expands the attack surface in this scenario. In order to ensure that adequate data exists for detection and analysis of events related to this type of compromise, we will also collect operating system and security logs, along with antivirus log data and host-based IDS alert data.

This planning produces this list of data sources:

- Edge Firewall Log Data
- DMZ Sensor – Full Packet Capture Data

- DMZ Sensor – Session Data
- DMZ Sensor – Packet String Data
- DMZ Sensor – Signature-Based NIDS
- DMZ Sensor – Anomaly-Based NIDS
- Web Server Application Log Data
- Database Server Application Log Data
- Mail Server Application Log Data
- Web and Mail Server OS and Security Log Data
- Web and Mail Server Antivirus Alert Data
- Web and Mail Server HIDS Alert Data

## Disruption of E-Commerce Server – Internal Asset Compromise

The next highest priority threat on our list is that an internal asset compromise will lead to a disruption of e-commerce services. Because the e-commerce web servers are still the final targets for the adversary, that part of the attack surface will remain the same, resulting in a furthered need for a DMZ sensor.

The only VLANs that have access to the DMZ from within the internal network are the servers in VLAN 200 and the developer users in VLAN 103. This provides another reason to deploy a sensor at the network core so that data from these devices can be collected.

If an attacker were to compromise a developer's machine, they would have access to the DMZ. This means that we should probably collect the relevant system and security logs from the developer workstations, along with HIDS and Antivirus alert data. We are also interested in what is actually traversing the link from the internal to DMZ network, so firewall logs from the core router are worth collecting.

If the attacker were able to compromise a machine on the internal network, one thing they would likely attempt to do is increase their foothold on the network by compromising the Windows Active Directory environment. As such, it is important that logs from the domain controller are collected as well. Assuming the primary domain controller is handling DNS for the enterprise, those logs are also incredibly useful in determining if clients are attempting to resolve potentially malicious hostnames related to an attacker downloading additional tools, or exerting some form of command and control on the network.

This planning produces this list of data sources:

### Network-Based

- Edge Firewall Log Data
- Core Firewall Log Data
- DMZ Sensor – Full Packet Capture Data
- DMZ Sensor – Session Data
- DMZ Sensor – Signature-Based NIDS
- DMZ Sensor – Anomaly-Based NIDS
- Internal Sensor – Full Packet Capture Data
- Internal Sensor – Session Data
- Internal Sensor – Packet String Data

- Internal Sensor – Signature-Based NIDS
- Internal Sensor – Anomaly-Based NIDS

**Host-Based**

- Web Server, Database Server, and Domain Controller Application Log Data
- Web Server, VLAN 200, and VLAN 103 OS and Security Log Data
- Web Server, VLAN 200, and VLAN 103 Antivirus Alert Data
- Web Server, VLAN 200, and VLAN 103 HIDS Alert Data

The lists of data sources generated from these perceived threats aren't meant to cover every possible scenario, but they do represent a fair number of potential defense scenarios.

Identifying a plethora of data sources that could be useful for NSM detection and analysis results in a modification of the original network diagram. This new diagram includes the placement of the DMZ and internal sensors, and outlines the visibility zones they create (Figure 2.3). We will talk more about sensor placement in the next chapter.

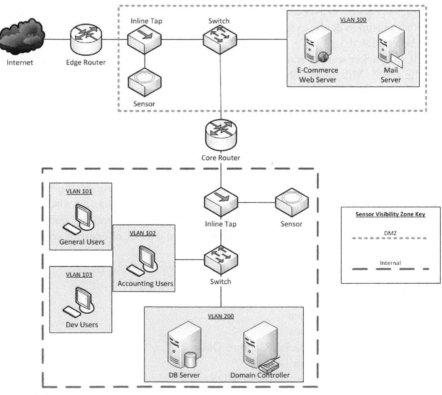

**FIGURE 2.3**

Updated Network Diagram Including Sensor Placement

## Narrow Focus

The last step in this process is to take the primary data sources that have been identified and refine those so that only useful aspects of that data are collected. There are limitless possible ways to approach this, but in this case, our fictitious company decided the following subsets of data were deemed to be feasible for collection based upon their own cost/benefit analysis.

For this scenario, the following refined set of data sources has resulted:

**Network-Based:**

- Edge Firewall Log Data
  - Internal → External Denies
- Core Firewall Log Data
  - External → Internal Permits/Denies
  - Internal → External Denies
- DMZ Sensor – Full Packet Capture Data
  - External → Internal Web Ports
  - External → Internal Mail Ports
  - Internal → External Mail Ports
- DMZ Sensor – Session Data
  - All Records
- DMZ Sensor – Signature-Based NIDS
  - Rules focusing on web application attacks: SQL injection, XSS, etc.
  - Rules focusing on web server attacks
  - Rules focusing on mail server attacks
- DMZ Sensor – Anomaly-Based NIDS
  - Rules focusing on web and mail content anomalies
- Internal Sensor – Full Packet Capture Data
  - Internal → Web Server IPs
  - Internal → Dev User VLAN 103
  - External → Server VLAN 200
- Internal Sensor – Session Data
  - All Records
- Internal Sensor – Packet String Data
  - Dev User VLAN 103 → External
- Internal Sensor – Signature-Based NIDS
  - Rules focusing on database attacks
  - Rules focusing on domain controller administration actions and attacks
  - General malware rules
- Internal Sensor – Anomaly-Based NIDS
  - Rules focusing on anomalous database interaction

**Host-Based:**

- Mail Server, Web Server, Database Server, and Domain Controller Application Log Data

- • Mail Server – Account Creation and Modification
  - • Web Server – Transactions from Billing Processing Subdomain
  - • Web Server – Transactions from Administration Subdomain
  - • Database Server – Account Creation and Modification
  - • Database Server – Billing Transactions
  - • Database Server – Administration Transactions
  - • Domain Controller – Account Creation and Modification
  - • Domain Controller – Computer Creation and Modification
- • Mail Server, Web Server, VLAN 200, and VLAN 103 OS and Security Log Data
  - • Account Creation and Modification
  - • Installed Software Notifications
  - • System Update Notifications
  - • System Reboot Notification
- • Mail Server, Web Server, VLAN 200, and VLAN 103 Antivirus Alert Data
  - • All Alert Data
- • Mail Server, Web Server, VLAN 200, and VLAN 103 HIDS Alert Data
  - • Alerts Related to Critical System File Changes
  - • Alerts Related to Account Creation/Modification

## CONCLUSION

In this chapter we introduced some of the driving forces behind data collection and discussed a framework for deciding what types of data should be collected. The case scenario here provides a high-level overview of the steps that an organization might take in determining what their data collection needs are, but this knowledge shouldn't be applied in a vacuum. The concepts presented in the remainder of this book will help to strengthen the decision-making that goes into defining collection requirements.

# The Sensor Platform

3

## CHAPTER CONTENTS

The most important non-human component of NSM is the sensor. By definition, a sensor is a device that detects or measures a physical property and records, indicates, or otherwise responds to it. In the NSM world, a sensor is a combination of hardware and software used to perform collection, detection, and analysis. Within the NSM Cycle, a sensor might perform the following actions:

- Collection
  - Collect PCAP
  - Collect Netflow
  - Generate PSTR Data from PCAP Data
  - Generate Throughput Graphs from Netflow Data
- Detection
  - Perform Signature-Based Detection
  - Perform Anomaly-Based Detection
  - Perform Reputation-Based Detection
  - Use Canary Honeypots for Detection
  - Detect Usage of Known-Bad PKI Credentials with a Custom Tool
  - Detect PDF Files with Potentially Malicious Strings with a Custom Tool
- Analysis
  - Provide Tools for Packet Analysis
  - Provide Tools for Review of Snort Alerts
  - Provide Tools for Netflow Analysis

Not every sensor performs all three functions of the NSM Cycle: however, the NSM sensor is the workhorse of the architecture and it is crucial that proper thought be put into how sensors are deployed and maintained. Having already stated how important collection is, it is necessary to respect that the sensor is the component that facilitates the collection. It doesn't matter how much time you spend defining the threats to your network if you hastily throw together sensors without due process.

There are four primary architectural concerns when defining how sensors should operate on your network. These are the type of sensor being deployed, the physical architecture of the hardware being used, the operating system platform being used, and the placement of the sensor on the network. The tools installed on the sensor that will perform collection, detection, and analysis tasks are also of importance, but those will be discussed in extensive detail in subsequent chapters.

# NSM DATA TYPES

Later chapters of this book will be devoted entirely to different NSM data types, but in order to provide the appropriate context for discussing sensor architecture, it becomes pertinent to provide a brief overview of the primary NSM data types that are collected for detection and analysis.

## Full Packet Capture (FPC) Data

FPC data provides a full accounting for every data packet transmitted between two endpoints. The most common form of FPC data is in the PCAP data format. While FPC data can be quite overwhelming due to its completeness, its high degree of granularity makes it very valuable for providing analytic context. Other data types, such as statistical data or packet string data, are often derived from FPC data.

## Session Data

Session data is the summary of the communication between two network devices. Also known as a conversation or a flow, this summary data is one of the most flexible and useful forms of NSM data. While session data doesn't provide the level of detail found in FPC data, its small size allows it to be retained for a much longer time, which is incredibly valuable when performing retrospective analysis.

## Statistical Data

Statistical data is the organization, analysis, interpretation, and presentation of other types of data. This can take a lot of different forms, such as statistics supporting the examination of outliers from a standard deviation, or data points identifying positive or negative relationships between two entities over time.

## Packet String (PSTR) Data

PSTR is derived from FPC data, and exists as an intermediate data form between FPC data and session data. This data format consists of clear text strings from specified protocol headers (for instance, HTTP header data). The result is a data type that provides granularity closer to that of FPC data, while maintaining a size that is much more manageable and allows increased data retention.

## Log Data

Log data refers to raw log files generated from devices, systems, or applications. This can include items such as web-proxy logs, router firewall logs, VPN authentication logs, Windows security logs, and SYSLOG data. This data type varies in size and usefulness depending upon its source.

## Alert Data

When a detection tool locates an anomaly within any of the data it is configured to examine, the notification it generates is referred to as alert data. This data typically contains a description of the alert, along with a pointer to the data that appears anomalous. Generally, alert data is incredibly small in size as it only contains pointers to other data. The analysis of NSM events is typically predicated on the generation of alert data.

When thinking about these data types holistically, its useful to be able to frame how their sizes compare. The largest data format is typically FPC data, followed by PSTR data, and then session data. Log, alert, and statistical data are generally miniscule compared to other data types, and can vary wildly based upon the types of data you are collecting and the sources you are utilizing.

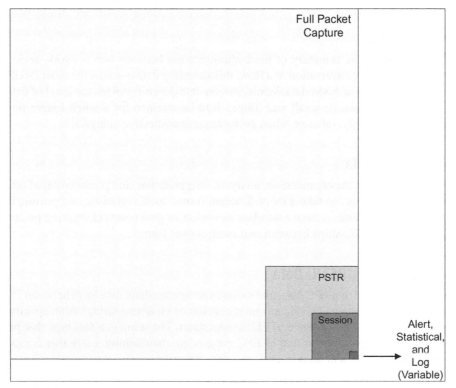

**FIGURE 3.1**

NSM Data Size Comparison

Quantifying these size differences can often be helpful, especially when attempting to determine sensor space requirements. This can vary drastically based upon the type of network environment. For instance, a user-heavy network might result in the generation of a lot more PSTR data than a server-heavy network segment. With that in mind, we have compiled the data from several different network types to generate some basic statistics regarding the size of particular data types given a static time period. Once again, log, alert, and statistical data are not included in this chart.

| Table 3.1 NSM Data Size Comparison | | | |
|---|---|---|---|
| | **FPC** | **PSTR** | **Flow** |
| Multiplier | 100 % | 4 % | 0.01 % |
| Data Size (MB) | 1024 | 40.96 | .1024 |

**CAUTION**

While the numbers shown in Table 3.1 provide a baseline of relative data sizes for the examples in this chapter, the relation between PSTR data, session data, and full packet capture data will vary wildly depending upon the types of network data you are capturing. Because of this, you should sample network traffic to determine the ratios that are accurate in your environment.

## SENSOR TYPE

Depending on the size and threats faced by a network, sensors may have varying roles within the phases of the NSM Cycle.

### Collection-Only

A collection-only sensor simply logs collected data such as FPC and session data to disk, and will sometimes generate other data (statistical and PSTR) based upon what has been collected. These are seen in larger organizations where detection tools access collected data remotely to perform their processing. Analysis is also done separately from the sensor, as relevant data is pulled to other devices as needed. A collection-only sensor is very barebones with no extra software installed, and analysts rarely have the ability to access it directly.

### Half-Cycle

A half-cycle sensor performs all of the functions of a collection-only sensor, with the addition of performing detection tasks. For instance, a half-cycle sensor will log PCAP data to disk, but will also run a NIDS (such as Snort) either in real-time from the NIC or in near-real-time against PCAP data that is written to disk. When analysis must occur, data is pulled back to another device rather than the analysis being performed on the sensor itself. This is the most common type of sensor deployment, with analysts accessing the sensor directly on occasion to interact with various detection tools.

## Full Cycle Detection

The last type of sensor is one in which collection, detection, and analysis are all performed on the sensor. This means that in addition to collection and detection tools, a full suite of analysis tools are installed on the sensor. This may include individual analysts profiles on the sensor, a graphical desktop environment, or the installation of a NIDS GUI such as Snorby. With a full cycle detection sensor, almost all NSM tasks are performed from the sensor. These types of sensors are most commonly seen in very small organizations where only a single sensor exists or where hardware resources are limited.

In most scenarios, a half cycle sensor is preferred. This is primarily due to the ease of implementing detection tools on the same system that data is collected. It is also much safer and more secure for analysts to pull copies of data back to dedicated analysis computers for their scrutiny ,rather than interacting with the raw data itself. This prevents mishandling of data, which may result in the loss of something important. Although analysts will need to interact with sensors at some level, they shouldn't be using them as a desktop analysis environment unless there is no other option. The sensor must be protected as a network asset of incredible importance.

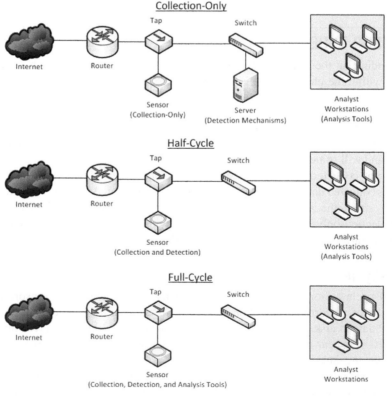

**FIGURE 3.2**

Sensor Types

# SENSOR HARDWARE

Once the proper planning has taken place, it becomes necessary to purchase sensor hardware. The most important thing to note here is that the sensor is, indeed, a server. This means that when deploying a sensor, server-grade hardware should be utilized. I've seen far too many instances where a sensor is thrown together from spare parts, or worse, I walk up to an equipment rack and see a workstation lying on its side being used as the sensor. This type of hardware is acceptable for a lab or testing scenario, but if you are taking NSM seriously, you should invest in reliable hardware.

A concerted engineering effort is required to determine the amount of hardware resources that will be needed. This effort must factor in the type of sensor being deployed, the amount of data being collected by the sensor, and the data retention desired.

We can examine the critical hardware components of the sensor individually. Before doing this, however, it helps to set up and configure a temporary sensor to help you determine your hardware requirements. This can be another server, a workstation, or even a laptop.

Prior to installing the temporary sensor, you should know where the sensor would be placed on the network. This includes the physical and logical placement that determines what network links the sensor will monitor. Determining sensor placement is discussed in depth later in this chapter.

Once the sensor has been placed on the network, you will utilize either a SPAN port or a network tap to get traffic to the device. Then you can install collection, detection, and analysis tools onto the sensor to determine the performance requirements of individual tools. Keep in mind that you don't necessarily need a temporary sensor that is so beefy that it will handle all of those tools being enabled at once. Instead, you will want to enable the tools individually to calculate their performance load, and then total the results from all of the tools you will be utilizing to assess the overall need.

## CPU

The amount of CPU resources required will mostly depend on the type of sensor being deployed. If you are deploying a collection-only sensor, then it is likely you will not need a significant amount of processing power, as these tasks aren't incredibly processing intensive. The most CPU intensive process is typically detection, therefore, if you are deploying a half or full cycle sensor, you should plan for additional CPUs or cores. If you expect significant growth, then a blade chassis might be an enticing option, as it allows for the addition of more blades to increase CPU resources.

An easy way to begin planning for your sensor deployment is to map the number of cores required on the system to the tools being deployed. The specific requirements will vary greatly from site to site depending on the total bandwidth to be monitored, the type of traffic being monitored, the ruleset(s) selected for signature-based detection mechanisms like Snort and Suricata, and the policies loaded into tools like Bro. We will examine some of the performance considerations and baselines for each of these tools in their respective sections.

If you've deployed a test sensor, you can monitor CPU usage with SNMP, or a Unix tool such as top (Figure 3.3) or htop.

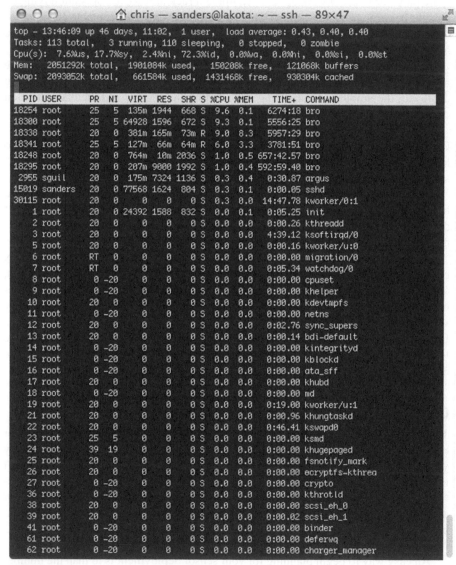

**FIGURE 3.3**

Monitoring Sensor CPU Usage with TOP

## Memory

The amount of memory required for collection and detection is usually smaller than for analysis. This is because analysis often results in multiple analysts running several instances of the same tools successively. Generally, a sensor should have an abundance of memory, but this amount should increase drastically if a full cycle sensor is being deployed. Since memory can be difficult to plan for, it is often best to purchase hardware with additional memory slots to allow for future growth.

Just like was discussed earlier regarding CPU usage, tools like top or htop can be used to determine exactly how much memory certain applications utilize (Figure 3.4). Remember that it is critical that this assessment be done while the sensor is seeing traffic throughput similar to the load it will experience while in production.

**FIGURE 3.4**

Monitoring Sensor Memory Utilization with HTOP

Practically speaking, memory is relatively inexpensive, and some of the latest network monitoring tools attempt to take advantage of that fact. Having a large amount of memory for your tools will help their performance under larger data loads.

## Hard Disk Storage

One of the areas organizations have the most difficulty planning for is hard disk storage. This is primarily because there are so many factors to consider. Effectively planning for storage needs requires you to determine the placement of your sensor and the types of traffic you will be collecting and generating with the sensor. Once you've figured all of this out, you have to estimate future needs as the network grows in size. With all of that to consider, it's not surprising that even after a sensor has been deployed, storage needs often have to be reevaluated.

The following series of steps can help you gauge the storage needs for a sensor. These steps should be performed for each sensor you are deploying.

### Step One: Calculate the Traffic Collected

Utilizing a temporary sensor, you should begin by calculating data storage needs by determining the amount of NSM data collected over certain intervals. I like to attempt to collect at least 24 hours of data in multiple collection periods, with one collection period on a weekday and another on a weekend. This will give you an accurate depiction of data flow encompassing both peak and off-peak network times for weekdays and weekends. Once you've collected multiple data sets, you should then be able to average these numbers to come up with an average amount of data generated per hour.

In one example, a sensor might generate 300 GB of data PCAP in a 24-hour period during the week (peak), and 25 GB of data on the weekend (off peak). In order to calculate the daily average, we multiply the peak data total with the number of weekdays (300 GB x 5 Days = 1500 GB), and multiply the off peak data total with the number of weekend days (25 GB x 2 Days = 50 GB). Next, we add the two totals (1500 GB + 50 GB = 1550 GB), and find the average daily total by dividing that number by the total number of days in a week (1550 GB / 7 Days = 221.43 GB). This can then be divided by the number of hours in a day to determine the average amount of PCAP data generated per hour (221.43 GB / 24 Hours = 9.23 GB).

The result of these calculations for multiple data formats can be formatted in a table like the one shown in Table 3.2.

| Table 3.2 Sensor Data Collection Numbers | | | | |
|---|---|---|---|---|
| | **Daily (Peak)** | **Daily (Off Peak)** | **Daily Average** | **Hourly Average** |
| **PCAP** | 300 GB | 25 GB | 221.43 GB | 9.23 GB |
| **Flow** | 30.72 MB | 2.56 MB | 16.64 MB | 0.69 MB |
| **PSTR** | 12 GB | 102.4 MB | 6.05 GB | 258.1 MB |
| | | | | **9.48 GB** |

### Step Two: Determine a Feasible Retention Period for Each Data Type

Every organization should define a set of operational minimum and ideal data retention periods for NSM data. The operational minimum is the minimal requirements for performing NSM services at an acceptable level. The operational ideal is set as a reasonable goal for performing NSM to the best extent possible. Determining these numbers depends on the sensitivity of your operations and the budget you have available for sensor hardware. When these numbers have been determined, you should be able to apply them to the amount of data collected to see how much space is required to meet the retention goals. We've taken the data from Table 3.2 and multiplied it with example minimum and ideal numbers. This data has been placed in Table 3.3.

**Table 3.3** Required Space for Data Retention Goals

|  | Daily Average | Operational Minimum | Minimum Requirement | Operational Ideal | Ideal Requirement |
|---|---|---|---|---|---|
| **PCAP** | 221.43 GB | 1 Day | 221.43 GB | 3 Days | 664.29 GB |
| **Flow** | 16.64 MB | 90 Days | 1.46 GB | 1 Year | 5.93 GB |
| **PSTR** | 6.05 GB | 90 Days | 544.50 GB | 1 Year | 2.16 TB |
|  |  |  | **2.21 GB** |  | **2.81 TB** |

### Step Three: Add Sensor Role Modifiers

In most production scenarios, the sensor operating system and tools will exist on one logical disk and the data that is collected and stored by the sensor will exist on another. However, in calculating total disk space required, you need to account for the operating system and the tools that will be installed. The storage numbers discussed up to this point assume a collection-only sensor. If you plan on deploying a half cycle sensor, then you should add an additional 10% to your storage requirements to accommodate for detection tools and the alert data generated from them. If you will be deploying a full cycle sensor, then you should add 25% for both detection and analysis tools and data. Once you've done this, you should add an additional 10-25% based upon the requirements for the operating system, as well as any anticipated future network growth. Keep in mind that these numbers are just general guidelines, and can vary wildly depending on the organization's goals and the individual network. These modifiers have been applied to our sample data in Table 3.4.

Although I didn't do this in Table 3.4, I always recommend rounding up when performing these calculations to give yourself plenty of breathing room. It is typically much easier to plan for additional storage before the deployment of a sensor rather than having to add more storage later.

While planning, it is important to keep in mind that there are numerous techniques for minimizing your storage requirements. The most common two techniques are varying your retention period for certain data types or simply excluding the

**Table 3.4** Completed Hard Disk Storage Assessment

|  | Minimum Requirement | Ideal Requirement |
| --- | --- | --- |
| **PCAP** | 221.43 GB | 664.29 GB |
| **Flow** | 1.46 GB | 5.93 GB |
| **PSTR** | 544.50 GB | 2.16 TB |
| **Sub-Total** | **2.21 GB** | **2.81 TB** |
| **+10% Half-Cycle Sensor** | 226.3 MB | 287.74 GB |
| **+15% Anticipated Growth** | 339.46 MB | 431.62 GB |
| **Total** | **2.76 GB** | **3.51 TB** |

collection of data associated with certain hosts or protocols. In the former, your organization might decide that since you are collecting three months of PSTR data, you only need twelve hours of FPC data. In the latter you may configure your full packet captures to ignore especially verbose traffic such as nightly backup routines or encrypted traffic such as SSL/TLS traffic. While both techniques have positives and negatives, they are the unfortunate outcome of making decisions in an imperfect world with limited resources. An initial tool you may use in the filtering of traffic to all of your sensor processes is the Berkeley Packet Filter (BPF). Techniques for using BPF's to filter traffic will be discussed in Chapter 13.

## Network Interfaces

The Network Interface Card (NIC) is potentially the most important hardware component in the sensor, because the NIC is responsible for collecting the data used for all three phases of the NSM Cycle.

A sensor should always have a minimum of two NICs. One NIC should be used for accessing the server, either for administration or analysis purposes. The other NIC should be dedicated to collection tasks. The NIC used for administration typically doesn't need to be anything special, as it will not be utilized beyond that of a typical server NIC. The degree of specialization required for the collection NIC depends upon the amount of traffic being captured. With quality commodity NICs, such as the popular Intel or Broadcom units, and the correct configuration of a load balancing network socket buffer, such as PF_Ring, it is rather trivial to monitor up to 1 Gbps of traffic without packet loss.

The number of NICs used will depend on the amount of bandwidth sent over the link and the types of taps selected. It is important to remember that there are two channels on a modern Ethernet: a Transmit (TX) channel and a Receive (RX) channel. A standard 1 Gbps NIC is cable of transporting an aggregate 2 Gbps; 1 Gpbs in each direction, TX and RX. If a NIC sees less than 500 Mbps (in each direction), you should be relatively safe specifying a single 1 Gbps NIC for monitoring. We say "relatively" though, because a 1 Gbps NIC connected to a router with a 500 Mbps/500 Mbps uplink could buffer traffic for transmission, allowing peaks in excess of the uplink throughput to happen. Advanced network taps can assist in mitigating these types of performance mismatches. We will provide more guidance on network taps in the next section.

In order to gauge exactly what throughput you will need for your collection NIC, you should perform an assessment of the traffic you will be collecting. The easiest method to assess the amount of traffic on a given link will be to inspect, or to set up, some simple aggregate monitoring on your router or switch. The two most important aggregate numbers are:

- Peak to peak traffic (Measured in Mbps)
- Average bandwidth (throughput) per day (Measured in Mbps)

For example, you may have an interface that you plan to monitor that is a 1 Gbps interface, with an average throughput of 225 Mbps, an average transmit of 100 Mbps, an average receive of 350 Mbps, and with sustained bursts to 450 Mbps. Whatever NIC you plan to utilize should be able to handle the sustained burst total as well as the average throughput.

---

**CAUTION**

Traffic is bi-directional! A 1 Gbps connection has a maximum throughput of 2 Gbps - 1 Gbps TX and 1 Gbps RX.

---

An additional input into your sensor design will be the composite types of network protocol traffic you will be seeing across the specific link. This may vary depending on the time of day (e.g. backup routines at night), the time of year (e.g. students in session), and other variables. To do this, configure the SPAN port or network tap the sensor will be plugged into, and then plug a temporary sensor into it that has a high throughput NIC to determine the type of data traversing this link. Suggested methods of analysis include capturing and analyzing NetFlow data, or capturing PCAP data to replay through analysis tools offline.

These measurements should be taken over time in order to determine the peak traffic levels and types of traffic to expect. This should help you to determine whether you will need a 100 Mbps, 1 Gbps, 10 Gbps, or larger throughput NIC. Even at low throughput levels, it is important that you purchase enterprise-level hardware in order to prevent packet loss. The 1 Gbps NIC on the shelf at Wal-Mart might only be $30, but when you try to extract a malicious PDF from a stream of packets only to find that you are missing a few segments of data, you will wish you had spent the extra money on something built with quality.

To capture traffic beyond 1 Gbps, or to maximize the performance of your sensor hardware, there are a variety of advanced high performance network cards available. The three most common vendors ,from most to least expensive, are Napatech, Endace, and Myricom. Each of these cards families provides various combinations of a variety of high performance features such as on card buffers, hardware time stamping, advanced network socket drivers, GBIC interface options, and more.

The enterprise NIC market is a very fast moving area. Currently, we recommend Myricom products, as they seem to be an incredible value and perform highly when paired with the propriety Myricom network socket buffer.

In cases where you find that your sensor is approaching the 10 Gbps throughput barrier, you will likely either have to reconsider the sensor placement, or look into some type of load-balancing solution. This amount of data being collected and written to disk could also cause some additional problems related to hard disk I/O.

## Load Balancing: Socket Buffer Requirements

Once the traffic has made its way to the network card, special consideration must be paid to balancing the traffic within a sensor across the various processes or application threads. The traditional Linux network socket buffer is not suited to high performance traffic analysis; enter Luca Deri's PF_Ring. The general goal of PF_Ring is to optimize the performance of network sockets through a variety of techniques such as a zero copy ring buffer where the NIC bypasses copying network traffic to kernel space by directly placing it in user space; thus saving the operating system an expensive context switch. This makes the data collection process faster and more efficient.

One way to conceptualize PF_Ring is to think of it taking your network traffic and fanning it out for delivery to a variety of tools. It can operate in two modes: either per packet round robin, or by ensuring an entire flow is delivered to a single process or thread within a sensor. In PF_Ring's current implementation, you can generate a 5-tuple hash consisting of the source host, destination host, source port, destination port and protocol. This algorithm ensures that all of the packets for a single TCP flow and mock UDP/ICMP flows are handled by a specific process or thread.

While PF_Ring isn't the only option for use with common detection tools like Bro, Snort, or Suricata, it is the most popular, and it is supported by all three of these.

For high performance sensor applications or designing sensors for operation in environments in excess of 1 Gbps, significant performance gains may be achieved through the use of aftermarket network sockets. With the sponsorship of Silicom, ntop.org now offers a high performance network socket designed for use with commodity Intel NICs called PF_Ring+DNA. Presently licensed per port, the PF_Ring+DNA performance tests are impressive and should be on your list of options to evaluate. Licensed per card, the Myricom after market driver for use with their own brand of card presently seems to be the best value.

## SPAN Ports vs. Network Taps

Although they are not a part of the physical server that acts as a sensor, the device you utilize to get packets to the sensor is considered a part of the sensor's architecture. Depending on where you place the sensor on your network, you will either choose to utilize a SPAN port or a Network Tap.

A SPAN port is the simplest way to get packets to your sensor because it utilizes preexisting hardware. A SPAN port is a function of an enterprise-level switch that allows you to mirror one or more physical switch ports to another port. In order to accomplish this, you must first identify the port(s) whose traffic is desirable to the sensor. This will most often be the port that connects an upstream router to the switch, but could also be several individual ports that important assets reside on. With this information in hand, you can configure the traffic inbound/outbound from this port to be mirrored to another port on the switch, either through a GUI or command line interface, depending on the switch manufacturer. When you connect your collection NIC on the sensor to this port, you will see the exact traffic from the source port you are mirroring from. This is depicted in Figure 3.5, where a sensor is configured to monitor all traffic from a group of network assets to a router by mirroring the port the router is attached to over to the sensor.

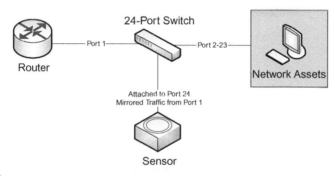

**FIGURE 3.5**

Using a SPAN Port to Capture Packets

---

**MORE INFORMATION**

While port mirror is a common feature on enterprise-level switches, it is a bit harder to find on small office and home (SOHO) switches. Miarec maintains a great listing of SOHO switches with this functionality at http://www.miarec.com/knowledge/switches-port-mirroring.

---

Most switches allow a many-to-one configuration, allowing you to mirror multiple ports to a single port for monitoring purposes. When doing this, it's important to consider the physical limits of the switch. For instance, if the ports on the switch are 100 Mbps, and you mirror 15 ports to one port for collection, then it is likely that the collection port will become overloaded with traffic, resulting in dropped packets. I've also seen some switches that, when sustaining a maximum load over a long time, will assume the port is caught in some type of denial of service or broadcast storm and will shut the port down. This is a worst-case scenario, as it means any collection processes attached to this port will stop receiving data.

Another method for getting packets to your sensor is the use of a network tap. A tap is a passive hardware device that is connected between two endpoints, and mirrors their traffic to another port designed for monitoring. As an example, consider a switch that is plugged into an upstream router. This connection utilizes a single cable with one end of the cable plugged into a port in the switch, and another cable plugged into a port on the router. Using a tap, there will be additional cabling involved. The end of one cable is plugged into a port on the switch, and the other end of that cable is plugged into a port on the tap. On the next cable, one end of the cable is plugged into a port on the tap, and the other end is plugged into a port on the router. This ensures that traffic is transmitted successfully between the router and the switch. This is shown in Figure 3.6.

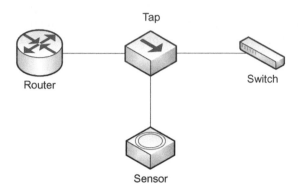

**FIGURE 3.6**

Using a Network Tap to Capture Packets

In order to monitor the traffic intercepted by the tap you must connect it to your sensor. The manner in which this happens depends on the type of tap being utilized. The most common type of tap is an aggregated tap. With an aggregated tap, a cable has one end plugged into a single monitor port on the tap, and the other end plugged into the collection NIC on the sensor. This will monitor bidirectional traffic between the router and switch. The other common variety of tap is the non-aggregated tap. This type will have two monitor ports on it, one for each direction of traffic flow. When using a non-aggregated tap, you must connect both monitor ports to individual NICs on the sensor. Both types of taps are shown in Figure 3.7.

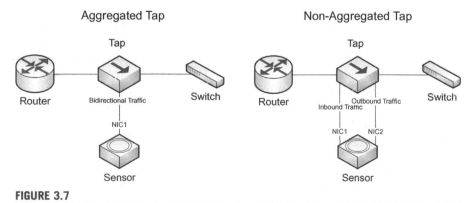

**FIGURE 3.7**

Aggregated and Non-Aggregated Taps

Taps are typically the preferred solution in high performance scenarios. They come in all shape and sizes and can scale up to high performance levels. You get what you pay for with taps, so you shouldn't spare expense when selecting a tap to be used to monitor critical links.

While both taps and SPAN ports can get the job done, in most scenarios, taps are preferred to SPAN ports due to their high performance and reliability.

### Bonding Interfaces

When using a non-aggregated tap, you will have at least two separate interfaces on your sensor. One interface monitors inbound traffic from the tap, and the other monitors outbound traffic. Although this gets the job done, having two separate data streams can make detection and analysis quite difficult. There are several different ways to combine these data streams using both hardware and software, but I prefer a technique called interface bonding. Interfacing bonding allows you to create a virtual network interface that combines the data streams of multiple interfaces into one. This can be done with software.

As an example, let's bond two interfaces together in Security Onion. As you can see by the output shown in Figure 3.8, the installation of Security Onion I'm using has three network interfaces. Eth2 is the management interface, and eth0 and eth1 are the collection interfaces.

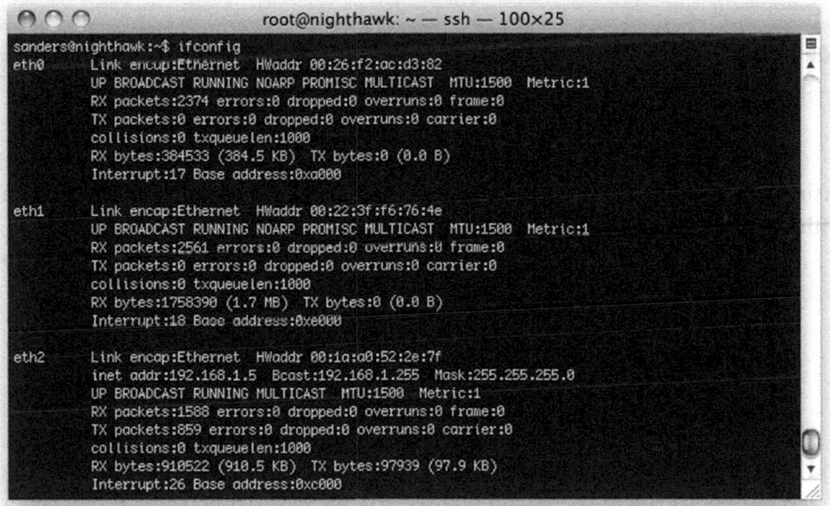

**FIGURE 3.8**

Network Interfaces on the System

For the purposes of this exercise, let's assume that eth0 and eth1 are connected to a non-aggregated tap, and that they are both seeing unidirectional traffic. An example of the same traffic stream sniffed from both interfaces can be seen in Figure 3.9.

In this figure, the results of an ICMP echo request and reply generated from the ping command are shown. In the top window, notice that only the traffic to 4.2.2.1 is seen, where as in the bottom window, only the traffic from 4.2.2.1 is seen.

```
root@nighthawk: ~ — ssh — 100×12
sanders@nighthawk:~$ sudo tcpdump -nni eth1 -c3 icmp
tcpdump: WARNING: eth1: no IPv4 address assigned
tcpdump: verbose output suppressed, use -v or -vv for full protocol decode
listening on eth1, link-type EN10MB (Ethernet), capture size 96 bytes
20:19:52.123419 IP 4.2.2.1 > 172.16.16.2: ICMP echo reply, id 56956, seq 0, length 64
20:19:53.124915 IP 4.2.2.1 > 172.16.16.2: ICMP echo reply, id 56956, seq 1, length 64
20:19:54.123288 IP 4.2.2.1 > 172.16.16.2: ICMP echo reply, id 56956, seq 2, length 64
3 packets captured
3 packets received by filter
0 packets dropped by kernel
sanders@nighthawk:~$
```

```
Terminal — ssh — 100×12
sanders@nighthawk:~$ sudo tcpdump -nni eth0 -c3 icmp
tcpdump: WARNING: eth0: no IPv4 address assigned
tcpdump: verbose output suppressed, use -v or -vv for full protocol decode
listening on eth0, link-type EN10MB (Ethernet), capture size 96 bytes
20:19:52.070332 IP 172.16.16.2 > 4.2.2.1: ICMP echo request, id 56956, seq 0, length 64
20:19:53.069423 IP 172.16.16.2 > 4.2.2.1: ICMP echo request, id 56956, seq 1, length 64
20:19:54.070685 IP 172.16.16.2 > 4.2.2.1: ICMP echo request, id 56956, seq 2, length 64
3 packets captured
3 packets received by filter
0 packets dropped by kernel
sanders@nighthawk:~$
```

**FIGURE 3.9**

Unidirectional Traffic Seen on Each Interface

Our goal is to combine these interfaces into their own interface to make analysis easier. In Security Onion this can be done using bridge-utils, which is now included with it. You can set up a temporary bridge using the following commands:

```
sudo ip addr flush dev eth0
sudo ip addr flush dev eth1
sudo brctl addbr br0
sudo brctl addif br0 eth0 eth1
sudo ip link set dev br0 up
```

This will create an interface named br0. If you sniff the traffic of this interface, you will see that the data from eth0 and eth1 are now combined. The end result is a single virtual interface. As seen in Figure 3.10, while sniffing traffic on this interface we see both sides of the communication occurring:

If you wish to make this change persistent after rebooting the operating system, you will need to make a few changes to Security Onion, including disabling the graphical network manager and configuring bridge-utils on the /etc/network/interfaces file. You can read more about those changes here:

- http://code.google.com/p/security-onion/wiki/NetworkConfiguration
- https://help.ubuntu.com/community/NetworkConnectionBridge

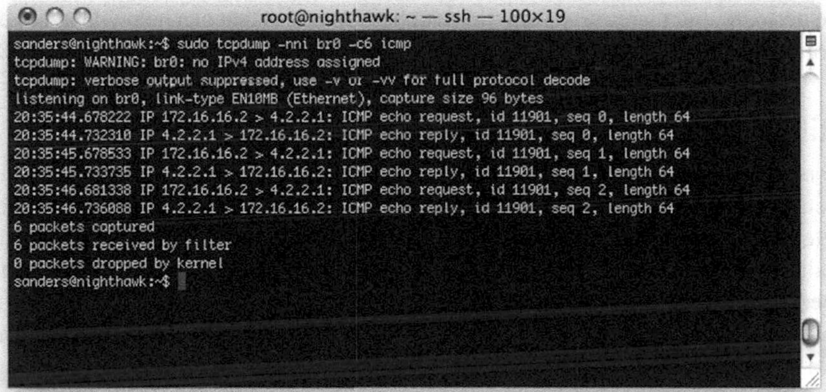

```
● ○ ○                    root@nighthawk: ~ — ssh — 100×19
sanders@nighthawk:~$ sudo tcpdump -nni br0 -c6 icmp
tcpdump: WARNING: br0: no IPv4 address assigned
tcpdump: verbose output suppressed, use -v or -vv for full protocol decode
listening on br0, link-type EN10MB (Ethernet), capture size 96 bytes
20:35:44.678222 IP 172.16.16.2 > 4.2.2.1: ICMP echo request, id 11901, seq 0, length 64
20:35:44.732310 IP 4.2.2.1 > 172.16.16.2: ICMP echo reply, id 11901, seq 0, length 64
20:35:45.678533 IP 172.16.16.2 > 4.2.2.1: ICMP echo request, id 11901, seq 1, length 64
20:35:45.733735 IP 4.2.2.1 > 172.16.16.2: ICMP echo reply, id 11901, seq 1, length 64
20:35:46.681338 IP 172.16.16.2 > 4.2.2.1: ICMP echo request, id 11901, seq 2, length 64
20:35:46.736088 IP 4.2.2.1 > 172.16.16.2: ICMP echo reply, id 11901, seq 2, length 64
6 packets captured
6 packets received by filter
0 packets dropped by kernel
sanders@nighthawk:~$
```

**FIGURE 3.10**

Bidirectonal Traffic from the Virtual Interface

# SENSOR OPERATING SYSTEM

The most common sensor deployments are usually some flavor of Linux or BSD. Every flavor has its upsides and downsides, but it usually boils down to personal preference. Most people who have DoD backgrounds prefer something Red Hat based such as CentOS or Fedora, because the DoD mostly utilizes Red Hat Linux. A lot of the more "old school" NSM practitioners prefer FreeBSD or OpenBSD due to their minimalistic nature. While the particular flavor you choose may not matter, it is very important that you use something *nix based. There are a variety of reasons for this, but the most prevalent is that most of the tools designed for collection, detection, and analysis are built to work specifically on these platforms. In 2013, Linux seems to be the most popular overall choice, as hardware manufactures seem to universally provide up to date Linux drivers for their hardware.

# SENSOR PLACEMENT

Perhaps the most important decision that must be made when planning for NSM data collection is the physical placement of the sensor on the network. This placement determines what data you will be able to capture, what detection ability you will have in relation to that data, and the extent of your analysis. The goal of sensor placement is to ensure proper visibility into the data feeds that have been established as critical to the NSM process within the organization. If you are using the methods described in this book to make that determination, then you likely decided what data was the most important for collection by going through the applied collection framework discussed in chapter two.

There is no tried and true method for determining where to best place a sensor on the network, but there are several tips and best practices that can help you avoid common pitfalls.

## Utilize the Proper Resources

Good security doesn't occur in a vacuum within an organization, and sensor placement shouldn't either. While the placement of a sensor is a goal of the security team, determining how to best integrate this device into the network is more within the realm of network engineering. With that in mind, the security team should make every effort to engage network engineering staff at an early stage of the placement process. Nobody knows the network better than the people who designed it and maintain it on a daily basis. They can help guide the process along by ensuring that the goals are realistic and achievable within the given network topology. Of course, in some cases the network engineering staff and the security team might consist of a solitary person, and that person might be you. In that case, it makes scheduling meetings a lot easier!

The document that is usually going to provide the most insight into the overall design of a network or individual network segment is the network diagram. These diagrams can vary wildly in detail and design, but they are critical to the process so that the network architecture can be visualized. If your organization doesn't have network diagrams, then this would be a good time to to make that happen. Not only will this be crucial in determining visibility of the sensor, but it will also help in the creation of visibility diagrams for use by your analysts. We will talk about those diagrams later in this section.

## Network Ingress/Egress Points

In the ideal case, and when the appropriate resources are available, a sensor should be placed at each distinct ingress/egress point into the network including Internet gateways, traditional VPNs, and partner links. In smaller networks, this may mean deploying a sensor at one border on the network edge. You will find that many large organizations have adopted a hub and spoke model where traffic from satellite offices are transported back to the main office via VPN, MPLS, or other point-to-point technology to centrally enforce network monitoring policies. This setup will require a wider dispersion of sensors for each of these ingress/egress points.

The diagram shown in Figure 3.11 represents a network architecture that might be found in a larger organization with many ingress/egress points. Note that all of the routers shown in this diagram are performing Network Address Translation (NAT) functions.

In this case, notice that there are four separate sensors deployed:

**A.** At the corporate network edge
**B.** At the research network edge
**C.** At the ingress point from a business partner network
**D.** At the edge of the wireless network

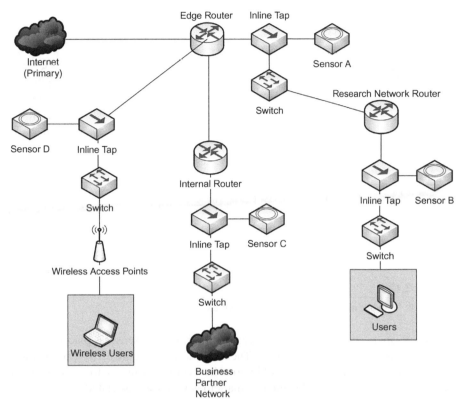

**FIGURE 3.11**

Placing Sensors at Network Ingress/Egress Points

Ultimately, any truly negative activity occurring on your network (except for physical theft of data) will involve data being communicated into or out of the network. With this in mind, sensors placed at these ingress/egress points will be positioned to capture this data.

## Visibility of Internal IP Addresses

When performing detection and analysis, it is critical to be able to determine which internal device is the subject of an alert. If your sensor is placed on the wrong side of a NAT device such as a router, you could be shielded from this information.

The diagram shown in Figure 3.12 shows two different scenarios for a single network. The network itself is relatively simple, in which the corporate network exists behind an internal router that forms a DMZ between itself and the edge router, which connects to the Internet.

The devices downstream from the internal router have IP addresses in the 172.16.16.0/24 range. The router has an internal LAN IP address of 172.16.16.1, and an external WAN interface of 192.168.1.254. This forms a DMZ between the internal router and the edge router.

Scenario A – External Placement

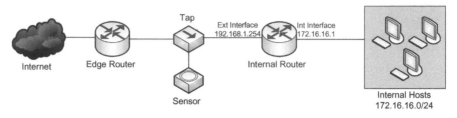

Scenario B – Internal Placement

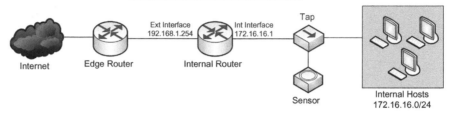

**FIGURE 3.12**

A Simple Network with Two Sensor Placement Examples

There are two scenarios shown here. In scenario A, the sensor is placed upstream from the internal router, in the DMZ. The alert shown in Figure 3.13 represents what happens when a user in the group of internal hosts falls victim to a drive-by download attack that causes them to download a malicious PDF file associated with the Phoenix exploit kit.

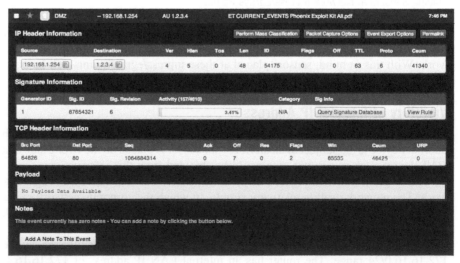

**FIGURE 3.13**

A User in Scenario A Generating an Alert

This alert indicates that the device at 192.168.1.254 attempted to download a PDF from the host at 1.2.3.4, and that this PDF is linked to the Phoenix exploit kit. The problem with this is that 192.168.1.254 is the external IP address of the internal router, and this doesn't give us any indication of which internal host actually initiated this communication. Pulling NetFlow data yields the results shown in in Figure 3.14.

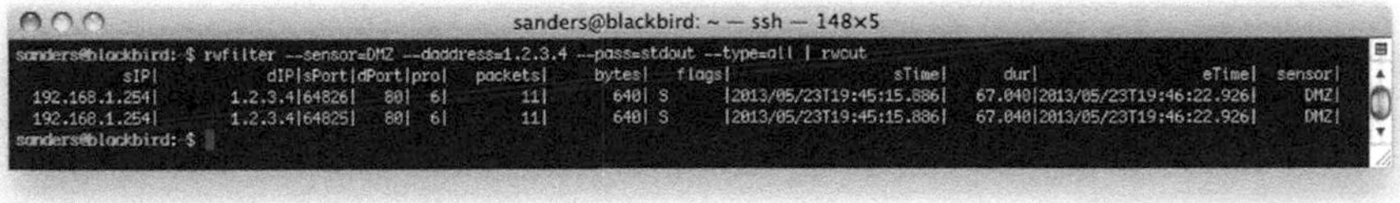

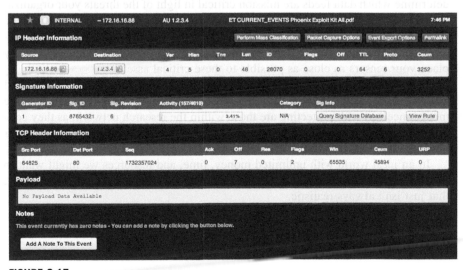

**FIGURE 3.14**

NetFlow Data from Scenario A

With this sensor placement, you will not see any internal IP addresses in the 172.16.16.0/24 range. This is because the internal router is utilizing NAT to mask the IP addresses of the hosts inside that network. The data collected by this sensor gives us absolutely no ability to adequately investigate the alert further. Even if you had other data sources available such as antivirus or HIDS logs, you wouldn't know where to begin looking. This becomes especially complex on a network with hundreds or thousands of hosts on a single network segment.

In scenario B, the sensor is placed downstream from the router. Figure 3.15 shows that the same malicious activity generates the same alert, but provides different information.

**FIGURE 3.15**

A User in Scenario B Generating an Alert

Here we can see the same external address of the site hosting the malicious file (1.2.3.4), but instead of the external IP of the internal router, we actually see the proper internal IP of the host that needs to be examined for further signs of infection. NetFlow data shows this as well in Figure 3.16.

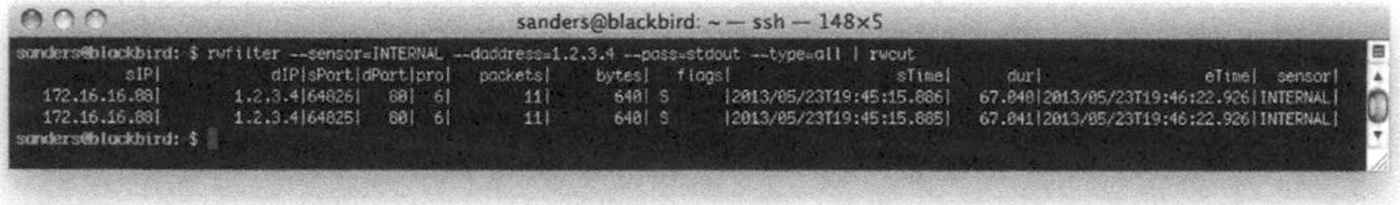

**FIGURE 3.16**

NetFlow Data from Scenario B

It is critical that your collected data serves an analytic purpose. This example applies just as much to sensors placed within internal network segments as it does to network segments that are only one hop away from the Internet. You should always ensure that you are on the right side of routing devices.

## Proximity to Critical Assets

In the introductory material of this book, we discussed how casting a wide net and attempting to collect as much data as possible can be problematic. This should be taken into account when you place your sensors. If you've taken the time to properly determine which data feeds are mission critical in light of the threats your organization faces, you should have defined which assets are the most important to protect. With this in mind, if you have limited resources and can't afford to perform collection and detection at all of your network's ingress/egress points, you can logically place your sensors as close as possible to these critical assets.

Figure 3.17 shows an example of a mid-sized network belonging to a biomedical research firm. In planning for collection, this firm decided that the devices they are most concerned with protecting are those within the research network, as they contain the organization's intellectual property. This image shows three possible sensor placements.

In an ideal world with unlimited money, time, and resources we might want to deploy all of these sensors in order gain the best visibility of the network. However, that just isn't always realistic.

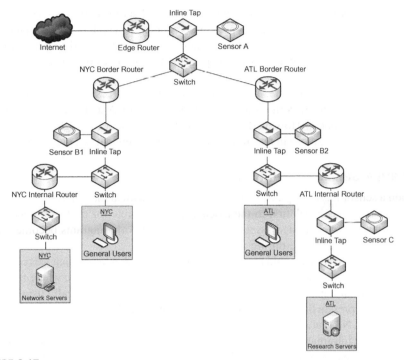

**FIGURE 3.17**

A Mid-Sized Network with Three Sensor Placement Examples

Our first thought might be to place a sensor on the network edge, which is what is depicted with sensor A. If this is the only sensor placed on this network, it becomes responsible for collection and detection for the entire enterprise. As we've already discussed, this model doesn't always scale well and ultimately results in incredibly expensive hardware and an inability to perform thorough collection, detection, and analysis.

Next, we might consider placing the sensors at the border of each physical site, as shown with sensors B1 and B2. This essentially splits the workload of sensor A in half, with a sensor for both the NYC and ATL locations. While this does have some performance benefits, we still have two sensors that are responsible for processing a wide variety of data. The sensor at the NYC site alone must have detection signatures that will encompass possible threats related to different servers on the network servers segment, as well as users. This still isn't focusing on the biggest perceived threat to the organization.

Finally, we come to sensor C, which is placed so that it has visibility into the research network at the ATL location. This segment contains users who are actively involved in research, and the servers where their data is stored. Based upon the risk analysis that was completed for this network, the biggest threat to the organization would be a compromise on this network segment. Therefore, this is where I would place my first sensor. Because this network is smaller in size, less powerful hardware can be used. Additionally, detection mechanisms can be deployed so that a trimmed down set of signatures that only encompass the technologies on this part of the network can be used.

In a scenario like this one, it would be ideal if the resources were available to place more than one sensor. Perhaps a combination of sensor A and C might be the best 'bang for your buck.' However, if the assets that represent the highest level of risk in the company are those in research server segment, then that is a great place to start.

## Creating Sensor Visibility Diagrams

When a sensor has been placed on the network, it is critical that analysts know where that sensor exists in relation to the assets it is responsible for protecting, as well as other trusted and untrusted assets. This is where network diagrams become incredibly useful for reference during an investigation.

Most organizations would be content to take a network diagram that was created by the systems administration or network engineering staff and point to where the sensor is physically or logically placed. While this can be useful, it isn't really the most efficient way to present this information to an NSM analyst. These diagrams aren't usually made for the NSM analyst, and can often induce a state of information overload where non-relevant information prevents the analyst from fully understanding the exact architecture as it relates to protected and trusted/untrusted assets. In other terms, I would consider giving an NSM analyst a network engineering diagram equivalent to providing a cook with the DNA sequence of a tomato. If the cook wants to know about the particulars of what comprises a tomato's flavor then he can reference that information, but in most cases, he just needs the recipe that tells him how to cook that tomato. With NSM analysis, it is always beneficial if detailed network diagrams are available to analysts, but in most cases a simplified diagram is better suited to their needs. The ultimate goal of the sensor visibility diagram is for an analyst to be able to quickly assess what assets a particular sensor protects, and what assets fall out of that scope.

A basic sensor visibility diagram should contain AT LEAST the following components:

- The high-level logical overview of the network
- All routing devices, proxies, or gateways that affect the flow of traffic
- External/Internal IP addresses of routing devices, proxies, and gateways
- Workstations, servers or other devices -- these should be displayed in groupings and not individually, unless they are particularly critical devices
- IP address ranges for workstation, server, and device groupings
- All NSM sensors, and appropriately placed boxes/areas that define the hosts the sensor is responsible for protecting. These boxes will usually be placed to define what hosts the sensor will actually collect traffic from. While the traffic from a nested subnet might only show the IP address of that subnet's router's external interface, the traffic will still be captured by the sensor unless otherwise excluded.

As an example, let's consider the network that was described in Figure 3.17 earlier. I've redrawn this image in Figure 3.18 to represent the visibility of each sensor, incorporating the items listed above. The differing zones can typically be most effectively defined by colored or shaded boxes, but since this book is printed in black and white, I've used boxes with different types of line dashes to represent each monitored zone. In this case, each sensor is monitoring all of the traffic in the subnets nested below its subnet, so each zone is overlapping the zone for the upstream network.

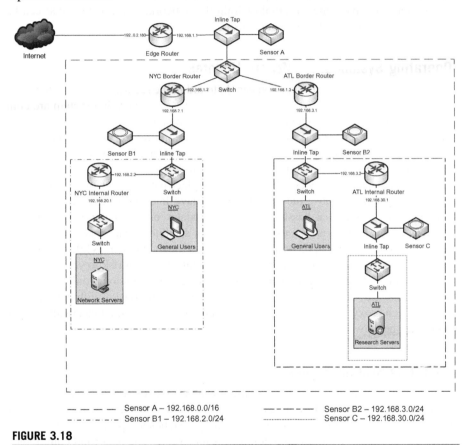

**FIGURE 3.18**

A Sensor Visibility Diagram

I would often have these diagrams laminated and placed at an analyst's desk for quick reference during an investigation. They work great for a quick reference document, and can be a launching point for an analyst to find or request additional documentation relevant to the investigation, such as a more detailed diagram of a specific network segment or information associated with a particular trusted host.

## SECURING THE SENSOR

In the realm of sensitive network devices, the security of the sensor should be considered paramount. If your sensor is storing full packet capture data, or even just PSTR data, it is very likely that these files will contain incredibly sensitive network information. Even an unskilled attacker could use these files to extract entire files, passwords, or other critical data. An attacker could even use a sensor that is only storing session data to help them garner information about the network that might allow them to expand their foothold within the network. Several steps that can be taken to ensure the sanctity of your sensors.

### Operating System and Software Updates

The single most important thing you can do to aid in the security of any system is to ensure that the software running on it and the underlying operating system are both up to date with the latest security patches. Even though your sensors shouldn't be visible from the Internet, if your network gets compromised through some other means and an attacker can move laterally to a sensor via a months-old remote code execution vulnerability in your operating system, it's game over.

I've seen many instances where people neglect patching sensor software and operating systems because the sensor doesn't have Internet access. As a result, it becomes too much of a hassle to perform updates on a regular basis. In such instances, one solution is to set up some type of satellite update server within your network to ensure these updates are occurring in a timely manner. While this is extra management overhead, it does reduce a significant amount of risk to your sensors if they are not being updated frequently enough. One other solution would be to limit access to those domains required for software and system updates with the use of an internal web proxy, but this may prove challenging based on the placement of your sensor in the network.

### Operating System Hardening

In addition to ensuring that the operating system of your sensor is up to date, it is critical that it is based upon secure configuration best practices before sensor software is even installed. There are several approaches to operating system security best practices. If your organization falls under any type of formal compliance standard such as HIPAA, NERC CIP, or PCI, then it is likely that you already employ some type of secure OS configuration standards. Federal and Defense sector agencies are also no stranger to these, as operating system security is enforced via any number of certification and accreditation processes, such as DIACAP or DITSCAP.

If you aren't guided by any formal compliance standard, there are several publicly available resources that can serve as a good starting point. Two of these that I really like are the Center for Internet Security (CIS) benchmarks (http://benchmarks.cisecurity.org/) and the NSA Security Guides for Operating Systems (http://www.nsa.gov/ia/mitigation_guidance/security_configuration_guides/operating_systems.shtml).

## Limit Internet Access

In most instances, your sensor should not have unfettered Interner access. If the sensor were to become compromised, this would make it trivially easy for an attacker to exfiltrate sensitive data from the sensor. I typically do not provide Internet access to sensors at all, although in some cases Internet access can be limited to only critically important domains (such as those required for software and system updates) with the use of an internal web proxy.

Importantly, your sensor processes will most likely be configured to download IDS signatures or reputation-based intelligence from the Internet at periodic intervals. Additionally, accessing data sources for intelligence services, such as Bro's real-time usage of the Team Cymru Malware Hash Registry and the International Computer Science Institutes SSL Observatory, is a growing trend. You should ensure that your sensor can receive this data, but it might be preferable to have a single system configured to download these updates, and have sensors pointed to that internal device for updates.

## Minimal Software Installation

A sensor is a specialized piece of hardware designed for a specific purpose. This specialization warrants that only necessary software be installed on the sensor. We recommend using a minimal operating system installation and only installing what software is needed to perform the required collection, detection, and analysis tasks for your type of sensor deployment. Furthermore, any unneeded services should be disabled and additional unused packages installed with the operating system should be removed. This ultimately increases sensor performancc, and minimizes the potential attack surface.

The most common mistake I see in slimming down a server installation is when a sensor administrator forgets to remove compilers from a sensor. It is often the case that a compiler will be required to install NSM tools, but under no circumstances should the compiler be left on this system, as it provides an additional tool for an attacker to use against your network should the sensor be compromised. In a best case scenario, sensor tools are actually compiled on another system and pushed out to the sensor rather than being compiled on the sensor itself.

## VLAN Segmentation

Most sensors should have at least two network connections. The first interface is used for the collection of network data, while the second will be used for the administration of the sensor, typically via SSH. While the collection interface shouldn't be assigned an IP address or be allowed to talk on the network at all, the administration interface will be required to exist logically on the network at some location. If the network environment supports the segmentation of traffic with Virtual Local Area Networks (VLANs), then this should be taken advantage of, and the sensor management interface placed into a secure VLAN that is only accessible by the sensor administrator.

## Host-Based IDS

The installation of some form of host-based intrusion detection (HIDS) on the sensor is critical. These systems provide detection of modifications to the host through a variety of means, including the monitoring of system logs and system file modification detection. Several commercial varieties of HIDS exist, but there are also free pieces of software available, such as OSSEC or the Advanced Intrusion Detection Environment (AIDE). Keep in mind that the HIDS software is used to detect a potential intrusion on the system it resides on, so the logs it generates should be sent to another server on the network. If they are stored locally and only periodically examined, this presents an opportunity for an attacker to modify or delete these logs before they can be examined.

## Two-Factor Authentication

As an attacker, an NSM sensor is a target of great value. The raw and processed network data found on a sensor can be used to orchestrate or further a variety of attacks. Therefore, it is important to protect the authentication process used to access the sensor. Using a password-only authentication presents a scenario in which an attacker could harvest that password from another source and then access the sensor. Because of this, having two forms of authentication for sensors is recommended.

## Network-Based IDS

It is crucial that the administration interface of the sensor be monitored as a high value network asset. It should come as no surprise that one of the best ways to do this is to subject this interface to the same NIDS detection used for the rest of the network. Of course, this software is probably running on the sensor itself. The easy solution is to mirror the administration interface's network traffic to the monitoring interface. This is an easy step to take, but one that is often overlooked.

One of the best things you can do to ensure that your sensor isn't communicating with any unauthorized hosts is to identify which hosts are permitted to talk to the sensor and create a Snort rule that will detect communication with any other device. For example, assuming that a sensor at 192.168.1.5 is only allowed to talk to the administrator's workstation at 192.168.1.50 and the local satellite update server at 192.168.1.150, the following rule would detect communication with any other host:

```
alert ip ![192.168.1.50,192.168.1.150] any <> 192.168.1.50 any (msg:
"Unauthorized Sensor Communication"; sid:5000000; rev:1;)
```

## CONCLUSION

There is a lot of planning and engineering that goes into proper sensor creation, placement, and capacity planning. Like many topics, this is something that could nearly be its own separate book. This chapter was intended to provide an overview of the main concepts that should be considered when performing those actions. In addition to the concepts introduced here, it is a good practice to speak with colleagues and other organizations to see how they've deployed their sensors in light of their organizational goals and network architecture. This will provide a good baseline knowledge for determining the who, what, when, where, and why of NSM sensors.

# Session Data

Session data is the summary of the communication between two network devices. Also known as a conversation or a flow, this summary data is one of the most flexible and useful forms of NSM data. If you consider full packet capture equivalent to a recording of every phone conversation someone makes from a their mobile phone, then you might consider session data to be equivalent to having a copy of the phone log on the bill associated with that mobile phone. Session data doesn't give you the "What", but it does give you the "Who, Where, and When".

When session or flow records are generated, the record will usually include the protocol, source IP address and port, the destination IP address and port, a timestamp of when the communication began and ended, and the amount of data transferred between the two devices. The various forms of session data that we will look at in this chapter will include other information, but these fields are generally common across all implementations of session data. A sample of flow data is shown in Figure 4.1.

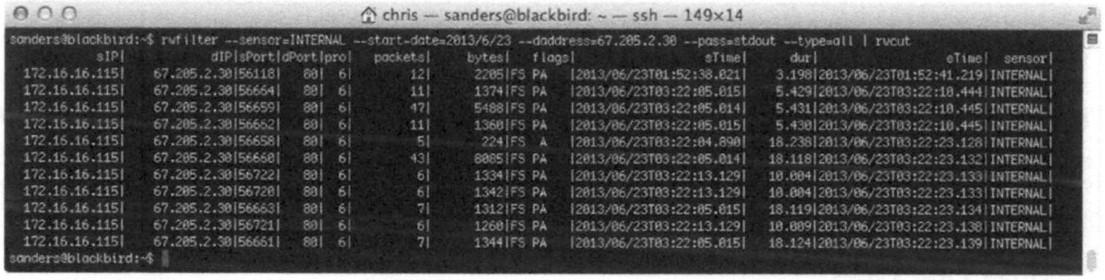

**FIGURE 4.1**

Sample Flow Records

While session data doesn't provide the level of detail found in full packet capture data, it does have some unique strengths that provide significant value to NSM analysts. As we will learn in the next chapter, the biggest challenge to FPC solutions is that the size of this data prohibits most organizations from retaining any significant amount of it. As such, this limits the ability to catch all types of traffic, or to perform retrospective analysis that might be relevant to current investigations. This weakness of FPC data is actually a strength of session data. Since session data is merely a collection of text records and statistics, it is incredibly small in size. The result is that it is easy to create large scale flow storage solutions. FPC data retention is generally thought of in terms of minutes or hours, but session data retention can be thought of in terms of months or years. I've even seen organizations choose to keep flow data indefinitely.

An additional benefit of session data and its smaller size is that it's much quicker to parse and analyze. This is convenient for both the analyst who is attempting to quickly comb through data, and analysis tools that are attempting to detect anomalies or generate statistics. Because of this, other data types, including statistical data that we will talk about in the Chapter 11, are often generated from session data.

In this chapter we will discuss how flows are generated, methods for session data collection, and explore two of the more popular session data analysis solutions, SiLK and Argus. However, before going into detail about the differences between analysis solutions, it's important to understand the differences between the types of flow data. This book will highlight the most commonly used flow types, NetFlow and IPFIX.

## FLOW RECORDS

A flow record is an aggregated record of packets. The aggregation can occur differently depending upon which tool is being used to generate and parse the data.

**ANALYST NOTE**

In this book, we concentrate mostly on SiLK, so this section describes how SiLK aggregates data to form flow records.

A flow record is identified based upon five attributes that make up the standard 5-tuple. The 5-tuple is a set of data whose attributes are source IP address, source port, destination IP address, destination port, and transport protocol. When a flow generator parses a packet, the 5-tuple attributes are examined and recorded, and a new flow record is created with 5-tuple data as well as any other fields defined by the flow type you are using (NetFlow v5, NetFlow v9, IPFIX, etc).

When a new packet is analyzed and contains the same 5-tuple attribute values, then that data is appended to the flow record that already exists. Data will be appended to this flow record for as long as packets matching the 5-tuple attribute values are observed. There are three conditions in which a flow record might be terminated (Figure 4.2):

1. Natural Timeout: Whenever communication naturally ends based upon the specification of the protocol. This is tracked for connection-oriented protocols, and will look for things like RST packets or FIN sequences in TCP.
2. Idle Timeout: When no data for a flow has been received within thirty seconds of the last packet, the flow record is terminated. Any new packets with the same 5-tuple attribute values after this thirty seconds has elapsed will result in the generation of a new flow record. This value is configurable.
3. Active Timeout: When a flow has been open for thirty minutes, the flow record is terminated and a new one is created with the same 5-tuple attribute values. This value is configurable.

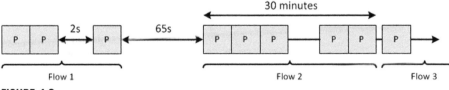

**FIGURE 4.2**

Flow Idle and Active Termination

Whenever packets are observed with new 5-tuple attribute values, a new flow record is created. There can be a large number of individual flow records open at any time.

I like to visualize this by imagining a man sitting on an assembly line. The man examines every packet that crosses in front of him. When he sees a packet with a unique set of 5-tuple attribute values, he writes those values on a can, collects the data he wants from the packet and places it into the can, and sits it to the side. Whenever a packet crosses the assembly line with values that match what is written on this can, he throws the data he wants from the packet into the can that is already sitting there. Whenever one of the three conditions for flow termination listed above are met, he puts a lid on the can, and sends it away.

As you might expect based upon this description, flows are generated in a unidirectional manner in most cases (some tools, such as YAF, can generate bidirectional flows). For instance, with unidirectional flows, TCP communication between 192.168.1.1 and 172.16.16.1 would typically spawn at least two flow records, one record for traffic from 192.168.1.1 to 172.16.16.1, and another for traffic from 172.16.16.1 to 192.168.1.1 (Table 4.1).

**Table 4.1** Two Unidirectional Flow Records for a Single Communication Sequence

| sIP | dIP | sPort | dPort | Pro | Packets | Bytes | Flags | Type |
|-----|-----|-------|-------|-----|---------|-------|-------|------|
| 192.168.1.1 | 172.16.16.1 | 3921 | 445 | 6 | 52 | 1331 | FS PA | Out |
| 172.16.16.1 | 192.168.1.1 | 445 | 3921 | 6 | 1230 | 310931 | FS PA | In |

A more realistic scenario might be to imagine a scenario where a workstation (192.168.1.50) is attempting to browse a web page on a remote server (192.0.2.75). This communication sequence is depicted in Figure 4.3.

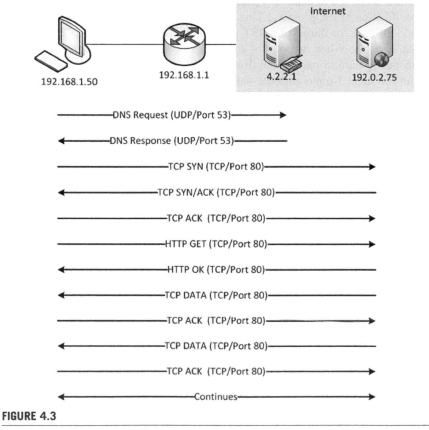

**FIGURE 4.3**

Web Server Communication Sequence

In this sequence, the client workstation (192.168.1.50) must first query a DNS server (4.2.2.1) located outside of his local network segment. Once a DNS response is received, the workstation can communicate with the web server. The flow records generated from this (as seen by the client workstation) would look like Table 4.2:

**Table 4.2** Flow Records Generated by Web Browsing

| sIP | dIP | sPort | dPort | Pro | Packets | Bytes | Flags | Type |
|-----|-----|-------|-------|-----|---------|-------|-------|------|
| 192.168. 1.50 | 4.2.2.1 | 9282 | 53 | 17 | 1 | 352 | | Out |
| 4.2.2.1 | 192.168. 1.50 | 53 | 9282 | 17 | 1 | 1332 | | In |
| 192.168. 1.50 | 192.0.2. 75 | 20239 | 80 | 6 | 1829 | 12283 | FS PA | Outweb |
| 192.0.2.75 | 192.168. 1.50 | 80 | 20239 | 6 | 2923 | 309103 | FS PA | Inweb |

A good practice to help wrap your mind around flow data is to compare flow records and packet data for the same time interval. Viewing the two data types and their representations of the same communication side-by-side will help you to learn exactly how flow data is derived. Next, we will look at a few of the major flow types.

## NetFlow

NetFlow was originally developed by Cisco in 1990 for use in streamlining routing processes on their network devices. In the initial specification, a flow record was generated when the router identified the first packet in new network conversations. This helped baseline network conversations and provided references for the router to compare to other devices and services on the network. These records were also used to identify and summarize larger amounts of traffic to simplify many processes, such as ACL comparisons. They also had the added benefit of being more easily parseable by technicians. Twenty-three years later, we have seen advancement of this specification through nine versions of NetFlow, including several derivative works. The features of these versions vary greatly and are used differently by individuals in various job functions, from infrastructure support and application development to security.

### NetFlow v5 and v9

The two most commonly used NetFlow standards are V5 and V9. NetFlow V5 is by far the most accessible NetFlow solution because most modern routing equipment supports NetFlow V5 export. NetFlow V5 flow records offer standard 5-tuple information as well all of the necessary statistics to define the flow aggregation of the packets being summarized. These statistics allow analysis engines to streamline the parsing of this information. Unlike NetFlow V9 and IPFIX, NetFlow V5 does not support the IPV6 protocol, which may limit its ability to be used in certain environments.

NetFlow V9 is everything V5 is, but so much more. NetFlow V9 provides a new template that offers quite a bit more detail in its logging. Whereas NetFlow V5 offers 20 data fields (two of those are padding), NetFlow V9 has 104 field type definitions. These modified field types can be sent via a templated output to comprise the configurable record. Thus, an administrator can use NetFlow V9 to generate records that resemble V5 records by configuring these templates. NetFlow V9 also provides IPV6 support. If you'd like to know more about the differences in NetFlow V5 and V9, consult Cisco's documentation.

Mike Patterson of Plixer provides one of the best and most entertaining examples on the comparison of NetFlow V5 and NetFlow V9 in a three-part blog at Plixer. com.[1] He states that the lack of V9 usage is almost entirely due to a lack of demand for the increased utility that V9 can offer. Mike argues that NetFlow V5 is like a generic hamburger. It will fulfill your needs, but generally do nothing more. However, depending on your situation, you might only desire sustenance. In that case, a generic hamburger is all you need. The generic hamburger is an easy and cheap way to satisfy hunger, providing only the bare minimum in features, but it is everything you need. NetFlow V9 on the other hand, is an Angus cheeseburger with all the trimmings. Most administrators either have minimal requirements from NetFlow data and don't require the extra trimmings that NetFlow V9 offers, or they don't have a method of interacting with the data as they did with NetFlow V5. Both of these reasons account for a lack of NetFlow V9 adoption.

## IPFIX

IPFIX has a lot in common with NetFlow V9 as it is built upon the same format. IPFIX is a template-based, record-oriented, binary export format.[2] The basic unit of data transfer in IPFIX is the message. A message contains a header and one or more sets, which contain records. A set may be either a template set or a data set. A data set references the template describing the data records within that set. IPFIX falls into a similar area as NetFlow V9 when it comes to adoption rate. The differences between NetFlow V9 and IPFIX are functional. For instance, IPFIX offers variable length fields to export custom information, where NetFlow V9 does not. It also has a scheme for exporting lists of formatted data. There are a number of differences between NetFlow V9 and IPFIX, but one word really defines them; IPFIX is "flexible". I use this word specifically because the extension to NetFlow V9 that makes it very similar to IPFIX is call "Flexible NetFlow", but that version falls out of the scope of this book.

---

[1] http://www.plixer.com/blog/general/cisco-netflow-v5-vs-netflow-v9-which-most-satisfies-your-hunger-pangs/
[2] http://www.tik.ee.ethz.ch/file/de367bc6c7868d1dc76753ea917b5690/Inacio.pdf

## Other Flow Types

Other flow technologies exist that could already be in use within your environment, but the question of accessibility and analysis might make them difficult to implement in a manner that is useful for NSM purposes. Juniper devices may offer Jflow while Citrix has AppFlow. One of the more common alternatives to NetFlow and IPFIX is sFlow, which uses flow sampling to reduce CPU overhead by only taking representative samplings of data across the wire. Variations of sFlow are becoming popular with vendors, with sFlow itself being integrated into multiple networking devices and hardware solutions. These other flow types leverage their own unique traits, but also consider that while you might have an accessible flow generator, be sure you have a means of collecting and parsing that flow data to make it an actionable data type.

In this book, we try our best to remain flow type agnostic. That is to say that when we talk about the analysis of flow data, it will be mostly focused on the standard 5-tuple that is included in all types of flow data.

## COLLECTING SESSION DATA

Session data can be collected in a number of different ways. Regardless of the method being used, a flow generator and collector will be required. A flow generator is the hardware or software component that creates the flow records. This can be done from either the parsing of other data, or by collecting network data directly from a network interface. A flow collector is software that receives flow records from the generator, and stores them in a retrievable format.

Those who are already performing FPC data collection will often choose to generate flow records from this FPC data. However, in most cases, the FPC data you are collecting will be filtered, which means you will be unable to generate flow records for the network traffic that isn't captured. Furthermore, if there is packet loss during your FPC capture, you will also lose valuable flow data. While this type of filtering is useful for maximizing disk utilization when capturing FPC data, the flow records associated with this traffic should be retained. This method of flow data generation isn't usually recommended.

The preferred method for session data generation is to capture it directly off of the wire in the same manner that FPC data or NIDS alert data might be generated. This can either be done by software on a server, or by a network device, like a router. For the purposes of this chapter, we will categorize generation by devices as "hardware generation" and generation by software as "software generation".

## Hardware Generation

In many scenarios, you will find that you already have the capability to generate some version of flow data by leveraging existing hardware. In these situations, you can simply configure a flow-enabled router with the network address of a destination collector and flow records from the router's interface will be sent to that destination.

While hardware collection may sound like a no-brainer, don't be surprised when your network administrator denies your request. On routing devices that are already being taxed by significant amounts of traffic, the additional processing required to generate and transmit flow records to an external collector can increase CPU utilization to the point of jeopardizing network bandwidth. While the processing overhead from flow generation is minimal, this can cause a significant impact in high traffic environments.

As you might expect, most Cisco devices inherently have the ability to generate NetFlow data. In order to configure NetFlow generation on a Cisco router, consult with the appropriate Cisco reference material. Cisco provides guides specifically for configuring NetFlow with Cisco IOS, which can be found here: http://www.cisco.com/en/US/docs/ios/netflow/command/reference/nf_cr_book.pdf.

## Software Generation

The majority of NSM practitioners rely on software generation. The use of software for flow generation has several distinct advantages, the best of which is the flexibility of the software deployment. It is much easier to deploy a server running flow generation software in a network segment than to re-architect that segment to place a flow generating router. Generating flow data with software involves executing a daemon on your sensor that collects and forwards flow records based upon a specific configuration. This flow data is generated from the data traversing the collection interface. In most configurations, this will be the same interface that other collection and detection software uses.

Now, we will examine some of the more common software generation solutions.

### Fprobe

Fprobe is an example of a minimalist NetFlow generation solution. Fprobe is available in most modern Linux distribution repositories and can be installed on a sensor easily via most package management systems, such as yum or apt.

If outside network connections are not available at your sensor location, the package can be compiled and installed manually with no odd caveats or obscure options. Once installed, Fprobe is initiated by issuing the fprobe command along with the network location and port where you are directing the flow data. As an example, if you wanted to generate flow data on the interface eth1, and send it to the collector listening on the host 192.168.1.15 at port 2888, you would issue the following command:

```
fprobe -i eth1 192.168.1.15:2888
```

### YAF

YAF (Yet Another Flowmeter) is a flow generation tool that offers IPFIX output. YAF was created by the CERT Network Situation Awareness (NetSA) team, who designed it for generating IPFIX records for use with SiLK (which will be discussed this later in this chapter).

As mentioned before, NetFlow v5 provides unidirectional flow information. This can result in redundant data in flow statistics that, on large distributed flow collection systems, can substantially affect data queries. To keep up with naturally increasing bandwidth and to provide bidirectional flow information for analysts, IPFIX was deemed to be a critical addition to SiLK, and YAF was created as an IPFIX generator. A bonus to using YAF is the ability to use the IPFIX template architecture with SiLK application labels for more refined analysis that you cannot get through the NetFlow V5 5-tuple.

Depending on your goals and the extent of your deployment, YAF might be a necessity in your IDS environment. If so, installing YAF is fairly straightforward. This book won't go into detail on this process, but there are a few details that can help streamline the process. Before compiling YAF, please make sure to review the NetSA documentation thoroughly. NetSA also has supplementary install tutorials that will take you through the installation and initialization of YAF. This documentation can be found here: https://tools.netsa.cert.org/confluence/pages/viewpage. action?pageId=23298051.

## COLLECTING AND ANALYZING FLOW DATA WITH SiLK

SiLK (System for Internet-Level Knowledge) is a toolset that allows for efficient manageable security analysis across networks. SiLK serves as a flow collector, and is also an easy way to quickly store, access, parse, and display flow data. SiLK is a project currently developed by the CERT NetSA group, but like most great security tools, it was the result of necessity being the mother of invention. Originally dubbed "Suresh's Work", SiLK was the result of an analyst needing to parse flow in a timely and efficient way, without the need for complex CPU intensive scripts. SiLK is a collection of C, Python, and Perl, and as such, works in almost any UNIX-based environment.

The importance of documentation is paramount. No matter how great of a tool, script, or device you create, it is nothing if it can only be used by the developer. The documentation for SiLK is second to none when it comes to truly helpful reference guides for an information security tool. To emphasize the importance of this documentation, the following sections will use this guide as both reference, and as part of a basic scenario in how to use SiLK.[3] It is not an overstatement to suggest that the SiLK documentation and the community that supports the tool are easily some of the best features of the SiLK project.

### SiLK Packing Toolset

The SiLK toolset operates via two components: the packing system and the analysis suite. The packing system is the method by which SiLK collects and stores flow data in a consistent, native format. The term "packing" refers to SiLK's ability to compress the flow data into a space-efficient binary format ideal for parsing via SiLK's

---

[3] http://tools.netsa.cert.org/silk/docs.html

analysis suite. The analysis suite is a collection of tools intended to filter, display, sort, count, group, mate, and more. The analysis tool suite is a collection of command line tools that provide an infinite level of flexibility. While each tool itself is incredibly powerful, each tool can also be chained together with other tools via pipes based on the logical output of the previous tool.

In order to utilize SiLK's collection and analysis features, you must get data to it from a flow generator. When the collector receives flow records from a generator, the records are logically separated out by flow type. Flow types are parsed based upon a configuration file that determines if the records are external-to-internal, internal-to-external, or internal-to-internal in relation to the network architecture.

In SiLK, the listening collection process is a tool known as rwflowpack. Rwflowpack is in charge of parsing the flow type, determining what sensor the data is coming from, and placing the refined flow data into its database for parsing by any of the tools within the analysis toolset. This workflow is shown in Figure 4.4.

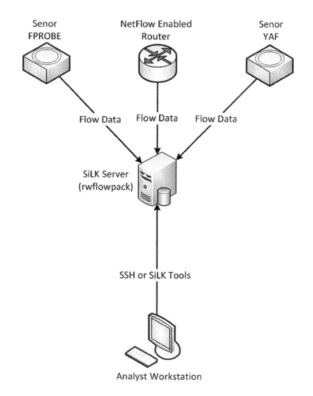

**FIGURE 4.4**

The SiLK Workflow

The execution of Rwflowpack is governed by a file named rwflowpack.conf, as well as optional command line arguments that can be issued during execution. The most common method to initiate rwflowpack is the command:

```
service rwflowpack start
```

Rwflowpack will confirm that the settings in the silk.conf and sensor.conf files are configured correctly and that all listening sockets identified by sensor.conf are available. If everything checks out, Rwflowpack will initialize and you will receive verification on screen.

While the packing process in SiLK is straightforward, it has more options that can be utilized outside of just receiving and optimizing flow data. The SiLK packing system has eight different tools used to accept and legitimize incoming flows. As previously mentioned, rwflowpack is a tool used to accept flow data from flow generators defined by SiLK's two primary configuration files, silk.conf and sensor.conf, and then convert and sort the data into specific binary files suitable for SiLK's analysis suite to parse. Forwarding flow data directly to an rwflowpack listener is the least complicated method of generating SiLK session data. Often the need arises for an intermediary to temporarily store and forward data between the generator and collector. For this, flowcap can be utilized. In most cases, flowcap can be considered a preprocessor to rwflowpack in that it first takes the flow data and sorts it into appropriate bins based on flow source and a unit or time variable. The SiLK documentation describes this as storing the data in "one file per source per quantum," with a quantum being either a timeout or a maximum file size. The packing system also has a number of postprocessing abilities with tools such as rwflowappend, rwpackchecker, and rwpollexec. Rwflowappend and Rwpackchecker do exactly what they say; rwflowappend will append SiLK records to existing records and rwpackchecker checks for data integrity and SiLK file corruptions. Rwpollexec will monitor the incoming SiLK data files and run a user-specified command against each one. Rwflowappend, rwpackchecker and rwpollexec can be referred to as postprocessors because they further massage the SiLK data after rwflowpack has converted the raw flows into binary SiLK files. The moral of this story is that there are more than enough ways to get your data to rwflowpack for conversion into SiLK binary files.

## SiLK Flow Types

SiLK organizes flows into one of several types that can be used for filtering and sorting flow records. This is handled based upon the network ranges provided for internal and external ipblocks in the sensor.conf configuration file used by rwflowpack (Figure 4.5). These flow types are:

- In: Inbound to a device on an internal network
- Out: Outbound to a device on an external network
- Int2int: From an internal network to the same, or another internal network
- Ext2ext: From an external network to the same, or another external network
- Inweb: Inbound to a device on an internal network using either port 80, 443, or 8080.

- Outweb: Outbound to a device on an external network using either port 80, 443, or 8080.
- Inicmp: Inbound to a device on an internal network using ICMP (IP Protocol 1)
- Outicmp: Outbound to a device on an external network using ICMP (IP Protocol 1)
- Innull: Inbound filtered traffic or inbound traffic to null-ipblocks specified in sensor.conf
- Outnull: Outbound filtered traffic or outbound traffic to null-ipblocks specified in sensor.conf
- Other: Source not internal or external, or destination not internal or external

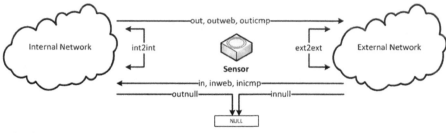

**FIGURE 4.5**

SiLK Flow Types

Understanding these flow types will be helpful when using some of the filtering tools we will talk about next.

## SiLK Analysis Toolset

The analysis toolset is where you will spend the majority of your time when working with flow data. There are over 55 tools included in the SiLK installation, all of which are useful, with some being used more frequently. These analysis tools are meant to work as a cohesive unit, with the ability to pipe data from one tool to another seamlessly. The most commonly used tool in the suite is rwfilter. Rwfilter takes the SiLK binary files and filters through them to provide only the specific data that the analyst requires. We've spoken at length about how the size of flow records allow you to store them for a significant time, so it becomes clear that there must be a convenient way to apply filters to this data in order to only see data that is relevant given your specific task. For instance, an analyst might only want to examine a week of data from a year ago, with only source IP addresses from a particular subnet, with all destination addresses existing in a specific country. Rwfilter makes that quick and easy. The output of rwfilter, unless specified, will be another SiLK binary file that can continue to be parsed or manipulated via pipes. The tool is very thoroughly covered in the SiLK documentation and covers categories for filtering, counting, grouping, and more. As this is the collection section of the book, we will only cover a few brief scenarios with the analysis toolset here.

## Installing SiLK in Security Onion

In this book, we don't go into the finer details of how to install each of these tools, as most of those processes are documented fairly well, and most of them come pre-installed on the Security Onion distribution if you want to test them. Unfortunately, at this time of this writing, SiLK doesn't come preinstalled on Security Onion like all of the other tools in this book. As such, you can find detailed instructions on this installation process on the Applied NSM blog at: http://www.appliednsm.com/silk-on-security-onion/.

## Filtering Flow Data with Rwfilter

The broad scope of flow collection and the speed of flow retrieval with SiLK makes a strong case for the inclusion of flow collection in any environment. With SiLK, virtually any analyst can focus the scope of a network incident with a speed unmatched by any other data type. The following scenarios present a series of common situations in which SiLK can be used to either resolve network incidents, or to filter down a large data set to a manageable size.

One of the first actions in most investigations is to examine the extent of the harassment perpetrated by an offending host with a single IP address. Narrowing this down from PCAP data can be extremely time consuming, if not impossible. With SiLK, this process can start by using the rwfilter command along with at least one input, output, and partitioning option. First is the --any-address option, which will query the data set for all flow records matching the identified IP address. This can be combined with the --start-date and --end-date options to narrow down the specific time frame we are concerned with. In addition to this, we will provide rwfilter with the –type = all options, which denotes that we want both inbound and outbound flows, and the --pass = stdout option, which allows us to pass the output to rwcut (via a pipe symbol) so that it can be displayed within the terminal window. This gives us an rwfilter command that looks like this:

```
rwfilter --any-address=1.2.3.4 --start-date=2013/06/22:11 --end-
date=2013/06/22:16 --type-all -pass=stdout | rwcut
```

Denoting only a start-date will limit your search to a specific quantum of time based on the smallest time value. For instance, --start-date = 2013/06/22:11 will display the entirety of the filter matched flow data for the 11th hour of that day. Similarly, if you have –start-date = 2013/06/22, you will receive the entire day's records. The combination of these options will allow you to more accurately correlate events across data types and also give you 1000 ft visibility on the situation itself.

For example, let's say that you have a number of events where a suspicious IP (6.6.6.6) is suddenly receiving significant encrypted data from a secure web server shortly after midnight. The easiest way to judge the extent of the suspicious traffic is to run the broad SiLK query:

```
rwfilter --start-date=2013/06/22:00 --any-address=6.6.6.6 --type
=all --pass=stdout | rwcut
```

If the data is too expansive, simply add in the partitioning option "--aport = 443" to the previous filter to narrow the search to just the events related to the interactions between the suspicious IP and any secure web servers. The --aport command will filter based upon any port that matches the provided value, which in this case is port 443 (the port most commonly associated with HTTPS communication).

```
rwfilter --start-date=2016/06/22:00 --any-address=6.6.6.6 --aport
=443 --type=all --pass=stdout | rwcut
```

After looking at that data, you might notice that the offending web server is communicating with several hosts on your network, but you want to zero in on the communication occurring from one specific internal host (192.168.1.100) to the suspicious IP. In that case, instead of using the --any-address option, we can use the --saddress and --daddress options, which allow you to filter on a particular source and destination address, respectively. This command would look like:

```
rwfilter --start-date=2013/06/22:00 --saddress=192.168.1.100
--daddress=6.6.6.6 --aport=443 --type=all --pass=stdout | rwcut
```

## Piping Data Between Rwtools

An analyst often diagnoses the integrity of the NSM data by evaluating the health of incoming traffic. This example will introduce a number of rwtools and the fundamentals of piping data from one rwtool to another.

It is important to understand that rwfilter strictly manipulates and narrows down data fed to it from binary files and reproduces other binary files based on those filter options. In previous examples we have included the --pass = stdout option to send the binary data which matches a filter to the terminal output. We piped this binary data to rwcut in order to convert it to human readable ASCII data in the terminal window. In this sense, we have already been piping data between rwtools. However, rwcut is the most basic rwtool, and the most essential because it is almost always used to translate data to an analyst in a readable form. It doesn't do calculations or sorting, it simply converts binary data into ASCII data and manipulates it for display at the user's discretion through additional rwcut options.

In order to perform calculations on the filtered data, you must pipe directly from the filtered data to an analysis rwtool. For this example, we'll evaluate rwcount, a tool used to summarize total network traffic over time. Analyzing the total amount of data that SiLK is receiving can provide an analyst with a better understanding of the networks that he/she is monitoring. Rwcount is commonly used for the initial inspection of new sensors. When a new sensor is brought online, it comes with many caveats. How many end users are you monitoring? When is traffic the busiest? What should you expect during late hours? Simply getting a summary of network traffic is what rwcount does. Rwcount works off of binary SiLK data. This means that piping data to it from rwfilter will give you an ASCII summary of any data matching your filter.

Consider a scenario where you want to evaluate how much data is being collected by your SiLK manager. We'll use rwfilter to output all of the data collected for an entire day, and we will pipe that data to rwcount:

```
rwfilter --start-date=2013/6/22 --proto=0-255 --pass=stdout --type
=all | rwcount --bin-size=60
```

This command will produce a summary of traffic over time in reference to total records, bytes, and packets per minute that match the single day filter described. This time interval is based upon the --bin-size option, which we set to 60 seconds. If you increase the bin size to 3600, you will get units per hour, which is shown in Figure 4.6. As mentioned before, rwfilter requires, at minimum, an input switch, a partitioning option, and an output switch. In this case, we want the input switch to identify all traffic (--type = all) occurring on 2013/6/22. In order to pass all data, we will specify that data matching all protocols (--proto = 0-255) should pass to stdout (--pass = stdout). This will give us all of the traffic for this time period.

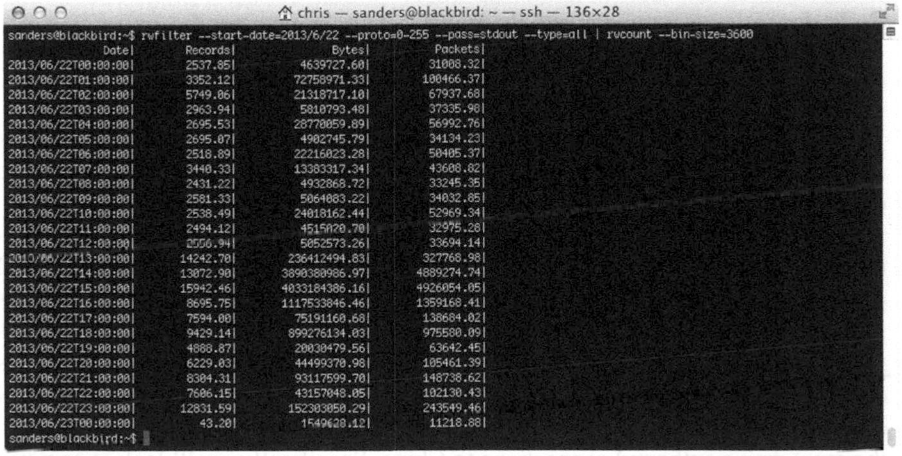

**FIGURE 4.6**

Output of Flow Data Parsed by Rwcount

You've now seen basic scenarios involving filtering flow records using rwfilter, and the use of rwcount, a tool that is of great use in profiling your networks at a high level. We'll now combine these two tools and add another rwtool called rwsetbuild. Rwsetbuild will allow you to build a binary file for SiLK to process using various partitioning options. Quite often, you'll find you need a query that will consider multiple IP addresses. While there are tools within SiLK to combine multiple queries, rwsetbuild makes this unnecessary as it will streamline the process by allowing you to generate a flat text list of IP addresses and/or subnets (we'll call it testIP-list.txt), and run them through rwsetbuild with the following command:

```
rwsetbuild testIPlist.txt testIPlist.set
```

Having done this, you can use the --anyset partitioning option with rwfilter to filter flow records where any of the IP addresses within the list appear in either source or destination address fields. The command would look like:

```
rwfilter --start-date=2014/06/22 --anyset=/home/user/testIPlist.set
--type=all --pass=stdout | rwcut
```

This ability can be leveraged to gather a trove of useful information. Imagine you have a list of malicious IP addresses that you're asked to compare with communication records for your internal networks. Of particular interest is how much data has been leaving the network and going to these "bad" IP addresses. Flow data is the best option for this, as you can couple what you've learned with rwsetbuild and rwcount to generate a quick statistic of outbound data to these malicious devices. The following process would quickly yield a summary of outbound data per hour:

1. Add IP addresses to a file called badhosts.txt.
2. Create the set file with the command:

```
rwsetbuild badhosts.txt badhosts.set
```

3. Perform the query and create the statistic with the command:

```
rwfilter --start-date=2013/06/22 --dipset=badhosts.set --type=all
--pass=stdout | rwcount --bin-size=3600
```

The next scenario is one that I run into every day, and one that people often ask about. This is a query for "top talkers", which are the hosts on the network that are communicating the most.

Top talker requests can have any number of variables involved as well, be it top-talkers outbound to a foreign country, top talking tor exit nodes inbound to local devices, or top talking local devices on ports 1-1024. In order to accomplish tasks such as these, we are interested in pulling summary statistics that match given filters for the data we want. If you haven't already guessed it, the tool we're going to use is creatively named rwstats. Piping rwfilter to rwstats will give Top-N or Bottom-N calculations based on the results of the given filter. In this example, we'll analyze the most active outbound connections to China. Specifically, we'll look at communications that are returning data on ephemeral ports (>1024). This can be accomplished with the following command:

```
rwfilter --start-date=2013/06/22 --dcc=cn --sport=1024-65535 --type=all
--pass=stdout | rwstats --top --count=20 --fields=sip --value=bytes
```

You will note that this rwfilter command uses an option we haven't discussed before, --dcc. This option can be used to specify that we want to filter based upon traffic to a particular destination country code. Likewise, we could also use the command --scc to filter based upon a particular source country. The ability to filter data based upon country code doesn't work with an out-of-the-box SiLK installation. In order to utilize this functionality and execute the command listed above, you will have to complete the following steps:

1. Download the MaxMind GeoIP database with wget:

```
wget http://geolite.maxmind.com/download/geoip/database/
GeoLiteCountry/GeoIP.dat.gz
```

2. Unzip the file and convert it into the appropriate format:

```
gzip -d -c GeoIP.dat.gz | rwgeoip2ccmap --encoded-
input > country_codes.pmap
```

3. Copy the resulting file into the appropriate location:

```
cp country_codes.pmap /usr/local/share/silk/
```

The results of this query take the form shown in Figure 4.7.

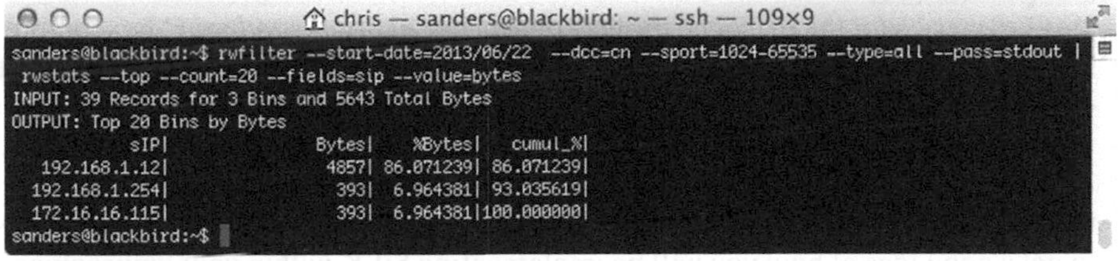

**FIGURE 4.7**

The Results of the Rwstats Query

In this example, rwstats only displays three addresses talking out to China, despite the --count = 20 option on rwstats that should show the top twenty IP addresses. This implies that there are only three total local IP addresses talking out to China in the given time interval. Had there been fifty addresses, you would have only seen the top 20 local IP addresses. The --bytes option specifies that the statistic should be generated based upon the number of bytes of traffic in the communication. Leaving off the –value option will default to displaying the statistic for total number of outbound flow records instead.

The next logical step in this scenario would be to find out who all of these addresses are talking to, and if it accepts the traffic. Narrowing down the results by augmenting the rwfilter portion of the command in conjunction with altering the fields in rwstats will provide you with the actual Chinese addresses that are being communicated with. We've also used the --saddress option to narrow this query down to only the traffic from the host who is exchanging the most traffic with China.

```
rwfilter --start-date=2013/06/22 --saddress=192.168.1.12 --dcc=cn
--sport=1024-65535 --type=all --pass=stdout | rwstats --top --
count=20 --fields=dip --value=bytes
```

Finally, utilizing the rwfilter commands in previous scenarios, you can retrieve the flow records for each host in order to gauge the type of data that is being transferred. You can these use this information, along with the appropriate timestamps, to retrieve other useful forms of data that might aid in the investigation, such as PCAP data.

## Other SiLK Resources

SiLK and YAF are only a small portion of the toolset that NetSA offers. I highly recommend that you check out the other public offerings that can work alongside SiLK. NetSA offers a supplementary tool to bring SiLK to the less unix-savvy with iSiLK, a graphical front-end for SiLK. Another excellent tool is the Analysis Pipeline, an actively developed flow analysis automation engine that can sit inline with flow collection. Once it has been made active with an appropriate rule configuration, the Analysis Pipeline can streamline blacklist, DDOS, and beacon detection from SiLK data so that you don't need to script these tools manually.

While the documentation is an excellent user reference for SiLK and is an invaluable resource for regular analysts, SiLK also has complementary handbooks and guides to help ignite the interests of amateur session data analysts or assist in generating queries for the seasoned professional. The '*Analyst Handbook*' is a comprehensive 107 page guide to many SiLK use cases.[4] This handbook serves as the official tutorial introduction into using SiLK for active analysis of flow data. Other reference documents pertain to analysis tips and tricks, installation information, and a full PySiLK starter guide for those wanting to implement SiLK as an extension to python. We highly recommended perusing the common installation scenarios to get a good idea of how you will be implementing SiLK within your environment.

## COLLECTING AND ANALYZING FLOW DATA WITH ARGUS

While Applied NSM will focus on SiLK as the flow analysis engine of choice, we would be remiss if we didn't at least mention Argus. Argus is a tool that also happens to be the product of some of CERT-CC's early endeavors in the field of flow analysis. Argus first went into government use in 1989, becoming the world's first real-time network flow analyzer.[5] Starting in 1991, CERT began officially supporting Argus. From there, Argus saw rapid development until 1995 when it was released to the public.

Argus defines itself as a definitive flow solution that encompasses more than just flow data, but instead provides a comprehensive systematic view of all network traffic in real time. Argus is a bi-directional flow analysis suite that tracks both sides of network conversations and reports metrics for the same flow record.[6] While offering many of the same features as other IPFIX flow analysis solutions, Argus has its own statistical analysis tools and detection/alerting mechanisms that attempt to separate it from other solutions. In the next few sections, I'll provide an overview of the basic solution architecture and how it is integrated within Security Onion. In doing so, I won't rehash a lot of concepts I've already covered, but instead, will focus on only

---

[4]http://tools.netsa.cert.org/silk/analysis-handbook.pdf
[5]http://www.qosient.com/argus/presentations/Argus.FloCon.2012.Tutorial.pdf
[6]http://qosient.com/argus/argusnetflow.shtml

the essentials to make sure you can capture and display data appropriately. As mentioned before, Argus sets itself apart in a few key ways, so I'll provide examples where these features might benefit your organization more than the competing flow analysis engines.

## Solution Architecture

Even though Argus comes packaged within Security Onion, it is important to understand the general workflow behind obtaining and verifying the data. Even with Security Onion, you might find yourself troubleshooting NSM collection issues, or you might desire to bring in data from external devices that aren't deployed as Security Onion sensors. In these events, this section should give you an understanding of the deployment of Argus and how its parts work together to give you a flow analysis package with little overhead.

We are going to frame this discussion with Argus as a standalone rollout. Argus consists of two main packages. This first package is simply known as the generic "Argus" package, which will record traffic seen at a given network interface on any device. That package can then either write the data to disk for intermittent transfer or maintain a socketed connection to the central security server for constant live transfer. This is the component that will typically reside on a sensor, and will transmit data back to a centralized logging server.

The second Argus package is referred to as the Argus Client package. This package, once deployed correctly, will read from log files, directories, or a constant socket connection for real-time analysis. These client tools do more than collect data from the external generator; they will serve as the main analysis tools for the duration of your Argus use. With that said, you will need the client tools on any device that you do Argus flow analysis from.

There isn't much difference in the workflow of Argus and other flow utilities. The basic idea is that a collection interface exists that has a flow-generating daemon on it. That daemon sees the traffic, generates flows, and forwards the flow data to a central collection platform where storage and analysis of that data can occur.

## Features

Argus is unique because it likely has more features built into it than most other flow analysis tools. A standalone deployment of Argus can do more than basic flow queries and statistics. Since partial application data can be retrieved with the collection of IPFIX flow data imported into Argus, it can be used to perform tasks such as filtering data based upon HTTP URLs. I mention that Argus is powerful by itself, because in today's NSM devices we generally have other tools to perform these additional tasks. This makes mechanisms like URL filtering redundant if it is working on top of other data types such as packet string data. Since we are referring to the basic installation of Argus within Security Onion, I will not be discussing the additional Argus application layer analysis. In Chapter 6 we will be talking about packet string data and how it can perform those tasks for you.

## Basic Data Retrieval

Data retrieval in different flow analysis tools can result in a déjà vu feeling due to the similarity in the data ingested by the tools. Ultimately, it is the query syntax and statistic creation abilities of these tools that differ. Argus has what appears to be a basic querying syntax on initial glance; however, the learning curve for Argus can be steep. Given the large number of query options and the vague documentation available for the tool online, the man pages for the tools will be your saving grace when tackling this learning curve.

The most useful tool within the Argus Client suite of tools is ra. This tool will provide you with the initial means to filter and browse raw data collected by Argus. Ra must be able to access a data set in order to function. This data can be provided through an Argus file from the –r option, from piped standard input, or from a remote feed. Since we are working so intimately with Security Onion, you can reference the storage directory for Argus files in /nsm/sensor_data/<interface>/argus/. At first glance, ra is a simple tool, and for the most part, you'll probably find yourself making basic queries using only a read option with a Berkeley Packet Filter (BPF) at the end. For example, you might have a suspicion that you have several geniuses on your network due to HTTP logs revealing visits to www.appliednsm.com. One way to view this data with Argus would be to run the command:

```
ra -r /nsm/sensor_data/<interface>/argus/<file>- port 80 and host
67.205.2.30
```

Sample output from this command is shown below in Figure 4.8.

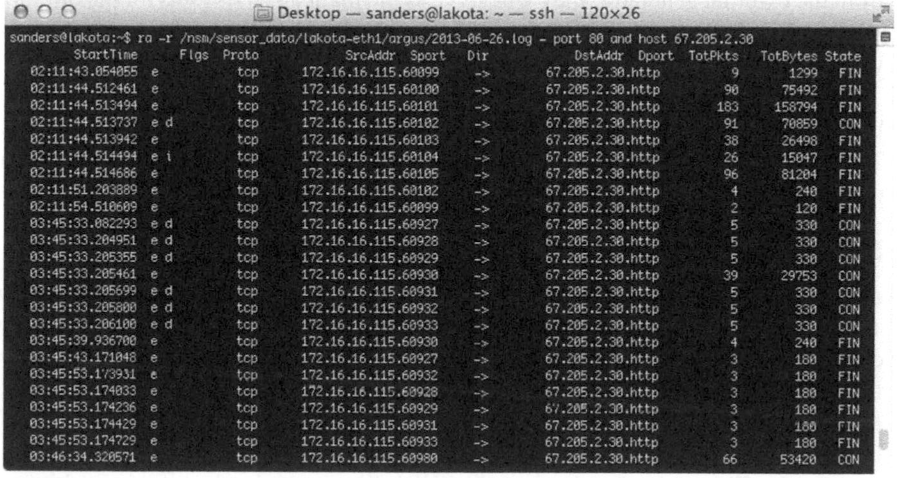

**FIGURE 4.8**

Sample Argus Output with ra

The nicest benefit of Argus over competing flow analysis platforms is its ability to parse logs using the same BPFs that tools like Tcpdump use. This allows for quick and effective use of the simplest functions of ra and Argus. After understanding the basic filter methodology for ra, you can advance the use of ra with additional options. As I stated before, ra can process standard input and feed other tools via standard output. In doing so, you can feed the data to other Argus tools. By default, ra will read from standard-in if the –r option is not present. Outputting ra results to a file can be done with the –w option. Using these concepts, we could create the following command:

```
cat /nsm/sensor_data/<interface>/argus/<file> | ra -w - - ip and host
67.205.2.30 | racluster -M rmon -m proto -s proto pkts bytes
```

This example will use ra to process raw standard input and send the output to standard out via the -w option. This output is then piped to the racluster tool. Racluster performs ra data aggregation for IP profiling. In the example, racluster is taking the result of the previous ra command and aggregating the results by protocol. A look at the manual page for ra reveals that it also accepts racluster options for parsing the output. The example command shown above would produce an output similar to what is shown in Figure 4.9.

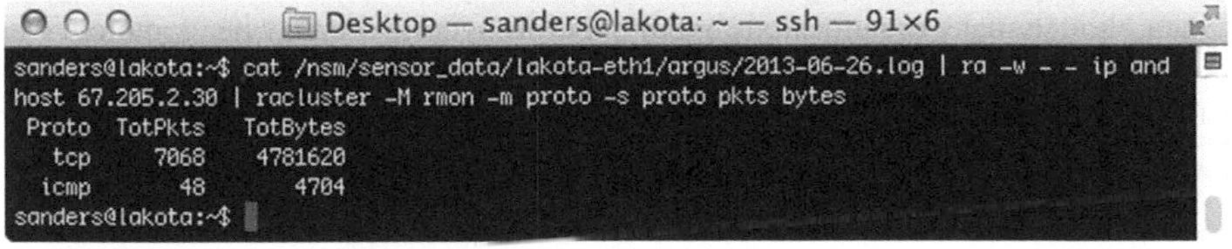

```
sanders@lakota:~$ cat /nsm/sensor_data/lakota-eth1/argus/2013-06-26.log | ra -w - - ip and
host 67.205.2.30 | racluster -M rmon -m proto -s proto pkts bytes
  Proto  TotPkts   TotBytes
   tcp     7068    4781620
   icmp      48       4704
sanders@lakota:~$
```

**FIGURE 4.9**

Sample Ra and Racluster Output

## Other Argus Resources

Though this book won't cover the extensive use of Argus from an analysis standpoint, it is still worth reviewing in comparison to other flow analysis suites like SiLK. When choosing a flow analysis tool each analyst must identify which tool best suits his/her existing skill set and environment. The ability to use BPFs in filtering data with ra makes Argus immediately comfortable to even the newest flow analysts. However, advanced analysis with Argus will require extensive parsing skills and a good understanding of the depth of ratools to be successful. If you want to learn more about Argus, you can visit http://qosient.com/argus/index.shtml, or for greater technical detail on how to work with Argus, go to http://nsmwiki.org/index.php?title=Argus.

## SESSION DATA STORAGE CONSIDERATIONS

Session data is miniscule in size compared to other data types. However, flow data storage cannot be an afterthought. I've seen situations where a group will set up flow as their only means of network log correlation, only to realize that after a month of data collection, they can't query their logs anymore. This results from improper flow rollover. Flow data can gradually increase in size to an unmanageable level if left unchecked. There is no specific recommendation on the amount of storage you'll need for flow data, as it depends on the data that is important to you, and how much throughput you have. With that said, just because are able to define a universal filter for all traffic you are collecting doesn't mean you should. Even though you might not be collecting FPC data for certain protocols, such as encrypted GRE tunnels or HTTPS traffic, you should still keep flow records of these communications.

To estimate the amount of storage space needed for flow data, the CERT NetSA team provides a SiLK provisioning worksheet that can help. It can be found at: http://tools.netsa.cert.org/releases/SiLK-Provisioning-v3.3.xlsx.

There are many ways to manage your network log records, but I find one of the simplest and easiest to maintain is a simple cron job that watches all of your data and does rollover as necessary or based upon a time interval. Many of your data capture tools will feature rollover features in the process of generating the data; however, you'll likely have to manage this rollover manually. This can be the case with flow data, though many organizations opt to only roll over flow data when required. One solution to limit the data is to simply create a cron job that cleans the flow data directory by purging files that are older that X days. One SiLK specific example of a cron job that will do this is:

```
30 12 * * * find /data/silk/* -mtime +29 -exec rm {} \;
```

In this example, the /data/silk/ directory will be purged of all data files 30 days or older. This purge will occur every day at 12:30 PM. However, be careful to make sure that you're not removing your configuration files if they are stored in the same directory as your data. Many organizations will also like to keep redundant storage of flow data. In that case, the following will move your data to a mounted external USB storage device.

```
*/30 * * * * rsync --update -vr /data/silk/ /mnt/usb/data/silk/ &> /dev/null
```

This command will copy all new flow files every 2 minutes. The method used to implement this cron job will vary depending on which operating system flavor you are using. In this spirit, it should be noted that SiLK also includes features to repeat data to other sites.

I like to include control commands like these in a general "watchdog" script that ensures services are restarted in the event of the occasional service failure or system reboot. In this watchdog script, I also include the periodic updating or removal of data, the transfer and copying of redundant data, status scripts that monitor sensor health, and the service health scripts that make sure processes stay alive. This has the added benefit of eliminating errors upon sensor startup, as the services in question will begin one the cron job starts rather than with all other kernel startup processes.

Ultimately, the greatest benefit of a centralized watchdog script is that it will provide a central point of reference for safely monitoring the health of your sensors, which includes ensuring that data is constantly flowing. The script below can be used to monitor YAF to make sure it is constantly running. Keep in mind that the script may require slight modifications to work correctly in your production environment.

```
#!/bin/bash
function SiLKSTART {
      sudo nohup /usr/local/bin/yaf --silk --ipfix=tcp --live=pcap --
out=192.168.1.10  --ipfix-port=18001  --in=eth1  --applabel  --max-
payload=384 --verbose --log=/var/log/yaf.log &
}
function watchdog {
      pidyaf=$(pidof yaf)
      if [ -z "$pidyaf" ]; then
            echo "YAF is not running."
            SiLKSTART
      fi
}
watchdog
```

Rwflowpack is another tool that you may want to monitor to ensure that it is always running and collecting flow data. You can use the following code to monitor its status:

```
#!/bin/bash

pidrwflowpack=$(pidof rwflowpack)

if [ -z "$pidrwflowpack" ]; then
echo "rwflowpack is not running."
sudo pidof rwflowpack | tr ' ' '\n' | xargs -i sudo kill -9 {}
sudo service rwflowpack restart
fi
```

# CONCLUSION

In this chapter we provided an overview of the fundamental concepts associated with the collection of session data. This included an overview of different types of session data like NetFlow and IPFIX, as well as a detailed overview of data collection and retrieval with SiLK, and a brief overview of Argus. I can't stress the importance of session data enough. If you are starting a new security program or beginning to develop an NSM capability within your organization, the collection of session data is the best place to start in order to get the most bang for your buck.

# Full Packet Capture Data

The type of NSM data with the most intrinsic value to the analyst is Full Packet Capture (FPC) data. FPC data provides a full accounting for every data packet transmitted between two endpoints. If we compare the investigation of computer-related crime to human focused crime, having FPC data from a device under investigation would be equivalent to having a surveillance-video recording of a human suspect under investigation. Ultimately, if an attacker accesses a system from the network, there will be evidence of it within FPC data.

FPC data can be quite overwhelming due to its completeness, but it is this high degree of granularity that is valuable when it comes to providing analytic context. It does come with a price, however, as it can be quite storage intensive to capture and store FPC data for an extended period of time. Some organizations find that they simply don't have the resources to effectively incorporate FPC data into their NSM infrastructure.

The most common form of FPC data is the PCAP data format (Figure 5.1). The PCAP format is supported by most open source collection, detection, and analysis tools and has been the gold standard for FPC data for quite a while. Several libraries exist for creating software that can generate and interact with PCAP files, but the most popular is Libpcap, which is an open source packet capture library that allows applications to interact with network interface cards to capture packets. Originally created in 1994, its main objective was to provide a platform-independent API that could be used to capture packets without the need for operating system specific modules. A large number of applications used in packet collection and analysis utilize Libpcap, including several of the tools discussed in this book, like Dumpcap, Tcpdump, Wireshark, and more. Since libraries like Libpcap make the manipulation of PCAP data so easy, often other NSM data types, such as statistical data or packet string data are generated from PCAP data.

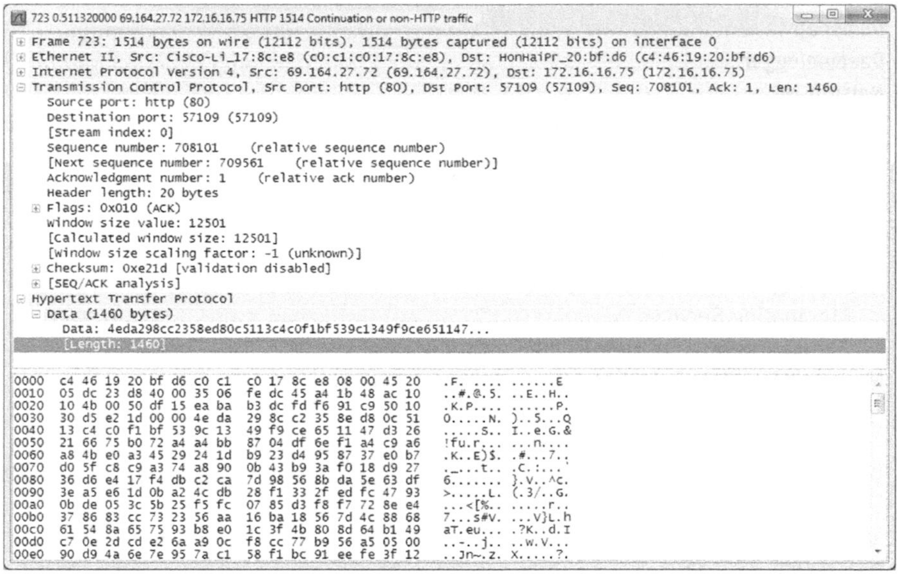

**FIGURE 5.1**

Sample PCAP Data as seen in Wireshark

Recently, the PCAP-NG format has evolved as the next version of the PCAP file format. PCAP-NG provides added flexibility to PCAP files, including allowing for comments to be inserted into packet captures (Figure 5.2). This feature is incredibly helpful to analysts when storing examined files for later analysis by themselves or other analysts. Most of the tools mentioned in this book support PCAP-NG.

---

**FROM THE TRENCHES**

You can determine the format of a packet capture file by using the capinfos tool that is provided with Wireshark (which we will talk about more in Chapter 13). To do this, execute the command capinfos -t < file >. If the file is just a PCAP file, capinfos will tell you that it is a "libpcap" file. If it is a PCAP-NG file, it will refer to it as "pcapng."

---

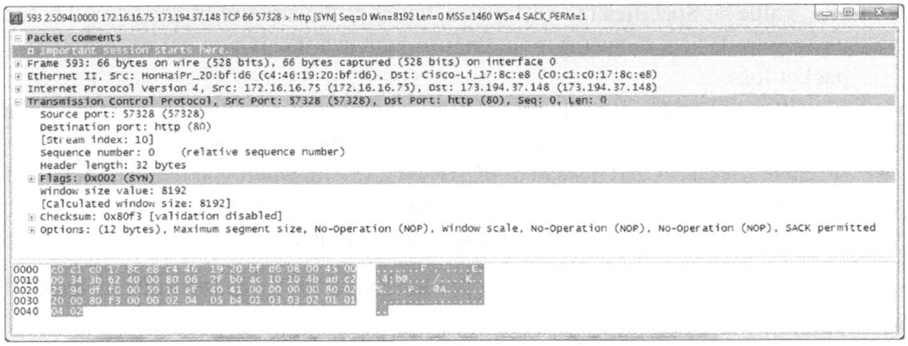

**FIGURE 5.2**

A Commented Packet Leveraging PCAP-NG

In this chapter we will explore several popular FPC collection solutions and high-light some of the benefits of each one. In addition to this, we will examine some strategies for implementing FPC solutions into your network in the most economical manner possible.

# DUMPCAP

One of the easiest ways to get up and running with full packet capture is by utilizing Dumpcap. The Dumpcap tool is included with Wireshark, which means that most analysts already have it on their system whether they know it or not. Dumpcap is a simple tool designed solely for the purpose of capturing packets from an interface and writing them to disk. Dumpcap utilizes the Libpcap packet capture library to capture packets and write them in PCAP-NG format.

If you are using Security Onion then Wireshark is already installed, which means that you already have Dumpcap. If not, then you can download the Wireshark suite from http://www.wireshark.org. Once you've downloaded and installed Wireshark (along with the bundled Libpcap driver, required for packet capture), you can begin logging packets by invoking the Dumpcap tool and specifying a capture interface, like this:

```
dumpcap -i eth1
```

This command will begin capturing packets and writing them to a randomly named file in the current working directory, and will continue to do so until stopped. Dumpcap provides some other useful options for crafting how packet data is stored and captured:

- -a < value >: Specifies when to stop writing to a capture file. This can be time duration, a file size, or a number of written files. Multiple conditions can be used together.
- -b < options >: Causes Dumpcap to write to multiple files based upon when certain criteria are met. This can be time duration, a file size, or a number of written files. Multiple conditions can be used together.

- -B < value >: Specifies the buffer size, which is the amount of data stored before writing to disk. It is useful to attempt to increase this if you are experiencing packet loss.
- -f < filter >: Berkeley Packet Filter (BPF) command(s) for filtering the capture file.
- -i < interface >: Capture packets from the specified interface
- -P: Save files as PCAP instead of PCAP-NG. Useful when you require backwards compatibility with tools that don't support PCAP-NG yet.
- -w < filename >: Used to specify the output file name.

In order to get this command more "production ready", we might invoke the command like this:

```
dumpcap -i eth1 -b duration:60 -b files:60 -w NYC01
```

This command will capture packets from the eth1 interface (-i eth1), and store them in 60 files (-b files:60), each containing 60 seconds worth of captured traffic (-b duration:60). When the 60th file has been written, the first file starts being overwritten. These files will be numbered using the string we specified and adding the number of the file, and a date time stamp (-w NYC01).

While Dumpcap is simple to get up and running, it does have its limitations. First of all, it doesn't always stand up well in high performance scenarios when reaching higher throughput levels, which may result in dropped packets. In addition, the simplicity of the tool limits its flexibility. This is evident in the limited number of configuration options in the tool. One example of this can be found in how Dumpcap outputs captured data. While it will allow you to specify text to prepend to packet capture filenames, it does not provide any additional flexibility in controlling the naming of these files. This could prove to be problematic if you require a specific naming convention for use with a custom parsing script or a third party or commercial detection or analysis tool that can read PCAP data.

Dumpcap is a decent FPC solution if you are looking to get up and running quickly with a minimal amount of effort. However, if you require a great degree of flexibility or are going to be capturing packets on a high throughput link, you will probably want to look elsewhere.

## DAEMONLOGGER

Designed by Marty Roesch, the original developer of the Snort IDS, Daemonlogger is a packet logging application designed specifically for use in NSM environments. It utilizes the Libpcap packet capture library to capture packets from the wire, and has two operating modes. Its primary operating mode is to capture packets from the wire and write them directly to disk. Its other mode of operation allows it to capture packets from the wire and rewrite them to a second interface, effectively acting as a soft tap.

The biggest benefit Daemonlogger provides is that, like Dumpcap, it is simple to use for capturing packets. In order to begin capturing, you need only to invoke the command and specify an interface.

```
daemonlogger -i eth1
```

This option, by default, will begin capturing packets and logging them to the current working directory. Packets will be collected until the capture file size reaches 2 GB, and then a new file will be created. This will continue indefinitely until the process is halted.

Daemonlogger provides a few useful options for customizing how packets are stored. Some of the more useful options include:

- -d: Run as a daemon
- -f <filename>: Load Berkeley Packet Filters (BPF's) from the specified file
- -g <group>: Run as the specified group
- -i <interface>: Capture packets from the specified interface
- -l <directory>: Log data to a specified directory
- -M <pct>: In ring buffer mode, log packet data to a specified percentage of volume capacity. To activate ring buffer mode, you'll also need to specify the -r option.
- -n <prefix>: Set a naming prefix for the output files (Useful for defining sensor name)
- -r: Activates ring buffer mode
- -t <value>: Roll over the log file on the specified time interval
- -u <user>: Run as the specified user

With these options available, a common production implementation might look like this:

```
daemonlogger -i eth1 -d -f filter.bpf -l /data/pcap/ -n NYC01
```

When this command is invoked, Daemonlogger will be executed as a daemon (-d) that logs packets captured from interface eth1 (-i eth1) to files in the directory /data/pcap (-l /data/pcap). These files will be prepended with the string NYC01 to indicate the sensor they were collected from (-n NYC01). The data that is collected will be filtered based upon the BPF statements contained in the file filter.bpf (-f filter.bpf).

Daemonlogger suffers from some of the same deficiencies as Dumpcap when it comes to performance. While Daemonlogger does perform better than Dumpcap at higher throughput levels, it can still suffer as throughput levels increase to those seen in some larger enterprise environments.

Daemonlogger also provides limited ability to control output file names. It will allow you to specify text to prepend to packet capture files, but it follows that text with the time the capture was created in epoch time format. There is no way to specify the date/time format that is included in the file name. Additional scripting can be done to rename these files after they've been created, but this is another process that will have to be managed.

Daemonlogger currently sets itself apart from the crowd by offering a ring buffer mode to eliminate the need for manual PCAP storage maintenance. By specifying the -r -M<pct> option in Daemonlogger, you can tell it to automatically remove older data when PCAP storage exceeds the specified percentage. In certain cases this might be essential, however if you're already gathering other types of data, this storage maintenance is probably already being taken care of by other custom processes, like the ones we will talk about later in this chapter.

Once again, Daemonlogger is a great FPC solution if you are looking to get up and running quickly with a minimal amount of effort. It is incredibly stable, and I've seen it used successfully in a variety of enterprise environments. The best way to determine if Daemonlogger is right for you is to give it a try on a network interface that you want to monitor and see if you experience any packet loss.

## NETSNIFF-NG

Netsniff-NG is a high-performance packet capture utility designed by Daniel Borkmann. While the utilities we've discussed to this point rely on Libpcap for capture, Netsniff-NG utilizes zero-copy mechanisms to capture packets. This is done with the intent to support full packet capture over high throughput links.

One of the neat features of Netsniff-NG is that it not only allows for packet capture with the RX_RING zero-copy mechanism, but also for packet transmission with TX_RING. This means that it provides the ability to read packets from one interface and redirect them to another interface. This feature is made more powerful with the ability to filter captured packets between the interfaces.

In order to begin capturing packets with Netsniff-NG, we have to specify an input and output. In most cases, the input will be a network interface, and the output will be a file or folder on disk.

```
netsniff-ng -i eth1 -o data.pcap
```

This command will capture packets from the eth0 interface (-i eth1) and write them to a file called data.pcap in the currently directory (-o data.pcap) until the application is stopped. If you execute this command, you'll also notice that your screen fills with the contents of the packets you are capturing. In order to prevent this behavior, you'll need to force Netsniff-NG into silent mode with the -s flag.

When you terminate the process (which can be done by pressing Ctrl+C), Netsniff-NG will generate some basic statistics related to the data it's captured. We see these statistics in Figure 5.3.

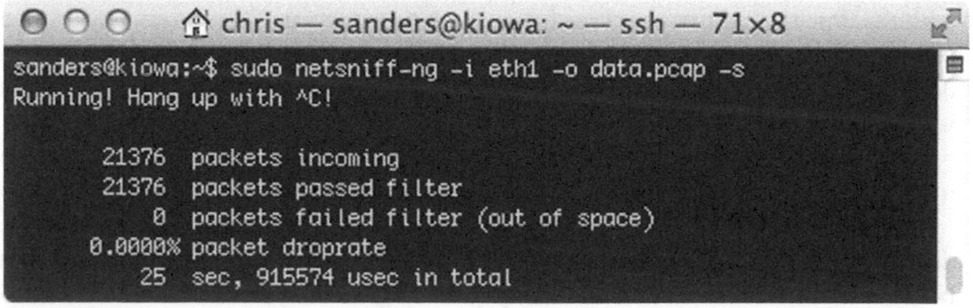

```
sanders@kiowa:~$ sudo netsniff-ng -i eth1 -o data.pcap -s
Running! Hang up with ^C!

   21376   packets incoming
   21376   packets passed filter
       0   packets failed filter (out of space)
 0.0000%   packet droprate
      25   sec, 915574 usec in total
```

**FIGURE 5.3**

Netsniff-NG Process Output

Netsniff-NG provides a lot of the features found in the other FPC applications we've discussed. Some of these options include:

- -g < group >: Run as the specified group
- -f < file name >: Load Berkeley Packet Filters (BPF's) from a specified file
- -F < value >: A size or time interval used to determine when to end capture in single-file mode, or roll over to the next file in ring buffer mode.
- -H: Sets the process priority to high
- -i < interface >: Capture packets from the specified interface
- -o < file >: Output data to the specified file
- -t < type >: Only handle packets of defined types (host, broadcast, multicast, outgoing)
- -P < prefix >: Set a naming prefix for the output files (Useful for defining sensor name)
- -s: Run silently. Don't print capture packets to screen
- -u < user >: Run as the specified user

With these options available, a common production implementation might look like this:

```
netsniff-ng -i eth1 -o /data/ -F 60 -P "NYC01"
```

This command will run Netsniff-NG in ring buffer mode, which is noted by the usage of an output directory instead of a file name in the –o parameter (-o /data/). This will generate a new PCAP file every 60 seconds (-F 60), and every file will be prefixed with the sensor name NYC01 (-P "NYC01").

In our testing, Netsniff-NG is the best performing FPC utilities in this book when it comes to very high throughput links. It performs so well, that it is included with Security Onion as the de facto FPC utility.

## CHOOSING THE RIGHT FPC COLLECTION TOOL

We have discussed three unique FPC solutions, and in each description mentioned the overall performance of each tool. While Dumpcap and Daemonlogger will generally work fine in most situations with little to no packet loss, you will need a tool like Netsniff-NG to operate in environments with extremely high sustained traffic rates. Without scaling up your collection tools to meet your throughput requirements, you will be wasting CPU cycles and gathering incomplete data. There is nothing more frustrating for an analyst than trying to reassemble a data stream only to find that a packet is missing and your efforts are all for naught.

The history of FPC collection tools mostly revolves around which can generate data "the best". While sometimes "best" is a reference to being feature rich, it has classically been that new FPC solutions are created to meet the requirements of newer, faster networks. This is not to say that the best FPC collection tool is the one that can ingest data the fastest, but instead the one that drops the least amount of packets on your sensor and that also contains enough features to ensure that data is stored in a format accessible by your detection and analysis tools.

The three tools mentioned earlier are included in this book because they are all proven to get the job done in various network environments, and are a few of the most well-known and widely deployed free solutions. With that in mind, you must choose the best fit for your organization based upon the criteria that are the most important to you.

## PLANNING FOR FPC COLLECTION

Collection of FPC data should take high priority when architecting your sensor for a multitude of reasons. One reason for this is that you can generate almost all other major data types from previously collected FPC data. With that said, FPC data is a "primary" data type that is always collected directly off the wire. FPC data will always be the largest of any data type per time quanta. This means that for any given amount of time, the amount of hard disk space that is consumed by FPC data will surpass that of any other data type. This is not to say that FPC data will always take up the vast percentage of your disk. Many organizations place an extraordinary amount of value in retrospective log analysis and correlation, and as such, can often devote an equal or larger amount of disk space to other types of logs, like Bro logs. Of course, the result might be that you can only store 24 hours of PCAP data compared to the 1 year of Bro logs. The takeaway here is that a lot of the data you collect will either be derived from PCAP data or will be affected by its expansive storage requirements.

The key consideration you must keep in mind when deploying an FPC solution is throughput, or the average rate of network traffic over the interface(s) that you're monitoring. Determining the throughput over a particular monitor port should be done before the first purchase of a sensor is made to ensure that the sensor will have the resources necessary to support collection and detection at the scale necessary. Attempting to engineer these requirements for a sensor after you've bought hardware is usually a recipe for disaster.

### Storage Considerations

The first and most obvious consideration when generating FPC data is storage. PCAP takes up a lot of space relative to all other data types; so determining the amount of FPC data you want to store is critical. This decision begins by choosing a retention strategy that is either time-based or size-based.

A time-based strategy says that you will retain PCAP data for at LEAST a specific time interval, for example, 24 hours. A size-based strategy says that you will retain a minimum amount of PCAP data, usually allocated by a specific hard drive volume, for example, 10 TB of PCAP data (limited by a 10 TB RAID array). With both of these strategies, your organization should attempt to define operational minimums and operational ideals. The operational minimum is the minimal requirement for performing NSM services at an acceptable level and defines the time or size unit representing the least amount of data you can store. The operational ideal is set as a reasonable goal for performing NSM to the best extent possible and defines the time or size unit representing the amount of data you would like to store in an ideal situation. In doing this, you should always have the minimum amount, but strive for the ideal amount.

Deciding between a time- or size-based FPC data collection can depend on a variety of factors. In some regulated industries where specific compliance standards must be met, an organization may choose to use time-based FPC collection to align with those regulations, or simply because their organization is more attuned to store data based upon time intervals. In organizations where budgets are tighter and hardware is limited, NSM staff may choose to use a size-based strategy due to hard limits on available space. It is also common to see organizations use a size-based strategy on networks that are very diverse or rapidly growing, due to an inability to accurately gauge the amount of storage required for time-focused collection.

When planning for time-based retention, in theory, gauging the average throughput across an interface can allow you to determine how much data, per time interval, that you can store given a fixed amount of drive space. For example, if you determine that your interface sees 100 MB/s throughput on average and you have 1 TB of hard drive space reserved, you can theoretically store over 24 days of FPC data. However, it is a common pitfall to rely solely on the average throughput measurement. This is because this measurement doesn't account for throughput spikes, which are short periods of time where throughput might dramatically increase. These spikes may occur for a number of reasons, and might be a result of regularly scheduled events like off site backups or application updates, or random events such as higher than average web browsing activity. Since FPC is a primary data type, these spikes can also result in an increase of other data that is derived from it. This compounds the effect of data spikes.

Due to the nature of network traffic, it is difficult to predict peak throughput levels. Because of this, organizations that choose a time-based retention plan are forced to choose a time interval that is considerably shorter than their hardware can handle in order to provide an overflow space. Without that overflow, you risk losing data or temporarily toppling your sensor.

Managing FPC data based on the total amount of stored data is a bit more straight forward and carries with it inherent safety features. With this method, you define the maximum amount of disk space that FPC data can occupy. Once the stored data reaches this limit, the oldest FPC data is removed to make room for newly collected data. As we saw before, Daemonlogger is an FPC solution that has this feature built in.

## Calculating Sensor Interface Throughput with Netsniff-NG and IFPPS

We've talked a lot about how the collection and storage of FPC data depends on being able to reliably determine the total throughput of a sensor's monitoring interface. Now, we will look at methods for calculating throughput statistics. The first method involves using a tool called ifpps, which is a part of the Netsniff-NG suite of tools. In Security Onion, Netsniff-NG is installed without ifpps, so if you want to follow along you will need to install it manually by following these steps:

1. Install the libncurses-dev prerequisite with APT

   ```
   sudo apt-get install libncurses-dev
   ```

2. Download Netsniff-NG with GIT

   ```
   git clone https://github.com/borkmann/netsniff-ng.git
   ```

3. Configure, Make, and Install only ifpps

   ```
   ./configure
   ```

   ```
   make && sudo make install ifpps_install
   ```

After installing ifpps, you can make sure it installed correctly by running it with the –h argument to see its possible arguments, or just cut to the chase and run this command, which will generate a list of continuously updating network statistics;

```
ifpps -d<INTERFACE>
```

Ifpps will generate statistics detailing the current throughput of the selected interface, as well as other data related to CPU, disk I/O and other system statistics. A sample of this output is shown in Figure 5.4.

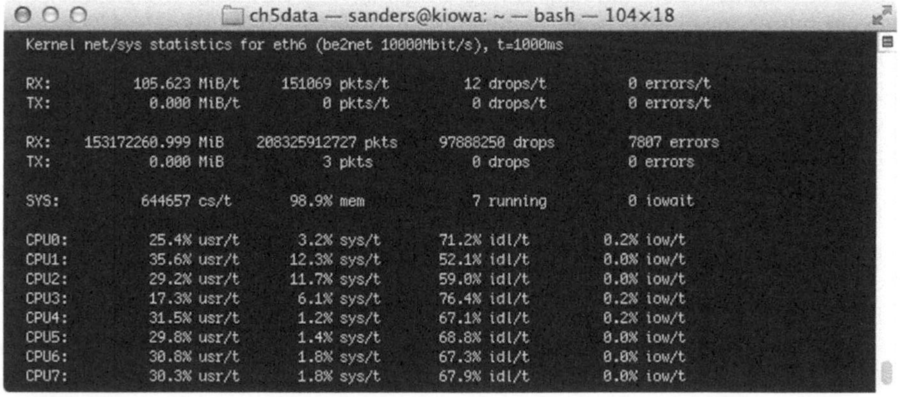

**FIGURE 5.4**

Generating Network Statistics with ifpps

The "/t" seen beside each statistic represents the time interval at the top right of the output and can be changed prior to execution using the -t option. The default time value is 1000ms.

Ifpps will give you a live snapshot of an interface's throughput at any given point in time, which can be a useful statistic when combined with a large sample size. Using this method, you want to ensure that you collect multiple peak and off-peak samples and average those together for accurate measurement of average throughput.

Unfortunately, ifpps is a bit limited in functionality. It doesn't provide any functionality for applying a filter to the interface you are capturing from, so if you are slimming down your FPC collection like we will talk about later, this might not be the best tool for the job.

## Calculating Sensor Interface Throughput with Session Data

Perhaps the most flexible way to calculate throughput statistics is to consult session data. Now we will walk through an example of calculating throughput using SiLK's rwfilter, rwcount, and rwstats tools that we referenced in the last chapter.

To begin, we will use rwfilter to select a specific time interval. The easiest way to do this is to with data from a single business day, which we will call "daily.rw"

```
rwfilter --start-date=2013/10/04 --proto=0- --type=all --pass=
daily.rw
```

This filter is basic, and will select all session data collected on October 4th and save it to the daily.rw file. You can verify that data exists in this file by using the following command to view a sample of it:

```
cat daily.rw | rwcut | head
```

Once you've confirmed that you have your day's worth of data, you can begin breaking it down to determine how much data you actually have coming across the wire. We will continue this example with a sample data set we've generated. To do this, we call on the rwcount tool:

```
cat daily.rw | rwcount --bin-size=60
```

This command will feed our data set to rwcount, which will provide a summary of the amount of data per minute traversing the sensor. This time interval is determined by the `--bin-size` setting, which instructs rwcount to group things in bins of 60 seconds. These results are shown in Figure 5.5.

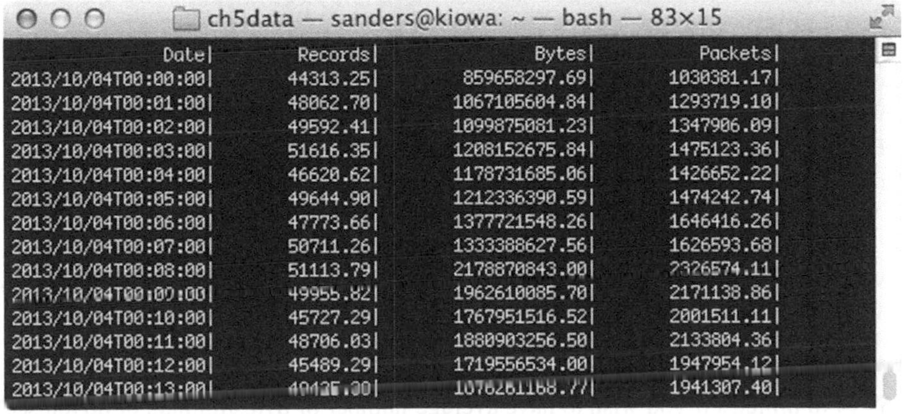

**FIGURE 5.5**

Data Throughput per Minute with Rwcount During Off-Peak Times

In the figure above you will notice that we see roughly 1.5 GB per minute traversing the sensor during off-peak hours at 00:00 UTC (which is 8 PM EST). However, if you look at the figure below (Figure 5.6) we see that traffic gets as high as 8-9 GB per minute during peak business hours at 17:00 UTC (which is 3 PM EST).

```
○ ○ ○        ch5data — sanders@kiowa: ~ — bash — 83×15
2013/10/04T17:00:00|      245936.33|      9047223014.56|      11452368.02|
2013/10/04T17:01:00|      235940.36|      8622123641.52|      11005983.02|
2013/10/04T17:02:00|      235221.40|      8311658855.48|      10556754.37|
2013/10/04T17:03:00|      235717.95|      8309323438.36|      10691004.55|
2013/10/04T17:04:00|      245585.77|      8427777053.55|      10875324.91|
2013/10/04T17:05:00|      242052.48|      8284062189.96|      10692829.75|
2013/10/04T17:06:00|      253800.12|      8766096605.52|      11278246.92|
2013/10/04T17:07:00|      238087.81|      8478673022.73|      10834914.19|
2013/10/04T17:08:00|      238097.17|      9041844500.38|      11127422.86|
2013/10/04T17:09:00|      235028.46|      8245354106.51|      10419034.95|
2013/10/04T17:10:00|      227160.69|      7698618756.96|       9627828.65|
2013/10/04T17:11:00|      248204.70|      8730988787.45|      11069068.46|
2013/10/04T17:12:00|      255120.64|      8979467783.83|      11467693.72|
2013/10/04T17:13:00|      239651.87|      8738665238.16|      11091686.19|
2013/10/04T17:14:00|      232305.00|      8500362290.98|      10798754.86|
```

**FIGURE 5.6**

Throughput per Minute with Rwcount During Peak Times

To calculate an average throughput for the day, you can increase the bin-size in the rwcount command to count the total data for a single day, which is 86400 seconds.

```
cat daily.rw | rwcount --bin-size=86400
```

Our results are shown in Figure 5.7.

```
○ ○ ○        ch5data — sanders@kiowa: ~ — bash — 83×5
                  Date|       Records|            Bytes|         Packets|
2013/10/04T00:00:00|  155413868.66|  4915977947088.87|   6010844467.93|
```

**FIGURE 5.7**

Calculating Average Throughput per Day

Using this calculation, we arrive at a total byte count of 4915977947088.87. We will want to get this number into something more manageable, so we can divide it by 1024 three times ($4915977947088.87 \times 1024^{-3}$) to arrive at a total of 4578.36 GB. To arrive at the average throughput for this link on this day, we can take this byte count and divide it by the time quanta whose average we want to ascertain. This is 1440 minutes if you wish to have average number of bytes/minute, or 86400 seconds if you wish to have average number of bytes/second. This yields 3.18 GB bytes per minute (4578.36 / 1440) or 54.26 MB per second ((4578.36 / 86400) × 1024). While doing these calculations, all numbers were rounded to two places after the decimal point.

## DECREASING THE FPC DATA STORAGE BURDEN

In an ideal world you could collect FPC data for every host, port, and protocol on your network and store it for a long time. In the real world, there are budgets and limitations that prevent that and sometimes we need to limit the amount of data we collect. Here we will talk about different strategies for eliminating the amount of FPC data you are retaining in order to get the best "bang for your buck" when it comes to data storage for NSM purposes.

### Eliminating Services

The first and easiest method of paring down the amount of FPC data that is retained is to eliminate traffic generated by individual services. One way we can identify services that are a good fit for this strategy is to use rwstats, which can provide us with great detail on exactly how much the retention of data related to various ports, protocols, and hosts can affect your FPC data storage footprint. Rwstats is covered in extensive detail in Chapter 11, but we will go ahead and dive into it a bit here too. We will use two different rwstats commands to determine the ports associated with the largest volume of inbound and outbound traffic.

First, we'll use rwstats to determine which ports are responsible for the most inbound communication within our example network. We will do that by calculating the source ports responsible for the most traffic, with this command:

```
cat daily.rw | rwstats --fields=sport --top --count=5 --value=bytes
```

This command takes our original data set and feeds it to rwstats, which calculates the top 5 (`--top --count=5`) source ports (`--fields=sport`) where the largest amount of data transfer occurred, by bytes (`--value==bytes`). The result is shown in Figure 5.8.

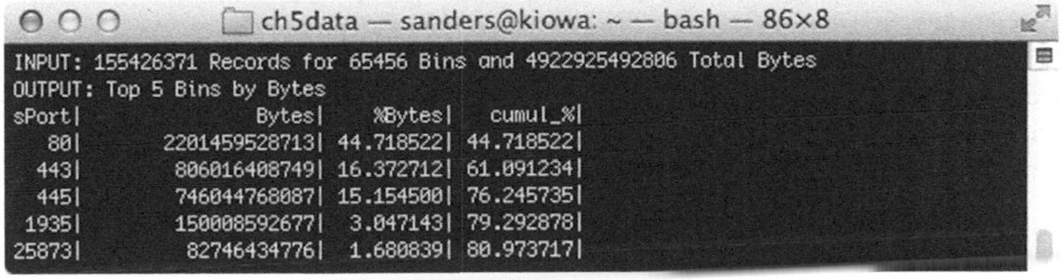

```
○ ○ ○          ch5data — sanders@kiowa: ~ — bash — 86×8
INPUT: 155426371 Records for 65456 Bins and 4922925492806 Total Bytes
OUTPUT: Top 5 Bins by Bytes
sPort|              Bytes|   %Bytes|   cumul_%|
   80|     2201459528713|  44.718522|  44.718522|
  443|      806016408749|  16.372712|  61.091234|
  445|      746044768087|  15.154500|  76.245735|
 1935|      150008592677|   3.047143|  79.292878|
25873|       82746434776|   1.680839|  80.973717|
```

**FIGURE 5.8**

Top Communicating Source Ports

As you can see in the figure above, the majority of the traffic on this network segment is port 80 traffic, which we will assume is related to HTTP traffic. Specifically, 44% of the observed traffic is HTTP. Of course, HTTP traffic is immensely valuable for NSM detection and analysis so we probably want to keep this for now. However, if you look at the next line you will see that more than 16% of the total data transferred over the course of a day originated from source port 443. For the complete picture, let's also take a look at the top 5 destination ports to get insight into outbound communication, using this command:

```
cat daily.rw | rwstats --fields=dport --top --count=5 --value=bytes
```

The output from this command is shown in Figure 5.9.

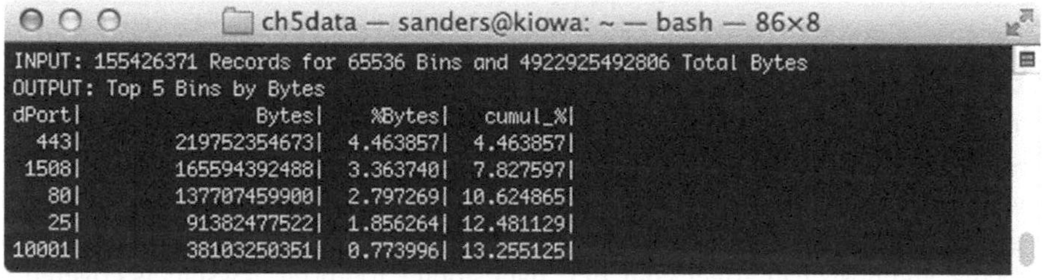

**FIGURE 5.9**

Top Communicating Destination Ports

The figure above shows that over 4% of traffic is destined to TCP/443, resulting in the conclusion that on a given business day, roughly 20.9% of all traffic traversing the monitoring interface of our sensor is TCP/443. Therefore, filtering out TCP/443 traffic will increase your total FPC data retention by 20.9% per business on average.

It is common for organizations to eliminate the collection of encrypted data that is a part of HTTPS communication. While the header information from encrypted data or statistics relating to it can be actionable, the encrypted data itself often isn't. This is a good example of maximizing your FPC data storage by eliminating retention of data that doesn't necessarily help you get the most bang for your buck when it comes to storage.

With TCP/443 traffic eliminated, we can revert back to our previous throughput calculation to see exactly how much of a dent it makes in those figures. We can modify our existing data set by using rwfilter to prune any TCP/443 traffic from our daily. rw file like this:

```
cat daily.rw | rwfilter --input-pipe=stdin --aport=443 --fail
=stdout| rwcount --bin-size=86400
```

This command takes the existing daily.rw dataset and passes that data to another filter that will "fail out" any records that have port 443 as a source or destination address. That data is piped directly to rwcount to again present a statistic that shows total data traversing the sensor based on the new filter (Figure 5.10).

**FIGURE 5.10**

Throughput Statistics for the Same Day without TCP/443 Traffic

The figure above represents the exact same data as before, however this time with any TCP/443 traffic taken out. When we calculate the throughput values, we can see that this yields statistics of 2.52 GB per minute, or 42.9 MB per second. The result shows that removing TCP/443 traffic has indeed reduced the total amount of data that would be collected by ~20.9% during a business day.

This type of action can be taken for other ports containing encrypted data as well, such as ports used for encrypted VPN tunnels. While it might not be a good fit for every organization to consider, starting with removing encrypted data from FPC collection is just one example of how to reduce the burden of FPC data storage by eliminating the retention of traffic from specific services This also pays dividends later when it is time to parse FPC data for the creation of secondary data types during collection, as well as when parsing data for detection and analysis. Let's look at some more ways that we can decrease the storage burden of FPC data.

## Eliminating Host to Host Communication

Another way to reduce the amount of FPC data being stored is to eliminate the storage of communication between specific hosts.

Since we've already evaluated how much traffic will be reduced by dropping TCP/443 communication, let's continue by removing that data from our next example. As you recall from earlier, we can "fail" anything that matches various criteria, so we will take advantage of that. In this example, we will look at the top-talking source and destination IP addresses remaining in the traffic after removing port 443 using this command:

```
cat daily.rw | rwfilter --input-pipe=stdin --aport=443 --fail-
=stdout| rwstats --fields=sip,dip --top --count=5 --value=bytes
```

This command sends our existing data set through another rwfilter command that removes any traffic matching TCP/443 on any port. This data is then piped to rwstats, which generates the top talking source and destination IP pairs (--fields=sip,dip) by the total amount of bytes transferred (--value=bytes). The result is shown in Figure 5.11.

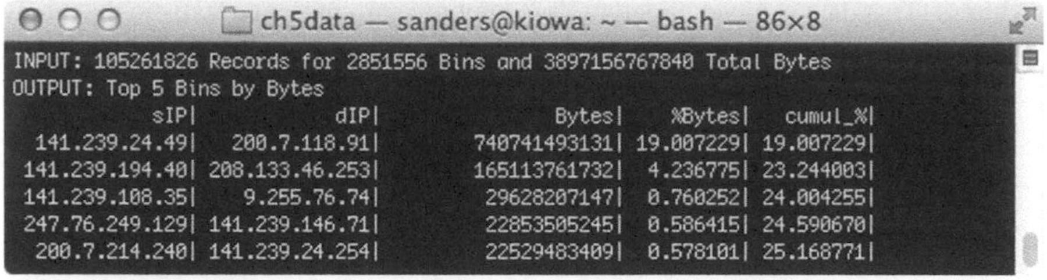

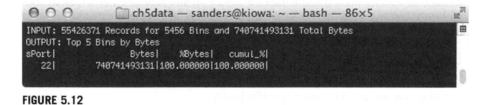

**FIGURE 5.11**

Identifying Top Talking IP Pairs

In the figure above we see that 19% of the communication on this network segment occurs between the hosts with the addresses 141.239.24.49 and 200.7.118.91. In order to determine whether this communication is a good candidate for exclusion from FPC data collection, you will have to dig a little deeper. Ideally, you would have friendly intelligence regarding the internal host you are responsible for, and would be able to identify the service that is responsible for this large amount of traffic. One way to do this with rwstats is to use the following query:

```
cat daily.rw | rwfilter --input-pipe=stdin --saddress=141.239.24.49
--daddress=200.7.118.91 --pass=stdout| rwstats --fields=sport --
top --count=10 --value=bytes
```

The results of this query are shown in Figure 5.12.

```
● ○ ○          ch5data — sanders@kiowa: ~ — bash — 86×5
INPUT: 55426371 Records for 5456 Bins and 740741493131 Total Bytes
OUTPUT: Top 5 Bins by Bytes
sPort|             Bytes|    %Bytes|   cumul_%|
   22|   740741493131|100.000000|100.000000|
```

**FIGURE 5.12**

Examining Communication Between These Hosts

In this case, it looks like all of this communication is occurring on port 22. Assuming this is a legitimate connection, this probably means that some form of SSH VPN exists between these two devices. If you don't have any ability to decrypt and monitor this traffic (such as through an intermediate proxy), then this would probably be a good candidate for exclusion from FPC data collection. This process can be repeated for other "top talkers" found on your network.

Using the strategies we've outlined here, we have successfully reduced the amount of FPC data being stored by around 40%. This means that your sensor can hold 40% more actionable data. Unfortunately, we can't provide clear-cut examples of things that can be eliminated from FPC data storage in every network, because every network and every organization's goals are so different. However, following the instructions provided in Chapter 2 for appropriately planning your data collection should help you make these determinations.

> **CAUTION**
>
> At the beginning of this chapter we mentioned that multiple other data types, such as PSTR, are often derived from FPC data. If your environment works in this manner, you should be aware of this when eliminating certain data types from FPC collection. For instance, if you generate PSTR data from FPC data and eliminate port 443 traffic, you won't be able to generate packet strings from the HTTPS handshake, which will create a gap in network visibility. This might not be avoidable when space is limited, but if you still wish to keep this PSTR data you will have to find another way to generate it, such as doing so with another process directly from the wire.

## MANAGING FPC DATA RETENTION

Since FPC data eats up more disk space than any other data type per second, it is likely that it will be FPC data that causes your sensor to go belly up if data retention and rollover isn't handled properly. I've seen even the most mature SOCs experience scenarios where a data spike occurs and it causes FPC data to be written to disk faster than it can be deleted. This can result in all sorts of bad things. Ideally, your FPC data storage exists on a volume that is separate from your operating system in order to prevent this from happening. However, even then I've even seen instances where FPC data was stored on shared dynamically expanding virtual storage, and a sustained spike in data led to other virtual devices being deprived of resources, ultimately leading to system crashes. There are dozens of other scenarios like this that can lead to the dreaded 2 AM phone call that nobody likes to make to systems administrators. With that in mind, this section is devoted to the management of FPC data; specifically, purging old data.

There are a number of ways to manage FPC data, but we will approach this from a simple perspective that only uses tools built in to most Linux distributions. This is because these tools are effective, and can be scripted easily. While some of the techniques we describe in this section might not fit your environment perfectly, we have confidence that they can be adapted fairly easily.

Earlier, we discussed the two most common strategies that organizations use for storing FPC data: time-based and size-based. The method for managing these two strategies varies.

### Time-Based Retention Management

Using a time-based retention strategy is fairly easy to manage in an automated fashion. The linux find utility can easily search for files with modify times that are of a certain age. For instance, in order to find files older than 60 minutes within the /data/pcap/ directory, simply run the following command;

```
find /data/pcap -type f -mtime +60
```

From that command you can generate a file list of PCAPs that you wish to delete. This command can be modified by pairing it with xargs in order to remove data that meets this criteria. The following one-liner will remove any data older than 60 minutes.

```
find /data/pcap -type f -mtime +60 | xargs -i rm {}
```

## Size-based Retention Management

Managing FPC data that is using a size-based retention strategy is a bit more difficult. This method of data retention deletes the oldest PCAP files once the storage volume exceeds a set percentage of utilized disk space. Depending on your FPC collection deployment, this method can be challenging to implement. If you are able to use Daemonlogger, it has the capability to do this type of data purging on its own, as was described earlier. If you are using a tool that doesn't have this feature built in, purging data in this manner requires a bit more critical thinking.

One way to handle this is through a BASH script. We've provided such a script here:

```
#!/bin/bash
## This script deletes excess PCAP when the "percentfull" reaches the pre-
defined limit.
## Excess PCAP is when the total amount of data within a particular PCAP
directory
## reaches the percent amount defined about, out of the total amount of
drive space
## on the drive that it occupies. For the purpose of consistency, the per-
centfull amount
## is uniform across all PCAP data sources.

## Refer to the "Data Removal Configuration (DRC)" at the bottom of this
script for settings.

#Example DRC:

## Data Removal Configuration
#dir="/data/pcap/eth1/"
#percentage=1
#datamanage $dir $percentage

#dir="/data/pcap/eth2/"
#percentage=3
#datamanage $dir $percentage
```

```
############################################################
## FUNCTION #################################################
############################################################

totaldiskspace=$(df | grep SOsensor-root | awk '{print $2}')

function datamanage {
# Initial data evaluation
        datadirectory="$1"
        datapercent="$2"
        datasize=$(du -s $datadirectory | awk '{print $1}')
        diskstatus=$(df | grep SOsensor-root | awk '{print $5}' | egrep
-o '[0-9]{1,3}')
        datapercentusage=$(echo "scale=2; $datasize / $totaldiskspace
* 100" | bc | sed 's/\..*//g')
         echo "Data usage in $datadirectory is at $datapercentusage% of
hard drive capacity)"
        # Data Removal Procedure
        while [ "$datapercentusage" -gt "$datapercent" ]; do
                filestodelete=$(ls -tr1 $datadirectory | head -
20)
                printf %s "$filestodelete" | while IFS=read -r ifile
                do
                        echo $ifile
                        if [ -z $datadirectory$ifile ]; then
                        exit
                        fi
                        echo "Data usage in $data directory
($datapercentusage%) is greater than your desired amount ($datapercent%
of hard drive)"
                        echo "Removing $datadirectory$ifile"
                        sudo rm -rf $datadirectory$ifile
                        du -s $datadirectory
#                       datasize=$(du -s $datadirectory | awk '{print
$1}')
                        done
                datasize=$(du -s $datadirectory | awk '{print $1}')
                datapercentusage=$(echo "scale=2; $datasize /
$totaldiskspace * 100" | bc | sed 's/\..*//g')
                du -s $datadirectory
                datasize=$(du -s $datadirectory | awk '{print $1}')
                datapercentusage=$(echo "scale=2; $datasize /
$totaldiskspace * 100" | bc | sed 's/\..*//g')
```

```
        done

}

# Data Removal Configuration
pidofdiskclean=$(ps aux | grep diskclean.sh | wc -l)
echo $pidofdiskclean

if [ "$pidofdiskclean" -le "4" ]; then
dir="/data/pcap/eth1/"
percentage=40
datamanage $dir $percentage

dir="/data/pcap/eth2/"
percentage=40
datamanage $dir $percentage
wait
echo ""
fi
```

To use the script above you must configure the volume name where data is stored by editing the `dir` variable. Additionally, you must configure the Data Removal Configuration section near the bottom of the script to indicate the directories where PCAP data is stored, and the amount of empty buffer space you wish to allow on the volume.

The script will take these variables and determine the percentage of utilized space that is taken up by the data within it. If it determines that this percentage is above the allowable amount, it will remove the oldest files until the percentage is at a suitable level.

This script can be placed in a scheduled cron job that runs on a regular basis, such as every hour, every 10 minutes, or every 60 seconds. How frequently it runs will depend on how much of an empty space buffer you allow, and how much throughput you have. For instance, if you only leave 5% of empty buffer space and have a large amount of throughput, you will want to ensure the script runs almost constantly to ensure that data spikes don't cause the drive to fill up. On the flip side, if you allow 30% of empty buffer space and the link you're monitoring has very little throughput, you might be fine only running this script every hour or so.

In a scenario where your sensor is under a high load and empty buffer space is very limited, your cron job has a chance of not running in time to remove the oldest files. However, if you run the script constantly, for instance on a sleep timer, you can still run the risk of slower script performance in calculating disk space requirements during execution. To split the difference, it is often ideal to require the script to calculate disk space, determine if the directory is too full, and then delete the 10 oldest files, instead of just the individual oldest file. This will increase script performance dramatically, but can result in less than maximum retention (but not by much). The script below will perform that task in a manner similar to the first script we looked at.

```
#!/bin/bash
## This script deletes excess pcap when the "percentfull" reaches the pre-
defined limit.
```

```
## Excess pcap is when the total amount of data within a particular pcap
directory
## reaches the percent amount defined about, out of the total amount of
drive space
## on the drive that it occupies. For the purpose of consistency, the per-
centful amount
## is uniform across all pcap data sources.

## Refer to the "Data Removal Configuration (DRC)" at the bottom of this
script for settings.

#Example DRC:

## Data Removal Configuration
#dir="/data/pcap/eth6/"
#percentage=1          ·
#datamanage $dir $percentage

#dir="/data/pcap/eth7/"
#percentage=3
#datamanage $dir $percentage

##################################################################
## FUNCTION ######################################################
##################################################################

totaldiskspace=$(df | grep SOsensor-root | awk '{print $2}')

function datamanage {
# Initial data evaluation
datadirectory="$1"
datapercent="$2"
datasize=$(du -s $datadirectory | awk '{print $1}')
diskstatus=$(df | grep SOsensor-root | awk '{print $5}' | egrep -o '[0-9]
{1,3}')
datapercentusage=$(echo "scale=2; $datasize / $totaldiskspace * 100" |
bc | sed 's/\..*//g')
echo "Data usage in $datadirectory is at $datapercentusage% of hard
drive capacity)"
        # Data Removal Procedure
        while [ "$datapercentusage" -gt "$datapercent" ]; do
                        filestodelete=$(ls -tr1 $datadirectory | head -
10)
                        echo $filestodelete
                printf %s "$filestodelete" | while IFS=read -r ifile
                do
                        echo $ifile
```

```
                if [ -z $datadirectory$ifile ]; then
                exit
                fi
                echo "Data usage in $datadirectory
($datapercentusage%) is greater than your desired amount ($datapercent%
of hard drive)"
                echo "Removing $datadirectory$ifile"
                sudo rm -rf $datadirectory$ifile
                done
            datasize=$(du -s $datadirectory | awk '{print $1}')
            datapercentusage=$(echo "scale=2; $datasize /
$totaldiskspace * 100" | bc | sed 's/\..*//g')
        done

}

# Data Removal Configuration
pidofdiskclean=$(ps aux | grep diskclean.sh | wc -l)
echo $pidofdiskclean

if [ "$pidofdiskclean" -le "4" ]; then
# Data Removal Configuration
dir='/data/pcap/eth1/'
percentage=10
datamanage $dir $percentage

dir="/data/pcap/eth2/"
percentage=10
datamanage $dir $percentage
wait
fi
```

While the code samples provided in this section might not plug directly into your environment and work perfectly, they certainly provide a foundation that will allow you to tweak them for your specific collection scenario. As another resource, consider examining the scripts that Security Onion uses to manage the retention of packet data. These scripts use similar techniques, but are orchestrated in a slightly different manner.

## CONCLUSION

FPC data is the most thorough and complete representation of network data that can be collected. As a primary data type, it is immensely useful by itself. However, its usefulness is compounded when you consider that so many other data types can be derived from it. In this chapter we examined different technologies that can be used for collecting and storing FPC data. We also discussed different techniques for collecting FPC data efficiently, paring down the amount of FPC data you are collecting, and methods for purging old data. As we move on through the remainder of the collection portion of this book, you will see how other data types can be derived from FPC data.

# Packet String Data

A dilemma that a lot of NSM teams run into is the inability to effectively search through large data sets in the course of retrospective analysis; that is, analysis on data older than a few days. In what many would consider the "best case scenario", an organization might be collecting both full packet capture data and session data, but it is likely that the FPC data is only kept for a few days, or a couple of weeks at most.

In this scenario, we have two problems. First, session data lacks the granularity needed to ascertain detailed information about what occurred in network traffic. Second, FPC data has such large storage requirements that it simply isn't reasonable to store enough of it to be able to perform retrospective analysis effectively.

This leaves us in a scenario where we must examine data older than our FPC data retention period, and where the session data that is available will leave a lot of unanswered questions. For instance, with only session data available, the following common retrospective analysis scenarios wouldn't be possible:

- Locating a unique HTTP User Agent that is associated with a newly attributed adversary
- Determine which users received a phishing e-mail that recently resulted in a compromise
- Searching for file download activity occurring after a newly identified and potentially malicious HTTP requests

One answer to this predicament is the collection of packet string data, or PSTR data (pronounced pee-stur), which is what this chapter is dedicated to. In this chapter, we will look at the defining qualities of PSTR data and how it can be collected manually or using tools like Httpry or Justniffer. While the collection of PSTR data is simple and its utility is limitless, the concept is fairly new, so there aren't a ton of organizations utilizing this data type just yet. However, with it having the wide contextual breadth of full packet capture and the speed, small storage footprint, and statistical parsing ability of session data, it is the closest solution you'll find to a suitable middle ground between FPC and session data that is useful in near real-time and retrospective analysis alike.

## DEFINING PACKET STRING DATA

Packet String Data is a term that is generally defined by the way you choose to use it. Loosely, it is a selection of important human-readable data that is derived from full packet capture data. This data can appear in many different forms. For instance, some SOCs choose to generate PSTR data that is specifically formatted to present header data from common application layer protocols (such as HTTP or SMTP), without unnecessary payload data involved. I carefully use the term "unnecessary" because in the analysis of PSTR data, the idea is not to extract files or analyze traffic byte by byte. The goal is to enable the analyst to get a snapshot view of the data to answer questions that might arise in retrospective analysis. An example of this type of PSTR data is shown in Figure 6.1.

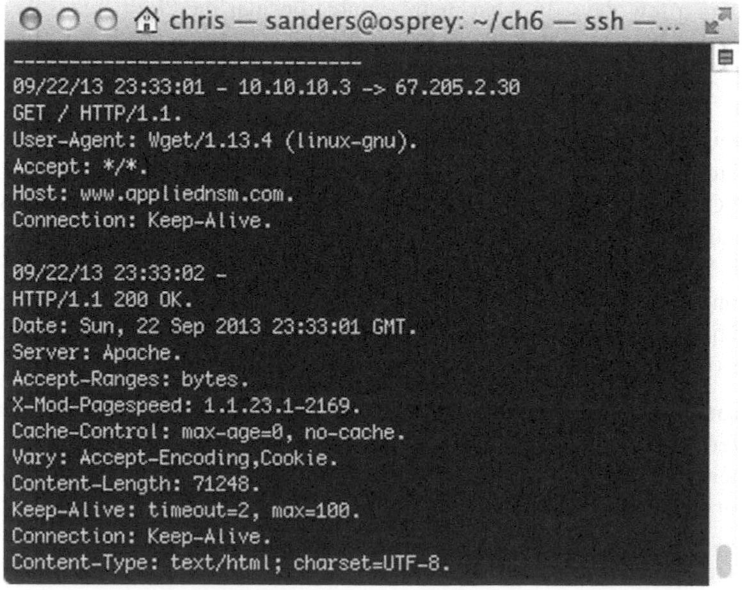

**FIGURE 6.1**

Log Style PSTR Data Showing an HTTP Request and Response

The example in Figure 6.1 represents data commonly accessed by analysts for use in retrospective analysis. Here there are two PSTR records showing the full HTTP request and response headers for an individual HTTP communication sequence. This is a fairly robust implementation where a great deal of the application layer header information is stored. Figure 6.2 shows an example where only a single field is stored.

```
○ ○ ○              ⌂ chris — sanders@osprey: ~/ch6 — ssh — 90×9
sanders@osprey:~/ch6$ sudo justniffer -f packets.pcap -p "tcp port 80" -u -l "%request.tim
estamp - %source.ip -> %dest.ip - %request.header.host%request.url"
09/22/13 23:41:02 - 10.10.10.3 -> 67.205.2.30 - www.appliednsm.com/
09/22/13 23:41:17 - 10.10.10.3 -> 157.166.240.13 - www.cnn.com/
09/22/13 23:41:22 - 10.10.10.3 -> 23.66.230.66 - www.foxnews.com/
09/22/13 23:41:27 - 10.10.10.3 -> 199.181.132.250 - www.espn.com/
09/22/13 23:41:42 - 10.10.10.3 -> 67.205.2.30 - www.appliednsm.com/
09/22/13 23:41:47 - 10.10.10.3 -> 67.205.2.30 - www.appliednsm.com/contributors
09/22/13 23:41:57 - 10.10.10.3 -> 67.205.2.30 - www.appliednsm.com/about-the-book
```

**FIGURE 6.2**

Log Style PSTR Data Showing a Requested HTTP URL

In this example, the PSTR data implementation only stores HTTP URL requests. While many organizations initially choose to store PSTR data for retrospective analysis, this example represents data that is collected on a near real-time basis. This allows the data to have multiple uses, including being more efficiently used by automated reputation detection mechanisms, discussed in Chapter 8. This can be much faster than attempting the same task while parsing FPC data.

A third common implementation of PSTR data is a payload focused deployment, and is concentrated entirely on the packet payload data occurring after the application layer protocol header. This data includes a limited number of non-binary bytes from the payload, which might provide a snapshot into the packet's purpose. In simpler terms, think of it as running the Unix strings tool against packet capture data. Figure 6.3 shows an example of this type of data.

The data shown in Figure 6.3 is a snapshot of the human readable data from a user's web browsing. Specifically, you can see the content of the page being visited without too much additional detail. This is efficient for data storage because unreadable characters aren't stored. The disadvantage of using payload style PSTR data is the overhead required to generate it. Further, there is a fair amount of excess data that comes along with it. Just because a byte can be translated into a readable ASCII character doesn't mean it necessarily makes sense. You can see this with the collection of random stray characters in the Figure above. The storage of these additional, but not very useful bytes, can become burdensome. Lastly, there are few streamlined ways of generating payload style PSTR data, so you will almost certainly be relying on a collection of custom written scripts and other utilities to generate it. Because of this, the overall efficiency might not be up to par when compared to other types of data

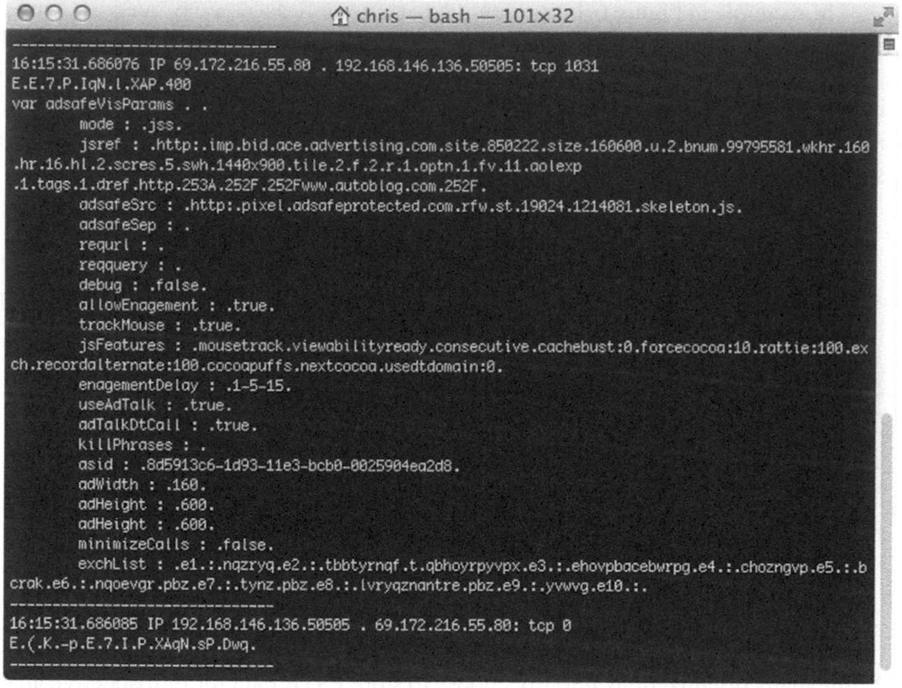

```
○ ○ ○                    ⌂ chris — bash — 101×32
------------------------------------------------
16:15:31.686076 IP 69.172.216.55.80 . 192.168.146.136.50505: tcp 1031
E.E.7.P.IqN.l.XAP.400
var adsafeVisParams . .
    mode : .jss.
    jsref : .http:.imp.bid.ace.advertising.com.site.850222.size.160600.u.2.bnum.99795581.wkhr.160
.hr.16.hl.2.scres.5.swh.1440x900.tile.2.f.2.r.1.optn.1.fv.11.aolexp
.1.tags.1.dref.http.253A.252F.252Fwww.autoblog.com.252F.
    adsafeSrc : .http:.pixel.adsafeprotected.com.rfw.st.19024.1214081.skeleton.js.
    adsafeSep : .
    requrl : .
    reqquery : .
    debug : .false.
    allowEnagement : .true.
    trackMouse : .true.
    jsFeatures : .mousetrack.viewabilityready.consecutive.cachebust:0.forcecocoa:10.rattie:100.ex
ch.recordalternate:100.cocoapuffs.nextcocoa.usedtdomain:0.
    enagementDelay : .1-5-15.
    useAdTalk : .true.
    adTalkDtCall : .true.
    killPhrases : .
    asid : .8d5913c6-1d93-11e3-bcb0-0025904ea2d8.
    adWidth : .160.
    adHeight : .600.
    adHeight : .600.
    minimizeCalls : .false.
    exchList : .e1.:.nqzryq.e2.:.tbbtyrnqf.t.qbhoyrpyvpx.e3.:.ehovpbacebwrpg.e4.:.chozngvp.e5.:.b
crok.e6.:.nqoevgr.pbz.e7.:.tynz.pbz.e8.:.lvryqznantre.pbz.e9.:.yvwvg.e10.:.
------------------------------------------------
16:15:31.686085 IP 192.168.146.136.50505 . 69.172.216.55.80: tcp 0
E.(.K.-p.E.7.I.P.XAqN.sP.Dwq.
------------------------------------------------
```

**FIGURE 6.3**

Payload Style PSTR Data

generated by more refined tools. In regard to multiline PSTR formats, the best bang for your buck is usually to opt for a log style format, such as that for request and response headers seen in Figure 6.1.

## PSTR DATA COLLECTION

We've already discussed FPC data at length, and with that in mind, you might consider PSTR data to be "partial packet capture." Because of this, it should come as no surprise that some organizations choose to generate PSTR data from FPC data that has already been collected. In contrast to this, it is also possible to collect PSTR data directly from the monitoring port on a sensor, in a manner similar to the way that FPC is collected.

Regardless of whether you choose to collect PSTR data from the wire, or generate it from FPC data, it is beneficial to perform this kind of collection from the same source that you're gathering other data from, which is the NSM sensor. This helps avoid data correlation errors with other data types during analysis. For instance, I've encountered some organizations that choose to generate PSTR data for HTTP communication from web content filtering devices. This can create a scenario where the segment that the web content filter is watching is not in the scope of the NSM visibility window analysts are concerned with, and thus, can't be used to enhance the analysis process. In addition, when you collect or generate PSTR data from your NSM sensor, you are ultimately in control of it. If you choose to generate this data from another device, especially those provided by third-party vendors, you would be required to accept only the data the vendor makes available, which might be subject to some additional parsing which isn't entirely clear. As with all NSM data, you should maintain a paranoid level of vigilance with how your data is created and parsed.

Before we start collecting or generating PSTR data, a few items must be considered. First, you must consider the extent of the PSTR data you wish to collect. The ideal solution is one that focuses on collecting as much essential application layer data from clear text protocols as long-term storage will permit. Since there are multiple variations of PSTR data that can be collected, the amount of storage space that this data will utilize is wildly variable. Thus, you should utilize some of the methods discussed in Chapter 3 to determine how much storage you can expect to be utilized by PSTR data, based upon the data format you've selected and the makeup of your network assets. This requires that you deploy a temporary sensor with PSTR data collection/generation tools installed on it so that you can sample data at multiple time intervals, and extrapolate that data over longer time periods. This may result in changing the extent of the PSTR data you wish to store in order to be able to retain this data for a longer time.

In parallel with determining the type of PSTR data you will create, you should also consider the time period for which it is retained. FPC data retention is often thought of in terms of hours or days, while session data retention is often thought of in terms of quarter years or years. PSTR data should fall somewhere in between, and should be thought of in terms of weeks or months to fill the void between FPC and session data.

When assessing the storage needs for PSTR data, you should take into account that it is wildly variable. For instance, during lunch time, you might see that the amount of HTTP traffic is at a peak and the amount of traffic generated from other protocols more closely associated with business processes has dipped. This might not impact the total amount of PCAP data being collected during this time period, but it will noticeably increase the amount of PSTR data being collected.

There are a number of free and open source applications that can perform both collection of PSTR data from the wire and generation of the data from FPC data. No matter how you choose to generate this data, it must be functional. When evaluating a PSTR data collection or generation solution, you should ensure that the resulting data is standardized such that it is usable in relation to your detection and analysis tools and processes. In the remainder of this section we will look at some of these tools.

## Manual Generation of PSTR Data

Before we look at some tools that can be used to automatically generate PSTR data, let's look at some alternative ways of generating PSTR data by utilizing tools built into the Linux BASH environment. To generate a baseline, we start by parsing the ASCII data from a PCAP file. With PSTR data, the only data you care to see are collections of human readable characters, so we limit our results by piping the data through the Linux utility "strings". From here, there are multiple variations of data that you can choose to generate, depending on whether you want to generate log or payload style PSTR data.

The log style script below will generate data similar to that show in Figure 6.2, with single line logs detailing the URI associated with the user's request.

```
#!/bin/bash
#Send the ASCII from the full packet capture to stdout
/usr/sbin/tcpdump -qnns 0 -A -r test.pcap | \

#Normalizes the PCAP
strings |\

#Parse out all timestamp headers and Host fields
grep    -e   '[0\-9][0\-9]\:[0\-9][0\-9]\:[0\-9][0\-9].[0\-9]\{6\}\|
Host:'| grep -B1 "Host:" |\

#Clean up the results
grep -v -- "--"| sed 's/\(Host.*$\)/\1\n/g'| \
tr "\n" "-" | sed 's/--/\n/g'| sed 's/-Host:/ -/g'
```

The payload style script below will generate multiline PSTR log data delimited by a series of dashes. This example extracts all readable strings from all protocols. There are currently few ways to generate this type of data outside of manually generating it.

```
#!/bin/bash
#Send the ASCII from the full packet capture to stdout
/usr/sbin/tcpdump -qnns 0 -A -r test.pcap |\

#Normalizes the PCAP
strings |\

#Remove all empty lines
sed '/o$/d' |\
#Splits each record with an empty line
sed '/[0-9][0-9]\:[0-9][0-9]\:[0-9][0-9].[0-9]\{6\} IP [0-9]\{1,3\}
\.[0-9]\{1,3\}.[0-9]\{1,3\}.[0-9]\{1,3\}/{x;p;x;}' |\

#Adds a delimiter between records by replacing the empty lines
sed 's/\^$/\-\-\-\-\-\-\-\-\-\-\-\-\-\-\-\-\-\-\-\-\-\-\-\-\-\-\-\-\-
\-\-\-\-/g' |\

#Removes duplicate special characters
sed 's/[\^[:alnum:][:space:]_():-]\+/./g'
```

While manual solutions are generally slower in processing data, there is no limit to the amount of customization you can perform on that incoming data. Now we will look at some tools that can be used to efficiently generate log style PSTR data.

## URLSnarf

The Dsniff suite is a collection of tools that can be useful for network security purposes. The collection of Dsniff tools can be separated into two classifications. Some of these tools are used for more offensive purposes, while the rest, and most significant for our purposes, are the snarf tools that are used to passively monitor the network for interesting information pertaining to files, emails, web requests and more. The tool that we are most interested in for this book is URLsnarf.

URLsnarf passively collects HTTP request data and stores it in common log format (CLF). The Dsniff suite holds a special place in my heart because its tools have been around for a long time, and due to the simplicity of installation and execution of all its tools. URLsnarf is no exception. In the most scenarios, you can install the Dsniff suite via your favorite package management solution. The Dsniff tool suite is not installed on Security Onion by default, so if you wish to use it you can install it with apt:

```
sudo apt-get install dsniff
```

With the Dsniff tools installed, you can verify the installation of URLsnarf by running the command with no arguments. Upon execution with no parameters specified, URLsnarf will passively listen on an interface and dump collected data to standard output, visible in your terminal window. By default, it will listen on interface eth0 and it is hardcoded to sniff for traffic on TCP port 80, 8080 and 3128.

URLsnarf only contains 4 options;

- -p: Allows the user to run URLsnarf against an already captured PCAP file
- -i: Specify a network interface
- -n: Parse data without resolving addresses DNS addresses
- -v < expression >: By default, you can specify a specific URL as an expression at run time to display only URLs matching that expression. The –v option allows you to specify an expression that will result in displaying all results that do NOT match the stated URL.

Due to the standard log output, I find it easier to parse the output by piping it to BASH command line tools such as grep, cut, and awk rather than specifying the expressions with the –v option. In Figure 6.4 below, I first captured the traffic using tcpdump and then fed it to URLsnarf with the -p option. Though reading from PCAP with tcpdump is not a requirement, it is likely that you will be utilizing existing FPC data in a production environment. By leaving off the -p option, you will be reading data off the wire.

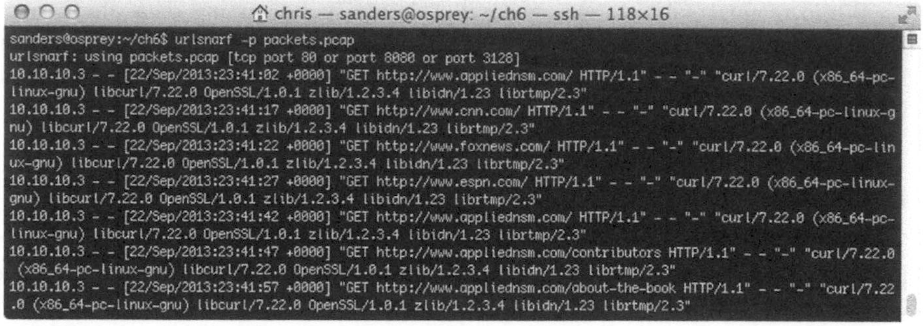

**FIGURE 6.4**

Sample Data from URLsnarf

The output shown in Figure 6.4 is a set of standardized logs detailing the HTTP requests from my visit to appliednsm.com. At first glance, the usefulness of this tool is limited to storing logs for retrospective analysis. However, with a careful application of command line kung-fu, this output can translate into serious on-the-fly examination of user traffic across a large network.

While URLsniff is incredibly simple to use, this simplicity can cause problems. If you desire less verbosity in its output, then the data must be manipulated with an external tool. If you desire more verbose output, you are out of luck; URLsnarf will not allow for multiline data output like some other tools do.

## Httpry

Httpry is a specialized packet sniffer for displaying and logging HTTP traffic. As you might ascertain from its name, httpry can only parse HTTP traffic. Unlike URLsnarf however, httpry has a lot more options when dealing with the data it can collect, parse, and output. It will allow for the capture and output of any HTTP header in any order. It is the ability to customize the output of each of these tools that make it useful in generating PSTR data that is useful in your environment. Due to the increased amount of customization and post processing that can be performed, the learning curve for httpry is a bit steeper than something like URLsnarf.

Httpry is not included on Security Onion by default, but can be installed fairly easily by building the application from source. In order to do this, you will complete the following steps:

1. Install the libpcap development library, a prerequisite for compiling Httpry

   ```
   sudo apt-get install libpcap-dev
   ```

2. Download the tarball from Jason Bittel's Httpry website

   ```
   wget http://dumpsterventures.com/jason/httpry/httpry-0.1.7.tar.gz
   ```

**3.** Extract the archive

```
tar -zxvf httpry-0.1.7.tar.gz
```

**4.** Change into the Httpry directory and then make and install the application

```
make && sudo make install
```

Once installation is completed, you can run the program with no arguments to start gathering HTTP traffic from port 80 on the lowest numbered network interface. In Figure 6.5 below, we show httpry reading traffic from a file using the –r argument and generating output.

**FIGURE 6.5**

Example Httpry Data

Httpry provides several command line arguments, but here are a few of the most useful for getting started:

- -r < file >: Read from an input PCAP file instead of performing a live capture
- -o < file >: Write to an httpry log file (needed for parsing scripts)
- -i < interface >: Capture data from a specified interface
- -d: Run httpry as a daemon
- -q: Run in quiet-mode, suppress non-critical output such as banners and statistics

The default logging format for httpry isn't always the ideal output for parsing in every environment. Fortunately, with very little command line magic, this data can be converted into something more easily parseable for detection mechanisms and analysis tools. Httpry has several built-in scripts that can manipulate the output to allow better analysis of the data output. By using the -o switch, you can force the data collected by httpry to be output by one of these plugins. Some of these plugins include the ability to output hostname statistics, HTTP log summary information, and the ability to convert output to common log formats, allowing you to generate similar results to what you would have seen from URI snarf. You'll notice that the fields are slightly different from URLsnarf output, and due to common log format varying slightly, parsers might see differences.

The ability to create parsing scripts allows for seamless integration of plugins that can automate a PSTR data solution based on httpry. To do the conversions, it requires a separate script called parse_log.pl. This script is located in the httpry scripts/plugins/ directory, and works by utilizing the plugins stored in that directory. As an example, the commands shown below can be utilized for a single parsing script. In this case, we are using the common log format for producing httpry data in a format that is versatile for parsing by detection and analysis tools.

1. Run Httptry and direct the output to a file

```
httpry -o test.txt
```

2. Parse the Output

```
perl scripts/parse_log.pl -p scripts/plugins/common_log.pm test.txt
```

This command works in a bit of an unexpected manner. If you attempt to generate output with httpry and then pipe it to something that modifies its output, the process will fail due to the lack of proper column headers. Instead, the httpry output must be written to a file first with the -o option. Then, the parse_log.pl script can be executed to parse the data. An example of this output is shown in Figure 6.6.

**FIGURE 6.6**

Example Httpry Output Parsed into a Common Format

Generating PSTR data with httpry is typically significantly faster than using URLsnarf to perform the same task. With that said, it is really the flexibility of data output that makes httpry a nice solution for many NSM environments.

## Justniffer

Justniffer is a full-fledged protocol analysis tool that allows for completely customizable output, making it useful for generating any TCP specific PSTR data beyond only HTTP traffic. Justniffer was primarily developed for streamlining the network troubleshooting process, and to focus on requests and responses in network traffic to provide only pertinent information used in narrowing down communication issues. This, of course, is exactly what we want to do with PSTR data generated for NSM purposes. In addition to capturing clear-text protocol headers, Justniffer can also be enhanced with simple scripts to do things like streaming its output directly from the wire to a local folder, sorted by host, with a BASH script. In another commonly used example; Justniffer includes a Python script called Justniffer-grab-http-traffic, which will extract files transferred during HTTP communication. Justniffer can also be extended to do performance measuring of response times, connection times, and more. The versatility of Justniffer makes it incredibly useful for a variety of PSTR data collection scenarios.

Justniffer is not included on Security Onion by default, so if you want to try it out then you are going to have to install it yourself. This can be done with these steps:

1. Add the appropriate PPA repository

```
sudo add-apt-repository ppa:oreste-notelli/ppa
```

2. Update the repository

```
sudo apt-get update
```

3. Install Justniffer with APT

```
sudo apt-get install justniffer
```

If you are installing Justniffer on a different distribution, the installation process might require additional steps. These installation steps can be found at http://justniffer.sourceforge.net/#!/install.

While getting started with Justniffer is fairly simple, getting the exact output you want can be tricky. With no command line arguments, Justniffer will function by capturing data on interface eth0, and displaying all HTTP traffic in a format nearly identical to the one used by URLsnarf. Justniffer provides some other useful command line arguments:

- -i < interface >: Select an interface to capture traffic on
- -f < file >: Read from a selected PCAP file
- -p < filter >: Apply a packet filter
- -l < format >: Specify how the output string will appear
- -u: Encode unprintable characters as dots

The output Justniffer generates by default is a good start, but let's generate some more interesting logs using the original examples in this chapter. If you recall, the first example we discussed was generating full request and response header data for HTTP communications, and was shown in Figure 6.1. Justniffer makes easy work of this with the request.header and response.header format keywords, utilized here:

```
sudo justniffer -f packets.pcap -p "tcp port 80" -u -l "%newline%request.
header%newline%response.header"
```

In this example we use the -f option to read a packet capture file (this could easily be substituted for –i < interface > to perform this action live from the wire), the -p option to specify a BPF, the -u option to convert unprintable characters to periods ( ), and the -l option to specify our own custom log format. The result of this command is shown in Figure 6.7, and displays two HTTP transactions.

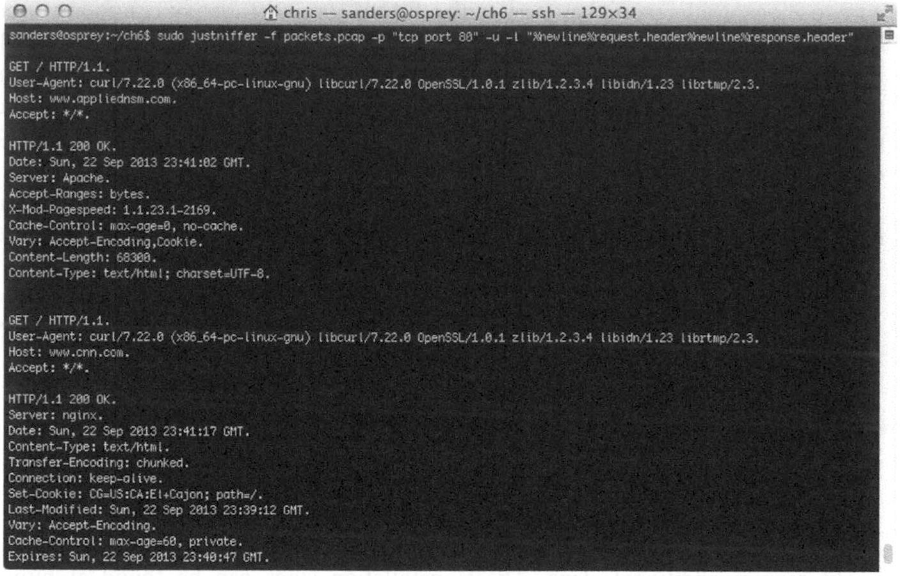

**FIGURE 6.7**

Sample Custom Justniffer Data

You'll notice that this example produces similar traffic to that of the original example, but it isn't entirely useful for analysis due to a critical lack of information. In order to analyze this data appropriately, we need to know the hosts responsible for the communication, and the timestamp indicating when the communication occurred. You have the "what", but you need the "who" and "when". We can extend this example by explicitly telling Justniffer to print those fields. Justniffer currently contains 85 different formatting options ranging from simple spacial delimiters to various elemental formatting options relating to requests, responses, and performance measurements. In order to get the formatting we desire, we're going to need a few more format keywords as well as a custom delimiter at the beginning of each multi-line log. This command is shown here:

```
sudo justniffer -f packets.pcap -p "tcp port 80" -u -l
"-------------------------------- %newline%request.timestamp - %
source.ip ->%dest.ip %newline%request.ader%newline%response.time-
stamp - %newline%response.header"
```

An example of output generated from this command is shown in Figure 6.8.

As you can see, we now have two entire HTTP transactions, complete with the hosts responsible for the communication and a timestamp detailing when the communication happened. We now have the who, the what, and the when. Later we'll discuss several methods of parsing this data, both with BASH scripts and free open source tools.

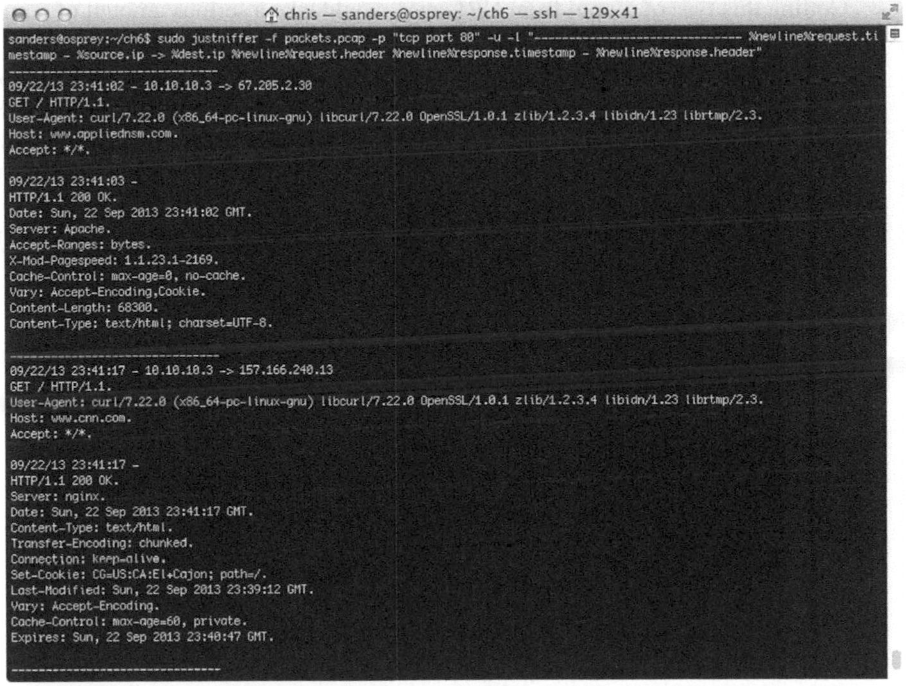

**FIGURE 6.8**

Multiple Line Justniffer Traffic Modified for Analysis

We can also use Justniffer to generate data similar to the example shown in Figure 6.2, which is a minimal single line log that shows only the communication timestamp, the source and destination IP address, and the URL requested. Using only a few special delimiters and the request.url variable, we generate this output with the following command:

```
sudo justniffer -f packets.pcap -p "tcp port 80" -u -l "%request.time-
stamp - %source.ip - >%dest.ip - %request.header.host%request.url"
```

The output of this command is shown in Figure 6.9.

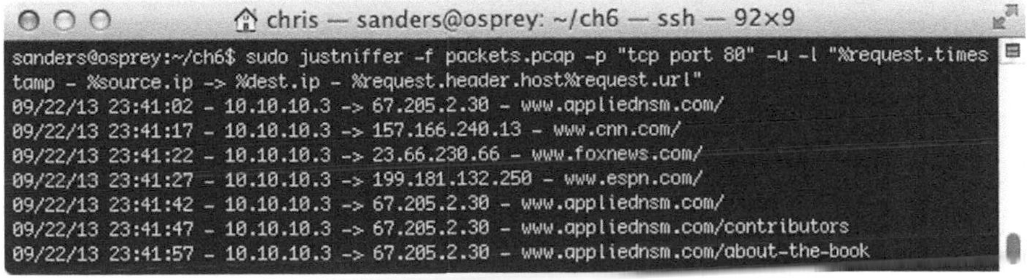

**FIGURE 6.9**

Single Line Justniffer Traffic Modified for Analysis

Getting this type of output from URLsnarf would take a serious amount of command line kung-fu.

So far, we've been focused on HTTP logs because some of these tools are only HTTP aware. Justniffer, however, is a fully functional TCP protocol analyzer, and as such, can parse other non-HTTP traffic with ease. For instance, Justniffer can also be used for pulling clear-text SMTP or POP mail records from FPC data or directly from the wire.

To get results similar to what we've already seen, but for SMTP mail data, we can tell Justniffer to look at port 25 traffic with this command:

```
justniffer -f packets.pcap -r -p "port 25"
```

An example of this data is shown in Figure 6.10.

```
chris — sanders@osprey: ~/ch6 — ssh — 87×38
220 mail.example.com ESMTP (41c61ac9c57d91073ede0da97e56d329)

EHLO amta03.example.com
250-mail.example.com Hello amta03.example.com [192.0.2.1], pleased to meet you
250-SIZE 100000000
250-PIPELINING
250-8BITMIME
250 HELP

MAIL From:<bounces@postmaster.example.com> SIZE=45468
250 Sender <bounces@postmaster.example.com> OK

RCPT To:<testuser@example.com>
DATA
250 Recipient <testuser@example.com> OK
354 Start mail input; end with <CRLF>.<CRLF>

Received: from app03.example.com (app03 [10.255.20.23])
        by amta03.example.com (8.13.8/8.13.8) with ESMTP id r8FDv2nw019441
        for <testuser@example.com>; Sun, 15 Sep 2013 06:57:03 -0700
DomainKey-Signature: a=rsa-sha1; s=mail; d=example.com; c=nofws; q=dns;
        b=fe07/sm14ZmxPwIyy4zJjt8FMN2EOtbVH9f/MpRF4QdJTV8Ark+xAv1tHyOms1A7k
        1Q6slfFrAO5kWc+XHCjh/qpkfB89tN2ygvlsieflkBs9StsqvEPEaMJ2JorQNJQbMp6
        i84BcG/JXD8T4FLzMGgBjfNJbgWcUgvTPqcFa/E=
DKIM-Signature: v=1; a=rsa-sha256; c=relaxed/relaxed; d=example.com;
        s=mail; t=1379233423;
        bh=YR0w43GoXOOHfGb0TCHbgjPuw+2up2qjkW56oY5Y/NY=;
        h=Message-Id:Date:From:Reply-To:To:Subject:Mime-Version:
         Content-Type:List-Unsubscribe;
        b=dteE9xK8WPsAdi2pzNvmCzyllpW9+41wMuEPpSAfasGFuQ0mQ7TT4l1kMr/6iCv9y+rx4
         O/OACBzg+WZ5YaUtCKWdi0JHFiniwEIwswmklsadRxbsqha0G4hHh/q0SSm8z6
         Y5J/qLNP69SruHlFeyQAXujFXZOTKOqB1bccpYnY=
Received: from app03.example.com (localhost [127.0.0.1])
        by app03.example.com (8.13.8/8.13.8) with ESMTP id r8FDuwLD002389
        for <testuser@example.com>; Sun, 15 Sep 2013 06:56:58 -0700
Received: (from example@localhost)
        by app03.example.com (8.13.8/8.13.8/Submit) id r8FDuw1n002331;
        Sun, 15 Sep 2013 06:56:58 -0700
```

**FIGURE 6.10**

Generating SMTP PSTR Data with Justniffer

# VIEWING PSTR DATA

As with all NSM data, a proper PSTR data solution requires a synergy between the collection and viewing mechanisms. A more customized collection mechanism can require more unique parsing methods. In this section we will examine potential solutions that can be used to parse, view, and interact with PSTR data using several of the data formatting examples we've already created.

## Logstash

Logstash is a popular log parsing engine that allows for both multi-line and single line logs of various types, including common formats like syslog and JSON formatted logs, as well as the ability to parse custom logs. As a free and open-source tool, it is an incredibly powerful log collector that is relatively easy to set up in large environments. As an example, we will configure Logstash to parse logs that are being collected with URLsnarf. Since Logstash 1.2.1 was released, it includes the Kibana interface for viewing logs, so we'll also discuss some of its features that can be used for querying the data you need, without getting the data you don't.

Logstash isn't included in Security Onion, so if you want to follow along you will need to download it from the project website at www.logstash.net. Logstash is contained entirely in one java package, so you'll need the Java Runtime Environment (JRE) installed (http://openjdk.java.net/install/, or simply `sudo apt-get install java-default`). At this point, you can simply execute the program.

In order to parse any type of data, Logstash requires a configuration file that defines how it will receive that data. In a real world scenario, you will probably have a steady stream of data rolling in from a logging source, so in this example, we'll look at data being written to a specific location. In this example, we'll call the configuration file urlsnarf-parse.conf. This is a very simple configuration:

```
input {
  file {
    type => "urlsnarf"
    path => "/home/idsusr/urlsnarf.log"
  }
}
output {
  elasticsearch { embedded => true }
}
```

This configuration tells Logstash to listen to data of any kind being written to /home/idsusr/urlsnarf.log and to consider any log written to that file to be a "urlsnarf" type of log, which is the log type we are defining. The output section of this configuration file starts an Elasticsearch instance inside of Logstash to allow for indexing and searching of the received data.

Once we have a configuration file, we can start up Logstash to initiate the log listener for when we start generating data. To begin Logstash with the Kibana web front end enabled, issue this command;

```
java -jar logstash-1.2.1-flatjar.jar agent -f urlsnarf-parse.conf -- web
```

The output of this command is shown in Figure 6.11.

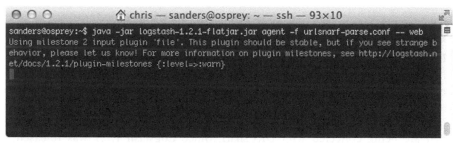

**FIGURE 6.11**

Executing Logstash

This command will initiate the agent, specifying urlsnarf-parse.conf with the –f option. Ending the command with " -- web " will ensure that Kibana is started along with the logging agent. The initial startup can take a minute, and since the Logstash output isn't too verbose, you can verify that Logstash is running by invoking netstat on the system.

```
sudo netstat -antp | grep java
```

If everything is running properly, you should see several ports initiated by the java service opened up. This is shown in Figure 6.12.

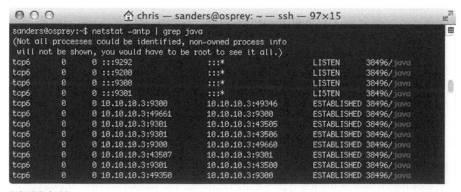

**FIGURE 6.12**

These Open Ports Indicate Logstash is Running Properly

Once these are running, go ahead and confirm that the Kibana front end is functioning by visiting http://127.0.0.1:9292 in your web browser, replacing 127.0.0.1 with the IP address of the system you've installed Logstash on. This will take you directly to the main Kibana dashboard.

---

**CAUTION**

If you've installed Logstash on a Security Onion system and are attempting to access the Kibana web interface from another system (such as your Virtual Machine host system), you will not be able to by default. This is because of the firewall enabled on the system. You can add an exception to the firewall with this command: `sudo ufw allow 9292/tcp`

---

Now that Logstash is listening and the Kibana front-end is functional, you can send data to the file specified in urlsnarf-parse.conf. To create data to parse, you can use your existing installation of the Dsniff tool set and start URLsnarf, sending its output data to a file.

```
sudo urlsnarf > /home/idsusr/urlsnarf.log
```

After URLsnarf is initialized, open a web browser (or use curl from the command line) and visit a few sites to generate some data. Once you've finished, use Ctrl + C to end the URLsnarf process. After stopping the data collection, go back to the Kibana front end and confirm that logs are arriving in the browser. If they are, you should see some data displayed on the screen, similar to Figure 6.13. If they are not, try making sure you've selected the correct time span towards the top of the dashboard.

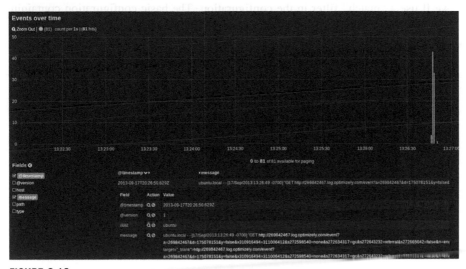

**FIGURE 6.13**

Viewing Log Data in Kibana

This figure represents "raw" log files that are being ingested, which are for the most part unparsed. So far, if you examine a log, only the timestamp in which it arrived and the hostname of the current device are present. This is because you haven't specified a filter in the Logstash configuration so that it knows how to parse the individual fields within each log entry. These filters make up the meat of the configuration and define how logs are indexed.

With that said, let's extend the flexibility of Logstash by defining custom filters to generate stateful information so that Kibana can really stretch its legs. Logstash uses GROK to combine text patterns and regular expressions to match log text in the order that you wish. GROK is a powerful language used by Logstash to make parsing easier than it would normally be when using regular expressions. We will address getting a stateful understanding of the URLsnarf log format shortly, but let's start with a simpler example in order to understand the syntax. In this example we'll create a filter that matches text fields in a log that we generated with Justniffer in Figure 6.14, but this time with the addition of a "sensor name" at the end.

**FIGURE 6.14**

Custom Justniffer Data with a Sensor Name to be Parsed

To show how Logstash handles basic matches as opposed to prebuilt patterns, we'll use a "match" filter in the configuration. The basic configuration containing match filters should look like this;

```
input {
  file {
    type => "Justniffer-Logs"
    path => "/home/idsusr/justniffer.log"
  }
}
filter {
  grok {
    type => "Justniffer-Logs"
    match => [ "message", "insertfilterhere" ]
  }
}
output {
  elasticsearch { embedded => true }
}
```

We'll use the existing built-in GROK patterns to generate the data we need for the configuration, which we'll call justniffer-parse.conf. These patterns can be found at https://github.com/logstash/logstash/blob/master/patterns/grok-patterns. But before we start examining which patterns we want to tie together, the first thing to do is look at the log format and define what fields we want to identify. This data format breaks down like this:

```
datestamp timestamp - IP -> IP - domain/path - sensorname SENSOR
```

Now we need to translate this into GROK, which is where the GROK debugger comes in. The debugger is located at http://grokdebug.herokuapp.com/. Here you simply place the log string you want to match in the top line, and in the pattern line enter the GROK pattern you think will match it. The application will show you which data is matched. The key when developing GROK formatted strings is to start with small patterns and extend them gradually to match the entire log line (Figure 6.15).

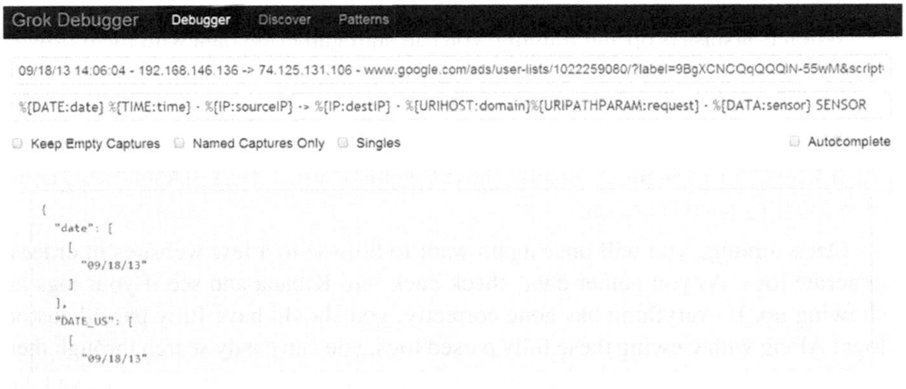

**FIGURE 6.15**

Using the Grok Debugger

In order to match the log line we are working with, we will use this pattern:

```
%{DATE:date} %{TIME:time} - %{IP:sourceIP} ->%{IP:destIP} - %{URI-
HOST:domain}%{URIPATHPARAM:request} - %{DATA:sensor} SENSOR
```

You'll notice we included field labels next to each field, which will identify the fields. Applying the filter to the full configuration file gives us a complete configuration that will parse all incoming Justniffer logs matching the format we specified earlier. This is our resulting configuration file:

```
input {
  file {
    type => "Justniffer-Logs"
    path => "/home/idsusr/justniffer.log"
  }
}
filter {
```

```
grok {
  type => "Justniffer-Logs"
  match => [ "message", "%{DATE:date} %{TIME:time} - %{IP:sourceIP}
->%{IP:destIP} - %{URIHOST:domain}%{URIPATHPARAM:request} - %{DATA:
sensor} SENSOR" ]
  }
}
output {
  elasticsearch { embedded => true }
}
```

Once you have this configuration, you can go ahead and start the Logstash collector with this command that uses our new configuration file:

```
java -jar logstash-1.2.1-flatjar.jar agent -f justniffer-parse.conf --
web
```

When Logstash is up and running, you can start gathering data with the following Justniffer command that will generate log data in the format matching the configuration we've just created:

```
sudo justniffer -p "tcp port 80" -u -l "%request.timestamp - %source.ip -
>%dest.ip - %request.header.host%request.url - IDS1 SENSOR" >> /home/
idsusr/justniffer.log
```

Once running, you will once again want to browse to a few websites in order to generate logs. As you gather data, check back into Kibana and see if your logs are showing up. If everything has gone correctly, you should have fully parsed custom logs! Along with viewing these fully parsed logs, you can easily search through them in Kibana's "Query" field at the bottom of the main dashboard page, or you can narrow down the display parameters to define only the fields you wish to see with the "Fields" Event filter to the left of the query field, shown in Figure 6.16.

**FIGURE 6.16**

Examining Individual Logs in Kibana

You can also examine metrics for a given field by clicking the field name in the list on the left side of the screen. Figure 6.17 shows field metrics for the Host field, which shows all of the hosts visited in the current logs.

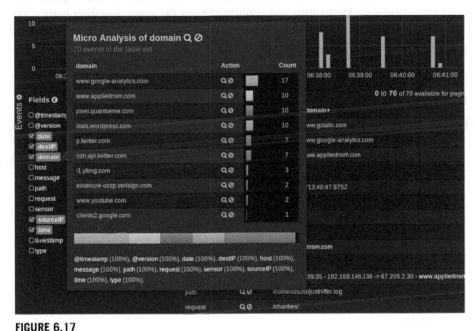

**FIGURE 6.17**

Examining Field Metrics in Kibana

This Justniffer log example provides an excellent way to dive into custom parsing of logs with Logstash. However, some log types will be more extensive and difficult to parse. For instance, if we examine URLsnarf logs, we see that they are nearly identical to Apache access logs, with the exception of a character or two. While Logstash would normally be able to handle Apache access logs with ease, these additional characters can break the built-in filters. For this example, we will look at creating our own GROK filter for replacing the existing filter pattern for Apache access logs in order to adequately parse the URLsnarf logs. Our new filter will take into account the difference and relieve the incongruity created by the additional hyphens. Since the filters are so similar to the built-in pattern, we can manipulate this pattern as needed. The latest GROK patterns can be found at the Logstash GIT repository, https://github.com/logstash/logstash/blob/master/patterns/grok-patterns. If you examine the COMBINEDAPACHELOG filter carefully, you'll see the issue falls with the lack of a simple hyphen, which has been added below.

```
COMBINEDAPACHELOG %{IPORHOST:clientip} %{USER:ident} %{USER:auth} \[%
{HTTPDATE:timestamp}\] "(?:%{WORD:verb} %{NOTSPACE:request}(?: HTTP/
```

```
%{NUMBER:httpversion})?|%{DATA:rawrequest})"    %{NUMBER:response}|-
(?:%{NUMBER:bytes}|-) %{QS:referrer} %{QS:agent}
```

The above filter looks complicated, and that's because it is. The break down of it is an exercise best left for the GROK debugger. Our changes to the original filter include correcting the hyphen and commented out the inner quotation marks. We can add this GROK filter into the base configuration we created earlier, resulting in this completed configuration file:

```
input {
  file {
    type => "urlsnarf"
    path => "/home/idsusr/urlsnarf.log"
  }
}
filter {
  grok {
    type => "urlsnarf"
    match => [ "message", "%{IPORHOST:clientip} %{USER:ident} %{USER:
auth}  \[%{HTTPDATE:timestamp}\]  \"(?:%{WORD:verb}   %{NOTSPACE:
request} (?: HTTP/%{NUMBER:httpversion})?|%{DATA:rawrequest})\" (%
{NUMBER:response}|-)  (?:%{NUMBER:bytes}|-)  %{QS:referrer}  %{QS:
agent}" ]
  }
}
output {
  elasticsearch { embedded => true }
}
```

Without using a GROK filter, these logs would look like Figure 6.18 in Kibana, with most of the data appearing as a single line that doesn't allow for any advanced analytics based upon fields.

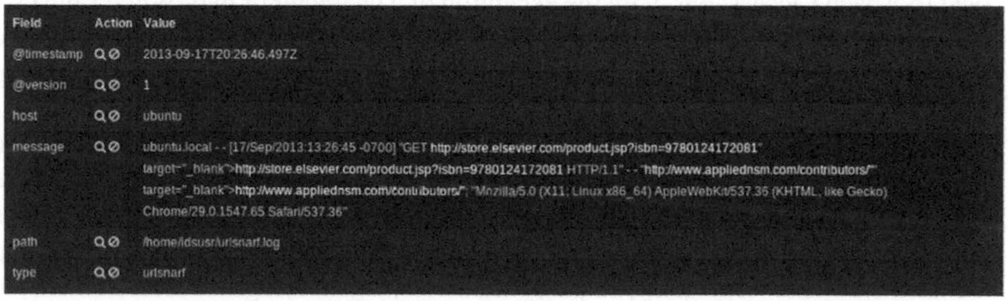

**FIGURE 6.18**

The Log Data Without GROK

The new log field description is fully parsed using the filter as seen in Figure 6.19.

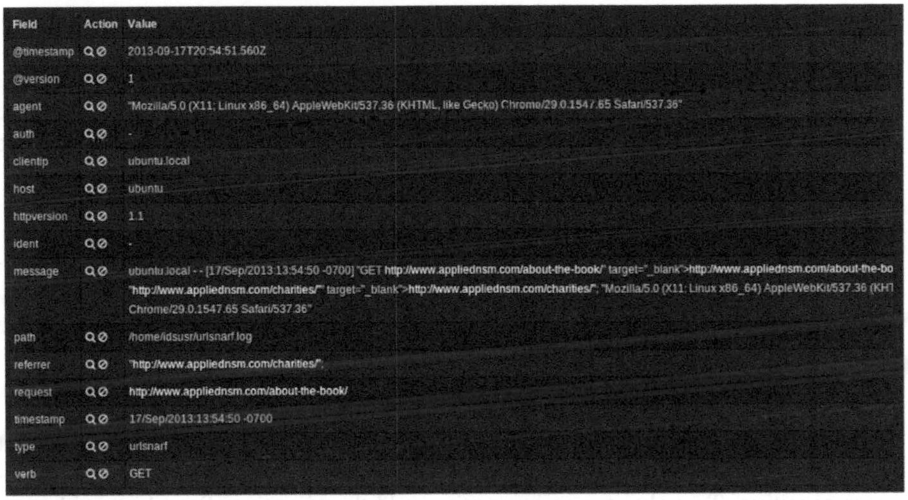

| Field | Action | Value |
|---|---|---|
| @timestamp | Q ⊘ | 2013-09-17T20:54:51.560Z |
| @version | Q ⊘ | 1 |
| agent | Q ⊘ | "Mozilla/5.0 (X11; Linux x86_64) AppleWebKit/537.36 (KHTML, like Gecko) Chrome/29.0.1547.65 Safari/537.36" |
| auth | Q ⊘ | - |
| clientip | Q ⊘ | ubuntu.local |
| host | Q ⊘ | ubuntu |
| httpversion | Q ⊘ | 1.1 |
| ident | Q ⊘ | - |
| message | Q ⊘ | ubuntu.local - - [17/Sep/2013:13:54:50 -0700] "GET http://www.appliednsm.com/about-the-book/" target="_blank">http://www.appliednsm.com/about-the-bo "http://www.appliednsm.com/charities/" target="_blank">http://www.appliednsm.com/charities/"; "Mozilla/5.0 (X11; Linux x86_64) AppleWebKit/537.36 (KHT Chrome/29.0.1547.65 Safari/537.36" |
| path | Q ⊘ | /home/idsusr/urlsnarf.log |
| referrer | Q ⊘ | "http://www.appliednsm.com/charities/"; |
| request | Q ⊘ | http://www.appliednsm.com/about-the-book/ |
| timestamp | Q ⊘ | 17/Sep/2013:13:54:50 -0700 |
| type | Q ⊘ | urlsnarf |
| verb | Q ⊘ | GET |

**FIGURE 6.19**

The New Log Data with GROK

As you can see, the combination of Logstash, Kibana, and GROK makes a powerful trio that is convenient for parsing logs like the ones generated by PSTR data. If you want to learn more about these tools, you should visit the Logstash website at http://logstash.net/.

## Raw Text Parsing with BASH Tools

The combination of Logstash and Kibana is an excellent way to parse single line PSTR data, but those tools might not be the best fit in every environment. Depending on how you are sourcing your data, you might find yourself in need of a broader toolset. Even in cases where log search utilities are present, I always recommend that whenever flat text logs are being used, they should be accessible by analysts directly in some form. In the following examples, we'll take a look at sample PSTR data that includes multi-line request and response headers.

Earlier we generated PSTR data with Justniffer, and for this example, we will start by doing it again:

```
sudo justniffer -i eth0 -p "tcp port 80" -u -l "-------
----------------------- %newline%request.timestamp - %source.ip -> 
%dest.ip %newline%request.header%newline%response.timestamp - %new-
line%response.header">pstrtest.log
```

This should generate data that looks similar to what is shown in Figure 6.7, and store that data in a file named pstrtest.log.

Parsing raw data with BASH tools such as sed, awk, and grep can sometimes carry a mystical aura of fear that is not entirely deserved. After all, parsing this kind of text is one of the most documented and discussed topics in Unix related forums, and I have yet to come across an unresolvable parsing issue. From the example data above, we can gather a significant amount of useful information for analysis. From a tool perspective, we can search and parse this with grep quite easily. For instance we can search for every Host seen in the data set by performing a simple search for the "Host" field, like this:

```
cat pstrtest.log | grep "Host:"
```

This will result in printing every line that contains the word "Host:" in any context, even if it is not the context you wish for. To make sure that it is looking for only lines beginning with the term "Host:", try extending grep with the –e option and the carrot (∧) symbol:.

```
cat pstrtest.log | grep -e "∧Host: "
```

The carrot symbol matches "beginning of a line", and for every line that has "Host: " after the beginning of the line, it will match. Currently, this search is case sensitive. To make it case insensitive, add the –i option. Searching with grep is the easiest and most common use for the tool, however, it can be extended to perform powerful regular expression searching, parsing, and massaging of data. For instance, let's consider searching for Etags of a very specific format, as shown in Figure 6.20.

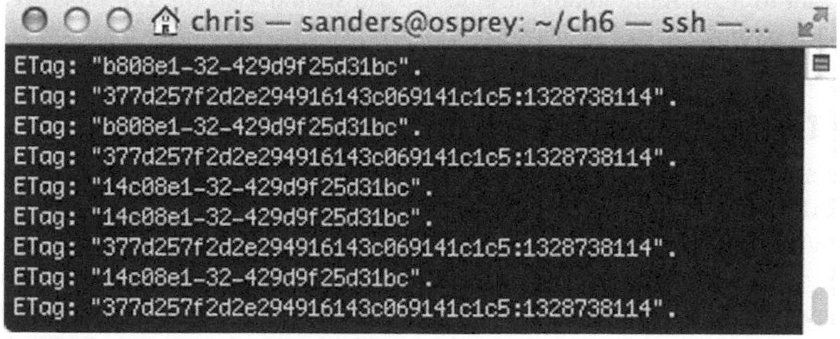

**FIGURE 6.20**

Using Grep to Search for Etags in PSTR Data

You'll notice that while most of these entries share similar formats, some will contain additional characters, such having more than one hyphen (-). The fifth line in Figure 6.14 is an example of this, so let's search for examples matching it. In theory, we are searching for all lines starting with the text "ETag", and followed by a specific value with two hyphens. We will print only the ETags themselves. The following command will accomplish this goal:

```
cat pstrtest.log | grep -e "∘ETag" | grep -oP "\".*?\-.*?\-.*?\"" | sed 's/
"//g'
```

Despite what appears to be a rather complicated command, it does exactly what we asked. Since this one-liner has multiple elements, let's break them down individually:

**1.** `cat pstrtest.log`

First, we dump to output of the pstrtest.log file to the screen (standard output)

**2.** `grep -e "^ETag"`

Next, we pipe the output of the file to grep, where we search for lines containing the text "ETag" at the beginning of a line.

**3.** `grep -oP "\".*?\-.*?\-.*?\""`

The ETags that are found are piped to another grep command that utilizes a regular expression to locate data in the proper format. This format is any number of characters (`.*?`) between a quote and a hyphen, followed by any number of characters between that hyphen and another, followed by any number of characters and another quote.

**4.** `sed 's/"//g'`

Next, we pipe the output of the last Grep command to Sed to remove any quotation marks from the output.

In this example, we introduced Sed into the equation. The sed command is useful for searching and replacing text. In this case, it looks at every line, and replaces every instance of double quotes (") with nothing. More simply put, it removes all double quotes. The output of this command is shown in Figure 6.21.

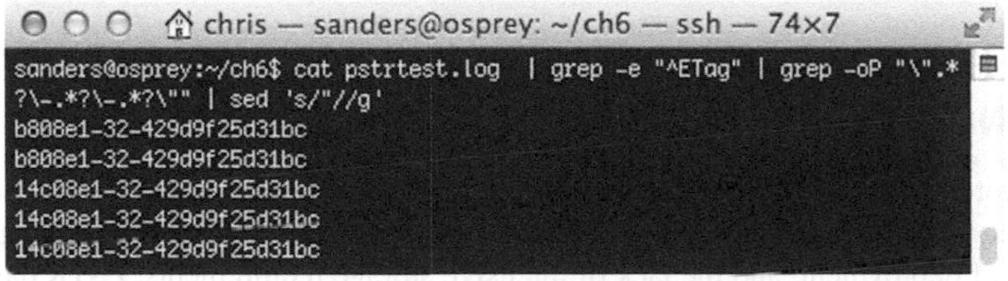

```
sanders@osprey:~/ch6$ cat pstrtest.log  | grep -e "^ETag" | grep -oP "\".*
?\-.*?\-.*?\""  | sed 's/"//g'
b808e1-32-429d9f25d31bc
b808e1-32-429d9f25d31bc
14c08e1-32-429d9f25d31bc
14c08e1-32-429d9f25d31bc
14c08e1-32-429d9f25d31bc
```

**FIGURE 6.21**

The Output of Specific ETag Results from PSTR Data

Another useful way to massage data is to simply sort and count what you have. This might sound like a simple task, and it is, but it is incredibly useful. For example, let's take a look at the User Agent string in the HTTP header information that can be contained within PSTR data. We can perform some rudimentary detection by sorting these User Agent strings from least to most visited. This can often times reveal suspicious activity and possible indicators due to user agent strings that are unexpected.

`cat pstrtest.log | grep -e "^User Agent: " | sort | uniq -c | sort -n`

In this example we have taken our PSTR data and outputted only lines beginning with "User Agent:". From here, we pipe this data to the sort command to order the results. This data is then piped to the uniq command, which parses the data by counting each uniq line and providing the total number of times it occurs in a left column. Finally, we pipe that data once more to the sort command and utilize the –n string to sort the data by the count of occurrences. We are left with the data shown in Figure 6.22.

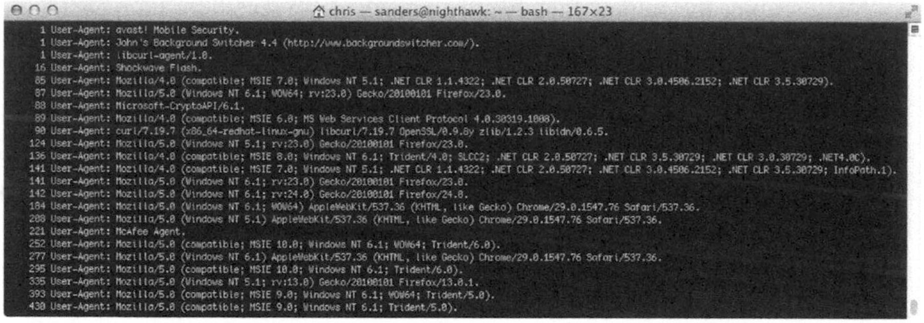

**FIGURE 6.22**

Sorted User Agent Data

Analyzing this data immediately reveals that a few unique and potentially suspicious user agents exist in this communication. From that point, you could perform a more thorough investigation surrounding this communication. This is an example of generating some basic statistical data from PSTR data.

## CONCLUSION

Packet String Data, in any of its possible forms, is critical for maximizing efficiency in detection and analysis. Given the speed of access, the depth of data, the general ease of deployment, and the lack of intensive storage requirements, PSTR data provides the perfect bridge between FPC and session data. In this chapter we defined PSTR data and discussed a number of ways to collect and parse this data type. In later chapters, we will reference instances in which analysis can be enhanced by referencing PSTR data.

# Detection

# Detection Mechanisms, Indicators of Compromise, and Signatures

# 7

## CHAPTER OUTLINE

The detection phase of Network Security Monitoring is all about knowing your detection capabilities, understanding adversarial tactics, and then applying those capabilities to detect when an adversary acts. This process occurs when collected data is examined and anomalies are identified.

In this first chapter of the Detection section of *Applied NSM*, we will define detection mechanisms, indicators of compromise (IOCs), and signatures, and then examine how the IOCs are comprised, and how they can be derived from network attacks. We will also look at several best practices for successful management of IOCs and signatures, and some common IOC and signature frameworks.

## DETECTION MECHANISMS

Generally, detection is a function of software that parses through collected data in order to generate alert data. This software is referred to as a detection mechanism. The alert data that is generated by the detection mechanism is presented to an analyst, and that's when detection ends and analysis begins. This process may sound hands-off, but that couldn't be farther from the truth. To perform detection successfully, you must take great care in choosing detection mechanisms and feeding them appropriately.

The majority of the detection mechanisms discussed in this book are network-based intrusion detection systems (NIDS). These can be divided into two primary categories: signature-based and anomaly-based detection.

Signature-based detection is the oldest form of intrusion detection, and it works by combing through data to find matches for specified patterns. Some patterns can be simple, like an IP address or a text string. Other patterns can be more complex, such as a particular number of null bytes occurring after a specific string while utilizing a specific protocol. When these patterns are broken down into objective platform-independent pieces of data, they become indicators of compromise. When they are expressed in the platform-specific language of a detection mechanism, they become signatures.

A subset of signature-based detection is reputation-based detection, which attempts to detect communication between friendly hosts on the network you are protecting and hosts on the Internet that are believed to be malicious based upon their participation in previous malicious actions. This essentially results in detection based upon a series of simple signatures that are usually based upon IP addresses or domain names.

We will cover several popular signature-based detection mechanisms, including Snort and Suricata in Chapter 9. We will also examine reputation-based detection mechanisms using multiple tools in Chapter 8.

Anomaly-based detection is a newer form of intrusion detection that is gaining popularity rapidly thanks to tools like Bro. Anomaly-based detection relies upon observing network occurrences and discerning anomalous traffic through heuristics and statistics. Instead of simply alerting whenever a specific pattern is seen, an anomaly-based detection mechanism has the ability to recognize attack patterns that deviate from normal network behavior. This type of detection is infinitely more powerful, but more difficult to implement. We will look into using Bro as an anomaly-based detection mechanism in Chapter 10, and performing statistical anomaly-based detection in Chapter 11.

A newly evolving subset of anomaly-based detection is the use of honeypot-based detection mechanisms. Honeypots have been used for many years to collect malware and attack samples for research purposes, but they have detection applications as well. This occurs by configuring honeypot systems to mirror production systems. These honeypots often contain known vulnerabilities, but have no actual confidential data on them. Instead, they are configured for an extensive level of logging, and often paired with other types of NIDS or HIDS. Detection with honeypots will be discussed in Chapter 12.

The detection mechanisms you will deploy depend on the maturity of your security program. Most SOCs start with only a signature-based mechanism and will wait to achieve confidence with that technology before moving on to something more advanced like an anomaly-based mechanism. This evolution lends itself well to the healthy development of a SOC. I've seen many organizations that try to implement the whole gamut of detection-mechanisms right off the bat, and end up failing because they just simply can't handle developing these capabilities simultaneously.

## INDICATORS OF COMPROMISE AND SIGNATURES

The detection mechanisms we just discussed are useless if they are not properly fed and cared for. This involves the development, maintenance, and implementation of IOCs and Signatures.

An IOC is any piece of information that can be used to objectively describe a network intrusion, expressed in a platform-independent manner. This could include a simple indicator such as the IP address of a command and control (C2) server or a complex set of behaviors that indicate that a mail server is being used as a malicious SMTP relay. IOCs can come in a variety of shapes and sizes, and can be formatted in different ways to be digested by various detection mechanisms. While one tool may be able to parse IP addresses in a comma-delimited list, another may require that they are inserted into a SQL database. Although the presentation of the IOC has changed, the IOC itself remains consistent. Furthermore, a single behavioral IOC may have to be broken down into several individual components and deployed to multiple detection mechanisms to be made actionable on a network. When an IOC is taken and used in a platform-specific language or format, such as a Snort Rule or a Bro-formatted file, it becomes part of a signature. A signature can contain one or more IOCs.

The remainder of this chapter is devoted to the classification and management of these indicators and signatures.

---

**ANALYST NOTE**

Throughout this book, the term IOC may simply be referred to as an indicator. It is important to understand that the term "indicator" can have varying definitions depending upon your audience. For instance, someone who works in the defense sector might think you are talking about behavioral or attribution indicators rather than objective pieces of information that describe an intrusion.

---

### Host and Network Indicators

The broadest and most common manner in which indicators are classified is either as host-based or network-based. This basic level of classification helps frame the indicator so you can plan the detection mechanism it will be used with.

A host-based IOC is a piece of information that is found on a host, and objectively describes an intrusion. Some common host-based indicators include:

- Registry Key
- File Name

- Text String
- Process Name
- Mutex
- File Hash
- User Account
- Directory Path

A network-based IOC is a piece of information that can be captured on the network between hosts, and objectively describes an intrusion. Some common network-based indicators include:

- IPv4 Address
- IPv6 Address
- X509 Certificate Hash
- Domain Name
- Text String
- Communication Protocol
- File Name
- URL

You could certainly argue that most of these indicators could be found on both the network and host levels at some point, but they are classified here based upon where they are primarily found. Some indicators are listed in both areas because they can be found equally as often in both locations, such as simple text strings and file names.

Dividing indicators into either host or network IOC's is a great way to initially classify them, but you can go a lot further in your classification efforts with the use of static and variable indicators, which are discussed next.

## Static Indicators

Static indicators are indicators for which values are explicitly defined. There are three variations of static indicators: Atomic, Computed, and Behavioral (Figure 7.1).

Atomic indicators are typically smaller and more specific indicators that cannot be broken down into smaller components, but still retain meaning in the context of an intrusion. This includes items such as IP addresses, text strings, hostnames, e-mail addresses, and file names.

Computed indicators are those that arc derived from incident data. This includes items such as hash values, regular expressions, and statistics.

Behavioral Indicators are collections of atomic and computed indicators that are paired together with some form of logic, often to provide some useful context. This might include a set of data containing file names and matching hash values, or a combination of a text string and a regular expression.

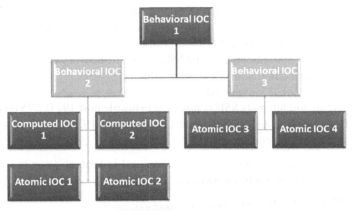

**FIGURE 7.1**

Atomic and Computed Indicators Comprise Behavioral Indicators

Consider a scenario in which we have determined that a device on our network has been compromised. An analysis of NSM data and host-based forensic data helps us determine that the following sequence of events occurred:

1. A user received an e-mail message from chris@appliednsm.com with the subject line "Payroll Information" and a PDF attachment called "Payroll.pdf." The PDF has an MD5 hash value of e0b359e171288512501f4c18ee64a6bd.
2. The user opened the PDF, triggering the download of a file called kerndel32. dll with the MD5 hash value da7140584983eccde51ab82404ba40db. The file is downloaded from http://www.appliednsm.com/kernel32.dll.
3. The file was used to overwrite C:/Windows/System32/kernel32.dll.
4. Code within the DLL was executed, and an SSH connection is established to a host with the IP address 192.0.2.75 on port 9966.
5. Once this connection is established, the malware searches for every DOC, DOCX, or PDF file from the friendly host and transmits it over the SSH connection to the hostile host.

The overall description of this incident could be described as a single large behavioral indicator. While this initial indicator does paint a broad picture of the incident, it does us little good in the context of NSM detection because it is far too complex.

To effectively tune signature, anomaly, and statistical based detection mechanisms, we must first break down the indicator into more useful pieces, ensuring that appropriate context remains. This could result in the creation of the following behavioral (B) indicators:

- B-1: A user receives an e-mail from chris@appliednsm.com with the subject line "Payroll Information" and a PDF attachment called "Payroll.pdf." The PDF file has an MD5 hash value of e0b359e171288512501f4c18ee64a6bd.

- B-2: The file kernel32.dll with the MD5 hash `da7140584983eccde51ab82404ba40db` is downloaded from the http://www. appliednsm.com/kernel32.dll.
- B-3: The file C:/Windows/System32/Kernel32.dll is overwritten by a malicious file of the same name with MD5 hash value `da7140584983eccde51ab82404ba40db`.
- B-4: Victim host attempts SSH connection to hostile host 192.0.2.75 on port 9966.
- B-5: DOC, DOCX, and PDF files are transmitted to 192.0.2.75 on port 9966 via an encrypted connection.

Next, we can attempt to break these behavioral indicators down into individual atomic (A) and computed (C) indicators. The following could result:

- C-1: MD5 Hash `e0b359e171288512501f4c18ee64a6bd`
- C-2: MD5 Hash `da7140584983eccde51ab82404ba40db`
- A-1: Hostile Domain: appliednsm.com
- A-2: E-Mail Address: chris@appliednsm.com
- A-3: Subject Line: "Payroll Information"
- A-4: File Name: Payroll.pdf
- A-5: File Name: Kernel32.dll
- A-6: Hostile IP 192.0.2.75
- A-7: Port 9966
- A-8: Protocol SSH
- A-9: File Types DOC, DOCX, and PDF
- A-10: File Name Kernel32.dll

This gives us a total of five behavioral indicators, one computed indicator, and ten atomic indicators that can be incorporated into our detection mechanisms. This could result in indicators being converted into signatures for use with a variety of detection mechanisms, such as in these examples:

- C-1/2: Antivirus signature to detect existence of hash value
- A-1: Snort/Suricata Signature to detect any communication with hostile domain
- A-2: Snort/Suricata Signature to detect mail received from hostile e-mail address
- A-3: Snort/Suricata Signature to detect subject line
- A-3: Bro script to detect subject line
- A-4/C-1: Bro script to detect file name or MD5 hash value being transmitted across the network
- A-5/C-2: Bro Script to Detect File Named Kernel32.dll or file with MD5 hash value transmitted over the network
- A-6: Snort/Suricata Signature to detect communication with IP address
- A-7/A-8: Snort/Suricata Signature to detect SSH communication to port 9966
- A-10: HIDS rule to detect modifications to Kernel32.dll

As you can see, there are different methods to approach detection of the various indicators we've generated from this single incident. With more detail, this scenario could present even more potential detection scenarios, such as the ability to detect certain malicious object calls within the PDF file itself, or characteristics of custom protocols that might be in use. Depending on the architecture of the network you're protecting, you might have multiple detection mechanisms that can be used to implement signatures for a single indicator, or alternatively, you might not have any capability to detect certain indicators. Deciding which method might be best for the detection of a certain IOC depends upon the infrastructure of the network, the nuances of the detection methods, and the nature of the intelligence related to the IOC.

---

**FROM THE TRENCHES**

Some organizations have multiple versions of the same detection mechanism in place to handle IOCs of varying importance. For instance, I've seen organizations that run multiple instances of the Snort IDS for signature-based detection. Snort can detect intrusions by analyzing packets live on the wire, or by periodically parsing existing PCAP data files. Here, priority is placed on the Snort instance analyzing live traffic on the wire. The real-time instance of Snort is then reserved for only highly efficient signatures that are related to IOCs supported by intelligence of the highest priority, where as lower confidence signatures or those signatures related to generic malware are handled by the periodic instance of Snort examining PCAP files. The result is that alert data related to critical indicators is generated faster so that analysts may react quicker.

---

## Variable Indicators

If the detection mechanisms used in your network were only configured to detect attacks where known indicators were used, then you would likely eventually miss detecting something bad. At some point, we have to account for variable indicators, which are indicators for which values are not known. These are usually derived by creating a sequence of events for which an attack might occur (forming a behavioral indicator), and identifying where variables exist. Essentially, it examines a theoretical attack, rather than one that has already occurred. This root-cause type of analysis is something performed on specific attack techniques, rather than instances of attacks executed by an individual adversary.

I like to think of variable indicators as resembling a movie script, where you know what will happen, but not who will play each particular role. Also, just like a movie script, there is always the potential for improvisation with a skilled actor. Variable indicators are not entirely useful for deployment to signature-based detection mechanisms, but find a great deal of use with solutions like Bro.

We can see an example of developing variable indicators by revisiting the scenario we looked at in the last section. Instead of basing the attack scenario on an attack that has actually occurred, we will base it on a theoretical attack. Restated, the attack scenario would broadly play out as follows:

1. A user received an e-mail message with a malicious attachment.
2. The user opens the attachment, triggering the download of a file from a malicious domain.
3. The file was used to overwrite a system file with the malicious version of that file.
4. Code within the malicious file was executed, triggering an encrypted connection to a malicious server.
5. Once the connection was established, a large amount of data was exfiltrated from the system.

These steps represent behavioral indicators that contain multiple variable atomic and computed indicators. We can enumerate some of these indicators here:

- VB-1: A user received an e-mail message with a malicious attachment.
  - VA-1: E-Mail Address
  - VA-2: E-Mail Subject
  - VA-3: Malicious E-Mail Source Domain
  - VA-4: Malicious E-Mail Source IP Address
  - VA-5: Malicious Attachment File Name
  - VC-1: Malicious Attachment MD5 Hash
- VB-2: The user opens the attachment, triggering the download of a file from a malicious domain.
  - VA-6: Malicious Redirection Domain/IP
  - VA-7: Malicious Downloaded File Name
  - VC-2: Malicious Downloaded File MD5 Hash
- VB-3: The file was used to overwrite a system file with the malicious version of that file.
- VB-4: Code within the malicious file was executed, triggering an encrypted connection to a malicious server on a non-standard port.
  - VA-8: External C2 IP Address
  - VA-9: External C2 Port
  - VA-10: External C2 Protocol
- VB-5: Once the connection was established, a large amount of data was exfiltrated from the system.

In this example, the V in the indicator names describes a variable component of the indicator. As we've laid it out, there are potentially ten variable atomic indicators, two variable computed indicators, and five variable behavioral indicators. Now, we can hypothesize methods in which these indicators can be built into signatures to be paired with detection mechanisms. Variable indicators will commonly be reused and combined in order to derive detection for broad attack scenarios.

- VB-1 (VA-3/VA-4) VB-2 (VA-6) VB-4 (VA-8) VB-5 (VA-8): Snort/Suricata rule to detect communication with known bad reputation IP addresses and domains
- VB-1 (VA-5/VC-1) VB-2 (VA-7/VC-2): Bro script to pull files off the wire and compare their names and MD5 hashes with a list of known bad reputation file names and MD5 hashes.
- VB-1 (VA-5/VC-1) VB-2 (VA-7/VC-2): Bro script to pull files off the wire and place them into a sandbox that performs rudimentary malware analysis.
- VB-2 (VA-6/VA-7/VC-2): HIDS signature to detect the browser being launched from a document
- VB-3: HIDS signature to detect a system file being overwritten
- VB-4 (VA-9/VA-10) VB-5: A Bro script to detect encrypted traffic occurring on a non-standard port
- VB-4 (VA-9/VA-10) VB-5: A Snort/Suricata rule to detect encrypted traffic occurring on a non-standard port

- VB-5: Custom written script that uses session data statistics to detect large volumes of outbound traffic from workstations

SOC analysts commonly monitor information security news sources like conference proceedings and the blogs and Twitter feeds from industry experts. This allows the SOC to stay abreast of new and emerging attack techniques so that the organization's defensive posture can be modeled around these techniques. When this happens, it becomes incredibly useful to break down the attack into variable indicators. When platform-specific signatures are provided, those can be reverse engineered into individual indicators so that they can be used in conjunction with the detection mechanisms in place on your network. These are incredibly useful exercise for NSM analysts. It helps the analyst to better understand how attacks work, and how detection mechanisms can be used to effectively detect the different phases of an attack.

The components of the variable indicator can be used for all varieties of detection, and they are most useful in determining how to detect things with unknown entities.

## Indicator and Signature Evolution

Software development usually goes through an evolution, in which the software is considered immature until it is fully tested. It then reaches a mature state while it is in production use before being retired once it is no longer useful. Indicators and signatures, just like software, have a shelf life. Indicator and signature evolution has the same steps: Immature, Mature, and Retired (Figure 7.2).

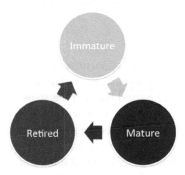

**FIGURE 7.2**

Indicator and Signature Evolution

An immature indicator or signature is one that has been newly discovered as the result of some form of intelligence, including intelligence gained from the internal investigation of an incident, or from a third-party source. This also includes newly created variable indicators that have not yet been evaluated fully within a detection mechanism signature. The confidence associated with immature indicators and signatures may vary initially, depending upon its source. An immature indicator or signature may change frequently, and might be deployed to a test environment before being deployed into production, which might include deployment to multiple detection mechanisms in order to determine which is the most appropriate. Because of this, analysts should closely monitor the deployed signature for false positives and false negatives. In some scenarios, it may be appropriate to only allow level two or three analysts to access the alerts generated from immature indicators and signatures, so that they can be taken with a grain of salt until being evaluated thoroughly.

Once an indicator or signature has proven that it is useful in the NSM environment, that it doesn't result in an excess of false positives, and that it doesn't result in missed activity through false negatives, it is considered to be mature. A mature indicator or signature doesn't usually undergo as many revisions as an immature one, and is considered reliable and stable. Mature indicators can also be more confidently combined with other indicators in order to make more granular behavioral indicators, resulting in more advanced signatures. Any change or revision to a mature indicator or signature should be documented.

Eventually, an indicator or signature may prove to no longer be effective, or the intelligence supporting it may call for its dismissal. This is especially common with items related to phishing campaigns, websites hosting drive-by downloads, and botnet C2. Proper record keeping and historical analysis dictates that you should never delete these items, so instead an indicator or signature that is no longer being actively used is considered retired. A retired indicator is no longer deployed within a signature to any detection mechanism. A retired signature isn't currently being utilized by a detection mechanism. If it is necessary that a retired indicator or signature be modified and reused, then it should be reverted into either an immature or a mature state.

## Tuning Signatures

A task that will be continuous for any security team is the tuning of signatures. This ensures that the indicators the signatures are based on are being used reliably and effectively, and that they are passed through the steps of indicator evolution appropriately. In some cases it can be easy to determine how effective a signature is. For instance, if you deploy a signature containing new indicators and it immediately starts filling up every analyst's screen with thousands of alerts, then there is a good chance that the signature is too broad and might need some work to eliminate false positives. However, not all signatures' performance is that easy to track. For example, if you had two signatures that detected the same thing, how would you compare them to determine which was more effective? This is where some statistics come in to play.

When determining the maturity and confidence level of a deployed signature, there are four data points that should be considered: true positives, false positives, true negatives, and false negatives.

*True Positive (TP)*. An alert that has correctly identified a specific activity. If a signature was designed to detect a certain type of malware, and an alert is generated when that malware is launched on a system, this would be a true positive, which is what we strive for with every deployed signature.

*False Positive (FP).* An alert has incorrectly identified a specific activity. If a signature was designed to detect a specific type of malware, and an alert is generated for an instance in which that malware was not present, this would be a false positive.

*True Negative (TN).* An alert has correctly not been generated when a specific activity has not occurred. If a signature was designed to detect a certain type of malware, and no alert is generated without that malware being launched, then this is a true negative, which is also desirable. This is difficult, if not impossible, to quantify in terms of NSM detection.

*False Negative (FN).* An alert has incorrectly not been generated when a specific activity has occurred. If a signature was designed to detect a certain type of malware, and no alert is generated when that malware is launched on a system, this would be a false negative. A false negative means that we aren't detecting something we should be detecting, which is the worst case scenario. False negatives can be incredibly difficult to calculate. After all, how do you detect false negatives if your signatures are missing the activities they were designed to detect? This is one of the many reasons why it is so important to do post-mortem analysis after an incident has occurred. It is here that you can step through an incident to systematically determine when a signature should have detected an activity, and record those results.

These data points are useful by themselves to determine how successful the signature is for detection. However, we can derive more value from these numbers by using them to calculate a signature's precision.

### Precision

The precision of a signature, also sometimes called the positive predictive value, refers to its ability to identify positive results. This is shown by determining the proportion of true positives against all positive results (both true positives and false positives) with the formula:

```
Precision = TP / (TP+FP)
```

This information can be used to determine the probability that, given an alert being generated, the activity that has been detected has truly occurred. Therefore, if a signature has a high precision and an alert is generated, then the activity has very likely occurred.

In a comparison scenario, consider that the same network traffic has generated two separate alerts, classifying the attack as two different pieces of malware. SID 1 in one of the alerts identifies Malware A, and SID 2 in the other alert identifies Malware B. If SID 1 has a precision of 90, and SID 2 has a precision of 40, then it is likely that SID 1 has actually correctly identified the malware.

---

**ANALYST NOTE**

A Signature Identifier (SID) Number is used to uniquely identify a signature.

---

High precision is desired for signatures, and should increase your confidence in a signature. If you find that a signature has low precision, then you can attempt to rectify this by refining the signature, adding additional indicators to the signature, or deploying it in conjunction with other signatures.

In lieu of a custom application, you can track these statistics fairly easily in a spreadsheet or CSV file. An example of how this could be done is shown in Table 7.1.

**Table 7.1** Tracking Signature Statistics

| Indicator GUID | Indicator Rev | Deployment | Modified | TP | FP | TN | FN |
|---|---|---|---|---|---|---|---|
| 60003023 | 1 | Snort Signature: 1000492 | 6/19/2013 | 1 | 432 | 0 | 0 |
| 60003023 | 2 | Snort Signature: 1000492 | 6/23/2013 | 5 | 3 | 0 | 0 |
| 60003024 | 1 | Snort Signature: 1000493 | 6/23/2013 | 2 | 17 | 0 | 0 |
| 60003025 | 1 | Snort Signature: 1000494 | 6/25/2013 | 1 | 2 | 0 | 0 |
| 60003026 | 1 | Snort Signature: 1000495 | 6/25/2013 | 3 | 0 | 0 | 1 |
| 60003026 | 2 | Snort Signature: 1000495 | 6/28/2013 | 1 | 0 | 0 | 0 |

The statistics presented here should help determine how much confidence you place in a signature, how you react when an alert from a signature is generated, and how much effort you place into tweaking a signature for better reliability. There are several other techniques and statistics that can be used for assessing the effectiveness of a signature, but precision has always worked consistently well for me in multiple SOC environments.

## Critical Indicator and Signature Criteria

An indicator or signature without context is not entirely useful. One of the first things an analyst should do when receiving a new alert is to examine the supporting context of the signature, along with the supporting context of any indicators contained in the signature. The context you can provide with a signature or indicator will vary, but it is critical in the investigation of a potential incident. It is important that you establish a standard that maintains a few critical criteria for each indicator and signature that you use. This is to ensure the indicators and signatures are unique, attributable, and able to be properly referenced in the event of an intrusion, an audit, or an instance where accuracy is called into question. These critical criteria are:

- *Unique Identifier:* A value that can be used to uniquely identify every indicator or signature. These should never be repeated. Most organizations will simply use an auto incrementing or randomly generated globally unique identifier (GUID) for indicators. The identifier that is used for signatures is usually dictated by the detection mechanism associated with the signature. This is most commonly a Signature ID (SID) number. This level of identification also has the benefit of allowing you to reference the indicator or signature in various forms of communication without actually listing the item itself. This will prevent false positives that might occur when indicators or signatures are mentioned in e-mail messages and similar forms of communication.

- *Author:* The analyst who created or added the indicator or signature. In the event that an alert is triggered and there is confusion regarding the indicator or signature itself or how it was implemented, this provides the opportunity to reach back to the individual who created, added, and deployed it.
- *Creation Date:* The original date the indicator or signature was created. In the event that it was drawn from another source, this would be the date that it was added to your internal management system.
- *Modified Date:* The most recent modification date of the indicator or signature. Ideally, you will track any time an indicator or signature is modified. This will be discussed later.
- *Source:* The original source of the indicator or signature. This can reference another organization, a URL, an internal case number, or even another indicator.
- *Type:* The type of indicator: Host or Network, Static or Variable, and Atomic, Computed, or Behavioral. Alternatively, the type of signature: Snort, Suricata, Bro, Antivirus, etc.
- *Classification:* The general classification type of the indicator or signature. This could be an IP Address, Hash Value, File Name, E-Mail Subject, DNS Name, or any other appropriate classification for an indicator. This could be the general category the signature is most closely associated with: malware activity, botnet C2, exploit activity, phishing, etc.
- *Evolution Stage:* The stage of the indicator or signature in relation to its evolution: Immature, Mature, or Retired.
- *Confidence:* A rating representing the amount of trust that can be placed in the indicator or signature. This is used to establish how reliable it is, and how much surety can be placed in its accuracy when it results in the generation of an alert. This can take several factors into account, including its precision, its source, or its evolutionary stage. It's not uncommon for an indicator or signature's confidence rating to change frequently over time. This is typically either a numerical value (1-100) or a relative value (low, medium, high, very high).
- *Indicator/Signature:* The indicator or signature itself, in its native format.

Along with the particulars of how you store and classify indicators and signatures, it is also tremendously important that you remain consistent in your efforts. The key to this consistency is ensuring the process is well-documented and frequently practiced within the organization.

## MANAGING INDICATORS AND SIGNATURES

The number of indicators and signatures being managed by an organization can grow large in a short time. It is critical that an organization adopts a strategy for storing, accessing, and sharing them.

Most organizations tend to store indicators and signatures solely within the detection mechanisms that they are being used with. For instance, if the organization is using Snort to detect and log access to known malicious domains (an atomic indicator), then those indicators will be stored as Snort signatures where they are directly accessed by Snort. While this is the easiest manner in which to store these items, this limits your ability to interact with and reference them. It can also prohibit easily sharing individual indicators or converting them to signatures designed for another detection mechanism. In order to get the most out of your indicators and signatures, it helps to manage them with these best practices in mind:

*Raw Data Format*. Indicators are the easiest to work with when they are in their native form. You should always be able to access an indicator without any additional content or extraneous processing. This ensures that indicators are portable and can be parsed easily by automated and custom tools, allowing them to be deployed within unique signatures to a variety of detection mechanisms. For example, this means that IP addresses and file hashes should be plain text, while binary data should exist in binary format.

*Ease of Access*. Analysts should be able to access and edit indicators and signatures with relative ease. If they have to go through many inconvenient steps in order to add new ones or find out the source of an existing one, this will eat up valuable time. This can discourage the analyst from interacting with the indicators and signatures, which is something you absolutely don't want to happen.

*Easily Searchable*. It won't take long before a directory or database full of indicators and signatures becomes too large to browse through manually. In order to facilitate the analysts' ability to quickly examine them, they should exist in a format that is searchable. This includes the ability to search the indicators or signatures themselves, along with any contextual data that is stored with them such as the date they were added, their source, or their type. If they are stored in a database, this can be done with database client access or a simple web front-end. If they are stored in flat files, then solutions can be created using a variety of Linux command line tools like grep.

*Revision Tracking*. It is common to revise signatures. This can occur when a signature results in the generation of too many false positives, or when it fails to detect the desired activity, resulting in false negatives. Signatures are also revised to reflect changes to adversarial strategy or attack techniques. Whenever this occurs, the revision, the person who made the change, and the date of the change should be recorded so that any issues arising from the modification can be addressed. Ideally, the reason for the change would also be noted.

*Deployment Tracking*. The purpose of any indicator is to eventually be able to utilize it within a signature in conjunction with a detection mechanism. When this happens, the pairing of the indicator and the detection mechanism should be noted.

This will help an analyst understand how the NSM infrastructure is being used with an indicator. This will also prevent duplication of effort so that indicators aren't deployed multiple times across redundant detection mechanisms. This is often done with a simple mapping of an indicator GUID to a SID.

*Data Backup.* At this point, you should realize just how important indicators and signatures are for NSM detection. This data should be considered critical for the success of the NSM mission, and should be backed up accordingly. This should include an off-site backup in the event of a catastrophic event affecting the main SOC facility.

## Simple Indicator and Signature Management with CSV Files

Organizations of differing sizes use a variety of techniques for the storage and management of indicators and signatures. Some organizations utilize commercial solutions, while others use custom-written web-front ends attached to some type of database. There is no question that these methods can be effective, but it generally takes a certain level of organizational maturity before their implementation can be feasible. That said, even smaller and more immature security teams still need to manage indicators and signatures.

While it may sound a bit rudimentary, these items can be managed very effectively with comma separated value (CSV) files. These are files containing data in rows and columns, with columns being separated by commas, and rows being separated by new lines. These files are a great format for a lot of types of data because they can be easily read and parsed via the command-line with built-in Linux tools like grep, cut, sed, awk, and sort. You can also interact with CSV files by using Microsoft Excel, Libre Office/Open Office Calc, or most other graphical spreadsheet editors.

In order to manage indicators and signatures effectively given the best practices discussed here, you should maintain at least three CSV files. This includes the statistics tracking file we discussed earlier (Table 7.1), a master list, and a tracking table.

### Master Indicator/Signature List

The primary CSV file used to store indicators and signatures is the Master IOC List. This contains fields for all of the critical criteria mentioned previously, as well as fields for tracking deployment. A sample of this is shown in Table 7.2

There are two simple ways to search this list. The first is to use a graphical spreadsheet editor like Microsoft Excel, where you can do simple sorting or Ctrl+F searches to find specific values. This might be appropriate for some users, but this becomes more difficult as the size of the CSV grows. Most commonly, analysts use Linux command line tools to query this list.

As an example, let's say that an alert that references SID 710031 has just been generated, and you'd like to gain additional context on that signature and any associated indicators. In order to do this, you could use grep to search the file for all instances of the SID using the following command:

```
grep 7100031 master_ioc_list.csv
```

**Table 7.2** Master Indicator/Signature List

| GUID | Author | Creation Date | Modified Date | Revision | Source | Classification | Type | Life Cycle Stage | Confidence | Indicator | Deployment |
|---|---|---|---|---|---|---|---|---|---|---|---|
| 10001 | Sanders | 3/17/2013 | 3/20/2013 | 2 | Case # 1492 | MD5 | Computed/ Static | Mature | Very High | e0b359e1712 88512501f4c 18ee64a6bd | Antivirus Signature 42039 |
| 10002 | Smith | 3/18/2013 | 3/18/2013 | 1 | Malware Domain List | Domain | Atomic/ Static | Mature | Moderate | appliednsm.com | Snort Signature 7100031 |
| 10003 | Sanders | 3/18/2013 | 3/18/2013 | 1 | Case # 1498 | E-Mail Address | Atomic/ Static | Mature | Very High | chris@appliednsm. com | Snort Signature 7100032 |
| 10004 | Sanders | 3/19/2013 | 3/19/2013 | 1 | Zeus Tracker | IP | Atomic/ Static | Mature | High | 192.0.2.99 | Custom SiLK Script |
| 10005 | Randall | 3/20/2013 | 3/24/2013 | 4 | Analyst | Protocol/Port | Behavioral/ Variable | Immature | Moderate | Encrypted Traffic over Non-Standard Port | Bro Script |
| 10006 | Sanders | 3/20/2013 | 3/20/2013 | 1 | RSS Feed | Protocol/Port | Behavioral/ Static | Mature | Moderate | SSH/9966 | Suricata Signature 7100038 |
| 10007 | Sanders | 3/21/2013 | 3/24/2013 | 3 | Internal Discussion | Statistical | Behavioral/ Variable | Immature | Low | Outbound Traffic Volume Ratio Greater than 4:1 | Custom SiLK Script |

The results of this command are shown in Figure 7.3. You will see that our search returns both a signature, and the indicator that is used in the signature.

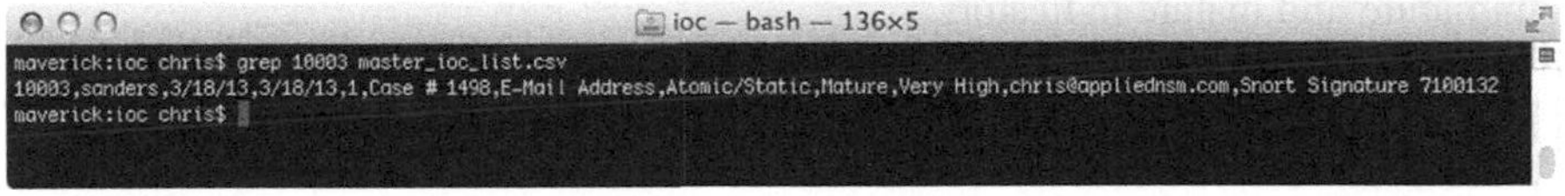

**FIGURE 7.3**

Search the CSV File for a SID

At some point it might come in handy to print column headers as well. Grep just sees data and isn't aware of columns, so it doesn't have this capability inherently. One option would be to use Sed or Awk for pattern matching, or you can just use the head command to print the first row of the file before performing your grep commands, like so:

```
head -1 master_ioc_list.csv && grep 7100031 master_ioc_list.csv
```

The commands are executed consecutively by combining them with two ampersands (&&). The output of this command is shown in Figure 7.4.

**FIGURE 7.4**

Output Results with Column Headers

Now, if we want to simply pull out the signature itself, we can redirect the results of the previous command (without the column headers) to another grep command that searches for lines that have the text "sid" in them, to only match signatures rather than indicators. Then, we can pipe that output to the cut command with the pipe 'l' symbol. Cut is used by specifying the comma delimiter with the –d flag, and selecting the eleventh column with the –f flag. This command would look like this:

```
grep 7100031 master_ioc_list.csv | grep sid | cut -d , -f11
```

Another method that will achieve the same goal is using the awk command. Awk, with the –F switch, can be directed to print a specified column, which we have done here:

```
grep 7100031 master_ioc_list.csv | grep sid | awk -F ' {print $11}'
```

These techniques can be expanded for more granular searches. For instance, you might want to retrieve every IP address within the list that is still active (not retired) so that you can deploy this to a detection mechanism. You can do this with the following command:

```
grep -v retired master_ioc_list.csv | grep IP | cut -d , -f11
```

In the first grep statement, you will notice the addition of the –v flag. This tells grep to match everything NOT matching the specified pattern. In this case, we are telling grep to list all of the indicators that are not retired, which will include both immature and mature indicators.

---

**CAUTION**

It is important to understand that even properly formatted CSV files can generate unexpected output when proper care isn't given to the data. For instance, what if a signature contains a comma? This will cause tools such as cut to identify columns incorrectly. You should be aware of misplaced delimiters in your CSV files, and perhaps do some type of substitution of certain characters if necessary to prevent parsing errors.

---

Next, we might want to search for all of the indicators that are domain names, and are actively deployed to the Snort IDS. This is done with this command:

```
head -1 master_ioc_list.csv && grep -v retired master_ioc_list.csv | grep Domain | grep Snort
```

You will notice the capitalization of the "Domain" and "Snort" searches that are used with grep. By default, grep is case sensitive, so we want to use this capitalization so that it matches our line entries appropriately, rather than matching any other instances of those words with other capitalizations. If you would like to make your searches not case-sensitive, you can use the –i command line argument. It is important to be aware of the case of items you are searching for so that grep can be used properly, with the –i switch if necessary.

Whenever the CSV file requires an addition or modification, this can be done with your favorite command line text editor, such as Vim, Emacs, or Nano. When doing this, be wary of accidentally creating new lines, which could negatively impact parsing of the file.

### Indicator/Signature Revision Table

Earlier, I mentioned that indicators and signatures often undergo revisions, and it was important to track those revisions. When you are using a master CSV file to manage these items, you can manage the modification of them with an additional file. This file is meant to be very simple, and it only contains the unique identifier for the indicator or signature, the date of the change, the author of the change, the new revision number, the column value that changed, the old and new versions of the changed data, and a note explaining why the change occurred. This will serve as an audit trail so that the evolution of an indicator or signature can be followed, and so that it can be referenced in the event that an error was made. You should note that a change isn't only recorded when the indicator or signature itself changes, but also when any of the contextual information associated with it changes, such as the detection method to which it is deployed. An example of this spreadsheet is shown in Table 7.3.

**Table 7.3** Indicator/Signature Revision Table

| GUID | Author | Date | Revision | Change Field | Old Value | New Value | Note |
|---|---|---|---|---|---|---|---|
| 10001 | Sanders | 3/20/2013 | 2 | Confidence | Moderate | High | Working very well. No false positives. |
| 10005 | Sanders | 3/21/2013 | 2 | Type \| Indicator | Port \| 9966 | Port/Protocol \| SSH/9966 | Added New Intel |
| 10005 | Randall | 3/21/2013 | 3 | Deployment | NULL | Bro Script | Developed Script |
| 10005 | Smith | 3/24/2013 | 4 | Life Cycle Stage \| Confidence | Immature \| Low | Mature \| Moderate | Few false positives. Continue to monitor. |
| 10007 | Sanders | 3/22/2013 | 2 | Indicator | Outbound Traffic Volume Ratio Greater than 2:1 | Outbound Traffic Volume Ratio Greater than 3:1 | Too many false positives. |
| 10007 | Sanders | 3/24/2013 | 3 | Indicator | Outbound Traffic Volume Ratio Greater than 3:1 | Outbound Traffic Volume Ratio Greater than 4:1 | Still too many false positives. |

This CSV file isn't meant to be all-encompassing, but rather, it should be used in conjunction with the Master Indicator/Signature List CSV file. You can then use similar commands to view the audit trail associated with an item:

```
head -1 master_ioc_list.csv && grep 10005 master_ios_list.csv
```

The results of this command illustrate the audit trail for indicator 10005, shown in Figure 7.5.

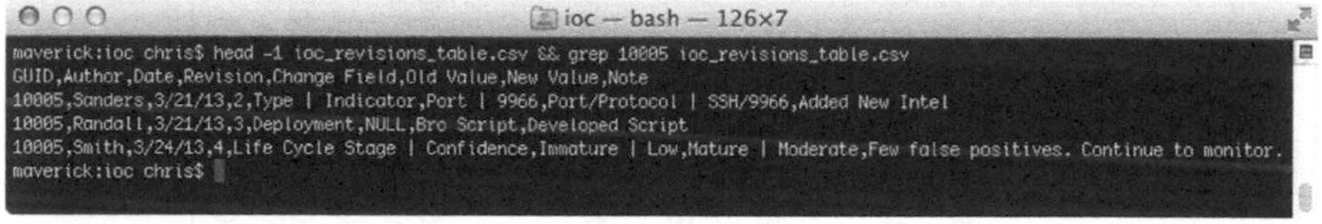

**FIGURE 7.5**

Audit Trail for Indicator 10005

If you've never interacted with data using Linux command-line tools, it may be a bit cumbersome at first, and even a little intimidating. However, as you do this more, it will become second nature. The best way to learn is to immerse yourself in the tools, and keep trying something until you figure it out. Eventually, you will encounter some of the limits of tools like grep, and begin using other tools such as sed and awk for different tasks. A strong knowledge of these tools is very important for any analyst. Eventually, you might even combine these tools into scripts to automate common tasks.

While CSV files are nice because of their simplicity, this same simplicity requires that extra attention be paid to the sanity of the data. Since most inputs or modifications to these files will be made with a text editor, there are no controls in place to ensure data remains in a proper format. This might result in an analyst accidentally messing up the formatting of the CSV file or placing data in the wrong column. This is why it is critical to maintain backups of these files. It is also highly recommended that the sanity of the data is checked frequently. If you depend upon these CSV files for the operation of your SOC, it is worth investing the time to write a custom script that can ensure no errors exist within the data. This can be done in relatively short order using something like the CSV library for the Python scripting language.

If you'd like to download templates for these CSV files you can do that at http://www.appliednsm.com/resources.

## INDICATOR AND SIGNATURE FRAMEWORKS

One of the biggest problems facing the information security and intelligence communities at large is the lack of a common framework for the creation, management, and distribution of indicators and signatures. While everybody uses them, most everyone tends to use their individual methods for organizing and storing the data. Because of this, the indicators and signatures are not portable, and can't easily be shared with other organizations. While sharing of the data itself can often be accomplished rather easily, such as with lists of IP addresses, sharing contextual information is where the real challenge arises.

In recent years, groups have made attempts to create frameworks for the sharing of indicator and signature data.

## OpenIOC

One of the biggest advancements towards a common framework for threat intelligence is Mandiant's OpenIOC project. This project, originally designed to enable Mandiant's products to codify intelligence to rapidly search for potential security breaches, was released in 2010 as a standardized and open source schema for communication of threat information.

At its core, OpenIOC is just an XML schema used to describe technical characteristics that identify adversarial activities. The OpenIOC scheme allows you to manage IOC's with a lot of the contextual information that is required in order to use the indicator efficiently. An example of an OpenIOC is shown in Figure 7.6.

```
9ad0ddec-dc4e-4432-9687-b7002806dcf8.ioc
<?xml version="1.0" encoding="us-ascii"?>
<ioc xmlns:xsi="http://www.w3.org/2001/XMLSchema-instance"
xmlns:xsd="http://www.w3.org/2001/XMLSchema" id="9ad0ddec-dc4e-4432-9687-
b7002806dcf8" last-modified="2013-02-20T02:07:40" xmlns="http://
schemas.mandiant.com/2010/ioc">
    <short_description>PHISH-UPS-218934</short_description>
    <description>Part of the UPS Phishing scheme reported on 12/4.</
description>
    <authored_by>Chris Sanders</authored_by>
    <authored_date>2013-02-20T02:02:00</authored_date>
    <links>
      <link rel="Source">http://www.appliednsm.com</link>
      <link rel="Stage">Mature</link>
    </links>
    <definition>
      <Indicator operator="OR" id="bea0030a-dddc-440b-9dd4-400cacc0e13d">
        <IndicatorItem id="16b2873b-a491-46b1-9f3e-805dd49f3cb0"
condition="contains">
          <Context document="Email" search="Email/Subject" type="mir" />
          <Content type="string">UPS Alert: Shipment Delayed</Content>
        </IndicatorItem>
      </Indicator>
    </definition>
</ioc>
```

**FIGURE 7.6**

A Simple IOC in OpenIOC XML Format

In this IOC, you can see several pieces of contextual information are stored, including:

- 9ad0ddec-dc4e-4432-9687-b7002806dcf8 – A unique identifier
- PHISH-UPS-218934 – A short description or additional identifier
- Part of the UPS Phishing scheme reported on 12/4. – A detailed description
- Chris Sanders – The author
- 2013-02-20 T01:02:00 – The date/time the indicator was created

- http://www.appliednsm.com - The source of the indicator
- Mature – The stage of the indicator in the IOC life cycle
- Atomic – The type of indicator
- E-Mail/Subject – The classification of the indicator
- UPS Alert: Shipment Delayed – The indicator itself. In this case, an e-mail subject line.

If you have a Windows computer available, one of the easiest ways to get up and running with creating and modifying IOCs using the OpenIOC format is to use Mandiant's free OpenIOC Editor tool. The tool is fairly simple, and allows you to create IOCs from scratch or modify existing IOCs.

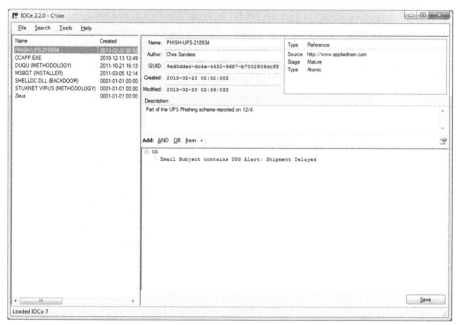

**FIGURE 7.7**

Mandiant's OpenIOC Editor for Windows

When you launch OpenIOC Editor for the first time you will be asked to select your IOC directory. Once you do this, you will be presented with a screen similar to what is shown in Figure 7.7. The OpenIOC Editor is broken into three separate areas. The left pane contains a list of IOCs in the IOC directory. If you click on one of these IOCs, it will populate the other two areas. In the upper right pane you will find all of the basic information about the IOC, including its name, the author, its GUID, its created/modified dates, a description, and any custom criteria that has been defined such as source, stage, or type. In the lower right pane, you will find the indicator itself, which may include multiple indicators linked with AND/OR logic statements.

OpenIOC Editor treats each IOC as a separate file, which is what you will find in the IOC directory you specified after you create new IOCs.

Unfortunately, OpenIOC Editor only exists for the Windows platform as of the writing of this chapter. Therefore, if you are using a *nix-based platform as most NSM analysts are, creating and editing IOC's in this format will have to be a manual endeavor. Alternatively, you can use a virtual machine or WINE to launch the Open-IOC Editor.

If you utilize any of Mandiant's commercial products then you can use the majority of those products to interact with indicators in this format. The OpenIOC standard is gaining a lot of popularity, and it is only a matter of time before more free publicly available tools for the management of OpenIOC indicators become available.

You can read more about the OpenIOC format, download the XML schema, and even download some sample IOCs at http://www.openioc.org.

## STIX

The Structured Threat Information eXpression (STIX) is an open source community-driven project developed by MITRE for the US Department of Homeland Security. STIX is designed to standardize threat intelligence information, and is gaining popularity within the government and defense arenas.

The STIX architecture is based upon independent constructs and how they are related (Figure 7.8).

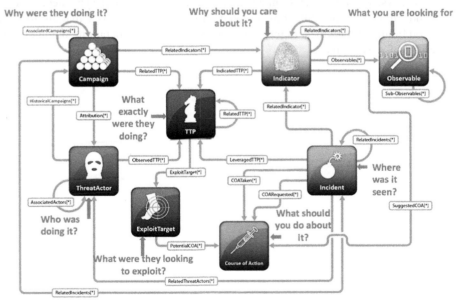

**FIGURE 7.8**

The STIX Architecture

At the core of this architecture are observables, which STIX defines as stateful properties or measurable events pertinent to the operation of computers and networks. This could be a service being stopped, a file name, a system rebooting, or a connection establishment. These observables are stored in an XML format that uses the CybOX language, another MITRE project, for representing observables. An example observable is shown in Figure 7.9. This observable represents an IPv4 address, with a few related objects. The objects are linked together through the use of globally unique identifiers.

**FIGURE 7.9**

A STIX Observable Representing an IP Address with Related Objects

Within the STIX framework, observables can be linked to indicators, incidents, TTPs, specific threat actors, adversary campaigns, specific targets, data markings, and courses of action. These entities come together to form more than a simple indicator management system, rather, they form a complete threat intelligence management system.

Indicators are representations of potentially anomalous activity that are formed by combining observables. Figure 7.10 shows an indicator containing domains that are part of a watch list.

**FIGURE 7.10**

A STIX Indicator with Domains in a Watch list

You should notice that this indicator is actually comprised of a single observable: a list of domain names. This would be an example of an atomic indicator within the STIX framework. An indicator can include as many observables as necessary, which means they are well suited for behavioral indicators as well. When these indicators are tied to the other constructs within STIX, there are a lot of possibilities.

As of the writing of this book, the only methods that exist for creating, editing, and managing STIX objects are the newly released set of Python bindings for writing custom Python applications, or using simple text or XML editors.

The STIX framework represents a lot of potential. Along with DHS, STIX is currently being evaluated by several organizations, including multiple government and defense agencies, defense contractors, and private organizations. While there aren't currently a lot of tools available to help with the management of STIX, this will likely change over time as the framework matures and expands.

You can learn more about STIX at http://stix.mitre.org.

## CONCLUSION

In this chapter we've looked at the fundamentals of detection mechanisms, indicators of compromise, and signatures along with the role they play in NSM detection. This includes indicator types, indicator and signature critical criteria, and some best practices for creating and managing them. We also looked at methods that smaller and younger security programs can use for the management of indicators and signatures, as well as the OpenIOC and STIX frameworks for IOC management. The remainder of the Detection portion of the book will be devoted to the applied use of several detection mechanisms that ingest indicators and signatures.

# Reputation-Based Detection

## CHAPTER CONTENTS

The most basic form of intrusion detection is reputation-based detection. This type of detection is performed by attempting to identify communication between friendly hosts on the network you are protecting, and hosts on the Internet that are believed to be malicious based upon a reputation for malicious actions.

By definition, reputation is a widespread belief that someone or something has a particular habit or characteristic. In the context of network defense, a host can have either a positive or negative reputation, or no reputation at all. Generally, hosts within your internal network have a positive reputation because they are trusted under the purview of your network security team. A host with a negative reputation is believed to be a potential threat to your trusted systems.

There can be several reasons that an organization will deem a host to have a negative reputation. The most common is that a publicly accessible system will be compromised and used to host malicious files, resulting in a negative reputation, as people who visit the site are often infected with some type of malware. In industries where corporate espionage is rampant, IP ranges associated with competitors may have a negative reputation because of the threat of intellectual property theft. In the realm of government and defense networks, hosts with negative reputations will often include those that are known to belong to unfriendly foreign governments, or devices that are known to have been compromised by the intelligence services of those governments.

In this chapter, we will examine public reputation lists and several ways that reputation-based detection can be performed. This will include an overview of performing reputation-based detection with BASH Scripts, CIF, Snort, Suricata, and Bro.

## PUBLIC REPUTATION LISTS

In reality, most organizations perform reputation-based detection by utilizing public lists of atomic indicators (most commonly IP addresses and domain names) with negative reputations. These blacklists are then fed into some type of detection mechanism so that analysts are alerted when a friendly hosts appears to communicate with an external device on one of these lists.

There are several benefits to using public reputation lists. First, most organizations simply don't have the visibility to create sizable reputation lists on their own. Even with sensors spread throughout offices globally, there are limitations to the number of attacks you will see, as well as your ability to investigate them all fully. Leveraging a public list takes advantage of larger networks of sensors that report up to the groups that maintain the lists. Additionally, most lists are reasonable well maintained. A significant number of the hosts that wind up on these lists are legitimate servers that were only temporarily compromised, such as systems used in "Watering Hole" attacks where a legitimate site is compromised in order to target its users. Because of this, it is just as important that negative reputation hosts are removed from these lists once they have proven to be more reputable.

There are also some negative aspects to using public reputation lists. In a lot of cases, the maintainers of these lists don't always provide context with the individual IP addresses or domains on the list. When an alert is generated based upon communication with a host on one of these lists, you don't really know why the host has a negative reputation. It could be because the host was at one time referring visitors to another malicious website thanks to a temporary persistent XSS flaw, or it could be because the host is a primary node in a major botnet. Some type of context is helpful in pointing the investigation in the right direction.

Ultimately, I believe that the positives of public lists outweigh the negatives, and that the problems with them can be dealt with provided due diligence is taken in vetting the lists and controlling how the list items are utilized. You should ensure that the lists you choose to incorporate into your detection architecture are consistent with organizational goals, and that analysts are properly trained in how to assess and investigate alerts generated from this intelligence. If leveraged properly, reputation-based detection can be one of the few "easy wins" an NSM practitioner can have when it comes to finding malicious activity on the network.

## Common Public Reputation Lists

There are many public reputation lists available. Here are a few of my favorites, along with some pros and cons of each, and how they can best be utilized.

### *Malware Domain List*

Regardless of the global concerns related to targeted attacks by sophisticated adversaries, the majority of an analyst's day will be spent investigating incidents related to malware infections on their systems. Because of this, it becomes pertinent to be able to detect malware at both the host and network level. One of the easiest ways to detect malware at the network level is to use public reputation lists that contain IP addresses and domain names that are known to be associated with malware-related communication.

Malware Domain List (MDL) is a non-commercial community project that maintains lists of malicious domains and IP addresses. The project is supported by an open community of volunteers, and relies upon those volunteers to both populate the list, and vet it to ensure that items are added and removed from the list as necessary.

MDL allows you to query its list on an individual basis, or download the list in a variety of formats. This includes CSV format, an RSS feed, and a hosts.txt formatted list. They also provide lists that include only new daily list entries, and lists of sites that were once on the list but have now been cleaned or taken offline. MDL is one of the largest and most used reputation lists available.

I've seen many organizations that have had a great deal of success detecting malware infections and botnet command and control (C2) by using MDL as an input for reputation-based detection. The vastness of MDL can sometimes result in false positives, so an alert generated from a friendly host visiting an entry found on MDL isn't enough by itself to automatically declare an incident. When one of these alerts is generated, you should investigate other data sources and a wider range of communication from the friendly host to attempt to determine if there are other signs of an infection or compromise.

You can learn more about MDL at http://www.malwaredomainlist.com.

### Abuse.ch ZeuS and SpyEye Trackers

ZeuS and SpyEye are incredibly popular crimeware kits that are used by attackers to infect systems and perform a variety of malicious tasks (Figure 8.1). The kits themselves provide the ability to create malware that infects machines via drive-by download, eventually joining them to a botnet that the kit can be used to control. At one time, ZeuS was the largest botnet in the world, with SpyEye being one of its biggest competitors. Even though the creator of ZeuS announced in 2010 that he was retiring the source code, its public release has ensured that ZeuS infections remain prevalent today. SpyEye infections are also still very common, even though the creator of the software was allegedly caught and jailed in 2013.

ZeuS Tracker and SpyEye Tracker are projects that track command and control servers on the Internet that are used to control Zeus and SpyEye infected machines. In addition to this, these services also track hosts that are infected with Zeus and SpyEye files, including those hosting drive-by download exploits. These lists allow for user submission, and list contents can be queried individually, or downloaded as a single list. These lists can be downloaded in a variety of formats, including by domain or IP only, or in the form of Squid, iptables, or host file block lists. They also maintain a list of recently removed entries.

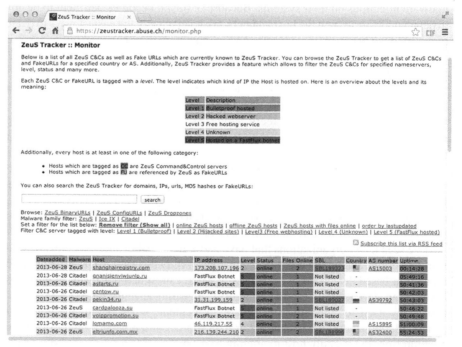

**FIGURE 8.1**

Zeus Tracker

I've found that both of these lists tend to be high quality with a minimal number of false positives when utilized for reputation-based detection. The way you handle the investigation of an alert generated by communication with a host on one of these lists depends upon the nature of the communication, and whether the friendly host appears to actually be infected with one of these types of malware.

You can learn more about the ZeuS Tracker at https://zeustracker.abuse.ch/, and SpyEye tracker at https://spyeyetracker.abuse.ch/.

### PhishTank

A great number of targeted attacks begin with some type of phishing as the initial attack vector. Most organizations have more success detecting these types of compromises after this initial stage, however, the ability to know when users are being redirected to known phishing websites can be useful for early detection of an incident that is currently happening, or for a retrospective investigation of an incident that has already occurred.

PhishTank, operated by OpenDNS, is a free community-driven website that allows for the sharing of phishing related data. Once registered, users can submit links they've found that appear to be associated with phishing attempts. PhishTank is unique because it relies on community verification in addition to community submission. In order for any URL to appear on its list, it must be verified by a certain number of registered PhishTank users. Users who have successfully verified more URLs have more weight to their verifications, so it takes a smaller number of verifications from these more trusted users.

One especially useful feature is their web-based search that allows you to search based upon the "Targeted Brand", or company name, that is being used for the phishing attack. If you happen to work for an organization that is frequently targeted for use in phishing schemes (such as a bank), then you can utilize the PhishTank list to derive adversaries who may be looking to prey on your customers.

PhishTank provides their list in a variety of formats, along with an API for integration with custom applications. While PhishTank doesn't have a web-based forum, it does have open mailing lists for users and developers.

If you deploy PhishTank listings into a detection mechanism on your network, then you should pay special attention to everything that occurs immediately following a device's initial visit to a known phishing site. Particularly, you will want to look for any additional redirections, the download of any executable content, or a user inputting their credentials into the site.

You can learn more about PhishTank at http://www.phishtank.com/.

### Tor Exit Node List

Normally, when you communicate with a device on the Internet, such as a web server, your client browses directly to that device. For the web server owner, this results in the web server generating a log of the communication containing the client's IP address. Additionally, if the web server is monitored by an NSM sensor, the client's IP address will appear in other data sources such as packet capture data or session data.

One method commonly used to prevent a client's true source IP address from showing up in these logs is a service like Tor. Tor is an open network that allows a user to mask their IP address so they can remain anonymous while accessing devices on the Internet.

When you browse to a web server utilizing a Tor client, your outbound traffic is routed to the Tor network instead of the destination web server. When this traffic is routed into the Tor network, it is eventually redirected to an exit node. It is the exit node that will actually initiate communication with the web server. This means that the logs generated by the web server and any NSM infrastructure will show the IP address associated with the Tor exit node rather than the actual client that initiated the communication. This process is illustrated in Figure 8.2.

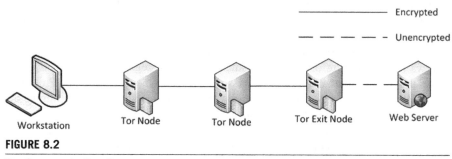

**FIGURE 8.2**

Tor Communication Process

If someone attempts to anonymize his or her activities while communicating with a device on your network, then this would constitute a suspicious action and might be worth investigating. With that said, plenty of individuals utilize Tor for legitimate anonymization. Traffic originating from a Tor exit node might warrant some suspicion, but this factor alone is not enough on its own to draw any sort of conclusion during an investigation.

The detection of traffic sourced from the Tor network can be accomplished by implementing a listing of Tor exit nodes into a detection mechanism. One such list exists at blutmagie.de, and can be queried from the browser or downloaded in a CSV file.

You can learn more about the Tor Exit Node list at http://torstatus.blutmagie.de/.

### Spamhaus Block Lists

Spamhaus is an international nonprofit organization that is devoted to tracking spam operations and sources on the Internet. They host multiple lists, including:

- Spamhaus Block List (SBL) – A database of IP addresses from which Spamhaus does not recommend accepting e-mail.
- Exploits Block List (XBL) – A database of IP addresses of hijacked systems infected by third party exploits, including open proxies, worms/viruses with built-in spam engines, and other types of exploits.

- Policy Block List (PBL) – A database of end-user IP address ranges that should not be delivering unauthenticated SMTP e-mail to any Internet mail server except those provided for specifically by an ISP for that customer's use. This essentially prevents hosts that shouldn't be sending mail from doing so. This is primarily used to help networks enforce their acceptable use policies.
- Domain Block List (DBL) – A database of domains found in spam messages.
- Don't Route or Peer (DROP) – A listing of hijacked network blocks of IP space that are directly allocated to spam hosting operations. These are blocks of IP addresses that are typically forgotten about by network owners that get reclaimed by spammers through a variety of techniques including the registration of abandoned domain names to accept point-of-contact e-mails, or by document forgery or social engineering tactics. Spamhaus also provides an Extended DROP (EDROP) list, which contains everything in the DROP list, as well as IP addresses that it believes to be more generally associated with cyber crime, but not directly allocated to spam distributors.

The SBL, XBL, PBL, and DBL lists are available for free for non-commercial use. If you don't meet these criteria, then you are required to purchase a subscription to these services. The DROP and EDROP lists, however, are free for use, which makes them good candidates for inclusion in reputation-based detection systems. The DROP/EDROP lists are well maintained as well, so they can be useful for detection of internal hosts who are communicating with known spam hosting systems.

Of particular interest is the DROP list's integration with the Emerging Threats (ET) signature repository. ET maintains a set of Spamhaus DROP list detection signatures for use with either the Snort or Suricata intrusion detection systems. This really simplifies the implementation of this list.

While it isn't entirely fruitful to utilize these lists to detect incoming spam, it might be worth knowing if a friendly host (other than a mail server) is communicating with systems that fall into the ranges typically used by spammers.

You can learn more about the Spamhaus lists at http://www.spamhaus.org/drop/.

## Other Lists
A plethora of other IP and Domain reputation lists are available. In fact, there are far too many to cover in this book. Others public lists you might want to look into include:

- AlientVault Labs IP Reputation Database: http://labs.alienvault.com/labs/index.php/projects/open-source-ip-reputation-portal/

- MalC0de Database http://malc0de.com/database/

- SRI Malware Threat Center http://www.mtc.sri.com/live_data/attackers/

- Project Honeypot
  https://www.projecthoneypot.org/list_of_ips.php

- Emerging Threats Rules
  http://www.emergingthreats.net/open-source/etopen-ruleset/

## Common Issues when Using Public Reputation Lists

While reputation-based detection can often be considered an "easy win," a few common pitfalls are associated with detecting malicious activity based upon communication with systems that have negative reputations.

### Automatic Blocking

It is generally never a good idea to utilize public blacklists in conjunction with automated blocking or intrusion prevention software without some form of manual vetting. This can lead to unintentional blocking of legitimate sites, or even potentially causing a denial of service condition on your network.

In one famous case, the US Navy enabled automatic blocking of hosts based upon a third-party reputation list that wasn't fully vetted. When this was turned on, the entire Navy found itself blocked from accessing a number of legitimate websites, including Google.

In another example, an organization was ingesting a public reputation list directly into its internal DNS servers in order to attempt to block access to malicious domains by redirecting name queries for them. This worked fine, until one day the list they were ingesting was populated with the company's own mail server. The result was that no users were able to send and receive mail, and it took the network administrators quite a while to figure out what was causing the problem.

There is nothing more embarrassing than causing a scenario like one of these in your own organization. Because of this, you should stick to using public reputation lists with detection-only mechanisms.

### Pruning of Lists

It is very common for Internet-facing servers to become compromised and temporarily used for the distribution of malware or other malicious content, ultimately resulting in the server's IP address or domain name being added to a blacklist. When this happens, usually the owners of these systems will eventually find out they have been compromised, and they will clean up the system. When this happens, the server isn't always removed from the blacklist in a timely manner. As a result, false positive alerts are generated for communication to this server.

These types of false positives are common, and are something you can never truly get away from when performing reputation-based detection. However, you should do your best to minimize these types of false positives so that you don't waste analysis time. The best way to do this is to ensure that the lists you are ingesting are as judicious about removing hosts from their lists as they are about adding them. Additionally, you should ensure that you pull updated lists from their sources on a frequent basis. I'd recommend doing this at least daily. There are a number of ways to automate this process, which we will look at later in this chapter.

### Shared Servers

It is incredibly common for IP addresses of shared servers to end up on public blacklists. In this scenario, a domain associated with a single user of a shared server, often one provided by an ISP or hosting provider, has become compromised and is hosting some type of malicious logic. The problem is that rather than the individual domain ending up on a blacklist, the IP address of the server is added. This means that whenever users visit another website hosted on this shared IP address, they will generate an alert when no malicious activity is actually occurring. This can be responsible for a large number of false positives.

With that said, if one website on a shared web server is compromised, it greatly increases the probability that other websites on that server are also compromised. With no additional context, you should still investigate every alert. If you start to find shared servers that appear on these lists because of issues that wouldn't affect all of the hosts on the server, such as cross-site scripting (XSS), then you might consider removing the IP address entry from the blacklist, and replacing it with an entry specific to the domain that is actually exhibiting malicious logic.

### Advertising Networks

Advertising networks allow their customers to submit ad code that is automatically placed onto the websites of the network subscribers. This is a huge industry, and it is how a lot of websites generate revenue. This appeals to attackers because it allows them to attempt to place malicious code into advertisements and have the ads distributed to popular websites automatically by the ad network. While most ad networks perform a review process that eliminates this practice, not all of them do, and sometimes attackers are able to subvert or slip through these processes.

This practice can result in domains associated with advertising networks being placed onto public blacklists. When this occurs and you are performing detection based upon a public blacklist, it will result in an alert being generated every time a user is presented with an advertisement from the ad network, whether it is malicious or not. This can be responsible for a massive number of false positives. If you don't believe me, try checking your organization's web logs for requests to the akamai.com or scorecardresearch.com domains, which both belong to major advertising networks. You will find that they are utilized by a large number of popular websites.

The most practical way to eliminate the excessive number of false positives generated by advertising networks is to remove any reference to these networks from the blacklists you are ingesting. These ads generally don't contain any malicious code, but rather, contain code that redirects the user somewhere else that contains the real malicious logic. It's better to rely on other detection mechanisms at this point, rather than having to deal with all of the false positives that could be generated otherwise.

### Further Reducing of False Positives with Whitelists

We've only talked about lists containing indicators with negative reputations (blacklists) to this point. However, there is merit to incorporating lists of indicators with positive reputations (whitelists) into your network as well. While blacklists can yield very positive results when paired with a detection mechanism, they are prone to false positives, especially when the lists aren't vetted well.

One tactic that can effectively minimize the amount of false positives associated with reputation-based detection is use of the Alexa Top Sites list as a whitelist. Their Top Sites list contains the top 1,000,000 visited sites on the Internet. This list can be pruned down to the top 100-500 sites, and then those results can be used in conjunction with blacklists to ensure that none of these whitelisted websites will trigger an alert if they are found on the blacklists. It is possible that one of these sites could become infected with some type of malware, but the chance of that occurring is small, and if it does occur, it is likely that the companies supporting the sites will quickly mitigate the infection.

## AUTOMATING REPUTATION-BASED DETECTION

To perform reputation-based detection, you need two components. First, you need at least one list of IPs or domains with negative reputations. We've already covered several of the publicly available blacklists, but this can also be supplemented with private, industry-specific, and internal lists. Once you have at least one list, you must feed the contents of that list into some type of mechanism for performing detection based upon the entries in the list. There are several options for automating and accomplishing these tasks.

### Manual Retrieval and Detection with BASH Scripts

The rest of this chapter will be devoted to using various free and open source tools for reputation-based detection. All of these tools can be effectively used in most organizations, but with that said, this provides the perfect opportunity to demonstrate just how simple reputation-based detection can be. It is so simple, in fact, that you can utilize basic Linux BASH scripting to interact with collected data to accomplish the entire process. In these next few examples, we will use BASH scripts to download and parse a public reputation list, and then use that list to detect malicious domains and IP addresses in network traffic.

#### Download and Parsing a List

As I stated above, the first thing you need to begin performing reputation-based detection is a list of things that are reputed to be bad. In this case, we will take one of the more popular public lists, Malware Domain List. MDL maintains both a domain and IP list, and we want to get both of them. Ultimately, we want each list to reside as a text file with entries delimited by new lines.

The IP address list can be downloaded using curl with the following command:

```
curl http://www.malwaredomainlist.com/hostslist/ip.txt > mdl.iplist
```

The greater than symbol (>) is used to redirect the output of the command to the file named mdl.iplist. If you examine this file, everything will look as you might expect. However, in order for us to parse the list properly later, we have to address one discrepancy.

If you run the command "file mdl.iplist," the tool will tell you that the file we've just created is of the type "ASCII text, with CRLF line terminators." Windows-based operating systems represent a new line with both the line feed

(\n in ASCII or 0x10 in hex) and carriage return (\r in ASCII or 0x0D in hex) characters. Unix-based operating systems represent a new line with only the line feed character. If we attempt to parse this file using Unix-based tools, the addition of the CR character at the end of every line will result in unexpected output.

There are several ways that the CR character can be stripped from each line in the file, but the easiest is to use the dos2unix utility. If dos2unix is not natively installed on the distribution you are using, it can be installed easily from most standard repositories (`apt-get install dos2unix`, `yum install dos2unix`, etc). We can pipe the output of the curl command directly to this utility before writing the output to a file. Our modified command looks like this:

```
curl http://www.malwaredomainlist.com/hostslist/ip.txt |
dos2unix > mdl.iplist
```

Now we need to accomplish the same task with the list of malicious domains from MDL. This command will initially look very similar (Figure 8.3):

```
curl http://www.malwaredomainlist.com/hostslist/hosts.txt |
dos2unix > mdl.domainlist
```

```
○ ○ ○   chris — sanders@nighthawk: ~ — ssh — 64×22
sanders@nighthawk:~$ head -20 mdl.domainlist
#                MalwareDomainList.com Hosts List         #
#     http://www.malwaredomainlist.com/hostslist/hosts.txt  #
#          Last updated: Wed, 07 Aug 13 20:36:19 +0000     #


127.0.0.1  localhost
127.0.0.1  0koryu0.easter.ne.jp
127.0.0.1  1.michaelwilsonmusic.com
127.0.0.1  11.lamarianella.info
127.0.0.1  125search.com
127.0.0.1  1364ih5d6.ni.net.tr
127.0.0.1  1k.pl
127.0.0.1  1wstdfgh.organiccrap.com
127.0.0.1  2.refiinc.com
127.0.0.1  2.wholesalepbm.com
127.0.0.1  2.zerocostfha.com
127.0.0.1  200mail.com
127.0.0.1  28ytls60.ni.net.tr
127.0.0.1  2wnpf.tld.cc
127.0.0.1  3.bluepointmortgage.com
sanders@nighthawk:~$
```

**FIGURE 8.3**

The Malware Domain List

If you run this command and then open the mdl.domainlist file, you will notice a few problems. At the top of the file, there are some extra lines of text, along with some blank lines that need to be removed. If we attempt to parse the file in its current state, those lines will generate errors. We can get rid of them by using sed, and instructing it to remove the first six lines of the file:

```
curl  http://www.malwaredomainlist.com/hostslist/hosts.txt  |  sed
'1,6d' | dos2unix > mdl.domainlist
```

Next, notice that each line has two values, with the first column containing the loopback IP address 127.0.0.1, and the second column containing the actual domain. This list is presented in this format so that the list can be easily copied and pasted into a host's file for redirection of requests to these hosts. This isn't something we are using the list for right now. This can be done by using awk to select only the data in the second column.

```
curl  http://www.malwaredomainlist.com/hostslist/hosts.txt  |  sed
'1,6d' | awk '{print $2}' | dos2unix > mdl.domainlist
```

The resulting output of this file is shown in Figure 8.4.

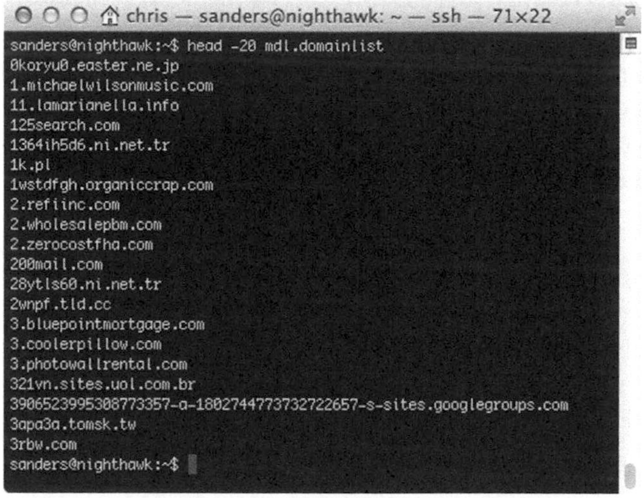

```
sanders@nighthawk:~$ head -20 mdl.domainlist
0koryu0.easter.ne.jp
1.michaelwilsonmusic.com
11.lamarianella.info
125search.com
1364ih5d6.ni.net.tr
1k.pl
1wstdfgh.organiccrap.com
2.refiinc.com
2.wholesalepbm.com
2.zerocostfha.com
200mail.com
28ytls60.ni.net.tr
2wnpf.tld.cc
3.bluepointmortgage.com
3.coolerpillow.com
3.photowallrental.com
321vn.sites.uol.com.br
3906523995308773357-a-1802744773732722657-s-sites.googlegroups.com
3apa3a.tomsk.tw
3rbw.com
sanders@nighthawk:~$
```

**FIGURE 8.4**

Our Modified Malware Domain List

We should now have two properly formatted files containing IP addresses and domains that we can use for detection. These lines can be placed into a single script, which can be run at a regular interval in order to ensure the lists are kept up to date. I'd recommend using a CRON job to schedule a new download of this data at least once per day. The following entry into /etc/crontab will run the update script once per day at 6:30 AM.

```
30 6 * * * /home/sanders/GatherMDL.sh
```

### Detection of Malicious IP Addresses in Session Data

With lists in hand, now we want to attempt to detect any communication between hosts on our network and hosts in the list of IP addresses from MDL. One of the most efficient ways to do this is to leverage session data. We will write a short script to perform detection leveraging SiLK.

First, we need to establish the time frame to examine. In this case, we will examine all traffic occurring within the past hour. We can use the date command to get the current date and time, as well as the date and time an hour ago. These will be set to variables.

```
start=$(date -ud '-60 minutes'+%Y/%m/%d:%T)
endd=$(date -ud+%Y/%m/%d:%T)
```

Next, we must take the line delimited list of IP addresses we generated earlier, and convert that into an IP set that can be iterated by SiLK's rwfilter tool. This is done with the rwsetbuild command. Here, we provide rwsetbuild with the name of the input file, and the name of the output file, which is mdl.domainlist.set:

```
rwsetbuild mdl.iplist mdl.iplist.set
```

Finally, we can use rwfilter to perform a query for any records matching the IP addresses in the list within the past hour. The command is:

```
rwfilter --start-date=$start --end-date=$end --anyset=mdl.iplist.set
--proto=0-255 --type=all --pass=stdout | rwcut
```

This command utilizes several of the same rwfilter options we examined in Chapter 4, along with the variable names created earlier as the value for that the --start-date and --end-date options. The --anyset option is where the input file is specified.

These elements combined will result in the following completed script:

```
#!/bin/bash

start=$(date -ud '-60 minutes'+%Y/%m/%d:%T)
end=$(date -ud+%Y/%m/%d:%T)

rwsetbuild mdl.iplist mdl.iplist.set

rwfilter      --active-time=$start-$end      --anyset=mdl.iplist.set
--proto=0-255 --type=all --pass=stdout | rwcut
```

This output of this script is shown in Figure 8.5.

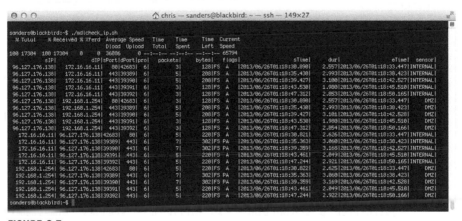

**FIGURE 8.5**

SiLK Output Matching Bad Reputation IP Addresses

### *Detection of Malicious Domains in Full Packet Capture Data*

Our next task is to attempt to detect any communication that is occurring between friendly hosts and potentially malicious domains found in the list that was pulled down from MDL. This data won't be found in session data, so instead, we will look to packet capture data.

This process will be a bit more involved than examining IP address with rwfilter, so we will be relying on BASH functions to organize each process. Before writing the first function, we need to tell the script that we will provide the PCAP file to parse as an argument within the command line when the script is executed. This is done with the statement:

```
pcapfile=$(echo $1)
```

The first function we will build utilizes Justniffer (discussed in Chapter 6) to parse the supplied PCAP file and extract all of the domain names found within HTTP communication occurring over TCP port 80 to a separate file called temp.domains:

```
ParsePCAP() {

        justniffer -p "tcp port 80" -f $pcapfile -u -l "%request.timestamp -
%source.ip ->%dest.ip - %request.header.host - %request.line">temp.
domains

}
```

Next, we can write the function that will actually examine the contents of the temp. domains file for matches from the MDL domain list using grep in a while loop. The output will display the portion of the HTTP request containing the match. The sed statement is used to add text to the end of the request that states what domain generated the match. In addition to outputting matches to the console, the tee command is used to output matches to a file called alert.txt.

```
DetectMDL() {
    while read blacklistterm; do
        grep -i $blacklistterm temp.domains | sed "s,$, -
Match\:$blacklistterm,g"| tee -a alert.txt
        done < "mdl.domainlist"
}
```

We can combine these functions into a single script, along with an additional function that cleans up the temporary file generated while parsing the PCAP:

```
#!/bin/bash

pcapfile=$(echo $1)
ParsePCAP() {

        justniffer -p "tcp port 80" -f $pcapfile -u -l "%request.timestamp -
%source.ip ->%dest.ip - %request.header.host - %request.line">temp.
domains

}
```

```
DetectMDL() {
    while read blacklistterm; do
        grep -i $blacklistterm temp.domains | sed "s,$, -
Match\:$blacklistterm,g" | tee -a alert.txt
        done < "mdl.domainlist"
}

CleanUp() {
    rm -rf temp.domains
}

ParsePCAP
DetectMDL
CleanUp
Exit
```

The final output of this script is shown in Figure 8.6.

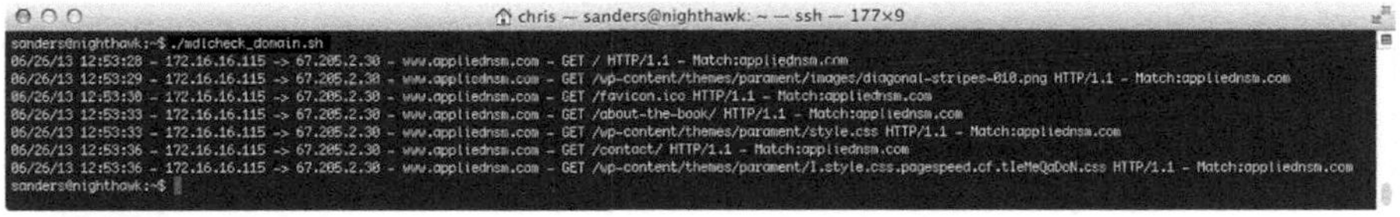

**FIGURE 8.6**

Matching Bad Reputation Domain Names from a PCAP File

The scripts shown here are very basic, and could be improved in a lot of ways. This includes:

- The ability to parse an entire directory instead of just a single PCAP file
- The ability to perform both strict and loose match checking
- Error checking
- Output to syslog, database, e-mail, etc.

We've provided a more full featured version of these scripts in a tool called Scruff, which can be found at http://www.appliednsm.com/scruff.

## The Collective Intelligence Framework (CIF)

The Collective Intelligence Framework (CIF) is a cyber threat intelligence management system developed by Wes Young at REN-ISAC. CIF allows analysts to define lists to ingest, and then automatically pulls in those lists on a regular basis. This data is then normalized and stored in the CIF database. Once this data is stored, it can be queried with CIF, or used in conjunction with a post process script to be deployed to a detection mechanism.

CIF comes with the ability to ingest several lists out of the box, including the Zeus/SpyEye tracker, the Spamhaus DROP list, and many more. Beyond that, it also provides the ability to write extensions so that you can parse lists that aren't preconfigured with the software. Once you've ingested these lists, you can utilize output plugins to send these indicators to whatever detection mechanisms you have in place.

CIF is not included by default in Security Onion. If you'd like to follow along with the examples in this chapter then you can install it by following the instructions at https://code.google.com/p/collective-intelligence-framework/wiki/ServerInstall_v1.

### Updating and Adding Indicator Lists

When you've installed CIF, the first thing you should do is issue commands that will force CIF to populate its database with entries from the lists it is already configured to parse. These are broken into two groups, hourly and daily. The lists in the hourly grouping are updated once every hour, and the lists in the daily grouping are updated once every day. First, you should update the hourly list with the command:

```
cif_crontool -d -p hourly
```

Next, you should update the daily lists, which are much larger. This could take quite some time depending upon your available bandwidth and the performance of the system you have CIF installed on. The command for the daily update is:

```
cif_crontool -d -p daily
```

Once completed, the CIF database should be populated with results from all of its preconfigured reputation lists.

CIF also provides a framework for ingesting and parsing additional lists, which comes in handy if you would like to utilize a reputation list that isn't already included with CIF. This is especially useful if you utilize a private reputation list that isn't publicly available, or isn't hosted on the Internet. CIF allows for parsing data in delimited or non-delimited text files, XML files, JSON files, and more.

The existing feed configuration files can be examined for examples of how to pull custom feeds into CIF. Figure 8.7 shows the configuration file used to ingest the list from malwaredomains.com, which are in a delimited text file.

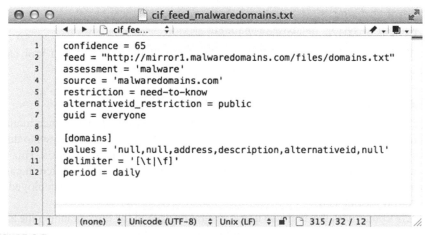

**FIGURE 8.7**

A CIF Feed Configuration File for a Delimited Text List

The configuration for this type of feed is fairly minimal. The first section of the configuration file identifies the location of the feed and sets several default values such as a confidence rating for the list (65) and an assessment value for classifying the indicators (malware). The second section of the configuration identifies how the values in the delimited text map to columns in the CIF database, how the text file is delimited, and how often the list should be updated. In this case, the text file is delimited by a tab and a form feed character (\t|\f), and the list is update daily.

You can read more about creating custom feed configuration files for varying data types on the CIF website.

### Querying Indicators

With CIF intelligence at our fingertips, we need the ability to query this data. There are two ways that data can be queried; the CIF Perl client and the web interface. The Perl client is the default mechanism for interacting with CIF data and the most stable. Using the CIF command, we can query for any indicator type that might be found within the CIF database. For example, if we wanted to perform a query for an IP address that we suspect to be associated with malicious activity, the following command will accomplish this:

```
cif -q 112.125.124.165
```

The –q command specifies a basic query of all CIF data available. CIF also allows you to search for IP address ranges using CIDR notation, such as 112.125.124.0/24. The results of this command are shown in Figure 8.8.

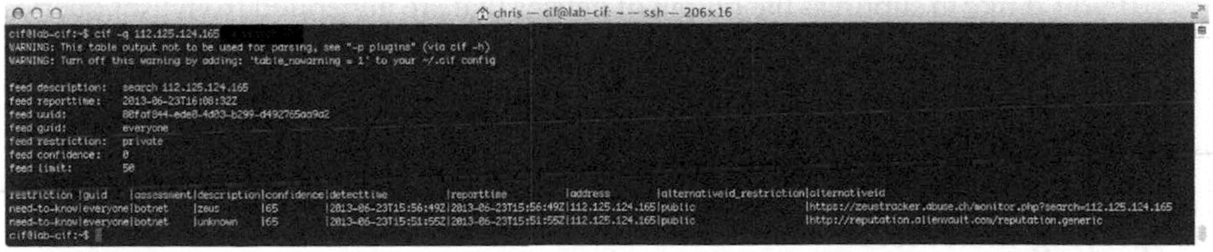

**FIGURE 8.8**

An IP Address Query in CIF

In this output, we can see that the IP address in question appears in both the Zeus Tracker and Alientvault Reputation lists, classified as being part of a botnet. The output provides a URL for both of these reputation lists so that you can get more context from the indicator. The output also provides information on restrictions and confidence associated with the indicator. These values are all configurable within the CIF configuration, as some lists are given a default restriction and confidence value.

If you run this command a second time, you will notice that an additional entry appears in the list with "search" listed under the assessment heading. Whenever someone searches for a particular indicator with CIF, it logs the search and will output this data in the search results. This is useful for knowing if other analysts are searching for the same indicator. In some cases, you may find that a particular indicator you are concerned about doesn't show up in any public reputation lists, but that multiple analysts within your group are searching repetitively for the same indicator. This probably means that activity associated with this indicator warrants further investigation if so many people suspect mischief. In the case of Figure 8.9, the output of the CIF query shows an indicator that has been searched for multiple times.

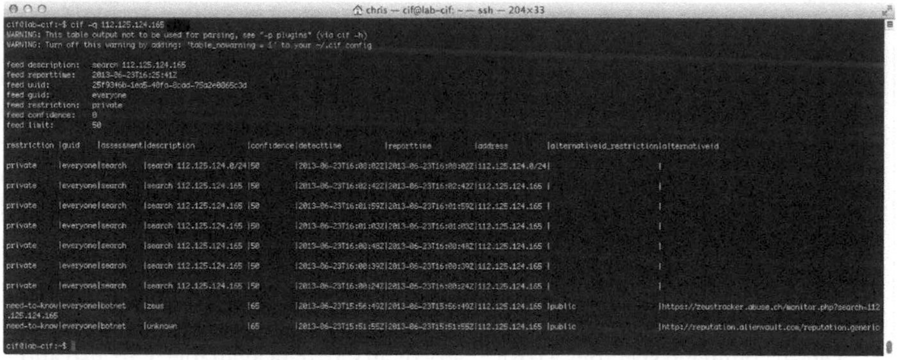

**FIGURE 8.9**

A CIF Query Identifying Multiple Historical Searches

If you'd like to suppress the output of entries that are generated from user queries, you can use the –e flag. This flag will allow you to specify any assessment type you do not want included in the query results. In this case, you could suppress search entries by appending "-e search" to the query.

### Deploying Indicators

One of my favorite features of CIF is the ability to create and utilize custom output plugins. These plugins allow you to output indicators contained within the CIF database to a format that is useful for deployment with various detection mechanisms. Currently, CIF supports the ability to output data to a variety of formats, including CSV files, ASCII tables, HTML tables, Iptables firewall rules, PCAP filters, Snort rules, and Bro input.

Be default, CIF will output results to a table format so that they can be read easily from a terminal window. If you'd like to use one of these other formats, you can the –p flag. If we wanted to output the results of our previous query to a Snort rule for detection, we would use the command:

```
cif -q 112.125.124.165 -p Snort
```

This command will output a Snort rule for each entry in the search output, which is shown in Figure 8.10.

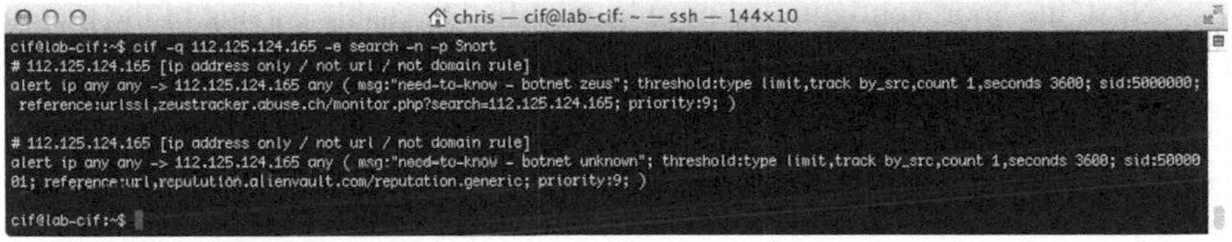

**FIGURE 8.10**

Snort Rule Output for the CIF Query

When utilizing CIF output to generate items like Snort rules, you should always double check the rules before deploying them to make sure they are optimized for performance and configured in a manner consistent with the standard you are using for deploying other IDS signatures within your organization. For instance, by default, CIF-generated Snort rules are only configured to detect traffic going to the listed IP addresses. In a lot of cases, you may want to reconfigure these rules to detect traffic to or from these addresses. Making this adjustment is pretty easy, and is addressed in the discussion of Snort Rules in the next chapter.

CIF is still in its infancy and isn't without a few quirks, but it represents a great deal of potential. The community support for the project has grown tremendously, with a great deal of users contributing configurations for a variety of list feeds and output plugins. I've also seen several use cases where organizations are using CIF to successfully manage their reputation-based detection capabilities. If you'd like to learn more about CIF, you can do so at the project website here: https://code.google.com/p/collective-intelligence-framework/.

## Snort IP Reputation Detection

Snort is one of the world's most popular signature-based IDS. We will talk about Snort in great detail in the next chapter, but for now we are going to look at its reputation-based detection capabilities by using its reputation preprocessor for detection of communication with potentially malicious IP addresses.

In the past, reputation-based detection for IP addresses with Snort was done with standard rules. In order to address performance concerns with that method, the reputation preprocessor was developed. This preprocessor runs before all of the other preprocessors, and does so in an efficient manner so that large lists of IP addresses can be managed.

The reputation preprocessor is enabled in Snort on Security Onion, but alerting for it is not. Before adding entries to the reputation preprocessor blacklist, we should enable alerting. In order to do this, you should first create a file called preprocessor_rules in the /etc/nsm/rules directory of your SO sensor. This rule should contain the following rule to allow for alerting of reputation preprocessor events:

```
alert ( msg; "REPUTATION_EVENT_BLACKLIST"; sid: 1; gid: 136; rev: 1;
metadata: rule-type preproc ; classtype:bad-unknown; )
```

Next, the Snort configuration must be modified to enable parsing of the preprocessor rule file that we just created. This is done by editing /etc/nsm/sensor_name/snort.conf, and uncommenting this line:

```
include $PREPROC_RULE_PATH/preprocessor.rules
```

Now, the only thing remaining is adding IP addresses to the reputation preprocessor blacklist. This file can be found at /etc/nsm/rules/black_list.rules. The file accepts both individual IP addresses, and IP address ranges in CIDR notation. You can also specify inline comments by appending the comment after the pound sign (#) following the IP entry. In order to test the preprocessor, you can add the following entry:

```
192.0.2.75 # Test Address
```

In order for these changes to take effect, you should restart Snort on the sensor, as shown in Figure 8.11.

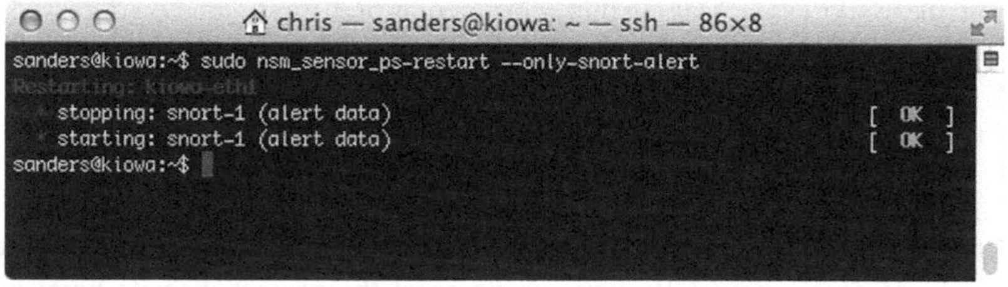

**FIGURE 8.11**

Restarting the Snort Process

In order to test the newly created rule, you can simply ping the address 192.0.2.75 from Security Onion itself, or from another device being monitored by it. Figure 8.12 shows an example of this rule generating an alert.

You can add a large number of IP addresses to the black_list.rules file without negatively affecting sensor performance. Since the alerts generated from this preprocessor aren't too verbose, you should make it a habit to add contextual comments regarding the indicators in the black list file so that analysts can reference this when an alert is generated.

Snort's reputation preprocessor doesn't have a lot of bells and whistles, but if you are already using Snort in your environment it makes it incredibly easy to implement reputation-based detection of IP addresses with only a few small changes. Unfortunately, this processor only handles IP addresses. If you would like to perform detection of communication with malicious domains using Snort, then you can use standard Snort rules, which are discussed in Chapter 9. Unfortunately, using standard rules for detection of a large number of malicious domains doesn't scale entirely well. You can read more about Snort's reputation preprocessor and its various configuration options at http://manual.snort.org/node175.html.

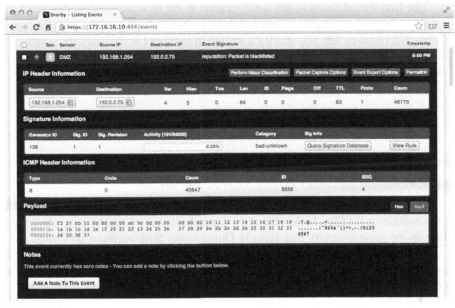

**FIGURE 8.12**

An Alert Generated by the Reputation Preprocessor

## Suricata IP Reputation Detection

Suricata is rapidly gaining popularity as an alternative to Snort for signature-based detection. This is primarily because of its ability to inspect traffic in a multithreaded manner, which makes it preferable for monitoring high throughput connections. It also utilizes the same rule syntax as Snort, so rules are portable between the two. We will examine Suricata in depth in Chapter 9, but for now we will look at Suricata's version of an IP reputation detection engine. It may help you to read that chapter first in order to gain a better understanding of how Suricata functions, and then come back to read this section.

Suricata's IP reputation capability functions in a manner that is designed to optimize the processing of a large number of entries. This works by utilizing the same API that is used for tagging and thresholding. To enable this functionality, you must first modify the Suricata.yaml configuration file. The following section is used to enable IP Reputation capabilities:

```
# IP Reputation
reputation-categories-file:  /etc/nsm/sensor-name/iprep/categories.
txt
default-reputation-path: /etc/nsm/rules
reputation-files:
   zeustracker.list
 - spyeyetracker.list
 - mdl.list
 - watch.list
```

The first item defined in this configuration is the reputation categories file. Categories allow you to organize lists and their alerts into manageable units. The categories file requires that you specify a unique id number for the category, a category name, and a description. Typically, categories will be organized by list source. These must take the format:

```
<id>,<short name>,<description>
```

An example category file might look like this:

```
1,ZeusTracker,Zeustracker IP Addresses
2,SpyEyeTracker,SpyEye Tracker IP Addresses
3,MDL,Malware Domain List IP Addresses
4,Watchlist,Internal Watch List IP Addresses
```

Next, you must define the default-reputation-path, which is the directory that contains reputation list files. In the case of the example above, we've chosen to place these files in the same directory that Security Onion stores Suricata/Snort IDS rules.

The last configuration item that is required is to define the actual list files to be parsed by Suricata. These files must exist within the default reputation path. The entries within these files must match the format:

```
<IP>,<category>,<confidence>
```

This format requires the IP address be in standard dotted-quad notation. In addition to this, the category number specified must exist in the category file mentioned earlier. Finally, you must include a numerical confidence value. An example reputation list file could look like this:

```
192.0.2.1,1,65
192.0.2.2,1,50
192.0.2.3,2,95
```

With IP reputation configured, all that remains is to create alerts so that analysts can be notified whenever communication with one of these IP addresses is detected. This is accomplished by adding a rule that utilizes the iprep directive. The iprep directive itself takes four options:

- Traffic Direction (any/src/dst/both): Used to specify the direction of the traffic to/from the IP.
- Category (Short Name): The short name of the category that you are attempting to match. The short name must match exactly what is listed in the categories file.
- Operator (>,<,=): The operator used in conjunction with the reputation value specified.
- Confidence Value (1-127): Will restrict matches to only those with confidence matching the operator and value specified.

This directive can be combined with any other features that might normally be used in a Suricata rule, allowing for a great deal of flexibility. However, the addition of any additional features such as content matching will decrease the speed in which IP reputation rules operate. A rule that only uses the iprep directive is an IP-only rule, and is the fastest way to implement a large number of IP reputation rules.

An example of a very basic IP-only rule is:

```
alert ip any any -> any any (msg:"IPREP Malware Domain List - High Confi-
dence"; iprep:dst,MDL,>,75; sid:1; rev:1;)
```

This rule will generate an alert whenever outbound communication is detected to an IP address listed on the MDL list, whose confidence value is greater than 75. An example alert generated by this rule is shown in Figure 8.13.

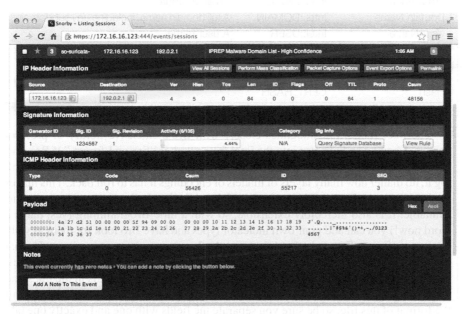

**FIGURE 8.13**

An Alert Generated by the Suricata Iprep Directive

Suricata has the ability to parse a large number of IP addresses using this method. I've heard of organizations testing this capability with up to a million addresses in lists being used with IP-only rules. Suricata is a very solid and efficient choice for reputation-based detection of IP addresses.

## Reputation Detection with Bro

The Bro IDS is easily one of the most powerful and flexible NSM detection tools available. We will talk about harnessing this power in depth in Chapter 10, but for now let's have a quick tour of Bro's reputation-based detection capabilities.

Bro is extremely well suited for the detection of several types of indicators, such as IP addresses, domains, email addresses and SSL certificates, using its built-in intelligence processing features collectively known as the intel framework. Table 8.1 lists the data types supported by the intel framework and what Bro calls them in its scripting language. We will confine ourselves the IP addresses, domains and email addresses for the purposes of this example.

**Table 8.1** Data Types Supported by the Bro Intel Framework

| Data Type | Bro Name | Description |
| --- | --- | --- |
| IP Address | Intel::ADDR | An IPv4 or IPv6 address or CIDR block |
| URL | Intel::URL | The complete URL, with the "http://" or "https://" prefix removed |
| Software Name | Intel::Software | The name of a specific piece of software |
| Email Address | Intel::EMAIL | An email address |
| Domain Name | Intel::DOMAIN | A full domain name, including any subdomains |
| User Name | Intel::USER | A user name |
| MD5, SHA-1 or SHA-256 File Hash | Intel::HASH | The hash of a file object (depends on the Bro File Analysis Framework) |
| SSL Certificate Hash | Intel::CERT_HASH | The SHA-1 hash of a specific SSL certificate |

The intel framework integrates closely with Bro's extensive library of protocol parsers. Loading an indicator into the intel framework is "fire-and-forget." If Bro ever sees that indicator while processing any of the protocols it knows how to decode, it will log it, no matter how many layers of tunnels or encodings it has to roll back. This makes the intel framework one of the most powerful and flexible indicator detection solutions available. It is also incredibly extensible, so with a little Brogramming (yes, that's a word now!) you can add your own indicator types and have Bro look for them as well.

In order to configure the intel framework, first you must create an input file that lists all your indicators, which is a simple tab-delimited text file. The first line is mandatory (even though it looks like a comment) and describes the fields in the lines that follow. Figure 8.14 shows the format of a sample input file. Bro is very picky about the format of this file, so be sure you separate the fields with one and exactly one tab, and that there are no blank lines.

**FIGURE 8.14**

Example Entries in a Bro Reputation List

Each line of data starts with the actual indicator value and its data type (according to Table 8.1 above). Although all of the remaining fields must be present in each line of data, their values are optional. If you don't wish to specify a value, just use a dash ("-") for that field.

The "meta.source" field is a place for you to name the intel feed that this indicator came from. The name can include spaces and punctuation, but no tabs. Depending on your intel management infrastructure, this could also be a database key or a URL into a web-based intel application. If the indicator shows up in traffic, Bro will log that data, and include the value of the source field in the log for a bit of context.

The "meta.do_notice" field is a Boolean, which can be either "T" (True) or "F" (False). It controls whether you want to also output any matches for that indicator to the Bro notice.log file. Notices are Bro's way of drawing extra attention to an event, even though it may already be logged somewhere else. We'll discuss notices and why you may want to do this in more detail in Chapter 10.

The "meta.if_in" field allows you to restrict notice logging to only certain contexts (e.g., "only if it appears in the HTTP Host: header"). No matter what you put here, the intel framework still logs all matches, it just doesn't create notices unless this condition matches. This may be useful, for example, when your intel says that the indicator is specifically related to HTTP traffic. If you see the indicator in DNS and Email traffic, Bro will still create entries for that activity in *intel.log*, but no notices will be created, since you're less concerned with activity in those contexts.

There are several ways to populate this list. If you are using CIF, then there is an option to output data in a format that is digestible by the Bro intel framework, so this is typically the easiest route. Alternatively, you could write your own script that will output list entries in this format. In order to test this functionality, we can just create entries by hand.

Now that we have a data file with our reputation data in it, we must deploy this file and a Bro script to load it up into the intelligence framework. The default installation of Bro keeps its configuration and script files in /usr/local/bro/share/bro, but the version of Bro included with Security Onion keeps its data files in /opt/bro/share/bro/site, so we'll use that. You can begin by creating a subdirectory there called Reputation, so that you can copy your data file there as /opt/bro/share/bro/site/Reputation/reputation.dat.

Next, you will need to add a few lines of code to Bro's default startup file, /opt/bro/share/bro/site/local.bro. Edit that file to include the following:

```
@load frameworks/intel/seen
@load frameworks/intel/do_notice
redef Intel::read_files+= {
        "/opt/bro/share/bro/site/Reputation/reputation.dat"
};
```

Chapter 10 will provide a lot more background that will be helpful for understanding Bro scripting in detail, but the code above should be reasonably decipherable as it is written. This code loads two Bro script modules from the intel framework (seen and do_notice), then adds your new intel data file to the (initially empty) list of data files it will read in when Bro starts. The framework handles everything else automatically. In fact, should you ever need to add or remove entries from your reputation list, you can just edit the reputation.dat file appropriately. Bro is smart enough to automatically notice the changes and update its internal state.

Finally, we need to let the running Bro know that we've changed its configuration by doing the following:

1. Execute `broctl check` – This will check the code for any errors.
2. Execute `broctl install` – This will install the new script
3. Execute `broctl restart` – This will restart Bro

With these changes made, you should be up and running. Whenever Bro observes any of the indicators listed in your data file, it will log this output to /usr/local/bro/logs/current/intel.log (default Bro installation) or /etc/nsm/bro/logs/current/intel.log (Security Onion). In addition, if you set the meta.do_notice on any of those indicators, those hits will also generate entries in the notice.log file in the same directory. An example intel.log file is shown in Figure 8.15.

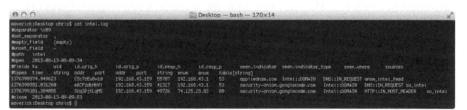

**FIGURE 8.15**

Sample Output of intel.log

We'll explain Bro's logging in more detail in Chapter 10, but for now, it's easy to see in the Intel log that someone did a DNS look up for appliednsm.com and visited the Security Onion web site on Google Code. Since the reputation data file specifies that indicator hits for appliednsm.com should also result in notices, the DNS activity for that domain also shows up in notice.log, as shown in Figure 8.16.

**FIGURE 8.16**

Sample Output of notice.log

For demonstration purposes, we're reading all this log output in raw format directly from the files, but in a production environment, they would probably be exported to some log management utility for alerting, like ELSA or Log Stash. Regardless of how you choose to view this data, Bro is an incredibly effective way to perform reputation-based detection.

## CONCLUSION

Reputation-based detection is one of the "easy wins" in NSM because it is so simple to accomplish effectively, and it always yields positive results. If you are just starting to build your NSM capability, then reputation-based detection is the easiest way to get the most bang for your buck right out of the gate.

In this chapter we discussed the importance of reputation-based detection, along with multiple sources for public reputation lists. We also looked at several methods for automating reputation-based detection, including the use of basic BASH scripting and the use of the Collective Intelligence Framework. We also looked at how Snort, Suricata, and Bro could be used for effective detection of potentially malicious communication with suspect IP addresses and domains. In the next few chapters we will take a much harder look at Snort, Suricata, and Bro, which will help extend your knowledge of these platforms.

# Signature-Based Detection with Snort and Suricata

The most common form of IDS is signature-based. These systems work by examining packet data for indicators of compromise. Indicators are combined with IDS platform-specific directives to form signatures (also called rules) that instruct the IDS how to efficiently locate the indicators within network data. Whenever a signature-based IDS locates data that matches content found in a signature, it generates alert data to notify analysts.

Signature-based detection has been the bread and butter of network-based defensive security for over a decade, partially because it is very similar to how malicious activity is detected at the host level with antivirus utilities. The formula is fairly simple: an analyst observes a malicious activity, derives indicators from the activity and develops them into signatures, and then those signatures will alert whenever the activity occurs again. This was incredibly effective in previous years when there were only a small number of malware strains to keep up with, but in the modern era using signature-based mechanisms as a means of "network-based antivirus" isn't entirely efficient. The popular malware sharing repository http://www.virusshare. com currently has over 11 million unique malware samples as of the writing of this book. This is only a sampling of all of the malware that can be found in the far reaches of the Internet, and attempting to create and maintain signatures for this number of malware samples isn't close to possible.

In the modern era, signature-based IDS can find itself efficiently positioned to detect malicious activity beyond just typical malware. This might include common post-exploitation activities such as the launch of a shell, the unexpected addition of a user account over the network, or policy violations such as the deployment of unauthorized servers or systems attempting to download updates from an unapproved server. Signature-based IDS can be used effectively for the detection of malware, but rather than attempting to use it to detect every instance of malicious code on your network, it is often best suited to detecting malware related to specific and current concerns. This might include detection of currently popular web-based exploit kits (Blackhole, Redkit, etc), or malware related to current world events. The ideal use of signature-based IDS will ultimately depend upon your network and the threats you are most concerned with, but it is a crucial component of an NSM deployment.

In this chapter we will introduce the two most popular signature-based detection IDS's, Snort and Suricata. Common configuration items relevant to both tools will be discussed. We will also take an in-depth look at how signatures are created, and look at a couple of popular methods for viewing alerts generated by Snort and Suricata. This chapter won't serve as an exhaustive resource on Snort and Suricata. Rather, it is meant to provide fundamental knowledge about how these technologies work, and how analysts can apply that knowledge to building effective signature-based detection.

## SNORT

The Snort IDS was originally developed by Martin Roesch in 1998 as a free and open source lightweight intrusion detection system, eventually leading to the creation of Sourcefire, Inc. In the years since Snort's inception, it has grown to be the most popular IDS in the world. With over four million downloads, this "lightweight" system has grown into a very powerful and flexible IDS that has set the standard for the IDS industry. You can find Snort deployed in universities, private companies, and governments throughout the world. In 2013, Cisco announced its intent to acquire Sourcefire (although the deal was not yet completed when this chapter was finalized).

Snort is installed on Security Onion by default, and is also easy to install manually. Sourcefire provides installation guides for several operating systems at http://snort.org/docs.

If you've gone through the Security Onion setup process and have chosen Snort as your IDS, then it is likely already running. You can verify this by running the command sudo nsm_sensor_ps-status. In the output shown in Figure 9.1, you will see that snort-1 (alert data) is listed as [OK].

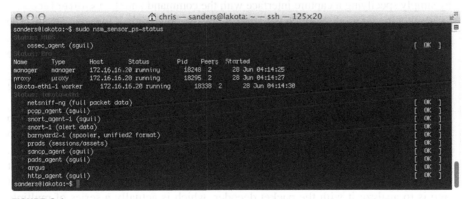

**FIGURE 9.1**

Checking Sensor Status

Snort itself is invoked from the command line. You can verify the version of Snort by running the command snort -V. The output of this command is shown in Figure 9.2.

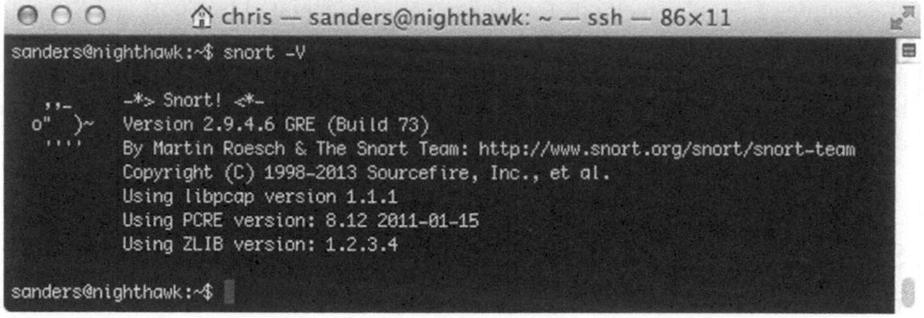

**FIGURE 9.2**

Verifying the Snort Version

## Snort Architecture

The way Snort functions will depend on which operating mode is specified at runtime. Snort has three primary operating modes: sniffer mode, packet logger mode, and NIDS mode.

Sniffer mode allows Snort to capture packets off the wire and outputs them to the screen in a human readable format, just as tcpdump might do (we will talk about tcpdump in Chapter 13). However, the its output is quite a bit nicer than tcpdump at baseline because of how it labels certain aspects of the traffic it sees. It will also provide some useful traffic statistics when the capture process is stopped. A sample of packet data as shown by Snort can bee seen in Figure 9.3.

Packet sniffer mode is how Snort runs by default, so you can execute Snort in this mode by simply specifying a capture interface with the command `snort -i<interface>`.

Packet logger mode is much the same as sniffer mode, only it logs packets to a file rather than the screen. This data is most commonly logged in binary PCAP format. You can enable this operation mode by specifying the logging directory with the addition of the –l switch, like this: `snort -l<log directory>`. At some point, you will probably want to read these PCAP files, which can be done by invoking Snort with the –r command: `snort -r<pcap file>`.

The mode we are primarily concerned about is NIDS mode, which is designed to read data captured from the network, with the ultimate goal of outputting alerts. To do this, packet data traverses different phases of Snort's architecture, shown in Figure 9.4.

Snort can receive data by parsing a manually specified PCAP file or by pulling it directly from a sensors monitoring interface. When Snort receives this data, its first step is to analyze it with the packet decoder, which is actually a series of multiple decoders that analyze packet data and normalize it into a state suitable for parsing by the preprocessors and detection engines.

When data has finished being processed by the packet decoder, it is sent to Snort's preprocessors. There are two types of preprocessors. The first type is used for detection purposes. The second type of preprocessor includes those that are used to modify packet data so that it can be better parsed by the detection engine.

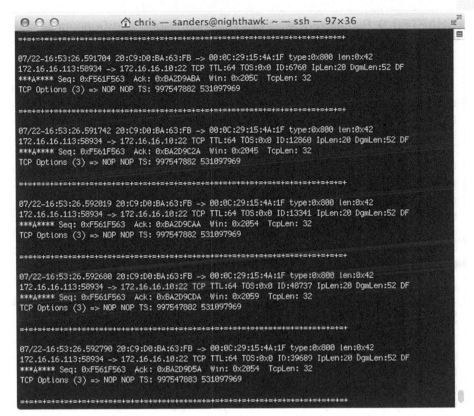

```
  ●  ○  ○                   ⌂ chris — sanders@nighthawk: ~ — ssh — 97×36

=+=+=+=+=+=+=+=+=+=+=+=+=+=+=+=+=+=+=+=+=+=+=+=+=+=+=+=+=+=+=+=+=+=+=+=+=+=+

07/22-16:53:26.591704 20:C9:D0:BA:63:FB -> 00:0C:29:15:4A:1F type:0x800 len:0x42
172.16.16.113:58934 -> 172.16.16.10:22 TCP TTL:64 TOS:0x0 ID:6760 IpLen:20 DgmLen:52 DF
***A**** Seq: 0xF561F563  Ack: 0xBA2D9ABA  Win: 0x205C  TcpLen: 32
TCP Options (3) => NOP NOP TS: 997547882 531097969

=+=+=+=+=+=+=+=+=+=+=+=+=+=+=+=+=+=+=+=+=+=+=+=+=+=+=+=+=+=+=+=+=+=+=+=+=+=+

07/22-16:53:26.591742 20:C9:D0:BA:63:FB -> 00:0C:29:15:4A:1F type:0x800 len:0x42
172.16.16.113:58934 -> 172.16.16.10:22 TCP TTL:64 TOS:0x0 ID:12860 IpLen:20 DgmLen:52 DF
***A**** Seq: 0xF561F563  Ack: 0xBA2D9C2A  Win: 0x2045  TcpLen: 32
TCP Options (3) => NOP NOP TS: 997547882 531097969

=+=+=+=+=+=+=+=+=+=+=+=+=+=+=+=+=+=+=+=+=+=+=+=+=+=+=+=+=+=+=+=+=+=+=+=+=+=+

07/22-16:53:26.592019 20:C9:D0:BA:63:FB -> 00:0C:29:15:4A:1F type:0x800 len:0x42
172.16.16.113:58934 -> 172.16.16.10:22 TCP TTL:64 TOS:0x0 ID:13341 IpLen:20 DgmLen:52 DF
***A**** Seq: 0xF561F563  Ack: 0xBA2D9CAA  Win: 0x2054  TcpLen: 32
TCP Options (3) => NOP NOP TS: 997547882 531097969

=+=+=+=+=+=+=+=+=+=+=+=+=+=+=+=+=+=+=+=+=+=+=+=+=+=+=+=+=+=+=+=+=+=+=+=+=+=+

07/22-16:53:26.592680 20:C9:D0:BA:63:FB -> 00:0C:29:15:4A:1F type:0x800 len:0x42
172.16.16.113:58934 -> 172.16.16.10:22 TCP TTL:64 TOS:0x0 ID:48737 IpLen:20 DgmLen:52 DF
***A**** Seq: 0xF561F563  Ack: 0xBA2D9CDA  Win: 0x2059  TcpLen: 32
TCP Options (3) => NOP NOP TS: 997547882 531097969

=+=+=+=+=+=+=+=+=+=+=+=+=+=+=+=+=+=+=+=+=+=+=+=+=+=+=+=+=+=+=+=+=+=+=+=+=+=+

07/22-16:53:26.592790 20:C9:D0:BA:63:FB -> 00:0C:29:15:4A:1F type:0x800 len:0x42
172.16.16.113:58934 -> 172.16.16.10:22 TCP TTL:64 TOS:0x0 ID:39689 IpLen:20 DgmLen:52 DF
***A**** Seq: 0xF561F563  Ack: 0xBA2D9D5A  Win: 0x2054  TcpLen: 32
TCP Options (3) => NOP NOP TS: 997547883 531097969

=+=+=+=+=+=+=+=+=+=+=+=+=+=+=+=+=+=+=+=+=+=+=+=+=+=+=+=+=+=+=+=+=+=+=+=+=+=+
```

**FIGURE 9.3**

Snort Packet Sniffer Output

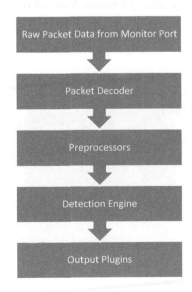

**FIGURE 9.4**

The Snort NIDS Mode Architecture

After preprocessing is finished, data is shipped to the workhorse of the Snort architecture, the detection engine. The detection engine is the portion of the architecture that is responsible for parsing rules and determining if the conditions identified in those rules match the traffic being analyzed.

When the detection engine determines that network traffic matches a rule, it hands that data over to the output plugins that are enabled in the Snort configuration file, so that an analyst can be notified of the alert. Snort can log to a variety of formats, including single line alerts in a text file, a CSV file, a PCAP format containing the traffic matching the rule, XML format, Syslog, and more. In many production environments, Snort is configured to log to Unified2 format, an open format that can be read by tools such as Barnyard2 or Pigsty, which can be used for more flexible output formats such as direct output to a database.

## SURICATA

While Snort is the most popular signature-based IDS in use today, another alternative that is gaining popularity is Suricata, an open source IDS developed by the Open Information Security Foundation (OISF) and initially funded by the Department of Homeland Security. Since its release in 2010, it has gained a large following. This is primarily due to its performance ability, made possible by its multi-threaded design. In truth, Suricata functions very similarly to Snort, so if you are familiar with its operation then you should have no trouble using Suricata.

If you've gone through the Security Onion setup process and you chose Suricata as your IDS, then it is likely already running. You can verify this by running the command `sudo nsm_sensor_ps-status`. In the output shown in Figure 9.5, you will see that Suricata (alert data) is listed as [OK].

**FIGURE 9.5**

Checking Sensor Status

If you are using a sensor platform other than Security Onion, then Suricata will have to be installed manually. The OISF provides installation guides for several operating systems at https://redmine.openinfosecfoundation.org/projects/suricata/wiki/Suricata_Installation

Suricata is invoked from the command line. You can verify the version of Suricata by running the command `suricata -V`. The output of this command is shown in Figure 9.6.

```
sanders@so-suricata:~$ suricata -V
This is Suricata version 1.4.2 RELEASE
sanders@so-suricata:~$
```

**FIGURE 9.6**

Verifying the Snort Version

## Suricata Architecture

Suricata is made up of several modules that can interact differently depending on how Suricata is initialized. The manner in which these modules and the threads and queues associated with them are arranged is referred to as Suricata's runmode. This runmode is chosen based upon where Suricata's processing priority should be placed.

The default runmode is one that is optimized for detection, which is typically the most resource intensive module. This runmode is depicted in Figure 9.7.

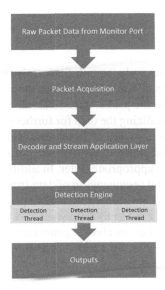

**FIGURE 9.7**

The Default Suricata Runmode

In another runmode, pfring is used to optimize packet acquisition and decoding for high throughput links. This runmode is shown in Figure 9.8.

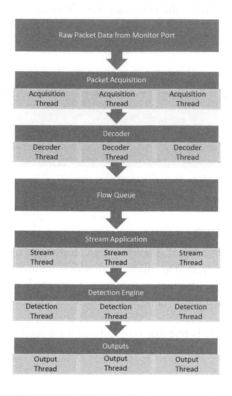

**FIGURE 9.8**

The Pfring Suricata Runmode

Regardless of which runmode is used, Suricata's first step is to collect packets with its Packet Acquisition module. This module gathers packets from the network interface and feeds them to the packet decoder, which is responsible for determining the link type then normalizing the data for further processing by other modules. Once completed, the data is passed to the stream module. The stream module is primarily responsible for tracking session-aware protocols (such as TCP) and reassembling packet data in the appropriate order. In addition to this, the stream module also does some handling and resequencing of data from application layer protocols such as HTTP. All of this data pampering leads up to the data being fed into the detection module, which is what analyzes packet data for matches based upon user-created signatures/rules. When an alert is generated, that alert and the associated data that caused it are sent to the output module, which can output data in a variety of formats.

## CHANGING IDS ENGINES IN SECURITY ONION

If you've already completed the Security Onion setup process and initially chose either Snort or Suricata as your IDS engine, but would like to try the other engine without reinstalling Security Onion, this can be done with a few quick changes.

**1.** Stop the NSM sensor processes:

```
sudo nsm_sensor_ps-stop
```

**2.** Modify the primary SO configuration file:

Switch from Snort to Suricata:

```
sudo sed -i 's|ENGINE=snort|ENGINE=suricata|g' /etc/nsm/
securityonion.conf
```

Switch from Suricata to Snort:

```
sudo sed -i 's|ENGINE=suricata|ENGINE=snort|g' /etc/nsm/
securityonion.conf
```

**3.** Update the sensor rule set for the appropriate IDS engine:

```
sudo rule-update
```

**4.** Start the NSM sensor processes:

```
sudo nsm_sensor_ps-start
```

If you've developed custom rules for your sensor, be sure that they are compatible with the IDS engine you are switching to in order to anticipate any issues that might prevent the IDS from initializing.

## INITIALIZING SNORT AND SURICATA FOR INTRUSION DETECTION

To invoke Snort or Suricata for the purpose of intrusion detection, all you have to do is specify the location of a valid configuration file with the −c command line option and a monitoring interface with the −i option.

Snort:

```
sudo snort -c snort.conf -i eth1
```

Suricata:

```
sudo suricata -c suricata.yaml i eth1
```

Before doing this however, it is important to verify that the configuration file is valid. This can be done by adding the −T argument, which will execute each IDS engine with the supplied configuration file to ensure that they can launch successfully with the provided configuration.

Snort:

```
sudo snort -Tc snort.conf -i eth1
```

Suricata:

```
sudo suricata -Tc suricata.yaml -i eth1
```

If everything checks out with Snort, you should see a message saying that it has successfully validated the configuration, as shown in Figure 9.9. Snort will exit when this test is completed.

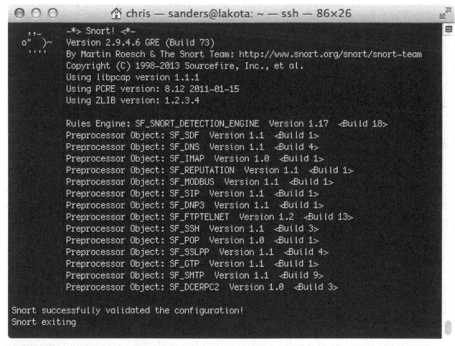

**FIGURE 9.9**

Snort Successfully Testing a Configuration File in NIDS Mode

If Suricata initializes successfully, you should see a message saying that the configuration provided was successfully loaded, as shown in Figure 9.10. Suricata will exit when this test is completed.

If any errors are reported with Snort or Suricata during these tests, they should be fixed before attempting to run the tools in production. One common error is forgetting to invoke the tools with the proper permissions to sniff network traffic, most commonly done by using the sudo command.

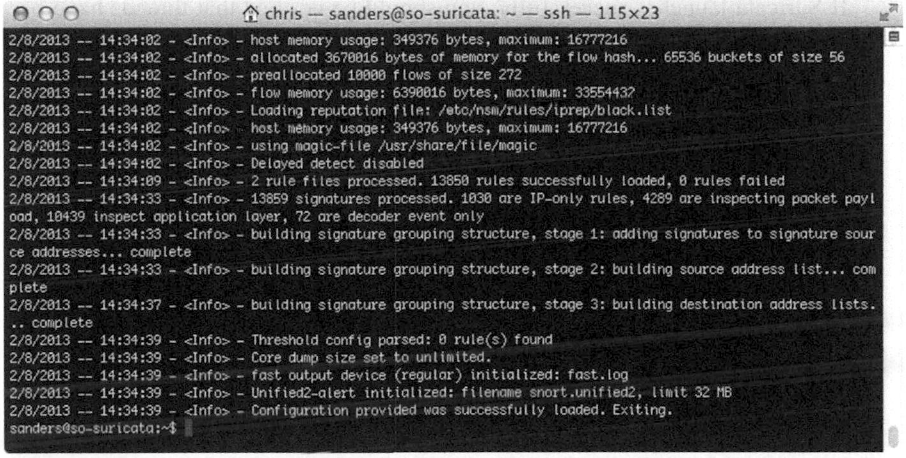

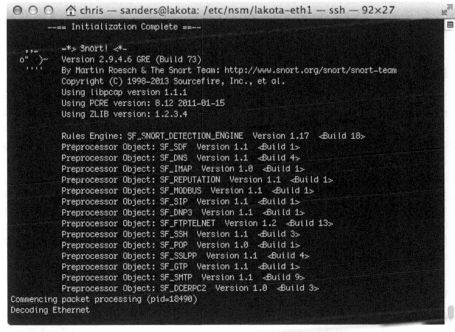

**FIGURE 9.10**

Suricata Successfully Testing a Configuration File in its Default Runmode

If Snort launches in NIDS mode successfully, you should be notified that Snort is commencing packet processing, and be provided with the process ID (PID) number, as shown in Figure 9.11.

**FIGURE 9.11**

Successfully Launching Snort in NIDS Mode

If Suricata launches successfully, you should be notified that threads have been initialized, and that the engine has been started, as shown in Figure 9.12.

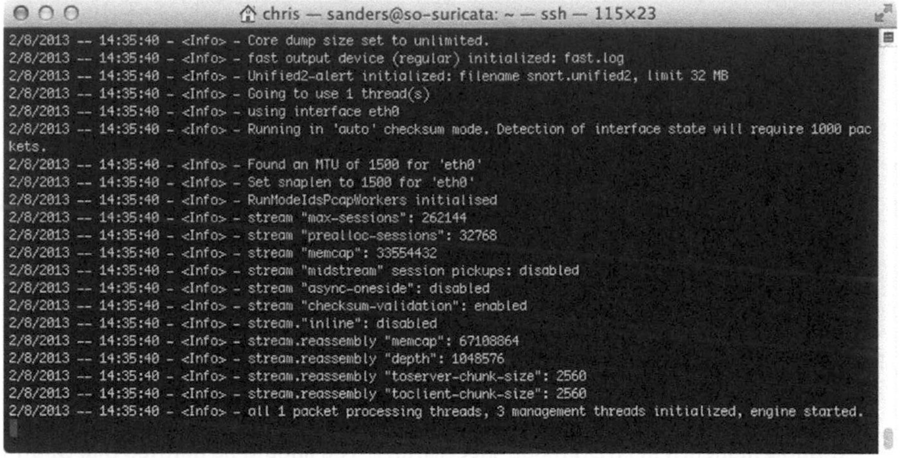

**FIGURE 9.12**

Successfully Launching Suricata in Default Runmode

In Security Onion, Snort and Suricata can be started by using the nsm_sensor_ ps-start script, which is described in Appendix 1.

## CONFIGURING SNORT AND SURICATA

Snort and Suricata both rely upon configuration files and/or command line arguments to control how they function. Snort uses a file called snort.conf, and Suricata uses one called suricata.yaml. These files can be used to control and tweak virtually every behavior in both applications, including the particulars of their detection engines, the location of rule files, and the declaration of variables used within those rules. If you are using Security Onion, these files are located in /etc/nsm/<sensor-interface>/. If you are responsible for managing a Snort or Suricata installation, or simply want to know more about how these tools function, you should take some time and step through the configuration files. They are commented incredibly well. Next, we will start stepping through some common configuration items that are applicable to both tools.

### Variables

In computing, variables are symbolic names that reference a stored value. Snort and Suricata both use variables within their respective configurations to add flexibility to

IDS rules and to ease their creation and maintenance. Snort also uses variables within its configuration file to reference common paths. A variable only has to be specified once so that it is loaded when Snort is executed, and then it can be referenced at any time within the configuration file or within Snort rules. There are three different types of variables used in this context: IP variables, port variables, and standard variables.

## IP Variables

IP variables are used to define network addresses or a range of addresses for use in IDS rules when referring to the source or destination of traffic being examined. By using variables to specify frequently referenced IP ranges, you only have to update the variable once to apply the change to any rule referencing that range.

With Snort, an IP variable is identified in snort.conf by the ipvar keyword, followed by the variable name and the IP address(es) that comprise the variable. For instance, you could specify the following variable to identify a DNS server on your network:

```
ipvar DNS_SERVERS 192.168.1.10
```

You can specify multiple IP addresses by enclosing the addresses in square brackets and separating them with commas. Here, we do this to identify several SMTP mail servers:

```
ipvar SMTP_SERVERS [192.168.1.75,192.168.1.76,192.168.1.77]
```

You can specify ranges of addresses using CIDR notation. These ranges can be combined in comma-separated lists, which must be enclosed in square brackets. Below, we identify two subnets that contain only web servers:

```
ipvar HTTP_SERVERS [192.168.2.0/24,192.168.12.0/24]
```

Suricata doesn't use a particular keyword to identify variables; instead, it requires that variables of particular types be defined in specific sections of suricata.yaml. Specifically, you must define all variables under the vars heading, and IP variables under the address-groups subheading. Apart from this, the same rules mentioned above regarding the formatting of addresses and the use of CIDR notation apply:

```
vars:
    address-groups:
    DNS_SERVERS 192.168.1.10
    SMTP_SERVERS [192.168.1.75,192.168.1.76,192.168.1.77]
    HTTP_SERVERS [192.168.2.0/24,192.168.12.0/24]
```

In order to use an IP variable in a rule you must refer to it with the dollar sign ($) followed by the variable name. In the case of the below rule, both the

$SMTP_SERVERS and $EXTERNAL_NET variables are used to attempt to detect SMTP AUTH LOGON brute forcing.

```
alert tcp $SMTP_SERVERS 25 - > $EXTERNAL_NET any (msg: "GPL SMTP AUTH LOGON
brute force attempt"; flow:from_server,established; content: "Authen-
tication unsuccessful"; offset:54; nocase; threshold:type threshold,
track by_dst, count 5, seconds 60; classtype:suspicious-login;
sid:2102275; rev:3;)
```

The two most important network variables are $HOME_NET and $EXTERNAL_NET.

The $HOME_NET variable is used to identify IP address ranges that Snort/Suricata is responsible for protecting. This will often be configured for internally used RFC1918 (non-routable) IP addresses, such as 10.0.0.0/8, 172.16.0.0/12, or 192.168.0.0/16m and will vary based upon the placement and visibility of the sensor.

A common $HOME_NET declaration may look like this:
Snort:

```
ipvar HOME_NET [192.168.0.0/16,10.0.0.0/8,172.16.0.0/12]
```

Suricata:

```
vars:
    address-groups:
    HOME_NET [192.168.0.0/16,10.0.0.0/8,172.16.0.0/12]
```

The $EXTERNAL_NET variable is used to identify IP address ranges that are not being protected by Snort/Suricata. This often includes any address range that doesn't belong to the organization and is considered exterior to the network perimeter. As you might imagine, this will generally include anything that is NOT a part of $HOME_NET. As such, it is common to set this variable to !$HOME_NET. The exclamation point can be used within a variable to negate the value specified. It is also quite common for this variable to be set to "any", which encompasses all IP addresses.

Snort:

```
ipvar EXTERNAL_NET !$HOME_NET
```

Suricata:

```
vars:
    address-groups:
    EXTERNAL_NET !$HOME_NET
```

The $HOME_NET and $EXTERNAL_NET network variables are required for Snort and Suricata, and most publicly available rules are written to use these values. The remainder of the network variables you will find already listed in snort.conf and suricata.yaml are optional, but are highly recommended as they allow for increased flexibility and granularity when writing rules. In addition, the public rule sets we will talk about later all make use of these variables. Some of them include:

- $HTTP_SERVERS – Useful for creating and deploying rules related to server-side or client-side web exploitation.
- $DNS_SERVERS – Useful for creating and deploying rules related to domain reputation or malware command and control.
- $SMTP_SERVERS – Useful for creating and deploying rules related to mail spam or malicious attachments.
- $SSH_SERVERS – Useful for logging activity related to the management of switches, routers, and other network devices over the SSH protocol.

You can also create your own variables using this syntax. This can be a useful tactic for grouping all sorts of devices, including:

- Mission Critical Systems
- VoIP Phones
- Printers
- Network-aware Televisions and Projectors
- Administrative Workstations
- Sensors

The possibilities are endless, and the more precise your groups are, the more flexibility you have when creating rules.

> **CAUTION**
>
> Be careful to fully evaluate each variable when using them to explicitly define things. For instance, it is easy to miss devices like printers and scanners that might contain built-in web servers when configuring the HTTP_SERVERS variable.

### Port Variables

Port variables define a layer four port or port range for use in IDS rules when referring to the source or destination ports of traffic being examined.

With Snort, these variables are created using the portvar keyword in snort.conf. This example is used to specify a single port that would be used by the SMTP service:

```
portvar SMTP_PORTS 25
```

You can specify a range of ports by using a semicolon in between the start and end of the range. This example identifies two ports that are commonly used by the FTP service:

```
portvar FTP_PORTS 20:21
```

When necessary, a list of ports can be declared using the same format as with IP variables, a comma-separated list surrounded by square brackets. Here we declare several ports that might be used for HTTP communication:

```
portvar  HTTP_PORTS  [80,81,82,83,84,85,86,87,88,89,311,383,591,593,
631,901,1220,1414,1741,1830,2301,2381,2809,3037,3057,3128,3702,4343,
```

```
4848,5250,6080,6988,7000,7001,7144,7145,7510,7777,7779,8000,8008,
8014,8028,
8080,8085,8088,8090,8118,8123,8180,8181,8222,8243,8280,8300,8500,
8800,8888,8899,9000,9060,9080,9090,9091,9443,9999,10000,11371,
34443,34444,41080,50002,55555]
```

Port variables are useful when writing rules for communication with a service that doesn't always use an expected port. For instance, while HTTP communication typically occurs over port 80, several web servers (especially those used for the management of specialized applications or devices) will use non-standard ports. Port variables can also come in handy if these services within your network are configured to use non-standard ports. This is a common practice for administrative protocols like SSH, where administrators will use something other than default port 22 to prevent automated scans from finding these services.

### Standard Variables

Standard variables are the last variable type that you will encounter, and they are only used by Snort. These variables are created by using the var keyword, and are typically used to specify directories. The default snort.conf file uses these frequently; for example, to specify the directories containing different types of Snort rules:

```
var RULE_PATH /etc/nsm/rules
var SO_RULE_PATH /etc/nsm/rules
var PREPROC_RULE_PATH /etc/nsm/rules
```

The majority of these variable declarations can be found in the first section of snort.conf. If you are going to create custom variables and you want to place them into snort.conf instead of including a separate file, it is a good practice to place those variables in this section so that you don't lose track of them.

## Defining Rule Sets

For Snort or Suricata to inspect network traffic for indicators of compromise, you must have rules in place. Snort and Suricata rules are platform-specific methods of implementing indicators of compromise. The rules essentially tell their detection engines how to locate the indicator within network traffic.

Rules exist in rule files, which are simply text files that contain rules in a line-delimited format. In order for Snort or Suricata to parse these rules, they must be included in their respective configuration files.

### Defining Snort Rule Files

In snort.conf, the last section of the configuration file is where rule declarations are usually made. You must specify a rule directory, typically done by using the include keyword, followed by the path and file name of the rule file. Typically, the rule path is specified using the $RULE_PATH variable, which is defined in the first section of snort.conf.

```
include $RULE_PATH/emerging-exploit.rules
```

> **FROM THE TRENCHES**
>
> Instead of constantly adding and removing rule file references in snort.conf, you can comment out a rule file you aren't using by appending the pound symbol (#) to the beginning of the line. Snort will not parse any line that begins with the pound symbol. This is useful for both temporarily disregarding individual's configuration lines, or for adding comment. The same principal applies to suricata.yaml.

Snort also allows for the use of non-standard rule types. These are:

- Preprocessor Rules: These rules are dependent upon functionality provided by preprocessors, and are parsed prior to rules parsed by the detection engine.
- Shared Object Rules: These rules are compiled rather than being interpreted from a line of text. They are useful for the creation of very advanced rules, or deploying rules without divulging the details of the indicators in the rule itself.

These rules may be located in different locations, so they have their own rule path variables. Rule files can be included using these variables:

```
include $PREPROC_RULE_PATH/preproc.rules
include $SO_RULE_PATH/sharedobj.rules
```

Snort loads its rules at initialization, but you can force a configuration update without completely restarting Snort. This is advantageous, because it means that you don't have to disable your detection for a few seconds every time you make a rule change. This assumes that Snort is compiled with the -enable-reload option. To perform a live reload, complete the following steps:

1. Find the process ID of the running Snort process. To list this process, use the ps command to list running processes and use grep to search for the Snort process:

```
ps aux | grep snort.conf
```

In this case, the process ID is 22859, shown in Figure 9.13:

**FIGURE 9.13**

Finding the Process ID of the Running Suricata Process

2. Finally, send a SIGHUP kill signal to the process to initiate a live rule reload. In this example, the command would be:

```
sudo kill -SIGHUP 22859
```

3. Snort should restart and parse the updated snort.conf file and the associated rules. Keep in mind that some configuration options are not supported by live reload. Those are listed here: http://manual.snort.org/node24.html.

### Defining Suricata Rule Files

With Suricata, rule files are identified by placing them into the appropriate section of suricata.yaml. To do this, the default rule path must be specified, then the rule files can be listed under the rule-files heading, with each file identified on a new line with a hyphen.

```
default-rule-path: /etc/nsm/rules/
    rule-files:
     - local.rules
     - downloaded.rules
```

Like Snort, Suricata does not have to be reloaded in order for new rules to take effect. The following steps will allow you to force rule additions, deletions, or modifications without restarting Suricata:

1. First, ensure that live rule reloads are enabled in Suricata.yaml:

```
# When rule-reload is enabled, sending a USR2 signal to the Suricata
process will trigger a live rule reload. Experimental feature, use with
care.
  - rule-reload: true
```

2. Next, find the process ID of the running Suricata process. In order to list this process, use the ps command to list running processes and use grep to search for the Suricata process:

```
ps aux | grep suricata.yaml
```

In this case, let's assume the process ID is 30577.

3. Finally, send a USR2 kill signal to the process to initiate a live rule reload. In this example, the command would be:

```
sudo kill –USR2 30577
```

This log output of this action is shown in Figure 9.14:

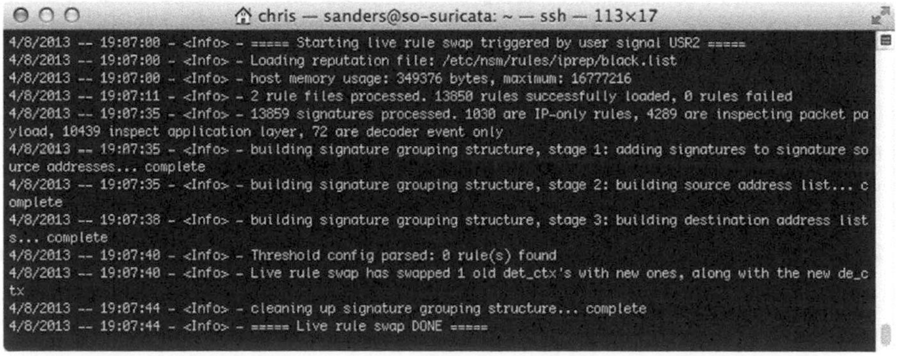

**FIGURE 9.14**

Forcing Suricata to Reload Rules with a USR2 Kill Signal

### Public Rule Sources

Rules can be created manually, shared between organizations, or retrieved from public sources. Building custom rules will be examined later in this chapter, but before that, there are two primary sources for Snort and Suricata rules that must be examined: Emerging Threats and the Sourcefire VRT.

Emerging Threats (ET), originally called Bleeding Snort, was originally launched in 2003 by Matt Jonkman, and was designed to serve as an open-source community for sharing IDS signatures. ET fostered the development of a large and active signature development community, and eventually received several grants that helped further their cause.

Now, the ET community is as strong as ever and provides rule sets for both Snort and Suricata. These come in the form of a free open rule set that is community-driven and maintained, and a paid subscription based "ETPro" rule set that is maintained by the Emerging Threats research team. You can read more about the ET rule set at http://www.emergingthreats.net/open-source/etopen-ruleset/. The ET team also has a blog that provides rule update notifications at http://www.emergingthreats.net/blog/.

The Sourcefire Vulnerability Research Team (VRT), from the same company that created Snort, is an elite team of security researchers who work proactively to develop detection capabilities for trending attack techniques, malware, and vulnerabilities. The VRT employs some very talented individuals, and they are responsible for the development and maintenance of rules in the official Snort.org rule set.

There are three official Snort rule sets. The VRT rule set is their premium offering. It requires a paid subscription, but provides immediate access to all VRT developed rules when they are released. Next is the Registered User release, which requires free registration on the snort.org website and provides access to VRT developed rules thirty days after they have been released. The third and final offering is the community rule set, which is a freely distributed subset of the subscriber rule set. The community rule set doesn't require registration, and is updated daily. All rules released in this rule set are licensed via GPLv2.

While the Sourcefire VRT doesn't provide a Suricata specific rule set, some of their rules will work with Suricata. However, Suricata doesn't support many of the rule options that are provided by Snort preprocessors. Therefore, if you are a Suricata user and would like to use VRT rules, it is recommended that you choose individual rules and test them with Suricata rather than attempting to implement the entire VRT rule set. By using this method, you can modify rules to work on a case-by-case basis.

You can download Snort VRT rules at http://www.snort.org/snort-rules/. You can also find the very informative VRT blog at http://vrt-blog.snort.org/, as well as find out about rule updates and the latest news for the ruleset at http://blog.snort.org.

### Managing Rule Updates with PulledPork

Both Emerging Threats and the Sourcefire VRT release new rules nearly every day. The task of checking for new rule updates, downloading those updates, placing them in the appropriate directory, and ensuring that they are put into production can be very tedious if done manually.

PulledPork was created to automate this process, and it can be used to ensure that your rules stay up to date. It provides a variety of features that make it useful for a number of scenarios. Among these, it provides mechanisms for downloading rule updates, the ability to manage and distribute custom rule files, and the ability to track rule changes. The configuration of PulledPork is beyond the scope of this book, but you can read more about it at https://code.google.com/p/pulledpork/.

### Managing Rules in Security Onion

By default, rules in Security Onion are placed in /etc/nsm/rules/. Rules that are downloaded from publicly available sources such as the Sourcefire VRT or Emerging Threats are placed into the downloaded.rules file, and custom created rules should be placed into the local.rules file. Additional rule files can be used, but they must first be specified in snort.conf or suricata.yaml.

If you are using Security Onion as your NSM platform, you should avoid updating your rules using the methods mentioned in the previous sections, and instead use the rule-update script. This script performs additional tasks required by other tools such as Barnyard2 and PulledPork. The script is run like this:

```
sudo rule-update
```

An excerpt of the output from the rule-update script is shown in Figure 9.15.

**FIGURE 9.15**

Running the Security Onion rule-update Script

There are two files that are especially important for the maintenance of rules in Security Onion: disablesid.conf and modifysid.conf. These files are part of Pulled-Pork and are used in the same way described in this chapter, even if you aren't running Security Onion.

The disablesid.conf file is used to persistently disable rules that you do not wish to use. This is especially important when interacting with publicly obtained rules because of their constant updates. As an example, let's say that you want to disable a rule that is identified by SID 12345. Your first inclination might be to either delete the rule from the rule file, or to disable it by commenting it out with a pound sign. This might work initially, but when PulledPork runs later that night and downloads a new rule update from Emerging Threats or Sourcefire, the rule that was deleted or disabled will be restored and put back into production. Because of this, the more appropriate way to disable rules is to use disablesid.conf. Whenever PulledPork downloads a new rule update, it parses this file so that it can go back and re-disable any rule that shouldn't be turned on. Entries are stored in this file with the format GID:SID. In this case, we can add the following entry to disablesid.conf to persistently disable this rule:

```
1:12345
```

The modifysid.conf file is used to persistently modify rules that are obtained from public sources. Just as with deleted rules, if we were to modify a rule obtained from a public source, the nightly PulledPork update would serve to replace that rule file and eliminate any changes that were made. Because of this, PulledPork parses modifysid. conf after every rule update so that it can go back and apply modifications to rules that have been customized.

As an example, let's modify the following rule:

```
alert ip any any ->any any (msg:"GPL ATTACK_RESPONSE id check returned
root"; content:"uid=0|28|root|29|"; fast_pattern:only; classtype:
bad-unknown; sid:2100498; rev:8;)
```

To modify this rule, we need to add an entry to modifysid.conf that specifies the SID of the rule we are modifying, the content we would like to change, and what we want the content changed to. In this case, we will replace "alert ip any any" with "alert ip $HOME_NET any". This will modify the signature so that it only alerts when the specified pattern occurs within traffic that is coming from an IP address that is external to the network the sensor is protecting. In order to make this change, we would add the following entry to modifysid.conf:

```
2100498 "alert ip any any" "alert ip $HOME_NET any"
```

Both disablesid.conf and modifysid.conf come with several examples listed in the respective files. You can read some more SO-specific examples here: https://code. google.com/p/security-onion/wiki/ManagingAlerts.

## Alert Output

Snort and Suricata both provide a lot of flexibility in how alert data can be output for analysis, which is useful for adapting them to a variety of scenarios.

In Snort, alert output is controlled in the output plugin section of snort.conf. To specify a particular output plugin you can use the output keyword, followed by the name of the plugin. This can be followed by any options required by the output plugin.

```
output <plugin name>: <options>
```

If it is not specified at runtime with the –l argument, Snort's default log directory is set to /var/log/snort.

In Suricata, alert output is controlled in the outputs section of Suricata.yaml. Underneath the outputs heading, each output option is listed, along with each one's relevant options.

```
outputs:
    -  <output type>:
        <options>
```

If it is not specified at runtime with the –l argument, Suricata's default log directory is set to /var/log/suricata.

---

**ANALYST NOTE**

Snort and Suricata allow for multiple output plugins to be used at once. When multiple plugins are used, they are called in order based upon how they are organized in snort.conf and suricata.yaml.

---

Now we will look at some of the more commonly used outputs. Remember, there are a lot more output options than those mentioned here, so if you are looking for something particular, refer to the Snort or Suricata documentation because it might already be available to you. For the alerting examples shown below, I visited http://www.testmyids.com in order to generate an alert based upon the rule identified by SID 2100498:

```
alert ip any any ->any any (msg:"GPL ATTACK_RESPONSE id check returned
root"; content:"uid=0|28|root|29|"; fast_pattern:only; classtype:
bad-unknown; sid:2100498; rev:8;)
```

### Fast

The fast alerting format will display alerts in a very simple one-line format. This is the most compact alerting format, and is easy for an analyst to digest visually from the command line. It provides the minimum amount of information needed to start reviewing data associated with the alert.

```
08/05-15:58:54.524545 [**] [1:2100498:8] GPL ATTACK_RESPONSE id check
returned root [**] [Classification: Potentially Bad Traffic] [Priority:
2] {TCP} 217.160.51.31:80 ->172.16.16.20:52316
```

### Full

The full alerting formatting will display everything that is shown in a fast alert, along with additional details from the packet header of the packet that generated the alert. This alerting format generates multi-line alerts, so it may not be as easy to parse with command line tools.

```
[**] [1:2100498:8] GPL ATTACK_RESPONSE id check returned root [**]
[Classification: Potentially Bad Traffic] [Priority: 2]
```

```
08/05-15:58:54.524545 217.160.51.31:80 ->172.16.16.20:52316
TCP TTL:40 TOS:0x20 ID:44920 IpLen:20 DgmLen:299 DF
***AP*** Seq: 0x6BD4465B Ack: 0xE811E4E6 Win: 0x36 TcpLen: 20
```

## Syslog

The syslog alerting format is designed to be sent to a syslog server that can either be running locally on the sensor, or on another device. Syslog is a very common logging format, thus it is supported by a wide variety of devices and can be digested by most log management and analysis tools. Syslog output is stored on a single line, and is easily searchable from a command line interface. The amount of information provided in this output is identical to the fast alerting format.

```
Aug 5 15:58:54 lakota snort: [1:2100498:8] GPL ATTACK_RESPONSE id check
returned root [Classification: Potentially Bad Traffic] [Priority: 2]:
{TCP} 217.160.51.31:80 ->172.16.16.20:52316
```

## Packet Logging

While text-based alerts are a great place to start, you will likely want to manually inspect the packet(s) that cause an alert to be generated. If you are utilizing a full packet capture solution like we discussed in Chapter 5, then that is probably where you will look. If not, you can also configure Snort and Suricata to log the packet(s) that generated the alert in PCAP format. The packet that generated the sample alert we have been working with is shown in Figure 9.16.

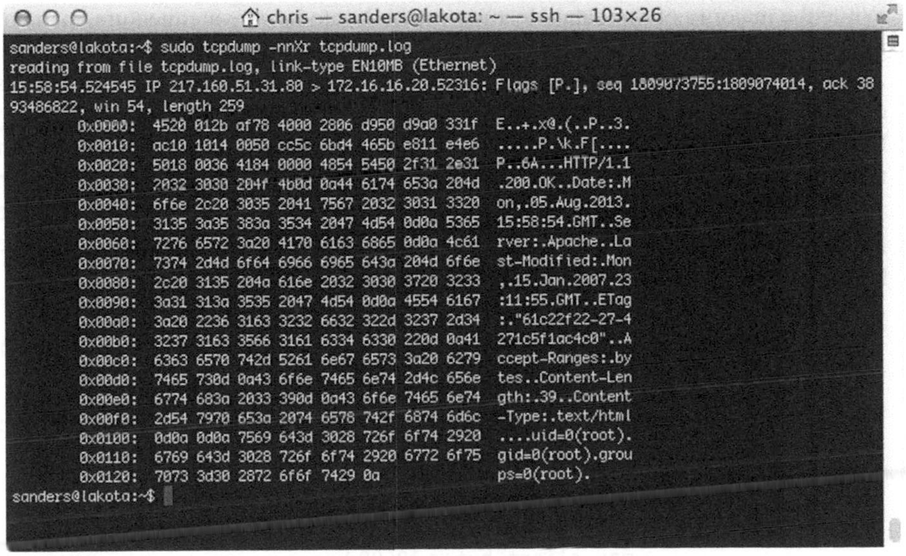

**FIGURE 9.16**

Packets Matching Rule SID 2100498

### *Unified2*

In an enterprise environment, the most commonly used log format is Unified2. This is a binary format capable of storing both the alert data and the packet data associated with it. If you attempt to examine one of these files manually you will find it isn't readable as it is stored. Unified2 output isn't designed to be read manually or via command line tools, but rather, it is meant to be used in conjunction with tools like Barnyard2 or Pigsty. These tools are used for interpreting Unified2 output and placing that alert data into a database, such a MySQL or Postgres SQL database. Snort also includes a tool called u2spewfoo that is able to read the unified2 format and dump it out on the command line.

Barnyard2 is the de facto standard tool for storing Unified2 alerts in database format for years, and works well. It also supports several other output modes. You can read more about Barnyard2 at https://github.com/firnsy/barnyard2.

Pigsty is a newer tool developed by the folks at Threat Stack, who brought us Snorby, which is discussed later in this chapter. Pigsty was written to achieve the same goals as Barnyard2, but in a more extensible way. It provides the ability to create custom output plugins to add even more flexibility to the wide array of output options for Snort and Suricata alert data. Along with database output plugins, Pigsty also supports other methods of output such as Websockets, Sguild, IRC, and REST output. You can read more about Pigsty at https://github.com/threatstack/pigsty.

If you'd like more information regarding the configuration of alert output, check out the appropriate sections of the Snort and Suricata online documentation.

## Snort Preprocessors

While the majority of Suricata's features are built into its core architecture, many of the features provided by Snort are made available by using individual preprocessors. As we discussed earlier when overviewing the Snort architecture, preprocessors come in two types and can be used for further normalizing data before it is parsed by the detection engine, or they can be used to provide additional flexibility for Snort rules used by the detection engine. Both types of preprocessors can be configured in snort.conf. A preprocessor is identified by the preprocessor keyword, followed by the preprocessor name and then its associated options. Some preprocessors, like the portscan detection preprocessor, only have a few configurable options.

```
# Portscan detection. For more information, see README.sfportscan
# preprocessor sfportscan: proto { all } memcap { 10000000 } sense_level
{ low }
```

Others, such as the SSH anomaly detection preprocessor, have several options:

```
# SSH anomaly detection. For more information, see README.ssh
preprocessor ssh: server_ports { 22 } \
                autodetect \
                max_client_bytes 19600 \
```

```
max_encrypted_packets 20 \
max_server_version_len 100 \
enable_respoverflow enable_ssh1crc32 \
enable_srvoverflow enable_protomismatch
```

It is important to realize that the preprocessors listed in the configuration file are executed in order. Because of this, they are ordered in accordance with the network layer they are associated with. Network layer preprocessors such as frag3, which deals with IP fragment assembly, come first. This is followed by transport layer protocols such as Stream 5, which handles TCP stream reassembly. This is followed by application layer preprocessors such as the SSH, HTTP, and SMTP anomaly detectors. This order is critical because application layer preprocessors might be unable to process data if it is fragmented, out of sequence, or received in an otherwise unexpected state.

When you begin using Snort, you likely won't take advantage of too many preprocessors, and you might not be aware of the ones you are using. However, you should definitely make the time to review all of the preprocessors listed in snort.conf and read the associated README files. There are several that will come in handy, and some that are completely necessary. You might even find yourself attempting to write complex rules that a preprocessor will make much simpler. A few of these include:

- Reputation: Used to do reputation-based detection and blocking of communication with certain IP addresses (we looked at this in Chapter 8).
- ARPSpoof: Designed to be able to detect the occurrence of ARP spoofing.
- SFportscan: Detects potential reconnaissance scans.
- Frag3: Performs defragmentation of IP packets and helps prevent IDS evasion.
- Stream5: Allows for state tracking of TCP connections and the creation of stateful rules.
- HTTP_Inspect: Normalizes HTTP traffic so that it can be properly parsed by the detection engine. Provides several directives that can be used within Snort rules.

You can learn more about each of Snort's preprocessors in the "Preprocessors" section of the Snort Users Guide, or by reviewing the README files for each preprocessor in the documentation included with Snort.

## Additional NIDS Mode Command Line Arguments

While most options can be configured in snort.conf and suricata.yaml, any options that are specified as command line arguments will be given preference over what is specified in the configuration files. It is common to execute Snort and Suricata with several of these arguments.

If you are using Security Onion, you can see an example of command line arguments being used by listing the running IDS engine process. In the case of Figure 9.17, we can see that Snort is running.

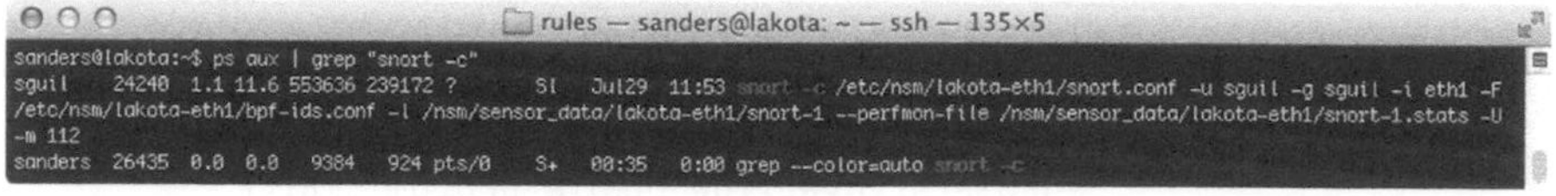

**FIGURE 9.17**

Snort Running with Command Line Options

Here we see several commonly used command line arguments for Snort. These, along with some other commonly used arguments are:

- -A < mode >: Specifies the level of alerting for plain text alerts. This can be set to fast, full, unsock, console, cmg, or none.
- -c < file >: Used to specify the path to the snort.conf configuration file used for NIDS mode.
- -D: Executes Snort as a daemon (in the background)
- -F < file >: Read Berkeley Packet Filters from a file. BPF's are discussed in depth in Chapter 13.
- -g < group >: Specifies the group Snort runs under after it has initialized. This can be used to allow Snort to drop root privileges after initializing.
- -i < interface >: Specifies a specific interface to use for monitoring traffic
- -l < directory >: Used to specify an output directory for text reporting of alerts.
- -L < directory >: Used to specify an output directory for binary reporting of alerts.
- -m < umask >: Forces the creation of new files to the specified umask permissions
- -u < user >: Specifies the user Snort runs under after it has initialized. This can be used to allow Snort to drop root privileges after initializing.
- -U: Changes the timestamps associated with all logs and alerts to UTC
- -T: Used to test a configuration file
- --perfmon-file < file >: Specifies the file used by the perfmon preprocessor for tracking Snort statistics.

In Figure 9.18, you can see an example of Suricata running with several command line arguments in Security Onion.

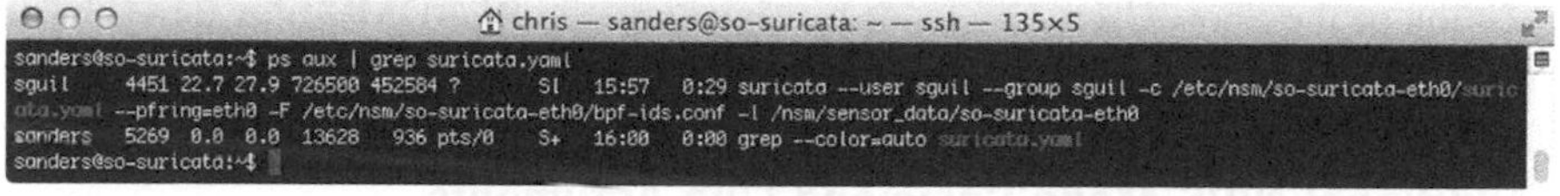

**FIGURE 9.18**

Suricata Running with Command Line Arguments

The command line arguments shown above, along with some other commonly used arguments are:

- -c < file >: Used to specify the path to the suricata.yaml configuration file
- -D: Executes Suricata as a daemon (in the background)

- --group < group >: Specifies the group Suricata runs under after it has initialized. This can be used to allow Suricata to drop root privileges after initializing.
- -F < file >: Read Berkeley Packet Filters from a file. BPF's are discussed in depth in Chapter 13.
- -i < interface >: Specifies a specific interface to use for monitoring traffic
- -l < directory >: Used to specify the default logging directory.
- -r < pcap file >: Parse a PCAP file in offline mode
- --runmode < mode id >: The ID of the runmode that Suricata will be initialized in.
- -s: Used to manually specify a file containing IDS signatures along with those specified in suricata.yaml.
- -T: Used to test a configuration file
- --user < user >: Specifies the user Suricata runs under after it has initialized. This can be used to allow Suricata to drop root privileges after initializing.

There are several other command line arguments that are available when initializing Snort and Suricata. You can view a full list of these options in each tool's respective manual pages, accessible by typing either `man snort` or `man suricata` at the command line of a system where the tools are installed.

## IDS RULES

We have already looked at how rules can be provided to Snort and Suricata, as well as some public rule sources and mechanisms for keeping those rules up to date. While these things are important, the primary interaction that an analyst will have with Snort or Suricata on a daily basis is the creation of new rules, and the modification of existing rules to make those rules more efficient, also referred to as "tuning". In this section we will look at how rules are built, some common rule options, and step through some practical rule creation scenarios.

The majority of the content in this section will apply to both Snort and Suricata rules, as they use the same basic syntax. Whenever a rule option is used that doesn't work with one of these technologies, I will explicitly say so.

### Rule Anatomy

The syntax used by Snort and Suricata rules is incredibly flexible, but it does require that certain conventions be followed. This is an example of a very simple rule:

```
alert tcp $EXTERNAL_NET 80 - >$HOME_NET any (msg:"Users Downloading
Evil); content:"evil"; sid:55555555; rev:1;)
```

This rule is very rudimentary, and would generate an alert if a user on your internal network downloaded data from a web server that contains the word "evil." Of course, detecting when users download evil things from the Internet isn't entirely that easy!

Before examining each specific component of this rule, you should recognize that rules have two distinct parts: the rule header and the rule options. The rule header is everything occurring before the parenthesis, and the rule options are everything occurring within the parenthesis. This breakdown is shown in figure 9.19.

alert tcp $EXTERNAL_NET 80 -> $HOME_NET any (content:"evil"; sid:55555555; rev:1;)

Rule Header                                    Rule Options

**FIGURE 9.19**

Basic Rule Anatomy

### *Rule Header*

The rule header is always the first portion of the rule and it is a required component of the rule. The header is responsible for defining "who" is involved in the traffic pattern than is attempting to be matched. Everything defined in the rule header can be found within the header of a packet, which is crucial in the parsing of these rules. The breakdown of the rule header is shown in Figure 9.20.

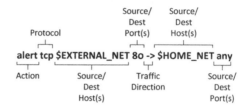

**FIGURE 9.20**

The IDS Rule Header

The rule header always consists of the same parts: rule action, protocol, source/dest hosts, source/dest ports, and the direction of the traffic.

### Rule Action

The first part of any rule is the action declaration which tells the IDS engine what to do when the alert fires. There are three possible actions:

- Alert: Tells the IDS engine to log the rule match, and the packet data associated with the match. This is the most common rule action.
- Log: Tells the IDS engine to log the rule match, but not the packet data associated with the match.
- Pass: Tells the IDS engine to do no further processing of the packet.

### Protocol

This field tells the IDS engine what protocol the rule will apply to. Valid options include tcp, idp, icmp, ip, and any. Note that only one of these can be selected, so if you wish to write a rule that applies to both TCP and UDP traffic, use the IP protocol option in the rule header. For the sake of performance, try to be specific to the traffic pattern you are attempting to match. In the sample rule, we are concerned about HTTP traffic, which sits on top of the TCP protocol, so that is what is specified.

### Source and Destination Hosts

In order to create a rule, you can specify the source and destination host for the traffic pattern you are trying to match. These hosts must be specified as IP addresses, which can be done in a variety of formats such as in lists or CIDR ranges, as was discussed earlier when discussing Snort and Suricata configuration. In the example rule we are working with, you will see that we opted to use the $HOME_NET and $EXTERNAL_NET variables to define IP addresses in this rule. If the rule cannot be limited to any particular grouping of hosts, the keyword "any" can be used to match any hosts.

### Source and Destination Ports

Along with specifying the hosts that we are concerned with matching our rule, we can also specify specific layer four ports. Remember, these can be specified as individual ports, lists, or ranges as we looked at earlier in this chapter. In cases when no specific ports are applicable, the keyword "any" can be used to match any ports. In the example rule, we have specified port 80 in association with the $EXTERNAL_NET IP variable and the any keyword with the $HOME_NEY IP variable.

### Traffic Direction

The final piece of the puzzle when creating a rule header is to specify the destination of the traffic. There are only two possible options here:

- ->: Defines unidirectional source to destination traffic
- <>: Defines bidirectional traffic

Because there are only two options here, when writing rules you must decide if the direction of the communication matters. If the direction of the communication doesn't matter, then the ordering of the source and destination hosts and port numbers in the header doesn't matter. However, if the direction does matter, then the source host and port number should be listed first.

In the case of the rule header shown in our sample rule, we are concerned about users downloading evil from an external web server. This means that the potential sources of the evil packets are external web servers, and the destination is one of our internal hosts. Therefore, the external hosts and ports are listed first ($EXTERNAL_NET 80), followed by the source to destination direction indicator (->), followed by the internal host and port ($HOME_NET any).

### *Rule Options*

While the rule header section is responsible for the "who", the rule options section is responsible for the "what." This section tells the IDS engine exactly what it is looking for in the packets it is examining, and how to find it. The contents of the rule options section are variable and can include several things, but no matter what you choose to include, the options section must always be enclosed in parenthesis. Within these parentheses, individual options take the form of:

```
<option>: <option values>;
```

The option name and its values are separated by a colon (:) and the option values are terminated with a semicolon (;). If the option values contain spaces, those values must be enclosed in quotes.

In some cases, options won't have values, and are simply invoked like this:

```
<option>;
```

Notice that the option name is terminated with a semicolon. If you fail to include colons or semicolons as required, the IDS engine you are using will fail to initialize when parsing that rule.

> **CAUTION**
>
> Don't forget the semicolon on the last option that is used in the rule options section. This is a common mistake, and it is easy to miss.

Now, we will look at several common rule options.

### Event Information Options

The event information options are used to provide contextual information about a rule. The more verbose you can be with event information, the more effective an analyst will be when investigating data associated with that alert. This includes:

*Message (msg).* Descriptive text associated with the rule. This is commonly thought of as the "name" of the rule, and it is what will be initially displayed to the analyst when they are reviewing alerts generated by an IDS engine. It is a good idea to make these as descriptive as possible. Some examples include:

- ET POLICY Outgoing Basic Auth Base64 HTTP Password detected unencrypted
- OS-WINDOWS SMB NTLM NULL session attempt
- EXPLOIT-KIT Blackholev2 exploit kit jar file downloaded

*Signature Identifier (sid).* Used to uniquely identify rules. Each rule must have a unique SID, which is simply a numeric value. It is important to note that some ranges are considered to be reserved. These are:

- 0-1000000: Reserved for the Sourcefire VRT
- 2000001-2999999: Used by Emerging Threats
- 3000000+: For public use

In order to avoid a conflict, you should use SIDs above 3000000. You should also track and maintain a listing of the local SIDs used on your sensors.

*Revision (rev).* The revision option is used to denote when a rule has been changed. When a new rule is created, it should be assigned rev:1; to indicate that it is the first revision of the rule. Instead of generating a new SID every time a rule is changed, you should retain the same SID and increment the revision number. In the event that Snort or Suricata encounter a duplicate SID, they will utilize the rule with the higher revision number.

**Reference.** The reference keyword provides the ability to link to external information sources to provide additional context to the rule. The most common way to do this is to simply include a reference to a URL, as shown in this rule:

```
alert tcp $HOME_NET any ->$EXTERNAL_NET $HTTP_PORTS (msg:"ET CURRENT
_EVENTS FakeAlert/FraudPack/FakeAV/Guzz/Dload/Vobfus/ZPack HTTP Post
2"; flow:established,to_server; content:"POST"; http_method; con-
tent:"/perce/"; nocase; http_uri; content:"/qwerce.gif"; nocase;
http_uri; content:"data="; nocase; reference:url,threatinfo.trendmi-
cro.com/vinfo/virusencyclo/default5.asp?VName=TROJ_AGENT.
GUZZ&VSect=T;    reference:url,www.threatexpert.com/threats/trojan-
fraudpack-sd6.html; reference:url,vil.nai.com/vil/content/v_157489.
htm; reference:url,doc.emergingthreats.net/2010235; classtype:tro-
jan-activity; sid:2010235; rev:6;)
```

The rule above is used to detect the presence of several pieces of malware that all make a similar type of HTTP POST to a remote server. In this case, the rule references that there are four individual references in the rule:

- reference:url,threatinfo.trendmicro.com/vinfo/virusencyclo/default5.asp? VName=TROJ_AGENT.GUZZ&VSect=T;
- reference:url,www.threatexpert.com/threats/trojan-fraudpack-sd6.html;
- reference:url,vil.nai.com/vil/content/v_157489.htm;
- reference:url,doc.emergingthreats.net/2010235;

Note that references take the following format:

```
reference: <reference name>,<reference>;
```

Reference types are defined in the reference.config file that is used by Snort and Suricata. The name and location of this file is configurable in snort.conf and suricata. yaml. In Security Onion, it is located in /etc/nsm/<sensor name>/reference.config. An example of this file is shown in Figure 9.21.

In reference.config, a reference type is defined with the following syntax:

```
config reference: <reference name><reference prefix>
```

The reference name can be any single word that you would like to use. The reference prefix is used to assign a URL value that will precede whatever is specified as the reference in the rule itself. This is done to keep rules concise, and to provide added flexibility to graphical front ends so that an analyst can click on the reference and be directed to the proper link.

Therefore, when specifying the URL reference:

```
reference:url,vil.nai.com/vil/content/v_157489.htm;
```

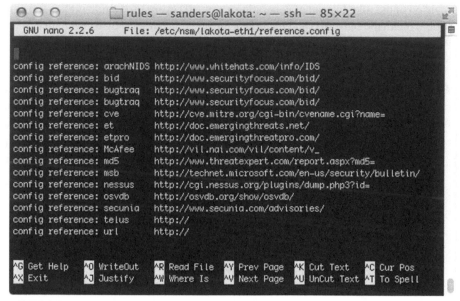

**FIGURE 9.21**

An Example reference.config File

The full reference will actually be:

```
http://url.vil.nai.com/vil/content/v_157489.htm
```

Other reference types utilize this feature more effectively. For example, consider the following rule that is used to detect an NTPDX overflow attempt:

```
alert udp $EXTERNAL_NET any ->$HOME_NET 123 (msg:"GPL EXPLOIT ntpdx
overflow attempt"; dsize:>128; reference:bugtraq,2540; reference:
cve,2001-0414; classtype:attempted-admin; sid:2100312; rev:7;)
```

In this rule, two references are specified; bugtraq and cve. If you examine the reference.config file shown in Figure 9.21, you will see that both of those reference types use special URL prefixes that allow that data to be referenced quickly:

```
config reference: bugtraq http://www.securityfocus.com/bid/
config reference: cve http://cve.mitre.org/cgi-bin/cvename.cgi?name=
```

Using this configuration, the actual reference associated with SID 2100312 would be:

- http://www.securityfocus.com/bid/2540
- http://cve.mitre.org/cgi-bin/cvename.cgi?name=2001-0414

As you can see, the ability to only include the reference name and value can greatly decrease the size of a rule, which makes them easier to edit and manage. The ability to create custom reference types adds quite a bit of flexibility to how you include contextual data with your rules.

***Priority.*** The priority field can be used to manually specify the priority for a rule, which can be used by analysts to help them best use their time when reviewing alerts. This option can be set to any integer value, but most public rule sets will only use a value of 1 through 10, with 1 being the highest priority and 10 being the lowest. The following syntax is used for this option:

```
priority:<value>;
```

If you have assigned a classification to a rule, then that rule will assume whatever default classification is specified for the rule in classification.config, but if you explicitly specify the priority, Snort uses that value instead.

***Classification.*** The classification option is used to assign rules to categories based upon the type of activity they are attempting to detect. The following rule shows the usage of the classification option:

```
alert tcp $HOME_NET any ->$EXTERNAL_NET $HTTP_PORTS (msg:"ET CURRENT_
EVENTS Potential Fast Flux Rogue Antivirus (Setup_245.exe)"; flow:
established,to_server; content:"GET"; nocase; http_method; con-
tent:"/Setup_"; nocase; http_uri; content:".exe"; nocase; http_uri;
pcre:"/\/Setup_\d+\.exe$/Ui"; reference:url,www.malwareurl.com/list
ing.php?domain=antivirus-live21.com;    classtype:trojan-activity;
sid:2012392; rev:3;)
```

Classification must be specified using the following syntax:

```
classtype:<classification name>;
```

Both Snort and Suricata draw classification names from the classification.config file. The name and path to this file is configurable in snort.conf and suricata.yaml. On Security Onion, the file can be found at /etc/nsm/<sensor name>/classification.config.

Entries within this file must use the following format:

```
config    classification:    <classification    name>,<classification
description>,<default priority>
```

The classification name is what is referenced within the rules, and it should be short and contain no spaces. The classification description can be longer and provide more detail related to the classification. The default priority specifies the baseline priority for any rules using this classification name.

Snort and Suricata both ship with some classification types built-in, and when you download rules from a public source such as Sourcefire VRT or Emerging Threats, those downloads will include a classification.config file containing all of the classifications used in the provided rules. Figure 9.22 shows an example classification.config file from Security Onion.

Generally, it is a good idea to strive to classify every rule in some form or another. If you are properly tracking the creation and modification of rules, then you have likely already established some form of classification that you can apply to your IDS rules. If you are just beginning to establish a signature-based detection capability, then the classification types provided by Snort and Suricata are a good starting point.

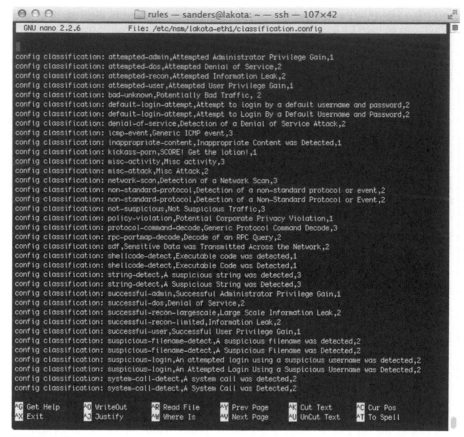

**FIGURE 9.22**

An Example classification.config File

## Content Inspection

The most basic action that can be taken within the options section of an IDS rule is to perform a basic content match. Using the content keyword, you can instruct the IDS engine to examine the application layer content (the payload) of a packet for the data you specify. Chapter 13 will go into detail on how to tell exactly where the payload area of a packet begins. This data can be expressed as text, binary data in hexadecimal format, or a combination of both.

For example, if we wanted to examine the content of a packet for the string "evilliveshere", then we could specify:

```
content:"evilliveshere";
```

You can also specify multiple content matches in a single rule, which will come in handy later when we talk about content modifiers and looking for content in specific places.

```
content:"evillives"; content:"here";
```

Negation can also be used in content matches with the exclamation character (!). For example, the following content matches could be combined to capture all login attempts, except for those associated with the anonymous user account:

```
content:"USER"; content:!"anonymous";
```

Binary data can also be matched by expressing that binary data as hexadecimal characters surrounded by pipe symbols (|). If we wanted to examine packet data for the existence of JPEG files by matching occurrences of the JPEG "magic numbers", we would express, as shown here:

```
content:"|FF D8|";
```

String data and binary data can be combined in content searches. In the following example, we are looking for three colons, followed by the text "evilliveshere", followed by three null bytes:

```
content:" |3A 3A 3A|evilliveshere|00 00 00|";
```

It is important to note that all content matches are case sensitive, and they will match content found anywhere in the packet.

---

**CAUTION**

When creating content rules, be aware that certain characters such as the semicolon, backslash, and quotation mark are reserved characters, and must be escaped or represented in hexadecimal format in order to be used for a content match.

---

## Content Inspection Modifiers

There are several modifiers that can be applied to content matches by placing them after the content being matched. These will allow you to specify exactly how the IDS engine will look for the content matches within network data. These modifiers help increase the accuracy of content matches in your rules, and they also help increase the performance of the detection process within the IDS engine, as they allow the engine to look in a specific location for specified content rather than having to examine the complete payload of every packet.

To apply a content modifier to a content match, it should be placed directly after the content match in the rule. We will look at several of these modifiers now.

***Nocase.*** Content matches are case sensitive by default. Therefore, if you specify a content match for the text "root" and a packet contains the string "ROOT", an alert will not be generated. To signify a content match as case insensitive, you can use the nocase modifier, like so:

```
content:"root"; nocase;
```

This content match will match any capitalization of the word "root."

***Offset and Depth.*** The offset modifier is used to match content occurring at a specific position with a packets payload, starting at the first byte of the payload. Note that the payload begins at byte 0, rather than byte 1. Therefore, if you specify offset 0, the detection engine will look for the content to start at the beginning of the payload. If you specify an offset of 1, the detection engine will look for the content to start at the second byte of the payload.

As an example, let's examine the following FTP packet:

```
14:51:44.824713 IP 172.16.16.139.57517 > 67.205.2.30.21: Flags [P.],
seq 1:15, ack 27, win 16421, length 14
        0x0000: 4510 0036 efe4 4000 4006 4847 ac10 108b  E..6..@.@.HG....
        0x0010: 43cd 021e e0ad 0015 0bcb 6f30 fcb2 e53c  C.........o0...<
        0x0020: 5018 4025 2efb 0000 5553 4552 2073 616e  P.@%....USER.san
        0x0030: 6465 7273 0d0a                           ders..
```

If we wanted to write a content matching rule that detected any time a user attempted to login to this external FTP server with this username, we could start with a rule like this:

```
alert tcp $HOME_NET any - >67.205.2.30 21 (msg:"Suspicious FTP Login";
content:"sanders"; sid:5000000; rev:1;)
```

This rule would definitely generate an alert for the given packet, but it is also prone to false positives. For instance, if someone were to login to another account on that FTP server and browse to a folder named "sanders", that would also generate an alert.

We can narrow the scope of this rule by specifying the offset where the username appears in the payload of the packet. In this case, the first byte of the packet payload is 0x55. The first character of the actual username appears at offset 5 (0x73). Don't forget, we are counting starting from zero. With this in mind, we can rewrite the rule to begin matching that content string at that offset:

```
alert tcp $HOME_NET any - >67.205.2.30 21 (msg:"Suspicious FTP Login"
content:"sanders"; offset:5; sid:5000000; rev:1;)
```

Not only will this rule yield less false positives, but it will also perform faster as it limits the number of bytes that the IDS engine must examine.

While the offset modifier can be used to specify where an IDS engine begins looking for a content match, the depth modifier can be used to specify where it will cease looking for a content match. This is done by specifying the byte offset relative to the first payload content byte being examined. If you aren't using the offset modifier, the depth will be relative to the first byte of the packet payload. If you are using the offset modifier, the depth will be relative to the byte specified in the offset value.

If we examine the Snort rule we created in the previous FTP login example, we can make our rule even more efficient by limiting its depth. Here, we've limited the depth to 6 bytes, which is the length of the string we are attempting to match (again, counting from 0). In this case, we have combined the offset and depth modifiers to specify the absolute location of the content we are attempting to match.

```
alert tcp $HOME_NET any - >67.205.2.30 21 (msg:"Suspicious FTP Login"
content:"sanders"; offset:5; depth:7; sid:5000000; rev:1;)
```

***Distance and Within.*** As we saw earlier, rules can be written so that they contain multiple content matches. When working with a rule like this, it can be incredibly useful to be able to specify how the content matches are positioned relative to each other. One way to do this is the distance rule modifier, which is used to specify the distance from the end of the previous content match to start the next content check.

The following rule makes use of the distance modifier:

```
alert tcp $HOME_NET 1024:->$EXTERNAL_NET 1024: (msg:"ET P2P Ares Server
Connection"; flow:established,to_
server; dsize:<70; content:"r|be|bloop|00|dV"; content:"Ares|00 0a|";
distance:16; reference:url,aresgalaxy
.sourceforge.net;    reference:url,doc.emergingthreats.net/bin/view/
Main/2008591; classtype:policy-violation;
sid:2008591; rev:3;)
```

The rule shown above is used to detect activity related to the Ares peer-to-peer file sharing network.

1. content:"r|be|bloop|00|dV";
   Match content occurring within any point of a packet payload
2. content:"Ares|00 0a|"; distance:16;

   Match content starting at least 16 bytes after the previous content match., counting from 1.
   The following packet payload will generate an alert from this rule:

```
0x0000: 72be 626c 6f6f 7000 6456 0000 0000 0000 r.bloop.dV.......
0x0010: 0000 0000 0000 0000 0000 0000 0000 0000 ................
0x0020: 4172 6573 000a Ares..
```

However, this payload will not match the rule, because the second content match does not occur at least 16 bytes after the first match:

```
0x0000: 72be 626c 6f6f 7000 6456 0000 0000 0000 r.bloop.dV.......
0x0010: 4172 6573 000a 0000 0000 0000 0000 0000 Ares............
```

**FROM THE TRENCHES**

A common misconception is that Snort or Suricata will look for content matches in the order they are listed within the rule. For example, if the rule states "content:one; content:two;", that the IDS engine would look for those content matches in that order. However, this isn't the case, and this rule would match on a packet whose payload contains "onetwo" or "twoone". To ensure that there is an order to these matches, you can pair them with a distance modifier of 0. This tells the IDS engine that the second content match should come after the first, but the distance between the matches doesn't matter. Therefore, we could amend the following content matches to be "content:one; content:two; distance:0;". This would match on "onetwo" but not on "twoone".

Another rule modifier that can be used to dictate how multiple content matches relate to each other is the within modifier. This modifier specifies the number of bytes from the end of the first content match that the second content match must occur within. The following rule combines both the distance and within modifiers with multiple content matches:

```
alert tcp $HOME_NET any -> $EXTERNAL_NET 3724 (msg:"ET GAMES World of
Warcraft connection"; flow:established,to_server; content:"|00|";
depth:1; content:"|25 00|WoW|00|"; distance:1; within:7; reference:
url,doc.emergingthreats.net/bin/view/Main/2002138;  classtype:pol-
icy-violation; sid:2002138; rev:9;)
```

This rule is designed to detect connections to the online World of Warcraft game by detecting two content matches occurring in the correct order:

**1.** content:"|00|"; depth:1;

> Match content occurring on the first or second byte of the packet payload.

**2.** content:"|25 00|WoW|00|"; distance:1; within:7;

> Start matching content 1 byte after the end of the previous content match, ending by the seventh byte.

Considering these criteria, the following packet payload would generate an alert from this rule:

```
0x0000: 0000 2500 576f 5700 0000 0000 0000 0000 ...WoW..........
0x0010: 0000 0000 0000 0000 0000 0000 0000 0000 ................
```

The following would not generate an alert, because the second content match falls outside of the values specified by the distance and within modifiers:

```
0x0000: 0000 0000 0000 0000 2500 576f 5700 0000 ..........WoW....
0x0010: 0000 0000 0000 0000 0000 0000 0000 0000 ................
```

***HTTP Content Modifiers.*** One of the most common types of rules you will be writing are ones that inspect HTTP traffic. This is because HTTP is a heavily used protocol for legitimate traffic, and malicious activity often tries to hide here. The content modifiers we've already discussed can be used to effectively detect actions occurring within HTTP traffic, but using this method can be a bit cumbersome.

As an example, consider the following HTTP packet:

```
11:23:39.483578 IP 172.16.16.139.64581 > 67.205.2.30.80: Flags [P.],
seq 1:806, ack 1, win 16384, length 805
                        0x0000: 4500 034d 532b 4000 4006 e1f9 ac10 108b E..MS+@.@.......
                        0x0010: 43cd 021e fc45 0050 2b1e 34a5 9140 5480 C....E.P+.4..@T.
                        0x0020: 5018 4000 5334 0000 4745 5420 2f20 4854 P.@.S4..GET./.HT
                        0x0030: 5450 2f31 2e31 0d0a 486f 7374 3a20 7777 TP/1.1..Host:.ww
                        0x0040: 772e 6170 706c 6965 646e 736d 2e63 6f6d w.appliednsm.com
                        0x0050: 0d0a 436f 6e6e 6563 7469 6f6e 3a20 6b65 ..Connection:.ke
                        0x0060: 6570 2d61 6c69 7665 0d0a 4163 6365 7074 ep-alive..Accept
                        0x0070: 3a20 7465 7874 2f68 746d 6c2c 6170 706c :.text/html,appl
```

```
0x0080: 6963 6174 696f 6e2f 7868 746d 6c2b 786d ication/xhtml+xm
0x0090: 6c2c 6170 706c 6963 6174 696f 6e2f 786d l,application/xm
0x00a0: 6c3b 713d 302e 392c 2a2f 2a3b 713d 302e l;q=0.9,*/*;q=0.
0x00b0: 380d 0a55 7365 722d 4167 656e 743a 204d 8..User-Agent: M
0x00c0: 6f7a 696c 6c61 2f35 2e30 2028 4d61 6369 ozilla/5.0.(Maci
0x00d0: 6e74 6f73 683b 2049 6e74 656c 204d 6163 ntosh;.Intel.Mac
0x00e0: 204f 5320 5820 3130 5f38 5f34 2920 4170 .OS.X.10_8_4).Ap
0x00f0: 706c 6557 6562 4b69 742f 3533 372e 3336 pleWebKit/537.36
0x0100: 2028 4b48 544d 4c2c 206c 696b 6520 4765 .(KHTML,.like.Ge
0x0110: 636b 6f29 2043 6872 6f6d 652f 3238 2e30 cko).Chrome/28.0
0x0120: 2e31 3530 302e 3935 2053 6166 6172 692f .1500.95.Safari/
0x0130: 3533 372e 3336 0d0a 4163 6365 7074 2d45 537.36..Accept-E
0x0140: 6e63 6f64 696e 673a 2067 7a69 702c 6465 ncoding:.gzip,de
0x0150: 666c 6174 652c 7364 6368 0d0a 4163 6365 flate,sdch..Acce
0x0160: 7074 2d4c 616e 6775 6167 653a 2065 6e2d pt-Language:.en-
0x0170: 5553 2c65 6e3b 713d 302e 380d 0a43 6f6f US,en;q=0.8..
```

If we considered the domain appliednsm.com to be malicious, then it would be reasonable that we might write an IDS rule that will attempt to detect users browsing to this domain with their browser. Using only the rule options that we've learned about so far, that rule might look like this:

```
alert tcp $HOME_NET any - > $EXTERNAL_NET any (msg:"Evil Domain www.appli
ednsm.com"; content:"GET "; offset:0; depth:4; content:"Host|3a 20|www.
appliednsm.com"; distance:0; sid:5000000; rev:1;)
```

This rule would do the following:

1. content:"GET "; offset:0; depth:4;

    Match content starting at the beginning of the packet payload and ending by the fourth byte of the payload.

2. content:"Host|3a 20|www.appliednsm.com";

    Match content occurring after the first content match.

While this would work perfectly fine, there is a better way. Both Snort and Suricata provide HTTP stream reassembly as well as a few rule modifiers that can be used to write more efficient rules related to this type of traffic. As an example, we could utilize the http_method and http_uri modifiers to rewrite the rule above:

```
alert tcp $HOME_NET any - > $EXTERNAL_NET any (msg:"Evil Domain www.appli
ednsm.com"; content:"GET"; http_method; content:"www.appliednsm.
com"; http_uri; sid:5000000; rev:1;)
```

As you can see, this rule is a lot easier to write, and it accomplishes the same objective in a more efficient manner. There are several of these HTTP modifiers available for use. Some of the more common HTTP modifiers are shown in Table 9.1.

**Table 9.1** HTTP Rule Modifiers

| HTTP Modifier | Description |
| --- | --- |
| http_client_body | Content in the body of an HTTP client request |
| http_cookie | Content in the "Cookie" HTTP header field |
| http_header | Content anywhere in the header of an HTTP request or response |
| http_method | The HTTP method being used by the client (GET, POST, etc) |
| http_uri | Content in the HTTP client request URI |
| http_stat_code | Content in the HTTP status field of a server response |
| http_stat_message | Content in the HTTP status message of a server response |
| http_encode | The type of encoding being used in the HTTP transation |

***Perl Compatible Regular Expressions (PCRE).*** At some point you might encounter a situation where it isn't possible to write a rule based upon the constructs provided by the IDS engine. In this case, rules can be extended with the use of a PCRE. Regular expressions are incredibly powerful and provide syntax that allows for matching any type of content you can think of.

PCRE's can be fairly simple, as seen in this rule that will detect credit card numbers:

```
alert ip any any ->any any (msg:"ET POLICY SSN Detected in Clear Text
(dashed)"; pcre:"/ ([0-6]\d\d|7[0-2
56]\d|73[0-3]|77[0-2])-\d{2}-\d{4} /"; reference:url,doc.emerging-
threats.net/2001328; classtype:policy-viol
ation; sid:2001328; rev:13;)
```

Or they can be very complex, as we see here in this rule that detects malicious java requests to dynamic DNS domains:

```
alert tcp $HOME_NET any ->$EXTERNAL_NET $HTTP_PORTS (msg:"ET CURRENT
_EVENTS SUSPICIOUS Java Request to Cha
ngeIP Dynamic DNS Domain"; flow:to_server,established; content:" Java/
1."; http_header; pcre:"/^Host\x3a\x2
0[○\r\n]+\.(?:m(?:y(?:p(?:op3\.(?:net|org)|icture\.info)|n(?:etav
\.(?:net|org)|umber\.org)|(?:secondarydns|
lftv|03)\.com|d(?:ad\.info|dns\.com)|ftp\.(?:info|name)|www\.biz|z
\.info)|(?:r(?:b(?:asic|onus)|(?:slov|fac
)e)|efound)\.com|oneyhome\.biz)|d(?:yn(?:amic(?:dns\.(?:(?:org|co|
me)\.uk|biz)|-dns\.net)|dns\.pro|ssl\.com
)|ns(?:(?:-(?:stuff|dns)|0[45]|et|rd)\.com|[12]\.us)|dns\.(?:m(?:e
\.uk|obi|s)|info|name|us)|(?:smtp|umb1)\.
com|hcp\.biz)|(?:j(?:u(?:ngleheart|stdied)|etos|kub)|y(?:ou(?:
dontcare|rtrap)|gto)|4(?:mydomain|dq|pu)|q(?:
```

```
high|poe)|2(?:waky|5u)|z(?:yns|zux)|vizvaz|1dumb)\.com|s(?:e(?:(?:
llclassics|rveusers?|ndsmtp)\.com|x(?:idu
de\.com|xxy\.biz))|quirly\.info|sl443\.org|ixth\.biz)|o(?:n(?:mypc
\.(?:info|biz|net|org|us)|edumb\.com)|(?:
(?:urhobb|cr)y|rganiccrap|tzo)\.com|f(?:ree(?:(?:ddns|tcp)\.com|
www\.(?:info|biz))|a(?:qserv|rtit)\.com|tp
(?:server|1)\.biz)|a(?:(?:(?:lmostm|cmeto)y|mericanunfinished)\.
com|uthorizeddns\.(?:net|org|us))|n(?:s(?:0
(?:1\.(?:info|biz|us)|2\.(?:info|biz|us))|[123]\.name)|inth\.biz)|
c(?:hangeip\.(?:n(?:ame|et)|org)|leansite
\.(?:info|biz|us)|ompress\.to)|i(?:(?:t(?:emdb|saol)|nstanthq|
sasecret|kwb)\.com|ownyour\.(?:biz|org))|p(?:
ort(?:relay\.com|25\.biz)|canywhere\.net|roxydns\.com)|g(?:r8(?:
domain|name)\.biz|ettrials\.com|ot-game\.or
g)|l(?:flink(?:up\.(?:com|net|org)|\.com)|ongmusic\.com)|t(?:o(?:
ythieves\.com|h\.info)|rickip\.(?:net|org)
)|x(?:x(?:xy\.(?:info|biz)|uz\.com)|24hr\.com)|w(?:ww(?:host|1)\.
biz|ikaba\.com|ha\.la)|e(?:(?:smtp|dns)\.b
iz|zua\.com|pac\.to)|(?:rebatesrule|3-a)\.net|https443\.(?:net|
org)|bigmoney\.biz)(\x3a\d{1,5})?\r$/Hmi"; c
lasstype:bad-unknown; sid:2016581; rev:1;)
```

As you can see in the rule examples shown above, a PCRE content match can be inserted into a rule using the following syntax:

```
pcre:<regular expression>;
```

Writing regular expressions is beyond the scope of this book, however, there are several online tutorials that provide a jump-start on the topic. If you are looking for a more thorough reference text, two books I like for varying skill levels are "Introducing Regular Expressions" by Michael Fitzgerald and "Mastering Regular Expressions" by Jeffrey E.F. Friedl.

## Communication Flow

Snort and Suricata both provide the ability to write rules based upon the state of communication flow for network traffic using the TCP protocol. While this may seem redundant when combined with the source or destination IP addresses and ports in the rule header, that is not actually the case. While that rule header information will help determine which direction the traffic is going (inbound or outbound), it does not always necessarily tell you who is responsible for which part of the communication.

To understand how flow options work and why they are important, you should understand what constitutes a TCP session. In a normal TCP session, there are a client and server that communicate. The client is the device that starts the connection to the server by sending a SYN packet to the server on a listening port. The server should, at that point, respond to the client with a SYN/ACK packet. Upon receipt, the client will respond back to the server with an ACK packet. At this point, a three-way handshake has been completed and the client and server can communicate until one of them terminates the connection, either abruptly with a RST packet, or more gracefully with a series of FIN packets known as a TCP teardown. We will examine this more in depth in Chapter 13, but this is the basic premise of what makes up a TCP session.

With this in mind, the flow rule option has several options of its own. These are broken down into three categories: state options, directional options, and traffic modeling state. These options are configured using the following format, where at least one option is required and additional ones are discretionary:

```
flow: <option>,<option>,<option>;
```

The two available state options are established and stateless. The established option will only match traffic where an established TCP session exists. The stateless option will match regardless of whether an established connection exists.

There are four directional options:

- to_server: Traffic from the client to the server
- from_server: Traffic from the server to the client
- to_client: Traffic from the server to the client
- from_client: Traffic from the client to the server

---

**ANALYST NOTE**

If you noticed that the to_server/from_client and to_client/from_server options are the same, then you can rest assured that your eyes aren't deceiving you and that it isn't a typo. These options are indeed the same, but are provided to make rules more readable.

---

The final two options are the no_stream and only_stream options that are used to define whether the data being matched is a reassembled stream or just a single packet.

As an example of flow option usage, let's examine the following rule:

```
alert tcp $HOME_NET any - > $EXTERNAL_NET 5222 (msg:"GPL CHAT MISC Jabber/
Google Talk Outgoing Traffic"; flo
w:to_server,established; content:"<stream"; nocase; reference:url,
www.google.com/talk/; classtype:policy-vi
olation; sid:100000230; rev:2;)
```

This rule is used to detect authentication to a Jabber/Google Talk chat server. In this case, we see that a simple content match is being used, but before that, the flow: to_server,established option is used. This increases the performance of Snort/Suricata by ensuring that only established TCP sessions are examined for this rule, and it increases the accuracy of the rule by ensuring that only traffic to the actual server as defined by the TCP session is detected.

While your rules might not always directly benefit from flow rules from an accuracy perspective, they can serve to increase performance when using flow state options, so I try to include this option whenever possible.

### Protocol Header Detection Options

Snort and Suricata provide the ability to detect values in the headers of the packets being examined. This includes most of the values in the ICMP, IP, TCP, and UDP headers. I won't rehash all of these values here as they can be found in the Snort and Suricata documentation, but some of the items I use most often include:

- TTL: Matches a specified TTL value. This can be specified as an exact value (=) or using a relational operator ($>, >=, <, <=$). This is useful for detecting certain types of operating system based upon their initial TTL value.
- dsize: Matches a packet with a specific payload size. This can be specified as an exact value (=) or using a relational operator ($>, <$). This is useful for increasing rule performance by combining it with content matching rules.
- itype: Matches a specific ICMP type value.
- icode: Matches a specific ICMP code value.
- ip_proto: Matches a specific IP protocol. This can be specified as either the protocol name (IGMP, GRE, etc) or number.

## Rule Tuning

In Chapter 7 we discussed techniques for determining the effectiveness of a signature through metrics like false positive rate and precision. There are several methods that can be used to enhance signatures when these become a concern. Some of these methods, and others, can also be used to increase the performance of certain rules. Now we will look at a few of these best practices for IDS rule tuning.

### Event Filtering

Sometimes rules may need to exist that generate an extremely high number of alerts by nature. An example of this would be a rule that detects a particular type of denial of service (DoS) attack. While it is important to be able to detect this type of attack, if the rule you've written matches every DoS packet sent, and you are receiving thousands of these packets per second, then you will receive thousands of alerts per second. This many alerts will eventually overwhelm your IDS engine or your analysts. The event filtering options provided by Snort and Suricata allow you to apply thresholds to rules to prevent this kind of alert explosion.

Instead of being placed inline with the rule as a rule option, event filters are designed to be placed in the threshold.conf file. The name and location of this file is configurable in snort.conf and suricata.yaml as needed. On Security Onion, this file is stored at /etc/nsm/<sensor name>/threshold.conf.

---

**ANALYST NOTE**

Previously, event filters were known as threshold rule options and were placed inline with the rule. As of the writing of this book, this method is still supported by Snort and Suricata, so you will find that a lot of publicly available rules still use this format. The syntax of the two formats is the same. Since this book uses rules from publicly available sources, you may find rules listed that utilize the older inline threshold options. However, it is recommended that the new method of placing event filter entries into the threshold.conf file be used.

---

There are three types of event filters:

- Limit: Generate an alert on the first number of specified matches (count) during the time interval (seconds), and then ignore the remaining alerts for the rest of the time interval.
- Threshold: Generate an alert every time there is a match (count) during this interval (seconds).
- Both: Generate an alert once per time interval (seconds) after the specified number of matches (count) has occurred, then ignore any further matches during the time interval.

Event filter entries use the following syntax:

```
event_filter gen_id<value>, sig_id<value>, type<limit|threshold|
both>, track<by_src|by_dst>, count<value>, seconds<value>
```

The options shown are broken down as:

- gen_id: Specifies the generator ID of the rule.
- sig_id: Specifies the SID of the rule
- type<limit|threshold|both>: Specifies the type of event filter being applied. These are described above.
- track<by_src/by_dst>: Specifies whether rule matches are tracked by unique source or unique destination address
- count: The number of rule matches occurring within the specified time that will cause the event filter limit to be exceeded
- seconds: The number of seconds that are used to track the count of rule matches

As an example of a usage scenario for event filtering, consider this rule:

```
alert tcp $HOME_NET any ->!$WSUS_SERVERS $HTTP_PORTS (msg:"ET POLICY
Windows Update in Progress"; flow:established,t
o_server;    content:"Windows-Update-Agent";    http_header;    con-
tent:"Host|3a|"; http_header; nocase; within:20;
pcre:"/User-Agent\x3a[^\n]+Windows-Update-Agent/i";
reference:url,windowsupdate.microsoft.com;  reference:url,doc.emer-
gingthreats.net/2002949; classtype:pol
icy-violation; sid:2002949; rev:8;)
```

The rule shown above is used to detect a device downloading Windows updates from a non-approved update server by matching a specific user agent string. When a Windows computer updates, this string can be seen in multiple packets and will result in a single host generating a significant number of alerts. If you have more than a few hosts exhibiting this behavior, the number of alerts can quickly overwhelm an analyst. This makes this rule a perfect candidate for an event filter. The following will do the trick:

```
event filter gen_id 1,sig_id 2002949,type limit,track by_s
rc,count 1, seconds 300
```

The event filter shown here will track the source address of the alert and count every event occurring over a 300 second interval. Since this is a limit filter and the count value is set to 1, only one alert per host will be generated for rule matches every 300 seconds.

Another great use of event filters is with rules associated with scanning. When scanning activity occurs, it will generate a lot of packets. Therefore, generating an alert for every packet matching the criteria specified in the rule could quickly overwhelm an analyst. In order to combat this, an event filter can be applied to notify an analyst of the scan without dominating their analysis console.

### Alert Suppression

I've seen many instances where an analyst has written a new rule that they've put a lot of work into, only to find that one or two hosts within the network generate some type of traffic that results in a plethora of false positives. This leads to frustration that eventually causes the analyst to scrap the rule all together. What those analysts typically don't know about is the alert suppression feature of Snort and Suricata. This feature allows you to specify a rule and an IP address (or group of IP addresses from a variable), and suppress alerts that would be generated from those hosts in relation to a rule.

Suppression entries are also included in the threshold.conf file, and take the following syntax:

```
suppress gen_id<value>,sig_id<value>,track<by_s
rc|by_dst>,ip<value>
```

The options shown are broken down as:

- gen_id: Specifies the generator ID of the rule.
- sig_id: Specify the SID of the rule
- track < by_src|by_dst >: Specifies whether suppression occurs for source or destination addresses generating traffic that matches a rule. This is optional.
- ip < value >: The IP address whose alerts from the specified rule are suppressed

The following entry would be used to suppress any alerts generated by SID 5000000 with the source IP address 192.168.1.100:

```
suppress gen_id 1, sig_id 5000000, track by_src, ip 192.168.1.100
```

Suppression is a useful tactic for eliminating individual hosts that are causing false positive issues with certain rules. This should be your first stop before removing a rule.

### Alert Detection Filters

Snort and Suricata provide the ability to use detection filters to set a threshold on the number of rule matches that must occur before an alert is generated. A detection filter can be applied to a rule based upon source or destination address of the traffic, and can apply its threshold based upon the number of rule matches that have been detected in a specified time interval.

The detection filter option is applied in line with a rule and takes the following format:

```
detection_filter: track<by_src|by_dst>, count<value>,
seconds<value>;
```

These options include:

- track < by_src|by_dst >: Specifies whether rule matches are tracked by unique source or unique destination address
- count: The number of rule matches in the specified time that will cause an alert to be generated
- seconds: The number of seconds that the specified number of rule matches must occur in order for an alert to be generated

As an example of detection filters in practice, let's look at this rule:

```
alert tcp $EXTERNAL_NET any ->$HTTP_SERVERS $HTTP_PORTS (msg:"ET SCAN
Sqlmap SQL Injection Scan"; flow:to_
server,established; content:"User-Agent|3a| sqlmap"; fast_pattern:
only; http_header; detection_filter:track
by_dst, count 4, seconds 20; reference:url,sqlmap.sourceforge.net; ref-
erence:url,doc.emergingthreats.net/2
008538; classtype:attempted-recon; sid:2008538; rev:8;)
```

This rule is used to detect scanning activity by the Sqlmap tool, which is used to detect and orchestrate SQL injection attacks. In this case, the rule matches content associated with the user agent that is used by Sqlmap. Generally, seeing this user agent only once or twice might not indicate any type of scanning activity since Sqlmap's scans are usually more verbose than that. As such, generating an alert every time this user agent is seen might generate a significant number of false positives. Because of this, the rule was configured with the following detection filter:

```
detection_filter:track by_dst, count 4, seconds 20;
```

This detection filter requires that a certain threshold be met before the detection engine will generate an alert from this rule. Specifically, the detection engine will track the number of rule matches to the destination address, and when this number exceeds four matches in a period of twenty seconds, it will generate an alert.

Detection filters are good for a variety of situations. They are especially useful when a little of something isn't a bad thing, but several could be. For instance, when a user is attempting to log into a web service and has one or two failed authentication attempts due to a forgotten password, we would consider this normal. However, when a user attempts to log into a web service a few hundred times within a couple of minutes, that might attempt a password guessing or brute force attempt that warrants further investigation.

### Eliminate Unwanted Traffic

A common misconception is that every option you add to a rule serves to decrease the performance of this rule, when in reality, the opposite is normally true. Whenever you add options to an IDS rule that limit the amount of traffic the IDS engine has to examine, you are increasing the performance of the rule. As such, you should do everything possible to add these options and limit the amount of traffic the IDS engine has to examine to evaluate traffic against a rule. A few ideas include:

- Always use protocol header detection options when possible. The detection engine will examine these first before examining the payload of a packet, so if you can exclude packets before content inspection this will save valuable processing cycles.
- Be selective with the use of the "any" keyword in the rule header. If you can limit the rule to a specific host or group of hosts, this will limit the amount of traffic that the IDS engine has to parse.
- Always specify exact locations of content being detected. For instance, if you know that a content string you are attempting to match always occurs at the same position within a packet payload, you should use the offset and depth options to keep the detection engine from having to inspect the entire content of the packet.
- Limit the size of the packets being examined based upon their payload size. Even if you don't know where the exact location of the content you are attempting to match will appear, if you know that it always occurs in packets of a certain size then you can limit the size of the packet that the detection engine will examine with the dsize option, which will increase performance.
- Always use flow options when possible. If the traffic you are attempting to match only exists inside of an established "to server" connection, then the detection engine can easily throw out all other traffic when attempting to match data to the rule. This can yield a significant performance increase.
- Select the appropriate protocol in the rule header. When you can specify TCP or UDP instead of simply IP, this will drastically reduce the number of packets that the detection engine will have to parse for the rule you are working with.

### Target the Vulnerability

When writing rules designed to catch exploitation of a service, it is often easier to write rules so that they catch specific exploits. While this is easier, it leaves a lot of room for false negatives. While a rule developed with an exploit in mind will catch that particular exploit, it will not catch other exploits targeting the same vulnerability. Because of this, it is always better to write a rule with the vulnerability in mind.

For example, consider a vulnerability that is exploited by way of a buffer overflow in the input field of a network application. It would be trivial to write a rule that detects the publicly available version of this exploit, but it would be equally as trivial for an attacker to modifier the exploit string to use different padding or a different shellcode or payload. Instead of content matching a string from the exploit, try writing a rule that content matches based upon the submission of that input field where there are an extraordinarily large number of characters. This rule will be harder to write and might yield some false positives, but it will more accurately detect attempts to exploit the vulnerable service.

While this strategy is more labor intensive, it will yield better results and will decrease your chances of missing malicious activity.

### Pair PCRE and Content Matches

While PCRE rules infinitely increase the flexibility of IDS rules, they also increase the performance load on the system. One strategy that can be used to decrease this load is to pair rules that utilize PCRE matching with content matching. The detection engine will parse the content match first, ensuring that only traffic that matches the content will be subjected to testing for the PCRE match.

As an example, consider the following rule:

```
alert tcp $EXTERNAL_NET any ->$HOME_NET any (msg:"ET TROJAN IRC poten-
tial reptile commands"; flow:establis
hed,from_server;  content:"PRIVMSG|20|";  depth:8;  content:"|3a|";
within:30; pcre:"/\.((testdlls|threads|nsp
|speed|uptime|installed|secure|sec|unsecure|unsec|process|ps|rand|
exploitftpd|eftpd|flusharp|farp|flushdns|
fdns|resolve|dns|pstore|pst|sysinfo|si|netinfo|ni|driveinfo|di|
currentip)\s*[\r\n]|(iestart|ies|login|l|mir
ccmd|system|file\s+(cat|exists|e|del|rm|rmdir|move|copy|attrib)|
down|dl\dx|update|reg\s+(query|delete|write
))\s+\w+|(banner|ban|advscan|asc|scanall|sa|ntscan|nts)\s*[\n\r])/
i"; reference:url,doc.emergingthreats.net
/2002363; classtype:trojan-activity; sid:2002363; rev:15;)
```

This rule is used to detect the presence of the "Reptile" malware strain when it attempts to execute commands via IRC. While this command does include a very CPU intensive regular expression, it also includes two individual content matches:

1. content:"PRIVMSG|20|"; depth:8;
2. content:"|3a|"; within:30;

These content matches will ensure that the IDS engine is only examining packets that already appear to be associated with IRC traffic before attempting to perform the PCRE match.

### Fast Pattern Matching

When multiple content matches are present within a rule, Snort and Suricata will attempt to match the most unique string first so that they can stop processing the data quickly if no match is found. Because of this, their default behavior is to attempt to match the longest content string first, as they assume that it will be the most unique string. While this strategy is typically effective, it doesn't always stand the test. Because of this, the Snort and Suricata detection engines provide the fast pattern matching content option modifier. This modifier can be specified with a shorter content option to instruct the detection engine to attempt to match this content first.

The following rule provides a good example of the fast pattern matching modifier in action:

```
alert tcp $EXTERNAL_NET any ->$HOME_NET $HTTP_PORTS (msg:"ET SCAN
Nessus User Agent"; flow: established,to
_server; content:"User-Agent|3a|"; http_header; nocase; content:"Nes-
sus"; http_header; fast_pattern; nocase
; pcre:"/oUser-Agent\:[o\n]+Nessus/Hmi"; threshold: type limit, track
by_src,count 1, seconds 60; reference
:url,www.nessus.org; reference:url,doc.emergingthreats.net/2002664;
classtype:attempted-recon; sid:2002664;
rev:12;)
```

As you can see, there are two content options here.

1. content:"User-Agentl3al"; http_header; nocase;
2. content:"Nessus"; http_header; fast_pattern; nocase

In this case, the "User-Agentl3al" content is the longest, but it is certainly not the most exclusive since this string is present in the standard HTTP client request header. Because of this, it makes more sense to match "Nessus" first, which is the shorter content option. This is why this option has the fast_pattern; modifier enabled.

> **ANALYST NOTE**
>
> The fast pattern modifier can only be used once in a rule, and it cannot be used in conjunction with the following HTTP content modifiers: http_cookie, http_raw_uri,http_raw_header, http_raw_cookie, http_method, http_stat_code, http_stat_msg.

### Manually Test Rules

When you've written a rule, it is important to test it thoroughly. We've already covered the process of testing rule syntax, but this is only one step of the process. You should also make sure that the rule detects the traffic it is supposed to match, and that it does not match on other similar traffic. Since recreating the attack or malicious activity itself can be incredibly time consuming, there are a couple of other options.

In the case of a SOC environment, for example, any analyst could be writing a rule based upon something that has already happened. If that is the case, and you have the packet capture of the activity, you can replay that activity to the monitoring interface of a sensor (preferably a test machine running an IDS engine with the newly deployed rule) to attempt to trigger an alert. Tcpreplay is a good option for replaying packet captures over a live interface. An example of Tcpreplay replaying a capture file is shown in Figure 9.23. You can learn more about Tcpreplay at http://tcpreplay. synfin.net/wiki/tcpreplay.

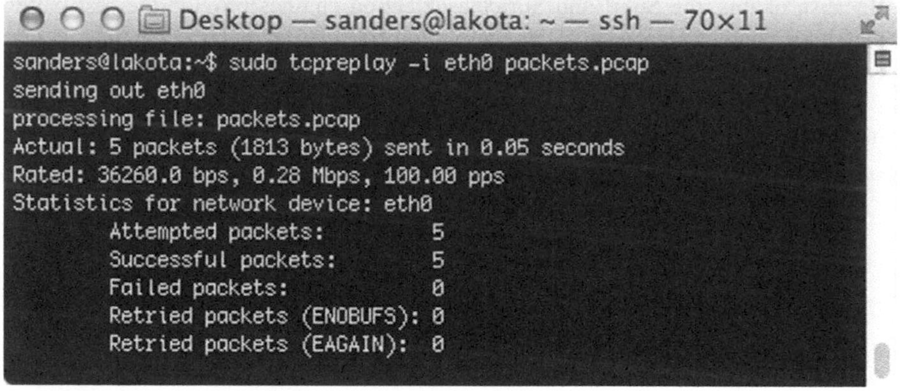

```
○ ○ ○ ▦ Desktop — sanders@lakota: ~ — ssh — 70×11
sanders@lakota:~$ sudo tcpreplay -i eth0 packets.pcap
sending out eth0
processing file: packets.pcap
Actual: 5 packets (1813 bytes) sent in 0.05 seconds
Rated: 36260.0 bps, 0.28 Mbps, 100.00 pps
Statistics for network device: eth0
        Attempted packets:          5
        Successful packets:         5
        Failed packets:             0
        Retried packets (ENOBUFS):  0
        Retried packets (EAGAIN):   0
```

**FIGURE 9.23**

Using Tcpreplay to Replay a PCAP File Over a Live Interface

If you don't have a capture file available for the activity associated with your rule, it is possible to manually generate the traffic using Scapy. Scapy is a powerful python library that can be used to generate and receive packets on the wire. While we don't cover Scapy in depth in this book, it is an incredibly valuable tool for an analyst to be familiar with. The sample shown below is a very basic Python script that uses Scapy to send a TCP packet with the payload "AppliedNSM" to the host at 192.168.1.200 on port 80.

```
ip=IP()
ip.dst="192.168.1.200"
ip.src="192.168.1.100"
tcp=TCP()
tcp.dport=80
tcp.sport=1234
payload="AppliedNSM"
send(ip/tcp/payload)
```

You can learn more about Scapy at http://www.secdev.org/projects/scapy/.

## VIEWING SNORT AND SURICATA ALERTS

Once your IDS engine of choice is configured on a sensor and you have downloaded or created IDS rules, all that is left is to sit back and wait for alerts to roll in. While these alerts can be read directly from the sensor and the files that Snort and Suricata generate, you will probably want to use a third-party graphical tool to help with this process. There are a variety of mechanisms available for viewing alerts that are generated by Snort or Suricata. Let's look at two of the most popular free and open source alert management interfaces: Snorby and Sguil. You will see these tools referenced through this book.

## Snorby

Snorby is a newer alert management console that is written in ruby on rails and operates in the web browser. Snorby was created by Dustin Weber, who has since founded a company called Threat Stack, which maintains Snorby as a free open source application. The overall goal of Snorby is to provide analysts a means of reviewing and analyzing alerts in a manner that is "all about simplicity," while providing all of the power needed to perform effective analysis.

You can access an online demo of Snorby at http://demo.snorby.org, using the username demo@snorby.org and the password snorby. In addition to this, if you are using Security Onion you can access Snorby by clicking the Snorby icon on your desktop, or by visiting https://<Security_Onion_IP>:444/. Figure 9.24 shows the main Snorby dashboard.

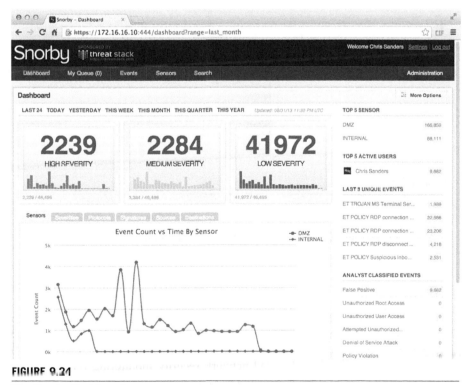

**FIGURE 9.24**

The Snorby Dashboard

You can read more about Snorby at http://www.snorby.org.

## Sguil

Sguil has been the de facto alert management console for NSM analysts for many years. Unlike Snorby, Sguil operates as a desktop application that connects back to a central data source. Sguil was written by Bamm Visscher, and is maintained as a free and open source application. It is installed on Security Onion by default, and can be accessed by clicking the Sguil icon on the desktop. Figure 9.25 shows the main Sguil interface.

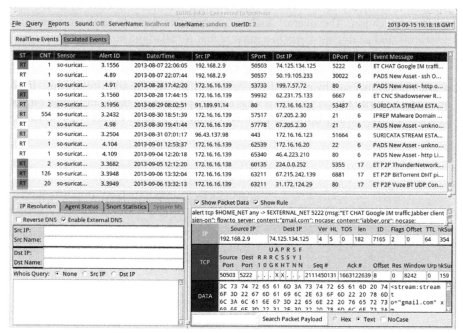

**FIGURE 9.25**

The main Sguil interface

You can read more about Sguil at http://sguil.sourceforge.net/.

## CONCLUSION

In this chapter, we've discussed signature-based detection with Snort and Suricata at length. We looked at how both IDS engines operate, what makes each one unique, and how to write detection rules for them. Signature-based detection has been the backbone of intrusion detection and network security monitoring for quite some time, and while it isn't always enough on its own, it is a critical capability of any NSM environment. Later in the analysis section, we will look at methods for viewing and analyzing alerts generated from Snort and Suricata.

# The Bro Platform

NSM is all about bringing network data together to provide context for detection and analysis. Most NSM systems already integrate the "big three" sources (IDS alerts, session data, full packet capture data), but as we've already seen in this book, these are not the only data sources you can use. One particularly rich source of this data is Bro.

Bro is often described as an IDS, though as we'll see in this chapter, that description hardly does it justice. Think of it, rather, as a development platform for network monitoring applications. It provides substantial "out-of-the-box" functionality for decoding and logging network traffic and provides an event-driven development model to allow you to watch for certain types of transactions and provide your own custom scripts to run when they happen.

In this chapter, we will see how to work with Bro's built-in logs to identify activity of interest on our network. We'll also see several examples of Bro programming that showcases some of its more important and useful features.

> **CAUTION**
>
> The examples in this chapter were written to use Bro 2.2, which is in beta release as of the writing of this book. As such, Bro 2.2 is not installed on Security Onion by default. If you'd like to follow along, you can install Bro 2.2 Beta on to Security Onion by following the instructions found at http://www.appliednsm.com/bro-22-on-seconion/.

## BASIC BRO CONCEPTS

Contrary to popular belief, Bro itself is not an IDS, even though you'll sometimes see it called "the Bro IDS". Bro is really a scripting platform that is designed for working with network traffic. As you will see in the examples in this chapter, Bro's scripting language (which, somewhat confusingly, is also called "Bro") offers features that are extremely useful for protocol analysis (IP addresses and ports are native data types, for example). It also offers a lot of out-of-the-box functionality for basic analysis tasks, such as robust protocol decoding, transaction logging and notifications for some common security events.

That said, Bro does actually make an excellent IDS platform, which is why it is included in this book. Bro is different than, and complimentary to, a signature-based IDS such as Snort or Suricata. The Snort rule language is well adapted to finding bytes in a network flow (and there are a lot of tasks that really just come down to that!), but Bro is often the best option for more complex tasks, such as those that require higher-level protocol knowledge, working across multiple network flows, or using a custom algorithm to compute something about the traffic in question.

One of Bro's strengths is that it inherently knows about all of the common Internet protocols, and even a number of the not-so-common ones. It can identify these protocols in network traffic even if they are running on non-standard ports, using a feature called Dynamic Protocol Detection (DPD). Just a few of the application and tunneling protocols that Bro supports include:

- DHCP
- DNS
- FTP
- HTTP
- IRC
- POP3
- SMTP
- SOCKS
- SSH
- SSL
- SYSLOG
- Teredo
- GTPv1

By default, when Bro sees network traffic using an application protocol it knows about, it will log the details of those transactions to a file. Of course, the logging is fully customizable, but Bro doesn't stop there. While it's parsing and decoding the protocol, Bro actually gives you a mechanism to create custom logic for processing the transactions in the traffic it is examining. It treats the actions taken by a protocol as a series of events, for which you can register event handlers written in Bro code. When you write and register a new event handler for a certain event, and when that event occurs in the network traffic, Bro will automatically call your code based upon the event handler you've written. You can do pretty much whatever you like in your handlers, and you can have as many as you like. You can even have multiple handlers for the same event. This might occur when you are inspecting the same protocol to find different types of behavior.

As an example, the Bro code below represents a very simple event handler for the http_request event. Bro generates this event whenever an HTTP client makes a request from a server. This code prints the original URL path requested by the client to the console (standard output). Of course, this isn't very useful in a production situation, but we'll see more real-world examples later in this chapter. For now, just know that simply adding this code to any script that is loaded into your running Bro (a process that will be explained later) is enough to register the event handler and have Bro call it when it sees an HTTP request.

```
#
# This is a sample event handler for HTTP requests.
#
event http_request(c: connection, method: string, orig_uri: string,
unescaped_uri: string, version: string) {
        print fmt("HTTP request found for %s", orig_uri);
}
```

## RUNNING BRO

The easiest way to run Bro is to execute it from the command line and have it process a PCAP file according to Bro's default configuration. This can be done with a command like:

```
bro -C -r file.pcap
```

The -r file.pcap argument tells Bro to read packets from the file specified, which in this case is file.pcap. The -C option is used to disable Bro's internal checksum verification. Every IP packet has a built-in checksum that allows the destination to determine if it was received correctly. This is absolutely critical to proper network transmission, and every host checks this by default. Increasingly, however, many network cards implement a feature called TCP checksum offloading, which implements this check in the NIC hardware, freeing the system's CPU from expending needless cycles. This can make a big difference at gigabit speeds or above, but often means that the checksum values are missing or incorrect when the packets make it to the operating system where libpcap (or another packet capture driver) can read them. By default, Bro simply ignores packets with invalid checksums, but the -C option forces Bro to skip the checksum validation and process all packets. You almost always want to use this, especially when processing PCAP files from systems where you don't know if checksum offloading is enabled or not. If you used Security Onion's setup script to automatically configure the network interfaces on your lab system, then it will disable offloading by default on your monitor interface, but most other systems have it on by default.

## BRO LOGS

A default Bro installation is configured to be very verbose in respect to logging. At this stage, Bro is not so much looking for bad things (a la IDS), but it does creates very detailed logs about the things it sees. Figure 10.1 shows a simple example of using Bro to process a single PCAP file. Notice that we started out with an empty directory, but Bro created several log files and a new directory as a result of parsing this file.

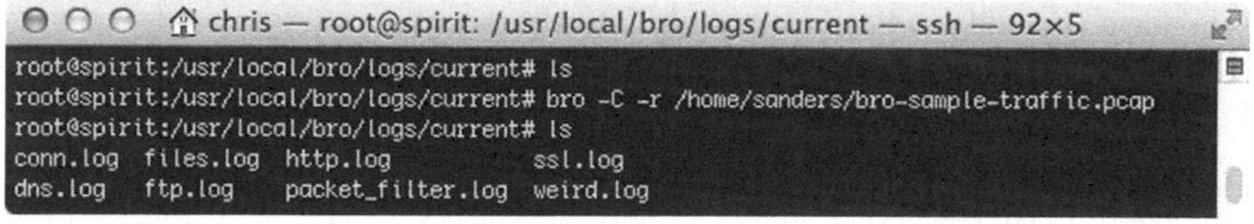

**FIGURE 10.1**

Bro Processing a PCAP and Creating Log Files

You can see by the names of the log files that Bro detected DNS, FTP, HTTP and SSL traffic in this capture file. We also have a few other files, whose contents may be a little less obvious. The conn.log file is a record of network connections (flows), and the files.log file is a record of all the files that were transferred (in this case, via HTTP or FTP, including all the HTML, images, and other embedded media that comprise the web traffic). Packet_filter.log simply contains the BPF filter Bro is using (the default is "ip or not ip", which is a roundabout way of saying "all packets"). Weird.log is where Bro logs unusual events from any of the protocols, though Bro's idea of what qualifies as "unusual" may or may not match your own. Finally, the extract_files directory is empty right now, but there will be more on this later.

If you open up one of these log files, you'll see that it is a tab-delimited text file. The first several lines are internal Bro metadata that describe the fields and their data types, when the log file was created, and other less useful information. Reading the lines marked fields and types is a great way to orient yourself when you need to familiarize yourself with the contents of a new type of Bro log file that you haven't dealt with before. The actual logs begin after the metadata. Each log is a single line of text.

Figure 10.2 shows a portion of the http.log file, and describes some of the HTTP transactions Bro saw in the PCAP file.

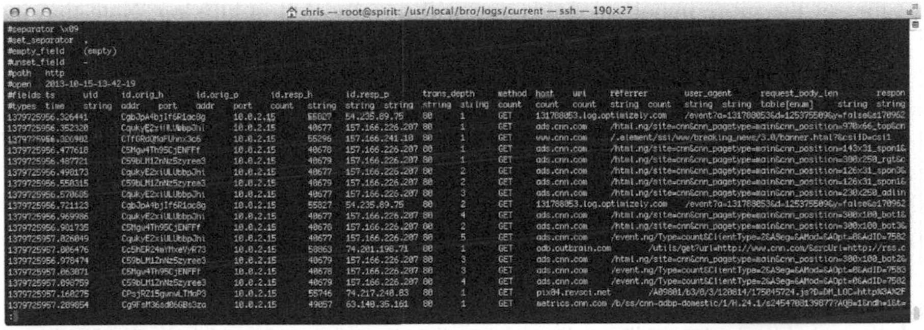

**FIGURE 10.2**

Partial http.log file contents

This is only a partial log file, for two reasons. First, there are too many records to fit in one window, so we're only seeing the top of the file. More importantly, though, the records are very long, and extend past the right side of the window. They're so long that it is hard to show a sample log file in print format. Table 10.1 summarizes

| Table 10.1 http.log fields | |
|---|---|
| **Field Name** | **Description** |
| ts | The event timestamp |
| uid | A unique ID for the flow containing this transaction |
| id.orig_h | Source host |
| id.orig_p | Source port |
| id.resp_h | Destination host |
| id.resp_p | Destination port |
| trans_depth | Position of transaction inside HTTP pipeline |
| method | HTTP verb for this transaction |
| host | HTTP Host header value |
| uri | The path of the request |
| referrer | HTTP Referrer header value |
| user_agent | HTTP User-Agent header value |
| request_body_len | Length of the body of the request |
| response_body_len | Length of the body of the response |
| status-code | Numeric HTTP response status |
| status_msg | Human-readable HTTP status message |
| filename | Downloaded filename, as specified by the server |
| username | HTTP Basic Authentication user name |
| password | HTTP Basic Authentication password |
| orig_fuids | List of unique file IDs in the request (cf. *files.log*) |
| orig_mime_types | MIME types for request objects |
| resp_fuids | List of unique file IDs in the response |
| resp_mime_types | MIME types for response objects |

some of the more important fields you will usually find in http.log. Note that it's possible, and even common, to extend standard Bro log files with extra fields, depending on the scripts you are running in your Bro instance.

> **FROM THE TRENCHES**
>
> If you're used to other packet or flow analysis tools like Tcpdump, Wireshark or Snort, you may be wondering where to find the source and destination IP addresses or ports in Bro. They are there, but Bro prefers to refer to them as originators and responders. In the log files, you'll see field names like orig_h and orig_p for the source IP addresses and port numbers, as well as resp_h and resp_p for the destination IP addresses and port numbers. In this chapter, as in the rest of the book, we will usually stick to calling them "source" and "destination" unless there's a reason to do otherwise.

If all this seems like an awful lot of info to stuff into a log file, you're right. And to be honest, most of the time you don't actually need all 25 + fields when you're just trying to find the answer to a specific question. Sometimes, it's far more convenient to just extract the fields you are interested in. Fortunately, there's a handy Bro command for this, bro-cut.

The simplest way to run bro-cut is to use the terminal to cat a log file into it with the pipe symbol. When you do this to pass this data to bro-cut, you can specify which fields you want to extract, as shown in Figure 10.3.

**FIGURE 10.3**

Simple bro-cut output

Here, we've specified that we only want to see the ts, uid, method, and host fields. In most cases, you will get more user-friendly output by using the -C (include all the log file metadata) and `-u` (decode timestamps into human-readable UTC time) options, as shown in Figure 10.4.

```
chris — root@spirit: /usr/local/bro/logs/current — ssh — 108×25
root@spirit:/usr/local/bro/logs/current# cat http.log | bro-cut -u ts uid method host
2013-09-21T01:12:36+0000	CcJaAH25rgacomA0df	GET	131788053.log.optimizely.com
2013-09-21T01:12:36+0000	CM341S1mCi9wwBNi3d	GET	ads.cnn.com
2013-09-21T01:12:36+0000	CkkK5a2ZTitgwP4dHb	GET	www.cnn.com
2013-09-21T01:12:36+0000	CTOhzaq5uhIyxTYo6	GET	ads.cnn.com
2013-09-21T01:12:36+0000	Cgf7A14WHFJ2e7n3g3	GET	ads.cnn.com
2013-09-21T01:12:36+0000	CM341S1mCi9wwBNi3d	GET	ads.cnn.com
2013-09-21T01:12:36+0000	Cgf7A14WHFJ2e7n3g3	GET	ads.cnn.com
2013-09-21T01:12:36+0000	CM341S1mCi9wwBNi3d	GET	ads.cnn.com
2013-09-21T01:12:36+0000	CcJaAH25rgacomA0df	GET	131788053.log.optimizely.com
2013-09-21T01:12:36+0000	CM341S1mCi9wwBNi3d	GET	ads.cnn.com
2013-09-21T01:12:36+0000	CTOhzaq5uhIyxTYo6	GET	ads.cnn.com
2013-09-21T01:12:37+0000	CM341S1mCi9wwBNi3d	GET	ads.cnn.com
2013-09-21T01:12:37+0000	CQVCXE2WGmmiFuNqd	GET	odb.outbrain.com
2013-09-21T01:12:36+0000	Cgf7A14WHFJ2e7n3g3	GET	ads.cnn.com
2013-09-21T01:12:37+0000	CTOhzaq5uhIyxTYo6	GET	ads.cnn.com
2013-09-21T01:12:37+0000	Cgf7A14WHFJ2e7n3g3	GET	ads.cnn.com
2013-09-21T01:12:37+0000	Co5CLO2hE6XKe2Yj5g	GET	pix04.revsci.net
2013-09-21T01:12:37+0000	CUVybV2Zqe66kBfzUi	GET	metrics.cnn.com
2013-09-21T01:12:37+0000	CPmGYeMX9b4XNuVRk	GET	ads.cnn.com
2013-09-21T01:12:37+0000	CWz9N11XaclhAm0R0b	GET	secure-us.imrworldwide.com
2013-09-21T01:12:37+0000	ClkIHb4j06BFs9xzJi	GET	b.scorecardresearch.com
2013-09-21T01:12:37+0000	Cgf7A14WHFJ2e7n3g3	GET	ads.cnn.com
2013-09-21T01:12:37+0000	CM341S1mCi9wwBNi3d	GET	ads.cnn.com
2013-09-21T01:12:37+0000	CTOhzaq5uhIyxTYo6	GET	ads.cnn.com
```

**FIGURE 10.4**

More useful bro-cut output

So far, we've been working with just one of the log files, but there are many others, and they are all related. For example, each of the HTTP transactions in http.log are tied to specific network flows in the conn.log file, and through that, many flows are also tied to DNS lookups for the destination hosts in the dns.log file. If you examine the last several screenshots closely, you'll see that the uid field is included. Bro uses these unique identifiers in several places to tie related log entries together, even though they may be in different files. Because of this, it is usually a good idea to include the uid field when reviewing Bro logs so that you can quickly pivot between log files.

As an example, let's say that we want to know more about the specific HTTP transaction listed on the first line in Figure 10.4. The second column lists the unique ID for the network flow containing this HTTP transaction. If you search for this string in all the log files, as shown in Figure 10.5, you will see that Bro found a number of different types of log entries. The `http.log` file shows that there were two HTTP transactions tied to this single flow record. This is a normal behavior for HTTP, which will often send multiple transactions through a single network connection to avoid having to take the time to set up and tear down quite so many TCP sessions. According to the `files.log` file, these transactions fetched a text file and a GIF image. The original network session itself is shown in `conn.log` as well, should you need to refer to it.

Many Bro logs contain more than one ID field. For example, the HTTP logs contain not only the first uid field, which ties them back to a specific connection, but also a resp_fuids field, which references a list of the IDs of the files that were downloaded in each transaction. Using these IDs allows you to associate transactions with each other, and to pivot between different types of transactions as you drill down through the logs.

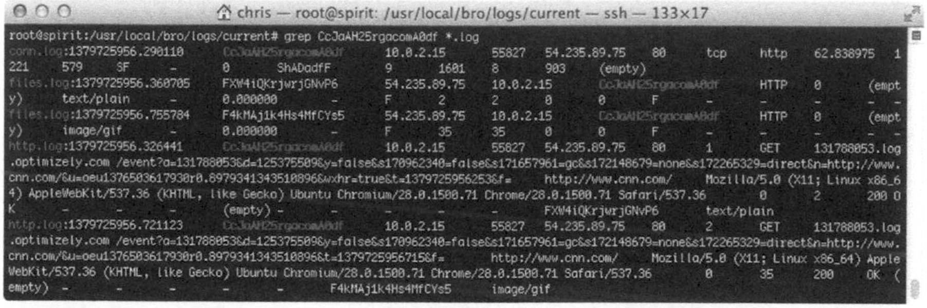

**FIGURE 10.5**

Pivoting through Bro log files based on a transaction uid

## CREATING CUSTOM DETECTION TOOLS WITH BRO

We started this chapter by drawing comparisons between Bro and scripting languages like Python or Perl, but so far, all we've been doing is looking at log files. Bro is more than just a logging platform, though. It's really a general purpose programming language that was consciously focused on reading and processing network traffic. All of its logging so far has just been a by-product of the extensive parsing and normalizing it performs in preparation for any programs you might write. So let's make things a bit more interesting, and write a tool with Bro that can aid in NSM collection, detection, and analysis.

We're going to spend the rest of the chapter talking about how wonderful Bro is, but this is probably a good time to talk about something that isn't so wonderful: Bro's documentation.

Although there has been somewhat of an improvement in the past year or so, the Bro team has traditionally spent almost all of its time on the platform itself, and not so much on documenting how to use it, except by example. This is especially true of the Bro programming language itself. While some basic reference documentation exists (an explanation of the built-in Bro data types, for example, or brief summaries of the events and functions that Bro ships with), there's really no comprehensive tutorial to aid the beginning Brogrammer.

Most people learn Bro scripting by examining existing code, either the large collection of scripts that ship with Bro's distribution (found in /opt/bro/share/bro and subdirectories in Security Onion) or by downloading them from mailing lists or code sharing sites like GitHub.

To try to prepare you for doing this yourself, the examples in this chapter take the same approach. Rather than an A-Z list of all the things you can do with Bro, we'll examine and dissect the code for a few useful scripts, covering some important Bro concepts as they show up in the code. You will find it helpful to refer to the online Bro documentation at http://www.bro.org/documentation/index.html as you go through the chapter. This closely mirrors the process you'll go through as you find new interesting pieces of Bro code and learn by figuring out what they do.

## File Carving

In an NSM environment, it is common to want to extract any files that were transferred from a session. If you have a PCAP file, there are tools that can do this (e.g., tcpxtract), but they usually operate on a byte level, without a lot of protocol knowledge. Once they recognize, say, the beginning of a PDF file, they can usually carve the next few thousand bytes and save them to disk, but this is only an approximation of the actual file that was transferred. This method may also require some manual carving after the fact to end up with the file you are looking for.

Bro, on the other hand, knows a lot about the protocols it decodes, and this knowledge makes all the difference. For our first example, we'll look at a method to extract files out of packet captures with Bro. We'll start by developing it as a tool we can call from the command line with a PCAP file, and then show how to integrate this into the Bro instance that runs with Security Onion so that it just runs all the time on our live network traffic.

First, let's create a quick prototype. Bro has a built-in mechanism for performing on-the-fly analysis of files it sees going over the wire, called the File Analysis Framework. One of the possible "analysis" types it knows how to perform is to write the file to disk. You just have to ask Bro to do this for each file you're interested in.

Fortunately, this is far easier to do than it probably sounds. Create a file called extract-files.bro that contains the following code:

```
# When Bro finds a file being transferred (via any protocol it knows about),
# write a basic message to stdout and then tell Bro to save the file to disk.
event file_new(f: fa_file)
{
    local fuid=f$id;
    local fsource=f$source;
    local ftype=f$mime_type;
    local fname=fmt("extract-%s-%s", fsource, fuid);

    print fmt("*** Found %s in %s. Saved as %s. File ID is %s", ftype,
fsource, fname, fuid);

    Files::add_analyzer(f, Files::ANALYZER EXTRACT,
[$extract_filename=fname]);
}
```

This Bro script creates a new event handler for the file_new event that Bro creates whenever it sees a new file transfer begin, regardless of the protocol. The single parameter Bro passes to this is called `f` and is of type `fa_file`, a record type defined by the framework. Notice Bro's use of the dollar sign character as the operator that refers to the fields in the record. The script references the id, source, and mime_type fields and uses those to construct and then print a short message about each file it finds. It then attaches the file extraction analyzer to that stream, which is the piece that actually tells Bro to save the file to disk. That's it! Now that the `ANALYZER_EXTRACT` analyzer is attached to the file, Bro will take care of the rest.

All that's left now is to actually run this against a PCAP file. Running a specific Bro script is very similar to the way we ran Bro before, but this time we just name the script file at the end of the command line. In fact, you can run multiple Bro scripts by just naming multiple scripts on the same command line, but we don't really need to do that here. The command we will run is:

```
bro -C -r ../pcaps/bro-sample-traffic.pcap ../scripts/extract-files.
bro
```

Figure 10.6 shows what our script looks like when it runs. Notice that each line contains the File ID, so you can find the corresponding log entry in files.log for more information if you need to.

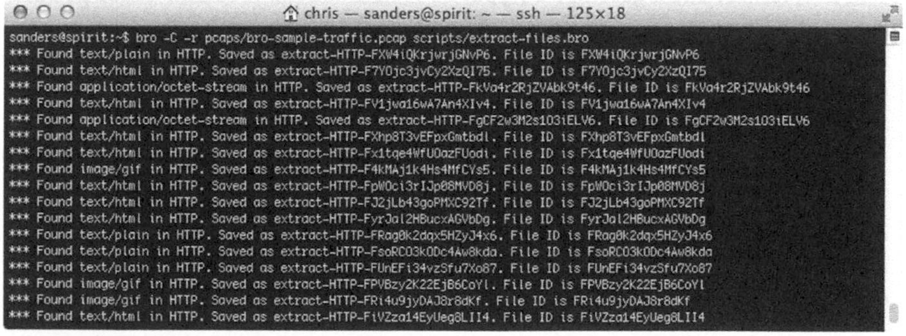

**FIGURE 10.6**

Simple file extractor output

After running the script, notice that you have all of the same log files that Bro generated in the previous examples. In fact, everything looks pretty much the same as before. But this time, there are files inside the extract_files subdirectory, as shown in Figure 10.7.

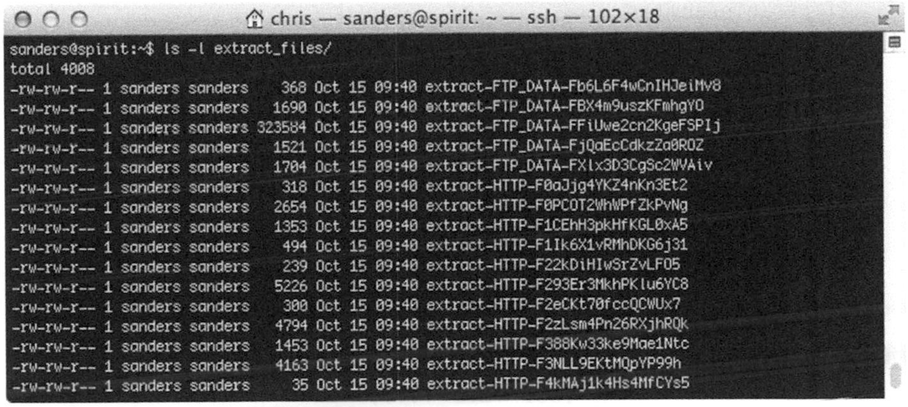

**FIGURE 10.7**

Extracted Files

## Selective file extraction

Looking at the output above, you can see there are a lot of GIF files in the PCAP I used for this example, and also some HTML text. These are all from web traffic, and not what most people think of when they think about "file downloads". What if you're not at all interested in those file types, and just want to extract only Windows executables? No problem! Notice from our earlier code sample that Bro actually knows the MIME type of each file. It figures that out by examining the file, rather than just trusting whatever the file transfer protocol said it was.

---

**FROM THE TRENCHES**

MIME stands for Multipurpose Internet Mail Extensions. Technically, MIME is a format used by email (and now HTTP and other protocols) to create a single message out of one or more message parts. If you've ever received an email with an attachment, you've received a MIME message, even if you never realized it.

Probably the most popular feature of the MIME specification is its use of types to describe what kind of content each message part consists of. MIME types are so popular, in fact, that many non-MIME applications actually use MIME's types to describe the data they work with.

HTTP uses MIME formatting for certain transactions that involve sending multiple pieces of data at once (for example, form submissions with the POST method). Even if it doesn't use the full MIME format, almost everything in HTTP is tagged with a MIME type. Common values here would be "text/html", "text/plain" and "image/gif". There are many others, and probably too many to actually try to list them all here.

---

We can modify our script to check the MIME type for each file before we attach the extraction analyzer.

```
#!/usr/bin/env bro
# When Bro finds an executable file being transferred (via any protocol it
# knows about), write a basic message to stdout and then tell Bro to save
# the file to disk.
event file_new(f: fa_file)
{
        # Check that we have a MIME type value in this record
        if (f?$mime_type) {
            # See if the type is one we care about
             if(f$mime_type == "application/x-dosexec" ||
                f$mime_type == "application/x-executable") {
                    local ftype=f$mime_type;
                    local fuid=f$id;
                    local fsource=f$source;
                    local fname=fmt("extract-%s-%s", fsource, fuid);
                    print fmt("*** Found %s in %s. Saved as %s. File ID
is %s", ftype, fsource, fname, fuid);
                    Files::add_analyzer(f,
Files::ANALYZER_EXTRACT, [$extract_filename=fname]);
                }
        }
}
```

This version is very similar to the first, but it adds an *if* statement to check whether the mime_type value exists in the file record (the f?$mime_type piece), and if so, checks the MIME type value before adding the extraction analyzer. Figure 10.8 shows the new output, skipping all the images and HTML content, and only processing executables.

**FIGURE 10.8**

Extracting only Windows executables

In order to demonstrate another way in which Bro code can be run, let's see a cool trick. So far, we've been explicitly running the Bro command and then naming the script we want to run. Notice the first line of the revised script starts with the typical Unix "shebang" (#!). As you might guess, this means that a standalone tool written in Bro can run from the command line just like any other scripting language. To do this, you must first change the permissions of the script to make it executable:

```
chmod 755 extract-exe-files.bro
```

Now, you can call the script like any other command, as shown in Figure 10.9. It still behaves the same way as before; creating log files and writing the extracted files to disk. It may be a more convenient way to run your code, though, especially if you're providing this tool to other team members who may not be familiar with Bro itself.

**FIGURE 10.9**

Calling the script as a command

## Extracting Files in Live Network Traffic

Now that we've enhanced our script as a standalone tool, let's take a look at what we can do to run it continually as part of Security Onion's Bro instance. This would be useful if you wanted to extract every occurrence of certain file types in near-real time as they came across the network, rather than interacting with individual PCAP files retrospectively.

Typically, once you have a working Bro script, getting it to run all the time isn't very difficult. When Security Onion runs Bro in sensor mode, Bro reads its configuration from /opt/bro/share/bro/site/local.bro by default. Of course, the term "configuration" is used pretty loosely here. Like everything else, local.bro is really just a script that Bro knows to load and run when it starts. The default version that ships with Security Onion really just loads other Bro scripts that perform some useful functions like detecting scans, logging applications in use on the network, adding GeoIP lookups to certain protocol logs, etc. Of course, local.bro really is just a "local" Bro configuration, and this is where you'll add all your own customizations, too. The easiest way to get our file extraction code into Bro is to just paste it verbatim into the bottom of the local.bro file, as shown in Figure 10.10.

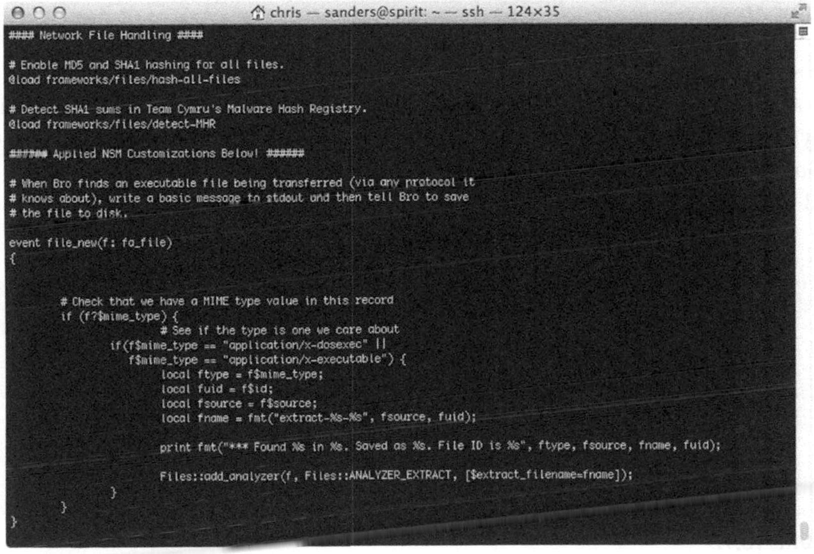

**FIGURE 10.10**

File extraction code added to local.bro

Whenever you make changes to local.bro, you need to run through a simple three-step process to make the running Bro instance aware of them. Each of the steps involves using the Bro control program broctl to perform a task. The commands for these steps are:

**1.** `broctl check`

Do quick syntax and sanity check of the entire configuration to make sure you haven't accidentally broken anything.

**2.** `broctl install`

Make the configuration changes active, also known as "installing" them.

**3.** `broctl restart`

Restart Bro to make it re-read the new changes.

These commands and their output are shown in Figure 10.11.

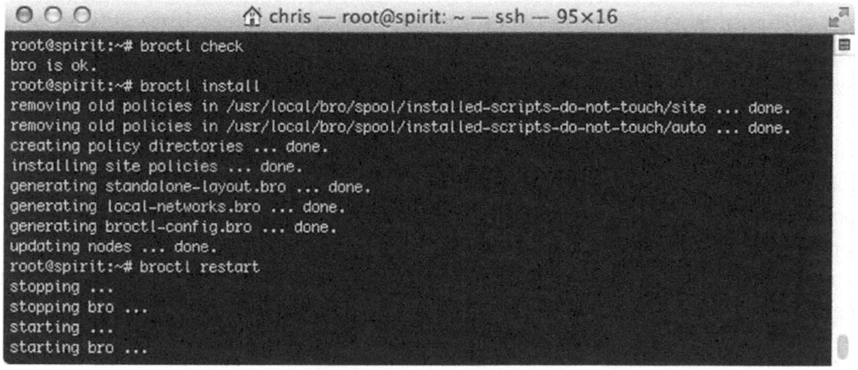

**FIGURE 10.11**

Making the new changes effective using broctl

After your new code has been running for a while, have a look in the Bro log directory /nsm/bro/logs/current. You can examine files.log to see what files were extracted. If any have been, you can look at the content of the "analyzers" field to see which files had the EXTRACT analyzer applied to them, as shown in Figure 10.12.

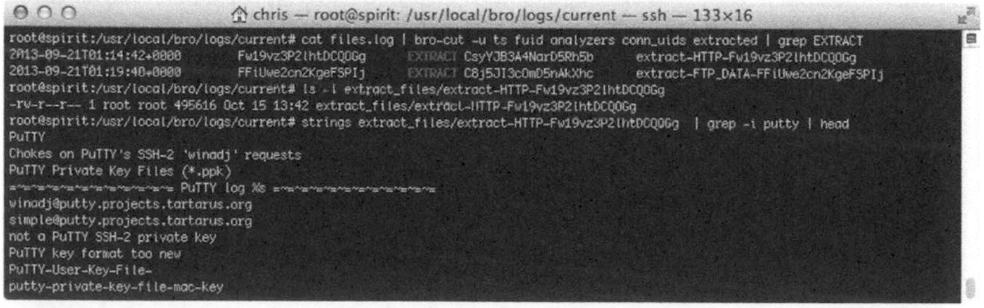

**FIGURE 10.12**

We extracted a file!

As you can see from the string's output on the extracted binary, this file appears to be a copy of the Windows SSH client PuTTY.

This is probably a good time to mention that restarting Bro also forces it to archive any logs currently in /nsm/bro/logs/current and create a fresh new set. This also happens automatically each night (at 00:00 GMT for Security Onion's configuration). If you're working through these examples, don't be surprised if some of your old logs disappear after you restart Bro, reboot the SO system, or even if you just leave things one day and come back the next. The logs are still there. Bro just moved them to a new date-coded subdirectory of /nsm/bro/logs.

## Packaging Bro Code

Right now, Bro is configured to extract executable files from the live network stream, which is incredibly useful. These files can be further analyzed for signs of malicious logic, compiled for statistical analysis, or even have information about them fed back into Bro for further analysis. With that said, everything is working, but we could do a little more to package up our code into its own separate file.

If you think about it, continually adding new code directly to local.bro will probably become unmanageable after a while. Not only that, but if you ever want to share your scripts with other Bro users, you'll have to comb through lots of unrelated modifications and make sure you get only the lines you need to share. This is likely to become a management pain after a while.

If you read the rest of local.bro (the parts we didn't edit), you'll see it really does nothing but load up other scripts, which are each stored in their own separate files. Let's do this with our code!

As it turns out, this is extremely simple. First, cut all of our custom code from local.bro and paste it into a new file called extract-interesting-files.bro, and copy that file into the /opt/bro/share/bro/site directory. This is in Bro's default load path, so we can just insert a statement like the following into local.bro to make our script run just like before:

```
@load extract-interesting files
```

If you use broctl to check, install and restart the Bro instance, you'll see everything is working just like before, but now our code is easier to find, manage, and share.

## Adding Configuration Options

While our code is stored in a much cleaner way, the only problem now is that if we ever want to extract different types of files for some reason, we would have to edit the script, possibly introducing new bugs and certainly making it more difficult to track changes to functionality.

For the final revision of our script, we're going to add a configuration parameter called interesting_types, which will be a set of MIME type strings we care about. Whenever Bro sees a file with one of those MIME types, it will extract it to disk. We will set up this parameter so that other scripts can modify its contents without actually editing the script file itself.

Here's the updated version of our extract-interesting-files.bro file:

```
#
# A module to find files of interest (according to their MIME types) and
# log them to disk.
#
module ExtractFiles;
export {
        const interesting_types: set[string]=[
"application/x-dosexec",
"application/x-executable"
                                                ] &redef;
}
event file_new(f: fa_file)
{
        # Check that we have a MIME type value in this record
        if (f?$mime_type) {
                # See if the type is one we care about
                if(f$mime_type in interesting_types) {
                        local ftype=f$mime_type;
                        local fuid=f$id;
                        local fsource=f$source;
                        local fname=fmt("extract-%s-%s", fsource, fuid);
                        print fmt("*** Found %s in %s. Saved as %s. File ID is %
s", ftype, fsource, fname, fuid);
                        Files::add_analyzer(f,
Files::ANALYZER_EXTRACT, [$extract_filename=fname]);
                }
        }
}
```

Right away, notice that we've declared this as a Bro "module" called Extra-ctFiles. Bro's modules are much like modules in other languages; they provide a new namespace for functions and variables, separate from the main namespace to avoid collisions. By default, these names are private to the module, so you see that we have to use the export directive around those variables and constants we want to make available to other namespaces.

We're only exporting one name here, the constant interesting_types, which is defined as a set of strings. A Bro set is an unordered collection of items of whatever type you specify. You can add and remove items, as well as check to see whether an item is a member of the set. There's only one real tricky part here. Even though this is a "constant", it has the &redef tag at the end of the declaration. That means you can actually explicitly change the contents of the constant, though you will have to use the special redef statement to do it. This is Bro's way of keeping you from accidentally modifying an important configuration parameter due to a bug in your code or any other type of mistake. We'll see how to do this intentionally in a short while.

The last change we made to our code was to replace the conditional that checks whether this is a MIME type we care about. Before, we had the types hard coded, like this:

```
if(f$mime_type == "application/x-dosexec" ||
    f$mime_type == "application/x-executable") {
```

Now we've simplified it to just check to see if the MIME type is part of our "interesting" set:

```
if(f$mime_type in interesting_types) {
```

Now, since we've already added the appropriate @load statement to local.bro, we should be nearly ready to go. Before we do that, though, let's see how you can add new file types to extract. In Security Onion, Bro's database of known MIME types can be found in the text files in the /opt/bro/share/bro/magic directory. Figure 10.13 shows how to modify local.bro to add new MIME types (GIF and HTML) to our "interesting types". Notice that we've used the redef keyword to add two new values to the "constant" set (which, from the main name space, we refer to as ExtractFiles::interesting_types).

```
chris — sanders@spirit: /usr/local/bro/share/bro/site — ssh —...
#### Network File Handling ####

# Enable MD5 and SHA1 hashing for all files.
@load frameworks/files/hash-all-files

# Detect SHA1 sums in Team Cymru's Malware Hash Registry.
@load frameworks/files/detect-MHR

##### Applied NSM Customizations Below! #####

# A module to find files of interest (according to their MIME types) and
# log them to disk.
@load extract-interesting-files

# Add some new interesting types to the list.
redef ExtractFiles::interesting_types += [
                              "image/gif",
                              "text/html"
                          ];
```

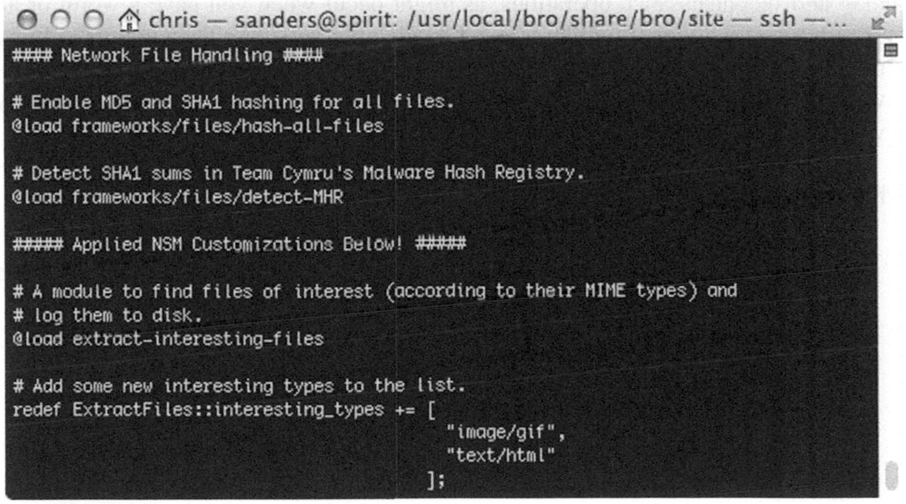

**FIGURE 10.13**

The Final File Extraction Config, with Additional Interesting MIME Types

If you use broctl to check, install and restart the Bro instance, you should start to see a lot of files being extracted very quickly if you are monitoring HTTP traffic at all, as is shown in Figure 10.14.

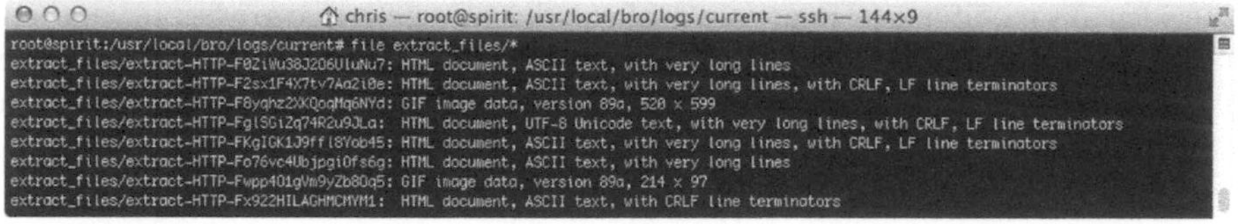

**FIGURE 10.14**

Extracted GIF and HTML files

## Using Bro to Monitor the "Dark" Side

Extracting files is a very useful task for a variety of purposes, but the question you will probably be asking yourself at this point is, "But how can I get Bro to let me know when something interesting happens?" Let's look at an example that asks Bro to look for a certain type of event and let us know when it finds one.

For this example, we'll use Bro to implement a darknet detector. A darknet is any subnet (or individual IP, technically) that is unused in your organization and that no other hosts should have any legitimate reason to interact with. For example, if your organization is allocated a /16 network, you may have several /24 networks that are unused. If you grab a few of those and guarantee they won't be allocated in the future, you just created a darknet.

Darknets are useful things to have, and are helpful for identifying internal scanning and reconnaissance operations, as might occur when you have a worm or an unauthorized individual running around inside your network. They are not entirely reliable, as it's easy for legitimate users to typo an IP address or for legitimate services to be misconfigured to point to your darknets, but they provide valuable early warning and are worth the time to set up and monitor.

To begin, create the file /opt/bro/share/bro/site/darknets.bro and place the following code into it:

```
#
# This module allows you to specify a set of unused netblocks or addresses
# that are part of your internal network but are not used. When Bro sees
# traffic to/from these netblocks, it will generate a notice.
#

@load base/frameworks/notice

module Darknets;

export {

        # Create a notice type for logging
        redef enum Notice::Type+= { Darknet_Traffic };

        # Your darknets. This is empty by default, so add some network
blocks
        # in local.bro. NOTE: You can add specific hosts here by
specifying
        # them as /32 subnets.
```

```
        const darknets: set[subnet]={} &redef;
}
# Check each new potential connection (successful or not, TCP/UDP/IP)
# against our darknet set
event new_connection(c:connection) {
        local darknet_conn=cat(c$id$orig_h, c$id$resp_h, c$id$resp_p);

        if(c$id$orig_h in darknets) {
          NOTICE([$note=Darknet_Traffic,
                $msg="Traffic detected FROM darknet",
                $conn=c,
                $identifier=darknet_conn]);
        }

        if(c$id$resp_h in darknets) {
          NOTICE([$note=Darknet_Traffic,
                $msg="Traffic detected TO darknet",
                $conn=c,
                $identifier=darknet_conn]);
        }

}
```

There are a few new things in here, so before we go on, let's examine this code more closely.

First, notice that the code starts by loading the base/frameworks/notice module. This module is the implementation of Bro's Notice Framework, a set of hooks that make it easy to create your own types of notices and to manage the notices of other modules. Before you can reference anything having to do with the Notice Framework, you have to make sure you've loaded it into your running Bro.

---

**FROM THE TRENCHES**

In reality, we probably don't absolutely have to load the Notice framework here because it is almost always loaded, since it is part of the default framework. However, if you reuse this code in special tools or non-default Bro instances, or if you distribute it to other Bro users, you may not be able to rely on the framework being preloaded. It's best practice to explicitly load anything you depend on. If it's already loaded, then there's no harm, and if it wasn't already loaded, your code will take care of doing that.

---

Next, you'll see that we created a new set, called *darknets*. This set contains members of type subnet, which is a built in Bro data type to store CIDR blocks, specified as literal values in the code, with the format x.x.x.x/y. By default, this set is empty, so just enabling this script won't really do anything. We don't know the allocated darknet subnet(s) in advance, of course, so this makes sense. We'll configure this later, in local.bro.

Next, you'll see that we provided an event handler for the new_connection event. Bro generates this event whenever it starts to track a new connection. The fact that this event was called doesn't imply that the connection attempt was successful, as this event is called too early in the process to know that; only that a new connection was attempted.

---

**FROM THE TRENCHES**

Bro tracks connections for all of the transport protocols it knows about. TCP has its own built-in concept of session establishment using the three-way handshake, and Bro will use that. For connectionless protocols like UDP and ICMP, however, Bro treats all communication between two unique endpoints as a "connection" until a period of time lapses with no communication, at which time the connection "ends". Additional communication between the same endpoints at a later time would generate a new connection.

---

The single parameter to the `new_connection` event is c, a record of type `connection`. Connection records are the kitchen sink of data that Bro tracks for connections. In addition to storing basic info like the source and destination addresses and ports, the connection state and Bro's connection IDs, it's common to find that other non-default or user-written scripts have stored additional data there, such as geotagging information, file hashes, etc.

Some of the most common pieces of data you will read from these records are the source and destination IPs and ports for the connection. Bro stores these as part of the id record, which is of type `conn_id` and a component of the `connection` type. `Conn_id` records have the following structure (Table 10.2):

**Table 10.2** The Structure of the conn_id Record Type

| Field Name | Description |
| --- | --- |
| orig_h | The IP address of the originator of the connection (the client) |
| orig_p | The originator's port number and protocol |
| resp_h | The IP address of the responder for the connection (the server) |
| resp_p | The responder's port number and protocol |

Although we don't need it for this example, it's worthwhile to note that ports in Bro are native data types, and include both a numeric and a protocol piece. For example, you could use the following piece of code to assign the normal SMTP port to a variable:

```
smtp_port=25/tcp;
```

For our example, though, we only care about the source and destination IP and the destination port, which we access through their nested data structures as c$id $orig_h, c$id$resp_h and c$id$resp_p respectively.

Our event handler starts by calling the `cat()` function, which simply takes the individual string representations of all of its arguments and returns them as a single string. Here, we're building a string that consists of the source and destination IPs and the destination port. This is an easy way of creating an identifier for this connection. We'll discuss why we need this shortly, but for now just know that we're assigning this value to the variable `darknet_conn`.

Next, we examine the source IP (and later, in a nearly identical piece of code, the destination IP) to see if it's in one of our darknets, like this:

```
if(c$id$orig_h in darknets) {
NOTICE([$note=Darknet_Traffic,
     $msg="Traffic detected FROM darknet",
     $conn=c,
     $identifier=darknet_conn]);
}
```

This code says "if the source IP is in the set called darknets, generate a notice." A notice is simply an entry in the notices.log file and is the most common way Bro draws extra attention to something. Bro also has the concept of alarms, which are like notices, except they go to the alarms.log file and are emailed out on a regular schedule. Notices can also be immediately emailed or paged for quick attention, but we won't do that in this example.

In our code, we're calling the NOTICE function, which takes exactly one argument: a record containing all the information about the notice. Although you can create a separate variable to hold the notice record, you will usually see code construct an implicit record using the [$field1=value1,$field2=value2,..., $fieldN=valueN] construct, which is the method we use here.

Each notice has a type, which is one of a set of enumerated values defined by the various modules loaded into Bro. The values themselves are not really important; they're just used to differentiate one type of notice from another. You just need to know their names so you can pass them as the value of the $note field in the notice record. Each module that creates its own notices defines its own new types. Our code defines one type called Darknet_Traffic, like this:

```
# Create a notice type for logging
redef enum Notice::Type+= { Darknet_Traffic };
```

Each notice also includes a human-readable message in the $msg field. We've defined one notice type with two different possible messages, according to whether the traffic is detected going into or coming out of the darknet.

Next, we add the information about the current network connection to the notice record as the $conn field. Because Bro now knows which connection this notice is associated with, it can properly log the connection ID into the notice.log file, which builds the pivot linkages into the conn.log file that we saw earlier in the chapter.

Finally, our code adds the identifier we created earlier as $identifier. The identifier is important for generating notices with this script.

## Notice Suppression

Consider what would happen if a system on your network were misconfigured, such that it tried to access the printer service on a host it thought was a print server, but was really an unused address in one of your darknets. Print jobs submitted by the faulty host would never print, but the system would keep submitting them, checking printer status, submitting them again, etc. It could do this for quite a long time until someone noticed and manually removed the jobs. You'd probably like to know about this activity, but you don't necessarily want to see a separate notice for every single network connection involved in this faulty printer communication.

Bro solves this problem by using notice suppression. In other words, it's smart enough to know that it's already sent a notice about a particular event, and if so, to hold off sending another one for a while. To do this, it examines each notice's type (`Darknet_Traffic`) and the unique identifier your code should supply. That's why we had to create that `darknet_conn` value.

`Darknet_conn` uses the source and destination IPs, plus the destination port, to create a "unique" identifier for that connection. In fact, this is not at all unique, because it leaves out the source port, but this is by design. Repeated connections to the same service would normally come from different source port numbers, so including this would make the identifier too specific and generate more notices. Instead, we're making the implicit assumption that once we know 10.0.2.15 talked to 192.168.1.1 on port 80 once, we can ignore the fact that it may have communicated several more times in the next few minutes. Once we have the original notice, we can always find the full list of connections in the conn.log file if we need to.

The default suppression interval is one hour, so for most things you should only get a max of 24 notices per day for the same event. You can adjust this up or down as you see fit, however. If you just want to change the default interval for all notices, you can add the following to local.bro:

```
# Change the default notice suppression interval for all notice types
redef Notice::default_suppression_interval = 30 min;
```

Bro has a built-in data type called `interval` that can be set to any number of `usec`, `msec`, `sec`, `min`, `hr`, or `day` values. This makes setting time intervals easier for this type of work.

You can also set the value differently for each type of notice. For example, if you want the keep the shorter value above for most notice types, but you want to set a longer value for our `Darknet_Traffic` types, you could add something like the following to local.bro:

```
Notice::type_suppression_intervals[Darknet_Traffic] = 2 hour;
```

As you become more familiar with Bro and how it works in your environment, you will almost certainly want to try your hand at tuning one or both of these types of suppression values.

### Using and Testing the Script

Now that we have our code installed as darknets.bro in the correct directory, all we need to do is to load it from local.bro and give it a real list of dark subnets. Figure 10.15 demonstrates how to do this.

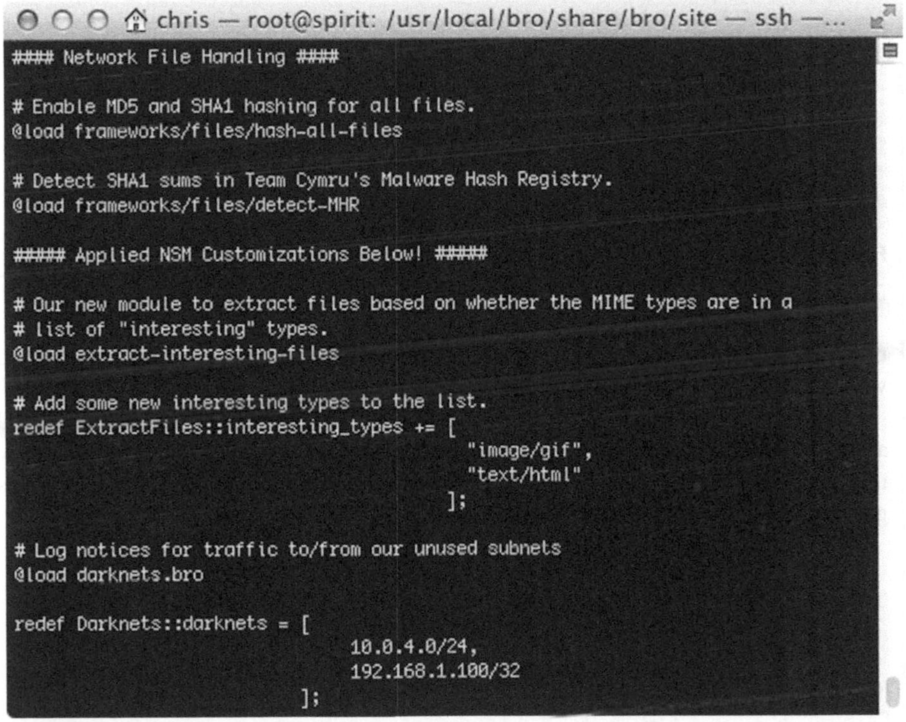

```
### Network File Handling ####

# Enable MD5 and SHA1 hashing for all files.
@load frameworks/files/hash-all-files

# Detect SHA1 sums in Team Cymru's Malware Hash Registry.
@load frameworks/files/detect-MHR

#### Applied NSM Customizations Below! ####

# Our new module to extract files based on whether the MIME types are in a
# list of "interesting" types.
@load extract-interesting-files

# Add some new interesting types to the list.
redef ExtractFiles::interesting_types += [
                                "image/gif",
                                "text/html"
                            ];

# Log notices for traffic to/from our unused subnets
@load darknets.bro

redef Darknets::darknets = [
                    10.0.4.0/24,
                    192.168.1.100/32
                ];
```

**FIGURE 10.15**

Darknet config in local.bro

For this example, I've specified the entire 10.0.4.0 – 10.0.4.255 range as a darknet, and also the individual IP address 192.168.1.100. Neither of those ranges are in use on my lab network, but in a real world scenario you should modify this list to fit your own environment.

After a quick round of `broctl check/install/restart`, the darknet code should be loaded into our running Bro instance. Ideally, since these are supposed to be "dark" nets, we shouldn't see any network traffic involving them. Since Bro doesn't create log files until it has something to write to them, this also means you may not see a notice.log file immediately. That's normal.

The next step is to create some test traffic to one of the configured darknets. For the first test, we'll try some simple ICMP traffic to a "dark" host. Here, I chose an arbitrary IP address in the 10.0.4.0/24 range I configured as a darknet above, then just used the ping command to send a few packets, as shown in Figure 10.16. This host doesn't exist on my network, so I didn't get any replies, but Bro doesn't care.

If you examine Figure 10.16, you'll see that Bro logged our notice as type `Darknets::Darknet_Traffic`, which makes it easy to find with grep or whatever other

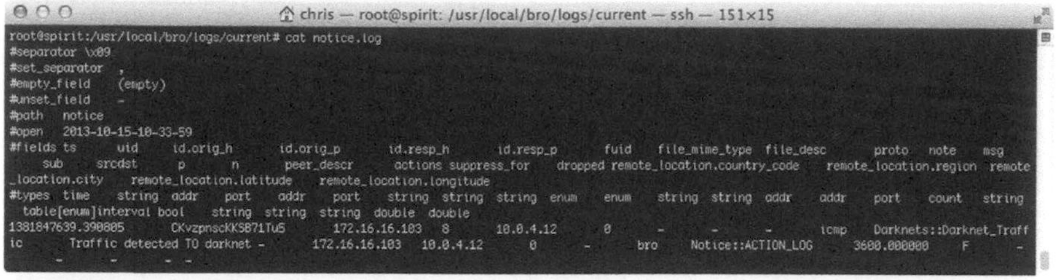

**FIGURE 10.16**

Darknet_Traffic notices generated by ICMP traffic

reporting tool you like. It also reported that it found "Traffic detected TO darknet" so we know that the connection was inbound to the dark subnet.

For another test, let's try a couple of TCP connections to the 192.168.1.100 address, which I previously configured as an individual dark host. I chose to try to connect on ports 80/tcp (HTTP) and 515/tcp (the Unix print spooler). The notices generated from this activity are shown in Figure 10.17.

**FIGURE 10.17**

Darknet_Traffic notices for a dark host

Reading Figure 10.17 closely, you can see that Bro logged a number of `Darknet_Traffic` notices for connection attempts to 192.168.1.100 on port 80, and one notice each for traffic to and from port 515. From this, we can deduce that the host did not respond at all to HTTP requests, but it is listening on the print spooler port. This might lead us to believe that someone may have misconfigured his or her printer.

## Extending the Darknet Script

With a little effort, the darknet module could be adapted to other uses as well. For example, if your security policy states that Active Directory servers should be on their own special subnet, and that the hosts on the network should not have access to the Internet, you could modify this code such that the list of "darknets" is replaced with a list of server subnets. In this case you would still expect to see a lot of traffic between your AD subnet and the rest of your internal network, so you can't simply just alert on everything you see. With this in mind, you could either run this on a Bro instance that sees only traffic as it passes to and from the Internet (and thus should never see AD traffic anyway) or modify the logic of the `new_connection` handler a bit to make sure that the other side of the connection is not a valid local subnet (perhaps using a set of `subnet` types).

You could also use a similar approach to detect unauthorized connections between your DMZ and sensitive parts of your internal network (e.g. "why is the DMZ talking to the CEO's computer?!") or even replace the list of subnets with a list of allowed ports and audit connections using unusual or out-of-policy services. The possibilities for customizing and adapting this simple example to your own network are nearly endless, and really demonstrate some of the power and flexibility of Bro as a framework for detecting bad things on the network.

## Overriding default notice processing

We've configured Bro to alert us whenever something tries to communicate with one of our darknets, but as written, our script isn't very particular about exactly *what* is communicating with the darknets. I said before that there should be no legitimate reason for any other host on our network to try to talk to a darknet, but there are a few exceptions to this rule., such as, internal network mapping.

An organization sometimes wants to know what's on its network, whether the purpose is to discover new devices that need to be managed or just to audit against unauthorized hosts being connected. Network engineers may do this on a regular basis, and it's also a normal feature of many vulnerability management packages. So clearly there are *some* hosts that try to talk to our darknets, even if just to verify that they still really are dark. We don't want to be alerted to all this legitimate activity, but as written, our script is likely to generate notices for an awful lot of this activity. Let's see if we can fix that.

There are a couple of ways we could address this problem. Using only techniques we've already seen, we could modify the darknets module to define another set of the addresses of our authorized network scanners, then include some logic in the `new_connection` handler to check for set membership before generating a notice. That would work just fine, and would probably be a useful addition to the script. In fact, it's probably the best way since we wrote the original darknets code ourselves. However, we've already seen all those techniques, so let's try something new.

Let's pretend that we originally got the darknet code from another Bro user. In that case, it might not make sense to directly modify the code, since we'd have to maintain a local patch, and apply and test it again with every new version of the module. That's a pain, and fortunately, there's another way. We can intercept Bro's notices before they are written to the disk, inspect them, and decide whether we want to log the notice, discard it, or potentially take some other action.

We could put our new code into its own file, as we have been doing for the other examples However, by loading our code directly into local.bro, we keep the code that loads the darknets module and the code that modifies its logging together, which probably makes it clearer and easier to maintain for the purposes of this example. Here's what the end of local.bro should look like, with both the previous darknets code and our new additions loaded in:

```
# Log notices for traffic to/from our unused subnets
@load darknets.bro

redef Darknets::darknets=[
                        10.0.4.0/24,
                192.168.1.100/32
                    ];

# These are our legitimate network scanners, which are allowed to talk to
# our darknets without logging notices.
const allowed_darknet_talkers: set[addr]={
                                10.0.2.15
                        };

#  Process  all  notices  at  high  priority,  looking  for  Darknets::
Darknet_Traffic
# types. When we find them and either the src or dst IP is an
#  allowed_darknet_talker,  remove  all  actions  from  the  notice,  which
causes
# Bro not to log, alarm, email or page it.
hook Notice::policy(n: Notice::Info) &priority=5 {
    if(n$note == Darknets::Darknet_Traffic &&
        (n$conn$id$orig_h in allowed_darknet_talkers ||
       n$conn$id$resp_h in allowed_darknet_talkers)) {

            # Remove all actions and assign it the empty set
            n$actions=set();
        }

}
```

The code starts by declaring a new constant, `allowed_darknet_talkers`, as a set of IP addresses (you could easily make this into a set of subnets if you have a particularly large number of network scanners or otherwise whitelisted IP addresses). I've added my scanning system's IP (10.0.2.15) as the only member of the set.

Next, I've declared a new type of function, called a *hook*. Hooks are similar to event handlers, in that Bro calls these hooks as it's processing traffic and doing work. The main difference is that events correspond to things Bro finds happening in network traffic, where hooks are called when Bro is performing its own internal processes.

In this case, when Bro generates a new notice, it calls the `Notice::policy` hook to allow you to perform local processing and modify how Bro will handle the notice (in other words, how it implements its notice policy for this notice). The single argument to this hook is *n*, a record of type `Notice::Info` that contains all the information Bro has about this notice.

One interesting thing about the hook declaration is that it uses the `&priority` keyword to assign a priority value of 5 to this hook function's execution. Because you can have multiple event handlers for each event and multiple hook functions for each hook, Bro allows you to set the order in which they are called. Valid priorities are any integer between 0 (default) and 5. Hooks and event handlers are called in priority order, with larger numbers being called before smaller numbers. In this case, `&priority=5` helps ensure that Bro calls our hook function before it does any other notice policy processing, to give us a chance to bail out on processing this notice early.

The first thing our hook has to do is to decide if it should process this notice or not. There are many types of notices that Bro can generate, but we only want to concern ourselves with `Darknets::Darknet_Traffic` here, and only if one of the two IPs is in our `allowed_darknet_talkers` set. In our original `Darknets` module code, we already saw how we could use the `Conn_id` record type to access the source and destination IP addresses of the connection in question. The `Notice::Info` type also stores a `Conn_id` record that refers to the original connection which generated the notice, which we can access as `n$conn`. Therefore, `n$conn$id$orig_h` would be the client's IP, and `n$conn$id$resp_h` would be the server's IP. All this processing goes into a simple `if` statement at the beginning of the hook to make sure we meet all the requirements. If not, we simply don't do anything, and Bro continues to log the notice as it normally would.

If, however, our conditional evaluates to true, Bro processes the body of the hook, a single line that assigns an empty set to the `n$actions` variable:

```
# Remove all actions and assign it the empty set
n$actions=set();
```

This requires some explanation. Bro decides what to do with a notice by examining the list of "actions" which have been assigned to it. Actions are just enumerated type values, and there are four to choose from. Table 10.3 lists these and explains what they do.

**Table 10.3** Bro Notice Actions

| Action | Description |
|---|---|
| `Notice:: ACTION_LOG` | Writes the notice to the notice.log file. |
| `Notice:: ACTION_ALARM` | Writes the notice to the alarm.log file. This file is emailed hourly to the address specified in the `Notice::mail_dest` variable. |
| `Notice:: ACTION_EMAIL` | Immediately emails the notice to the address specified in the `Notice::mail_dest` variable. |
| `Notice:: ACTION_PAGE` | Immediately sends the notice to the address specified in the `Notice::mail_page_dest` variable. This is normally an email-to-SMS gateway of some sort, but could be any email address. |

The underlying purpose of the `Notice::policy` hook is to allow you to change the set of default actions to be applied to the notice before Bro starts to implement those actions. In our code, since we removed all of the actions by assigning the empty set, we're effectively telling Bro "do nothing with this notice."

Now it's time to try our new code. Recall that after restarting Bro, our log directory starts fresh and clean, so there are no notices. From our scanning host, we then ping one of the darknets (unsuccessfully) and connect to the printer port of the dark host we defined (successfully). But if we look at the log files, there are still no more notices (Figure 10.18). This indicates that our hook is working successfully, and will help us to avoid generating notices from traffic sources from approved internal scanning devices.

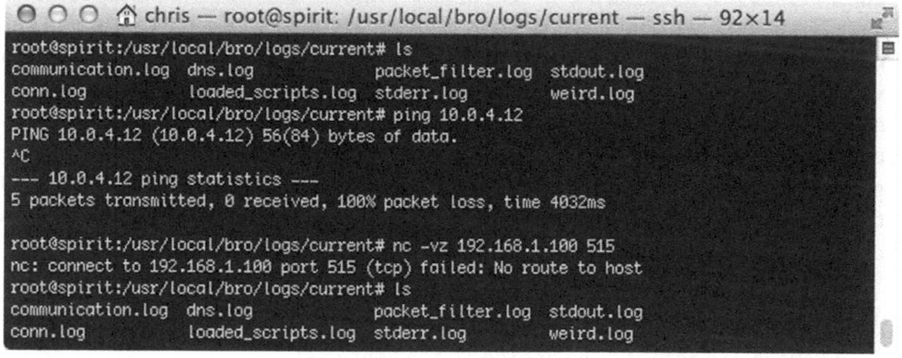

**FIGURE 10.18**

Communication from an Approved Device Does Not Generate Notices

### Generating E-Mail Notices from Darknet Events

As with the other examples in this chapter, you could easily repurpose the code that disables logging of `Darknets::Darknet_Traffic` notices for other useful purposes. For example, if there are no authorized network scanners in your organization, maybe you really want to know about darknet notices immediately. It would be quite simple to modify this code to elevate the processing such that the notice is logged and also emailed. Just take the checks for `n$conn$id$orig_h` and `n$conn$id$dest_h` out of the `if` statement, and replace these lines:

```
# Remove all actions and assign it the empty set
n$actions = set();
```

With these:

```
# In addition to the default Notice::ACTION_LOG which is already assigned
# to this event, add the Notice::ACTION_EMAIL action, so the notice will be
# emailed immediately.
add n$actions[Notice::ACTION_EMAIL];
```

You'll need to also supply the email address as the value of `Notice::mail_dest` in your local.bro file like so:

```
redef Notice::mail_dest = "admin@appliednsm.com";
```

After restarting Bro, you should start receiving email alerts any time a system tries to communicate with one of your defined darknets.

## Suppressing, E-Mailing, and Alarming - The Easy Way

In the last section, we saw how to hook into Bro's notice processing to provide detailed, granular customizations that allowed you to make decisions about how to process each individual notice. This surgical precision is nice, but sometimes all you need is a big hammer.

Bro provides a number of convenient shortcuts for changing the notice processing policy. These shortcuts take the form of constants you can modify to change the policy for all events of a certain type.

For example, suppose you have only a single SSH server on your network, and it's exposed to the Internet. It has a legitimate business use (secure remote file transfers for your business partners), but the fact that it's directly accessible from the Internet and needs to use the default SSH port means it's going to be the constant target of password guessing attacks. Bro's support for the SSH protocol logs the `SSH::Password_Guessing` notice each time it sees this type of activity, but you could get hundreds of these notices each day. This can be annoying since there's nothing you can do to prevent these attacks. You won't want to turn off Bro's SSH protocol support entirely, but there is another option.

The answer is to add the `SSH::Password_Guessing` notice type to the list of notices which should just never be logged. Bro still tracks them (other notice types still depend on knowing when password guessing attacks are going on) but you'll never see them. You can do this by adding the following to local.bro:

```
# Don't generate any notices for SSH password guessing attempts.
redef Notice::ignored_types += { SSH::Password_Guessing };
```

After you restart Bro, the password guessing notices will no longer show up in the logs. This affects all such notices from any host, so if you want to see notices from some hosts and not others, this mechanism is not for you. In our example, though, we have only a single SSH server anyway, so this is perfect.

The opposite example would be to escalate the processing of certain types of notices to alarms (alert data), or to email alerts. Assume you have at least one Internet-facing web server and are especially concerned with SQL injection attacks. Bro can detect SQL injection if you load the `detect-sqli` script (which is likely on by default), and will generate `HTTP::SQL_Injection_Attacker` notices whenever it sees a host performing such an attack against one of your servers (it also generates an `HTTP::SQL_Injection_Victim` notice for the target server, but we can ignore that for now).

The problem is, by default, these just go into the notice.log file with everything else, but you'd like them to go into alerts.log so you'll get an automatic email summary every hour. You can accomplish this with the following code in local.bro:

```
# Alarm on any SQLi attempts
redef Notice::alarmed_types+= { HTTP::SQL_Injection_Attacker };
```

Alternatively, you can escalate even further, and turn these into immediate email alerts, like this:

```
# Send email immediately for any SQLi attempts
redef Notice::emailed_types+= { HTTP::SQL_Injection_Attacker };
```

Of course, for either of these last two to work, you'll have to make sure you have defined the `Notice::mail_dest` variable discussed earlier. Otherwise Bro won't know where to send the messages.

## Adding New Fields to Bro's Logs

For our final example, let's circle back to the beginning of the chapter and talk a little more about logs. We've already seen that Bro does an excellent job of logging different types of transactions, but sometimes even Bro's logging falls short. Perhaps you need to track an additional piece of information for certain transactions, or you maybe you just want to provide extra context around some events. Adding new fields to existing Bro logs is quite easy, and is a common thing to do.

Suppose you work for an organization that is concerned about where its Internet traffic is coming from or going to. One simple thing you can do to track this is have Bro look up the country codes for all network connections it sees (both sources and destinations) and add them to the conn.log file as new fields.

To start, paste the following code into a file called conn-geoip.bro:

```
redef record Conn::Info+= {
     orig_cc: string &optional &log;
     resp_cc: string &optional &log;
};

event connection_state_remove (c: connection)
{
    local client_geo_data=lookup_location(c$id$orig_h);
    local server_geo_data=lookup_location(c$id$resp_h);

    if(client_geo_data?$country_code) {
        c$conn$orig_cc=client_geo_data$country_code;
    }
    if(server_geo_data?$country_code) {
        c$conn$resp_cc=server_geo_data$country_code;
    }
}
```

The script begins by adding two fields to the `Conn::Info` record type. This is the data type Bro uses to store information about each connection it sees. It typically records things like the connection timestamp, uid, endpoints, application-layer protocol, and so on. In our case, we're adding two new fields to store country codes for the endpoints, `orig_cc` and `resp_cc`.

Notice that each of the new fields is tagged with a couple of options. These tags are not part of the record itself, but rather, they tell Bro how to treat these fields in various circumstances. The `&log` option tells Bro to make sure to write the value of this field to the log file when it creates the conn.log entry. If you leave this out, Bro will track the data but you'll never see it in the log file. The `&optional` tag specifies that it's OK for this field to have no value (for example, if one of the endpoints is an RFC 1918 address and thus has no specific geographic ties). In this case, Bro will just log a "-" in that field, which is the default behavior for any field in any log if there is no value to record. Technically, you could replace `&optional` with `&default="None"` (or some other string) if you wanted to log a different value in that case, but "-" is the standard everywhere else, so we'll stick with that for consistency.

Next, we set up a simple event handler for the `connection_state_remove` event, which Bro generates just before it's ready to remove an active connection from its state table and write the log to disk. We're using the `lookup_location()` function, which is built in to Bro. It takes an IP address as its argument, and returns a geo_location record, which Bro defines like so:

```
type geo_location: record {
    country_code: string;
    region: string;
    city: string;
    latitude: double;
    longitude: double;
}
```

Our script generates two lookup requests, one for each side of the connection, with the IPs stored in the connection record:

```
local client_geo_data=lookup_location(c$id$orig_h);
local server_geo_data=lookup_location(c$id$resp_h);
```

Next, it checks each return value to see if the resulting record includes country code information. If so, it assigns the country code to the appropriate field in the newly redefined connection info record. Otherwise it does nothing.

```
if(client_geo_data?$country_code) {
    c$conn$orig_cc=client_geo_data$country_code;
}
```

That's it! Once we added the two new fields to the `Conn::Info` record and set the `&log` parameter, we guaranteed that those values would be logged to the conn.log file. All the `connection_state_remove` handler had to do was to look them up and insert them into the connection info record. Bro handled all the rest.

Now it's time to run our script. For demonstration purposes, we're going to go back to testing it from the command line with a PCAP file, though you now know enough to permanently add this to your running Bro instance, if you wish. Figure 10.19 shows the tail end of our connection log now, extracting IP address and geographic data for each endpoint.

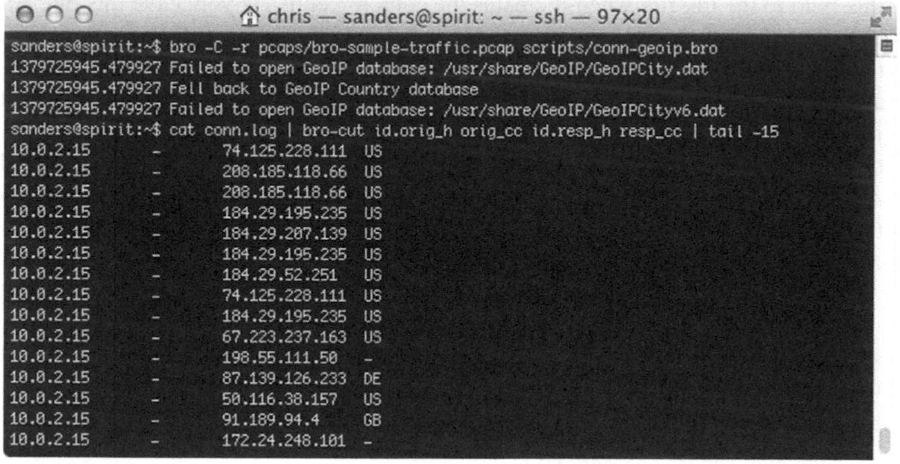

**FIGURE 10.19**

Connection logs with GeoIP info included

---

**CAUTION**

There's one very important prerequisite for this example that we haven't covered yet: the GeoIP database! Bro doesn't actually know about all possible IP addresses and country codes. It relies on the third party GeoIPLite database by MaxMind (http://www.maxmind.com) to provide this mapping. This database is installed by default on Security Onion, but if you are running the example on a different system, you may need to install it yourself. Fortunately, GeoIPLite is widely available as an installable package on most Linux or *BSD platforms.

MaxMind also provides other databases with more detailed information. The default GeoIPLite database only provides country codes, and only for IPv4 addresses, so Bro is not able to fill in any of the other fields in the `geo_location` structure except the country code. However, other MaxMind databases include city and latitude/longitude information as well, for both IPv4 and IPv6. If you need more granular location information or if you deal with a lot of IPv6-capable hosts, visit the GeoIPLite web page at http://dev.maxmind.com/geoip/legacy/geolite/ for instructions on how to download and install these additional databases.

If you choose not to install these additional databases, geographic lookups will still work, but most of the values in the `geo_location` structure will be undefined. You might also see non-fatal warnings similar to the ones shown in Figure 10.19 as Bro tries and fails to use these additional databases, but you can ignore these.

# CONCLUSION

We started this chapter with a quick overview of some essential Bro concepts and a tour through the log files, but quickly got down to a very hands-on, incremental primer on coding for Bro. So far, we've done some simple but very useful things, like extracting files and monitoring darknets. We've also seen several techniques you can use over and over again in your Bro journey, such as notice handling, alarming, tweaking configuration and logging settings, and creating your own modules.

Despite all we've just covered, we've barely scratched the surface. Even though we tried our best, it's impossible to do justice to Bro in a single chapter. Bro really deserves its own book, but until we get that, keep a close eye on the web site at http://bro.org, especially their email lists. There is a lively and rapidly growing community of other Bro users out there answering questions, publishing scripts, and pushing the envelope of what you can do with it as a platform. For more real-time help, you can also tune into Freenode IRC's #bro channel, where there is often someone around to help answer your questions or just to chat about cool things they are doing with Bro. It is the opinion of the authors of this book, and a lot of individuals in the NSM community, that Bro is the future of efficient NSM detection.

# Anomaly-Based Detection with Statistical Data

# 11

## CHAPTER CONTENTS

Network Security Monitoring is based upon the collection of data to perform detection and analysis. With the collection of a large amount of data, it makes sense that a SOC should have the ability to generate statistical data from existing data, and that these statistics can be used for detection and analysis. In this chapter we will discuss methods for generating statistical data that can be used to support detection, including near real-time detection and retrospective detection.

Statistical data is data derived from the collection, organization, analysis, interpretation and presentation of existing data[1]. With the immense amount of data that an NSM team is tasked with parsing, statistical data can play a large role in detection and analysis, from the analysis of the traffic generated by a particularly hostile host, to revealing the total visibility for a new sensor. In the current NSM landscape, the big name vendors most prominently push statistical data in the form of dashboards within dashboards. While this is used partly for justifying wall mounting 70 inch plasma TV's in your SOC and to wow your superior's superior, it turns out that this data can actually be immensely useful if it is applied in the right way.

## TOP TALKERS WITH SiLK

A simple example of statistical data is a list of top talkers on your network. This list identifies the friendly devices that are responsible for the largest amount of communication on a monitored network segment. The NSM team within a SOC can use top talker statistics to identify things like devices that have a suspiciously large amount

---

[1]Dodge, Y. (2006) The Oxford Dictionary of Statistical Terms, OUP. ISBN 0-19-920613-9

of outbound traffic to external hosts, or perhaps to find friendly hosts that are infected with malware connecting to a large number of suspicious external IP addresses. This is providing detection that signatures cannot, because this is a true network anomaly.

The ability to generate a top talkers list can be challenging without the right tools and access to network data. However, session data analysis tools like SiLK and Argus make this task trivial.

In Chapter 4, we discussed various methods for collection of session data and basic methods of parsing it. There we discussed SiLK, a tool used for the efficient collection, storage and analysis of flow data. Within SiLK there are a number of tools that are useful for generating statistics and metrics for many scenarios. SiLK operates by requiring the user to identify the data they want to use as the source of a data set, then allowing the user to choose from a variety of tools that can be used for displaying, sorting, counting, grouping, and mating data from that set. From these tools, we can use rwstats and rwcount to generate a top talkers list. Let's look at how we can do this.

While many people will use SiLK for directly viewing flow data, rwstats is one of the most powerful ways to really utilize session data for gaining a better understanding of your environment, conducting incident response, and finding evil. In every environment that I've seen SiLK deployed, rwstats is always the most frequently used statistical data source. We will start by using rwstats to output a list of top talkers.

As with all uses of SiLK, I recommend that you begin by generating an rwfilter command that you can use to verify the data set you intend to use to generate statistics. Generally, this can be as easy as making the filter and piping the resultant data to rwcut. This will output the results of the rwfilter command so that you can be sure the data set you are working with is correct. If you aren't familiar with rwfilter usage and piping output between rwtools, then now might be a good time to review Chapter 4 before reading further. For the majority of these examples, we'll be using basic examples of rwfilter queries so that anyone can follow along using their current "out of the box" SiLK deployment.

Rwstats only requires that you specify three things: an input parameter, a set of fields that you wish to generate statistics for, and the stopping condition by which you wish to limit the results. The input parameter can either be a filename listed on the command line, or in the more common case, data being read from standard input from the result of an rwfilter command. This input should be fed straight from rwfilter without being parsed by the rwcut command. The set of fields that you specify represents a user-defined key by which SiLK flow records are to be grouped. Data that matches that key is stored in bins for each unique match. The volume of these bins (be it total bytes, records, packets, or number of distinct communication records) is then used to generate a list ordered by that volume size from top to bottom (default), or from bottom to top, depending on the user's choosing. The stopping condition is used to limit the results that you're generating and can be limited by defining a total count (print 20 bins), a value threshold (print bins whose byte count is less than 400), or a percentage of total specified volume (print bins that contain at least 10% of all the packets).

Now that we have an understanding of how rwstats works, the first step toward generating a list of top talkers is to make a functional rwfilter command that will generate the data that we want to examine. Following that, we use the pipe symbol to send that data to rwstats. That command looks like this:

```
rwfilter --start-date=2013/08/26:14 --any-address=102.123.0.0/16 --
type=all --pass=stdout | rwstats --top --count=20 --fields=sip,dip --
value=bytes
```

In this example, the rwfilter command gathers all of the flow records collected during the 1400 hour of August 8th, and only examines traffic in the 102.123.0.0/16 IP range. That data is piped to rwstats, which will generate a list of the top 20 (--count=20) source and destination IP address combinations (--fields=sip,dip) for the data in that filter, sorted by bytes (--value=bytes).

Another way to achieve the same results is to pass the results of the rwfilter command to a file, and then use rwstats to parse that file. These two commands will do this, using a file named test.rwf:

```
rwfilter --start-date=2013/08/26:14 --any-address=102.123.0.0/16 --
type=all --pass=stdout > test.rwf
```

```
rwstats test.rwf --top --count=20 --fields=sip,dip --value=bytes
```

The results from these commands are shown in Figure 11.1.

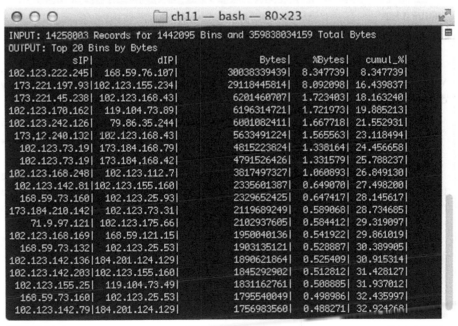

**FIGURE 11.1**

Top Talkers Generated by Rwstats

In the data shown in Figure 11.1, there are several extremely busy devices on the local network. In cases where this is unexpected, this should lead to further examination. Here, we see that the host 102.123.222.245 appears to be responsible for a large amount of traffic being generated. We can generate more statistics to help narrow down its communication.

By running the same command, this time substituting the CIDR range for our top talkers IP address in the rwfilter statement, we can see the hosts that it is communicating with that are responsible for generating all of this traffic.

```
rwfilter --start-date=2013/08/26:14 --any-address=102.123.222.245
--type=all --pass=stdout | rwstats --top --count=5 --fields=sip,dip
--value=bytes
```

The statistics generated by this query are shown in Figure 11.2.

```
● ○ ○                    ch11 — bash — 80×8
INPUT: 128837 Records for 8511 Bins and 32059683554 Total Bytes
OUTPUT: Top 5 Bins by Bytes
            sIP|          dIP|          Bytes|   %Bytes|   cumul_%|
102.123.222.245| 168.59.76.107|    30038339439| 93.695059| 93.695059|
 168.59.76.107|102.123.222.245|      418907922|  1.306650| 95.001709|
102.123.222.245|102.123.231.154|       81795975|  0.255137| 95.256846|
102.123.222.245| 102.123.168.62|       60875215|  0.189881| 95.446727|
 102.123.168.62|102.123.222.245|       24694805|  0.077028| 95.523754|
```

**FIGURE 11.2**

Focusing in on Top Communication Partners for a Single Host

This helps identify the "who" in relation to this anomalous high amount of traffic. We can identify the "what" by changing our search criteria to attempt to identify common services observed from the communication between these devices.

```
rwfilter --start-date=2013/08/26:14 --any-address=102.123.222.245
--type=all --pass=stdout | rwstats --top --count=5 --fields=sip,
sport,dip --value=bytes
```

In this command, we use the same set of data, but tell rwstats to use the source port field as another criterion for statistics generation. Figure 11.3 shows us the results of this query.

```
● ○ ○                    ch11 — bash — 82×5
INPUT: 128837 Records for 32092 Bins and 32059683554 Total Bytes
OUTPUT: Top 5 Bins by Bytes
            sIP|sPort|          dIP|          Bytes|   %Bytes|   cumul_%|
102.123.222.245|  22| 168.59.76.107|    15257159577| 47.589863| 47.589863|
maverick:ch11 chris$
```

**FIGURE 11.3**

Using Statistics to Identify Service Usage

It appears that our culprit is associated with some type of SSH connection, but before consulting with the user or another data source to verify, let's generate some more statistics that can help us identify the "when" regarding the timing of this communication. In order to do this, we're going to step away from rwstats briefly and use rwcount to identify the time period when this communication was taking place. Rwcount is a tool in the SiLK analysis package that summarizes SiLK flow records across time. It does this by counting the records in the input stream and grouping their bytes and packet totals into time bins. By default, piping an rwfilter command directly to rwcount will provide a table that represents the volume of records, bytes, and packets seen in every 30 second interval within your rwfilter results. Using the --bin-size option will allow you to change that by specifying a different second value. With that in mind, we will use the following command:

```
rwfilter --start-date=2013/08/26:14 --any-address=102.123.222.245
--sport=22 --type=all --pass=stdout | rwcount --bin-size=600
```

Since we're trying to identify when this port 22 traffic occurred, we have edited the rwfilter to use the --sport=22 option, and we have replaced rwstats with rwcount to evaluate the time unit where the data exists. We'll talk more about rwcount later in this chapter, but for now we have used the --bin-size option to examine the traffic with 10 minute (600 second) bins. The results of this command are shown in Figure 11.4.

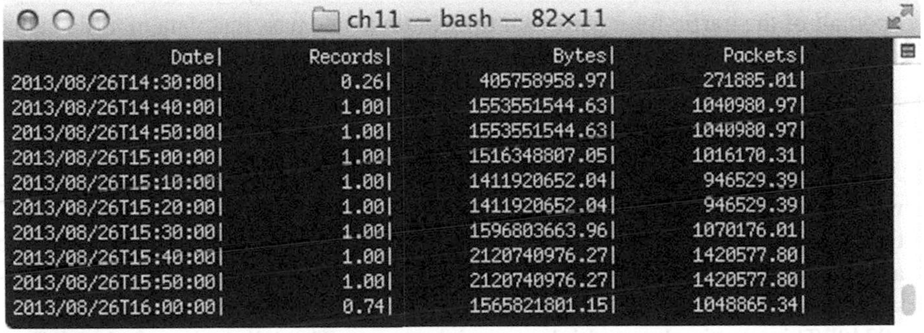

| Date | Records | Bytes | Packets |
| --- | --- | --- | --- |
| 2013/08/26T14:30:00 | 0.26 | 405758958.97 | 271885.01 |
| 2013/08/26T14:40:00 | 1.00 | 1553551544.63 | 1040980.97 |
| 2013/08/26T14:50:00 | 1.00 | 1553551544.63 | 1040980.97 |
| 2013/08/26T15:00:00 | 1.00 | 1516348807.05 | 1016170.31 |
| 2013/08/26T15:10:00 | 1.00 | 1411920652.04 | 946529.39 |
| 2013/08/26T15:20:00 | 1.00 | 1411920652.04 | 946529.39 |
| 2013/08/26T15:30:00 | 1.00 | 1596803663.96 | 1070176.01 |
| 2013/08/26T15:40:00 | 1.00 | 2120740976.27 | 1420577.80 |
| 2013/08/26T15:50:00 | 1.00 | 2120740976.27 | 1420577.80 |
| 2013/08/26T16:00:00 | 0.74 | 1565821801.15 | 1048865.34 |

**FIGURE 11.4**

Rwcount Results Detailing When Communication Occurred

We can see here that the data transfer appears to be relatively consistent over time. This would indicate that the SSH tunnel was probably being used to transfer a large chunk data. This could be something malicious such as data exfiltration, or something as simple as a user using the SCP tool to transfer something to another system for backup purposes. Determining the true answer to this question would require the analysis of additional data sources, but the statistics we've generated here should give the analyst an idea of where to look next.

## SERVICE DISCOVERY WITH SiLK

Rwstats can also be used for performing discovery activities for friendly assets on your own local network. In an ideal situation, the SOC is notified any time a new server is placed on a production network that the SOC is responsible for protecting. In reality, analysts are rarely presented with this documentation in a timely manner. However, as long as these servers fall into the same range as what you are responsible for protecting, you should have mechanisms in place to detect their presence. This will not only help you keep tabs on friendly devices that have been deployed, but also on unauthorized and rogue servers that might be deployed by internal users, or the adversary.

We can use rwstats can identify these servers with relative ease. In this example, I'll identify a number of key servers that regularly communicate to devices outside of the local network. This process begins with creating an rwfilter to gather the data set you would like to generate statistics from. In an ideal scenario, this type of query is run on a periodic basis and examined continually. This can help to catch rogue servers that might be put in place only temporarily, but then are shut down.

In this example, we will be working with a file generated by rwfilter so that we can simply pass it to rwstats rather than continually generating the data set and piping it over. To do this, we can use a filter like this that will generate a data set based upon all of the traffic for a particular time interval and pass that data to a file called sample.rw.

```
rwfilter --start-date=2013/08/28:00 --end-date=2013/08/28:23 --
type=all --protocol=0- --pass=sample.rw
```

With a data set ready for parsing, now we have to determine what statistic we want to generate. When generating statistics, it is a good idea to begin with a question. Then, you can write out the question and "convert" it to rwstats syntax to achieve the data you are looking for. As a sample of this methodology, let's ask ourselves, "What local devices communicate the most from the common server ports, 1-1024?" This question has multiple potential answers. The delineation of what defines "top" in "top talker" can be a determining factor in getting the real results you want. In this example we'll rephrase the question to say, "What are the top 20 local devices that talk from source ports 1-1024 to the most distinctly different destination IP addresses outside of my local network?" Converted to an rwstats command, this question looks like this:

```
rwfilter sample.rw --type=out,outweb --sport=1-1024 --pass=stdout |
rwstats --fields=sip,sport --count=20 --value=dip-distinct
```

The results of this query are shown in Figure 11.5.

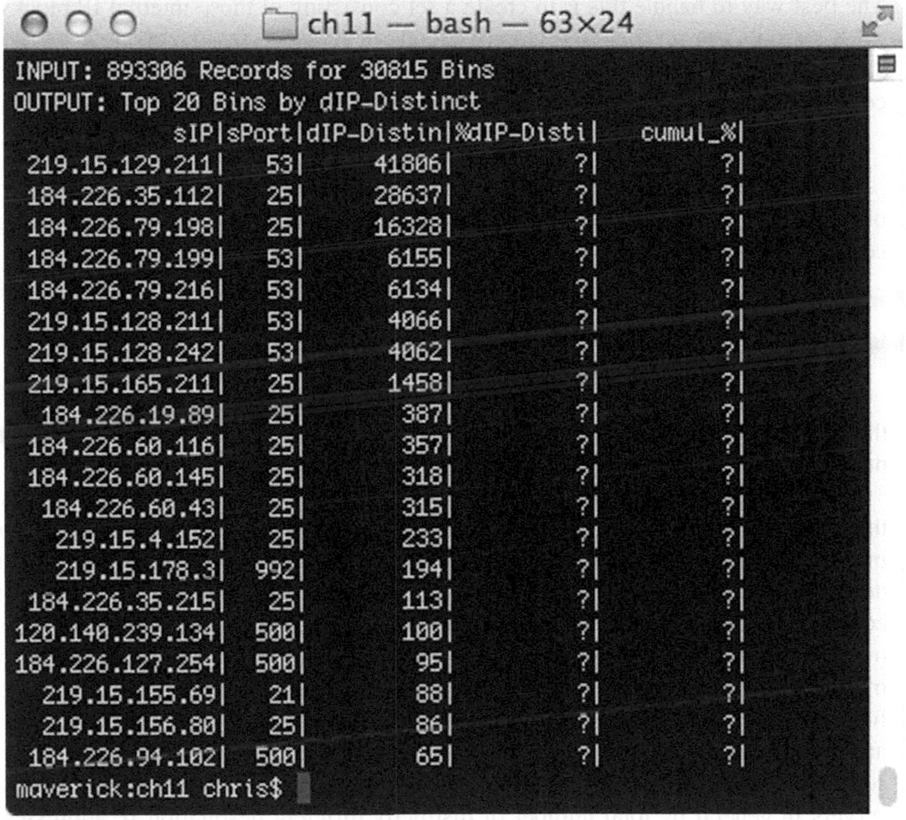

```
○ ○ ○           ⬜ ch11 — bash — 63×24              ⬐
INPUT: 893306 Records for 30815 Bins                    ☰
OUTPUT: Top 20 Bins by dIP-Distinct
          sIP|sPort|dIP-Distin|%dIP-Disti|   cumul_%|
  219.15.129.211|  53|    41806|        ?|        ?|
  184.226.35.112|  25|    28637|        ?|        ?|
  184.226.79.198|  25|    16328|        ?|        ?|
  184.226.79.199|  53|     6155|        ?|        ?|
  184.226.79.216|  53|     6134|        ?|        ?|
  219.15.128.211|  53|     4066|        ?|        ?|
  219.15.128.242|  53|     4062|        ?|        ?|
  219.15.165.211|  25|     1458|        ?|        ?|
   184.226.19.89|  25|      387|        ?|        ?|
  184.226.60.116|  25|      357|        ?|        ?|
  184.226.60.145|  25|      318|        ?|        ?|
   184.226.60.43|  25|      315|        ?|        ?|
    219.15.4.152|  25|      233|        ?|        ?|
    219.15.178.3| 992|      194|        ?|        ?|
  184.226.35.215|  25|      113|        ?|        ?|
 120.140.239.134| 500|      100|        ?|        ?|
 184.226.127.254| 500|       95|        ?|        ?|
   219.15.155.69|  21|       88|        ?|        ?|
   219.15.156.80|  25|       86|        ?|        ?|
  184.226.94.102| 500|       65|        ?|        ?|
maverick:ch11 chris$ ▌
```

**FIGURE 11.5**

Top Communicating Server Ports

This query provides results showing the top 20 local servers (`--count=20`) by Source IP address and port (`- fields=sip,sport`) as determined by recognizing the amount of external devices that these servers communicated with (`--value=dip-distinct`). The data set this query is pulled from is limited by running rwfilter on the sample.rw data set we've already generated, and only passing the outbound traffic from ports 1-1024 to rwstats (`--type=out,outweb --sport=1-1024`).

This gives us some of the data we want, but what about server traffic that doesn't involve communication from external hosts? If your flow collector (a sensor or a router) is position to collect internal to internal traffic, we can include this as well by adding int2int to the –type option.

Another thing we can do to enhance the quality of this data and to set us up better for statistical data we will generate later, is to limit it to only source IP addresses that exist within the network ranges we are responsible for protecting. This will usually be the values that are defined in the SiLK sensor.conf file as the internal IP blocks.

The best way to handle this is to create a set consisting of those internal IP blocks. SiLK rwtools use set files to reference groups of IP addresses. To create a set file, simply place all of the IP addresses (including CIDR ranges) in a text file, and then convert it to a set file using this rwsetbuild command:

```
rwsetbuild local.txt local.set
```

Here, rwsetbuild takes in the list of IP blocks specified in the local.txt file, and outputs the set file named local.set. With the set file created, we can use the following command to get the data we want:

```
rwfilter sample.rw --sipset=local.set --type=int2int,out,outweb --
sport=1-1024 --pass=stdout | rwstats --fields=sip,sport --count=20
--value=dip-distinct
```

Notice here that the `--sipset` option is used with the rwfilter command to limit the data appropriately to only source IP addresses that fall within the scope of the network we are responsible for protecting.

With minimal modifications to the methods we've already used, you can narrow these commands to fit into your own environment with incredible precision. For instance, while we're only examining the top 20 matches for each query, you might determine that any device resembling a server should be considered in your query if it communicates with at least 10 unique devices. In order to get a list of devices matching that criteria, simply change `--count=20` to `--threshold=10`. You can manipulate the results more by focusing the port range or making new set files to focus on. It is important to note here that we're searching with a focus on the service, and in specifying `--fields=sip,sport`, it means that you are displaying the top source address and source port combinations. If the idea is to identify top talking servers in general by total number of distinctly different destination IP addresses, it is important to remove the `sport` field delimiter in the previous rwstats command in order to sum up the total amount of connections that each particular device talks to entirely, like this:

```
rwfilter sample.rw --sipset=local.set --type=all --sport=1-1024 --
pass=stdout| rwstats --fields=sip --count=20 --value=dip-distinct
```

Taking the results of this query and performing additional rwstats commands to drill down on specific addresses (as seen in previous examples) will yield more information regarding what services are running on devices appearing in the lists we've generated. For instance, if you wanted to drill down on the services running on 192.168.1.21, you could identify a "service" by individual source ports with at least 10 unique outbound communications. You can narrow the rwfilter to include this address and change the rwstats command to consider this threshold parameter:

```
rwfilter sample.rw --saddress=192.168.1.21 --type=all --pass=std-
out| rwstats --fields=sport --threshold=10 --value=dip-distinct
```

The output from this command is shown in Figure 11.6.

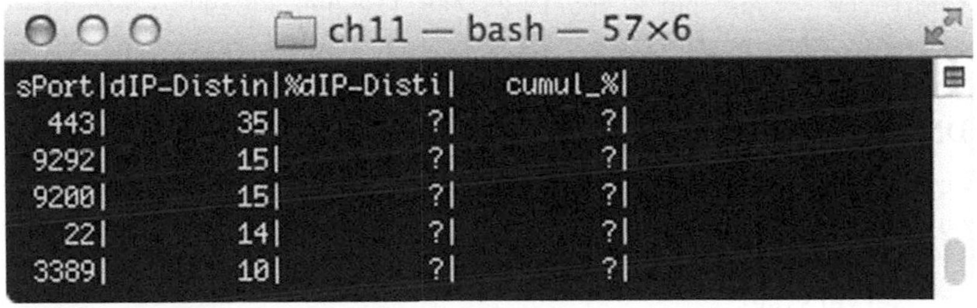

**FIGURE 11.6**

Drilling Down on Services Running on a Specific Device

There is an excellent article about performing this type of asset identification using session data written by Austin Whisnant and Sid Faber[2]. In their article, "Network Profiling Using Flow", they walk the SiLK user through a very detailed methodology for obtaining a network profile of critical assets and servers via a number of SiLK tools, primarily leveraging rwstats for discovery. They even provide a series of scripts that will allow you to automate this discovery by creating a sample of data via rwfilter (as seen above in creating sample.rw). Following their whitepaper will result in the development of an accurate asset model as well as specific sets to aid in further SiLK queries. This is useful for building friendly intelligence (which is discussed in Chapter 14) and for detection. Their paper serves as a great compliment to this chapter.

The examples Whisnant and Faber provide also do a good job of making sure that what you're seeing is relevant data with high accuracy. As an example of this accuracy, I've converted some of the query statements from "Network Profiling Using Flow" into quick one-liners. Give these a try to obtain detail on services hosted by your network:

### Web Servers

```
rwfilter sample.rw --type=outweb --sport=80,443,8080 --protocol=6 --
packets=4- --ack-flag=1 --pass=stdout|rwstats --fields=sip --
percentage=1 --bytes --no-titles|cut -f 1 -d "|"|rwsetbuild>web_ser-
vers.set ; echo Potential Web Servers:;rwfilter sample.rw --type=outweb
--sport=80,443,8080 --protocol=6 --packets=4- --ack-flag=1 --sip-
set=web_servers.set --pass=stdout|rwuniq --fields=sip,sport --
bytes --sort-output
```

### Email Servers

```
echo Potential SMTP servers ;rwfilter sample.rw --type=out --
sport=25,465,110,995,143,993 --protocol=6 --packets=4- --ack-
flag=1 --pass=stdout|rwset --sip-file=smtpservers.set ;rwfilter
```

---

[2]http://www.sei.cmu.edu/reports/12tr006.pdf

```
sample.rw --type=out --sport=25,465,110,995,143,993 --sipset=smtp-
servers.set --protocol=6 --packets=4- --ack-flag=1 --pass=stdout|
rwuniq --fields=sip --bytes --sort-output
```

### DNS Servers

```
echo DNS Servers: ;rwfilter sample.rw --type=out --sport=53 --proto-
col=17 --pass=stdout|rwstats --fields=sip --percentage=1 --packets
--no-titles|cut -f 1 -d "|"| rwsetbuild>dns_servers.set ;rwsetcat
dns_servers.set
```

### VPN Servers

```
echo   Potential   VPNs:   ;rwfilter   sample.rw   --type=out   --proto-
col=47,50,51 --pass=stdout|rwuniq --fields=sip --no-titles|cut -f 1
-d "|" |rwsetbuild>vpn.set ;rwfilter sample.rw --type=out --sip-
set=vpn.set --pass=stdout|rwuniq --fields=sip,protocol --bytes --
sort-output
```

### FTP Servers

```
echo -e "\nPotential FTP Servers"; rwfilter sample.rw --type=out --pro-
tocol=6 --packets=4- --ack-flag=1 --sport=21 --pass=stdout|rwstats
--fields=sip --percentage=1 --bytes --no-titles|cut -f 1 -d "|"|rwset-
build>ftpservers.set ;rwsetcat ftpservers.set ; echo FTP Servers mak-
ing   active   connections:   ;rwfilter   sample.rw   --type=out   --
sipset=ftpservers.set   --sport=20   --flags-initial=S/SAFR   --
pass=stdout|rwuniq --fields=sip
```

### SSH Servers

```
echo -e "\nPotential SSH Servers"; rwfilter sample.rw --type=out --pro-
tocol=6 --packets=4- --ack-flag=1 --sport=22 --pass=stdout|rwstats
--fields=sip --percentage=1 --bytes --no-titles|cut -f 1 -d "|"|rwset-
build>ssh_servers.set ;rwsetcat ssh_servers.set
```

### TELNET Servers

```
echo -e "\nPotential Telnet Servers"; rwfilter sample.rw --type=out --
protocol=6  --packets=4-  --ack-flag=1  --sport=23  --pass=stdout|
rwstats --fields=sip --percentage=1 --bytes --no-titles|cut -f 1 -d
"|"|rwsetbuild>telnet_servers.set ;rwsetcat telnet_servers.set
```

### Leftover Servers

```
echo Leftover Servers: ;rwfilter sample.rw --type=out --sport=1-
19,24,26-52,54-499,501-1023 --pass=stdout|rwstats --fields=sport
--percentage=1
```

In a detection scenario, these commands would be run on a routine basis. The results of each run should be compared with previous runs, and when a new device running as a server pops up, it should be investigated.

## FURTHERING DETECTION WITH STATISTICS

For most organizations, alert data and near real-time analysis provides the majority of reportable incidents on a network. When a new alert is generated, it is can be useful to generate statistical queries using session data that might help to detect the existence of similar indicators on other hosts.

As an example, let's consider the alert shown in Figure 11.7.

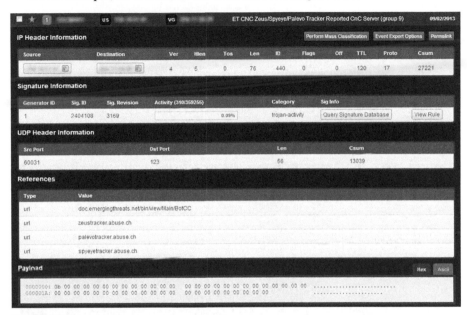

**FIGURE 11.7**

A Zeus Alert Generated by Snort

This alert was generated due to evidence of communications with a device known to be associated with Zeus botnet command and control. At first glance, this traffic looks like it might only be NTP traffic since the communication occurs as UDP traffic over port 123.

If you don't have access to the packet payload (which might be the case in a retrospective analysis), then this event might be glossed over by some analysts because there are no other immediate indicators of a positive infection. There is a potential that this traffic is merely masking its communication by using the common NTP port. However, without additional detail this can't be confirmed. For more detail, we need to dig down into the other communication of the host. To do this we'll simply take the unique details of the alert and determine if the host is talking to additional "NTP servers" that might appear suspicious. We also add the destination country code field into this query, since we only expect our devices to be communicating with US-based NTP servers. The yields the following command:

```
rwfilter --start-date=2013/09/02 --end-date=2013/09/02 --any-address=192.168.1.17 --aport=123 --proto=17 --type=all --pass=stdout | rwstats --top --fields=dip,dcc,dport --count=20
```

This command utilizes rwstats to display the devices that 192.168.1.17 is communicating with over port 123. The results are shown in Figure 11.8. In this figure, some IP addresses have been anonymized.

```
ch11 — bash — 72×23
INPUT: 2042 Records for 44 Bins and 2042 Total Records
OUTPUT: Top 20 Bins by Records
             dIP|dcc|dPort|    Records|  %Records|    cumul_%|
    192.5.xxxxxx| us|   123|        128|  6.268364|   6.268364|
   192.36.xxxxxx| se|   123|         86|  4.211557|  10.479922|
   192.36.xxxxxx| se|   123|         85|  4.162586|  14.642507|
   192.36.xxxxxx| se|   123|         84|  4.113614|  18.756121|
  150.254.xxxxxx| pl|   123|         84|  4.113614|  22.869736|
   129.242xxxxxx| no|   123|         83|  4.064643|  26.934378|
   192.36.xxxxxx| se|   123|         81|  3.966699|  30.901077|
    62.119xxxxxx| se|   123|         81|  3.966699|  34.867777|
    62.119xxxxxx| se|   123|         80|  3.917728|  38.785504|
   192.36.xxxxxx| se|   123|         77|  3.770813|  42.556317|
  192.36.1xxxxxx| se|   123|         75|  3.672870|  46.229187|
  203.117.xxxxxx| sg|   123|         75|  3.672870|  49.902057|
   192.36.xxxxxx| se|   123|         73|  3.574927|  53.476983|
       193xxxxxx| si|   123|         72|  3.525955|  57.002938|
    204.11xxxxxx| vg|   123|         67|  3.281097|  60.284035|
  192.36.1xxxxxx| se|   123|         67|  3.281097|  63.565132|
    128.9.xxxxxx| us|   123|         64|  3.134182|  66.699314|
    192.16xxxxxx| us| 60059|         60|  2.938296|  69.637610|
    193.62xxxxxx| gb|   123|         59|  2.889324|  72.526934|
    192.16xxxxxx| us| 60060|         58|  2.840353|  75.367287|
```

**FIGURE 11.8**

The Friendly Host Communicating with Multiple Hosts on Port 123

As you can see, the internal host in question appears to be communicating with multiple external hosts over port 123. The number of records associated with each host and the sheer amount of communication likely indicate that something malicious is occurring here, or at the very least, that this isn't actually NTP traffic. In a typical scenario, a host will only synchronize NTP settings with one or a few easily identifiable hosts. The malicious nature of this traffic can be confirmed by the existence of foreign (Non-US) results, which wouldn't be typical of NTP synchronization from a US-based host/network.

At this point, we have an incident that can be escalated. With that said, we also have an interesting indicator that can give us insight into detecting more than our IDS rules can provide. As before, we need to evaluate what we want before we jump into the data head first. In this event, we searched for all session data where 192.168.1.17

was a source address and where communication was occurring over UDP port 123. The overwhelming amount of UDP/123 traffic to so many external hosts led us to conclude that there was evil afoot. We can create a filter that matches these characteristics for any local address. That filter looks like this:

```
rwfilter --start-date=2013/09/02 --end-date=2013/09/02 --not-dip-
set=local.set --dport=123 --proto=17 --type=all --pass=stdout |
rwstats --top --fields=sip --count=20 --value=dip-distinct
```

The command above says to only examine data from 2013/09/02, what is not destined for the local network, and what is destined for port 123 using the UDP protocol. This data is sent to rwstats, which generates statistics for the top 20 distinct local IP addresses meeting these criteria (Figure 11.9).

```
● ○ ○                    ch11 — bash — 72×23
INPUT: 19279 Records for 95 Bins
OUTPUT: Top 20 Bins by dIP-Distinct
          sIP|dIP-Distin|%dIP-Disti|   cumul_%|
   192.16.xxxxxx|    596|       ?|       ?|
    192.16xxxxxx|    500|       ?|       ?|
  192.16.1xxxxxx|    471|       ?|       ?|
   192.16.xxxxxx|    130|       ?|       ?|
    192.26xxxxxx|     93|       ?|       ?|
    10.20.xxxxxx|     46|       ?|       ?|
    192.16xxxxxx|     22|       ?|       ?|
    10.49xxxxxx|      21|       ?|       ?|
    10.49xxxxxx|      21|       ?|       ?|
  205.204xxxxxx|     12|       ?|       ?|
  192.24.1xxxxxx|    10|       ?|       ?|
    192.25xxxxxx|      7|       ?|       ?|
   10.242.xxxxxx|      5|       ?|       ?|
   10.240.xxxxxx|      5|       ?|       ?|
    192.16xxxxxx|      3|       ?|       ?|
   192.24.xxxxxx|      3|       ?|       ?|
   192.24.xxxxxx|      3|       ?|       ?|
  192.24.1xxxxxx|      3|       ?|       ?|
   10.240.xxxxxx|      3|       ?|       ?|
   10.43.1xxxxxx|      3|       ?|       ?|
```

**FIGURE 11.9**

Showing Multiple Devices Exhibiting Similar Communication Patterns

We can narrow this filter down a bit more by giving it the ability to match only records where UDP/123 communication is observed going to non-US hosts, which was one of the criteria that indicated the original communication was suspicious. This query builds upon the previous one, but also passes the output of the first rwfilter instance to a second rwfilter instance that says to "fail" any records that contain a destination code of "us", ensuring that we will only see data that is going to foreign countries.

```
rwfilter --start-date=2013/09/02 --end-date=2013/09/02 --not-dip-
set=local.set --dport=123 --proto=17 --type=all --pass=stdout |
rwfilter --input-pipe=stdin --dcc=us --fail=stdout | rwstats --top
--fields=sip --count=20 --value=dip-distinct
```

Further examination of these results can lead to the successful discovery of malicious logic on other systems that are exhibiting a similar behavior as the original IDS alert. While an IDS alert might catch some instances of something malicious, it will catch all of them, which is where statistical analysis can come in handy. The example shown here was taken from a real world investigation where the analysis here yielded 9 additional infected hosts that the original IDS alert didn't catch.

## VISUALIZING STATISTICS WITH GNUPLOT

The ability to visualize statistics provides useful insight that can't always be as easily ascertained from raw numbers. One globally useful statistic that lends itself well to detection and the visualization of statistics is graphing throughput statistics. Being able to generate statistics and graph the total amount of throughput across a sensor interface or between two hosts is useful for detection on a number of fronts. Primarily, it can serve as a means of anomaly-based detection that will alert an analyst when a device generates or receives a significantly larger amount of traffic than normal. This can be useful for detecting outbound data exfiltration, an internal host being used to serve malware over the Internet, or an inbound Denial of Service attack. Throughput graphs can also help analysts narrow down their data queries to a more manageable time period, ultimately speeding up the analysis process.

One of the more useful tools for summarizing data across specific time intervals and generating relevant statistics is rwcount. Earlier, we used rwcount briefly to narrow down a specific time period where certain activity was occurring. Beyond this, rwcount can be used to provide an idea of how much data exists in any communication sequence(s). The simplest example of this would be to see how much data traverses a monitored network segment in a given day. As with almost all SiLK queries, this will start with an rwfilter command to focus on only the time interval you're interested in. In this case, we'll pipe that data to rwcount which will send the data into bins of a user-specified time interval in seconds. For example, to examine the total amount of Records, Bytes, and Packets per minute (--bin-size = 60) traversing your interface over a given hour, you can use the following command:

```
rwfilter --start-date=2013/09/02:14 --proto=0- --pass=stdout --
type=all | rwcount --bin-size=60
```

Variations of the original rwfilter will allow you to get creative in determining more specific metrics to base these throughput numbers on. These tables are pretty useful alone, but it can be easier to make sense of this data if you can visualize it.

As an example, let's look back to the example in the previous section with the suspicious NTP traffic. If we dig further into the results shown in Figure 11.9 by using rwcount like the command above, we can see that multiple external IP addresses in the 204.2.134.0/24 IP range are also soliciting NTP client communications, which might indicate rogue devices configured to use non-local NTP servers. If we dig down further and examine the traffic over the course of the day, we just see equivalent amounts of data per minute (Figure 11.10); a table that doesn't give much support in explaining the traffic:

```
○ ○ ○                    ☐ ch11 — bash — 82×11
            Date|    Records|            Bytes|         Packets|
2013/09/02T00:20:00|  2848.12|      3881203.67|        28537.12|
2013/09/02T00:21:00|  3565.92|      5550209.88|        41936.87|
2013/09/02T00:22:00|  3371.62|      5296400.96|        39838.18|
2013/09/02T00:23:00|  3014.70|      4507246.46|        34867.01|
2013/09/02T00:24:00|  2983.83|      4713578.12|        36133.11|
2013/09/02T00:25:00|   390.33|       663388.40|         5114.80|
2013/09/02T00:26:00|     1.41|         1714.79|            6.62|
2013/09/02T00:27:00|     0.96|          847.26|            3.95|
2013/09/02T00:28:00|     0.61|          152.66|            1.82|
2013/09/02T00:29:00|     0.51|          128.79|            1.53|
```

**FIGURE 11.10**

Rwcount Shows Data Spread Evenly Across Time Intervals

In order to really visualize this data on a broad scale, we can literally draw the big picture. Since SiLK doesn't possess the capability of doing this, we'll massage the results of the SiLK query and pipe it to gnuplot for graphing. Gnuplot (http://www.gnuplot.info/) is a portable command-line driven graphing application. It isn't the most intuitive plotting interface, but once you have a configuration to read from existing data, it is easily scripted into other tools.

To make the data shown above more useful, our goal is to build a graph that represents the volume of bytes per hour for session data containing any address from the 204.2.134.0/24 IP range. We begin by using the same rwcount command as above, but with a bin size of 3600 to yield "per hour" results. The output of the rwcount command is sent through some command line massaging to generate a CSV file containing only the timestamp and the byte value for each timestamp. The command looks like this:

```
rwfilter --start-date=2013/09/02 --any-address=204.2.134.0/24 --
proto=0- --pass=stdout --type=all | rwcount --bin-size=3600 -
delimited=, --no-titles| cut -d "," -f1,3>hourly.csv
```

The resulting data look like this:

```
2013/09/02T13:00:00,146847.07
2013/09/02T14:00:00,38546884.51
2013/09/02T15:00:00,1420679.53
2013/09/02T16:00:00,19317394.19
2013/09/02T17:00:00,16165505.44
2013/09/02T18:00:00,14211784.42
2013/09/02T19:00:00,14724860.35
2013/09/02T20:00:00,26819890.91
2013/09/02T21:00:00,29361327.78
```

```
2013/09/02T22:00:00,15644357.97
2013/09/02T23:00:00,10523834.82
```

Next, we need to tell Gnuplot how to graph these statistics. This is done by creating a Gnuplot script. This script is read line-by-line, similar to a BASH script, but instead relies on Gnuplot parameters. You will also notice that it calls Gnuplot as its interpreter on the first line of the script. The script we will use for this example looks like this:

```
#! /usr/bin/gnuplot
set terminal postscript enhanced color solid
set output "hourly.ps"
set title "Traffic for 204.2.134.0/24 (09/02/2013)"
set xlabel "Time (UTC)"
set ylabel "Bytes"
set datafile separator ","
set timefmt '%Y/%m/%dT%H:%M:%S'
set xdata time
plot 'hourly.csv' using 1:2 with lines title "Bytes"
```

If the postscript image format won't work for you, then you can convert the image to a JPG in Linux via the convert command:

```
convert hourly.ps hourly.jpg
```

Finally, you are left with a completed Gnuplot throughput graph, shown in Figure 11.11.

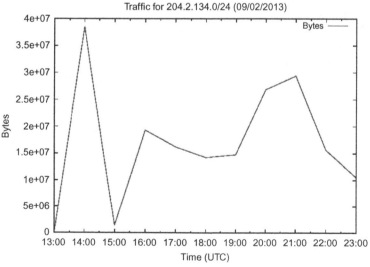

**FIGURE 11.11**

A Gnuplot Throughput Graph

You could easily use this example to create a BASH script to automatically pull data based on a date and host and generate a Gnuplot graph. An example of this might look like this:

```
#!/bin/bash

#traffic.plotter
echo "Enter Date: (Example:2013/09/02)"
read theday
echo "Enter Host: (Example:192.168.5.0/24)"
read thehost

if [ -z "theday" ]; then
echo "You forgot to enter the date."
exit
fi
if [ -z "thehost" ]; then
echo "You forgot to enter a host to examine."
exit
fi

rm hourly.csv
rm hourly.ps
rm hourly.jpg

rwfilter --start-date=$theday --any-address=$thehost --proto=0- --
pass=stdout --type=all -- | rwcount --bin-size=3600 --delimited=,
--no-titles| cut -d "," -f1,3>hourly.csv

gnuplot<< EOF
set terminal postscript enhanced color solid
set output "hourly.ps"
set title "Traffic for $thehost ($theday)"
set xlabel "Time (UTC)"
set ylabel "Bytes"
set datafile separator ","
set timefmt '%Y/%m/%dT%H:%M:%S'
set xdata time
plot 'hourly.csv' using 1:2 with lines title "Bytes"
EOF

convert hourly.ps hourly.jpg
exit
```

This script will allow you to pick a particular date to generate a "bytes per hour" throughput graph for any given IP address or IP range. This script should be fairly easy to edit for your environment.

## VISUALIZING STATISTICS WITH GOOGLE CHARTS

Another way to display throughput data and more is to leverage the Google Charts API (https://developers.google.com/chart/). Google offers a wide array of charts for conveying just about any data you can think of in an understandable and interactive fashion. Most of the charts generated with the API are cross-browser compatible and the Google Charts API is 100% free to use.

The biggest difference between Google Charts and Gnuplot for plotting SiLK records across time is the abundance of relevant examples. Gnuplot has been supported and under active development since 1986, and as such will do just about anything you could ever want as long as you're able to gain an understanding of the Gnuplot language. Because Gnuplot has been the go-to plotting and charting utility for so long, there are endless examples of how to get what you want out of it. However, Google Charts is fairly new, so fewer examples exist for showing how to use it. Luckily, it is rapidly growing in popularity, and it is designed to easily fit what people want out of the box. In order to aid in adoption, Google created the Google Charts Workshop, which allows a user to browse and edit existing examples to try data inline before going through the effort of coding it manually. The term "coding" is used loosely with Google Charts in that its syntax is relatively simple. For our purposes, we're going to use simple examples where we take data from rwcount and port it to an HTML file that leverages the Google Charts API file. Most modern browsers should be able to display the results of these examples without the use of any add-ons or extensions.

As an example, let's look at the same data that we just used in the previous Gnuplot example. We will use this data to generate a line chart. The first thing that you'll notice when you examine the Google Charts API for creating a line chart is that the data it ingests isn't as simple as a standard CSV file. The API will accept both JavaScript and Object Literal (OL) notation data tables. These data formats can be generated with various tools and libraries, but to keep this simple, we'll go back to using some command line Kung Fu to convert our CSV output into OL data table format.

In the previous example we had a small CSV file with only 11 data points. In addition to that data, we need to add in column headings to define the independent and dependent variable names for each data point. In other words, we need to add "Data,Bytes" to the top of our csv file to denote the two columns, like this:

```
Date,Bytes
2013/09/02T13:00:00,146847.07
2013/09/02T14:00:00,38546884.51
2013/09/02T15:00:00,1420679.53
2013/09/02T16:00:00,19317394.19
2013/09/02T17:00:00,16165505.44
2013/09/02T18:00:00,14211784.42
2013/09/02T19:00:00,14724860.35
2013/09/02T20:00:00,26819890.91
2013/09/02T21:00:00,29361327.78
```

```
2013/09/02T22:00:00,15644357.97
2013/09/02T23:00:00,10523834.82
```

Now, we can reformat this CSV file into the correct OL data table format using a bit of sed replacement magic:

```
cat hourly.csv | sed "s/\(.*\),\(.*\)/['\1', \2],/g"|sed '$s/,$//'| sed
"s/,\([A-Za-z].*\)],/, '\1'],/g"
```

At this point, our data look like this, and is ready to be ingested by the API:

```
['Date', 'Bytes'],
['2013/09/02T13:00:00', 146847.07],
['2013/09/02T14:00:00', 38546884.51],
['2013/09/02T15:00:00', 1420679.53],
['2013/09/02T16:00:00', 19317394.19],
['2013/09/02T17:00:00', 16165505.44],
['2013/09/02T18:00:00', 14211784.42],
['2013/09/02T19:00:00', 14724860.35],
['2013/09/02T20:00:00', 26819890.91],
['2013/09/02T21:00:00', 29361327.78],
['2013/09/02T22:00:00', 15644357.97],
['2013/09/02T23:00:00', 10523834.82]
```

Now we can place this data into an HTML file that calls the API. The easiest way to do this is to refer back to Google's documentation on the line chart and grab the sample code provided there. We've done this in the code below:

```
<html>
  <head>
    <script type="text/javascript" src="https://www.google.com/
jsapi"></script>
    <script type="text/javascript">
      google.load("visualization", "1", {packages:["corechart"]});
      google.setOnLoadCallback(drawChart);
      function drawChart() {
        var data=google.visualization.arrayToDataTable([
['Date', 'Bytes'],
['2013/09/02 T13:00:00', 146847.07],
['2013/09/02 T14:00:00', 38546884.51],
['2013/09/02 T15:00:00', 1420679.53],
['2013/09/02 T16:00:00', 19317394.19],
['2013/09/02 T17:00:00', 16165505.44],
['2013/09/02 T18:00:00', 14211784.42],
['2013/09/02 T19:00:00', 14724860.35],
['2013/09/02 T20:00:00', 26819890.91],
['2013/09/02 T21:00:00', 29361327.78],
['2013/09/02 T22:00:00', 15644357.97],
['2013/09/02 T23:00:00', 10523834.82]
```

```
    ]);
    var options={
       title: 'Traffic for 204.2.134.0-255'
    };
    var  chart=new  google.visualization.LineChart(document.
getElementById('chart_div'));
    chart.draw(data, options);
    }
  </script>
</head>
<body>
  <div id="chart_div" style="width: 900px; height: 500px;"> </div>
  </body>
</html>
```

Figure 11.12 shows the resulting graph in a browser, complete with mouse overs.

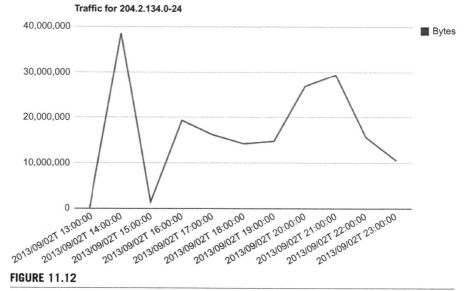

**FIGURE 11.12**

A Google Charts API Throughput Graph

Just as we were able to script the previous Gnuplot example, we can also auto-mate this Google Chart visualization. The methods shown below for automating this are crude for the sake of brevity, however, they work with little extra interaction.

From a working directory, we've created a directory called "googlecharts". Within this directory we plan to build a number of templates that we can insert data into. The first template will be called linechart.html.

```html
<html>
  <head>
    <script  type="text/javascript"  src="https://www.google.com/
jsapi"></script>
    <script type="text/javascript">
      google.load("visualization", "1", {packages:["corechart"]});
      google.setOnLoadCallback(drawChart);
      function drawChart() {
        var data=google.visualization.arrayToDataTable([
        dataplaceholder
        ]);

        var options={
          title: 'titleplaceholder'
        };
        var chart=new google.visualization.LineChart(document.get
ElementById('chart_div'));
        chart.draw(data, options);
      }
    </script>
  </head>
  <body>
    <div id="chart_div" style="width: 900px; height: 500px;"></div>
  </body>
</html>
```

You'll notice that our linechart.html has two unique placeholders; one for the data table we'll create (dataplaceholder) and one for the title that we want (titleplaceholder).

Now, in the root working directory, we'll create our plotting utility, aptly named plotter.sh. The plotter utility is a BASH script that will generate graphs based on a user supplied rwfilter and rwcount command. It will take the output of these commands and parse it into the proper OL data table format and insert the data into a temporary file. The contents of that temporary file will be used to replace the data place holder in the googlecharts/linechart.html template. Since we also have a title place holder in the template, there is a variable in the plotter script where that can be defined.

```
##EDIT THIS##################################
title='Traffic for 204.2.134.0-255'
rwfilter --start-date=2013/09/02 T1 --any-address=204.2.134.0/24 --
type=all --proto=0- --pass=stdout | rwcount --bin-size=300 --
delimited=, |\
cut -d "," -f1,3 |\
############################################
```

```
sed "s/\(.*\),\(.*\)/['\1', \2],/g"|sed 's/$s/,$//'| sed "s/,\([A-Za-z].
*\)],/, '\1'],/g">temp.test
sed '/dataplaceholder/{
    s/dataplaceholder//g
    r temp.test
}' googlechart/linechart.html | sed "s/titleplaceholder/${title}/g"
rm temp.test
}
linechart
```

When you run plotter.sh, it will use the template and insert the appropriate data into linechart.html.

The script we've shown here is simple and crude, but can be expanded to allow for rapid generation of Google Charts for detection and analysis use.

## VISUALIZING STATISTICS WITH AFTERGLOW

It is easy to get deep enough into data that it becomes a challenge to effectively communicate to others what that data represents. In fact, sometimes it is only in stepping back from the data that you can see really what is going on yourself. Afterglow is a Perl tool that facilitates the generation of link graphs that allow you to see a pictorial representation of how "things in lists" relate to each other. Afterglow takes two or three column CSV files as input and generates either a dot attributed graph language file (required by the graphviz library) or a GDF file that can be parsed by Gephi. The key thing to note is that Afterglow takes input data and generates output data that can be used for the generation of link graphs. The actual creation of those link graphs is left to third party tools, such as Graphviz which we will use here. There are numerous examples of how to use Afterglow to find relationships in a number of datasets on the Internet; PCAP and Sendmail are examples shown on Afterglow's main webpage.

Before getting started with Afterglow, it is a good idea to first visit http://afterglow.sourceforge.net/ to read the user manual and get an idea of how it functions. Essentially, all you need to get going is a CSV file with data that you want to use, and if you pipe it to Afterglow correctly, you'll have a link graph in no time.

First, download Afterglow and place it in a working directory. For this example, you'll want to make sure you have access to SiLK tools in order to make these examples seamless. After downloading and unzipping Afterglow, you might need to install a Perl module (depending on your current installation). If you do need it, run the following:

```
sudo /usr/bin/perl -MCPAN -e 'install Text::CSV'
```

We'll be using visualization tools provided by Graphviz, which can be installed with the package management utility used by your Linux distribution. Graphviz is an open source visualization software from AT&T Research that contains numerous graphing utilities that can each be used to provide their own interpretation of link graphs. For documentation on each graphing tool included with Graphviz, visit http://www.graphviz.org/Documentation.php. To install Graphviz in Security Onion, we can use APT:

```
sudo apt-get install graphviz
```

At this point you should be in the Afterglow working directory. Afterglow will require that you use a configuration file, but a sample.properties file has been included. I recommend adding the line `xlabels=0` to this file to ensure that labels show up properly. While generating data, be mindful of the two "modes" mentioned before, two-column and three-column. In two-column mode, you only have a "source" (source IP address) and a "target" (destination IP address). If a third column is present, the arrangement now becomes "source, event, target".

To begin generating a link graph, let's start by generating a CSV file of data traversing your local network over the course of an hour using SiLK. For this example, we'll use 184.201.190.0/24 as the network that we are examining. To generate this data with SiLK, we'll use some additional rwcut options to limit the amount of data massaging that we have to do:

```
rwfilter --start-date=2013/09/06:15 --saddress=184.201.190.0/24 -
type=all --pass=stdout | rwcut --fields=sip,dip --no-titles --
delimited=, | sort -u>test.data
```

After running the command shown above, examine the file "test.data" to confirm that you have data containing "source IP, destination IP" combinations in each line. If data is present, you've completed the hard part. To generate the link graph you can do one of two things. The first option is to run your data through Afterglow and generate a DOT file with the `-w` argument, which Graphviz utilities such as Neato will parse for graph creation. Another option is to pipe the output of Afterglow straight to Neato. Since you're likely going to be utilizing Afterglow exclusively for feeding data to a graphing utility of your choice, our example will focus on piping the output of Afterglow straight to Graphviz utilities.

To generate our graph, run the following command:

```
cat test.data | perl afterglow.pl -e 5 -c sample.properties -t | neato -
Tgif -o test.gif
```

The -e argument defines how "large" the graph will be. The -c argument specifies a configuration file to use, which in this case is the sample file that is included with Afterglow. The -t argument allows you to specify that you're using "two-column" mode. Finally, that data is piped to neato, which uses the –T argument to specify that a GIF file should be created, and the –o argument that allows the file name to be specific. The result is test.gif, which is shown in Figure 11.13.

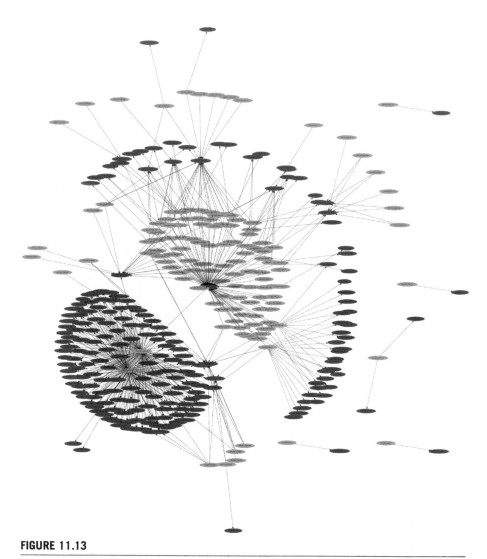

**FIGURE 11.13**

A Link Graph Created from NetFlow Data

If you are following along at home, you should now have something similar to the figure above, although possibly with different colors. The colors used by Afterglow are defined in the sample.properties file. This sample file is preconfigured to use specific colors for RFC 1918 addresses. In the event that you're not using one of these ranges (as in with our example), the "source" nodes will show up in red. Examine the sample configuration carefully as you'll no doubt be making changes to color codes for your local ranges. Keep in mind that the configuration file works on a "first match wins" basis regarding the color-coding. For instance, all source nodes will be blue if your source color configuration lines read as below, due to the fact that the top statement is read as "true", and thus matches first;

```
color.source="blue"
color.source="greenyellow" if ($fields[0]=~/∧192\.168\.1\..*/);
color.source="lightyellow4" if ($fields[0]=~/∧172\.16\..*/);
```

Now that you've been able to create some pretty data, let's generate some useful data. In this next example we'll generate our own configuration file and utilize three-column mode. In this scenario, we'll take a look at the outbound connections from your local address range during non-business hours. We'll generate a configuration file that will allow us to visually identify several anomalies. In this scenario, we don't expect end users to be doing any browsing after hours, and we don't expect a lot of outbound server chatter outside of a few responses from external hosts connecting in. As before, we need to have an idea of what we're using as our data set moving forward. We're going to be identifying several things with this graph, so I'll explain the columns as I walk through the configuration. In this example, I'll also show you how this can be streamlined into a one-line command to generate the graph.

We will begin by creating a configuration file. To make sure that our labels don't get mangled, we'll start with the line `xlabels=0`. In this scenario, we're going to generate a link graph that gives us a good picture of how local devices are communicating out of the network, whether it is through initiating communication or by responding to communication. In doing so we'll assume that all local addresses are "good" and define `color.source` to be "green".

To pick out the anomalies, our goal is to have the target node color be based on certain conditions. For one, we want to identify if the communication is occurring from a source port that is above 1024 in order to try and narrow down the difference between typical server responses and unexpected high port responses. If we see that, we'll color those target nodes orange with `color.target="orange" if ($fields[1]>1024)`. This statement tells Afterglow to color the node from the third column (target node) orange if it determines that the value from the second column (event node) is a number over 1024. Referencing the columns in the CSV file is best done by referencing fields, with field 0 being the first column, field 1 being the second column, and so on.

Next, we'd like to see what foreign entities are receiving communications from our hosts after hours. In this case, we'll try to identify the devices communicating out to China specifically. Since these could very well be legitimate connections, we'll color these Chinese nodes yellow with `color.target="yellow" if ($fields[3]=~/cn/)`. Remember that based on the way Afterglow numbers columns, field 3 implies that we're sourcing some information from the fourth column in the CSV file. While the fourth column isn't used as a node, it is used to make references to other nodes in the same line, and in this case we're saying that we're going to color the node generated from the third column yellow if we see that the fourth column of that same row contains "cn" in the text.

We'd also like to escalate certain nodes to our attention if they meet BOTH of the previous scenarios. If we identify that local devices are communicating outbound to Chinese addresses from ephemeral ports, we will highlight these nodes as red. In order to do that, we identify if the source port is above 1024 AND if the fourth column of the same row contains "cn" in the text. In order to make this AND operator, we'll use `color.target="red" if (grep($fields[1]>1024,$fields[3]=~/cn/))`. As mentioned before, it is the order of these configuration lines that will make or break your link graph. My recommendation is that you order these from the most strict to the most lenient. In this case our entire configuration file (which we'll call config.properties) will look like this:

```
##Place all labels within the nodes themselves.
xlabels=0
##Color all source nodes (first column addresses) green
color.source="green"
##Color target nodes red if the source port is above 1024 and ##4th column
reads "cn"
color.target="red" if (grep($fields[1]>1024,$fields[3]=~/cn/))
##Color target nodes yellow if the 4th column reads "cn"
color.target="yellow" if ($fields[3]=~/cn/)
##Color target nodes orange if the source port is above 1024
color.target="orange" if ($fields[1]>1024)
##Color target nodes blue if they don't match the above statements
color.target="blue"
##Color event nodes from the second column white
color.event="white"
##Color connecting lines black with a thickness of "1"
color.edge="black"
size.edge=1;
```

To generate the data we need for this graph, we will use the following command:

```
rwfilter --start-date=2013/09/06:15 --saddress=184.201.190.0/24 --
type=out,outweb --pass=stdout |\
rwcut --fields=sip,sport,dip,dcc --no-titles --delimited=,|\ sort -u
|perl afterglow.pl -e 5 -c config.properties -v |\
neato -Tgif -o test.gif
```

Notice that the type argument in the rwfilter command specifies only outbound traffic with the out and outweb options. We also generate the four columns we need with the `--fields=sip,sport,dip,dcc` argument. The output of this data is piped directly to Afterglow and Neato to create test.gif, shown in Figure 11.14.

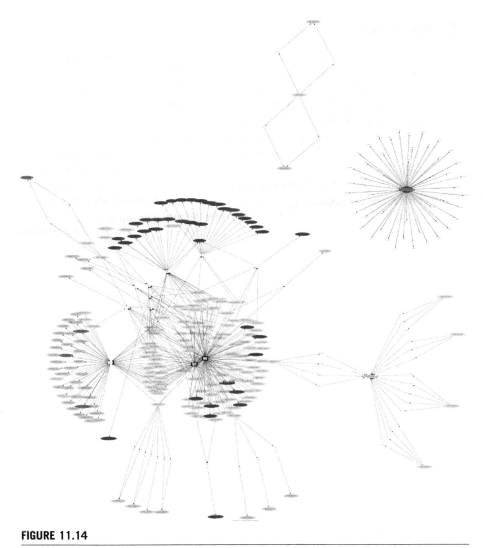

**FIGURE 11.14**

A Customized Link Graph Showing Outbound Communication

The power and flexibility that Afterglow provides allow for the creation of a number of link style graphs that are useful in a variety of situations where you need to examine the relationships between entities. Hopefully this exercise has shown you some of that power, and will give you a jump start on creating link graphs of your own.

## CONCLUSION

Understanding the gradual flow of data in your environment as it relates to the user and the network as a whole is challenging. However, there are a number of statistical data measures that can be taken to ensure that as your organization matures, so does your knowledge of its data network and the communication occurring on it. The overarching theme of this chapter is that you can make better data out of the data you already have. This new data revolves around stepping back a few feet in order to refocus and see the big picture. Sometimes the big picture is making lists that generalize large quantities of data. Other times, the big picture is really just a big picture. While the direction provided here doesn't tell you how to create statistics or visualizations for all of the scenarios you might face when performing NSM detection or analysis, our hope is that it will help you get over the initial hump of learning some of these tools, and that it will plant a seed that will allow you to generate useful statistics for your environment.

# Using Canary Honeypots for Detection

## CHAPTER CONTENTS

By definition, a honeypot is a security resource whose value lies in being probed, attacked, or compromised. In practice, a honeypot often takes the form of either a system or a piece of software that mimics a system or service that is intentionally vulnerable. This system is placed so that an attacker will find the system and exploit it. What the attacker is usually unaware of however, is that the honeypot contains no real data of value and is isolated from other network devices. Network defenders can then use the detailed logging information collected by the honeypot to derive tools, tactics, and procedures used by the attacker.

It is rare to find honeypots on production networks, as it can seem counterintuitive to place a device on a production network that is designed to be breached by an attacker. As a matter of fact, most honeypots are only found in research or academic environments. However, some organizations with mature NSM capabilities have looked to honeypots as an advanced form of detection in their environments. In this chapter we will define the canary honeypot and take a look at different types of honeypots that can be used for NSM purposes. In addition, we will discuss the issue of canary honeypot placement, logging, and best practices for implementation. We will also look at some popular honeypot software solutions.

Before going any further, I should make it absolutely clear that this chapter will discuss some controversial defense tactics. Some organizations steer away from the use of honeypots for legal reasons, which we won't address here (that's between you and your lawyer). Other organizations simply don't understand how to properly secure their environments to ensure that an attacker can't leverage a compromised honeypot in an unexpected manner, or they just don't understand how a honeypot can have operational value. Regardless of your disposition towards honeypots, I must stress that the implementation of honeypots for NSM can be a labor-intensive process and is generally only suited for mature SOC environments with $24 \times 7$ monitoring.

## CANARY HONEYPOTS

Canaries were originally used as an early warning system by the mining industry. Before technology could be used to gauge the severity of lethal gases in mineshafts, miners would place canaries in cages in these shafts. The canary was more susceptible to lethal gases such as methane, so if the canary became ill or died, the miners knew they were in danger and they should evacuate the mine shaft or take some other type of corrective action, such as opening more ventilation shafts. This same concept helps define the canary honeypot.

A canary honeypot is a system that mimics a production system and is deployed so that it can serve as an early detection mechanism in the event of a network breach. These honeypots can operate in two different formats; either as an exploitable or non-exploitable honeypot.

An exploitable canary honeypot is one that actually uses software to mimic real services, but in a manner that presents some form of vulnerability to an attacker. When the attacker exploits this vulnerability, they are usually provided some limited access to a simulated environment designed to make them believe that they are interacting with a real system. While this is occurring, the honeypot software also generates extensive logs detailing the method the attacker used to breach the faux-service, and their actions within the simulated operating environment. This alerting can also be combined with other forms of detection, including IDS signatures, to aid analysts in utilizing the canary honeypots as a detection resource.

A non-exploitable canary honeypot provides the same legitimate services as the production box it is mirroring, but isn't designed to be exploited by an attacker in the traditional sense. The only difference between these honeypots and a legitimate production system is that no other legitimate systems are actually communicating with the honeypot. This means that any connection initiated with this system is suspicious. While an attacker won't actually be able to access this system, if they attempt to log on to it, scan it, or otherwise interact with it, then any signature, anomaly, or statistical detection mechanisms that are deployed in the environment should be configured to generate alerts based upon the attacker actions. This is a similar concept to the Darknet example we looked at with Bro in chapter 10.

Because neither of these honeypot types represents a real business-related service, there is no legitimate reason for anyone to connect to them. While it wouldn't be possible to utilize this level of extensive logging and alerting with a real production system due to the number of false positives that would be generated, this is a great solution for a system that nobody should ever be communicating with in the first place.

It is important to realize that a canary honeypot isn't designed to detect an attacker who is gaining initial access into your network. Instead, they are designed to detect the actions of an attacker who has already gained an initial foothold in the network and is attempting to further their level of access. Regardless of how sophisticated attackers might be, they will still take the path of least resistance towards their goals, maintaining only as much stealth as necessary. The prevalence of social engineering and targeted phishing attacks has made defending the perimeter and performing detection across this boundary difficult.

## TYPES OF HONEYPOTS

Honeypots are categorized by the level of interaction they provide and are most commonly designated as either low interaction or high interaction. Organizational goals, the assets you are protecting, and the services you wish to emulate will help define the level of interaction needed for your honeypot deployment.

A low interaction honeypot is software-based, and is designed to emulate one or more services. The level of interaction they provide is dependent upon the service being emulated and the software itself. For instance, Kippo is a low interaction honeypot that mimics the SSH service. It allows an attacker to log in to the service and even to browse a fake file system. However, it never allows an attacker to access a real component of the underlying operating system.

A high interaction honeypot is actually configured to mirror a production system, and is designed to give an attacker full reign of an operating system in the event that they are lured into compromising it. This system will be configured to utilize extensive system and file system logging, and will also be subject to a very exhaustive set of IDS rules and monitoring. High interaction honeypots will often exist as virtual machines so that they can be reverted back to a known clean snapshot with relative ease.

When implementing a high interaction honeypot, special precautions must be taken to limit the attacker's ability to use the system as a staging point for attacks against the production system. They must be allowed to compromise the machine and perform some level of activity without being able to use their control of the system to take advantage of legitimate systems on the network.

---

**CAUTION**

Some honeypots will claim to be medium interaction honeypots, existing as a middle ground between low and high interaction solutions. For example, Kippo is a medium interaction honeypot because it is software that simulates a service, but it also simulates a fake file system that an attacker can actually interact with. This is in contrast to something like Tom's Honeypot, which is a true low interaction honeypot because it simulates services using software, but doesn't provide any type of simulated environment that an attacker can interact with post-compromise. While medium-interaction honeypots are a valid classification in some instances, this book groups medium interaction honeypots with low interaction honeypots because they are typically still applications that run on a system rather than an actual operating system.

---

High interaction honeypots are useful for intelligence gathering in relation to sophisticated adversaries. However, they require an incredible amount of labor and diligence in their setup, and require constant and rigorous monitoring.

Overall, low interaction honeypots are easier to configure and maintain. They also introduce the least amount of risk into an environment because of their simplicity. If your goal is detection, as it would be in an NSM environment, low interaction honeypots are usually the best fit. This book will focus on low interaction honeypots for NSM detection.

## CANARY HONEYPOT ARCHITECTURE

As with all aspects of NSM, the deployment of canary honeypots should be thoroughly planned in relation to the threats faced by your organization, as discussed with the Applied Collection Framework in Chapter 2. With those results in hand, planning the deployment of one or more canary honeypot systems should involve three major steps:

1. Identify the devices and services to be mimicked
2. Determine Canary Honeypot Placement
3. Develop Alerting and Logging

Let's examine each of these phases in depth.

### Phase One: Identify Devices and Services to be Mimicked

Based upon the risk assessment you completed while planning for your NSM collection needs, you should have an idea of which network assets are considered high priority. These are prime targets for having their services replicated with a honeypot system. The goal of this deployment is that a canary honeypot will generate an alert when it has been compromised, serving as an early warning indicator that similar high priority services might be targeted next, or in a worse scenario, that they have already been compromised.

This strategy is best served by deploying honeypot software that will emulate services offered by critical systems. Realistically, software doesn't exist that will emulate EVERY service that might be critical to your organization, but there are solutions that will emulate a lot of the more common services found in organizations.

As an example, let's consider an environment in which the most critical network assets were identified as a group of Windows servers that are not externally accessible, and host a proprietary internal application used by the finance department. These Windows servers are part of a domain, and are managed via the Remote Desktop Protocol (RDP). Mimicking the internal application as a honeypot might be difficult to do, but the RDP service is a perfect candidate for being emulated with a honeypot. Tom's Honeypot, which we will discuss later, provides the ability to mimic an RDP server and will generate an alert when someone even attempts to log in to this server. While it may not be feasible to actively log and examine every RDP login for the other Windows servers, actively reviewing alerts generated from the RDP honeypot is certainly feasible. This is because nobody should ever try to log on to this system since it is not exposed to the Internet.

In another scenario, we have an organization that has several Linux servers that host the back end databases associated with their public facing e-commerce site. The Linux servers are not public facing, and the only services they have running internally are SSH for server management and MySQL for the databases. In this case, both services can be mimicked as honeypots. The SSH service can be mimicked with an SSH honeypot like Kippo, and the MySQL service can be mimicked with a tool like Tom's Honeypot. Again, nobody should ever log into these particular honeypot systems, so any access to these systems should generate an alert and serve as a warning of a potential internal compromise or an impending attack against your critical systems.

## Phase Two: Determine Canary Honeypot Placement

Once you've determined which services you intend to emulate, you must place honeypot systems within your network. While placement may seem as simple as deploying the honeypot applications on a host and plugging it into the network, there are other considerations that must be accounted for.

First, you should ensure that the honeypot is placed on the same network segment as the assets it is mimicking. If the honeypot is placed in another segment, then its compromise might not actually indicate that an attacker has made their way into the segment you are trying to protect. As an example, consider Figure 12.1.

In this figure, multiple network segments are shown. The network segment containing the most critical network assets from a threat perspective is the research segment. This is where the canary honeypot systems are placed. Legitimate servers have complementary honeypot systems placed in the network segment alongside them. The Linux File Servers are accompanied by an SSH honeypot, the Windows Application Servers are accompanied by an RDP honeypot, and the Web Servers are paired with an HTTP honeypot.

The primary goal of the honeypot system is to generate alert and log data when someone attempts to access the system or service. With that in mind, you should be certain that your placement of the honeypot allows data to be transmitted to an NSM sensor or log collection device. In Figure 12.1, Sensor B would be responsible for performing detection for this network segment by analyzing data entering and leaving the segment.

Beyond the mechanics of ensuring that the honeypot is functioning properly for its role, you should also ensure that the amount of actual communication that the honeypot can participate in is limited. While the honeypot should be able to respond to the same types of requests as the legitimate assets it mimics it should be prevented from actually initiating communication with other hosts. This can be done with thorough firewall rules on the router that is upstream from the honeypot. In figure 12.1, this upstream router would be the Research Network Router.

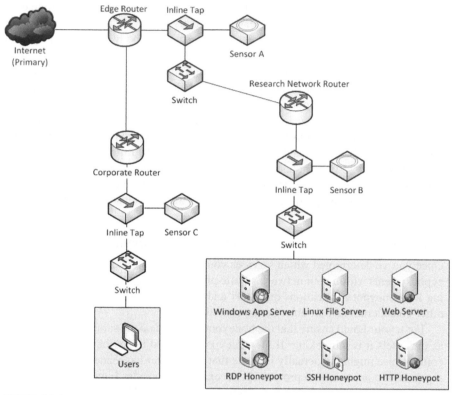

**FIGURE 12.1**

Canary Honeypot Placement Near Protected Assets

## Phase Three: Develop Alerting and Logging

The final step in canary honeypot deployment is developing the logging and alerting that will notify analysts that an attacker is interacting with the honeypot system.

First and foremost, you should always be aware of the capabilities of the honeypot software you are using. In some cases, you may find the software has the ability to generate data that can serve as an alert. This might include the ability to generate something like a MySQL database entry or a Syslog event. If this isn't an option, then you might need to combine the honeypot software with another detection mechanism to generate an alert.

When considering how to best generate alerts from a canary honeypot without using the honeypot software itself, you must consider where the NSM sensor is placed in relation to the honeypot systems. In Figure 12.1, a sensor is placed directly upstream from the critical network segment where the honeypots exist. If an attacker accesses those honeypots from another internal network segment, you can utilize the network detection mechanisms used by that sensor, such as Snort/Suricata, Bro, or a statistical detection tool to generate alerts for honeypot interaction.

Since any interaction with the honeypot should be considered abnormal, you can generate alerts from normal communication sequences in the context of the service being mimicked. For example, IDS signatures for the following events would be appropriate for Figure 12.1:

1. **SSH Honeypot** – Detecting SSH server banner being transmitted
2. **RDP Honeypot** – Detecting an RDP login
3. **HTTP Honeypot** – Detecting an HTTP GET/POST/etc request

In a scenario where an attacker is interacting with a honeypot system from a device that they control inside the critical network segment, this sensor would probably not be able to detect the attacker's actions since that communication wouldn't traverse the sensor boundary. This can be remedied by configuring a host-based detection mechanism on the honeypot host itself so that alert data can still be generated. This might be a capability inherent to the honeypot software, or might require a third party tool such as OSSEC for host-based detection, or even a custom script. In our example, the host based mechanism could report directly to Sensor B, or another upstream system that is collecting log data.

Once an alert has been generated, an analyst should have the ability to access the logs generated by the honeypot system to determine what the potential attacker did with the system. The amount of detail available in these logs will usually be dependent upon the honeypot software itself, but you should strive to make these logs as verbose as possible. Since the potential for false positives while using canary honey pots is so low, this results in fewer logs, so there isn't much danger of exceeding your storage capacity or generating an overwhelming flood of log data. Remember that any activity occurring on a honeypot is considered suspicious, because no legitimate user should ever attempt to communicate with it.

With that said false positives can be generated. This is commonly the case with network auto discovery type services, and legitimate internal scanning. This phase of honeypot deployment should also include tuning out false positives, which can be done by excluding honeypot IP addresses from scanning services, or tweaking the detection mechanisms used in conjunction with the honeypot systems.

## HONEYPOT PLATFORMS

There are several freely available low interaction honeypots. The remainder of this chapter will be devoted to discussing how a few of these tools can be used as canary honeypots for NSM.

### Honeyd

When someone brings up the history of honeypot software, the discussion typically begins with Honeyd. The Honeyd utility was developed by Niels Provos over ten years ago, and provides the ability to emulate hosts as a low-interaction honeypot. Honeyd has been the de facto low-interaction honeypot solution for years, and is so popular that a lot of modern honeypot solutions borrow from its functionality.

While it hasn't been significantly updated in some time, it is still very functional and serves a great purpose as a canary honeypot utility. While there has been more than one version of Honeyd on Windows, the original Honeyd runs exclusively on Unix based operating systems, and that is the version that we will cover here.

The flexibility of Honeyd lies in its ability to emulate a large number of systems and services with a simple configuration file. A single Honeyd instance can spawn dozens, hundreds, and even thousands of honeypot systems. Not only this, but Honeyd will utilize operating system fingerprinting information to mimic the characteristics of the OS down to the layer three and four characteristics that might be expected. When an attacker attempts to determine the operating system of the device they are interacting with, most automated tools will tell them that it is whatever OS you have specified in the Honeyd configuration file, even if that isn't the true OS that the Honeyd honeypots are running on.

The best way to show the functionality of Honeyd is to demonstrate it in practice. Installing Honeyd can be accomplished via building from source, or using a package manager like APT, with the following command:

```
apt-get install honeyd
```

To run Honeyd, we will have to create a configuration file. A default configuration file that contains a few different examples of how the file is structured is provided at /etc/honeypot/honeyd.conf. We will create our own configuration file that is a bit simpler and build upon it. In this example, let's try to configure a honeypot that mimics a Windows Server 2003 device with only typical Windows ports (135, 139, and 445) open.

First, we must configure a few default settings for Honeyd. These lines are:

```
create default
set default default tcp action block
set default default udp action block
set default default icmp action block
```

These first four lines tell Honeyd block all inbound communication to its honeypots unless otherwise specified. Think of this as a default deny rule on a firewall.

Next, we can create a honeypot by using the create command and specifying the name of the honeypot. In this case we will call it ansm_winserver_1:

```
create ansm_winserver_1
```

We want to emulate a Windows Server 2003 device, so we will use the set command along with the personality option to accomplish this.

```
set ansm_winserver_1 personality "Microsoft Windows Server 2003 Stan-
dard Edition"
```

The personality reference is drawn from the fingerprints database used by the popular Nmap port and vulnerability scanning application. The default installation of Honeyd uses the file /etc/honeypot/nmap.prints for these fingerprints, but this file isn't even close to being up to date. If you'd like to reference the personality of a modern operating system that isn't including in the default nmap.prints file, you can create your own entry from the updated Nmap fingerprint database at https://svn.nmap.org/nmap/nmap-os-db. Keep in mind that fingerprints from modern versions of Nmap might require some modification to work properly with Honeyd.

Now that we have created the honeypot itself, we have to configure the ports we want to appear open. In this case we want the three ports that are typically indicative of a Windows system, which are TCP ports 135, 139, and 445.

```
add ansm_winserver_1 tcp port 135 open
add ansm_winserver_1 tcp port 139 open
add ansm_winserver_1 tcp port 445 open
```

Our last step is to provide our honeypot with a MAC address and an IP address so that it can communicate on the network. This is done with the set and bind commands, respectively.

```
set ansm_winserver_1 ethernet "d3:ad:b3:3f:11:11"
bind 172.16.16.202 ansm_winserver_1
```

At this point, we've created everything we need to get this simple honeypot up and running. Assuming you've saved these configuration lines into a file named ansm.conf, you can execute Honeyd with the following command:

```
sudo honeyd -d -f /etc/honeypot/ansm.conf
```

The –d switch is used to tell Honeyd not to run in daemon mode. This is done so that we can see its output on the screen. The –f switch is used to specify the location of the configuration file we've created. Now, we can test Honeyd by port scanning the honeypot we created in the configuration file. The output of this scan is shown in Figure 12.2.

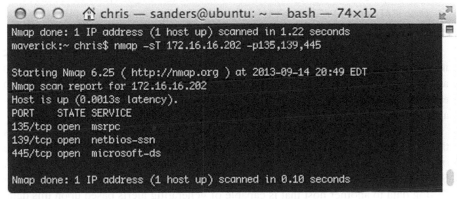

**FIGURE 12.2**

Port Scanning Shows Open Ports on the Honeypot

As you might expect, Honeyd has performed extensive logging of this scanning. These logs are stored in Syslog format in /var/log/syslog by default, which makes it incredibly easy to ship this log data to a third party tool like ELSA or Logstash. The log output of our scanning activity is shown in Figure 12.3:

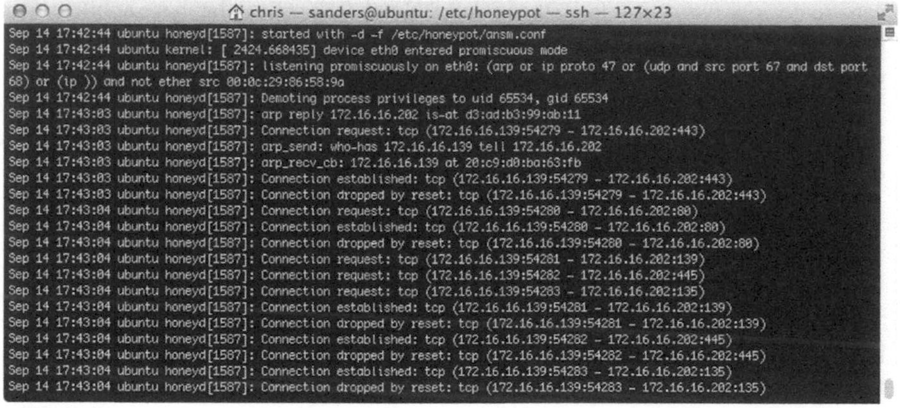

**FIGURE 12.3**

Honeyd Log Output to Syslog Showing our Scanning

At this point, our honeypot is extremely limited in functionality. While an attacker can scan this host and find open ports (the result of a TCP three-way hand-shake), they will not actually be able to interact with the host. In cases where you would like to emulate a Windows host that doesn't provide any services beyond that of a domain controller or file sharing server, the functionality we have now would suffice perfectly for a canary honeypot. Since nobody should ever be communicating with this system, you could place it under the visibility of an IDS sensor that uses a rule like this:

```
alert ip !$TRUSTED_MS_HOSTS any - > $MS_HONEYPOT_SERVERS [135,139,445]
(msg:"Attempted Communication with Windows Honeypot on MS Ports";
sid:5000000; rev:1;)
```

This rule will detect any TCP or UDP communication to this honeypot (assuming it is included in the $MS_HONEYPOT_SERVERS variable), except for systems in an approved $TRUSTED_MS_HOSTS variable. This variable should be used to exclude communication from devices like domain controllers, or update and management servers such as WSUS and SMS.

To be prepared for scenarios in which a system in the same network segment as this honeypot might attempt to communicate with it, you should also use some type of detection mechanism that can generate alert data from the honeypot server itself. Since Honeyd generates log data in Syslog format, this can be done easily by pushing Syslog data to another host that is capable of generating alerts based upon this data, or by using a host-based IDS tool like OSSEC.

While the current configuration works great for mimicking simple services, the functionality of Honeyd doesn't stop there. It can also emulate more advanced services by invoking scripts that are tied to specific open ports. As an example, let's edit our Windows 2003 honeypot so that it will emulate a web server. To do this, add the following line after the other open port designations:

```
add ansm_winserver_1 tcp port 80 "sh /usr/share/honeyd/scripts/win32/
web.sh"
```

If an attacker attempts to port scan this device now, they would see that port 80 is open, indicating that a web server is present on this system. If that same attacker then actually connects to the system with a web browser, they would actually be presented with a web page. This page is contained with the web.sh script that is called, and can be customized to resemble another web server in your environment. In addition to its standard logging to syslog, Honeyd will log the HTTP client request header of the attacker attempting to connect to the fake web server. This is shown in Figure 12.4.

```
sanders@ubuntu:/var/log/honeypot$ cat iis.log
GET / HTTP/1.1
Host: 172.16.16.202
Connection: keep-alive
Cache-Control: max-age=0
Accept: text/html,application/xhtml+xml,application/xml;q=0.9,*/*;q=0.8
User-Agent: Mozilla/5.0 (Macintosh; Intel Mac OS X 10_8_4) AppleWebKit/537.36 (KHTML, like Gecko) Chrome/29.0
.1547.65 Safari/537.36
Accept-Encoding: gzip,deflate,sdch
Accept-Language: en-US,en;q=0.8
sanders@ubuntu:/var/log/honeypot$
```

**FIGURE 12.4**

The HTTP Client Header of an Attacker Connecting to the Honeypot Web Server

This level of logging allows you to profile the tools that the attacker is using while attempting to access your infrastructure. For instance, in Figure 12.4 you can see that the attacker is using the Chrome browser (User-Agent: Mozilla/5.0 (Macintosh; Intel Mac OS X 10_8_4) AppleWebKit/537.36 (KHTML, like Gecko) Chrome/29.0.1547.65 Safari/537.36) and the US English character set (Accept-Language: en-US,en;q$=0.8$).

In this case, the following IDS rule would detect communication with this canary honeypot:

```
alert tcp any any ->$WEB_HONEYPOT_SERVERS 80 (msg:"HTTP GET Request to
Web Honeypot"; content:"GET"; http_method; sid:5000000; rev:1;)
```

This rule will generate an alert for any HTTP GET request to this host, assuming it is included in the $WEB_HONEYPOT_SERVERS variable in the IDS engine you are using. If you want to make a more content-specific rule, embed a particular content string in the HTML of the honeypot website, and create a rule that detects that specific string. Honeyd has several scripts that emulate a variety of services in a similar manner, including scripts to emulate SMTP, SNMP, TELNET, POP, and other services. These scripts all provide varying levels of interaction, so you should test them thoroughly to see if they might be a good fit in your environment.

In this chapter we only scratched the surface of Honeyd's capabilities. In addition to what we've shown here, Honeyd also has to ability to redirect an attacker to another system, or even masquerade as a routing device. While it isn't necessarily as robust as some other honeypot solutions that focus on emulating a single service, its ability to spawn dozens of honeypot systems makes it immensely useful as a canary honeypot for NSM detection. If you want to experiment more with Honeyd, you should check out their documentation at http://honeyd.org/.

## Kippo SSH Honeypot

The next platform we will look at is one that I've already mentioned a few times in this chapter, the Kippo SSH honeypot. Kippo is a low interaction honeypot that simulates an SSH server, and it is designed to detect brute force attempts and log attacker interaction with a simulated shell environment.

Kippo is useful as a canary honeypot because the SSH protocol is commonly used to manage both Unix-based devices and network devices like switches and routers. When an attacker gains a foothold onto the network, a couple of scenarios exist where the attacker might try to access devices using the SSH service:

1. The attacker will attempt a brute force or dictionary attack against the SSH server to gain access
2. The attacker will attempt to guess the password of a user to gain access
3. The attacker will attempt to log into the service with credentials already obtained through some other means

The first scenario might be detectable if the attacker performs these attacks across a sensor boundary where alerts might be triggered. However, if an attacker attempts to perform the brute force attack against a device on the same network segment, then network-based detection won't be possible. The same applies for the second scenario, but a lower volume of authentication attempts further complicates that scenario. While a brute force or dictionary attack will generate a great deal of traffic that could easily be detected by an IDS signature or some type of statistical detection, an attacker simply guessing passwords for a user might not meet the thresholds for alert generation. In the third scenario, network based detection is nearly impossible through traditional means, because an attacker using legitimate credentials would look almost identical to a user authenticating normally. Our only chance of detecting this type of activity would be through some type of anomaly based detection that notices a user logging into this service from a system they don't normally use.

As a defender, we can gain leverage against this type of attack by deploying an SSH honeypot like Kippo into a network segment where high priority assets exist. Since nobody should ever log into this system, any login attempt or exchange of network traffic beyond standard broadcast or update traffic should trigger an alert. This places us in a situation where all three scenarios above are detectable, and the canary honeypot can effectively serve as an early warning that someone is in the network performing an unauthorized activity. As an added advantage, if the attacker attempts to use credentials they have obtained through other means, this will become clear to us and incident response can occur, assuming that other services that user has access to might be compromised. The only false positives here might occur when an admin accidentally attempts to log into one of these systems.

You can download Kippo from https://code.google.com/p/kippo/. Since Kippo is a Python script, no compiling or installation is required, and you can run Kippo by executing the start.sh file that is contained in the Kippo directory. Kippo is highly configurable via the kippo.cfg file, but for our purposes here, we will leave the default configuration file intact.

---

**FROM THE TRENCHES**

If you are deploying Kippo into a production environment, you should take time to modify settings that an attacker could use to identify the system as a honeypot. This includes items like the hostname and the contents of the false file system. Ideally, these things will be configured similarly to production devices.

---

If you are following along and have executed Kippo, then you should be able to connect back in to its faux SSH environment. The default configuration has Kippo launch its SSH service on port 2222. You should set up your honeypot to use whatever port is common within your environment, such as the default port 22.

At baseline, Kippo will log any attempt to log into the service, complete with the username and password used in the attempt. These files are logged by default in the log/kippo.log directory. A sample output from this log is shown in Figure 12.5.

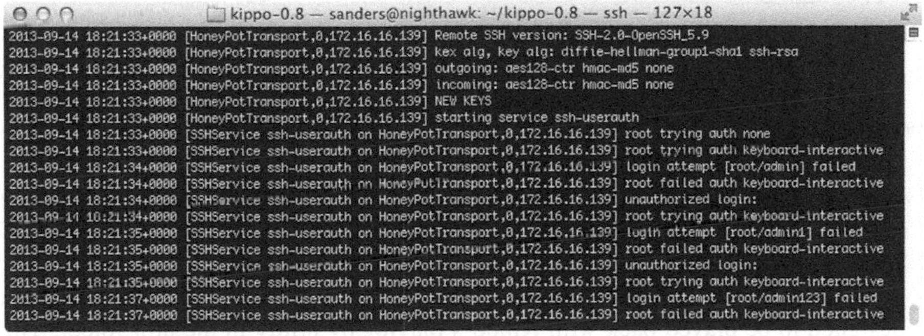

**FIGURE 12.5**

Kippo Logging Authentication Attempts

Kippo can be configured to allow a potential attacker to log into its simulated file system by specifying a user account and password that will allow for successful authentication. This username and password is specified in the data/userdb.txt file, and is username "root" and password "123456" by default. If an attacker utilizes this username and password combination, they will be presented with a fake file system that they can browse around in, and that even allows them to create and delete files, shown in Figure 12.6.

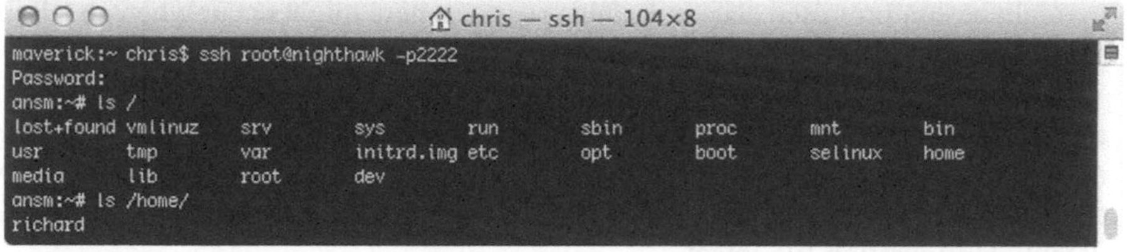

**FIGURE 12.6**

Browsing Kippo's Fake File System

As you might expect, the attacker's actions in this environment are logged thoroughly as well. An example of one of these logs is shown in Figure 12.7.

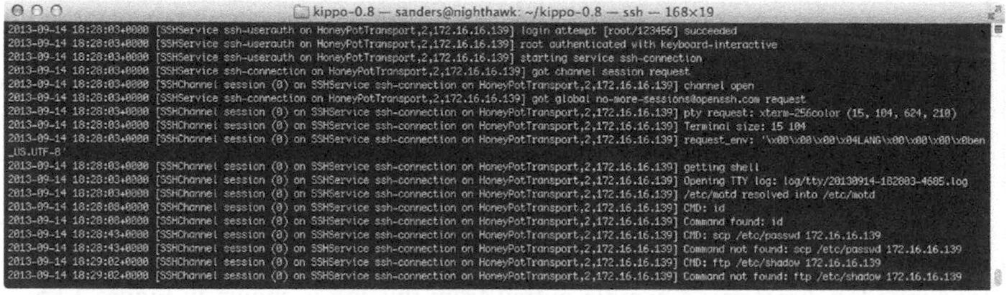

**FIGURE 12.7**

Kippo Logging an Attacker's Actions at the Terminal

In the example above, we can see that the attacker attempts to send the /etc/passwd file back to the host they logged in from the SCP and FTP commands. The SCP and FTP clients aren't available in this environment, so the system indicates that the commands aren't found. The default kippo.log file doesn't show verbose output of these commands, but this information can be found in the log/tty folder. This folder contains a detailed binary log file of the actions taken in every terminal spawned by the software. Each file name is based upon the timestamp of when the terminal is initialized. These files aren't easily viewable in plaintext, and are designed to be played back with Kippo's playlog.py utility in the util/ folder. This utility will replay as if you were sitting over the attacker's shoulder watching their interaction with the terminal. This shows the command input in real time, and captures every keystroke, backspace, and pause. This output is very impressive when used in presentations. Figure 12.8 shows the playlog.py output for the attack sequence shown in Figure 12.7. You can see the more verbose output of the id command that isn't shown in the base kippo.log file.

The additional level of interaction that Kippo provides with its fake file system is useful for gaining intelligence related to an attacker's motives or tactics. Often, the first thing an attacker does when they gain access to a system is to download additional files from an external site. This might include malware, a keylogger, a backdoor, or a rootkit that will further their attack goals. When they attempt to download these tools in the Kippo environment, you can see the remote host they are attempting to access and the tools they attempt to download. This incredibly useful intelligence can be used to help shape collection, detection, and analysis strategy.

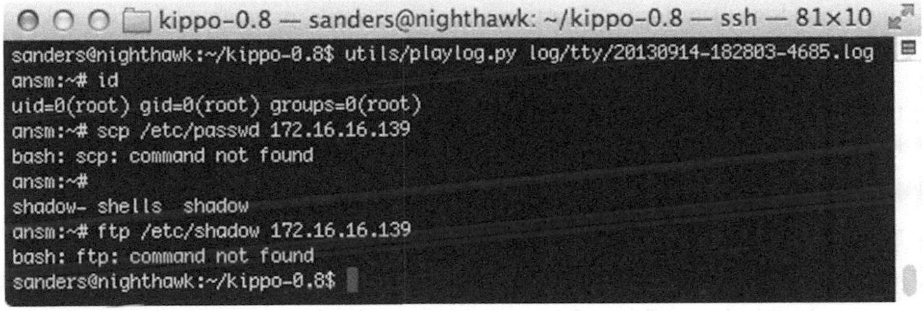

**FIGURE 12.8**

Replayed Attacked Sequence in the Kippo TTY Log

The native Kippo logging format is fairly easily parseable by other tools, and it also provides the option to log to a MySQL database, which can be useful for incorporating Kippo data into another tool. To enhance detection, IDS signatures and other detection mechanisms can be paired with the honeypot server itself. This is generally the preferred method for alerting on honeypot interaction. For instance, the following Snort/Suricata IDS rules can be used to indicate an attempt to authenticate to a honeypot system.

```
alert tcp $HONEYPOT_SERVERS $SSH_PORTS ->any any (msg:"ET POLICY SSH
Server Banner Detected on Expected Port - Honeypot System"; flow: from_
server,established; content:"SSH-"; offset: 0; depth: 4; byte_test:
1,>,48,0,relative; byte_test:1,<,51,0,relative; byte_test:1,=,46,1,
relative; reference:url,doc.emergingthreats.net/2001973; classtype:
misc-activity; sid:2001973; rev:8;)
```

```
alert tcp any any <> $HONEYPOT_SERVERS $SSH_PORTS (msg:"ET POLICY SSH
session in progress on Expected Port - Honeypot System"; threshold: type
both, track by_src, count 2, seconds 300; reference:url,doc.emerging-
threats.net/2001978; classtype:misc-activity; sid:2001978; rev:7;)
```

The first rule shown above (SID 2001973) detects the SSH server banner being transmitted to a client. The second rule (SID 2001978) detects an SSH session in progress. These rules are provided by Emerging Threats, and you should note that I've modified them here to only detect traffic occurring to systems identified by the $HONEYPOT_SERVERS variable, which would have to be configured on your sensor for these rules to work.

Utilizing rules like these, you should be alerted whenever a sensor detects that someone has interacted with the SSH service on the honeypot system. At this point, you can reference the log data generated by Kippo to assess the extent of the interaction. Remember, this activity can only be detected if an attacker accesses the honeypot in a manner where the sensor can see it. To perform detection against events occurring from within the same network segment, you would have to generate alerts from the Honeypot system itself. There are a couple of ways to do this, such as sending Kippo logs to syslog and alerting on certain events, or using a host-based detection program such as OSSEC.

Kippo has a few more features that aren't covered here, and a number of additional utilities and third party enhancements that are worth looking into. You can learn more about all of this at https://code.google.com/p/kippo/.

## Tom's Honeypot

The last honeypot we will look at is Tom's Honeypot, which was developed by Tom Liston, the developer of one of the earliest production honeypots, the LaBrea Tar Pit. Tom's Honeypot is a low interaction Python honeypot that is designed to mimic a few specific services that are commonly targeted by attackers. These services include:

- Remote Desktop Protocol (RDP) (TCP/3389)
- Microsoft SQL Server (MSSQL) (TCP/1433, UDP/1434)
- Virtual Network Computer (VNC) (TCP/5900)
- RAdmin (Remote Administration) (TCP/4899)
- Session Initiation Protocol (SIP) (UDP/5060)

Tom's Honeypot listens on specified ports for communication related to these services. When an attacker attempts to access one of these services, an alert is generated in the tomshoneypot.log file.

Since Tom's Honeypot is just a Python script, all you need to do to run it is install a prerequisite (the Python Twisted module) and then use Python to run it. The following command will install the prerequisite in Security Onion:

```
sudo apt-get install python-twisted
```

The script can be obtained from http://labs.inguardians.com/tomshoneypot. It can be executed by running the following command:

```
python tomshoneypot.py
```

By default, Tom's Honeypot runs with all of its available services turned on. If you only want to run a subset of these services, you will have to manually edit the script and comment the appropriate sections out. These sections are:

```
reactor.listenTCP(1433, fMSSQL, interface=interface)
reactor.listenTCP(3389, fTS, interface=interface)
reactor.listenTCP(5900, fVNC, interface=interface)
reactor.listenTCP(22292, fDump, interface=interface)
reactor.listenTCP(4899, fRAdmind, interface=interface)
```

```
reactor.listenUDP(1434, uFakeMSSQL(), interface=interface)
reactor.listenUDP(5060, uFakeSIP(), interface=interface)
```

If you don't want to run a particular service, simple place a pound symbol at the beginning of that services line. This will cause the Python interpreter to skip this line and forgo starting a listener on the ports tied to these services.

As an example, let's take a look at one of these services. The RDP protocol is used for remote desktop administration of Windows hosts. In a common attack scenario where an attacker has gained a foothold onto the network, they will typically do some scanning to determining what other targets they can access. The RDP service typically utilizes port 3389, and when an attacker sees this port open they will usually try to connect to it with an RDP client. If the attacker has gained users' credentials through some other means, the RDP service could allow them to take control of the server and begin pillaging data. Even if the attacker doesn't have a user's credentials, they could still use the RDP server to attempt to guess a user's password, or simply to enumerate the version of Windows running on the machine.

In this case of Tom's Honeypot, a fake RDP server will run over port 3389 to entice an attacker to interact with the service. When the attacker attempts this, the device they are attacking from will complete a three-way TCP handshake with the honeypot, and will then initiate an RDP connection request; however, the honeypot will not generate a response back. A typical attacker will usually assume this is because some type of host restriction is in place, or that the service is simply malfunctioning. However, this is occurring because there is no legitimate RDP service to log into, and instead of providing an RDP server to log into, Tom's Honeypot simply logs the access to the fake system. An example of such a log is shown in Figure 12.9.

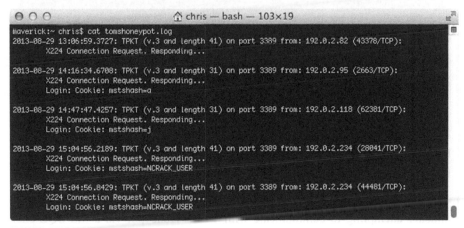

**FIGURE 12.9**

An Example Tom's Honeypot RDP Access Attempt Log

In the logs shown above, you'll notice five individual entries. Four of these entries include a "Login" field. While Tom's Honeypot won't generate an interactive screen that an attacker can attempt to log into, it takes advantage of the fact that an RDP client will attempt to transmit a cookie during its initial negotiation request. This RDP cookie doesn't have anything to do with authentication, but it does contain a username that is used for terminal services identification. The first log in Figure 12.9 doesn't show any result for this field because no RDP cookie was present during that connection attempt, but the following four log entries have values present. The second and third entries show two different IP addresses attempting to make connections to the honeypot with RDP cookie usernames values of "a" and "j". The last two log entries show two attempts from the IP address 192.0.2.234, using the RDP cookie username "NCRACK_USER." The Ncrack tool is an authentication-cracking tool that can be used to attack RDP servers. This would indicate that 192.0.2.234 is attempting to obtain unauthorized access to the honeypot system.

The other fake services provided by Tom's Honeypot work in a similar manner. Figure 12.10 shows an example of logs generated from the MSSQL and SIP honeypot services.

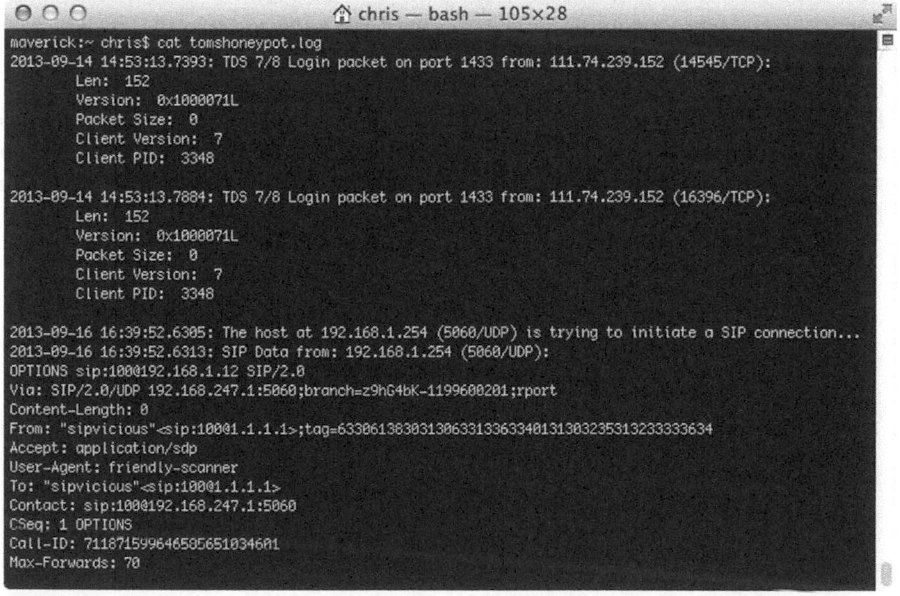

**FIGURE 12.10**

Example Tom's Honeypot Logs for MSSQL and SIP Protocols

Two logs are shown in Figure 12.10. The first log shows data obtained from an attacker attempting to communicate with Tom's Honeypot via a MS SQL client (TCP port 1433). Note that this output shows information about the client used to connect to the fake MS SQL service.

The second log shows someone attempting to communicate with the honeypot via the SIP protocol (UDP 5060), which is commonly used by Voice over IP (VoIP) services. In this case, we see that this traffic is associated with the Sipvicious tool, which is used for scanning, enumerating, and auditing SIP services.

Tom's Honeypot is an actively developed project, and it is likely that by the time this book is published, even more features will have been added. If you want to learn more about Tom's Honeypot, you can visit the project site at http://labs.inguardians.com/tomshoneypot/.

## Honeydocs

When conceptualizing information security, we often focus on protecting systems and processes. While this is certainly a worthwhile venture, it usually isn't the systems and processes that we are actually trying to protect; it is the data that resides within them. That is where a honeydoc comes into play.

A honeydoc is a specialized form of "honey technology." Instead of mimicking a legitimate system and logging access to that system, a honeydoc mimics a legitimate document, and logs access to that document.

In a typical deployment, a honeydoc containing a bunch of false data is created and placed alongside legitimate data. Along with the false data, the honeydoc will contain some type of hidden code that references a third party server. The goal here is that an attacker who succeeds in accessing secure data will eventually open this honeydoc, and their system will connect to the third party system. The third party system will, of course, log any details it can about the client that has opened to document.

There are a number of ways to create a honeydoc, but the most common method involves including code in the document that will force the generation of an HTTP request when the document is opened. While these requests can be blocked or subverted, they are often fairly successful when dealing with an inexperienced or hasty attacker.

As an example, let's create a honeydoc using a Microsoft Word document. The quickest way to do this is to create a plain text document devoid of any special formatting. This can be done from the terminal or from a tool like Notepad or Textedit. This document should contain a set of fake data that might be of interest to an attacker, like a list of fake users or password hashes. With the data in place, you should surround the data with the $<$html$>$ and $</$html$>$ tags to designate it as web content. As a last step, we can place the content that will generate the request to our web server. This can be done by using the HTML $<$img$>$ tag, but instead of providing the URL location of an image, we will provide a serialized URL to our web server, like this:

```
<img src="http://172.16.16.202/doc123456">
```

In a real world scenario, this URL would point towards a public IP address or domain name. It is important that each honeydoc is serialized, so that you can keep track of requests generated from each document. The resulting honeydoc you've created should look similar to Figure 12.11.

```
◀ | ▶ | 🗋 honeydoc.docx ⁝
1    <html>
2    1,Sanders,Chris
3    2,Sanders,Ellen
4    3,Sanders,Rocky
5    4,Sanders,Dorie
6    5,Smith,Jason
7    6,Bianco,David
8    7,Randall,Liam
9    8,Vader,Darth
10   9,Alderson,Jimmy
11   10,Skywalker,Anakin
12   <br/>
13   <br/>
14   <br/>
15   <br/>
16   <br/>
17   <br/>
18   <br/>
19   <br/>
20   <br/>
21   <br/>
22   <br/>
23   <br/>
24   <br/>
25   <br/>
26   <br/>
27   <br/>
28   <br/>
29   <br/>
30   <img src="http://172.16.16.202/doc123456">
31   </html>
```

**FIGURE 12.11**

A Honeydoc in Raw HTML

The last step in this process is to save this document in the appropriate format. This is usually going to be a .doc or .docx file for compatibility with an application like Microsoft Word. Now, when you open this document Word will attempt to download the image file referenced in the <img> tag, but instead, will generate a GET request to your web server. For the purposes of this example, I pointed a honeydoc to a Honeyd server, which generated the output in Figure 12.12.

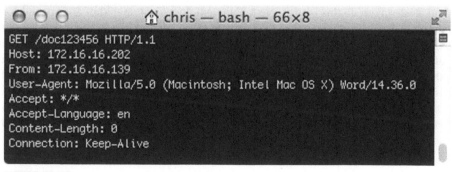

**FIGURE 12.12**

Honeyd Log Output from the Honeydoc

With this log data, you could easily generate an alert that will notify analysts that a honeydoc has been accessed. Since honeydocs will often reside next to real data, it is always possible that a legitimate user could access a honeydoc mistakenly, but this shouldn't be a common occurrence.

Honeydocs aren't restricted to text documents. This scenario could be applied to other types of files including HTML pages, PDF files, or even XLS files. If you want to experiment with the creation and tracking of a Honeydoc without setting up a web server, the Honeydocs.com service was launched with the goal to automate the creation of Honeydocs, as well as the tracking of honeydoc campaigns (or stings, as they call them). You can register at honeydocs.com for free, which allows for the creation of a single sting that can contain multiple honeydocs. For a fee, you can create more stings and utilize the Honeydoc service to generate e-mail or SMS alerts whenever a honeydoc you've created is accessed. Figure 12.13 shows an example of the Honeydocs.com web interface.

**FIGURE 12.13**

The Honeydocs.com Web Interface

I've seen honeydocs of various types used in a variety of detection and response scenarios with great success. However, I must provide the warning that honeydocs aren't entirely covert, and even a relatively unskilled attacker will be able to notice a document attempting to communicate with an external host. This could expose the third party server to probes by the attacker, so you should ensure that this host is secure, and ideally, located away from your corporate network. It should also be unattributable to your organization. In a best case scenario, the attacker doesn't notice the honeydoc "phoning home" at all. If they do notice, you will want to minimize risk as much as possible. With all of this said, great care should be taken when implementing honeydocs, as with the other technologies discussed in this chapter.

## CONCLUSION

In this chapter we've taken a look at the application of canary honeypots in an NSM environment. This includes the placement of canary honeypots, alerting and logging considerations, and a few different honeypot software solutions that can serve this purpose. We also took a quick look at honeydocs and how they can be used for NSM detection. While honeypots have traditionally been reserved for research purposes, the strategies discussed here can make canary honeypots an incredibly useful detection mechanism in the fight against the adversary.

# Analysis

# Packet Analysis

# 13

## CHAPTER CONTENTS

The analysis phase of Network Security Monitoring is predicated on the analysis of data to determine if an incident has occurred. Since most of the data that is collected by NSM tools is related to network activity, it should come as no surprise that the ability to analyze and interpret packet data is one of the most important skills an analyst can have. In this first chapter of the analysis section of this book, we will dive into the world of packet analysis from the perspective of the NSM analyst. This chapter will assume that the reader is somewhat familiar with how computers communicate over the network, but will assume no prior packet analysis knowledge. We will examine how to interpret packets using "packet math" and protocol header maps, and look at ways packet filtering can be performed. While discussing these topics we will use both tcpdump and Wireshark to interact with packets.

The main goal of this chapter is to equip you with the knowledge you need to understand packets at a fundamental level, while providing a framework for understanding the protocols that aren't covered here.

---

**MORE INFORMATION**

While this book is designed for analysts of all skill levels, it does assume at least some knowledge of how network devices communicate with each other. Before proceeding you should have a basic understanding of the OSI or TCP/IP model and how encapsulation and decapsulation work. If you want to refresh yourself before reading this chapter, I recommend reading my other book, "Practical Packet Analysis." You don't have to read the whole thing before diving in here, but an understanding of the first chapter should suffice.

---

## ENTER THE PACKET

The heterogeneous nature of computing is what allows a multitude of devices developed and manufactured by a variety of companies to interoperate with each other on a given network. Whether that network is a small network like the one in your house, a large network like a corporation might have, or a global network like the Internet, devices can communicate on it as long as they speak the right protocol.

A networking protocol is similar to a spoken or written language. A language has rules, such as how nouns must be positioned, how verbs should be conjugated, and even how individuals should formally begin and end conversations. Protocols work in a similar fashion, but instead of dictating how humans communicate, they dictate how network devices can communicate. Regardless of who manufactures a networking device, if it speaks TCP/IP, then it can most likely communicate with any other devices that speak TCP/IP. Of course, protocols come in a variety of forms, with some being more simple and others being more complex. Also, the combined efforts of multiple protocols are required for normal network communication to take place.

The evidence of a protocol in action is the packet that is created to conform to its standards. The term packet refers to a specially formatted unit of data that is transmitted across a network from one device to another. These packets are the building blocks of how computers communicate, and the purest essence of network security monitoring.

For a packet to be formed, it requires the combination of data from multiple protocols. For instance, a typical HTTP GET request actually requires the use of at least four protocols to ensure that the request gets from your web browser to a web server (HTTP, TCP, IP, and Ethernet). If you've looked at packets before, then you may have seen the packet displayed in a format similar to what is shown in Figure 13.1, where Wireshark is used to display information about the packets contents.

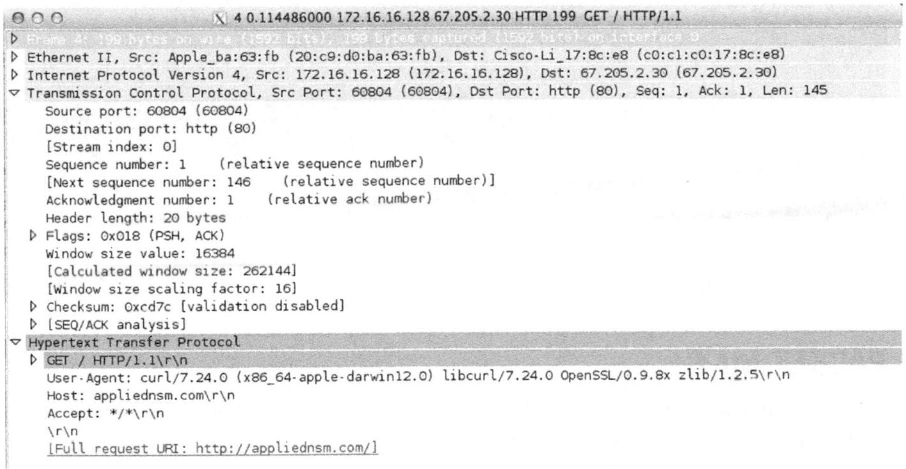

**FIGURE 13.1**

A Simple HTTP GET Request Packet Shown in Wireshark

Wireshark is a great tool for interacting with and analyzing packets, but to really understand packets at a fundamental level, we are going to start with a much more fundamental tool, tcpdump (or its Windows alternative, Windump). While Wireshark is a great tool, it is GUI based and does a lot of the legwork for you in regards to packet dissection. On the other hand, tcpdump relies on you to do a lot of the interpretation for individual packets on your own. While this may seem a bit counterintuitive, it really challenges the analyst to think more about the packets they are seeing, and provides a fundamental understanding that can be better applied to any packet analysis tool, or even the raw parsing of packet data.

Now that we've seen Wireshark break down an HTTP GET Request packet, let's look at the same packet in hexadecimal form. This output is achieved by using the command:

```
tcpdump -nnxr ansm-13-httpget.pcapng
```

We will discuss tcpdump later in this chapter, but for now, the packet is shown in Figure 13.2.

If you've never attempted to interpret a packet from raw hex before, then the output in Figure 13.2 can be a bit intimidating. However, it isn't very hard to read this data if we break it down by protocol. We are going to do that, but first, let's explore some basic packet math that will be necessary to proceed.

```
000                    ⌂ chris — bash — 113×17
maverick:~ chris$ tcpdump -nnexxr ansm-13-httpget.pcapng
reading from file ansm-13-httpget.pcapng, link-type EN10MB (Ethernet)
10:21:55.026074 20:c9:d0:ba:63:fb > c8:c1:c8:17:8c:e8, ethertype IPv4 (0x0800), length 199: 172.16.16.128.60804 >
  67.205.2.30.80: Flags [P.], seq 430817104:430817249, ack 2543215990, win 16384, length 145
        0x0000:  c0c1 c017 8ce8 20c9 d0ba 63fb 0800 4500
        0x0010:  00b9 3d2a 4000 4006 fa99 ac10 1080 43cd
        0x0020:  021e ed84 0050 19ad bf50 9796 6576 5018
        0x0030:  4000 cd7c 0000 4745 5420 2f20 4854 5450
        0x0040:  2f31 2e31 0d0a 5573 6572 2d41 6765 6e74
        0x0050:  3a20 6375 726c 2f37 2e32 342e 3020 2878
        0x0060:  3836 5f36 342d 6170 706c 652d 6461 7277
        0x0070:  696e 3132 2e30 2920 6c69 6263 7572 6c2f
        0x0080:  372e 3234 2e30 204f 7065 6e53 534c 2f30
        0x0090:  2e39 2e38 7820 7a6c 6962 2f31 2e32 2e35
        0x00a0:  0d0a 486f 7374 3a20 6170 706c 6965 646e
        0x00b0:  736d 2e63 6f6d 0d0a 4163 6365 7074 3a20
        0x00c0:  2a2f 2a0d 0a0d 0a
```

**FIGURE 13.2**

A Simple HTTP Get Request Packet Shown in tcpdump

# PACKET MATH

If you are anything like me, then the title of this section might get your blood boiling hotter than two dollar grits on the back burner of a twenty dollar stove. After all, there was no warning that math would be required! Don't worry though, packet math is actually pretty easy, and if you can do basic addition and multiplication, then you should be fine.

## Understanding Bytes in Hex

When examining packets at a lower level, such as with tcpdump, you will usually be looking at packet data represented in hexadecimal form. This hex format is derived from the binary representation of a byte. A byte is made up of 8 bits, which can either be a 1 or a 0. A single byte looks like this: 01000101.

To make this byte more readable, we can convert it to hex. This starts by splitting the byte into two halves, called nibbles (Figure 13.3). The first four bits is referred to as the higher order nibble, because it represents the larger valued portion of the byte. The second four bits is referred to as the lower order nibble, because it represents the lower valued portion of the byte.

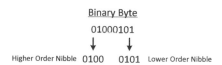

**FIGURE 13.3**

A Byte Split into Nibbles

Each nibble of this byte is converted into a hex character to form a two character byte. For most beginners, the fastest way to calculate the hex value of a byte is to first calculate the decimal value of each nibble, shown in Figure 13.4.

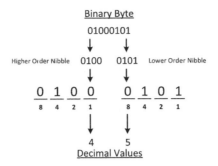

**FIGURE 13.4**

Calculating the Decimal Value of Each Nibble

While doing this calculation, notice that each position in the binary byte represents a value, and that this value increases from right to left, which is also how these positions are identified with the first position being the rightmost. The positions represent powers of 2, so the right most position is $2^0$, followed by $2^1$, $2^2$, and $2^3$. I find it easiest to use their decimal equivalents of 1, 2, 4, and 8 for performing calculations. With that said, if the position has a value of 1, then the value is added to a total. In the higher order nibble shown in Figure 13.4, there is only a value of 1 in the 3rd position, resulting in a total of 4. In the lower order nibble, there is a 1 in the 1st and 3rd positions, resulting in a total of 5 (1 + 4). The decimal values 4 and 5 represent this byte.

A hex character can range from 0-F, where 0-9 is equal to 0-9 in decimal, and A-F is equal to 10-15 in decimal. This means that 4 and 5 in decimal are equivalent to 4 and 5 in hexadecimal, meaning that 45 is the accurate hex representation of the byte 01000101. This entire process is shown in Figure 13.5.

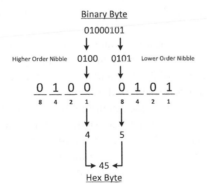

**FIGURE 13.5**

Converting a Binary Byte to Hex

Let's try this one more time, but with a different byte. Figure 13.6 shows this example.

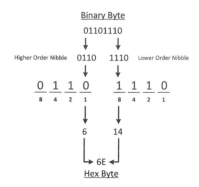

**FIGURE 13.6**

Converting Another Binary Byte to Hex

In this example, the higher order nibble has a 1 in the $2^{nd}$ and $3^{rd}$ position, resulting in a total of 6 $(2+4)$. The lower order nibble has a 1 in the $2^{nd}$, $3^{rd}$, and $4^{th}$ positions. This yields a decimal value of 14 $(2+4+8)$. Converting these numbers to hex, 6 in decimal is equivalent to 6 in hex, and 14 in decimal is equivalent to E in hex. This means that 6E is the hex representation of 01101110.

## Converting Hex to Binary and Decimal

We've discussed how to convert a binary number to hex, but later we will also need to know how to convert from hex values to decimal, so let's approach that subject quickly. First, we will convert a hex number back into binary, and then into decimal. We will use the same example as earlier, and attempt to convert 0x6E to a decimal number.

As we now know, a two digit hex value represents a single byte, which is 8 bits. Each digit of the hex value represents a nibble of the byte. This means that 6 represents the higher order nibble of the byte and E represents the lower order nibble. First, we need to convert each of these hex digits back into their binary equivalent. The manner I like to use is to convert each digit into its decimal equivalent first. Remembering that hex is base 16, this means that 6 in hex is equivalent to 6 in decimal, and E is equivalent to 12 in decimal. Once we've determined those values, we can convert them to binary by placing 1's in the appropriate bit positions (based on powers of 2) of each nibble. The result is a higher order nibble with the value 0100 and the lower order nibble of 1110.

Next, we can combine these nibbles to form a single byte, and consider each position as a power of 2 relative to the entire byte. Finally, we add up the values of the positions where the bit value is set to 1, yielding a decimal value of 110. This process is shown in Figure 13.7.

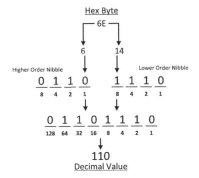

**FIGURE 13.7**

Converting Hexadecimal to Binary and Decimal

---

**MORE INFORMATION**

There are charts in Appendix 4 that can be used for quickly converting hex to ASCII or decimal representations. There are also several online converters that can help you perform these conversions quickly.

---

## Counting Bytes

Now that you understand how to interpret bytes in hex, let's talk about counting bytes. When examining packets at the hex level, you will spend a lot of time counting bytes. Although counting is pretty easy (no shame in using your fingers and toes!), there is an extra consideration when counting bytes in a packet.

As humans, we are used to counting starting from 1. When counting bytes, however, you must count starting from 0. This is because we are counting from an offset relative position.

---

**FROM THE TRENCHES**

When we say that we are counting from an offset relative position, this usually means that the position is relative to the 0 byte in the current protocol header, not the 0 byte at the beginning of the packet.

---

To explain this, let's consider the packet shown in in Figure 13.8.

This figure shows a basic IP packet, spaced so that it is easier to read the individual bytes. In order to figure out what makes this packet tick, we might want to evaluate values in certain fields of this packet. The best way to do this is to "map" each field in the protocols contained within this packet. This book contains several protocol field maps in Appendix 3 that can be used to dissect fields within individual protocols. In this case, since we know this is an IP packet, let's evaluate some of the values in the IP header. For convenience, it is shown in Figure 13.9:

45 00 00 40 fd 0d 40 00 40 06 3b 2f ac 10 10 80

43 cd 02 1e ed 84 00 50 19 ad bf 4f 00 00 00 00

b0 02 ff ff 45 1f 00 00 02 04 05 b4 01 03 03 04

01 01 08 0a 31 4e f7 43 00 00 00 00 04 02 00 00

**FIGURE 13.8**

A Basic IP Packet in Hex

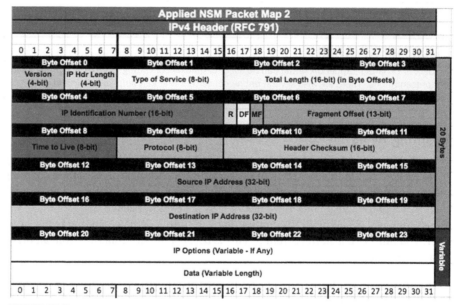

**FIGURE 13.9**

Packet Map for the IP Header

One useful piece of information that could help us dissect this packet further would be the embedded protocol that is riding on top of the IP header. The protocol map for IP indicates that this value is at byte 9. If you were to count bytes in this packet starting from 1, you would determine that the value of the embedded protocol field is 40, but this would be incorrect. When referring to a byte in this manner, it is actually referred to as byte offset 9, the ninth byte offset from 0, or more simply, 0x9. This means that we should be counting from 0, which shows that the true value of this field would be 06. This protocol value designates that TCP is the embedded protocol here. This is shown in Figure 13.10

Byte 0x9: Protocol
06 = TCP
↑
45 00 00 40 fd 0d 40 00 40 <u>06</u> 3b 2f ac 10 10 80

43 cd 02 1e ed 84 00 50 19 ad bf 4f 00 00 00 00

b0 02 ff ff 45 1f 00 00 02 04 05 b4 01 03 03 04

01 01 08 0a 31 4e f7 43 00 00 00 00 04 02 00 00

**FIGURE 13.10**

Locating the Protocol Field in the IP Header at 0 × 9

Applying this knowledge to another field, the IP protocol map tells us that the Time-to-Live (TTL) field is in the eighth byte offset from 0. Counting from 0 at the beginning of the packet, you should see that the value for this field is 40, or 64 in decimal.

Looking at the protocol map, you will notice that some fields are less than a byte in size. For example, the 0x0 byte in this packet contains two fields: IP Version and IP Header Length. In this example, the IP Version field is only the higher order nibble of this byte, while the IP Header Length field is the lower order nibble of this byte. Referencing Figure 13.9, this means that the IP Version is 4. The IP header length is displayed as 5, but this field is actually a bit tricky. The IP header length field actually has a calculated value, and must be multiplied by four. In this case, we multiply the value 5 times 4, and end up at an IP header length of 20 bytes. With this knowledge, you ascertain that the maximum length of an IP header is 60 bytes, because the highest possible value in the IP header length field is F (15 in decimal), and 15 × 4 is 60 bytes. These fields are shown in Figure 13.11.

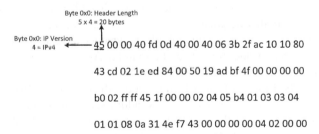

Byte 0x0: Header Length
5 x 4 = 20 bytes
Byte 0x0: IP Version
4 = IPv4
4 5 00 00 40 fd 0d 40 00 40 06 3b 2f ac 10 10 80

43 cd 02 1e ed 84 00 50 19 ad bf 4f 00 00 00 00

b0 02 ff ff 45 1f 00 00 02 04 05 b4 01 03 03 04

01 01 08 0a 31 4e f7 43 00 00 00 00 04 02 00 00

**FIGURE 13.11**

The IP Version and Header Length Fields at 0 × 0

In a final example, you will notice that some fields span more than one byte. One such example of this is the source and destination IP address fields, which are each 4 bytes in length, and occur at positions 0×12 and 0×16 in the IP header, respectively. In our example packet, the source IP address breaks down as ac 10 10 80 (172.16.16.128 in decimal), and the destination IP address is 43 cd 02 1e (67.205.2.30 in decimal). This is shown in Figure 13.12

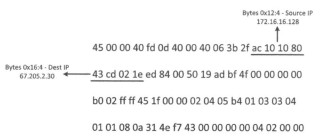

**FIGURE 13.12**

The Source and Destination IP Address Fields at 0x12 and 0x16

Take note of the special notation used in this figure to denote a field that is multiple bytes in length. When byte 0x16:4 is noted, this means to start at the sixteenth byte offset from 0, and then select four bytes from this point. This notation will come in handy later when we start writing packet filters.

At this point, we've looked at enough packet math to start dissecting packets at a low level. Hopefully it wasn't too painful.

# DISSECTING PACKETS

With some math out of the way, let's return to the packet shown in Figure 13.2 and break it down by each individual protocol. If you have an understanding of how packets are built, you know that a packet is built starting with the application layer data, and headers from protocols operating on lower layers are added as the packet is being built, moving from top to bottom. This means that the last protocol header that is added is at the Data Link layer, which means that we should encounter this header first. The most common data link layer protocol is Ethernet, but let's verify that this is what's being used here.

In order to verify that we are indeed seeing Ethernet traffic, we can compare what we know an Ethernet header should look like to what we have at the beginning of this packet. The Ethernet header format can be found in Appendix 3, but we've included it here in Figure 13.13 for convenience.

Looking at the Ethernet header format, you will see that the first 6 bytes of the packet are reserved for the destination MAC address, and the second six bytes, starting at 0x6, are reserved for the source MAC address. Figure 13.14 shows that these bytes do correspond to the MAC addresses of the two hosts in our example. The only other field that is included in the Ethernet header is the two-byte Type field at 0x12, which is used to tell us what protocol to expect after the Ethernet header. In this case, the type field has a hex value of 08 00, which means that the next embedded protocol that should be expected is IP. The length of the Ethernet header is static at 14 bytes, so we know that 00 is the last byte of the header.

---

**FROM THE TRENCHES**

While I've included the Ethernet header in this example, the data link layer header is not printed by tcpdump by default. Because all of the examples in this book use Ethernet, the examples moving forward won't show this header, and will instead begin from the network layer protocol instead.

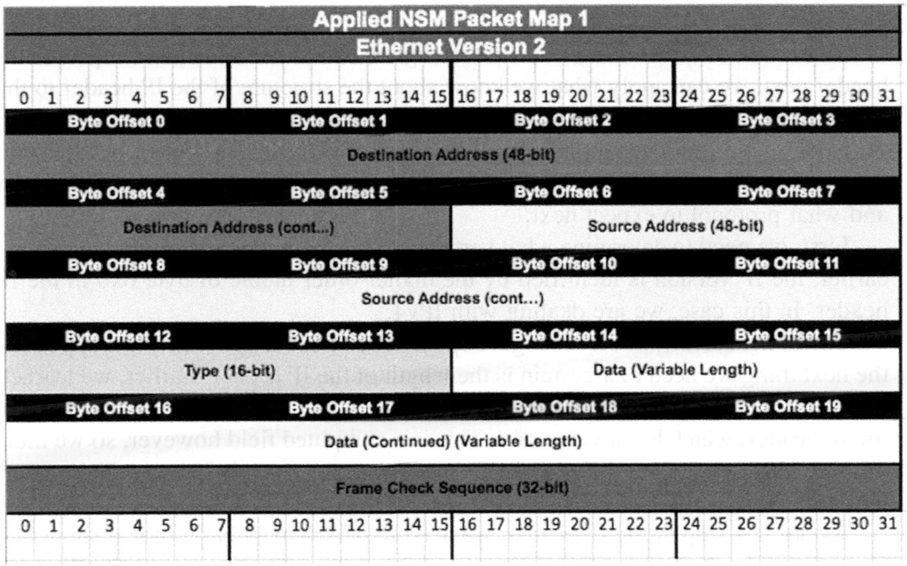

**Applied NSM Packet Map 1**
**Ethernet Version 2**

| 0 1 2 3 4 5 6 7 | 8 9 10 11 12 13 14 15 | 16 17 18 19 20 21 22 23 | 24 25 26 27 28 29 30 31 |
|---|---|---|---|
| Byte Offset 0 | Byte Offset 1 | Byte Offset 2 | Byte Offset 3 |
| Destination Address (48-bit) | | | |
| Byte Offset 4 | Byte Offset 5 | Byte Offset 6 | Byte Offset 7 |
| Destination Address (cont...) | | Source Address (48-bit) | |
| Byte Offset 8 | Byte Offset 9 | Byte Offset 10 | Byte Offset 11 |
| Source Address (cont...) | | | |
| Byte Offset 12 | Byte Offset 13 | Byte Offset 14 | Byte Offset 15 |
| Type (16-bit) | | Data (Variable Length) | |
| Byte Offset 16 | Byte Offset 17 | Byte Offset 18 | Byte Offset 19 |
| Data (Continued) (Variable Length) | | | |
| Frame Check Sequence (32-bit) | | | |
| 0 1 2 3 4 5 6 7 | 8 9 10 11 12 13 14 15 | 16 17 18 19 20 21 22 23 | 24 25 26 27 28 29 30 31 |

**FIGURE 13.13**

Packet Map for the Ethernet Header

Ethernet Header

c0 c1 c0 17 8c e8 20 c9 d0 ba 63 fb 08 00 45 00

00 b9 3d 2a 40 00 40 06 fa 99 ac 10 10 80 43 cd

02 1e ed 84 00 50 19 ad bf 50 97 96 65 76 50 18

40 00 cd 7c 00 00 47 45 54 20 2f 20 48 54 54 50

2f 31 2e 31 0d 0a 55 73 65 72 2d 41 67 65 6e 74

3a 20 63 75 72 6c 2f 37 2e 32 34 2e 30 20 28 78

38 36 5f 36 34 2d 61 70 70 6c 65 2d 64 61 72 77

69 6e 31 32 2e 30 29 20 6c 69 62 63 75 72 6c 2f

37 2e 32 34 2e 30 20 4f 70 65 6e 53 53 4c 2f 30

2e 39 2e 38 78 20 7a 6c 69 62 2f 31 2e 32 2e 35

0d 0a 48 6f 73 74 3a 20 61 70 70 6c 69 65 64 6e

73 6d 2e 63 6f 6d 0d 0a 41 63 63 65 70 74 3a 20

2a 2f 2a 0d 0a 0d 0a

**FIGURE 13.14**

The Ethernet Header Identified

Since the Ethernet header was kind enough to tell us that we should expect an IP header next, we can apply what we know about the structure of the IP header to the next portion of the packet. We are attempting to break this packet down by individual protocol, so we aren't concerned about every single value in this header, but there are a few values we will have to evaluate in order to determine the length of the IP header and what protocol to expect next.

First, we need to determine what version of IP is being used here. As we learned earlier, the IP version is identified by the higher order nibble of byte 0x0 in the IP header. In this case, we are dealing with IPv4.

The IP header is variable in length depending on a set of options it can support, so the next thing we need to ascertain is the length of the IP header. Earlier, we learned that the IP header length field is contained in the lower order nibble of byte 0×0 in the IP header, which has a value of 4. This is a computed field however, so we must multiply this field by 5 to arrive at the IP header length, which is 20 bytes. This means that the last two bytes of the IP header are 02 1e.

As our last stop in the IP header, we need to determine what protocol should be expected next in the packet. The IP header gives us this information with the Protocol field at 0x9. Here, this value is 06, which is the value assigned to the TCP protocol (Figure 13.15).

| Ethernet Header | c0 c1 c0 17 8c e8 20 c9 d0 ba 63 fb 08 00\|45 00 |
| IP Header | 00 b9 3d 2a 40 00 40 06 fa 99 ac 10 10 80 43 cd |
| | 02 1e ed 84 00 50 19 ad bf 50 97 96 65 76 50 18 |
| | 40 00 cd 7c 00 00 47 45 54 20 2f 20 48 54 54 50 |
| | 2f 31 2e 31 0d 0a 55 73 65 72 2d 41 67 65 6e 74 |
| | 3a 20 63 75 72 6c 2f 37 2e 32 34 2e 30 20 28 78 |
| | 38 36 5f 36 34 2d 61 70 70 6c 65 2d 64 61 72 77 |
| | 69 6e 31 32 2e 30 29 20 6c 69 62 63 75 72 6c 2f |
| | 37 2e 32 34 2e 30 20 4f 70 65 6e 53 53 4c 2f 30 |
| | 2e 39 2e 38 78 20 7a 6c 69 62 2f 31 2e 32 2e 35 |
| | 0d 0a 48 6f 73 74 3a 20 61 70 70 6c 69 65 64 6e |
| | 73 6d 2e 63 6f 6d 0d 0a 41 63 63 65 70 74 3a 20 |
| | 2a 2f 2a 0d 0a 0d 0a |

**FIGURE 13.15**

The IP Header Identified

Now that we've made our way to the TCP protocol, we must determine whether or not any application layer data is present. To do this, we must determine the length of the TCP header (Figure 13.16), which like the IP header, is variable depending on the options that are used.

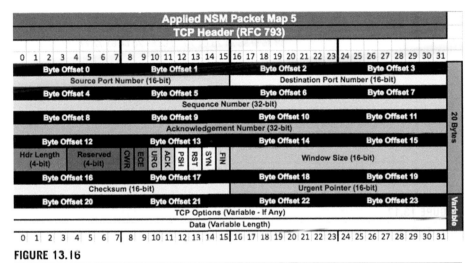

**FIGURE 13.16**

Packet Map for the TCP Header

This is achieved by examining the TCP data offset field at the higher order nibble of $0\times12$. The value for this field is 5, but again, this is a computed field and must be multiplied by four to arrive at the real value. This means that the TCP header length is really 20 bytes.

If you count off 20 bytes from the beginning of the TCP header, you will find that there is still data after the end of the header. This is application layer data. Unfortunately, TCP doesn't have any sort of field that will tell us what application layer protocol to expect in the application, but something we can do is take a look at the destination port field (assuming that this is client to server traffic, otherwise we would look at the source port field) at $0\times2:2$ in the TCP header. This field has a value of 00 50, which converts to 80 in decimal. Since port 80 is typically used by the HTTP protocol, it might be the case that the data that follows is HTTP data. You could verify this by comparing the hex data with a protocol map of the HTTP protocol, or by just taking that data, from the end of the TCP header to the end of the packet, and converting it to ASCII text (Figure 13.17).

| | |
|---|---|
| Ethernet Header | c0 c1 c0 17 8c e8 20 c9 d0 ba 63 fb 08 00\|45 00 |
| IP Header | 00 b9 3d 2a 40 00 40 06 fa 99 ac 10 10 80 43 cd |
| TCP Header | 02 1e\|ed 84 00 50 19 ad bf 50 97 96 65 76 50 18 |
| | 40 00 cd 7c 00 00 47 45 54 20 2f 20 48 54 54 50 |
| | 2f 31 2e 31 0d 0a 55 73 65 72 2d 41 67 65 6e 74 |
| | 3a 20 63 75 72 6c 2f 37 2e 32 34 2e 30 20 28 78 |
| | 38 36 5f 36 34 2d 61 70 70 6c 65 2d 64 61 72 77 |
| | 69 6e 31 32 2e 30 29 20 6c 69 62 63 75 72 6c 2f |
| | 37 2e 32 34 2e 30 20 4f 70 65 6e 53 53 4c 2f 30 |
| | 2e 39 2e 38 78 20 7a 6c 69 62 2f 31 2e 32 2e 35 |
| | 0d 0a 48 6f 73 74 3a 20 61 70 70 6c 69 65 64 6e |
| | 73 6d 2e 63 6f 6d 0d 0a 41 63 63 65 70 74 3a 20 |
| | 2a 2f 2a 0d 0a 0d 0a |

**FIGURE 13.17**

The TCP Header Identified

**CAUTION**

Just because you find data on a port that is typically associated with a particular service, such as port 80 and HTTP or port 22 and SSH, you shouldn't always make the assumption that these services are explicitly responsible for the traffic you're seeing. The fact of the matter is that any service can be configured to run on any port, and attackers will often use this tactic. For instance, it is very common for attackers to run custom protocols used for command and control over port 80. This provides many benefits to the attacker, including the ability to get traffic out of the network since port 80 is almost always allowed out of egress firewalls, and the ability to hide amongst traffic that is erratic and unpredictable because of user-driven HTTP traffic.

The protocol level break down of the packet we've just dissected is now shown in Figure 13.18.

Now, let's talk about some tools that you can use to display and interact with packets.

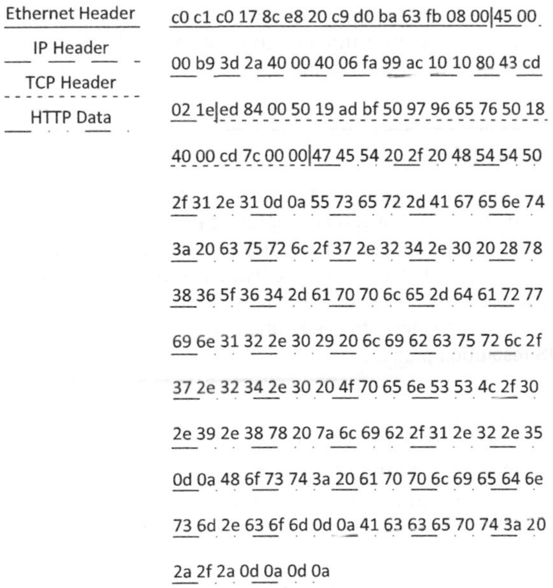

| Ethernet Header | c0 c1 c0 17 8c e8 20 c9 d0 ba 63 fb 08 00|45 00 |
| --- | --- |
| IP Header | 00 b9 3d 2a 40 00 40 06 fa 99 ac 10 10 80 43 cd |
| TCP Header | 02 1e|ed 84 00 50 19 ad bf 50 97 96 65 76 50 18 |
| HTTP Data | 40 00 cd 7c 00 00|47 45 54 20 2f 20 48 54 54 50 |
| | 2f 31 2e 31 0d 0a 55 73 65 72 2d 41 67 65 6e 74 |
| | 3a 20 63 75 72 6c 2f 37 2e 32 34 2e 30 20 28 78 |
| | 38 36 5f 36 34 2d 61 70 70 6c 65 2d 64 61 72 77 |
| | 69 6e 31 32 2e 30 29 20 6c 69 62 63 75 72 6c 2f |
| | 37 2e 32 34 2e 30 20 4f 70 65 6e 53 53 4c 2f 30 |
| | 2e 39 2e 38 78 20 7a 6c 69 62 2f 31 2e 32 2e 35 |
| | 0d 0a 48 6f 73 74 3a 20 61 70 70 6c 69 65 64 6e |
| | 73 6d 2e 63 6f 6d 0d 0a 41 63 63 65 70 74 3a 20 |
| | 2a 2f 2a 0d 0a 0d 0a |

**FIGURE 13.18**

The Protocol Level Break Down of an HTTP Packet

# TCPDUMP FOR NSM ANALYSIS

Tcpdump is a packet capture and analysis tool that is the de facto standard for command line packet analysis in Unix environments. It is incredibly useful as a packet analysis tool because it gets you straight to the data quickly, without a bunch of fuss. This makes it ideal for examining individual packets or communication sequences. It also provides consistent output, so packet data can be manipulated with scripts easily. Tcpdump is also included with a large number of Unix-based distributions, and can be installed easily via the operating systems packet manager software when it is not. Security Onion includes tcpdump out of the box.

The downside to tcpdump is that its simplicity means that it lacks some of the fancier analysis features that are included in a graphical tool like Wireshark. It has no concept of state, and it also doesn't provide any ability to interpret application layer protocols.

In this section we won't provide an extensive guide to every feature tcpdump has to offer, but we will provide the necessary jumpstart that a new NSM analyst needs to get moving in the right direction.

To start with, tcpdump has the ability to capture packets directly from the wire. This can be done by running tcpdump with no command line arguments, which will instruct tcpdump to capture packets from the lowest numbered network interface. In this case, tcpdump will output each packet it captures as a single summary line in the current terminal. To gain a bit more control over this process, we will use the –i argument so that we can specify the interface to capture packet on, and the –nn switch to turn off host and protocol name resolution.

---

**FROM THE TRENCHES**

When capturing packets, it is a best practice to be as stealthy as possible. This isn't because you are trying to hide the fact that you are capturing packets (unless you are a penetration tester), but more so because you don't want to generate any additional traffic that you might have to filter out or weed through while you are trying to investigate an event. Because of this, I always use at least one –n switch when running tcpdump in order to prevent name resolution from happening, as this can cause the generation of additional packets on the network to perform the DNS resolution process.

---

If you'd like to save the packets you are capturing for analysis later, you can use the –w switch to specify the name of an output file where the data can be saved. Combining all of these arguments, we are left with the following command:

```
sudo tcpdump -nni eth1 -w packets.pcap
```

Now, if you want to read this file you can specify the –r command with the file name, shown in Figure 13.19.

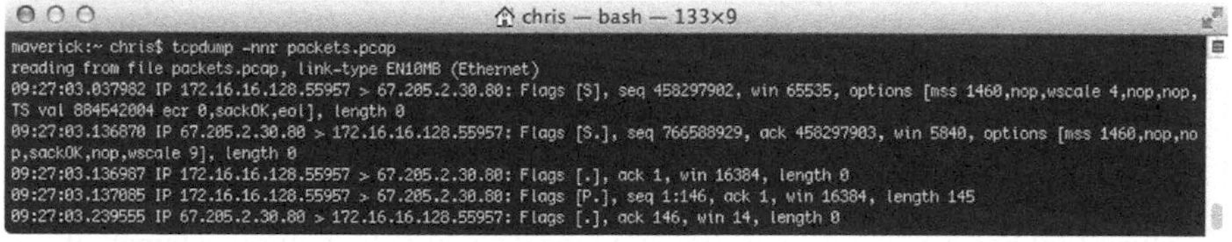

**FIGURE 13.19**

Reading Packets from a File with tcpdump

The output tcpdump provides by default gives some basic information about each packet. The formatting of this output will vary based upon what protocols are in use, but the most common formats are:

TCP:

```
[Timestamp] [Layer 3 Protocol] [Source IP].[Source Port]>[Destination
IP].[Destination Port]: [TCP Flags], [TCP Sequence Number], [TCP
Acknowledgement Number], [TCP Windows Size], [Data Length]
```

UDP:

```
[Timestamp] [Layer 3 Protocol] [Source IP].[Source Port]>[Destination
IP].[Destination Port]: [Layer 4 Protocol], [Data Length]
```

You can force tcpdump to provide more information in this summary line by adding the –v tag to increase its verbosity. You can further the verbosity by adding additional v's, up to a total of three. Figure 13.20 shows the same packet from above, but with –vvv verbosity.

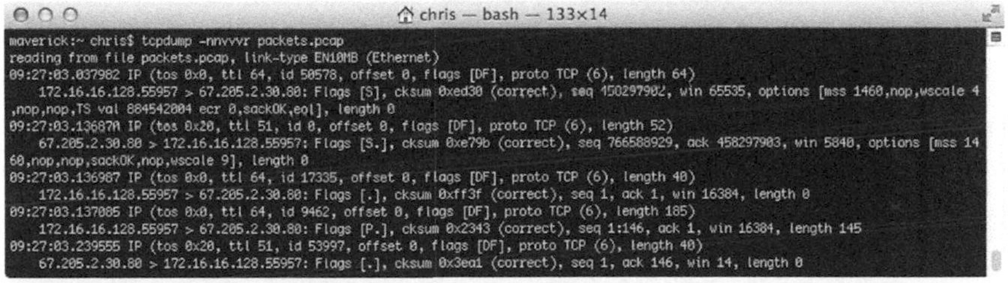

**FIGURE 13.20**

Reading Packets with Increased Verbosity

This is all very useful data, but it doesn't give us the entire picture.

One way to display the entirety of each packet is to instruct tcpdump to output packets in hex format, with the –x switch, shown in Figure 13.21.

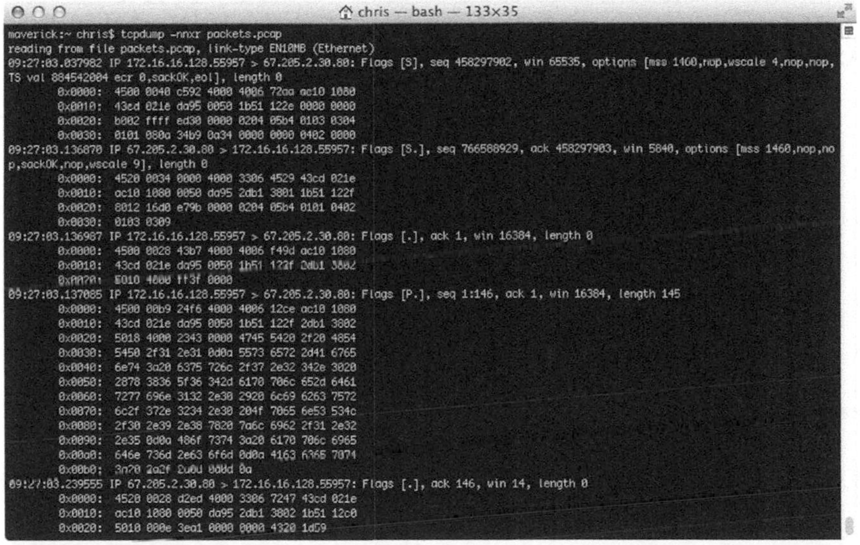

**FIGURE 13.21**

Viewing Full Packets in Hex

---

**CAUTION**

In a lot of tcpdump documentation, you will see mention of the default snapshot length (snaplen) denoted by the –s argument. The snaplen argument instructs tcpdump how much of a packet should be captured. In older versions of tcpdump, it would only capture the first 68 bytes (of an IPv4) packet. Because of this, you would have to specify a larger snaplen if you wanted to capture the entire packet, or simply specify a snaplen of 0, which will capture an entire packet regardless of its size. In tcpdump 4.0 and later, the default snaplen has been increased to 65535 bytes, so the –s 0 command isn't typically needed if you are running a newer version.

---

Another method is to display packets in ASCII, with the –A argument (Figure 13.22).

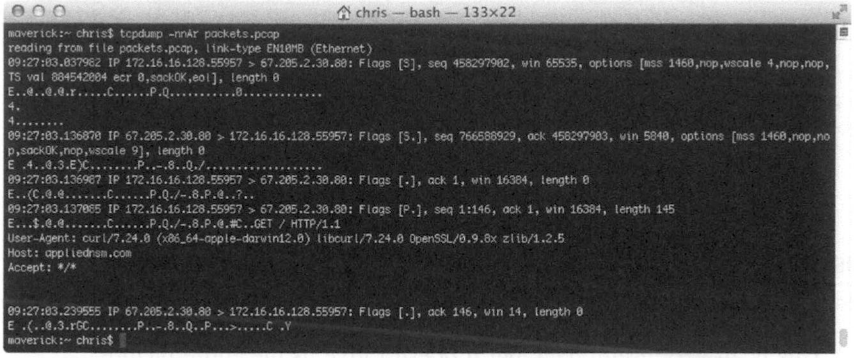

**FIGURE 13.22**

Viewing Full Packets in ASCII

My personal favorite is the –X argument, which displays packets in both hex and ASCII, side by side (Figure 13.23).

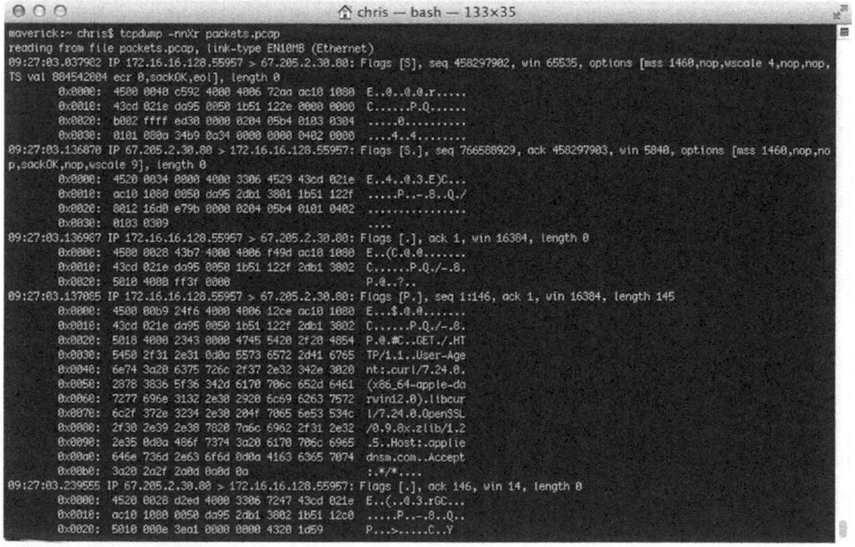

**FIGURE 13.23**

Viewing Full Packets in ASCII and Hex

In many cases, you will be dealing with larger PCAP files and it may become necessary to use filters to select only the data you wish to examine, or to purge data that isn't valuable to the current investigation. Tcpdump utilizes the Berkeley Packet Filter (BPF) format. A filter can be invoked by tcpdump by adding it to the end of the tcpdump command. For easier readability, it is recommended that these filters be enclosed in single quotes. With this in mind, if we wanted to view only packets with the destination port TCP/8080, we could invoke this command:

```
tcpdump -nnr packets.pcap 'tcp dst port 8080'
```

We could also take advantage of the –w argument to create a new file containing only the packets matching this filter:

```
tcpdump -nnr packets.pcap 'tcp dst port 8080' -w packets_tcp8080.pcap
```

In some cases, you might be using a large number of filtering options when parsing a packet capture. This commonly happens when an analyst is reviewing traffic and weeding out traffic from a large number of hosts and protocols that aren't relevant to the current investigation. When this happens, it isn't easy to edit these filters in the command line argument. Because of this, tcpdump allows for the use of the –F argument, which allows the user to specify a filter file that contains BPF arguments.

---

**CAUTION**

A tcpdump filter file must only contain filtering statements, and cannot contain any comments. Since comments are helpful in deciphering larger filters, I maintain two filter files: one for production without comments, and one for reference with comments.

---

This command designates a filter file with the –F argument:

```
tcpdump -nnr packets.pcap -F known_good_hosts.bpf
```

We will talk about creating custom filters later in this chapter.

While this isn't an exhaustive reference on tcpdump, it covers all of the primary uses that an analyst will usually encounter in the day-to-day parsing of packet data. If you want to learn more about tcpdump, you can visit http://www.tcpdump.org, or view the tcpdump manual pages by typing man tcpdump on a system with tcpdump installed.

## TSHARK FOR PACKET ANALYSIS

The tshark utility is packaged with the Wireshark graphical packet analysis application as a command-line based alternative. It has a lot of the same abilities as tcpdump, but it has the added advantage of leveraging Wireshark's protocol dissectors, which can be used to perform additional automated analysis of application layer protocols. This also allows for the use of Wireshark's display filtering syntax, which adds some flexibility beyond that of Berkeley Packet Filters. This strength can also be a weakness in some cases, as the additional processing required to support these features means that tshark is generally slower than tcpdump when parsing data.

If you are using a system that has Wireshark installed, like Security Onion, then tshark is already installed and can be invoked by running the tshark command. The following command can be used to capture packets with tshark:

```
sudo tshark -i eth1
```

This command will display captured packets in the current terminal window, and will display a single one-line summary for each packet. If you'd like to save the packets you are capturing for analysis later, you can use the –w switch to specify an output file where the data can be saved. Combining all of these arguments, we are left with the following command:

```
sudo tshark -i eth1 -w packets.pcap
```

Now, if you want to read this file you can specify the –r command with the file name, shown in Figure 13.24.

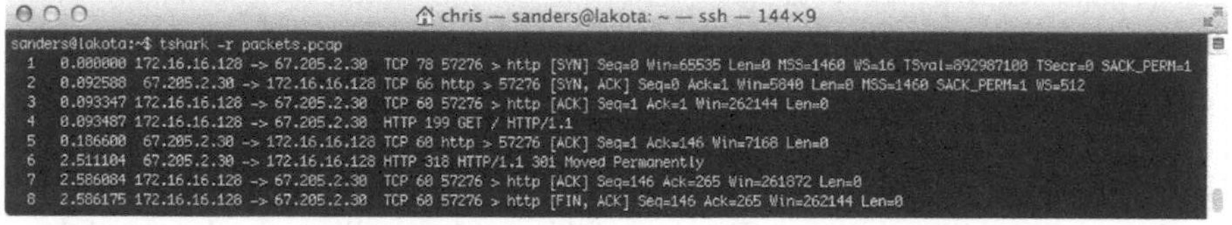

**FIGURE 13.24**

Displaying Captured Packets with tshark

The formatting of this output will vary based upon what protocols are in use. In this case, notice that tshark is able to provide the additional functionality of showing application layer data in packets 4 and 6. This is possible because of its extensive collection of protocol dissectors. If you'd like a significantly more verbose output, including information obtained from tshark's application layer protocol dissectors, you can add the –V argument. Figure 13.25 shows a portion of this output for a single packet.

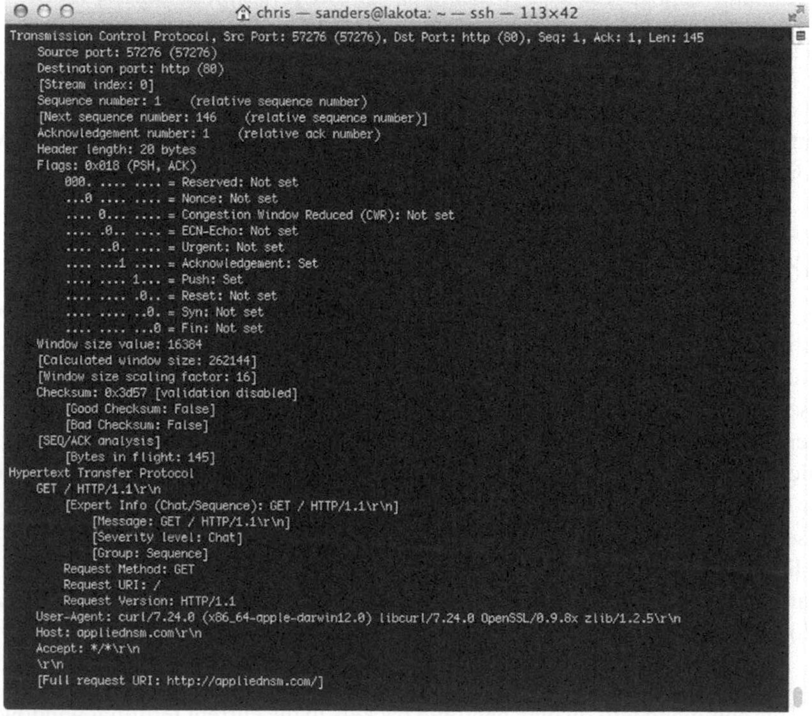

**FIGURE 13.25**

Reading Packets with Increased Verbosity

Looking closely at the normal tshark output shown in Figure 13.20, you will notice that the timestamps look a little funny. Tshark's default behavior is to display timestamps that are in relation to the beginning of the packet capture. To provide more flexibility, tshark provides the –t option so that you can specify alternate ways to display the timestamp. In order to print packets with timestamps that show the actual date and time the packet was captured, similar to tcpdump, use the –t ad option, as shown in Figure 13.26.

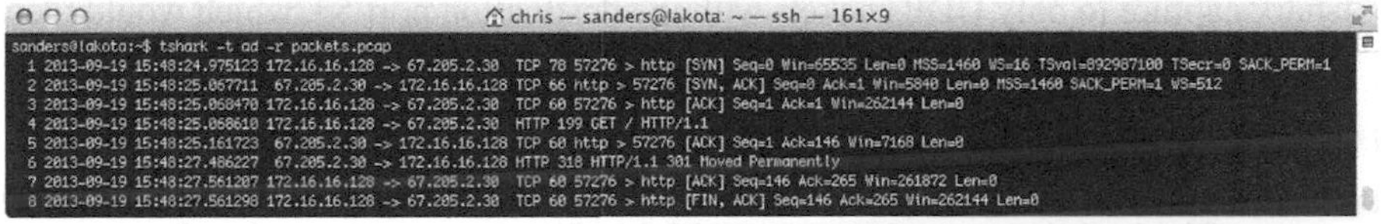

**FIGURE 13.26**

Displaying Packets with an Absolute Data and Time

Using this feature, you can also choose to display packet timestamps as a delta, which is the time since the previous captured packet, using the –t d argument.

If you'd like to examine the raw packet data in a capture file, you can instruct tshark to output packets in hex and ASCII format using the –x argument, shown in Figure 13.27.

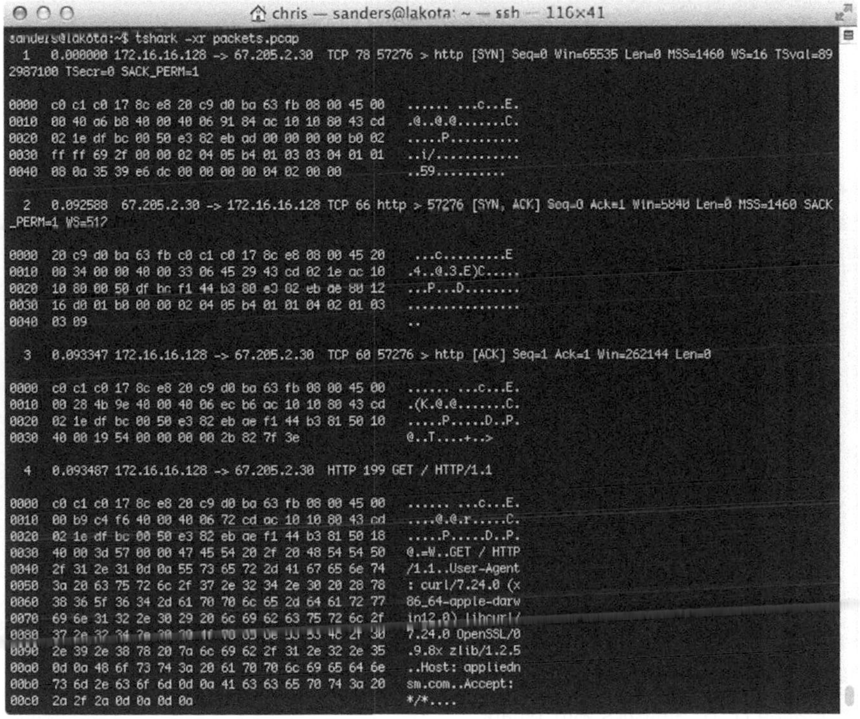

**FIGURE 13.27**

Displaying Packets in Hex and ASCII Format with Tshark

Tshark provides the ability to use both capture filters that use the same BPF syntax you are used to with tcpdump, and display filters that leverage tshark's packet dissectors. The key distinction here is that capture filters can only be used while capturing packets, whereas display filters can also be used when reading packets from a file. To use capture filters, invoke the –f argument, followed by the filter you'd like to use. For example, the following command would limit a tshark capture to only UDP packets with the destination port 53, which would identify DNS traffic:

```
sudo tshark -I eth1 -f 'udp && dst port 53'
```

If you'd like to use a display filter to perform the same filtering action on a capture file that's being read, you can add this filter by specifying the –R argument, like this:

```
tshark -r packets.pcap -R 'udp && dst.port == 53'
```

We will discuss tshark and Wireshark's display filter syntax later in this chapter.

Another really useful feature provided by tshark is its ability to generate statistics based on the packet data that it sees. You can instruct tshark to generate statistics from a packet capture by invoking the –z option with the name of the statistic you wish to generate. A complete list of the statistical options is available by viewing the tshark manual page. This command uses the http,tree option, which displays a breakdown of HTTP status codes and request methods identified in the packet capture.

```
tshark -r packets.pcap -z http.tree
```

The output of this command is shown in Figure 13.28.

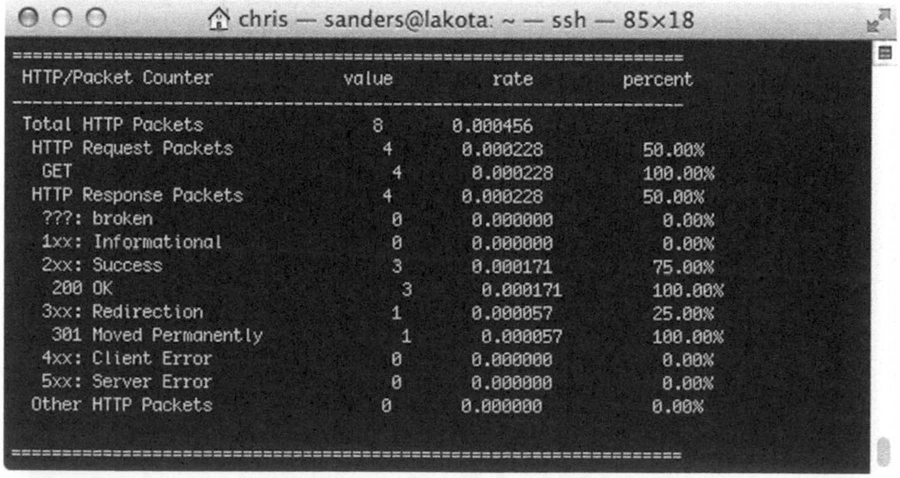

**FIGURE 13.28**

Generating HTTP Statistics with Tshark

A few of my favorite statistical options available here are:

- io,phs: Displays a protocol hierarchy showing all protocols found within the capture file.
- http,tree: Displays statistics related to the types of HTTP Request and Response packets.
- http_req,tree: Displays statistics for every HTTP Request made.
- smb,srt: Displays statistics related to SMB commands. Useful for analyzing Windows SMB traffic.

Tshark is incredibly powerful, and is a useful tool for an NSM analyst in addition to tcpdump. In my analysis, I typically start with tcpdump so that I can filter through packets quickly based upon their layer three and four attributes. When I need to remain at the command line level and get more detail about a communication sequence in relation to application layer information, or to generate some basic statistics, I will usually call upon tshark. You can learn more about tshark by visiting http://www.wireshark.org or by viewing the tshark manual page by running `man tshark` on a system with tshark installed.

## WIRESHARK FOR NSM ANALYSIS

While command-line based packet analysis tools are ideal for interacting with packets at a fundamental level, some analysis tasks are best accomplished with a graphical packet analysis application like Wireshark. Wireshark was developed by Gerald Combs in 1998 under the project name Ethereal. The project was renamed Wireshark in 2006, and has grown tremendously thanks to the help of over 500 contributors since its inception. Wireshark is the gold standard for graphical packet analysis applications, and comes preinstalled on Security Onion.

If you aren't using Security Onion, you can find instructions for installing Wireshark on to your platform at http://www.wireshark.org. Wireshark is a multi-platform tool, and works on Windows, Mac, and Linux systems. If you are using Security Onion, you can launch Wireshark from the command line by simply typing `wireshark`, or by clicking the Wireshark icon under the Security Onion heading in the desktop menu. If you need to be able to capture packets in addition to analyzing them, you will have to run Wireshark with elevated privileges using the command `sudo wireshark`. The Wireshark window is devoid of any useful information when it first opens, so we need to collect some packet data to look at.

### Capturing Packets

To capture packets from the wire, you can select Capture > Interfaces from the main drop-down menu. This will show all of the interfaces on the system (Figure 13.29). Here you can choose to capture packets from a sensor interface or another interface. To begin capturing packets from a particular interface, click Start next to that interface.

**FIGURE 13.29**

Capturing Packets in Wireshark

---

> **CAUTION**
>
> Be careful if you decide to start capturing packets with Wireshark on a very busy sensor interface. While Wireshark is a great tool, it can get overwhelmed if you attempt to load too much data into it at once, since it will attempt to load all of the packets into memory. This is why it is often best to start analyzing large data sets with a command-line based tool, and then filter down the data you are examining before loading it into a tool like Wireshark.

When you've finished collecting packets, click the Stop button under the Capture drop-down menu. At this point, you should be presented with data to be analyzed. In Figure 13.30, we've opened up one of the many packet capture files that come with Security Onion under the /opt/samples/ directory.

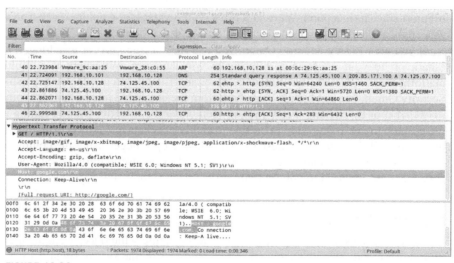

**FIGURE 13.30**

Viewing Packets in Wireshark

Looking at the image above, you will notice that Wireshark is divided into three panes. The uppermost is the packet list pane, which shows each packet summarized into a single line, with individual fields separated as columns. The default columns include a packet number, a timestamp (defaulting to the time since the beginning of the capture), source and destination address, protocol, packet length, and an info column that contains protocol-specific information.

The middle pane is the packet details pane, and shows detailed information about the data fields contained within the packet that is selected in the packet list pane. The bottom pane is the packet bytes pane, and details the individual bytes that comprise a packet, shown in hex and ASCII format, similar to tcpdump's –X option.

The important thing to note when interacting with these three panes is that the data that each one displays is linked to actions taken in the other panes. When you click on a packet in the packet list pane, it shows data related to that packet in the packet details and packet bytes panes. Furthermore, when you click on a field in the packet details pane, it will highlight the bytes associated with that field in the packet bytes pane. This is ideal for visually bouncing around to different packets and determining their properties quickly.

Wireshark has a ton of features that are useful for analyzing packets. So many, as a matter of fact, that there is no way that we can cover them all in this chapter. If you want to read something that more exhaustively covers Wireshark and its features, I recommend my other book, "Practical Packet Analysis", or Laura Chappell's book, "Wireshark Network Analysis." Both of these books cover packet analysis and TCP/IP protocols from a very broad perspective. With that said, there are a few nice features that are worth highlighting here. We will cover these briefly.

## Changing Time Display Formats

Just like with Tshark, Wireshark will default to displaying packets with a timestamp that shows each packet relative to the number of seconds since the beginning of the packet capture. While this can be useful in certain situations, I typically prefer to see packets in relation to absolute time. You can change this setting from the main drop-down menu by selecting View > Time Display Format > Date and Time of Day. If the capture file you are working with contains packets from a single day, you can compact the size of your time column by selecting Time of Day instead.

Instead of having to change the time display format every time you open Wireshark, you can change the default setting by following these steps:

1. From the main drop-down menu, select Edit > Preferences.
2. Select the Columns heading, and select the Time field.
3. Change the Field Type to Absolute Date and Time.

Another time display format I find useful from time to time is the Seconds Since Previous Displayed Packet option. This can be useful when analyzing a solitary communication sequence and attempting to determine the time intervals between specific actions. This can be handy for determining if the actions of a process are being caused by human input or a script. Human actions are unpredictable, where as a script's actions can be aligned with precise intervals.

Finally, in some cases it might be useful to know how long something has occurred after a previous event occurs. In these instances, Wireshark allows you to toggle an individual packet as time reference. This can be done by right clicking on a packet and selecting Set Time Reference (toggle). With this set, change your time display format back to Seconds Since Beginning of Capture, and packets following the packet you've toggled will reference the number of seconds since that packet has occurred. Multiple packets can be selected as time reference packets.

## Capture Summary

The first thing I typically do when I open any packet capture in Wireshark is to open the Summary window by selecting Statistics > Summary from the main drop-down menu. This screen, shown in Figure 13.31, provides a wealth of information and statistics about the packet capture and the data contained within it.

**FIGURE 13.31**

Wireshark's Summary Window

The important items on this screen for the analyst include:

- Format: The format of the file. If you are dealing with a PCAP-NG file, you know that you can add comments to packets.
- Time: This section includes the time the first packet was captured, the time the last packet was captured, and the duration between those times. This is critical in confirming that the capture contains the time frame associated with the current investigation.
- Bytes: The size of the data in the capture file. This gives you an idea of how much data you are looking at.
- Avg. Packet Size: The average size of the packets in the capture file. In some cases, this number can be used to ascertain the makeup of the traffic in the capture file. For instance, a larger average would indicate more packets containing data, and a smaller average would indicate more control/command packets generated at the protocol level. Keep in mind that this isn't always the most reliable indicator, and is something that can vary wildly depending on a variety of factors.
- Avg. Bytes/sec and Avg. Mbit/sec: The average number of bytes/megabits per second occurring in the capture. This is useful for determining the rate at which communication is occurring.

## Protocol Hierarchy

The protocol hierarchy screen is accessible by selecting Statistics > Protocol Hierarchy from the main drop-down menu. It will provide a snapshot of every protocol

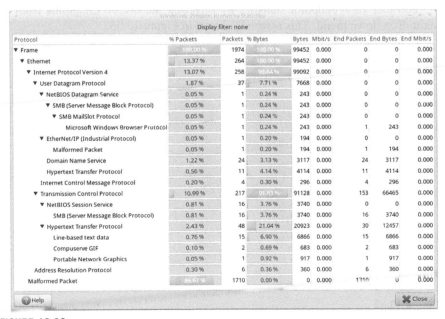

| Protocol | % Packets | Packets | % Bytes | Bytes | Mbit/s | End Packets | End Bytes | End Mbit/s |
|---|---|---|---|---|---|---|---|---|
| ▼ Frame | 100.00 % | 1974 | 100.00 % | 99452 | 0.000 | 0 | 0 | 0.000 |
| ▼ Ethernet | 13.37 % | 264 | 100.00 % | 99452 | 0.000 | 0 | 0 | 0.000 |
| ▼ Internet Protocol Version 4 | 13.07 % | 258 | 99.64 % | 99092 | 0.000 | 0 | 0 | 0.000 |
| ▼ User Datagram Protocol | 1.87 % | 37 | 7.71 % | 7668 | 0.000 | 0 | 0 | 0.000 |
| ▼ NetBIOS Datagram Service | 0.05 % | 1 | 0.24 % | 243 | 0.000 | 0 | 0 | 0.000 |
| ▼ SMB (Server Message Block Protocol) | 0.05 % | 1 | 0.24 % | 243 | 0.000 | 0 | 0 | 0.000 |
| ▼ SMB MailSlot Protocol | 0.05 % | 1 | 0.24 % | 243 | 0.000 | 0 | 0 | 0.000 |
| Microsoft Windows Browser Protocol | 0.05 % | 1 | 0.24 % | 243 | 0.000 | 1 | 243 | 0.000 |
| ▼ EtherNet/IP (Industrial Protocol) | 0.05 % | 1 | 0.20 % | 194 | 0.000 | 0 | 0 | 0.000 |
| Malformed Packet | 0.05 % | 1 | 0.20 % | 194 | 0.000 | 1 | 194 | 0.000 |
| Domain Name Service | 1.22 % | 24 | 3.13 % | 3117 | 0.000 | 24 | 3117 | 0.000 |
| Hypertext Transfer Protocol | 0.56 % | 11 | 4.14 % | 4114 | 0.000 | 11 | 4114 | 0.000 |
| Internet Control Message Protocol | 0.20 % | 4 | 0.30 % | 296 | 0.000 | 4 | 296 | 0.000 |
| ▼ Transmission Control Protocol | 10.99 % | 217 | 91.63 % | 91128 | 0.000 | 153 | 66465 | 0.000 |
| ▼ NetBIOS Session Service | 0.81 % | 16 | 3.76 % | 3740 | 0.000 | 0 | 0 | 0.000 |
| SMB (Server Message Block Protocol) | 0.81 % | 16 | 3.76 % | 3740 | 0.000 | 16 | 3740 | 0.000 |
| ▼ Hypertext Transfer Protocol | 2.43 % | 48 | 21.04 % | 20923 | 0.000 | 30 | 12457 | 0.000 |
| Line-based text data | 0.76 % | 15 | 6.90 % | 6866 | 0.000 | 15 | 6866 | 0.000 |
| Compuserve GIF | 0.10 % | 2 | 0.69 % | 683 | 0.000 | 2 | 683 | 0.000 |
| Portable Network Graphics | 0.05 % | 1 | 0.92 % | 917 | 0.000 | 1 | 917 | 0.000 |
| Address Resolution Protocol | 0.30 % | 6 | 0.36 % | 360 | 0.000 | 6 | 360 | 0.000 |
| Malformed Packet | 86.63 % | 1710 | 0.00 % | 0 | 0.000 | 1710 | 0 | 0.000 |

**FIGURE 13.32**

Wireshark's Protocol Hierarchy Window

found within the capture file, along with a statistical breakdown that will help you to determine the percentage of traffic associated with each protocol in the capture file.

This statistical feature is often another first stop when performing analysis of a packet capture. Because of its concise view of the data, you can quickly identify abnormal or unexpected protocols that warrant further analysis, such as an instance where you see SMB traffic, but you have no Windows or Samba hosts on a network segment. You can also use this feature to find odd ratios of expected protocols. For instance, seeing that the packet capture contains an unusually high percentage of DNS or ICMP traffic might mean those packets warrant further investigation.

You can create display filters directly from this window by right clicking on a protocol, selecting Apply As Filter, and then selecting a filter option. The Selected option will only show packets utilizing that protocol, where as the Not Selected option will show packets not utilizing that protocol. Several other options are available that can be used to build compound display filters.

## Endpoints and Conversations

In Wireshark terms, a device that communicates on the network is considered to be an endpoint, and when two endpoints communicate they are said to be having a conversation. Wireshark provides the ability to view communication statistics for individual endpoints and for communication between endpoints.

You can view endpoint statistics by selecting Statistics > Endpoints from the main drop-down menu. This screen is shown in Figure 13.33.

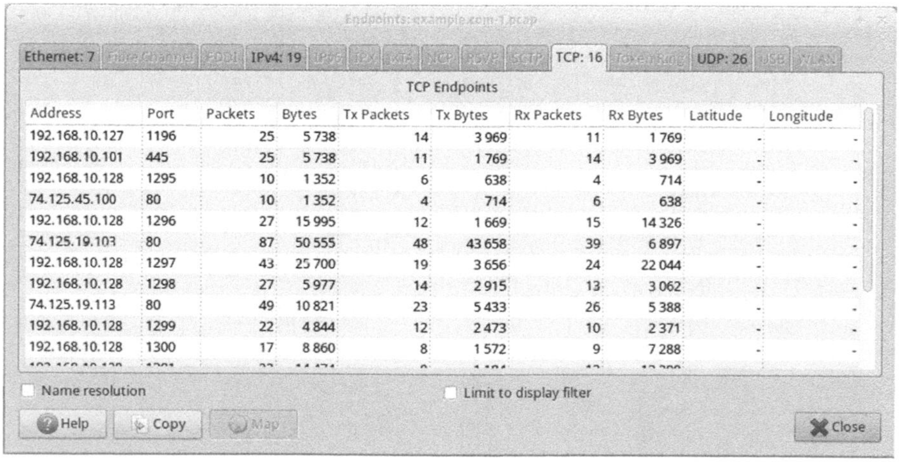

Endpoints: example.com-1.pcap

Ethernet: 7 | Fibre Channel | FDDI | IPv4: 19 | IPv6 | IPX | JXTA | NCP | RSVP | SCTP | TCP: 16 | Token Ring | UDP: 26 | USB | WLAN

### TCP Endpoints

| Address | Port | Packets | Bytes | Tx Packets | Tx Bytes | Rx Packets | Rx Bytes | Latitude | Longitude |
|---------|------|---------|-------|-----------|----------|-----------|----------|----------|-----------|
| 192.168.10.127 | 1196 | 25 | 5 738 | 14 | 3 969 | 11 | 1 769 | - | - |
| 192.168.10.101 | 445 | 25 | 5 738 | 11 | 1 769 | 14 | 3 969 | - | - |
| 192.168.10.128 | 1295 | 10 | 1 352 | 6 | 638 | 4 | 714 | - | - |
| 74.125.45.100 | 80 | 10 | 1 352 | 4 | 714 | 6 | 638 | - | - |
| 192.168.10.128 | 1296 | 27 | 15 995 | 12 | 1 669 | 15 | 14 326 | - | - |
| 74.125.19.103 | 80 | 87 | 50 555 | 48 | 43 658 | 39 | 6 897 | - | - |
| 192.168.10.128 | 1297 | 43 | 25 700 | 19 | 3 656 | 24 | 22 044 | - | - |
| 192.168.10.128 | 1298 | 27 | 5 977 | 14 | 2 915 | 13 | 3 062 | - | - |
| 74.125.19.113 | 80 | 49 | 10 821 | 23 | 5 433 | 26 | 5 388 | - | - |
| 192.168.10.128 | 1299 | 22 | 4 844 | 12 | 2 473 | 10 | 2 371 | - | - |
| 192.168.10.128 | 1300 | 17 | 8 860 | 8 | 1 572 | 9 | 7 288 | - | - |

Name resolution          Limit to display filter

Help | Copy | Map | Close

**FIGURE 13.33**

Wireshark's Endpoints Window

Conversations can be accessed in a similar manner by selecting Statistics > Conversations from the main drop-down menu. This screen is shown in Figure 13.34.

| Address A | Address B | Packets | Bytes | Packets A→B | Bytes A→B | Packets A←B | Bytes A←B | Rel Start | Duration | bps A→B | bps A←B |
|---|---|---|---|---|---|---|---|---|---|---|---|
| 192.168.10.101 | 192.168.10.255 | 1 | 243 | 1 | 243 | 0 | 0 | 0.000000000 | 0.0000 | N/A | N/A |
| 192.168.10.101 | 192.168.10.127 | 29 | 6034 | 13 | 1917 | 16 | 4117 | 2.690156000 | 11.3699 | 1348.82 | 2896.76 |
| 192.168.10.120 | 255.255.255.255 | 1 | 194 | 1 | 194 | 0 | 0 | 12.669128000 | 0.0000 | N/A | N/A |
| 192.168.10.101 | 192.168.10.128 | 8 | 1020 | 4 | 721 | 4 | 299 | 22.218498000 | 15.9239 | 362.22 | 150.21 |
| 192.168.10.101 | 216.239.34.10 | 4 | 730 | 2 | 149 | 2 | 581 | 22.219424000 | 2.3012 | 518.00 | 2019.84 |
| 74.125.45.100 | 192.168.10.128 | 10 | 1352 | 4 | 714 | 6 | 638 | 22.725147000 | 10.5226 | 542.83 | 485.05 |
| 72.14.235.9 | 192.168.10.101 | 2 | 216 | 1 | 140 | 1 | 76 | 23.013902000 | 0.3073 | N/A | N/A |
| 74.125.19.103 | 192.168.10.128 | 87 | 50555 | 48 | 43658 | 39 | 6897 | 23.322510000 | 14.5924 | 23934.58 | 3781.13 |
| 74.125.77.9 | 192.168.10.101 | 2 | 224 | 1 | 144 | 1 | 80 | 24.520895000 | 0.0618 | N/A | N/A |
| 74.125.19.113 | 192.168.10.128 | 49 | 10821 | 23 | 5433 | 26 | 5388 | 24.583768000 | 8.6854 | 5004.28 | 4962.83 |
| 192.168.10.100 | 239.255.255.250 | 11 | 4114 | 11 | 4114 | 0 | 0 | 27.673618000 | 0.0009 | 374000000.00 | N/A |

**FIGURE 13.34**

Wireshark's Conversations Window

Both of these windows have a similar layout, and list each endpoint or conversation on a new line, complete with statistics regarding the number of packets and bytes transmitted in each direction. You should also notice that each window has a number of tabs across the top that represent different protocols operating on multiple layers. Wireshark breaks down endpoints and conversations by these protocols and the addresses used on these layers. Because of this, a single Ethernet endpoint could actually be tied to multiple IPv4 endpoints. Likewise, a conversation between several IP addresses could actually be limited to only two physical devices, each having a single Ethernet MAC address.

The endpoints and conversations windows are useful for determining who the key role players are in a capture file. Here you can see which hosts transmit and receive the most or least amount of traffic, which can help you narrow down the scope of your investigation. Just like with the protocol hierarchy window, you can create filters directly from these screens by right clicking on an endpoint or conversation.

## Following Streams

We've already seen how Wireshark can delineate traffic that occurs as a part of a conversation between two endpoints, but often we are more concerned about the content of the data being exchanged between these devices rather than merely the list of packets associated with the communication sequence. Once you've created a filter that only shows the traffic in a conversation, you can use Wireshark's stream following options to get a different viewpoint on the application layer data contained in those packets. In this case, this can be done by right clicking on a TCP packet, and selecting Follow TCP Stream.

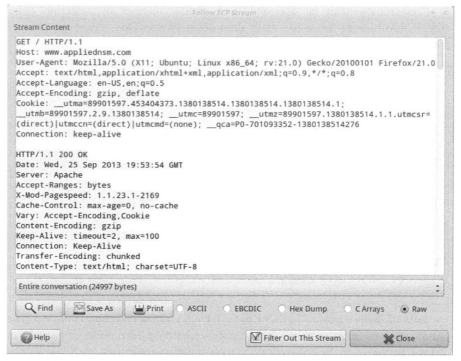

**FIGURE 13.35**

Following a TCP Stream

The figure above shows the TCP Stream output of an HTTP connection. As you can see, Wireshark has taken the application layer data contained in this conversation's packets and has reassembled them in a manner that excludes all of the lower layer information. This allows us to quickly see what is going on in this HTTP transaction. You can choose to output this information in a variety of formats, and you can also only show communication from a single direction if you choose.

Wireshark also provides the functionality to perform this same action with UDP and SSL streams. The amount of value you will obtain from following streams varies depending upon the application layer protocol in use, and of course, following encrypted streams like HTTPS or SSH connection often won't yield a ton of value.

## IO Graph

You are able to see the average throughput of the data contained in a packet capture by using the Wireshark Summary dialog that we looked at earlier. This is great for an overall average throughput measurement, but if you want to ascertain the throughput of packets in a capture at any given point in time, you will need to use Wireshark to generate an IO graph. These graphs allow you to display the throughput of data in a capture file over time (Figure 13.36).

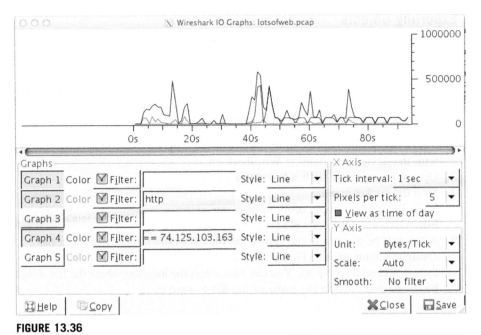

**FIGURE 13.36**

Viewing Capture Throughput with an IO Graph

The figure above shows a basic throughput graph for a single packet capture. In this case, there is a line showing throughput for all of the packets contained in the capture file (Graph 1), and two more lines showing throughput for packets that match display filters. One of these display filters shows all HTTP traffic contained in the capture (Graph 3), and the other shows traffic generated from a specific host with the IP address 74.125.103.164 (Graph 4).

> **CAUTION**
>
> In the print version of this book, it will be hard to distinguish the lines in Figure 13.32 because Wireshark identifies these by color, but the book is in black and white. Graph 3 was also skipped in this image because the color of the line didn't show up at all in print

The IO graph provides the ability to change the units and intervals used by the graph. I tend to use Bytes/tick as my unit, and will scale the unit intervals with the size of the data I'm looking at.

IO Graphs are useful for examining the amount of traffic generated by certain devices or protocols, or for quickly identifying spikes in the amount of traffic associated with a particular type of communication.

## Exporting Objects

Wireshark has the ability to detect the transfer of individual files inside of certain protocols. Because of this, it also has the ability to export these files from the packet capture, assuming the capture includes the entire data stream that contains the file. As of the writing of this book, Wireshark supports exporting objects from HTTP, SMB, and DICOM streams.

If you'd like to experiment with this functionality, you can try the following steps:

1. Start a new packet capture in Wireshark. Choose the network interface associated with the device you running Wireshark on.
2. Open a browser and visit a few different websites.
3. Stop the packet capture.
4. From Wireshark's main drop-down menu, select
   File > Export > Objects > HTTP
5. A list will be displayed that shows the files Wireshark has detected in the communication stream (Figure 13.37). Click on the object you would like to export, and select Save As. You can then select the location where the file should be stored and provide the name of the file to save it.

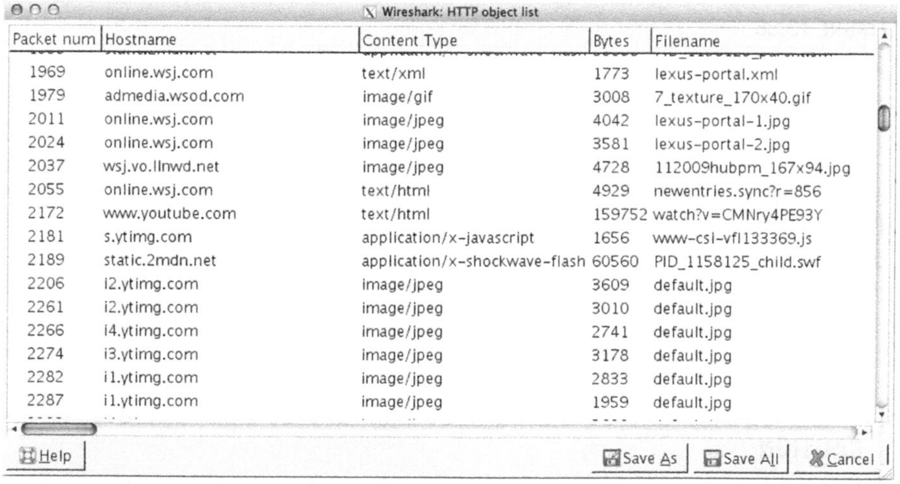

| Packet num | Hostname | Content Type | Bytes | Filename |
|---|---|---|---|---|
| 1969 | online.wsj.com | text/xml | 1773 | lexus-portal.xml |
| 1979 | admedia.wsod.com | image/gif | 3008 | 7_texture_170x40.gif |
| 2011 | online.wsj.com | image/jpeg | 4042 | lexus-portal-1.jpg |
| 2024 | online.wsj.com | image/jpeg | 3581 | lexus-portal-2.jpg |
| 2037 | wsj.vo.llnwd.net | image/jpeg | 4728 | 112009hubpm_167x94.jpg |
| 2055 | online.wsj.com | text/html | 4929 | newentries.sync?r=856 |
| 2172 | www.youtube.com | text/html | 159752 | watch?v=CMNry4PE93Y |
| 2181 | s.ytimg.com | application/x-javascript | 1656 | www-csi-vfl133369.js |
| 2189 | static.2mdn.net | application/x-shockwave-flash | 60560 | PID_1158125_child.swf |
| 2206 | i2.ytimg.com | image/jpeg | 3609 | default.jpg |
| 2261 | i2.ytimg.com | image/jpeg | 3010 | default.jpg |
| 2266 | i4.ytimg.com | image/jpeg | 2741 | default.jpg |
| 2274 | i3.ytimg.com | image/jpeg | 3178 | default.jpg |
| 2282 | i1.ytimg.com | image/jpeg | 2833 | default.jpg |
| 2287 | i1.ytimg.com | image/jpeg | 1959 | default.jpg |

**FIGURE 13.37**

Selecting an HTTP Object to Export

Remember that to be able to extract a file properly from a packet capture, you must have every packet associated with that file's transfer across the network.

This feature of Wireshark is incredibly valuable. While there are other options for exporting files from packet data streams, such as Bro's File Analysis Framework, being able to do this directly from Wireshark is very convenient. I use this feature often when I see a suspicious file going across the wire. Just be careful with any file you export, as it could be malicious and you might end up infecting yourself with some type of malware or something else that might cause other harm to your system.

## Adding Custom Columns

In a default installation, Wireshark provides 7 columns in the packet list pane. These are the packet number, time stamp, source address, destination address, protocol, length, and info fields. These are certainly essentials, but it is often the case that adding additional columns to this pane can enhance analysis. There are a couple of ways to do this, and to demonstrate both methods we will add three new columns to the packet list pane: source and destination port number and HTTP method.

We will begin by adding the source and destination port number. While the source and destination port number values are generally shown in the Info field, having them as their own column so that you can identify and sort by them easily is convenient. This is also useful for identifying different streams.

We will add these columns using the Wireshark Preferences dialog, which involves these steps:

1. From Wireshark's main drop-down menu, select Edit > Preferences.
2. Select the Columns option on the left side of the screen.
3. Click the Add button, and select the Source Port (unresolved) option in the Field Type dialog.
4. Double click "New Column" on the newly added field, and replace that title with "SPort."
5. Click the Add button, and select the Dest Port (unresolved) option.
6. Double click "New Column" on the newly added field, and replace that title with "DPort".
7. Drag the SPort field so that it is placed after the Source field.
8. Drag the DPort field so that it is placed after the Destination field
9. Select the OK button.
10. When you are finished, the Columns screen should look similar to Figure 13.38.

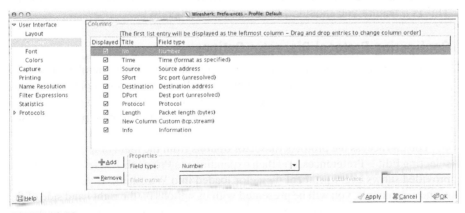

**FIGURE 13.38**

The Columns Screen with Newly Added Fields

Next, we will add the HTTP Method column. This field isn't something that you will want taking up screen real estate all the time, but it is useful when analyzing HTTP traffic so that you can quickly identify packets representing HTTP GET or POST commands. Instead of adding this field using the same method as before, we will add it from the main Wireshark window using the following steps:

1. Start a new packet capture in Wireshark. Choose the network interface associated with the device you running Wireshark on.
2. Open a browser and visit a few different websites.
3. Stop the packet capture.
4. Find an HTTP packet that contains an HTTP Request Method, such as a GET or POST packet. This can be done manually, or with the help of the display filter http.request.
5. Select the packet in the packet list pane, and then expand the HTTP protocol header information portion of the packet in the packet details pane. Drill down until you find the Request Method field.
6. Right click the Request Method field and select "Apply as Column".

The Request Method column should now be inserted right before the Info column. If you'd like to change the position of the column, you can click and drag it to the left or right of the other columns. You can edit the name and other attributes of the column by right clicking it and selecting Edit Column Details. If you decide that you want to get rid of a column you can remove it by right clicking the column header and choosing Remove Column.

Columns added using either of these methods will be added to the profile currently in use, so when you close Wireshark and relaunch it, the columns you have added will remain. Some columns, such as source and destination port, are something I use in most every scenario. Other columns like the HTTP Request Method are situational, and I will usually add and remove those at will depending on the type of traffic I am examining. You can turn virtually any field from a dissected packet into a column in Wireshark by right-clicking that field and choosing Apply as Column. This is a feature you shouldn't be afraid to use liberally!

## Configuring Protocol Dissector Options

Perhaps the most exciting feature offered by Wireshark is the vast number of protocol dissectors. Protocol dissectors are modules that Wireshark uses to parse individual protocols so that they can be interpreted on a field-by-field basis. This allows the user to create filters based upon specific protocol criteria. Some of these protocol dissectors have options that can be useful in changing the way that analysis is performed.

You can access the protocol dissector options from the main drop-down menu by selecting Edit > Preferences, and then expanding the Protocols header. The list that is provided shows every protocol dissector loaded into Wireshark. If you click on one of these protocols, you will be presented with its options on the right hand side of this window. Figure 13.39 shows the protocol dissector options for the TCP protocol.

Examining the protocol dissector options for common protocols is a useful way to gain insight into how Wireshark obtains some of the information it presents. For

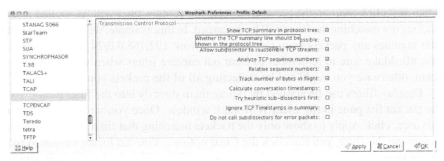

**FIGURE 13.39**

Protocol Dissector Options for the TCP Protocol

instance, in the figure above you will notice that, by default, Wireshark will display relative sequence numbers for TCP connections rather than absolute sequence numbers. If you didn't know this and were to look at the same set of packets in another application expecting to locate a particular sequence number, you might be alarmed to find that the number you were expecting doesn't exist. In that case, you could disable relative sequence numbers here to get the real TCP sequence numbers. If you spend a lot of time at the packet level, then you will probably want to take some time to examine the protocol dissector options for the major TCP/IP protocols and other protocols you work with on a regular basis.

## Capture and Display Filters

Wireshark allows for the use of BPF formatted capture filters, as well as display filters that use its own custom syntax designed to interact with fields generated by protocol dissectors.

Capture filters in BPF format can be applied to Wireshark only while capturing data. To use a capture filter, select Capture > Options from the main drop-down menu. Then, double-click the interface you plan to perform the capture on. Finally, place your capture filter into the Capture Filter dialog area (Figure 13.40) and click OK. Now,

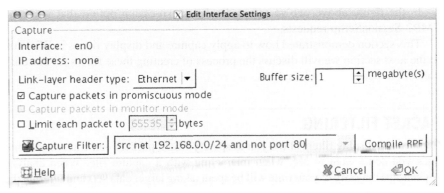

**FIGURE 13.40**

Specifying a Capture Filter

when you click Start on the previous screen, the capture filter will be applied and the packets not matching the filter will be discarded. In this example, we've applied a filter that matches any packets from the source network 192.168.0.0/24 that are not using port 80. Make sure to remember to clear out capture filters when you are done with them, otherwise you might not be collecting all of the packets you expect.

Display filters can be applied by typing them directly into the filter dialog above the packet list pane in the main Wireshark window. Once you've typed a filter into this area, click Apply to show only the packets matching that filter. When you'd like to remove the filter, you can click the Clear options. You can locate advanced filtering options by using Wireshark's expression filter. This is done by clicking the Expression button next to the display filter dialog box (Figure 13.41).

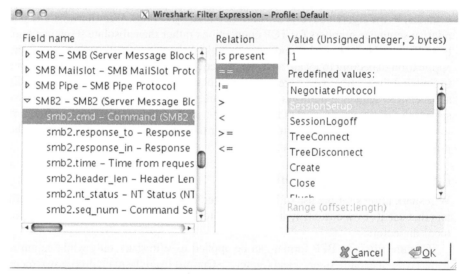

**FIGURE 13.41**

Building Display Filters with the Expression Builder

In the figure above, we've selected a filter expression option that will match SMB2 SessionSetup requests.

This section demonstrated how to apply capture and display filters in Wireshark. In the next section we will discuss the process of creating these filters for use during collection, detection, and analysis.

## PACKET FILTERING

Capture and display filters allow you to specify which packets you want to see, or the ones you don't want to see, when interacting with a capture file. When analyzing packets, the majority of your time will be spent taking larger data sets and filtering them down into manageable chunks that are valuable in the context of an investigation.

Because of this, it is critical that you understand packet filtering and how it can be applied to a variety of situations. In this section we will look at two types of packet filtering syntaxes: Berkeley Packet Filters (Capture Filters) and Wireshark/tshark Display Filters.

## Berkeley Packet Filters (BPFs)

The BPF syntax is the most commonly used packet filtering syntax, and is used by a number of packet processing applications. Tcpdump uses BPF syntax exclusively, and Wireshark and tshark can use BPF syntax while capturing packets from the network. BPFs can be used during collection in order to eliminate unwanted traffic, or traffic that isn't useful for detection and analysis (as discussed in Chapter 4), or they can be used while analyzing traffic that has already been collected by a sensor.

### BPF Anatomy

A filter created using the BPF syntax is called an expression. These expressions have a particular anatomy and structure, consisting of one or more primitives that can be combined with operators. A primitive can be thought of as a single filtering statement, and they consist of one or more qualifiers, followed by a value in the form of an ID name or number. An example of this expression format is shown in Figure 13.42, with each component labeled accordingly.

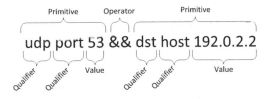

**FIGURE 13.42**

A Sample BPF Expression

In the example shown above, we have an expression that consists of two primitives, udp port 53 and dst host 192.0.2.2. The first primitive uses the qualifiers udp and port, and the value 53. This primitive will match any traffic to or from port 53 using the UDP transport layer protocol. The second primitive uses the qualifiers dst and host, and the value 192.0.2.2. This primitive will match any traffic destined to the host with the IP address 192.0.2.2. Both primitives are combined with the concatenation operator (&&) to form a single expression that evaluates to true when a packet matches both primitives.

BPF qualifiers come in three different types. These types, along with an example of qualifiers for each type are shown in Table 13.1.

As you can see in the example shown in Figure 13.1, qualifiers can be combined in relation to a specific value. For example, you can specify a primitive with a single qualifier like host 192.0.2.2, which will match any traffic to or from that IP address. Alternatively, you can use multiple qualifiers like src host 192.0.2.2, which will match only traffic sourced from that IP address.

**Table 13.1** BPF Qualifiers

| Qualifier Type | Qualifier | Description |
| --- | --- | --- |
| Type | | Identifies what the value refers to. "What are you looking for?" |
| | host | Specify a host by IP address |
| | net | Specify a network in CIDR notation |
| | port | Specify a port |
| Dir | | Identifies the transfer direction to or from the value. "What direction is it going?" |
| | src | Identify a value as the communication source |
| | dst | Identify a value as the communication destination |
| Proto | | Identifies the protocol in use. "What protocol is it using?" |
| | ip | Specify the IP protocol |
| | tcp | Specify the TCP protocol |
| | udp | Specify the UDP protocol |

When combining primitives, there are three logical operators that can be used, shown here (Table 13.2):

**Table 13.2** BPF Logical Operators

| Operator | Symbol | Description |
| --- | --- | --- |
| Concatenation (AND) | && | Evaluates to true when both conditions are true |
| Alternation Operator (OR) | \|\| | Evaluates to true when either condition is true |
| Negation Operator (NOT) | ! | Evaluates to true when a condition is NOT met |

Now that we understand how to create basic BPF expressions, I've created a few basic examples in Table 13.3.

**Table 13.3** Example BPF Expressions

| Expression | Description |
| --- | --- |
| host 192.0.2.100 | Matches traffic to or from the IPv4 address specified |
| dst host 2001:db8:85a3::8a2e:370:7334 | Matches traffic to the IPv6 address specified |
| ether host 00:1a:a0:52:e2:a0 | Matches traffic to the MAC address specified |
| port 53 | Matches traffic to or from port 53 (DNS) |
| tcp port 53 | Matches traffic to or from TCP port 53 (Large DNS responses and zone transfers) |
| !port 22 | Matches any traffic not to or from port 22 (SSH) |
| icmp | Matches all ICMP traffic |
| !ip6 | Matches everything that is not IPv6 |

## Filtering Individual Protocol Fields

You can do some pretty useful filtering using the syntax we've learned up until this point, but using this syntax alone limits you to only examining a few specific protocol fields. One of the real benefits of the BPF syntax is that it can be used to look at ANY field within the headers of the TCP/IP protocols.

As an example, let's say that you would like to examine the Time to Live (TTL) value in the IPv4 header to attempt to filter based upon the operating system architecture of a device that is generating packets. While it isn't always an exact science and it can certainly be fooled, Windows devices will generally use a default initial TTL of 128, and Linux devices will generally use a TTL of 64. This means that we can do some rudimentary passive operating system detection with packets. To do this, we will create a BPF expression that looks for values in the TTL field that are greater than 64.

To create this filter, we have to identify the offset where the TTL field begins in the IP header. Using a packet map, we can determine that this field begins at 0x8 (remember to start counting from 0). With this information, we can create a filter expression by telling tcpdump which protocol header to look in, and then specifying the byte offset where the value exists inside of square brackets. This can be combined with the greater than (>) logical operator and the value we've selected. The end result is this BPF expression:

```
ip[8]>64
```

The expression above will instruct tcpdump (or whatever BPF-aware application you are using) to read the value of the eighth byte offset from 0 in the TCP header. If the value of this field is greater than 64, it will match. Now, let's look at a similar example where we want to examine a field that spans multiple bytes.

The Window Size field in the TCP header is used to control the flow of data between two communicating hosts. If one host becomes too overloaded with data and its buffer space fills up, it will send a packet to the other host with a window size value of 0 to instruct that host to stop sending data so that it can catch up. This process helps ensure reliable delivery of data. We can detect the TCP zero window packets by creating a filter to examine this field.

Using the same strategy as before, we have to look at a packet map to determine where this field is located in the TCP header. In this case, the field occurs at byte 0x14. In this case, note that this field is actually two bytes in length. We can tell tcpdump that this is a two byte field by specifying the offset number and byte length inside of the square brackets, separated by a colon. Doing this, we are left with this expression:

```
tcp[14:2]=0
```

This expression tells tcpdump to look at the TCP header and to examine the 2 bytes occurring starting at the fourteenth byte offset from 0. If the value of this field is 0, the filter expression will match. Now that we know how to examine a field longer than a byte, let's look at examining fields shorter than a byte.

The TCP protocol uses various flags to indicate the purpose of each packet. For instance, the SYN flag is used by packets that initialize a connection, while the RST and FIN packets are used for terminating a connection in an abrupt or graceful manner, respectively. These flags are individual 1-bit fields contained within byte 0x13 in the TCP header.

To demonstrate how to create filters matching fields smaller than a byte, let's create an expression that matches any TCP packet that has only the RST flag enabled. This will require a few steps toward the creation of a bit masked expression.

First, we should identify the value we want to examine within the packet header. In this case, the RST flag is in byte 0x13 in the TCP header, in the third position in this byte (counting from right to left). With that knowledge in mind, it becomes necessary to create a binary mask that tells tcpdump which bits in this field we actually care about.

The field we want to examine in this byte is in the third position, so we place a 1 in the third position of our bit mask and place 0's in the remaining fields. The result is the binary value 00000100.

Next, we have to translate this value into its hexadecimal representation. In this case, 00000100 breaks down as 0x04 in hex.

Now we can build our expression by specifying the protocol and byte offset value for 0x13, followed by an ampersand (&) and the byte mask value we just created.

```
tcp[13] & 0x04
```

Finally, we can provide the value we want to match in this field. In this case, we want any packet that has a 1 set in this field. Since a 1 in the third position of a byte equals 4, we can simply use 4 as the value to match.

```
tcp[13] & 0x04 = 4
```

This expression will match any packet with only the TCP RST bit set.

There are a number of different applications for BPF expressions that examine individual protocol fields. For example, the expression `icmp[0] == 8 || icmp[0] == 0` can be used to match ICMP echo requests or replies. Given the examples in this section, you should be able to create filter expressions for virtually any protocol field that is of interest to you. Next, we will look at display filters.

## Wireshark Display Filters

Wireshark and tshark both provide the ability to use display filters. These are different than capture filters, because they leverage the protocol dissectors these tools use to capture information about individual protocol fields. Because of this, they are a lot more powerful. As of version 1.10, Wireshark supports around 1000 protocols and nearly 141000 protocol fields, and you can create filter expressions using any of them. Unlike capture filters, display filters are applied to a packet capture after data has been collected.

Earlier we discussed how to use display filters in Wireshark and tshark, but let's take a closer look at how these expressions are built, along with some examples.

A typical display filter expression consists of a field name, a comparison operator, and a value.

A field name can be a protocol, a field within a protocol, or a field that a protocol dissector provides in relation to a protocol. Some example field names might include the protocol icmp, or the protocol fields icmp.type and icmp.code. A complete list of field names can be found by accessing the display filter expression builder (described in the Wireshark section of this chapter) or by accessing the Wireshark help file. Simply put, any field that you see in Wireshark's packet details pane can be used in a filter expression.

Next is the comparison operator (sometimes called a relational operator), which determines how Wireshark compares the specified value in relation to the data it interprets in the field. The comparison operators Wireshark supports are shown in Table 13.4. You can alternate use of the English and C-like operators based upon what you are comfortable with.

**Table 13.4** Display Filter Comparison Operators

| Operator (English) | Operator (C-Like) | Description | Example |
|---|---|---|---|
| eq | == | Matches values equal to the specified value | ip.addr == 192.168.1.155 |
| ne | != | Matches values not equal to the specified value | ip.addr != 192.168.1.155 |
| gt | > | Matches values greater than the specified value | tcp.port gt 1023 |
| lt | < | Matches values less than the specified value | tcp.port < 1024 |
| ge | >= | Matches values greater than or equal to the specified value | udp.length >= 75 |
| le | <= | Matches values less than or equal to the specified value | udp.length le 75 |
| contains | | Matches values where the specified value is contained within the field | smtp.req. parameter contains "FROM" |

The last element in the expression is the value, which is what you want to match in relation to the comparison operator. Values also come in different types as well, which are shown in Table 13.5.

**Table 13.5** Value Types

| Value Type | Description | Example |
|---|---|---|
| Integer (Signed or Unsigned) | Expressed in decimal, octal, or hexadecimal | `tcp.port == 443`<br>`ip.proto == 0x06` |
| Boolean | Expressed as true (1) or False (0) | `tcp.flags.syn == 1`<br>`ip.frags.mf == 0` |
| String | Expressed as ASCII text | `http.request.uri == "http://www.`<br>`appliednsm.com"`<br>`smtp.req.parameter contains "FROM"` |
| Address | Expressed as any number of addresses: IPv4, IPv6, MAC, etc. | `ip.src == 192.168.1.155`<br>`ip.dst == 192.168.1.0/24`<br>`ether.dst == ff:ff:ff:ff:ff:ff` |

Now that we understand how filters are constructed, let's build a few of our own. Starting simple, we can create a filter expression that only shows packets using the IP protocol by simply stating the protocol name:

```
ip
```

Now, we can match based upon a specific source IP address by adding the src keyword to the expression:

```
ip.src == 192.168.1.155
```

Alternatively, we could match based upon packets with the destination IP address instead:

```
ip.dst == 192.168.1.155
```

Wireshark also includes custom fields that will incorporate values from multiple other fields. For instance, if we want to match packets with a specific IP address in either the source or destination fields, we could use this filter, which will examine both the ip.src and ip.dst fields:

```
ip.addr == 192.168.1.155
```

Multiple expressions can be combined using logical operators. These are shown in Table 13.6.

**Table 13.6** Display Filter Logical Operators

| Operator (English) | Operator (C-Like) | Description |
|---|---|---|
| and | && | Evaluates to true when both conditions are true |
| or | \|\| | Evaluates to true when either condition is true |
| xor | oo | Evaluates to true when one and only one condition is true |
| not | ! | Evaluates to true when a condition is NOT met |

We can combine a previous expression with another expression to make a compound expression. This will match any packets sourced from 192.168.1.155 that are not destined for port 80:

```
ip.src == 192.168.1.155 && !tcp.dstport == 80
```

Once again, the key thing to keep in mind when creating display filters is that anything you see in the packet details pane in Wireshark can be used in a filter expression. Table 13.7 contains a few more example display filter expressions.

**Table 13.7** Example Display Filter Expressions

| Filter Expression | Description |
|---|---|
| eth.addr != <MAC address> | Match packets not to or from the specified MAC address. Useful for excluding traffic from the host you are using. |
| ipv6 | Match IPv6 packets |
| ip.geoip.country ==<country> | Match packets to or from a specified country |
| ip.ttl <=<value> | Match packets with a TTL less than or equal to the specified value. This can be useful for some loose OS fingerprinting. |
| ip.checksum_bad == 1 | Match packets with an invalid IP checksum. Can be used for TCP and UDP checksums as well by replacing ip in the expression with udp or tcp. Useful for finding poorly forged packets. |
| tcp.stream ==<value> | Match packets associated with a specific TCP stream. Useful for narrowing down specific communication transactions. |
| tcp.flags.syn == 1 | Match packets with the SYN flag set. This filter can be used with any TCP flag by replacing the "syn" portion of the expression with the appropriate flag abbreviation. |
| tcp.analysis. zero_window | Match packets that indicate a TCP window size of 0. Useful for finding hosts whose resources have become exhausted. |
| http.request == 1 | Match packets that are HTTP requests. |
| http.request.uri == "<value>" | Match HTTP request packets with a specified URI in the request. |
| http.response.code ==<value> | Match HTTP response packets with the specified code. |
| http.user_agent == "value" | Match HTTP packets with a specified user agent string. |
| http.host == "value" | Match HTTP packets with a specified host value. |
| smtp.req.command == "<value>" | Match SMTP request packets with a specified command |
| smtp.rsp.code ==<value> | Match SMTP response packets with a specified code |
| smtp.message == "value" | Match packets with a specified SMTP message. |

*Continued*

**Table 13.7** Example Display Filter Expressions—cont'd

| Filter Expression | Description |
|---|---|
| bootp.dchp | Match DHCP packets. |
| !arp | Match any packets that are not ARP. |
| ssh.encrypted_packet | Match encrypted SSH packets. |
| ssh.protocol == "<value>" | Match SSH packets of a specified protocol value. |
| dns.qry.type ==<value> | Match DNS query packets of a specified type (A, MX, NS, SOA, etc). |
| dns.resp.type ==<value> | Match DNS response packets of a specified type (A, MX, NS, SOA, etc). |
| dns.qry.name == "<value>" | Match DNS query packets containing the specified name. |
| dns.resp.name == "<value>" | Match DNS response packets containing the specified name. |

You should spend some time experimenting with display filter expressions and attempting to create useful ones. A quick perusal of the expression builder in Wireshark can point you in the right direction.

## CONCLUSION

In this chapter we discussed the basics of packet analysis from a fundamental level. This journey began with an introduction to reading packets in hex with a primer in packet math. This led into an overview of tcpdump and tshark for packet analysis from the command line, and Wireshark as a graphical packet analysis platform. Finally, we discussed the anatomy and syntax of capture and display filters. Packet analysis is one of the most important skills an NSM analyst can have, so the knowledge in this chapter is incredibly important. Once you've mastered these concepts, you can look into some of the additional packet analysis resources mentioned at the start of the chapter to gain a deeper understanding of how packets work and the TCP/IP protocols.

## CHAPTER CONTENTS

Intelligence has many definitions depending on the application. The definition that most closely aligns to NSM and information security is drawn from Department of Defense Joint Publication 1-02, and says that "intelligence is a product resulting from the collection, processing, integration, evaluation, analysis, and interpretation of available information concerning foreign nations, hostile or potentially hostile forces or elements, or areas of actual or potential operations.[1] "

While this definition might not fit perfectly for a traditional SOC performing NSM services (particularly the part about information concerning foreign nations), it does provide the all-important framing required to begin thinking about generating intelligence. The key component of this definition is that intelligence is a product. This doesn't mean that it is bought or sold for profit, but more specifically, that it

---

[1]http://www.dtic.mil/doctrine/new_pubs/jp1_02.pdf

is produced from collected data, based upon a specific requirement. This means that an IP address, or the registered owner of that address, or the common characteristics of the network traffic generated by that IP address are not intelligence products. When those things are combined with context through the analysis process and delivered to meet a specific requirement, they become an intelligence product.

Most SOC environments are generally concerned with the development of two types of intelligence products: friendly intelligence and threat intelligence. In this chapter, we will take a look at the traditional intelligence cycle and methods that can be used to generate these intelligence products. This includes the creation of friendly intelligence products, as well as threat products associated with tactical threat intelligence. While reading, you should keep in mind that there are many components to intelligence as a whole, and we are only covering a small subset of that here.

## THE INTELLIGENCE CYCLE FOR NSM

The generation of intelligence products in a SOC requires the coordinated effort of multiple stakeholders within the organization. Because there are so many moving parts to the process, it helps to be able to organize the intelligence generation process into an organized, repeatable framework. The framework that the government and military intelligence community (IC) have relied on for years is called the Intelligence Cycle.

Depending on the source you reference, the intelligence cycle can be broken down into any number of steps. For the purposes of this book, we will look at a model that uses six steps: defining requirements, planning, collection, processing, analysis, and dissemination. These steps form a cycle that can continually feed itself, ultimately allowing its products to shape how newer products are developed (Figure 14.1).

**FIGURE 14.1**

The Traditional Intelligence Cycle

Let's go through each of these steps to illustrate how this cycle applies to the development of friendly and hostile intelligence for NSM.

## Defining Requirements

An intelligence product is generated based upon a defined requirement. This requirement is what all other phases of the intelligence cycle are derived from. Just like a movie can't be produced without a script, an intelligence product can't be produced without a clearly defined intelligence requirement.

In terms of information security and NSM, that requirement is generally focused on a need for information related to assets you are responsible for protecting (friendly intelligence), or focused on information related to hosts that pose a potential threat to friendly assets (hostile intelligence).

These requirements are, essentially, requests for information and context that can help NSM analysts make judgments relevant to their investigations. This phase is ultimately all about asking the right questions, and those questions depend on whether the intelligence requirement is continual or situational. For instance, the development of a friendly intelligence product is a continual process, meaning that questions should be phrased in a broad, repeatable manner.

Some examples of questions designed to create baselines for friendly communication patterns might be:

- What are the normal communication patterns occurring between friendly hosts?
- What are the normal communication patterns occurring between sensitive friendly hosts and unknown external entities?
- What services are normally provided by friendly hosts?
- What is the normal ratio of inbound to outbound communication for friendly hosts?

On the other end of the spectrum, the development of a threat intelligence product is a situational process, meaning that questions are often specific, and designed to generate a single intelligence product for a current investigation:

- Has the specific hostile host ever communicated with friendly hosts before, and if so, to what extent?
- Is the specific hostile host registered to an ISP where previous hostile activity has originated?
- How does the content of the traffic generated by the specific hostile host compare to activity that is known to be associated with currently identified hostile entities?
- Can the timing of this specific event be tied to the goals of any particular organization?

Once you have asked the right question, the rest of the cards should begin to fall into place. We will delve further into the nature of friendly and threat intelligence requirements later in their respective sections.

## Planning

With an intelligence requirement defined, appropriate planning can ensure that the remaining steps of the intelligence cycle can be completed. This involves planning each of these steps and assigning resources to them. In NSM terms, this means different things for different steps. For instance, during the collection phase this may mean assigning level three analysts (thinking back to our Chapter 1 discussion of classifying analysts) and systems administrators to work with sensors and collection tools. In the processing and analysis phase this may mean assigning level one and two analysts to these processes and sectioning off a portion of their time to work on this task.

Of course, the types of resources, both human and technical, that you assign to these tasks will vary depending upon your environment and the makeup of your technical teams. In larger organizations you may have a separate team specifically for generating intelligence products. In smaller organizations, you might be a one-man show responsible for the entirety of intelligence product creation. No matter how large or small your organization, you can participate in the development of friendly and threat intelligence.

## Collection

The collection phase of the intelligence cycle deals with the mechanisms used for collecting the data that supports the outlined requirements. This data will eventually be processed, analyzed, and disseminated as the intelligence product.

In a SOC environment, you may find that your collection needs for intelligence purposes will force you to modify your overall collection plan. For the purposes of continual friendly intelligence collection, this can include the collection of useful statistics, like those discussed in Chapter 11, or the collection of passive real-time asset data, like the data generated with a tool we will discuss later, called PRADS.

When it comes to situational threat intelligence collection, data will typically be collected from existing NSM data sources like FPC or session data. This data will generally be focused on what interaction the potentially hostile entity had with trusted network assets. In addition, open source intelligence gathering processes are utilized to ascertain publicly available information related to the potentially hostile entity. This might include items like information about the registrant of an IP address, or known intelligence surrounding a mysterious suspicious file.

In order for intelligence collection to occur in an efficient manner, collection processes for certain types of data (FPC, PSTR, Session, etc.) should be well-documented and easily accessible.

## Processing

Once data has been collected, some types of data must be further processed to become useful for analysis. This can mean a lot of different things for a lot of different types of data.

At a higher level, processing can mean just paring down the collected data set into something more immediately useful. This might mean applying filters to a PCAP file to shrink the total working data set, or selecting log files of only a certain type from a larger log file collection.

At a more granular level, this might mean taking the output from a third party or custom tool and using some BASH commands to format the output of those tools into something more easily readable. In cases where an organization is using a custom tool or database for intelligence collection, it might mean writing queries to insert data into this format, or pull it out of that format into something more easily readable.

Ultimately, processing can sometimes be seen as an extension of collection where collected data is pared down, massaged, and tweaked into a form that is ideal for the analyst.

## Analysis

The analysis phase is where multiple collected and processed items are examined, correlated, and given the necessary context the make them useful. This is where intelligence goes from just being loosely related pieces of data to a finished product that is useful for decision-making.

In the analysis and generation of both friendly and threat intelligence products, the analyst will take the output of several tools and data sources and combine those data points on a per host basis, painting a picture of an individual host. A great deal more intelligence will be available for local hosts, and might allow this picture to include details about the tendencies and normal communication partners of the host. The analysis of potentially hostile hosts will be generated from a much smaller data set, and require the incorporation of open source intelligence into the analysis process.

What ultimately results from this process is the intelligence product, ready to be parsed by the analyst.

## Dissemination

In most practical cases, an organization won't have a dedicated intelligence team, meaning the NSM analysts will be generating intelligence products for their own use. This is a unique advantage, because the consumer of the intelligence will usually be the same person who generated it, or will at least be in the same room or under the same command structure. In the final phase of the intelligence cycle, the intelligence product is disseminated to the individual or group who initially identified the intelligence requirement.

In most cases, the intelligence product is constantly being evaluated and improved. The positive and negative aspects of the final product are critiqued, and this critique goes back into defining intelligence requirements and planning the product creation process. This is what makes this an intelligence cycle, rather than just an intelligence chain.

The remainder of this chapter is devoted to the friendly and threat intelligence products, and ways to generate and obtain that data. While the intelligence framework might not be referenced exclusively, the actions described in these sections will most certainly fit into this framework in a manner that can be adapted to nearly any organization.

## GENERATING FRIENDLY INTELLIGENCE

You cannot effectively defend your network if you do not know what is on it, and how it communicates. This statement cannot be emphasized enough. No matter how simple or sophisticated an attack may be, if you don't know the roles of the devices on your network, especially those where critical data exists, then you won't be able to effectively identify when an incident has occurred, contain that incident, or eradicate the attacker from the network. That's why the development of friendly intelligence is so important.

In the context of this book, we present friendly intelligence as a continually evolving product that can be referenced to obtain information about hosts an analyst is responsible for protecting. This information should include everything the analyst needs to aid in the event of an investigation, and should be able to be referenced at any given time. Generally, an analyst might be expected to reference friendly intelligence about a single host any time they are investigating alert data associated with that host. This would typically be when the friendly host appears to be the target of an attack. Because of that, it isn't uncommon for an analyst to reference this data dozens of times per shift for a variety of hosts. Beyond this, you should also consider that the analysis of friendly intelligence could also result in the manual observance of anomalies that can spawn investigations. Let's look at a few ways to create friendly intelligence from network data.

### The Network Asset History and Physical

When a physician assesses a new patient, the first thing they perform is an evaluation of the medical history and physical condition of the patient. This is called a patient history and physical, or an H&P. This concept provides a useful framework that can be applied the friendly intelligence of network assets.

The patient history assessment includes current and previous medical conditions that could impact the patient's current or future health. This also usually includes a history of the patient's family's health conditions, so that risk factors for those conditions in the patient can be identified and mitigated.

Shifting this concept to a network asset, we can translate a network asset's medical history to its connection history. This involves assessing previous communication transactions between the friendly host and other hosts on the network, as well as hosts outside of the network. This connection profiling extends beyond the hosts involved in this communication, but also to the services used by the host, both as a client and a server. If we can assess this connection history, we can make educated guesses about the validity of new connections a friendly host makes in the context of an investigation.

The patient physical exam captures the current state of a patient's physical health, and measures items such as the patient's demographic information, their height and weight, their blood pressure, and so on. This product of the physical exam is an overall assessment of a patient's health. Often physical exams will be conducted with a targeted goal, such as assessments that are completed for the purposes of health insurance, or for clearance to play a sport.

When we think about a friendly network asset in terms of the patient physical exam, we can begin to identify criteria that help define the state the asset on the network, opposed to a state of health in a patient. These criteria include items such as the IP address and DNS name of the asset, the VLAN it is located in, the role of the device (workstation, web server, etc.), the operating system architecture of the device, or its physical network location. The product of this assessment on the friendly network asset is a state of its operation on the network, which can be used to make determinations about the activity the host is presenting in the context of an investigation.

Now, we will talk about some methods that can be used to create a network asset H&P. This will include using tools like Nmap to define the "physical exam" portion of an H&P through the creation of an asset model, as well as the use of PRADS to help with the "history" portion of the H&P by collecting passive real-time asset data.

## Defining a Network Asset Model

A network asset model is, very simply, a list of every host on your network and the critical information associated with it. This includes things like the host's IP address, DNS name, general role (server, workstation, router, etc), the services it provides (web server, SSH server, proxy server, etc), and the operating system architecture. This is the most basic form of friendly intelligence, and something all SOC environments should strive to generate.

As you might imagine, there are a number of ways to build a network asset model. Most organizations will employ some form of enterprise asset management software, and this software often has the capacity to provide this data. If that is true for your organization, then that is often the easiest way to get this data to your analysts.

If your organization doesn't have anything like that in place, then you may be left to generate this type of data yourself. In my experience, there is no discrete formula for creating an asset model. If you walk into a dozen organizations, you will likely find a dozen different methods used to generate the asset model and a dozen more ways to access and view that data. The point of this section isn't to tell you exactly how to generate this data, because that is something that will really have to be adapted from the technologies that exist in your organization. The goal here is simply to provide an idea of what an asset model looks like, and to provide some idea of how you might start generating this data in the short term.

> **CAUTION**
>
> Realistically, asset inventories are rarely 100% accurate. In larger organizations with millions of devices, it just isn't feasible to create asset models that are complete and always up to date. That said, you shouldn't strive to achieve a 100% solution if it just isn't possible. In this case, sometimes it's acceptable to shoot for an 80% solution because it is still 80% better than 0%. If anything, do your best to generate asset models of critical devices that are identified while doing collection planning.

One way to actively generate asset data is through internal port scanning. This can be done with commercial software, or with free software like Nmap. For instance, you can run a basic SYN scan with this command:

```
nmap -sn 172.16.16.0/24
```

This command will perform a basic ICMP (ping) scan against all hosts in the 172.16.16.0/24 network range, and generate output similar to Figure 14.2.

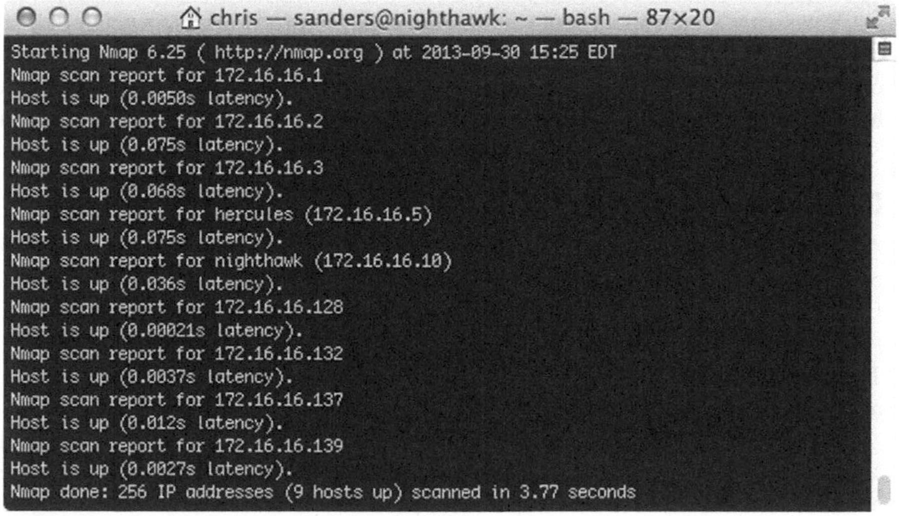

```
Starting Nmap 6.25 ( http://nmap.org ) at 2013-09-30 15:25 EDT
Nmap scan report for 172.16.16.1
Host is up (0.0050s latency).
Nmap scan report for 172.16.16.2
Host is up (0.075s latency).
Nmap scan report for 172.16.16.3
Host is up (0.068s latency).
Nmap scan report for hercules (172.16.16.5)
Host is up (0.075s latency).
Nmap scan report for nighthawk (172.16.16.10)
Host is up (0.036s latency).
Nmap scan report for 172.16.16.128
Host is up (0.00021s latency).
Nmap scan report for 172.16.16.132
Host is up (0.0037s latency).
Nmap scan report for 172.16.16.137
Host is up (0.012s latency).
Nmap scan report for 172.16.16.139
Host is up (0.0027s latency).
Nmap done: 256 IP addresses (9 hosts up) scanned in 3.77 seconds
```

**FIGURE 14.2**

Ping Scan Output from Nmap

As you can see in the data shown above, any host that is allowed to respond to ICMP echo request packets will respond with an ICMP echo reply. Assuming all of the hosts on your network are configured to respond to ICMP traffic (or they have an exclusion in a host-based firewall), this should allow you to map the active hosts on the network. The information provided to us is a basic list of IP addresses.

We can take this a step farther by utilizing more advanced scans. A SYN scan will attempt to communicate with any host on the network that has an open TCP port. This command can be used to initiate a SYN scan:

```
nmap -sS 172.16.16.0/24
```

This command will send a TCP SYN packet to the top 1000 most commonly used ports of every host on the 172.16.16.0/24 network. The output is shown in Figure 14.3.

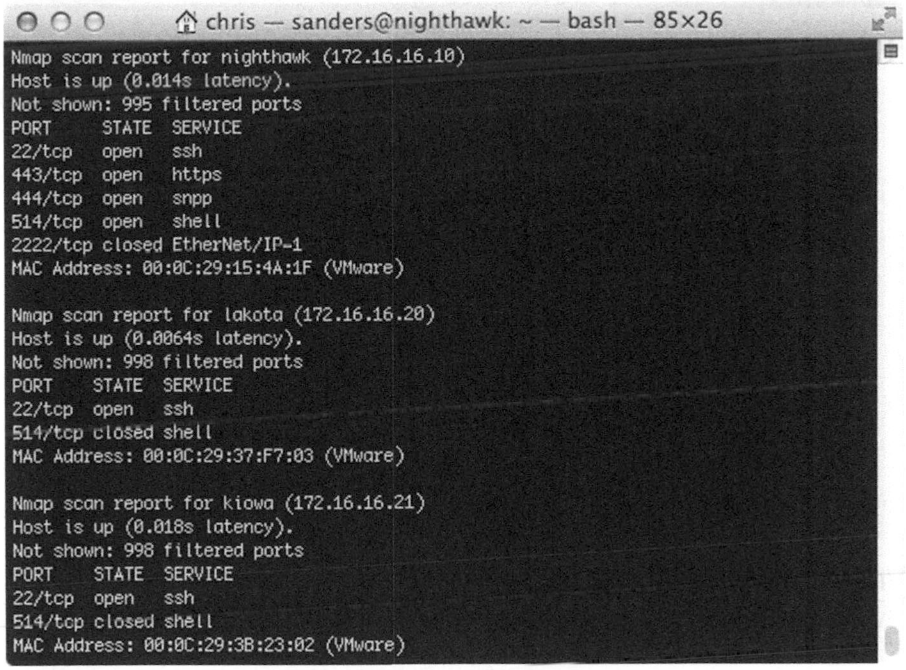

**FIGURE 14.3**

SYN Scan Output from Nmap

This SYN scan gives us a bit more information. So now, in addition to IP addresses of live hosts on the network, we also have a listing of open ports on these devices, which can indicate the services they provide.

We can extend this even farther by using the version detection and operating system fingerprinting features of nmap:

```
nmap -sV -O 172.16.16.0/24
```

The command will perform a standard SYN port scan, followed by tests that will attempt to assess the services listening on open ports, and a variety of tests that will attempt to guess the operating system architecture of the device. This output is shown in Figure 14.4.

```
○ ○ ○                    ⌂ chris — sanders@nighthawk: ~ — nmap — 121×48
Nmap scan report for nighthawk (172.16.16.10)
Host is up (0.036s latency).
Not shown: 995 filtered ports
PORT     STATE  SERVICE        VERSION
22/tcp   open   ssh            OpenSSH 5.9p1 Debian 5ubuntu1.1 (Ubuntu Linux; protocol 2.0)
443/tcp  open   ssl/http       Apache httpd 2.2.22 ((Ubuntu))
444/tcp  open   ssl/http       Apache httpd 2.2.22 ((Ubuntu))
514/tcp  open   shell?
2222/tcp closed EtherNet/IP-1
MAC Address: 00:0C:29:15:4A:1F (VMware)
Device type: general purpose|storage-misc|WAP|media device
Running (JUST GUESSING): Linux 3.X|2.6.X (98%), HP embedded (91%), Netgear embedded (89%), Western Digital embedded (89%)
OS CPE: cpe:/o:linux:linux_kernel:3 cpe:/o:linux:linux_kernel:2.6 cpe:/h:hp:p2000_g3 cpe:/h:netgear:dg834g cpe:/o:western
digital:wd_tv
Aggressive OS guesses: Linux 3.1 - 3.4 (98%), Linux 2.6.32 - 2.6.39 (97%), Linux 2.6.32 - 3.6 (96%), Linux 2.6.32 - 2.6.3
5 (96%), Linux 3.0 (94%), Linux 2.6.23 - 2.6.38 (93%), Linux 2.6.37 (93%), Linux 2.6.39 (93%), Linux 2.6.32 - 3.2 (93%),
HP P2000 G3 NAS device (91%)
No exact OS matches for host (test conditions non-ideal).
Network Distance: 1 hop
Service Info: OS: Linux; CPE: cpe:/o:linux:linux_kernel

Nmap scan report for lakota (172.16.16.20)
Host is up (0.041s latency).
Not shown: 998 filtered ports
PORT     STATE SERVICE VERSION
22/tcp   open  ssh     OpenSSH 5.9p1 Debian 5ubuntu1.1 (Ubuntu Linux; protocol 2.0)
514/tcp  closed shell
MAC Address: 00:0C:29:37:F7:03 (VMware)
Aggressive OS guesses: Linux 3.0 (93%), HP P2000 G3 NAS device (91%), Linux 3.1 - 3.4 (90%), Linux 2.6.32 - 2.6.35 (90%),
 Linux 2.6.32 - 2.6.39 (89%), OpenWrt Kamikaze 7.09 (Linux 2.6.22) (89%), Netgear DG834G WAP or Western Digital WD TV med
ia player (89%), Linux 2.6.23 - 2.6.38 (88%), Linux 2.6.37 (88%), Linux 2.6.22 (88%)
No exact OS matches for host (test conditions non-ideal).
Network Distance: 1 hop
Service Info: OS: Linux; CPE: cpe:/o:linux:linux_kernel

Nmap scan report for kiowa (172.16.16.21)
Host is up (0.046s latency).
Not shown: 998 filtered ports
PORT     STATE SERVICE VERSION
22/tcp   open  ssh     OpenSSH 5.9p1 Debian 5ubuntu1.1 (Ubuntu Linux; protocol 2.0)
514/tcp  closed shell
MAC Address: 00:0C:29:3B:23:02 (VMware)
Aggressive OS guesses: Linux 3.0 (96%), HP P2000 G3 NAS device (91%), Linux 3.1 - 3.4 (91%), Linux 2.6.32 - 2.6.35 (91%),
 Linux 2.6.32 - 3.4.1 (90%), Linux 2.6.32 - 2.6.39 (89%), Netgear DG834G WAP or Western Digital WD TV media player (89%),
 Linux 2.6.23 - 2.6.38 (88%), Linux 2.6.37 (88%), Linux 2.6.22 (88%)
No exact OS matches for host (test conditions non-ideal).
Network Distance: 1 hop
Service Info: OS: Linux; CPE: cpe:/o:linux:linux_kernel
```

**FIGURE 14.4**

Version and Operating System Detection Scan Output

This type of scan will generate quite a bit of additional traffic on the network, but it will help round out the asset model by providing the operating system architecture and helping clarify the services running on open ports.

The data shown in the screenshots above is very easily readable when it is output by Nmap in its default format, however, it isn't the easiest the search through. We can fix this by forcing Nmap to output its results in a single line format. This format is easily searchable with the grep tool, and very practical for analysts to reference. To force nmap to output its results in this format, simply add -oG < filename > at the end of any of the commands shown above. In figure 14.5, we use the grep command to search for data associated with a specific IP address (172.16.16.10) in a file that is generated using this format (data.scan).

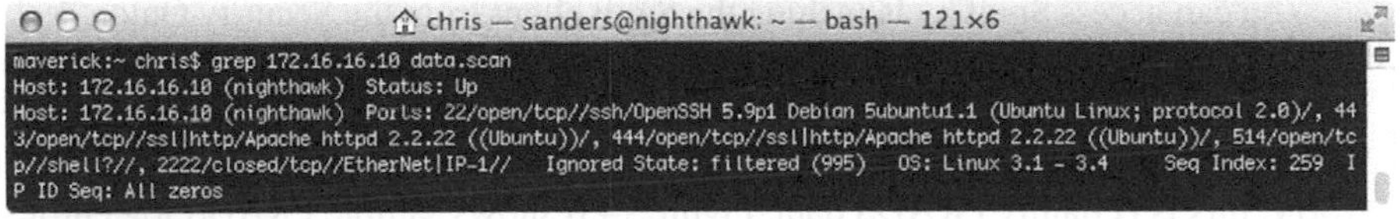

```
○ ○ ○              ⌂ chris — sanders@nighthawk: ~ — bash — 121×6
maverick:~ chris$ grep 172.16.16.10 data.scan
Host: 172.16.16.10 (nighthawk)  Status: Up
Host: 172.16.16.10 (nighthawk)  Ports: 22/open/tcp//ssh/OpenSSH 5.9p1 Debian 5ubuntu1.1 (Ubuntu Linux; protocol 2.0)/, 44
3/open/tcp//ssl|http/Apache httpd 2.2.22 ((Ubuntu))/, 444/open/tcp//ssl|http/Apache httpd 2.2.22 ((Ubuntu))/, 514/open/tc
p//shell?//, 2222/closed/tcp//EtherNet|IP-1//  Ignored State: filtered (995)  OS: Linux 3.1 - 3.4   Seq Index: 259  I
P ID Seq: All zeros
```

**FIGURE 14.5**

Greppable Nmap Output

You should keep in mind that using a scanner like nmap isn't always the most conclusive way to build friendly intelligence. Most organizations schedule noisy scans like these in the evening, and this creates a scenario where devices might be missed in the scan because they are turned off. This also doesn't account for mobile devices that are only periodically connected to the network, like laptops that employees take home at night, or laptops belonging to traveling staff. Because of this, intelligence built from network scan data should combine the results of multiple scans taking at different time periods. You may also need to use multiple scan types to ensure that all devices are detected. Generating an asset model with scan data is much more difficult than firing off a single scan and storing the results. It requires a concerted effort and may take quite a bit of finessing in order to get the results you are looking for on a consistent basis.

No matter how reliable your scan data may seem, it should be combined with another data source that can be used to validate the results. This can be something that is already generated on your network, like DNS transaction logs, or something that is part of your NSM data set, like session data. Chapter 4 and 11 describe some useful techniques for generating friendly host data with session data using SiLK. Another option is to use a passive tool, like PRADS, which we will talk about next.

## Passive Real-time Asset Detection System (PRADS)

PRADS is a tool that is designed to listen to network traffic and gather data about hosts and services that can be used to map your network. It is based upon two other very successful tools, PADS, the Passive Asset Detection System, and P0f, the passive OS fingerprinting tool. PRADS combines the functionality of these tools into a single service that is effective for building friendly intelligence. It does this by generating data that can be loosely compared to session data that might be used by SiLK or Argus.

PRADS is included in Security Onion by default, so we can examine this data by creating a query in Sguil. We will talk more about Sguil in the next chapter, but if you remember our brief mention of Sguil in Chapter 9, then you know that it is an analyst console that can be used for viewing alerts from detection mechanisms and data from other NSM collection and detection tools.

You can access Sguil by launching the Sguil client from the Security Onion desktop, or by launching the client from another device and connecting remotely. Once there, you can sort the visible alerts by the Event Message column to find PRADS entries. You may notice that Sguil still references PADS for these events, but don't worry, this is certainly PRADS data. Figure 14.6 shows sample PRADS log entries.

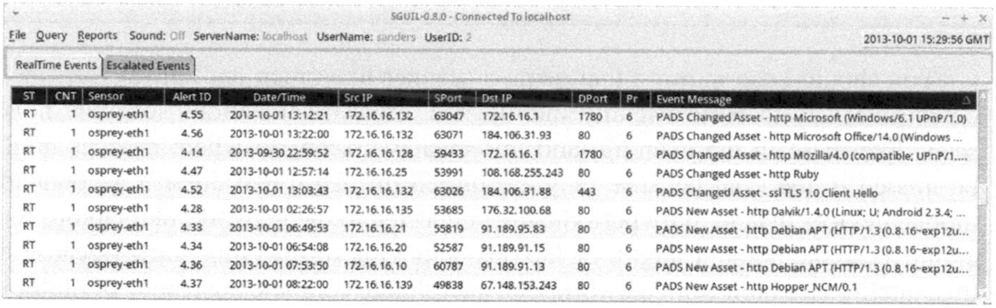

**FIGURE 14.6**

PRADS Data in Sguil

There are a couple of different types of entries shown in this image. New Asset alerts are generated when a host that hasn't been seen communicating on the network before is observed. Changed Asset alerts are generated when a host that has been seen before exhibits a communication behavior that hasn't been observed, such as a new HTTP user agent, or a new service.

To better understand how these determinations are made, let's look at an example of PRADS log data. In a default Security Onion installation, PRADS runs with a command similar to this one:

```
prads -i eth1 -c /etc/nsm/<sensor-name>/prads.conf -u sguil -g sguil -L /
nsm/sensor_data/<sensor-name>/sancp/ -f /nsm/sensor_data/<sensor-
name>/pads.fifo -b ip or (vlan and ip)
```

This arguments shown here, along with a few other useful PRADS command-line arguments are:

- -b < filter >: Listen to network traffic based upon BPFs.
- -c < config file >: The PRADS configuration file.
- -D: Run as a daemon.
- -f < file >: Logs assets to a FIFO (first in, first out) file.
- -g < group >: The group that PRADS will run as.
- -i < interface >: The interface to listen on. PRADS will default to the lowest numbered interface if this is not specified.
- -L < directory >: Logs cxtracker type output to the specified directory.
- -l < file >: Logs assets to a flat file.
- -r < file >: Read from a PCAP file instead of listening on the wire.

- -u < username >: The user that PRADS will run as.
- -v: Increase the verbosity of PRADS output.

In the case of SO, PRADS runs as the Sguil user and listens for data on the wire. Collected data is stored in a FIFO file so that it can be sucked into a database that Sguil can access.

Since most of the runtime options for PRADS in SO are configured with command-line arguments, the only real purpose that prads.conf serves is to identify the home_nets IP range variable (Figure 14.7). This variable tells PRADS which networks it should consider assets that it should monitor. In most situations you will configure this similarly to the $HOME_NET variable used by Snort or Suricata, since it is used in a similar manner.

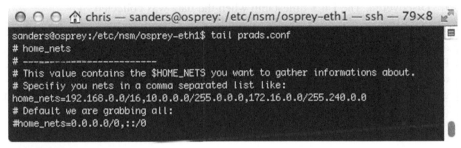

```
sanders@osprey:/etc/nsm/osprey-eth1$ tail prads.conf
# home_nets
# --------------------------------
# This value contains the $HOME_NETS you want to gather informations about.
# Specifiy you nets in a comma separated list like:
home_nets=192.168.0.0/16,10.0.0.0/255.0.0.0,172.16.0.0/255.240.0.0
# Default we are grabbing all:
#home_nets=0.0.0.0/0,::/0
```

**FIGURE 14.7**

Configuring the home_nets Variable in prads.conf

PRADS data stored in a database format is really convenient for querying asset data or writing tools that leverage this data, but it isn't the greatest for viewing it in its raw form. Fortunately, asset data is also stored as a flat text file at /var/log/prads-assets.log. A sample of this file is shown in Figure 14.8.

```
sanders@osprey:/nsm/sensor_data/osprey-eth1$ head -15 prads.log
asset,vlan,port,proto,service,[service-info],distance,discovered
172.16.16.128,0,63538,6,SYN,[65535:64:1:64:M1460,N,W4,N,N,T,S,E,E:P:unknown:unknown:link:ethernet/modem:uptime:2342hrs],0,1380640852
172.16.16.132,0,443,6,CLIENT,[unknown:@https],0,1380640853
172.16.16.140,0,443,6,CLIENT,[unknown:@https],0,1380640858
172.16.16.130,0,443,6,CLIENT,[unknown:@https],0,1380640859
172.16.16.140,0,53,17,CLIENT,[unknown:@domain],0,1380640859
172.16.16.140,0,59083,6,RST,[0:64:1:40::.:.:FreeBSD:4.8 (Linux?) (dropped)],0,1380640859
172.16.16.128,0,63538,6,SYN,[65535:64:1:48:M1460,S,E,E:P:MacOS:iPhone OS 3.1.3 (UC):link:ethernet/modem],0,1380640859
172.16.16.128,0,53,17,CLIENT,[unknown:@domain],0,1380640859
172.16.16.20,0,53,17,CLIENT,[unknown:@domain],0,1380640860
172.16.16.21,0,53,17,CLIENT,[unknown:@domain],0,1380640860
172.16.16.128,0,443,6,CLIENT,[unknown:@https],0,1380640860
172.16.16.130,0,58903,6,FIN,[8192:64:1:52:N,N,T:ATFN:unknown:unknown:uptime:955hrs],0,1380640861
172.16.16.130,0,58904,6,SYN,[65535:64:1:64:M1460,N,W4,N,N,T,S,E,E:P:unknown:unknown:link:ethernet/modem],0,1380640861
172.16.16.128,0,443,6,CLIENT,[ssl:SSL 2.0 Client Hello],0,1380640861
```

**FIGURE 14.8**

The PRADS Log File

The first line of this file defines the format for log entries. This is:

```
asset,vlan,port,proto,service,[service-info],distance,discovered
```

These fields break down as such:

- Asset: The IP address of asset in the home_nets variable that is detected
- VLAN: The VLAN tag of the asset
- Port: The port number of the detected service
- Proto: The protocol number of the detected service
- Service: The service PRADS has identified as being in use. This can involve the asset interacting the service as a CLIENT or a SERVER.
- Service Info: The fingerprint that matches the identifying service, along with its output.
- Distance: The distance to the asset based upon a guessed initial time-to-live value
- Discovered: The Unix timestamp when the data was collected

Based upon this log data, you can see that PRADS itself doesn't actually make the determination we saw earlier in Sguil of whether or not an asset is new or changed. PRADS simply logs the data it observes and leaves any additional processing to the user or other third party scripts or applications. This means that the New and Changed Asset alerts we were seeing in Sguil are actually generated by Sguil itself based on PRADS data, and not by PRADS itself.

### Making PRADS Data Actionable

There are a couple of ways that we can use PRADS for friendly intelligence. The first method is to actually use Sguil and its notification of New and Changed assets. As an example, consider Figure 14.9.

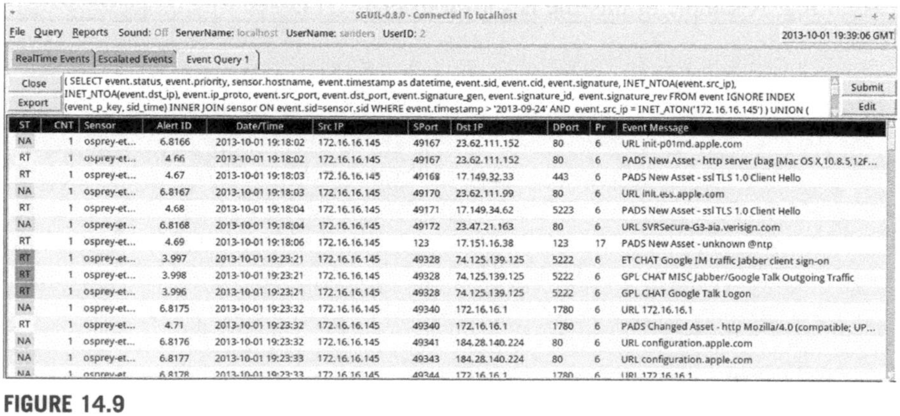

**FIGURE 14.9**

Sguil Query for a Single Host

In the figure above, I've made a Sguil query for all of the events related to a single alert. This can be done pretty easily in Sguil by right-clicking an event associated with a host, hovering over Quick Query, then Query Event Table, and selecting the SrcIP or DstIP option depending on which IP address you want events for. Here, we see a number of events associated with the host at 172.16.16.145. This includes some Snort alerts, visited URLs, and more PRADS alerts.

Of the PRADS alerts shown, there are 4 New Asset Alerts that showsthe first time this host has ever connected to each of the individual destination IP addresses listed in the alert:

- Alert ID 4.66: HTTP Connection to 23.62.111.152
- Alert ID 4.67: HTTPS Connection to 17.149.32.33
- Alert ID 4.68: HTTPS Connection to 17.149.34.62
- Alert ID 4.69: NTP Connection to 17.151.16.38

When investigating this event, this provides useful context that can help you immediately determine whether a friendly device has ever connected to a specific remote device. In a case where you are seeing suspicious traffic going to an unknown address, the fact that the friendly device has never communicated with this address before might be an indicator that something suspicious is going on, and more investigation is required.

The figure also shows 1 Change Asset Alert showing the use of a new HTTP client user agent string.

- Alert ID 4.71: Mozilla/4.0 (compatible; UPnP/1.0; Windows NT/5.1)

This type of context demonstrates that a friendly host is doing something that it has never done before. While this can mean something as simple as a user downloading a new browser, this can also be an indicator of malicious activity. You should take extra notice of devices that begin offering new services, especially when those devices are user workstations that shouldn't be acting as servers.

At this point, we have the ability to discern any new behavior or change in behavior for a friendly host, which is an incredibly powerful form of friendly intelligence. While it may take some time for PRADS to "learn" your network when you first configure it, eventually, it can provide a wealth of information that would otherwise require a fair bit of session data analysis to accomplish.

Another way to make PRADS data actionable is to use it to define a baseline asset model. Since PRADS stores all of the asset information it collects for assets defined in the home_nets variable, this data can be parsed to show all of the data it has gathered on a per host basis. This is accomplished by using the prads-asset-report script, which is a Perl script that is included with PRADS. This script will take the output from a PRADS asset log file, and output a listing of all of the information it knows about each IP address. If you are using PRADS to log data to /var/log/prads-asset.log, then you can simply run the command prads-asset-report to generate this data. Otherwise, you can specify the location of PRADS asset data by using the − r < file > argument. A sample of this data is shown in Figure 14.10.

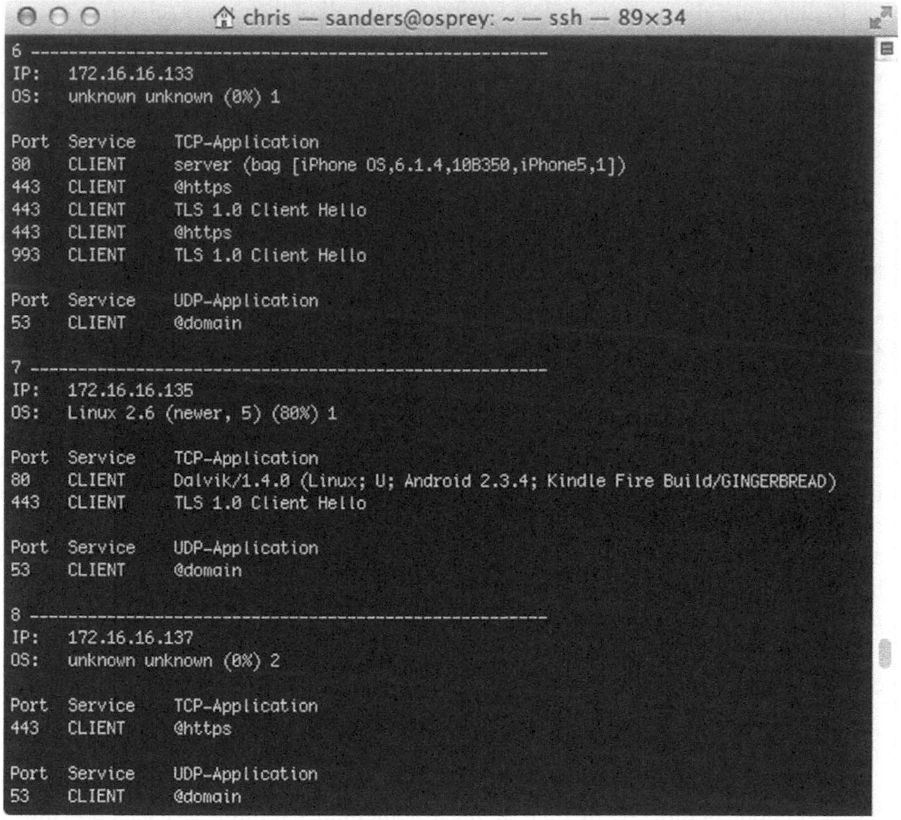

**FIGURE 14.10**

PRADS Asset Report Data

Notice in this output that PRADS also makes its best guess at the operating system architecture of each device. In the figure above, it can only identify a single device. PRADS is able to guess more accurately the more it can observe devices communicating on the network.

In some cases it might make the most sense to generate this report regularly and provide it in a format where analysts can access and search it easily. You can save the file that this script generates by adding the −w < filename > argument. In other cases, analysts might have direct access to the PRADS log data, which means they can use the prads-asset-report script itself to generate near real-time data. This can be done on the basis of an individual IP address, using the −i switch like this:

```
prads-asset-data -i 172.16.16.145
```

The output of this command is shown in Figure 14.11.

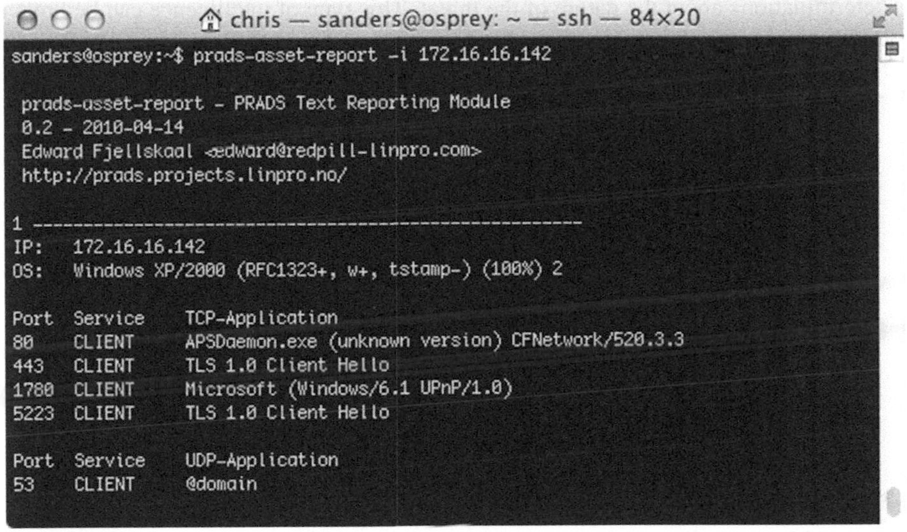

```
  ○ ○ ○        ⌂ chris — sanders@osprey: ~ — ssh — 84×20

sanders@osprey:~$ prads-asset-report -i 172.16.16.142

prads-asset-report - PRADS Text Reporting Module
0.2 - 2010-04-14
Edward Fjellskaal <edward@redpill-linpro.com>
http://prads.projects.linpro.no/


1 _____
IP:    172.16.16.142
OS:    Windows XP/2000 (RFC1323+, w+, tstamp-) (100%) 2


Port  Service   TCP-Application
80    CLIENT    APSDaemon.exe (unknown version) CFNetwork/520.3.3
443   CLIENT    TLS 1.0 Client Hello
1780  CLIENT    Microsoft (Windows/6.1 UPnP/1.0)
5223  CLIENT    TLS 1.0 Client Hello


Port  Service   UDP-Application
53    CLIENT    @domain
```

**FIGURE 14.11**

Searching for Individual IP Addresses in PRADS Asset Data

When generating an asset model from PRADS, remember it is a passive tool that can only report on devices it sees communicate across a sensor boundary. This means that devices that only communicate within a particular network segment and never talk upstream through a link that a sensor is monitoring will never be observed by PRADS. Because of this, you should pair PRADS with another technique like active scanning to ensure that you are accurately defining network assets.

PRADS is an incredibly powerful but eloquently simple tool that can be used to build friendly intelligence. Because of its minimal requirements and flexibility, it can find its way into most SOC environments. You can read more about PRADS at http://gamelinux.github.io/prads/.

## GENERATING THREAT INTELLIGENCE

Once you know your network, you are prepared to begin to know your adversary. With this in mind, we begin to dive into threat intelligence. If you work in information security then you are no stranger to this term. With the prevalence of targeted attacks occurring daily, most every vendor claims to offer a solution that will allow you to "generate threat intelligence to stop the APT." While this is typically a bunch of vendor sales garbage gone awry, the generation of threat intelligence is a critical component of analysis in NSM, and pivotal for the success of a SOC.

Threat intelligence is a subset of intelligence as we defined it earlier in this chapter. This subset focuses exclusively on the hostile component of that definition, and seeks to gather data to support the creation of an intelligence product that can be used to make determinations about the nature of the threat. This type of intelligence can be broken down into three sub categories: strategic, operational, and tactical threat intelligence (Figure 14.12).

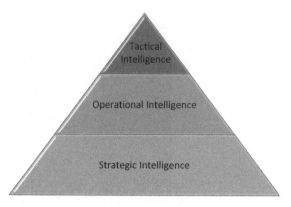

**FIGURE 14.12**

Types of Threat Intelligence

Strategic Intelligence is information related to the strategy, policy, and plans of an attacker at a high level. Typically, intelligence collection and analysis at this level only occurs by government or military organizations in response to threats from other governments or militaries. With that said, larger organizations are now developing these capabilities, and some of these organizations now sell strategic intelligence as a service. This is focused on the long-term goals of the force supporting the individual attacker or unit. Artifacts of this type of intelligence can include policy documents, war doctrine, position statements, and government, military, or group objectives.

Operational Intelligence is information related to how an attacker or group of attackers plans and supports the operations that support strategic objectives. This is different from strategic intelligence because it focuses on narrower goals, often more timed for short-term objectives that are only a part of the big picture. While this is, once again, usually more within the purview of government or military organizations, it is common that individual organizations will fall victim to attackers who are performing actions aimed at satisfying operational goals. Because of this, some public organizations will have visibility into these attacks, with an ability to generate operational intelligence. Artifacts of this type of intelligence are similar, but often more focused versions of artifacts used for the creation of strategic intelligence.

Tactical Intelligence refers to the information regarding specific actions taken in conducting operations at the mission or task level. This is where we dive into the tools, tactics, and procedures used by an attacker, and where 99% of SOCs performing NSM will focus their efforts. It is here that the individual actions of an attacker or group of attackers are analyzed and collected. This often includes artifacts such as indicators of compromise (IP addresses, file names, text strings) or listings of attacker specific tools. This intelligence is the most transient, and becomes outdated quickly.

---

**FROM THE TRENCHES**

The discussion of threat intelligence often leads to a discussion of attribution, where the actions of an adversary are actually tied back to a physical person or group. It is important to realize that detection and attribution aren't the same thing, and because of this, detection indicators and attribution indicators aren't the same thing. Detection involves discovering incidents, where as attribution involves tying those incidents back to an actual person or group. While attribution is most certainly a positive thing, it cannot be done successfully without the correlation of strategic, operational, and tactical intelligence data. Generally speaking, this type of intelligence collection and analysis capability is not present within most private sector organizations without an incredibly large amount of visibility or data sharing from other organizations. The collection of indicators of compromise from multiple network attacks to generate tactical intelligence is an achievable goal. However, collecting and analyzing data from other traditional sources such as human intelligence (HUMINT), signals intelligence (SIGINT), and geospatial intelligence (GEOINT) isn't within the practical capability of most businesses. Furthermore, even organizations that might have this practical capability are often limited in their actions by law.

---

When analyzing tactical intelligence, the threat will typically begin as an IP address that shows up in an IDS alert or some other detection mechanism. Other times, it may manifest as a suspicious file downloaded by a client. Tactical threat intelligence is generated by researching this data and tying it together in an investigation. The remainder of this chapter is devoted to providing strategies for generating tactical threat intelligence about adversarial items that typically manifest in an NSM environment.

## Researching Hostile Hosts

When an alert is generated for suspicious communication between a friendly host and a potentially hostile host, one of the steps an analyst should take is to generate tactical threat intelligence related to the potentially hostile host. After all, the most the IDS alert will typically provide you with is the host's IP address and a sample of the communication that tripped the alert. In this section we will look at information that can be gained from having only the host's IP address or a domain name.

### Internal Data Sources

The quickest way to obtain information about external and potentially hostile hosts is to examine the internal data sources you already have available. If you are concerned about a potentially hostile host, this is likely because it has already communicated with one of your hosts. If that is the case, then you should have collected some of this data. The questions you want to answer with this data are:

1. Has the hostile host ever communicated with this friendly host before?
2. What is the nature of this host's communication with the friendly host?
3. Has the hostile host ever communicated with other friendly hosts on the network?

The answers to these questions can lie within different data sources.

Question 1 can be answered easily if you have the appropriate friendly intelligence available, such as the PRADS data we examined earlier. With this in place, you should be able to determine if this is the first time these hosts began communicating, or if it occurred at an earlier time. You might even be able to determine the operating system architecture of the host. If this data isn't available, then session data is probably the quickest way to get this answer.

Question 2 is something that can only be answered by a data source with a higher level of granularity. While session data can tell you some basics of when the communication occurred and the ports that are in use, it doesn't provide the depth necessary to accurately describe exactly what is occurring. In some cases, the detection tool that generated the initial alert will provide this detail. Snort and Suricata will typically provide the offending packet that tripped one of their signatures, and tools like Bro will provide as much additional data as you've configured it to. In other scenarios, you may need to look to FPC data or PSTR data to find answers. In these cases, packet analysis skills will come in handy.

Answering Question 3 will typically begin with session data, as it is the quickest way to get information pertaining to communication records between hosts. With that said, if you find that communication has occurred between the hostile host and other friendly devices then you will probably want to turn to another data source like FPC or PSTR data to determine the exact nature of the communication. If this data isn't available, then PRADS data is another way to arrive at an answer.

The internal analysis performed at this level is all about connecting the dots and looking for patterns. At a high level, these patterns might include a hostile host communicating with devices using a specific service, at specific time intervals, or in conjunction with other real world or technical events. At a more granular level, you might find patterns that indicate the hostile host is using a custom C2 protocol, or that the communication is responsible for several clients downloading suspicious files from other hosts.

The combined answers to these three questions will help you build threat intelligence surrounding the behaviors of the hostile host on your network. Often, analyzing the behavior of the hostile host in relation to a single event or communication sequence won't provide the evidence necessary to further an investigation, but that same analysis applied to communication across the network could be the key to determining whether an incident has occurred.

### Open Source Intelligence

Once you've looked inward, it is time to examine other available intelligence sources. Open source intelligence (OSINT) is a classification given to intelligence that is collected from publicly available resources. In NSM, this typically refers to intelligence gathered from open websites. The key distinction with OSINT is that it allows you to gather information about a hostile entity without ever directly sending packets to them.

Now we will look at a few websites that can be used to perform OSINT research related to IP addresses, domain names, and malicious files. This is a broad topic with a variety of different approaches, and the topic of OSINT research could easily have its own book. If you'd like a much more detailed list of websites that can be used to perform OSINT research, then check out http://www.appliednsm.com/osint-resources.

### IP and Domain Registration

The International Assigned Numbers Authority (IANA) is a department of the Internet Corporation for Assigned Names and Numbers (ICANN) that is responsible for overseeing the allocation of IP addresses, autonomous system number (ASN) allocation, DNS root zone management, and more. IANA delegates the allocation of addresses based upon region, to 5 individual Regional Internet Registries (RIRs). These organizations are responsible for maintaining records that associate each IP address with its registered owner. They are listed in Table 14.1.

**Table 14.1** Regional Internet Registries

| RIR Name | Abbreviation | Service | Website |
| --- | --- | --- | --- |
| African Network Information Centre | AfriNIC | Continental Africa | http://www.afrinic.net/ |
| American Registry for Internet Numbers | ARIN | United States, Canada, parts of the Caribbean region, and Antarctica | https://www.arin.net/ |
| Asia-Pacific Netowrk Information Centre | APNIC | Asia, Australia, New Zealand, and neighboring countries | http://www.apnic.net/ |
| Latin America and Caribbean Network Information Centre | LACNIC | Latin America and parts of the Caribbean region | http://www.lacnic.net/ |
| Reseaux IP Europeens Network Coordination Centre | RIPE NCC | Europe, Russia, the Middle East, and Central Asia | http://www.ripe.net/ |

Each of these registries allows you to query them for the registration records associated with an IP address. Figure 14.13 shows the results from querying the ARIN database for the registration records associated with an IP address in the 50.128.0.0/9 range. This was done from http://whois.arin.net/ui/advanced.jsp.

In this case, we can see that this block of IP addresses is allocated to Comcast. We can also click on links that will provide contact information for representatives at this organization, including abuse, technical, and administrative Points of Contact (POCs). This is useful when you detect a hostile device in IP space that is owned by a reputable company attempting to break into your network. In a lot of cases this will indicate that the hostile device has been compromised by another adversary and is being used as a hop point for launching an attack. When this occurs, it's a common practice to notify the abuse contact for the organization that the attack appears to be coming from.

| Network | |
| --- | --- |
| NetRange | 50.128.0.0 - 50.255.255.255 |
| CIDR | 50.128.0.0/9 |
| Name | CCCH3-4 |
| Handle | NET-50-128-0-0-1 |
| Parent | NET50 (NET-50-0-0-0-0) |
| Net Type | Direct Allocation |
| Origin AS | AS7922 |
| Organization | Comcast Cable Communications Holdings, Inc (CCCH-3) |
| Registration Date | 2010-10-21 |
| Last Updated | 2010-10-21 |
| Comments | |
| RESTful Link | http://whois.arin.net/rest/net/NET-50-128-0-0-1 |
| See Also | Related POC records. |
| See Also | Related organization's POC records. |
| See Also | Related delegations. |

**FIGURE 14.13**

Querying the ARIN RIR

---

**FROM THE TRENCHES**

Notifying other organizations that one of their hosts might be compromised can be a bit of a struggle sometimes. In some cases, the organization won't believe you, and in some more extreme scenarios, the organization might even accuse you of taking some type of adversarial action against them. Because this is a delicate process, there is proper etiquette involved in notifying someone else that their network might be compromised. This article written by Tom Liston for the SANS Internet Storm Center provides a good overview of some lessons learned from this process: http://www.dshield.org/diary.html?storyid=9325.

---

In a lot of cases, you will find that an IP address is registered to an ISP. In that case, you may have luck contacting the ISP if someone on their IP address space is attempting to attack your network, but in most cases I've experienced, this isn't usually very fruitful. This is especially true when dealing with ISP's outside of the jurisdiction of the US.

Because IP addresses are divided amongst the 5 RIR's, you won't necessarily know which one is responsible for a specific IP until you search for it. Fortunately, if you search for an IP address at an RIR's website and the RIR isn't responsible for that IP address, it will point you towards the correct RIR so that you can complete your search there. Another solution is to use a service that will make this determination for you, like Robtex, which we will look at in a moment.

Another useful piece of information that the registry record gives us is the Autonomous System Number (ASN) associated with the IP address. An ASN is a number used to identify a single network or group of networks controlled by a common entity. These are commonly assigned to ISPs, large corporations, or universities. While two IP address might be registered to two different entities, their sharing the same ASN might allow you to conclude that there is some relationship between the two addresses, though this is something to be evaluated on a case-by-case basis. You can search for ASN information specifically from each registry.

Just like with IP addresses, researching domain names usually begins with finding the registered owner of the domain. However, it is important to remember to distinguish between an actual physical host and a domain name. IP space is finite and exists with certain limitations. In general, if you see an IP address in your logs then you can usually assume that the data you have collected in relation to that host actually did come from that IP address (at least, for session-oriented communication). You can also have a reasonable amount of faith that the IP address does exist under the ownership of the entity that registered it, even though that machine might have been compromised and be controlled by someone else.

A domain name serves as a pointer to a location. When you see a domain name in your logs, usually because one of your friendly hosts is accessing that domain in some way, the truth is that the domain can be configured to point to any address at any given time. This means that the domain name you are researching from yesterday's logs might point to a different IP address now. For that matter, the domain you research now may not point to anything later. It is common for attackers to compromise a host and then reassign domain names to the IP addresses of those hosts to serve malware or act in another malicious capacity. When the owner of that host discovers that it has been compromised and eradicates the attacker's presence, the attacker will reassign the domain name to another compromised IP address. Even further to this point, malware now has the ability to use domain name generation algorithms to randomly register domains that can be used for command and control. Because of all this, a domain isn't compromised; the IP address the domain points to is compromised. However, a domain name can be used for malicious purposes. This should be considered when researching potentially malicious domain names.

With that said, domain name registration is managed by ICANN, who delegates this authority to domain name registries. Whenever someone registers a domain name, they are required to provide contact information that is associated with this domain. Unfortunately, this process usually involves very little verification, so there is nothing to say that the domain registration information for any particular domain is actually valid. Furthermore, a lot of registries provide anonymous registration services, where they will mask the actual registered owner of the domain and provide their own information. With that said, there are plenty of instances where useful information can be obtained from domain name registration.

Domain information can be queried in a number of ways. One way is to simply pick any domain name registry such as GoDaddy or Network Solutions and perform a whois query from their website. Another method is to use the whois command from a Unix command line (Figure 14.14). This uses the simple syntax:

```
whois <domain name>
```

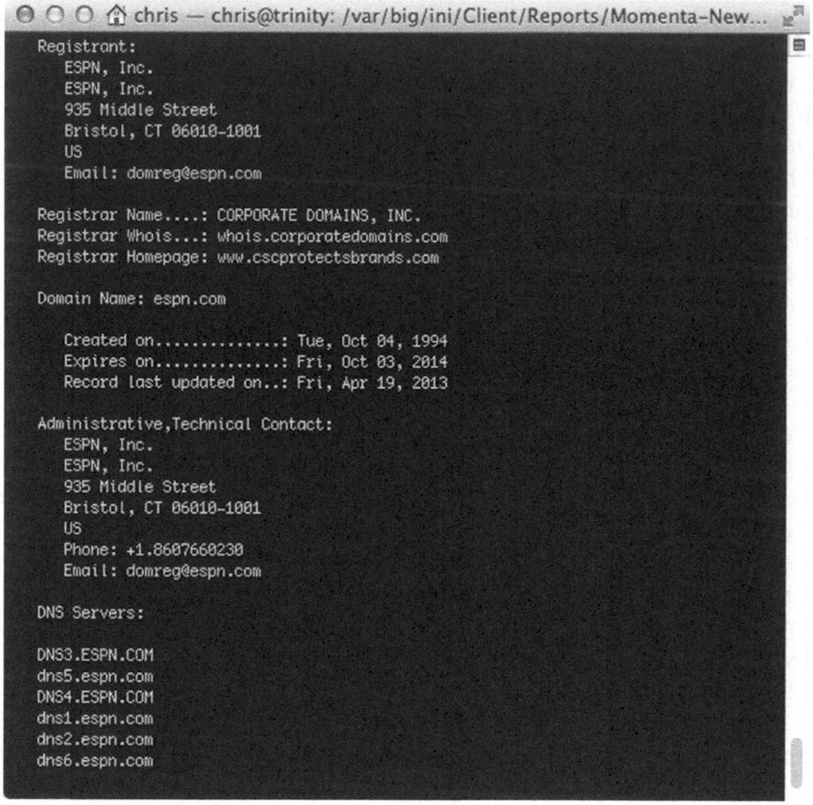

```
⊖ ⊖ ⊖  ⌂ chris — chris@trinity: /var/big/ini/Client/Reports/Momenta-New...

Registrant:
    ESPN, Inc.
    ESPN, Inc.
    935 Middle Street
    Bristol, CT 06010-1001
    US
    Email: domreg@espn.com

Registrar Name....: CORPORATE DOMAINS, INC.
Registrar Whois...: whois.corporatedomains.com
Registrar Homepage: www.cscprotectsbrands.com

Domain Name: espn.com

    Created on.............: Tue, Oct 04, 1994
    Expires on.............: Fri, Oct 03, 2014
    Record last updated on..: Fri, Apr 19, 2013

Administrative,Technical Contact:
    ESPN, Inc.
    ESPN, Inc.
    935 Middle Street
    Bristol, CT 06010-1001
    US
    Phone: +1.8607660230
    Email: domreg@espn.com

DNS Servers:

DNS3.ESPN.COM
dns5.espn.com
DNS4.ESPN.COM
dns1.espn.com
dns2.espn.com
dns6.espn.com
```

**FIGURE 14.14**

Whois Query Results for ESPN.com

You can see that this tells us the registrant information, as well as a few other useful pieces of information. The registration dates can be helpful in determining the validity of a domain. If you suspect that a domain you've seen one of your hosts communicating with is hosting malicious content and you find that the domain was registered only a couple of days ago, this would indicate a higher potential for malicious activity actually occurring.

This output also lists the DNS servers associated with the domain, which can be used to find correlation between multiple suspicious domains. You can also use some additional DNS Kung Fu to attempt various techniques (like zone transfers) to enumerate subdomains and DNS host names, but this isn't recommended in most instances since it will involve actually interacting with potential DNS servers. If you want to know more about doing this, there are a fair number of guides on the Internet, as well as videos at http://www.securitytube.net.

Rather than going around to all of these different websites in order to research IP addresses and domain name registration information, I tend to use publicly available websites that will provide all of this information at a single stop. One of my favorites is Robtex (http://www.robtex.com). Robtex provides a lot of useful information, including everything we've discussed up until this point summarized in a very useful interface. In Figure 14.15 I've done a search for espn.com and browsed Robtex's Records tab.

**FIGURE 14.15**

Robtex's Records Tab

In this image, you can see that Robtex provides all of the DNS information that was obtained, the associated IP addresses, and the ASN's tied to those IP addresses. The interface provided help to quickly build a picture that an analyst can use quickly.

---

**CAUTION**

In this chapter we discuss a lot of web-based services that collect or provide OSINT information. While these sites can be useful, you should always be aware of exactly how they interact with the information you give them in relation to the hostile IP or domain. Some of these services will interact with the IP address or domain you are researching for one reason or another, and the last thing you want is for them to disclose your IP address to the potentially hostile host. I've seen plenty of scenarios where web services will forward the requesting client's IP address in those requests in an HTTP header. You can test for this type of functionality by using these tools against your own network or a test network and then analyzing the data associated with the connections from the web service.

---

## IP and Domain Reputation

In Chapter 8, we discussed IP and domain reputation at length. While reputation can be useful for detection, it is also immensely useful for analysis. If an IP address or domain has been associated with malicious activity in the past, then there is a good chance that it might be associated with malicious activity in the present.

I listed a few of my favorite sources of reputation information for detection purposes in Chapter 8. Those sites were optimized for detection because they generate lists that can be fed into detection mechanisms. Those sites can also be used for analysis of IP addresses and domain names, but I won't rehash those here. Instead, I'll discuss a couple of my other favorite reputation websites that are more suited for post-detection analysis: IPVoid and URLVoid.

IPVoid (http://www.ipvoid.com/) and URLVoid (http://www.urlvoid.com/) are two sites that were developed as free services by a company called NoVirusThanks. These services connect to multiple other reputation lists (including a few of those discussed in this book) and provide results that indicate whether or not the IP or domain you've entered is found on any of those lists. Figures 14.16 and 14.17 show example output from both services.

**Domain Information**

| | |
|---|---|
| Analyzed On | 2013-10-03 15:29 GMT |
| Website Address | ████████.eu |
| Blacklist Status | BLACKLISTED |
| Detection Ratio | 3 / 28 (11 %) |
| Domain 1st Registered | Unknown |
| Google Page Rank | PAGE RANK 4 |
| Alexa Rank | Unknown |

**Website Blacklist Report**

| Engine | Status | Info |
|---|---|---|
| SCUMWARE | ⚠ DETECTED | ↗ |
| B BitDefender | ⚠ DETECTED | ↗ |
| ⟨⟩ GoogleSafeBrowsing | ⚠ DETECTED | ↗ |
| S SpamhausDBL | ✓ NOT FOUND | ↗ |
| MyWOT | ✓ NOT FOUND | ↗ |
| MalwareDomainList | ✓ NOT FOUND | ↗ |

**FIGURE 14.16**

URLVoid Output Excerpt

**IP Blacklist Report**

| Engine | Status | Info |
|---|---|---|
| TornevallNET | ⚠ DETECTED | ↗ |
| Spamhaus | ⚠ DETECTED | ↗ |
| DNSBL_AbuseCH | ⚠ DETECTED | ↗ |
| SpamCop | ⚠ DETECTED | ↗ |
| PSBL | ⚠ DETECTED | ↗ |
| WPBL | ⚠ DETECTED | ↗ |
| ProjectHoneypot | ⚠ DETECTED | ↗ |
| CBL_AbuseAt | ⚠ DETECTED | ↗ |
| SORBS | ⚠ DETECTED | ↗ |
| NiX_Spam | ⚠ DETECTED | ↗ |
| Swinog_DNSRBL | ⚠ DETECTED | ↗ |
| BlockList_de | ✓ NOT FOUND | ↗ |
| MyWOT | ✓ NOT FOUND | ↗ |

**FIGURE 14.17**

IPVoid Output Excerpt

In both outputs, the services will provide a header with basic information about the IP or domain, along with a statistic of the number of blacklists that match your search. In the case of Figure 14.16 you can see that the domain was found on 3/28 (11%) of the blacklists that were searched by URLVoid. Those 3 blacklists are listed at the top of the report, and each blacklist has a link in the Info column that will take you directly to the reference to this domain name at those sites. The output shown in Figure 14.17 has had the IP address information from IPVoid trimmed off for size, but shows several of the IP blacklist services that are used.

IPVoid and URLVoid are a great one-stop shop for determining whether an IP address or domain has found its way onto a reputation blacklist somewhere. While this isn't always a clear-cut indicator of malicious activity, it frequently points in that direction.

When performing analysis, keep in mind that sometimes multiple domains exist on a single IP address. While you may find that a single domain appears on multiple public blacklists, that doesn't necessarily mean that every other domain whose content is hosted on the same IP address is also malicious. This is especially true of shared hosting servers. On these servers, it is typically a web application flaw that results in one site being compromised. More often than not, this compromised is limited to just the affected domain. With that said, there are certainly exceptions to this line of thought, but this is something you should keep in mind when analyzing IP and domain reputation.

One way to quickly identify domains that are hosted on an IP address while ensuring that you aren't communicating with any remote DNS servers yourself is to use the Domains by IP service (http://www.domainsbyip.com/). The output of this tool is shown in Figure 14.18.

**FIGURE 14.18**

Results of a Domain by IP Query

In the image above, the results tell us that four different domains are hosted on this IP address. This looks like it is probably a shared hosting server based upon the number of domains with no clear link between them. We can also see that the service provides a listing of "nearby" IP addresses. These are addresses that are numerically close to the IP address we searched for, and also host domains. This service is very useful, but it isn't all-inclusive, so your mileage may vary when using it.

Now that we've looked at a few ways to get OSINT information on hosts, let's look at OSINT sources for files.

## Researching Hostile Files

After IP addresses and host names, the next most common artifacts you will encounter while performing NSM analysis are files. Sometimes this might just be a file name, other times it could include an MD5 hash, and in the best of scenarios you may have access to the entire file. Suspicious files are usually observed being downloaded from suspicious hosts, or in relation to an alert generated by a detection mechanism, such as an IDS. Regardless of how much of this information you have or where it came from, intelligence related to files can be used to build tactical intelligence about the threat you are investigating.

---

**FROM THE TRENCHES**

There are a number of ways to pull suspicious files off the wire. If you know of certain file types you want to pull of the wire in real time, then you can use Bro for this task. We talk about how to do this in Chapter 10. If you are performing an investigation and have access to full packet capture data, then you can use a tool like Wireshark to pull files out of a communication stream. This is discussed in Chapter 13.

---

### Open Source Intelligence

Just like with host intelligence, there are a number of sources available on the Internet that can be used for researching suspicious files. Let's take a look at a few of these resources.

If you have the actual file that you suspect to be malicious, the easiest thing to do is perform a behavioral analysis of this file. This is something that can be done in house, but if you don't have that capability, you may be better off submitting the file to an online malware sandbox. These sandboxes allow users to submit files and automatically perform a behavioral analysis based upon the changes the malware makes to the system and the type of actions it tries to take. Let's take a look at a few of these sandboxes.

---

**CAUTION**

A large number of public malware sandboxes index the malware you submit so that other people can search for it. This saves processing cycles on the sandbox itself, so that it doesn't have to reanalyze the file if someone else submits the same thing. While this helps the site owners save resources, it can be an operational security concern. If normal users can search for malware on public sandboxes, then so can the individuals or groups who create the malware. In a targeted situation, it may be possible that the adversary has created a strain of malware specifically targeted at your organization. At that point, the adversary can do periodic queries against public sandboxes for the file name or MD5 hash of that malware. If the malware shows up in their search results, they will know that you have found the malware and that they need to change their tactics or create new malware that is harder to detect. This should be considered before submitting malware to a public site, especially if you work in a high security environment that is often the target of attacks.

---

### Virustotal

Perhaps the easiest way to determine if a file is malicious is to run an antivirus tool against it. Unfortunately, the detection rate for antivirus in the modern security landscape is very low, and the chances that a single antivirus product will be able to detect a strain of malware are 50/50 or less. Because of this, the chances of detecting malware are increased by submitting a malware sample to multiple antivirus engines. It isn't entirely feasible to configure a single system with multiple AV engines, nor is it cheap to license it. However, there is an online solution called VirusTotal.

VirusTotal (http://www.virustotal.com) is a free service that was bought by Google in 2012, and analyzes suspicious files and URLs using multiple antivirus engines. There are multiple ways to submit files to VirusTotal, including their website, by e-mail, or by any tool that uses their API. My preferred mechanism is their Google Chrome extension. Once you submit the file, VirusTotal will perform its analysis and generate a report indicating which antivirus engines detected a match for the file or its content, and the name of the string(s) that match.

An example of this output is shown in Figure 14.19. As of now, VirusTotal currently supports 49 different antivirus engines, including all of those from the larger and more popular antivirus providers.

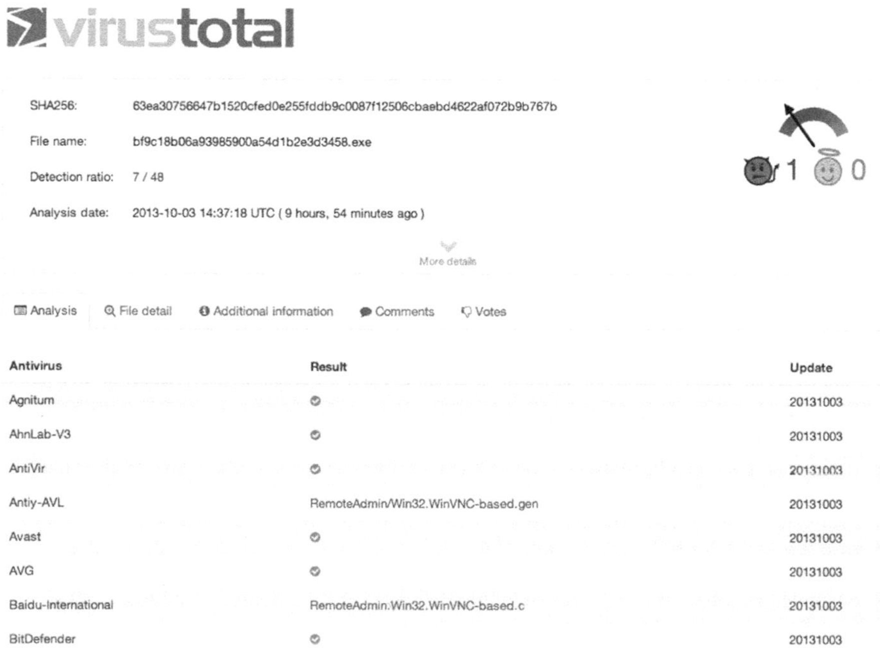

| SHA256: | 63ea30756647b1520cfed0e255fddb9c0087f12506cbaebd4622af072b9b767b |
| File name: | bf9c18b06a93985900a54d1b2e3d3458.exe |
| Detection ratio: | 7 / 48 |
| Analysis date: | 2013-10-03 14:37:18 UTC ( 9 hours, 54 minutes ago ) |

More details

Analysis    File detail    Additional information    Comments    Votes

| Antivirus | Result | Update |
| --- | --- | --- |
| Agnitum | | 20131003 |
| AhnLab-V3 | | 20131003 |
| AntiVir | | 20131003 |
| Antiy-AVL | RemoteAdmin/Win32.WinVNC-based.gen | 20131003 |
| Avast | | 20131003 |
| AVG | | 20131003 |
| Baidu-International | RemoteAdmin.Win32.WinVNC-based.c | 20131003 |
| BitDefender | | 20131003 |

**FIGURE 14.19**

A Sample VirusTotal Report

In the example above, you can see that this report indicates the file that was submitted was detected as malware by 7 out of 48 different antivirus engines. Two of the engines that detected this are shown; the antiy-AVL and Baidu-International engines. They both detect this file as some sort of VNC-based application, which can be used to remotely control a system. The meter at the top right of the screen shows an indication of whether the file is actually malicious based upon the number of matches and a few other factors. In this case, it thinks that the file we've submitted is probably malicious.

While VirusTotal doesn't share submitted samples publicly, it does share samples that match at least one antivirus engine with antivirus companies. Keep this in mind when submitting files that might be highly sensitive or involved in targeted attacks.

### Cuckoo Sandbox and Malwr.com

One of the most popular sandbox environments for malware analysis is Cuckoo. Cuckoo (http://www.cuckoosandbox.org) will launch an instance of a virtual machine, execute malware, and perform a variety of analysis tasks. This includes recording the changes and actions the malware makes, any changes to the system that occur, Windows API calls, and files that are created or deleted. Beyond this, Cuckoo can also create a full memory dump of the system or selected processes, and takes screenshots of the virtual machine as the malware is executing. All of this goes into a final report that Cuckoo can generate. Cuckoo is designed around a modular system that allows the user to customize exactly what occurs during the processing of malware and the reporting of findings.

Cuckoo sandbox is a tool that you can download and deploy internally, and one that I've seen used successfully in a lot of environments. However, this section is about online malware analysis sandboxes, and that is what exists at http://www.malwr.com. Malwr is a website that utilizes Cuckoo to perform malware analysis services for free. It is operated as a non-commercial site that is run by volunteer security professionals with the exclusive intent to help the community. The files you submit are not shared publicly or privately unless you specify that this is allowed when you submit.

Figures 14.20 and 14.21 shows an excerpt of a Cuckoo report from Malwr.

In these figures, the first image shows Cuckoo providing information about signatures that the malware has matched, indicating that those sections of the report should be examined in more detail. This also shows screenshots from the virtual machine where the malware was executed. Figure 14.21 shows results form the behavioral analysis performed by Cuckoo. In this case, we see some of the actions taken by the file mypcbackup0529.exe.

Malwr publishes shared analysis reports on its home page, so you can go there and view these reports to get a real idea of the power that Cuckoo provides. You can also search these reports based on the MD5 hash of a malware sample to see if a report already exists for the file. This will get you to the results you want to see faster without waiting for analysis to be completed.

**Signatures**

Starts servers listening on 0.0.0.0:0

File has been identified by at least one AntiVirus on VirusTotal as malicious

Performs some HTTP requests

Retrieves Windows ProductID, probably to fingerprint the sandbox

Collects information to fingerprint the system (MachineGuid, DigitalProductId, SystemBiosDate)

**Screenshots**

**FIGURE 14.20**

Cuckoo Report Showing Matching Signatures and Screenshots

- **mypcbackup0529.exe** 1088
  - **BackupSetup.exe** 376
    - **dotnetfx.exe** 180
      - **setup.exe** 1928
        - **clwireg.exe** 1244

mypcbackup0529.exe    BackupSetup.exe    dotnetfx.exe    setup.exe    clwireg.exe

mypcbackup0529.exe, PID: **1088**, Parent PID: 1824

1  2  3  ...  80

network   filesystem   registry   process   services   synchronization

| TIME | API | ARGUMENTS | STATUS | RETURN | REPEATED |
|------|-----|-----------|--------|--------|----------|
| 2013-10-03 04:54:58,143 | **LdrGetDllHandle** | FileName: C:\WINDOWS\system32\rpcss.dll ModuleHandle: 0x00000000 | failed | 0xc0000135 | 1 time |
| 2013-10-03 04:54:58,143 | **DeviceIoControl** | DeviceHandle: 0x00000048 IoControlCode: 3735560 InBuffer: E\x10p\xeb-~X2\xcb\xaa\x97I\xbe\x16g\xfd,YA6L | success | 0x00000001 | |

**FIGURE 14.21**

Cuckoo Report Showing Behavioral Analysis Results

If you have the capacity to do so, setting up a Cuckoo sandbox internally is a useful venture for any SOC or NSM environment. The setup is a bit long and complicated, but that provides much more flexibility than you will find from the online service, including the ability to customize analysis routines and reporting. I think that you will find that Cuckoo is a very full-featured malware analysis sandbox that can come in handy in a variety of situations during daily analysis.

### ThreatExpert

ThreatExpert is another online sandbox that provides similar functionality to Cuckoo and Malwr. ThreatExpert (http://www.threatexpert.com) allows for the submission of suspicious files via its website. It will execute submitted files in a sandbox environment to perform a limited behavioral analysis of the file. The end result of this analysis is a report that details the actions that the suspicious file took in relation to the file system, system registry, and more. Figures 14.22 and 14.23 show excerpts from a ThreatExpert Report.

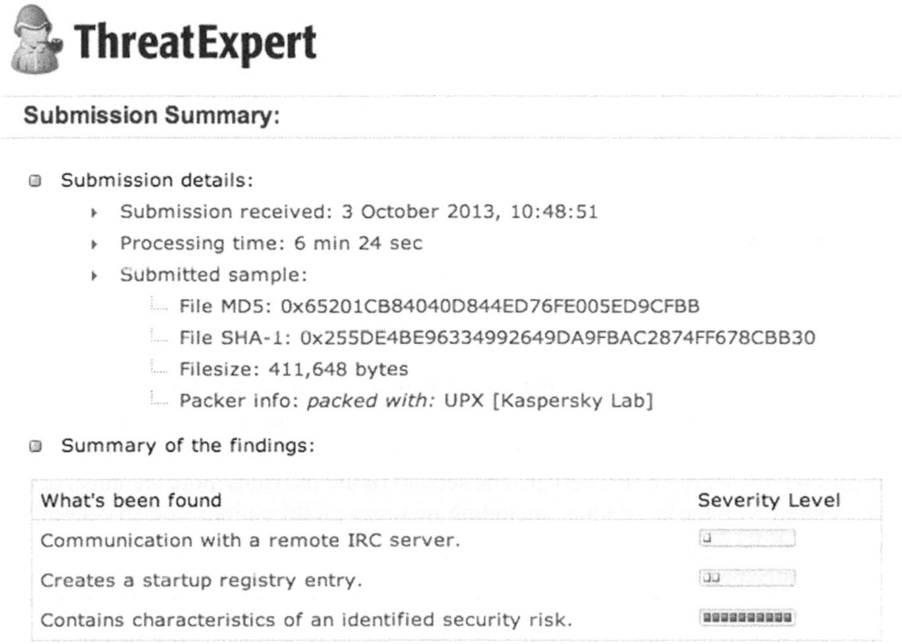

**Submission Summary:**

- Submission details:
  - ▸ Submission received: 3 October 2013, 10:48:51
  - ▸ Processing time: 6 min 24 sec
  - ▸ Submitted sample:
    - File MD5: 0x65201CB84040D844ED76FE005ED9CFBB
    - File SHA-1: 0x255DE4BE96334992649DA9FBAC2874FF678CBB30
    - Filesize: 411,648 bytes
    - Packer info: *packed with:* UPX [Kaspersky Lab]

- Summary of the findings:

| What's been found | Severity Level |
| --- | --- |
| Communication with a remote IRC server. | |
| Creates a startup registry entry. | |
| Contains characteristics of an identified security risk. | |

**FIGURE 14.22**

ThreatExpert Report Submission Summary

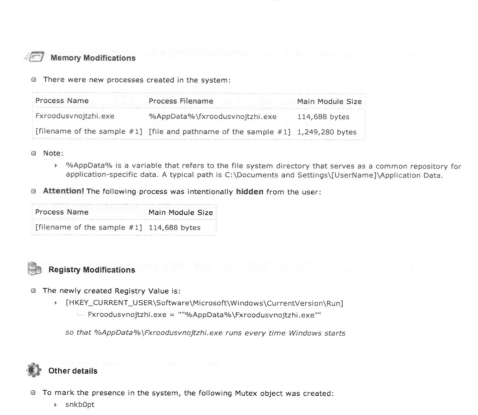

**Memory Modifications**

There were new processes created in the system:

| Process Name | Process Filename | Main Module Size |
|---|---|---|
| Fxroodusvnojtzhi.exe | %AppData%\fxroodusvnojtzhi.exe | 114,688 bytes |
| [filename of the sample #1] | [file and pathname of the sample #1] | 1,249,280 bytes |

Note:

▸ %AppData% is a variable that refers to the file system directory that serves as a common repository for application-specific data. A typical path is C:\Documents and Settings\[UserName]\Application Data.

**Attention!** The following process was intentionally **hidden** from the user:

| Process Name | Main Module Size |
|---|---|
| [filename of the sample #1] | 114,688 bytes |

**Registry Modifications**

The newly created Registry Value is:

▸ [HKEY_CURRENT_USER\Software\Microsoft\Windows\CurrentVersion\Run]
    └ Fxroodusvnojtzhi.exe = ""%AppData%\Fxroodusvnojtzhi.exe""

*so that %AppData%\Fxroodusvnojtzhi.exe runs every time Windows starts*

**Other details**

To mark the presence in the system, the following Mutex object was created:
▸ snkb0pt

The following port was open in the system:

| Port | Protocol | Process |
|---|---|---|
| 1033 | TCP | Fxroodusvnojtzhi.exe (%AppData%\Fxroodusvnojtzhi.exe) |

**FIGURE 14.23**

ThreatExpert Report Detailing Multiple Actions

In the first image, we can see that the file that was submitted appears to be packed with UPX, and that ThreatExpert thinks that this file contain characteristics that represent a security risk, including the creation of a startup registry entry, and communication with a remote IRC server. The second figure provides more technical details associated with these findings, including memory modifications, registry modifications, and the creation of a mutex and opening of a port.

ThreatExpert also has a very robust search feature. It will allow you to search for files that have already been analyzed by searching based upon the files' MD5 or SHA1 hash, so that you don't have to wait for it to re-analyze a file that may have already be submitted. Its most powerful feature, however, is the ability to search for terms within reports. This means that you can search for arbitrary text, file names, IP addresses, or domain names that you have found elsewhere on your network to see if they show up in relation to any of ThreatExpert's malware analysis reports. I've been involved in many investigations where the only intelligence I was able to find regarding a certain address was within a ThreatExpert malware report, and many of those times that has been enough to lead me down the right path towards figuring out whether an incident had occurred.

While ThreatExpert is an efficient sandbox, it doesn't go into quite as much detail as Cuckoo, and it doesn't have the option of being downloaded and installed locally. With that said, in a lot of instances it will get the job done just fine, and its search feature makes it incredibly valuable for NSM analysis.

## Team Cymru Malware Hash Registry

The quickest way to identify any file is by its cryptographic hash. Because of this, most files are uniquely identified by their file hash; typically MD5, but sometimes SHA1. This is advantageous because a single hash value can be used to identify a file regardless of its name. We've already seen instances where both Malwr and ThreatExpert identify files using these hashes, so it makes sense that it would be relatively easy for someone to compile a list of known malicious malware hashes. That is exactly what Team Cymru did.

The Team Cymru Malware Hash Registry (http://www.team-cymru.org/Services/MHR/) is a database containing known malware hashes from multiple sources. This database can be queried in a lot of ways, and provides a quick and efficient way to determine if a file you've collected during detection or analysis is malicious.

The easiest way to query the registry is actually with the WHOIS command. This may seem a bit odd, but it works surprisingly well. You can query the database by issuing a WHOIS command in the following format:

```
whois -h hash.cymru.com<hash>
```

The results of two of these queries are shown in Figure 14.24.

**FIGURE 14.24**

Querying the Team Cymru Malware Hash Registry

In the figure above, we complete two queries that each return three columns. The first column contains the hash value itself. The second column contains the timestamp (in epoch format, which you can convert to local time by using the date -d command) of the last time that the hash was observed. The third column shows a percentage number of antivirus detection engines that classified the file as malicious. In the first submission we see that the file was detected as malicious by 79% of antivirus engines. The second submission lists NO_DATA for this field, which means that the hash registry has no record for that hash value. The malware hash registry will not keep records on hash values that have below a 5% detection rate.

The Team Cymru Malware Hash Registry can be useful for the individual analysis of suspicious files, but because of the extensive number of ways you can query the database, it also lends itself well to automated analysis. For instance, Bro provides functionality to use its file extraction framework (Chapter 10) in conjunction with its intelligence framework (Chapter 8) to selectively extract files and automatically compare their hashes against the hash registry. This is incredibly valuable from a detection perspective, and can ease the analysis burden of an event.

You can read more about the malware hash registry and the numerous ways you can query it by visiting its website, listed above.

Combining all of the IP and domain name intelligence we've discussed here with the observations that you've made from your own network data should give you the resources you need to begin building a tactical intelligence product.

## CONCLUSION

Know your network, know your adversary, and you will be able to get to the bottom of any investigation. The capability to collect and generate intelligence for friendly assets combined with the ability to research and derive information about potentially hostile entities is critical for the successful analysis of any network security event. In this chapter we discussed methods for doing all of these things. While there are a number of ways to approach intelligence, it is key that intelligence is approached as a product that is designed to help analysts make decisions that lead to escalation. In the next chapter we will discuss the analysis process, which will draw upon information gained during the analysis collection and generation process.

# The Analysis Process

# 15

## CHAPTER CONTENTS

The most important component of NSM is the analysis process. This is where the analyst takes the output from a detection mechanism and accesses various data sources to collect information that can help them determine whether something detrimental to the network or the information stored on it has actually happened. The process the analyst goes through in order to accomplish this is called the analysis process.

In almost every SOC I've visited and with nearly every analyst I've spoken to, the analysis process is an ad-hoc, subjective series of loosely defined steps that every individual defines on their own. Of course, everyone has their own individual style and everyone parses information differently, so this is expected to some degree. However, a codified, systematic analysis process on which all analysts can base their efforts is valuable. The adoption of such a process supports faster decision making, more efficient teamwork, and clearer incident reporting. Most of all, it helps an analyst solve an investigation quicker.

In this chapter, we will look at two different analysis methods that can serve as a framework for performing NSM analysis. One of these methods is taken from a system police investigators use to solve criminal investigations, while the other is taken from a process that doctors use to solve medical investigations. As of the writing of this book, a written framework for the NSM analysis process is something I've yet to see in existence. Because of that, if you take nothing else from this book, my hope is that this chapter will provide you with the knowledge necessary to apply one of these two analysis methods to your daily analysis process, and that it serves to hone your analysis skills so that you can achieve better, faster, more accurate results in your investigations.

Once we've discussed these analysis methods, I will provide a number of analysis best practices that I've learned from my own experience as an NSM analyst and from my colleagues. Finally, we will discuss the incident "morbidity and mortality" process, which can be used for refining collection, detection, and analysis after an investigation has concluded.

## ANALYSIS METHODS

In general, a method is simply a way of doing something. While there are hundreds of ways to do the "something" that is NSM analysis, every analysis process requires three things: an input, an investigation, and an output. The way these things are done and organized is what defines an analysis method, which is simply a systematic approach to determining if an incident has occurred. In this case, the input is usually some type of IDS alert or another anomaly that catches an analyst's eye, and the output is the decision of whether an incident has occurred. The steps that occur between those two things during the investigation stage are what we are going to talk about here in defining analysis methods.

## Relational Investigation

The term "investigation" is most closely associated with a police investigation. This isn't just because some information security engineer decided to steal this term twenty years ago; it's because the processes of investigating an information security breach and investigating a crime are quite similar. As a matter of fact, the approach that police investigators often use to get to the bottom of a crime is something we can use as a framework for an analysis method. This is called a relational investigation.

The relational method is based upon defining linear relationships between entities. If you've ever seen an episode of "CSI" or "NYPD Blue" where detectives stick pieces of paper to a corkboard and then connect those items with pieces of yarn, then you've seen an example of a relational investigation. This type of investigation relies on the relationships that exist between clues and individuals associated with the crime. A network of computers is not unlike a network of people. Everything is connected, and every action that is taken can result in another action occurring. This means that if we as analysts can identify the relationships between entities well enough, we should be able to create a web that allows us to see the full picture of what is occurring during the investigation of a potential incident.

The relational investigation process flows through four steps (Figure 15.1).

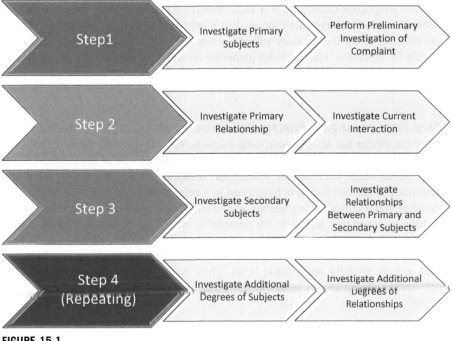

Step1 — Investigate Primary Subjects — Perform Preliminary Investigation of Complaint

Step 2 — Investigate Primary Relationship — Investigate Current Interaction

Step 3 — Investigate Secondary Subjects — Investigate Relationships Between Primary and Secondary Subjects

Step 4 (Repeating) — Investigate Additional Degrees of Subjects — Investigate Additional Degrees of Relationships

**FIGURE 15.1**

The Relational Investigation Analysis Method

### Step One: Investigate Primary Subjects and Perform Preliminary Investigation of the Complaint

In a police investigation, law enforcement is typically notified of an event because of a complaint, which is usually dispatched from the police station. When they receive this complaint, they are given information about the subjects involved with the complaint and the nature of the complaint itself.

When arriving on the scene, the first thing an officer does is identify the subjects involved (the primary subject) and determine if the complaint is worth further investigation. This determination is made based on the law, and the officer's initial judgement of whether there is the potential for a law to have been broken. If the officer thinks that this potential exists, he will begin collecting information from each of the subjects involved. This might include verifying that they have legitimate identification, viewing the prior criminal history, and performing a pat down to determine if they are in possession of any weapons or illegal items.

In an NSM investigation, the analyst is typically notified of an event by means of alert data, including alerts generated by an IDS. This alert typically includes the hosts involved with the event and the nature of the alert. In this case, the alert is similar to an officer's complaint, and the hosts are similar to an officer's subjects. In a similar chain of events, the NSM analyst must make an initial determination of whether the alert is worth further investigation. Usually, this means examining the details of the rule or detection mechanism that caused the generation of the alert, and determining if the traffic associated with it actually matches that alert. Essentially, this is an attempt to quickly determine if a false positive has occurred. If the alert can't be deemed a false positive, then the analyst's next step should be to begin collecting information about the primary subjects associated with the alert: the friendly and hostile IP addresses. This includes gathering friendly and tactical threat intelligence like we discussed in Chapter 14.

### Step Two: Investigate Primary Relationships and Current Interaction

Once an officer has investigated both subjects, he will investigate the relationship between them. This includes the previous relationship as well as the current interaction. As an example, consider a domestic complaint. The officer will attempt to determine if the two subjects have been in a relationship, the duration of that relationship, if the subjects live together, and so on. Then, the officer will determine what actions occurred that led up to the complaint, when that escalated into the current situation, and what happened afterwards.

The NSM analyst will do the same thing to investigate the primary relationship between the friendly and hostile hosts. They begin by determining the nature of previous communication between the hosts. The following questions might me asked:

- Have these two hosts ever communicated before?
- If yes, what ports, protocols, and services were involved?

Next, the analyst will thoroughly investigate the communication associated with the initial alert. This is where data from multiple sources is retrieved and analyzed to look for connections. This will include actions like:

- Gathering PCAP data
- Performing packet analysis
- Gathering PSTR data
- Extracting files and performing malware analysis
- Generating statistics from session data

In some cases the analyst will be able to determine if an incident has occurred at this point. When this happens, the investigation may end here. If the incident is not clearly defined at this point or no concrete determination has been made, then it is time to proceed to the next step.

### Step Three: Investigate Secondary Subjects and Relationships

When a police officer is investigating primary subjects and the relationship between them, secondary subjects will often be identified. These are individuals that are related to the complaint in some way, and may include associates of the subject making the complaint, associates of the subject the complaint is made against, or other witnesses. When these subjects are identified, the investigation is typically aided by performing the same investigative steps outlined in the first two steps. This includes an investigation of these subjects, as well as the relationships between them and the primary subjects.

In an NSM investigation, this happens often. For instance, while investigating the relationship between two hosts an analyst may find that the friendly host is communicating with other hostile hosts in the same manner or that the hostile host is communicating with other friendly hosts. Furthermore, analysis of malicious files may yield IP addresses revealing other sources of suspicious communication. These hosts are all considered secondary subjects.

When secondary subjects are identified, they should be investigated in the same manner as primary subjects. Following this, the relationships between secondary subjects and primary subjects should be examined.

### Step Four: Investigate Additional Degrees of Subjects Relation

At this point, the investigation of subjects and relationships should repeat as many times as necessary, and may require the inclusion of tertiary and even quaternary subjects. As you go, you should fully evaluate subjects and relationships on a per-level basis, fully exhausting each layer of interaction before moving on to the next. Otherwise, it is easy to get lost down the rabbit hole and miss earlier connections that could impact how you view other hosts. When you are finished, you should be able to describe the relationships between the subjects and how malicious activities have occurred, if at all.

### Relational Investigation Scenario

Now that we've explained the relational investigation process, let's go through an example to demonstrate how it might work in a real NSM environment.

### Step One: Investigate Primary Subjects and Perform Preliminary Investigation of the Complaint

Analysts are notified that an anomaly was detected with the following Snort alert:

```
ET WEB_CLIENT PDF With Embedded File
```

In this alert, the source IP is 192.0.2.5 (Hostile Host A) and the destination IP address is 172.16.16.20 (Friendly Host B). These are the primary subjects. The preliminary examination of the traffic associated with this activity indicates that there does appear to be a PDF file being downloaded. The PCAP data for the communication sequence is obtained, and the PDF is extracted from the file using Wireshark. The MD5 hash of the PDF file is submitted to the Team Cymru Malware Hash Registry, and it determines that 23% of antivirus detection engines think that this file is malicious. Based on this, you should make the decision that further investigation is warranted.

The next step is to gather friendly and tactical threat intelligence related to both hosts. This process determines the following:

Friendly Intelligence for 172.16.16.20:

- This system is a user workstation running Windows 7
- The system has no listening services or open ports
- The user of this system browses the web frequently, and multiple New Asset Notifications exist in PRADS data

Hostile Intelligence for 192.0.2.5:

- IPVoid returns 0 matches on public blacklists for this IP address
- URLVoid returns 5 matches on public blacklists for the domain name the PDF file was downloaded from
- NetFlow data indicates that this IP address has not communicated with any other devices on the friendly network

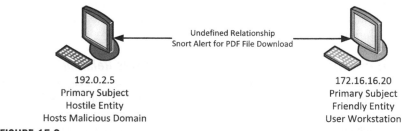

Undefined Relationship
Snort Alert for PDF File Download

| 192.0.2.5 | 172.16.16.20 |
|---|---|
| Primary Subject | Primary Subject |
| Hostile Entity | Friendly Entity |
| Hosts Malicious Domain | User Workstation |

**FIGURE 15.2**

Initial Primary Subjects

### Step Two: Investigate Primary Relationships and Current Interaction

In order to investigate the relationship between 172.16.16.20 and 192.0.2.5, the first action that is performed is an analysis of packet data for the communication occurring around the time of the alert. Packet data is downloaded for communication between these two hosts with the time interval set to retrieve data from 10 minutes before the alert happened to 10 minutes after the alert happened. After performing packet analysis on this data, it is determined that the friendly host was redirected to the malicious host from a third-party advertisement on a legitimate website. The friendly host downloaded the file, and the communication with the hostile host ceased.

The next step taken to investigate the relationship between 172.16.16.20 and 192.0.2.5 is to inspect the PDF file that was downloaded. This PDF file is submitted to a Cuckoo sandbox in order to perform automated malware analysis. The behavioral analysis of this file indicates that this PDF contains an executable file. The executable file contains the IP address 192.0.2.6 hard coded in its configuration. No other information was able to be determined from the malware analysis of these files.

At this point, you've exhausted your investigation of the primary subjects and the relationship between them. While everything points to this being an incident, you can't quite make this determination for sure yet. However, we have identified a secondary subject, so we will move on to the next step of our investigation with that data in hand.

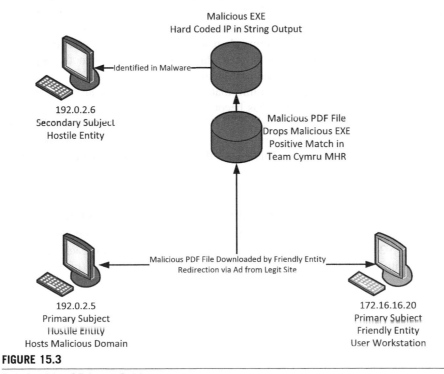

**FIGURE 15.3**

Relationship of Primary Subjects

### Step Three: Investigate Secondary Subjects and Relationships

We have identified the secondary subject 192.0.2.6 coded into the executable that was dropped by the PDF file downloaded by the primary subject. Now, we must investigate that subject by collecting hostile intelligence for this IP address:

Hostile Intelligence for 192.0.2.6:

- IPVoid returns 2 matches on public blacklists for this IP Address.
- NetFlow data indicates that the primary subject 172.16.16.20 has communicated with this host. This communication occurred approximately thirty minutes after the initial alert.
- NetFlow data indicates that two other friendly hosts on our network have been communicating with this IP address on a periodic basis with low volumes of traffic for the past several days. Their addresses are 172.16.16.30 and 172.16.16.40.

Based upon this information, it appears as though this issue might be larger than we originally thought. Next, we need to determine the relationship between our secondary subject 192.0.2.6 and our primary subject 172.16.16.20. Based upon our hostile intelligence, we already know that communication occurred between these two devices. The next step is to gather PCAP data for communication occurring between these hosts. Once this data is collected, analysis reveals that although these devices are communicating on Port 80, they are not using the HTTP protocol. Instead, they are using a custom protocol, and you can see that commands are being issued to this system. These commands result in the friendly system transmitting system information to the hostile host. At this point that you also notice a periodic call back that is transmitted to the hostile host.

At this point, we have enough information to determine that an incident can be declared, and that 172.16.16.20 has become compromised (Figure 15.4). In some cases, the investigation could end here. However, remember that we identified two additional hosts (now identified as tertiary hosts) that were communicating with the hostile IP 192.0.2.6. This means that there is a good chance those might also be infected.

### Step Four: Investigate Additional Degrees of Subjects' Relation

An examination of the packet data transmitted between these tertiary hosts and 172.16.16.20 reveals that it is also participating in the same call back behavior as was identified in the primary friendly host (Figure 15.5). Because of this, you can determine that the tertiary friendly hosts are also compromised.

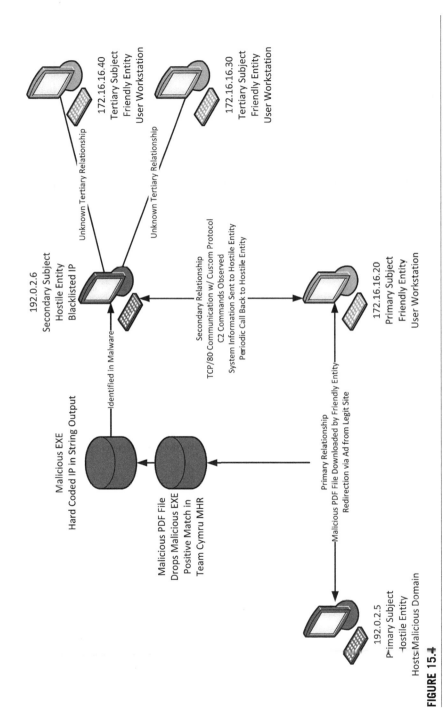

**FIGURE 15.4**

Relationship of Primary and Secondary Subjects

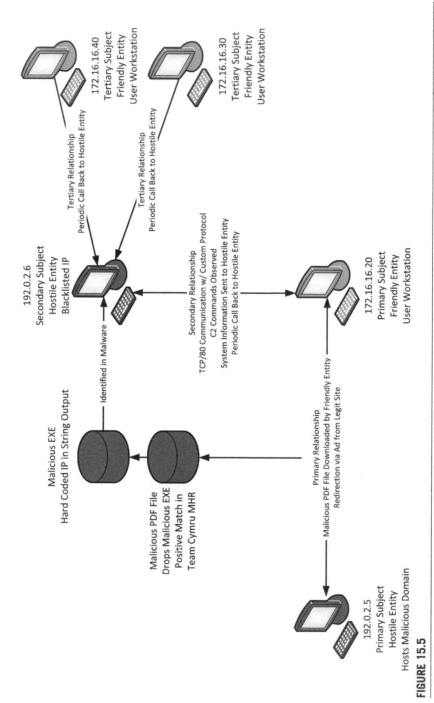

**FIGURE 15.5**

Relationship of All Subjects

## Summarizing the Incident

This scenario was based on a real incident that occurred in a SOC. Using a systematic analysis process to identify hosts and build relationships between them not only allowed us to determine if a compromise occurred, it also allowed us to find other hosts that were also compromised but weren't identified in the original alert that tipped us off. This is a great example of how a structured process can help an analyst get from A to Z without getting detoured or being overloaded with information. It is very easy to get buried in the weeds in a scenario like this one. The key is approaching each step as it is intended and not venturing too far off the path you are on. If you trust the path, it will eventually get you where you want to go.

# Differential Diagnosis

The goal of an NSM analyst is to digest the alerts generated by various detection mechanisms and investigate multiple data sources to perform relevant tests and research to see if a network security breach has happened. This is very similar to the goals of a physician, which is to digest the symptoms a patient presents with and investigate multiple data sources and perform relevant tests and research to see if their findings represent a breach in the person's immune system. Both practitioners share a similar of goal of connecting the dots to find out if something bad has happened and/or is still happening.

Although NSM has only been around a short while, medicine has been around for centuries. This means that they've got a head start on us when it comes to developing their diagnostic method. One of the most common diagnostic methods used in clinical medicine is one called differential diagnosis. If you've ever seen an episode of "House" then chances are you've seen this process in action. The group of doctors will be presented with a set of symptoms and they will create a list of potential diagnoses on a whiteboard. The remainder of the show is spent doing research and performing various tests to eliminate each of these potential conclusions until only one is left. Although the methods used in the show are often a bit unconventional, they still fit the bill of the differential diagnosis process.

The differential method is based upon a process of elimination. It consists of five distinct steps, although in some cases only two will be necessary. The differential process exists as follows:

### Step One: Identify and list the symptoms

In medicine, symptoms are typically conveyed verbally by the individual experiencing them. In NSM, a symptom is most commonly an alert generated by some form of intrusion detection system or other detection software. Although this step focuses primarily on the initial symptoms, more symptoms may be added to this list as additional tests or investigations are conducted.

### Step Two: Consider and evaluate the most common diagnosis first

A maxim every first year medical student learns is "If you hear hoof beats, look for horses...not zebras." That is, the most common diagnosis is likely the correct one. As a result, this diagnosis should be evaluated first. The analyst should focus his investigation on doing what is necessary to quickly confirm this diagnosis. If this common diagnosis cannot confirmed during this initial step, then the analyst should proceed to the next step.

### Step Three: List all possible diagnosis for the given symptoms

The next step in the differential process is to list every possible diagnosis based upon the information currently available with the initially assessed symptoms. This step requires some creative thinking and is often most successful when multiple analysts participate in generating ideas. Although you may not have been able to completely confirm the most common diagnosis in the previous step, if you weren't able to rule it out completely then it should be carried over into the list generated in this step. Each potential diagnosis on this list is referred to as a candidate condition.

### Step Four: Prioritize the list of candidate conditions by their severity

Once a list of candidate conditions is created, a physician will prioritize these by listing the condition that is the largest threat to human life at the top. In the case of an NSM analyst you should also prioritize this list, but the prioritization should focus on which condition is the biggest threat to your organization's network security. This will be highly dependent upon the nature of your organization. For instance, if "MySQL Database Root Compromise" is a candidate condition then a company whose databases contains social security numbers would prioritize this condition much more highly than a company who uses a simple database to store a list of its sales staff's on-call schedule.

### Step Five: Eliminate the candidate conditions, starting with the most severe

The final step is where the majority of the action occurs. Based upon the prioritized list created in the previous step, the analyst should begin doing what is necessary to eliminate candidate conditions, starting with the condition that poses the greatest threat to network security. This process of elimination requires considering each candidate condition and performing tests, conducting research, and investigating other data sources in an effort to rule them out as a possibility. In some cases, investigation of one candidate condition may rule out multiple candidate conditions, speeding up this process. Alternatively, investigation of other candidate conditions may prove inconclusive, leaving one or two conditions that are unable to be definitively eliminated as possibilities. This is acceptable, since sometimes in network security monitoring (as in medicine) there are anomalies that can't be explained and require more observation before determining a diagnosis. Ultimately, the goal of this final step is to be left with one diagnosis so that an incident can be declared or the alert can be dismissed as a false positive. It's very important to remember that "Normal Communication" is a perfectly acceptable diagnosis, and will be the most common diagnosis an NSM analyst arrives at.

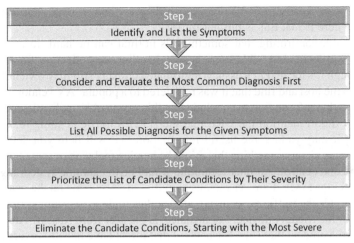

**FIGURE 15.6**

The Differential Diagnosis Analysis Process

### Differential Diagnosis Scenarios

Now that we've explained the differential diagnosis process, let's go through a couple of practical examples to demonstrate how it might work in a real NSM environment. Since we paint with such broad strokes when performing differential diagnosis, we will look at two unique scenarios.

### Scenario 1

***Step 1: Identify and List the Symptoms.*** The following symptoms were observed through IDS alerts and investigation of immediately available data:

1. A friendly host appears to be sending outbound traffic to a Russian IP address
2. The traffic is occurring at regular intervals, every 10 minutes
3. The traffic is HTTPS over port 443, and as such is encrypted and unreadable

***Step 2: Consider and Evaluate the Most Common Diagnosis First.*** Based on these symptoms, it might appear that the most logical assumption is that this machine is infected with some form of malware and is phoning home for further instructions. After all, the traffic is going to a Russian IP address at regular 10 minute intervals. Although those things are worth noting (I wouldn't have listed them if they weren't), I don't think we should buy into the malware theory so hastily. All too often, too much emphasis is placed on the geographic location of IP addresses, so the fact that the remote IP address is Russian means little right off the bat. Additionally, there are a lot of normal communication mechanisms that communicate on regular periodic intervals. This includes things like web-based chat, RSS feeds, web-based e-mail, stock tickers, software update processes, and more. Operating on the principal that all packets are good unless you can prove they are bad, I think the most common diagnosis here is that this is normal traffic.

That said, confirming that something is normal can be hard. In this particular instance we could start with some hostile intelligence collection for the Russian IP. Although it's located in Russia, a legitimate company still may own it. If we were to look up the host and find that it was registered to a popular AV vendor we might be able to use that information to conclude that this was an AV application checking for updates. I didn't mention the URL that the HTTPS traffic is going to, but quickly Googling it may yield some useful information that will help you determine if it is a legitimate site or something that might be hosting malware or some type of botnet command and control. Another technique would be to examine system logs or host-based IDS logs to see if any suspicious activities are occurring on the machine at the same intervals the traffic is occurring at. Another route is to examine friendly intelligence for the friendly device. For instance, is the user from Russia? Are they using an Antivirus product that (like Kaspersky) that might have update servers in Russia? Those things might help to determine if the traffic is normal.

For the purposes of this exercise, let's assume that we weren't able to make a final determination on whether this was normal communication.

***Step 3: List all Possible Diagnoses for the Given Symptoms.*** There are several potential candidate conditions within the realm of possibility for the current scenario. For the sake of brevity, we've only listed a few of those here:

*Normal Communication.* We weren't able to rule this out completely in the previous step so we carry it over to this step.

*Malware Infection / Installed Malicious Logic.* This is used as a broad category. We typically don't care about the specific strain of malware until we determine that malware may actually exist. If you are concerned about a specific strain then it can be listed separately. Think of this category as a doctor listing "bacterial infection" as a candidate condition knowing that they can narrow it down further once more information has been obtained.

*Data Exfiltration from Compromised Host.* This condition represents the potential that the host could be sending proprietary or confidential information out of the network in small intervals. This type of event would often be part of a coordinated or targeted attack.

*Misconfiguration.* It's well within the realm of possibilities that a system administrator mistyped an IP address and a piece of software that should be trying to communicate periodically with an internal system is now trying to do so with a Russian IP address. This is really quite common.

***Step 4: Prioritize the List of Candidate Conditions by their Severity.*** With candidate conditions identified, we can prioritize these based upon their severity. This prioritization will vary depending on the risk profile for an organization. As a generalization, we've selected the following priorities, with priority 1 being the highest:

**Priority 1: Data Exfiltration from Compromised Host**
**Priority 2: Malware Infection / Installed Malicious Logic**
**Priority 3: Misconfiguration**
**Priority 4: Normal Communication**

**Step 5: Eliminate the Candidate Conditions, Starting with the Most Severe.** Now we can gather data and perform tests to eliminate each potential candidate condition. Once you've identified the correct diagnosis you would stop this process, but for this scenario we've gone through the motions with every condition.

*Priority 1: Data Exfiltration from Compromised Host.* This one can be a bit tricky to eliminate as a possibility. Full packet capture won't provide a lot of help since the traffic is encrypted. If you have session data available, you should be able to determine the amount of data going out. If only a few bytes are going out every 10 minutes then it's likely that this is not data exfiltration, since this would probably involve a larger amount of outbound data. It would also be valuable to determine if any other hosts on your network are communicating with this IP address or any other IPs in the same address space. Finally, baselining normal communication for your internal host and comparing it with the potentially malicious traffic may provide some useful insight. This can be done with friendly intelligence data, like data collected by PRADS.

*Priority 2: Malware Infection / Installed Malicious Logic.* At this point the research you've already done should give you a really good idea of whether or not this condition is true. It is likely that by examining the potential for data exfiltration, you will rule this condition out as a result or will have already been able to confirm that it is true. In addition to things listed in those steps, you could examine network antivirus or HIDS logs in detail.

*Priority 3: Misconfiguration.* This condition can best be approached by comparing the traffic of the friendly host against the traffic of one or more hosts with a similar role on the network. If every other workstation on that same subnet has the same traffic pattern, but to a different IP address, then it's likely that the wrong IP address was entered into a piece of software somewhere. Having access to host-based logs can also be useful in figuring out if a misconfiguration exists since records of the misconfiguration might exist in Windows or Unix system logs.

*Priority 4: Normal Communication.* If you've gotten this far, then the diagnosis of normal communication should be all that remains on your list of candidate conditions.

**Making a Diagnosis.** At this point you have to use your experience as an analyst and your intuition to decide if you think something malicious is really occurring. If you were able to complete the previous analysis thoroughly, then operating on the assumption that all packets are good unless you can prove they are bad would mean your final diagnosis here should be that this is normal communication. If you still have a hunch something quirky is happening though, there is no shame in monitoring the host further and reassessing once more data has been collected.

## Scenario 2

***Step 1: Identify and List the Symptoms.*** The following symptoms were observed through IDS alerts and investigation of immediately available data:

1. A web server in the DMZ is receiving massive amounts of inbound traffic
2. The inbound traffic is unreadable and potentially encrypted or obfuscated
3. The inbound traffic is coming to multiple destination ports on the internal host
4. The inbound traffic is UDP based

***Step 2: Consider and Evaluate the Most Common Diagnosis First.*** With the amount of traffic received by the internal host being abundant and the packets using the UDP protocol with random destination ports, my inclination would be that this is some form of denial of service attack.

The quickest way to determine whether something is a denial of service is to assess the amount of traffic being received compared with the normal amount of traffic received on that host. This is something that is really easy to do with session data using the throughput calculation statistics we discussed in Chapter 11. If the host is only receiving 20% more traffic than it normally would, then I would consider alternatives to a DoS. However, if the host is receiving 10 or 100 times its normal amount of traffic then DoS is very likely. It's important to remember that a DoS is still a DoS even if it is unintentional.

Once again, for the sake of this scenario we will continue as though we weren't able to make a clear determination of whether a DoS condition exists.

***Step 3: List all Possible Diagnoses for the Given Symptoms.*** There are several candidate conditions within the realm of possibility for the current scenario. For the sake of brevity, we've only listed a few of those here:

***Denial of Service.*** We weren't able to rule this out completely in the previous step so we carry it over to this step.

***Normal Communication.*** It doesn't seem incredibly likely, but there is potential that is normal traffic being generated by a legitimate service.

***Misdirected Attacks.*** When a third party chooses to attack another they will often spoof their source address for the sake of anonymity and to prevent getting DoS'd themselves. This will result in the owner of the spoofed IP they are using seeing that traffic. This web server could be seeing the effects of this.

***Misconfigured External Host.*** A misconfiguration could have happened on someone else's network just as easily as it could on yours. This misconfiguration could result in an external host generating this traffic and sending it to the web server.

***SPAM Mail Relay.*** The server could be misconfigured or compromised in a manner that allows it to be used for relaying SPAM mail across the Internet.

***Step 4: Prioritize the List of Candidate Conditions by their Severity.*** With candidate conditions identified, we can prioritize these based upon their severity. This prioritization will vary depending on the risk profile for an organization. As a generalization, we've selected the following priorities, with priority 1 being the highest:

> **Priority 1: Denial of Service**
> **Priority 2: SPAM Mail Relay**
> **Priority 3: Misconfigured External Host**
> **Priority 4: Misdirected Attacks**
> **Priority 5: Normal Communication**

***Step 5: Eliminate the Candidate Conditions, Starting with the Most Severe.*** Now we can gather data and perform tests to eliminate each potential candidate condition. Once you've identified the correct diagnosis you would stop this process, but for this scenario we've gone through the motions with every condition.

*Priority 1: Denial of Service.* We've already gone through our paces on this one without being able to identify that it is the definitive diagnosis. Even though this is the most severe we would have to proceed to attempt to eliminate other candidate conditions to help in figuring out if a DoS is occurring. Of course, depending on the effect of the attack it may make the most sense to contain the issue by blocking the traffic before spending more time investigating the root cause.

*Priority 2: SPAM Mail Relay.* This one is relatively easy to eliminate. If the server were being used as a mail relay then you would have a proportionate amount of traffic going out as you do going in. If that's not the case and you don't see any abnormal traffic leaving the server then it is likely that it is not relaying SPAM. You can determine this by generating throughput statistics from session data, like we discussed in Chapter 11. If the web server is also running mail services then you can examine the appropriate logs here as well. If it is not supposed to be running mail services, you can examine the host to see if it is doing so in an unauthorized manner.

*Priority 3: Misconfigured External Host.* This one is typically pretty tricky. Unless you can identify the owner of the IP address and communicate with them directly then the most you can hope to do is block the traffic locally or report abuse at the ISP level.

*Priority 4: Misdirected Attacks.* This is another tricky one along the same lines as the previous candidate condition. If it's an attacker somewhere else whose antics are causing traffic redirection to your server then the most you can do is report the issue to the ISP responsible for the IP address and block the traffic locally.

*Priority 5: Normal Communication.* This doesn't seem likely, but you can't say this for sure without baselining the normal traffic for the host. Using friendly intelligence gathered from a tool like PRADS combined with session data review, you can compare the host's traffic at similar times on previous days to see if you can draw any conclusions. Is the pattern normal and it's just the amount of traffic that anomalous? Is it both the pattern and the amount that's anomalous? Does the server ever talk to the offending IP prior to this? These questions should lead you in the right direction.

*Making a Diagnosis.* In this scenario, it's very possible that you are left with as many as three candidate conditions that you cannot rule out. The good thing here is that even though you can't rule these out, the containment and remediation methods would be the same for all of them. This means that you still have gotten to a state of diagnosis that allows the network to recover from whatever is occurring. This is just like when a doctor knows that an infection is occurring with a patient. Even if the doctor doesn't know the exact nature of the infection, they know that treating it with antibiotics will help solve the problem.

If the amount of traffic isn't so large that it is actually preventing services from being delivered, then you may not need to block the activity. This will allow you to continue monitoring it in order to attempt to collect more symptoms that may be useful in making a more accurate diagnosis.

## Implementing Analysis Methods

The two analysis methods we've described here are very different. There really is no clear-cut formula for choosing the right method as they each have their strengths and weaknesses depending on the current scenario and the strengths and weaknesses of the analyst. From my experience, the relational investigation method tends to work best in complex scenarios where more than a few hosts are involved. This is because it better allows you to keep track of a large number of entities and relationships without getting overwhelmed or going off on an odd tangent. The differential diagnosis method tends to work best in scenarios where you have a smaller number of hosts involved and you are fixated on a few distinct symptoms in route to a singular diagnosis.

The important thing to take away from this section isn't that you should use one of these analysis methods to the letter. They are merely provided as frameworks that you might be able to adapt to your environment. The thing to take away here is that all analysis is improved through the use of some systematic method that allows the analyst to work through an investigation efficiently.

## ANALYSIS BEST PRACTICES

Throughout this book we've mentioned several "best practices" for analysis. While everyone performs analysis in their own unique way, there are certain truths that I have found to be beneficial to remember when performing analysis. These best practices are compiled through years of experience from the authors of this book, as well as our colleagues.

## Unless You Created the Packet Yourself, There Are No Absolutes

Analysis happens in a world of assumptions and best guesses. Most of the decisions you will make are centered on a packet or a log entry, and then honed based upon the review of additional data or intelligence. Because of this, the assumptions and guesses you make will be constantly shifting as new information comes to light. Don't worry though; there is nothing wrong with that. Ask your friendly neighborhood chemist or physicist. Most of their work is based upon assumptions and they have great success.

The takeaway here is that there are rarely absolutes in analysis, and it is healthy to question assumptions and guesses constantly. Is that IP address REALLY a known legitimate host? Does that domain REALLY belong to XYZ company? Is that DNS server REALLY supposed to be communicating with that database server? Always question yourself and stay on your toes.

## Be Mindful of Your Abstraction from the Data

An analyst depends on data to perform their job. This data can come in the form of a PCAP file, a PSTR record, or an IIS file. Since most of your time will be spent using various tools to interact with data it's crucial to be mindful of how that tool interacts with the data. Humans are imperfect and because they make tools, sometimes "features" can cloud data and prevent proper analysis.

In one scenario, I worked for a SOC that used a very popular commercial SIEM solution. One day, we started seeing weird log entries in the SIEM console that indicated a large amount of internal traffic was going to the IP address 255.255.255.255 on port 80. Investigating the data at a more intimate level uncovered that the traffic generating these logs was actually internal HTTP requests that were being blocked by a web proxy. An update to the parser the SIEM was using to ingest records from that proxy resulting in it not knowing how to handle the destination IP address field, yielding the improper value 255.255.255.255. This is a prime example where knowing your data and being aware of how far abstracted from it you are is crucial.

In a job where reliance upon data is critical, you can't afford to not understand exactly how your tools interact with that data.

## Two Sets of Eyes are Always Better than One

There is a reason that authors have editors, policemen have partners, and there are two guys sitting in every nuclear silo. No matter how much experience you have and how good you are, you will always miss things. This is expected because different people come from different backgrounds, and nobody is operates at 100% efficiency all the time. After all, we are only human.

I come from a military network defense background, so the first thing I look at when examining network traffic is the source and destination country. Now, I know that in most cases geolocation data doesn't matter much since those values can easily be spoofed or represent another compromised host being used by someone in a differing country. However, it's just how I'm programed. On the flip side, several of my colleagues come from a systems administration backgrounds and as a result, will look at the port number of the traffic first. As another example, I've worked with people who have a number crunching background, who will look at the amount of data transferred in a communication sequence first. This subtle technique helps demonstrate that our experiences help to shape our tactics a bit differently. This means that the numbers guy might see something that the sysadmin didn't see, or that the military guy might have insight that the numbers guy doesn't.

Whenever possible it's always a good idea to have a second set of eyes look at the issue you are facing. In any SOC I manage, I usually implement a two-person rule stating that at least two analyst are required to confirm an incident.

## Never Invite an Attacker to Dance

My coworker, SANS Senior Instructor, and packet ninja master Mike Poor phrased it best when I first heard him say, "Never invite an attacker to dance." As an analyst, it's very tempting to want to investigate a hostile IP address a bit beyond conventional means. Trust me, there have been many occasions where I've been tempted to port scan a hostile entity that kept sending me poorly crafted UDP packets. Even more so, any time someone attempts to DoS a network I'm responsible for defending, I wish for nothing more than to be able to unleash the full fury of a /8 network on their poor unsuspecting DSL connection.

The problem with this is that 99% of the time we don't know who or what we are dealing with. Although you may just be seeing scanning activity, the host that is originating the traffic could be operated by a large group of attackers or even a military division of another country. Even something as simple as a ping could tip off an attacker that you know they exist, prompting them to change their tactics, change source hosts, or even amplify their efforts. You don't know who you are dealing with, what their motivation is, and what their capabilities are, so you should never invite them to dance. The simple fact of the matter is that you don't know if you are capable of handling the repercussions.

## Packets are Inherently Good

The ultimate argument in life is whether people are inherently good or inherently evil. This same argument can be had for packets as well. You can either be the analyst that believes all packets are inherently evil or the analyst that believes all packets are inherently good.

In my experience, I've noticed that most analysts typically start their career assuming that packets are inherently evil, but eventually progress to assuming that packets are inherently good. That's because it's simply not feasible to approach every single piece of network evidence as something that could be a potential root-level compromise. If you do this, you'll eventually get fired because you spent your entire day running down a single alert or you'll just get burnt out. There is something to be said for being thorough, but the fact of the matter is that most of the traffic that occurs on a network isn't going to be evil, and as such, packets should be treated as innocent until proven guilty.

## Analysis is No More About Wireshark than Astronomy is About a Telescope

Whenever I interview someone for any analyst position (above entry level), I always ask that person to describe how he or she would investigate a typical IDS alert so that I can understand their thought process. A common answer that I hear sometimes goes like this: "I use Wireshark, Network Miner, Netwitness, and Arcsight." That's it.

Although there are processes and sciences in the practice of NSM, it is so much more than that. If this weren't the case then it wouldn't even be necessary to have humans in the loop. An effective analyst has to understand that while different tools may be an important part of the job, those things are merely pieces of the puzzle. Just like an astronomer's telescope is just another tool that allows him to figure out what makes the planets orbit the sun, Wireshark is just another tool in an analyst's arsenal that allows him to figure out what makes a packet get from point A to point B.

Start with the science, add in a few tools and processes, stay cognizant of the big picture, keep an attention to detail, and eventually the combination of all of those things and the experience you gain over time will help you develop your own analysis technique.

## Classification is Your Friend

It won't be long before you encounter a situation where you have more than one significant event to analyze at a time. When this occurs, it helps to have a system in place that can help you to determine which incident takes precedence for investigation and notification. In most SOC's, this is an incident classification system. There are several of these in existence, but the one I've grown accustomed to using is the DoD Cyber Incident and Cyber Event Categorization system,[1] outlined by CJCSM 6510. Table 15.1 outlines these categories, ordered by the precedence each category should take.

**Table 15.1** DOD Cyber Incident and Cyber Event Categorization

| Precedence | Category | Name | Incident/Event |
| --- | --- | --- | --- |
| 0 | 0 | Training and Exercise | N/A |
| 1 | 1 | Root-Level Intrusion | Incident |
| 2 | 2 | User-Level Intrusion | Incident |
| 3 | 4 | Denial of Service | Incident |
| 4 | 7 | [Installed/Executed] Malicious Logic | Incident |
| 5 | 3 | Unsuccessful Activity Attempt | Event |
| 6 | 5 | Non-Compliance Activity | Event |
| 7 | 6 | Reconnaissance | Event |
| 8 | 8 | Investigating | Event |
| 9 | 9 | Explained Anomaly | Event |

---

[1]http://www.dtic.mil/cjcs_directives/cdata/unlimit/m651001.pdf

> **FROM THE TRENCHES**
>
> Malicious Logic (Category 7) events trip up new analysts all of the time. Any time they see any evidence of malicious code they will tend to classify the event as a CAT 7. However, the key factor to note about CAT 7 incidents is that they only represent installed or executed malicious logic. This means that is isn't enough to observe a system downloading malicious code. In order to truly classify something as a CAT 7, you have to find evidence that this malicious code was installed or executed on the machine.

While this exact model might not be the best fit for your organization, I think that any group can benefit from implementing a categorization system. Any time an analyst performs a preliminary review of an event and determines that it warrants more investigation, that event should be assigned a category, even if that category is "Investigating " (CAT 8 Above). The category an investigation is assigned to can change multiple times throughout the investigation, and it is equally as common for the severity of an event to be downgraded as it is for it to be escalated. These things can be tracked in whatever internal ticketing/tracking system the SOC is using, and any change to the category of an event should be accompanied by an explanation by the analyst making that determination.

## The Rule of 10's

New analysts usually have a habit of grabbing too much data or too little data when investigating an event occurring at a specific point in time. On one extreme, the analyst will see an event occurring on 7 October 08:35 and will attempt to retrieve NSM data associated with that host for all of 7 October. This creates a scenario where the analyst has far too much data to analyze efficiently. On the other extreme, the analyst retrieves only data occurring on 7 October 08:35 to the minute. This creates a scenario where the analyst doesn't have enough information to determine exactly what happened.

To prevent either of these scenarios from occurring with my analysts, I created the rule of 10's. This rule states that any time you need to perform analysis on an event occurring at a single point in time, you should begin by retrieving data occurring 10 minutes before the event occurred to 10 minutes after the event occurred. I've found that this time frame sits in the "sweet spot" where the analyst has enough data to determine what led up to the event and what occurred after the event happened. Once the analyst has analyzed this data, they can make the decision to retrieve more data as necessary. Of course, this rule doesn't fit every situation, but I've found it effective for new analysts in 99% of the investigations they perform.

## When you Hear Hoof Beats, Look for Horses – Not Zebras

This is another concept borrowed from the medical community that is drilled into the heads of medical students for the duration of their education. If you see a patient who has a stomachache, it doesn't make a lot of sense to start performing tests for a lot of obscure diseases and conditions. Instead, ask the patient what they ate last night. If it happens to be two-dozen tacos and half a pizza, then you've probably found the problem.

Similarly, we should always consider the most obvious solution first when investigating events. If a system appears to be sending periodic communication to an unknown web server, then you shouldn't immediately assume that this is a callback to some adversary-run command and control infrastructure. Instead, it might just be a webpage they have open to check sports scores or stock ticker information.

This concept relies upon accepting the principle I spoke of earlier that all packets are inherently good. It also lends itself well to the differential diagnosis analysis method we looked at earlier.

## INCIDENT MORBIDITY AND MORTALITY

It may be a bit cliché, but encouraging the team dynamic within a group of analysts ensures mutual success over individual success. There are a lot of ways to do this, including items we discussed before in Chapter 1, such as fostering the development of infosec superstars or encouraging servant leadership. Beyond these things, there is no better way to ensure team success within your group than to create a culture of learning. Creating this type of culture goes well beyond sending analysts to formalized courses or paying for certifications. It relies upon adopting the mindset that in every action an analyst takes, they should either be teaching or learning, with no exceptions. Once every analyst begins seeing every part of their daily job as an opportunity to learn something new or teach something new to their peers, then a culture of learning is flourishing.

A part of this type of organizational culture is learning from both successes and failures. NSM is centered on technical investigations and cases, and when something bad eventually happens, an incident. This is not unlike medicine, which is also focused on medical investigations and patient cases, and when something bad eventually happens, death.

### Medical M&M

When death occurs in medicine, it can usually be classified as something that was either avoidable or inevitable from both a patient standpoint and also as it related to the medical care that was provided. Whenever a death is seen as something that may have been prevented or delayed with modifications to the medical care that was provided, the treating physician will often be asked to participate in something called a Morbidity and Mortality Conference, or "M&M" as they are often referred to casually. In an M&M, the treating physician will present the case from the initial visit, including the presenting symptoms and the patient's initial history and physical assessment. This presentation will continue through the diagnostic and treatment steps that were taken all the way through the patient's eventual death.

The M&M presentation is given to an audience of peers, including any other physicians who may have participated in the care of the patient. The audience will also include physicians who had nothing to do with the patient. The general premise is that these peers will question the treatment process in order to uncover any mistakes that may have been made, processes that could be improved upon, or situations that could have been handled differently.

The ultimate goal of the medical M&M is for the team to learn from any complications or errors, to modify behavior and judgment based upon experiences gained, and to prevent repetition of errors leading to complications. This is something that has occurred within medicine for over one hundred years and has proven to be wildly successful.[2]

## Information Security M&M

Earlier, we discussed how the concept of differential diagnosis can be translated from the medical field to information security. The concept of M&M is also something that I think transitions well to information security.

As information security professionals, it is easy to miss things. Since we know that prevention eventually fails, we can't be expected to live in a world free from compromise. Rather, we must be positioned so that when an incident does occur, it can be detected and responded to quickly. Once that is done, we can learn from whatever mistakes occurred that allowed the intrusion, and be better prepared to prevent, detect, and respond next time.

When an incident occurs we want it to be because of something out of our hands, such as a very sophisticated adversary or an attacker who is using an unknown zero day exploit. The truth of the matter is that not all incidents are that complex and often times there are ways in which detection, analysis, and response could occur faster. The information security M&M is a way to collect that information and put it to work. In order to understand how we can improve from mistakes, we have to understand why they are made. Uzi Arad summarizes this very well in the book, "Managing Strategic Surprise", a must read for information security professionals.[3] In this book, he cites three problems that lead to failures in intelligence management, which also apply to information security:

- The problem of misperception of the material, which stems from the difficulty of understanding the objective reality, or the reality as it is perceived by the opponent.
- The problems stemming form the prevalence of pre-existing mindsets among the analysts that do not allow an objective professional interpretation of the reality that emerges from the intelligence material.

---

[2]Campbell, W. (1988). *"Surgical morbidity and mortality meetings"*. Annals of the Royal College of Surgeons of England 70 (6): 363–365. PMC 2498614.PMID 3207327.

[3]Arad, Uzi (2008). *Intelligence Management as Risk Management*. Paul Bracken, Ian Bremmer, David Gordon (Eds.), *Managing Strategic Surprise* (43-77). Cambridge: Cambridge University Press.

- Group pressures, groupthink, or social-political considerations that bias professional assessment and analysis.

The information security M&M aims to provide a forum for overcoming these problems through strategic questioning of incidents that have occurred.

### When to Convene an M&M

In an Information Security M&M, the conference should be initiated after an incident has occurred and been remediated. Selecting which incidents are appropriate for M&M is a task that is usually handled by a team lead or member of management who has the ability to recognize when an investigation could have been handled better. This should occur reasonably soon after the incident so important details are fresh on the minds of those involved, but far enough out from the incident that those involved have time to analyze the incident as a whole, post-mortem. An acceptable time frame can usually be about a week after the incident has occurred.

### M&M Presenter(s)

The presentation of the investigation will often involve multiple individuals. In medicine, this may include an initial treating emergency room physician, an operating surgeon, and a primary care physician. In information security, this could include an NSM analyst who detected the incident, the incident responder who contained and remediated the incident, the forensic investigator who performed an analysis of a compromised machine, or the malware analyst who reverse engineered the malware associated with the incident.

### M&M Peers

The peers involved with the M&M should include at least one counterpart from each particular specialty, at minimum. This means that for every NSM analyst directly involved with the case, there should be at least one other NSM analyst who had nothing to do with it. This aims to get fresh outside views that aren't tainted by feeling the need to support any actions that were taken in relation to the specific investigation. In larger organizations and more ideal situations, it is nice to have at least two counterparts from each specialty, with one having less experience than the presenter and one having more experience.

### The Presentation

The presenting individual or group should be given at least a few days notice before their presentation. Although the M&M isn't considered a formal affair, a reasonable presentation is expected to include a timeline overview of the incident, along with any supporting data. The presenter should go through the detection, investigation, and remediation of the incident chronologically and present new findings only as they were discovered during this progression. Once this chronological presentation is given, the incident can then be examined holistically.

During the presentation, peers are expected to ask questions as they arise. Of course, this should be done respectfully by raising your hand as the presenter is speaking, but questions should NOT be saved for after the presentation. This is in order to frame the questions to the presenter as a peer would arrive at them during the investigation process.

### Strategic Questioning

Questions should be asked to presenters in such a way as to determine why something was handled in a particular manner, or why it wasn't handled in an alternative manner. As you may expect, it is very easy to offend someone when providing these types of questions, therefore, it is critical that participants enter the M&M with an open mind and both presenters and peers ask and respond to questions in a professional manner and with due respect.

Initially, it may be difficult for peers to develop questions that are entirely constructive and helpful in overcoming the three problems identified earlier. There are several methods that can be used to stimulate the appropriate type of questioning.

### Devils Advocate

One method that Uzi Arad mentions in his contribution to "Managing Strategic Surprise" is the Devils Advocate method. In this method, peers attempt to oppose most every analytical conclusion made by the presenter. This is done by first determining which conclusions can be challenged, then collecting information from the incident that supports the alternative assertion. It is then up to the presenter to support their own conclusions and debunk competing thoughts.

### Alternative Analysis (AA)

R.J. Heuer presents several methods for strategic questioning in his paper, "The Limits of Intelligence Analysis". These methods are part of a set of analytic tools called Alternative Analysis (AA).[4] Some of these more commonly used methods are:

### Group A / Group B

This analysis involves two groups of experts analyzing the incident separately based upon the same information. This requires that the presenters (Group A) provide supporting data related to the incident prior to the M&M so that the peers (Group B) can work collaboratively to come up with their own analysis to be compared and contrasted during the M&M. The goal is to establish to individual centers of thought. Whenever points arise where the two groups reach a different conclusion, additional discussion is required to find out why the conclusions differ.

### Red Cell Analysis

This method focuses on the adversarial viewpoint, where peers assume the role of the adversary involved with the particular incident. They will question the presenter regarding how their investigative steps were completed in reaction to the attacker's actions. For instance, a typical defender may solely be focused on finding out how to

---

[4]Heuer, Richards J., Jr. *Limits of Intelligence Analysis.* Orbis 49, no. 1 (2005)

stop malware from communicating back to the attacker, but the attacker may be more concerned with whether the defender was able to decipher the communication that was occurring. This could lead to a very positive line of questioning that results in new analytic methods that help to better assess the impact of the attacker, ultimately benefiting the incident containment process.

## What If Analysis

This method is focused on the potential causes and effects of events that may not have actually occurred. During detection, a peer may ask a question related to how the attack might have been detected if the mechanism that did detect it hadn't been functioning correctly. In the response to the event, a peer might question what the presenter would have done had the attacker been caught during the data exfiltration process rather than after it had already occurred. These questions don't always relate directly to the incident at hand, but provide incredibly valuable thought-provoking discussion that will better prepare your team for future incidents.

## Analysis of Competing Hypotheses

This method is similar to what occurs during a differential diagnosis, where peers create an exhaustive list of alternative assessments of symptoms that may have been presented. This is most effectively done by utilizing a whiteboard to list every potential diagnosis and then ruling those out based on testing and review of additional data.

## Key Assumptions Check

Most all sciences tend to make assumptions based on generally accepted facts. This method of questioning is designed to challenge key assumptions and how they affect the investigation of a scenario. This most often pairs with the What If analysis method. As an example, in the spread of malware, it's been the assumption that when operating within a virtual machine, the malware doesn't have the ability to escape to the host or other virtual machines residing on it. Given an incident being presented where a virtual machine has been infected with malware, a peer might pose the question of what action might be taken if this malware did indeed escape the virtual environment and infect other virtual machines on the host, or the host itself.

### M&M Outcome

During the M&M, all participants should actively take notes. Once the M&M is completed, the presenting individuals should take their notes and combine them into a final report that accompanies their presentation materials and supporting data. This reporting should include a listing of any points which could have been handled differently, and any improvements that could be made to the organization as a whole, either technically or procedurally. This report should be attached to the case file associated with the investigation of the incident. This information ultimately serves as the "lessons learned" for the incident.

### Additional M&M Tips

Having organized and participated in several of these conferences and reviews of similar scope, I have a few other pointers that help ensure that they provide value.

- M&M conferences should be held only sporadically, with no more than one per week and no more than three per month.
- It should be stressed that the purpose of the M&M isn't to grade or judge an individual, but rather, to encourage the culture of learning.
- M&M conferences should be moderated by someone at a team lead or lower management level to ensure that the conversation doesn't get too heated and to steer questions in the right direction. It is important that this person is technical, and not at an upper management level so that they can fully understand the implications of what is being discussed.
- If you make the decision to institute M&M conferences, it should be a requirement that everybody participates at some point, either as a presenter or a peer.
- The final report that is generated from the M&M should be shared with all technical staff, as well as management.
- Information security professionals, not unlike doctors, tend to have big egos. The first several conferences might introduce some contention and heated debates. This is to be expected initially, but will work itself out over time with proper direction and moderation.
- The M&M should be seen as a casual event. It is a great opportunity to provide food and coordinate other activities before and after the conference to take the edge off.
- Be wary of inviting upper management into these conferences. Their presence will often inhibit open questioning and response and they often don't have the appropriate technical mindset to gain or provide value to the presentation.
- If you don't have a lot of real incidents to base your M&M's on, make some up! This is a great framework for performing tabletop exercises where hypothetical scenarios are discussed. You can also employ red teams to assist in these efforts by generating real attack scenarios.

It is absolutely critical that initiating these conferences is done with care. The medical M&M was actually started in the early 1900s by a surgeon named Dr. Ernest Codman at Massachusetts General Hospital in Boston. MGH was so appalled that Dr. Codman suggested that the competence of surgeons should be evaluated that he eventually lost his staff privileges. Now, M&M is a mainstay in modern medicine and something that is done in all of the best hospitals in the world, including MGH. I've seen instances where similar types of shunning can occur in information security when these types of peer review opportunities are suggested. As NSM practitioners it is crucial that we are accepting of this type of peer review and that we encourage group learning and the refinement of our skills.

## CONCLUSION

In this chapter we discussed the analysis process, and two different methods that can be used for performing analysis in a structured, systematic manner. We also looked at a few analysis scenarios using these methods, as well as some analysis best practices. Finally, we covered methods for performing post-mortem lessons learned events.

No matter how hard you try, there will come a point where the network you are defending gets successfully attacked and compromised. In the modern security landscape, it's inevitable and there isn't a lot you can do about it because prevention eventually fails. Because of this, you need to be prepared when it happens.

An incident won't be remembered for how an intrusion occurred, but rather how it was responded to, the amount of downtime that occurred, the amount of information that was lost, and ultimately the amount of money it costs the organization. What recommendations can you make to management to ensure a similar incident doesn't occur again? What can you show your superiors to explain why the attack wasn't detected? What shortcomings do your tools have? These are questions that can't fully be answered until an intrusion has occurred and you have the context of an attack. However, these are questions you should constantly be asking yourself as you seek to improve your collection, detection, and analysis processes. Every event and incident flows through the NSM cycle and the lessons learned from each one will help to improve the process for the next time.

You will get caught off guard, you will be blind sided, and sometimes you will lose the fight. This chapter, and this book, is about equipping you with the right tools and techniques to be prepared when it happens.

# Security Onion Control Scripts

This appendix contains a listing of scripts used to control and interact with Security Onion services and data. All of these scripts (with the exception of rule-update) are located in the /usr/sbin/ directory and are required to be executed with elevated privileges using the sudo command. While we won't cover every available option for every single script, you can learn more about each script by running it with the --help argument.

## HIGH LEVEL COMMANDS

### nsm

This script is used to pass options to underlying scripts, such as nsm_server and nsm_sensor. This script can be used to check the status of an SO system by using this command:

```
sudo nsm --all --status
```

### nsm_all_del

This script will delete all SO server and sensor data, including configuration data. This script will prompt for confirmation before performing this action. The script is executed with no arguments, like this:

```
sudo nsm_all_del
```

### nsm_all_del_quick

This script will delete all SO server and sensor data, including configuration data. This script will NOT prompt for confirmation before performing this action. This script should be executed with care. This script is executed with no arguments, like this:

```
sudo nsm_all_del_quick
```

## SERVER CONTROL COMMANDS

### nsm_server

This script is used to pass options to underlying scripts. The script can be used to check the status of an SO system's server components with this command:

```
sudo nsm_server --status
```

### nsm_server_add

This script is used to create a new Sguil server. This script is executed during the SO setup process and shouldn't need to be run manually.

### nsm_server_backup-config

This script is used to back up the Sguil configuration files. This example will back up the configuration to an archive file in my home directory:

```
sudo nsm_server_backup-config --backup-file=/home/sanders/config-backup.tar.gz
```

### nsm_server_backup-data

This script is used to back up Sguil data. This example will back up data to an archive file in my home directory:

```
sudo nsm_server_backup-data --backup-file=/home/sanders/data-backup.tar.gz
```

### nsm_server_clear

This script will delete all Sguil data. This example will clear data for the current Sguil server:

```
sudo nsm_server_clear
```

### nsm_server_del

This script will permanently delete the Sguil server. This example will delete the current Sguil server:

```
sudo nsm_server_del
```

### nsm_server_edit

This script is used to modify specific Sguil configuration settings. All of these settings can be listed by running this command:

```
sudo nsm_server_edit --help
```

This example command would change the server sensor port:

```
sudo nsm_server_edit --server-name=<server> --new-server-sensor-port=<port>
```

### nsm_server_ps-status

This script is used to check the status of the Sguild service. This script is usually executed with no options, like this:

```
sudo nsm_server_ps-status
```

### nsm_server_ps-start

This script starts the Sguild service. This script is usually executed with no options, like this:

```
sudo nsm_server_ps-start
```

### nsm_server_ps-stop

This script stops the Sguild service. This script is usually executed with no options, like this:

```
sudo nsm_server_ps-stop
```

### nsm_server_ps-restart

This script restarts the Sguild service. This script is usually executed with no options, like this:

```
sudo nsm_server_ps-restart
```

### nsm_server_sensor-add

This script is used to add a sensor to the Sguil configuration. If this script is launched without arguments, it will provide a dialog for completing this action. Otherwise, this command will add a sensor to a Sguil server:

```
sudo    nsm_server_sensor-add    --server-name=<server>--sensor-
name=<sensor>
```

### nsm_server_sensor-del

This script is used to remove a sensor from the Sguil configuration. If this script is launched without arguments, it will provide a dialog for completing this action. Otherwise, this command will delete a sensor from a Sguil server:

```
sudo    nsm_server_sensor-del    --server-name=<server>--sensor-
name=<sensor>
```

### nsm_server_user-add

This script is used to add a new user to the Sguil configuration. If this script is launched without arguments, it will provide a dialog for completing this action. Otherwise, this command will add a user to a Sguil server:

```
sudo    nsm_server_user-add    --server-name=<server>--user-name
=<username>--user-pass=<password>
```

## SENSOR CONTROL COMMANDS

### nsm_sensor

This script is used to pass options to underlying scripts. The script can be used to check the status of an SO system's sensor components with this command:

```
sudo nsm_sensor --status
```

### nsm_sensor_add

This script is used to create a new sensor. This script is executed during the SO setup process and shouldn't need to be run manually.

### nsm_sensor_backup-config

This script is used to back up the sensor configuration files. This example will back up the configuration to an archive file in my home directory:

```
sudo nsm_sensor_backup-config --backup-file=/home/sanders/config-backup.tar.gz
```

### nsm_sensor_backup-data

This script is used to back up collected sensor data. This example will back up data to an archive file in my home directory:

```
sudo    nsm_sensor_backup-data    --backup-file=/home/sanders/data-backup.tar.gz
```

### nsm_sensor_clean

This script is used to remove collected sensor data when the total disk utilization is above 90%. When executed, the oldest sensor data is removed until disk utilization falls below this threshold. The script is run hourly as a cron job. It can be executed manually by running it without any arguments:

```
sudo nsm_sensor_clean
```

### nsm_sensor_clear

This script is used to remove all collected sensor data. If this script is launched without arguments, it will provide a dialog for completing this action. This command will remove all collected data for a specified sensor:

```
sudo nsm_sensor_clear --sensor-name=<sensor>
```

### nsm_sensor_del

This script removes all collected sensor data and configuration information. If this script is launched without arguments, it will provide a dialog for completing this action. This command will remove all collected sensor data and configuration information for a specified sensor:

```
sudo nsm_sensor_clear --sensor-name=<sensor>
```

### nsm_sensor_edit

This script is used to modify specific sensor configuration settings. All of these settings can be listed by running this command:

```
sudo nsm_sensor_edit --help
```

This example command would change the IP address of the server that the sensor reports to:

```
sudo  nsm_sensor_edit  --sensor-name=<sensor> --new-sensor-server-
host=<server>
```

## nsm_sensor_ps-daily-restart

This script is used with a cron job to perform a daily restart of certain sensor services at midnight. It should not need to be run manually.

## nsm_sensor_ps-status

This script is used to check the status of sensor services. If it is executed with no options, it will display the status of all sensor services. However, you can also use it to display the status of individual services. You can list these services by running the following command:

```
sudo nsm_sensor_ps-status --help
```

This example command will only display the status for Bro:

```
sudo nsm_sensor_ps-status --only-bro
```

## nsm_sensor_ps-start

This script is used to start sensor services. If it is executed with no options, it will start all sensor services, unless they are already running. However, you can also use it to start individual services. You can list these services by running the following command:

```
sudo nsm_sensor_ps-start --help
```

This example command will only start Snort:

```
sudo nsm_sensor_ps-start --only-snort-alert
```

## nsm_sensor_ps-stop

This script is used to stop sensor services. If it is executed with no options, it will stop all sensor services, unless they are already running. However, you can also use it to stop individual services. You can list these services by running the following command:

```
sudo nsm_sensor_ps-stop --help
```

This example command will only stop Netsniff-NG:

```
sudo nsm_sensor_ps-stop --only-pcap
```

## nsm_sensor_ps-restart

This script is used to restart sensor services. If it is executed with no options, it will restart all sensor services, unless they are already running. However, you can also use it to restart individual services. You can list these services by running the following command:

```
sudo nsm_sensor_ps-restart --help
```

This example command will only restart PRADS:

```
sudo nsm_sensor_ps-stop --only-prads
```

### rule-update

This script is used to update sensor IDS rules. In a standalone or server installation, it will download these rules from the Internet. Once a sensor installs, it will download these rules from the configured server. It runs automatically at 7:01 AM UTC every day. It can be executed manually by running it without any arguments:

```
sudo rule-update
```

For more information on these scripts, visit the Security Onion wiki at https://code.google.com/p/security-onion/w/list.

# Important Security Onion Files and Directories

2

This appendix contains a listing of important Security Onion files and directories. Some of these refer to areas where data is stored, while others point to configuration files that can be modified to change how Security Onion interacts with various tools. We've also included the location of many configuration files used by Security Onion tools, since they might be in a different location on an SO system than where they would be if you installed the tool manually on another operating system.

## APPLICATION DIRECTORIES AND CONFIGURATION FILES

This listing describes the location of configuration files for multiple tools included with Security Onion, as well as configuration files for SO itself. This listing is short and only includes files that are commonly accessed or modified.

### Security Onion

- General SO settings can be modified at /etc/nsm/securityonion.conf
- Template configurations for tools used on SO are stored at /etc/nsm/templates/
- Packet filtering can be applied by editing the /etc/nsm/rules/bpf.conf file
- Status checking and maintenance scripts are stored in /etc/cron.d/

### Snort/Suricata

- If you are using Snort, its configuration file is located at /etc/nsm/<sensor>/ snort.conf.
- If you are using Suricata, its configuration file is located at /etc/nsm/< sensor >/ suricata.yaml.
- IDS rules are stored at /etc/nsm/rules/
  - Downloaded rules are stored in the downloaded.rules file
  - Custom rules can be added to the local.rules file
  - Rule threshold entries can be added to the threshold.conf file

### PulledPork

- The PulledPork configuration file is located at /etc/nsm/pulledpork/pulledpork. conf

- Rule modifications using PulledPork are accomplished with these files:
  - /etc/nsm/pulledpork/disablesid.conf
  - /etc/nsm/pulledpork/dropsid.conf
  - /etc/nsm/pulledpork/enablesid.conf
  - /etc/nsm/pulledpork/modifysid.conf

## PRADS

- The PRADS configuration file is located at /etc/nsm/< sensor-interface >/prads.conf

## Bro

- The Bro configuration files are located at /opt/bro/

## ELSA

- In standalone and server installations, the ELSA web interface configuration file is located at /etc/elsa_web.conf
- In standalone and sensor installations, the ELSA node configuration file is located at /etc/elsa_node.conf

## Snorby

Snorby configuration files are located at /opt/snorby/config/.

## Syslog-NG

Syslog-NG configuration files are located at /etc/syslog-ng/.

## Sguil

- Sguil configuration files are located at /etc/nsm/securityonion/
  - Access to Sguil can be controlled with sguild.access
  - Automatic categorization of events is handled by autocat.conf
  - E-Mail alerts can be configured with sguild.email
  - Queries for Sguil can be created with sguild.queries

---

## SENSOR DATA DIRECTORIES

This listing contains locations where sensor tools store raw data:

| Data Type | Application | Location |
|---|---|---|
| FPC Data | Netsniff-NG | /nsm/sensor_data/< sensor >/dailylogs/ |
| Session Data | Argus | /nsm/sensor_data/< sensor >/argus/ |
| Alert Data | Snort/Suricata | /nsm/sensor_data/< sensor >/snort-1/ |
| Network Log Data / Alert Data | Bro | /nsm/bro/ |
| Host Data | PRADS | /var/log/prads-asset.log |

# Packet Headers

| Applied NSM Packet Map 1 | | | |
| Ethernet Version 2 | | | |

| 0 1 2 3 4 5 6 7 | 8 9 10 11 12 13 14 15 | 16 17 18 19 20 21 22 23 | 24 25 26 27 28 29 30 31 |
| --- | --- | --- | --- |
| Byte Offset 0 | Byte Offset 1 | Byte Offset 2 | Byte Offset 3 |
| Destination Address (48-bit) | | | |
| Byte Offset 4 | Byte Offset 5 | Byte Offset 6 | Byte Offset 7 |
| Destination Address (cont...) | | Source Address (48-bit) | |
| Byte Offset 8 | Byte Offset 9 | Byte Offset 10 | Byte Offset 11 |
| Source Address (cont...) | | | |
| Byte Offset 12 | Byte Offset 13 | Byte Offset 14 | Byte Offset 15 |
| Type (16-bit) | | Data (Variable Length) | |
| Byte Offset 16 | Byte Offset 17 | Byte Offset 18 | Byte Offset 19 |
| Data (Continued) (Variable Length) | | | |
| Frame Check Sequence (32-bit) | | | |

| 0 1 2 3 4 5 6 7 | 8 9 10 11 12 13 14 15 | 16 17 18 19 20 21 22 23 | 24 25 26 27 28 29 30 31 |

Type | IPv4 | 0x0800
| ARP | 0x0806
| IPv6 | 0x86DD

459

## Applied NSM Packet Map 2
## IPv4 Header (RFC 791)

| 0 1 2 3 4 5 6 7 | 8 9 10 11 12 13 14 15 | 16 17 18 19 20 21 22 23 | 24 25 26 27 28 29 30 31 |
|---|---|---|---|
| Byte Offset 0 | Byte Offset 1 | Byte Offset 2 | Byte Offset 3 |
| Version (4-bit) / IP Hdr Length (4-bit) | Type of Service (8-bit) | Total Length (16-bit) (in Byte Offsets) | |
| Byte Offset 4 | Byte Offset 5 | Byte Offset 6 | Byte Offset 7 |
| IP Identification Number (16-bit) | R DF MF | Fragment Offset (13-bit) | |
| Byte Offset 8 | Byte Offset 9 | Byte Offset 10 | Byte Offset 11 |
| Time to Live (8-bit) | Protocol (8-bit) | Header Checksum (16-bit) | |
| Byte Offset 12 | Byte Offset 13 | Byte Offset 14 | Byte Offset 15 |
| Source IP Address (32-bit) | | | |
| Byte Offset 16 | Byte Offset 17 | Byte Offset 18 | Byte Offset 19 |
| Destination IP Address (32-bit) | | | |
| Byte Offset 20 | Byte Offset 21 | Byte Offset 22 | Byte Offset 23 |
| IP Options (Variable - If Any) | | | |
| Data (Variable Length) | | | |

(20 Bytes for header; IP Options and Data are Variable)

| 0 1 2 3 4 5 6 7 | 8 9 10 11 12 13 14 15 | 16 17 18 19 20 21 22 23 | 24 25 26 27 28 29 30 31 |

**IP Version Number**   Valid values are:      4 for IPv4      6 for IPv6

**IP Header Length**   4 Byte Multiplier      Min Value 5 (20 bytes)   Max Value 15 (60 bytes)

**Total Length**      No Multiplier      Max Length 65535

**Flags**      R - Reserved   D - Don't Fragment      MF - More Fragments (1=Yes 0=No)

**Fragment Offset**   8 Byte Multiplier      Max Size 65528

| IP Protocol | Dec | Hex | Proto | Dec | Hex | Proto |
|---|---|---|---|---|---|---|
| | 1 | 0x01 | ICMP | 17 | 0x11 | UDP |
| | 2 | 0x02 | IGMP | 47 | 0x2F | GRE |
| | 6 | 0x06 | TCP | 50 | 0x32 | ESP |
| | 9 | 0x09 | IGRP | 51 | 0x33 | AH |

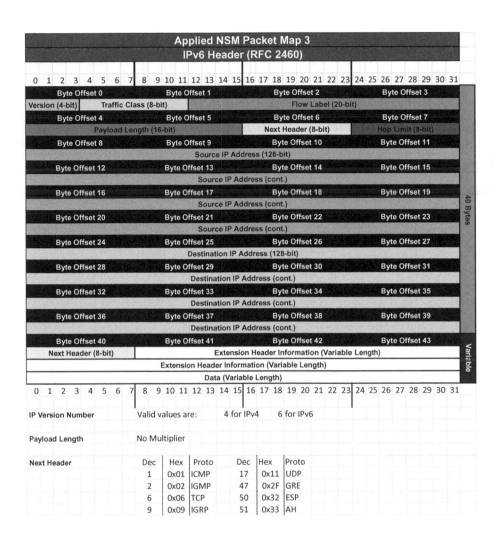

| | | | |
|---|---|---|---|
| IP Version Number | Valid values are: | 4 for IPv4 | 6 for IPv6 |
| Payload Length | No Multiplier | | |

| Next Header | Dec | Hex | Proto | Dec | Hex | Proto |
|---|---|---|---|---|---|---|
| | 1 | 0x01 | ICMP | 17 | 0x11 | UDP |
| | 2 | 0x02 | IGMP | 47 | 0x2F | GRE |
| | 6 | 0x06 | TCP | 50 | 0x32 | ESP |
| | 9 | 0x09 | IGRP | 51 | 0x33 | AH |

**Applied NSM Packet Map 4**
**ICMP Header (RFC 792)**

| 0 1 2 3 4 5 6 7 | 8 9 10 11 12 13 14 15 | 16 17 18 19 20 21 22 23 | 24 25 26 27 28 29 30 31 | |
|---|---|---|---|---|
| Byte Offset 0 | Byte Offset 1 | Byte Offset 2 | Byte Offset 3 | 4 Bytes |
| Message Type (8-bit) | Message Code (8-bit) | Checksum (16-bit) | | |
| Byte Offset 4 | Byte Offset 5 | Byte Offset 6 | Byte Offset 7 | Variable |
| (Variable Contents Depending on Type and Code) | | | | |

| 0 1 2 3 4 5 6 7 | 8 9 10 11 12 13 14 15 | 16 17 18 19 20 21 22 23 | 24 25 26 27 28 29 30 31 |
|---|---|---|---|

**Common Types & Codes**

| T | C | |
|---|---|---|
| 0 | 0 | Echo reply |
| 3 | 0 | Destination Unreachable |
| | 0 | Net Unreachable |
| | 1 | Host Unreacheable |
| | 2 | Protocol Unreachable |
| | 3 | Port Unreachable |
| 5 | 0 | Redirect |
| 8 | 0 | Echo Request |
| 11 | 0 | Time Exceeded |
| | 0 | Time to Live Exceeded in Transit |
| | 1 | Fragment Reassembly Time Exceeded |
| 13 | 0 | Timestamp Request |
| 14 | 0 | Timestamp Reply |
| 15 | 0 | Information Request |
| 16 | 0 | Information Reply |
| 17 | 0 | Address Mask Request |
| 18 | 0 | Address Mask Reply |

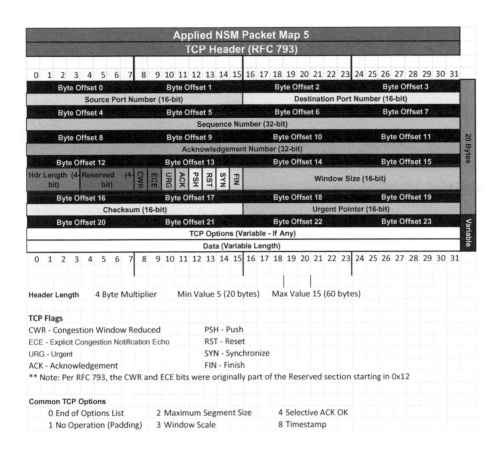

Header Length    4 Byte Multiplier    Min Value 5 (20 bytes)    Max Value 15 (60 bytes)

**TCP Flags**

CWR - Congestion Window Reduced          PSH - Push
ECE - Explicit Congestion Notification Echo      RST - Reset
URG - Urgent                             SYN - Synchronize
ACK - Acknowledgement                    FIN - Finish
** Note: Per RFC 793, the CWR and ECE bits were originally part of the Reserved section starting in 0x12

**Common TCP Options**

| 0 End of Options List | 2 Maximum Segment Size | 4 Selective ACK OK |
|---|---|---|
| 1 No Operation (Padding) | 3 Window Scale | 8 Timestamp |

| Applied NSM Packet Map 6 | | | | | | | | | | | | | | | | | | | | | | | | | | | | | | | |
|---|---|---|---|---|---|---|---|---|---|---|---|---|---|---|---|---|---|---|---|---|---|---|---|---|---|---|---|---|---|---|---|
| UDP Header (RFC 768) | | | | | | | | | | | | | | | | | | | | | | | | | | | | | | | |
| 0 | 1 | 2 | 3 | 4 | 5 | 6 | 7 | 8 | 9 | 10 | 11 | 12 | 13 | 14 | 15 | 16 | 17 | 18 | 19 | 20 | 21 | 22 | 23 | 24 | 25 | 26 | 27 | 28 | 29 | 30 | 31 |
| Byte Offset 0 | | | | | | | | Byte Offset 1 | | | | | | | | Byte Offset 2 | | | | | | | | Byte Offset 3 | | | | | | | |
| Source Port Number (16-bit) | | | | | | | | | | | | | | | | Destination Port Number (16-bit) | | | | | | | | | | | | | | | |
| Byte Offset 4 | | | | | | | | Byte Offset 5 | | | | | | | | Byte Offset 6 | | | | | | | | Byte Offset 7 | | | | | | | |
| Length (16-bit) | | | | | | | | | | | | | | | | Checksum (16-bit) | | | | | | | | | | | | | | | |
| Byte Offset 8 | | | | | | | | Byte Offset 9 | | | | | | | | Byte Offset 10 | | | | | | | | Byte Offset 11 | | | | | | | |
| Data (Variable Length) | | | | | | | | | | | | | | | | | | | | | | | | | | | | | | | |
| 0 | 1 | 2 | 3 | 4 | 5 | 6 | 7 | 8 | 9 | 10 | 11 | 12 | 13 | 14 | 15 | 16 | 17 | 18 | 19 | 20 | 21 | 22 | 23 | 24 | 25 | 26 | 27 | 28 | 29 | 30 | 31 |

Length     No Multiplier     Max Length 65515

# Decimal / Hex / ASCII Conversion Chart

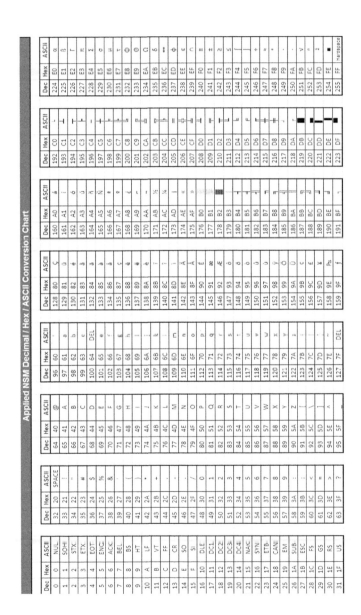

Applied NSM Decimal / Hex / ASCII Conversion Chart

# Index

Note: Page numbers followed by *b* indicate boxes, *f* indicate figures and *t* indicate tables.

**467**